HANDBOOK OF TRUST RESEARCH

Handbook of Trust Research

Edited by

Reinhard Bachmann

Associate Professor of Management, Birkbeck College, University of London, UK

Akbar Zaheer

Curtis L. Carlson Professor of Strategic Management and Organization and Director, Strategic Management Research Center, Carlson School of Management, University of Minnesota, USA

Edward Elgar
Cheltenham, UK • Northampton, MA, USA

Published by
Edward Elgar Publishing Limited
Glensanda House
Montpellier Parade
Cheltenham
Glos GL50 1UA
UK

Edward Elgar Publishing, Inc.
136 West Street
Suite 202
Northampton
Massachusetts 01060
USA

A catalogue record for this book
is available from the British Library

Library of Congress Cataloguing in Publication Data
Handbook of trust research / edited by Reinhard Bachmann, Akbar Zaheer.
    p. cm. – (Elgar original reference)
    Includes bibliographical references and index.
    1. Organizational behavior—Research. 2. Trust—Research. 3.
    Interpersonal relations—Research. 4. Interorganizational
    relations—Research. 5. Organizational sociology—Research. I. Bachmann,
    Reinhard, 1961– II. Zaheer, Akbar, 1952– III. Series.
    HD58.7.H366 2006
    302.3′5—dc22   2006004280

ISBN-13: 978 1 84376 754 1 (cased)
ISBN-10: 1 84376 754 6 (cased)

Printed and bound in Great Britain by the MPG Books Group

Contents

PART III CROSS-LEVEL APPROACHES

PART IV TRUST AT THE LEVEL OF SOCIETY AND THE ECONOMY

List of contributors

Richard Arena is Professor at the University of Nice Sophia Antipolis. His research focuses on issues of economic and social analyses of industrial organizations. He has published in journals such as *Cambridge Journal of Economics, History of Economic Ideas* etc. Together with C. Dangel-Hagnauer, he is the editor of *The Contribution of J.A. Schumpeter to Economics Development* (Routledge, 2002).

Reinhard Bachmann is Associate Professor (Reader) in Management at the University of London, Birkbeck College. He has published widely in journals such as *Organization Studies, British Journal of Sociology, Cambridge Journal of Economics* etc. Together with Christel Lane, he edited *Trust Within and Between Organizations* (Oxford University Press, 1998/2000). In 2001 he edited a special issue of *Organization Studies* on 'Trust and Control in Organizational Relations' (with David Knights and Jörg Sydow). He is a member of the Editorial Boards of *Organization* and *Organization Studies*. His work emphasizes the role of social mechanisms (trust, power etc.) and societal influences (institutional arrangements, cultural traditions) on the structure and quality of organizational relationships and business strategies.

Sanjay Banerjee is a PhD student in Accounting at the University of Minnesota. His research interests include information economics, financial reporting and disclosure. He has a BS in aerospace engineering from the Indian Institute of Technology, an MBA from XLRI, India, and an MSc in service management from the University of Buckingham, London. In his last corporate assignment with a global travel company, he was looking after new projects and business development.

Jens Beckert is Professor of Sociology and Director of the Max-Planck-Institute for the Study of Societies in Cologne. Previously he was Professor of Sociology at the Georg-August-University, Göttingen. He was a Visting Fellow at the sociology department of Princeton University in 1994/95 and at the Center for European Studies of Harvard University in 2001/02. He is the author of *Beyond the Market. The Social Foundations of Economic Efficiency* (Princeton University Press, 2002). Together with Milan Zafirovski, he is the editor of the *International Encyclopedia of Economic Sociology* (Routledge, 2005). He has published in journals such as *Theory and Society, Journal of Economic Issues* and *Organization Studies*.

Cristina Bicchieri is Carol and Michael Lowenstein Endowed Term Chair and Professor of Philosophy and Director of the Philosophy, Politics and Economics Program at the University of Pennsylvania. Previously she was Professor of Philosophy and Social and Decision Sciences, Carnegie Mellon University. She is the author of *Rationality and Coordination* (1993/97) and *The Grammar of Society: the Nature and Dynamics of Social Norms* (2006), both by Cambridge University Press. Her research includes work on the logical foundations of game theory, applications of game-theoretic and evolutionary models to distributed artificial intelligence, and social norms and impersonal trust.

Norman E. Bowie is the Elmer L. Andersen Professor in Corporate Responsibility at the University of Minnesota. He is the author or editor of 15 books and over 75 scholarly articles in business ethics and related fields. His most recent book is *Management Ethics* (Blackwell, 2004) and his most recent edited book is *Blackwell Guide to Business Ethics* (2002). His authoritative co-edited text *Ethical Theory and Business* (Prentice Hall, 2003) is in its seventh edition. He has held a position as Dixons Professor of Business Ethics and Social Responsibility at the London Business School and been a fellow at Harvard's Program in Ethics and the Professions.

Philip Bromiley is Professor in Organization and Strategic Management at the Merage School of the University of California, Irvine. Previously he held the Curtis L. Carlson Chair in Strategic Management and chaired the Department of Strategic Management and Organization at the University of Minnesota. He has published widely on organizational decision-making and strategic risk-taking. He served on the Editorial Boards of *Academy of Management Journal* and *Organization Science*, and as associate editor for *Management Science*. He currently serves on the boards of *Strategic Management Journal* and *Strategic Organization*. He also edits the Blackwell series on *Theories of Strategic Management*.

Mark Casson is Professor of Economics and Director of the Centre for Institutional Performance at the University of Reading, UK. He has published widely on the economics of the multinational enterprise, entrepreneurship and business culture, in addition to publishing over 30 books in these areas, including *The Economics of Business Culture* (Oxford University Press, 1991), *Enterprise and Leadership* (Edward Elgar, 2000) and *Economics of International Business: A New Research Agenda* (Edward Elgar, 2000). He is particularly interested in the economic costs and benefits of institutional investments in trust-building.

Norman L. Chervany is Carlson Professor of Information and Decision Sciences at the Carlson School of Management, University of Minnesota. He received his doctorate in decision sciences from Indiana University. His research focuses on human issues in the use of technology. His specific research interests revolve around the relationships among information technology/systems and organizational strategy, the role of trust in an organization's information management enterprise, work design issues in systems development, and the implementation of systems projects. His work is widely published in such outlets as *MIS Quarterly, Management Science* and *Decision Sciences*.

Steven C. Currall is Professor of Enterprise and the Management of Innovation and Director of the Centre for Enterprise and the Management of Innovation at University College London and Visiting Professor at London Business School. Previously he was William and Stephanie Sick Professor of Entrepreneurship at Rice University. He conducts research in the areas of emerging technology companies, trust and corporate governance. He serves on the Editorial Review Boards of the *Journal of Organizational Behavior* and *Academy of Management Perspectives*.

Simon Deakin is the Robert Monks Professor of Corporate Governance in the Judge Institute of Management Studies, University of Cambridge. In addition he is a Fellow of

Peterhouse and Yorke Professorial Research Fellow in the Faculty of Law at Cambridge. He is co-author of *Markesinis and Deakin's Tort Law* (Clarendon Press, 5th edition, 2003) and of *Labour Law* (Butterworths, 2nd edition, 1998) (with G. Morris). Also, he has published widely in journals such as the *Cambridge Journal of Economics*, *Organization* and *Industrial Relations Journal*. Present research includes work on corporate law and economic performance, reflexive law and democratic governance, and the modernization of employment institutions.

Marina Della Giusta is a Lecturer in Economics at the University of Reading, UK. Her research interests lie in the field of institutional economics, focusing particularly on the roles of institutions and social mechanisms in market access. Her main publications are in the areas of micro-finance and social capital as well as the institutional design of development organizations. She is currently doing work on the economics of trust, on social capital and well-being, the economics of prostitution, and the responses of institutions to changes in development models. She has an active interest in fair trade and trade regulation issues, on which she works with an NGO based in Reading.

Kurt T. Dirks is currently Associate Professor at the John M. Olin School of Business at Washington University in St Louis. He has published in the *Journal of Applied Psychology*, *Academy of Management Review*, *Organization Science* etc. He is on the Editorial Board of *Organization Science*. His research is focused on trust in the workplace, including its antecedents, consequences and processes. He also conducts research on feelings of ownership.

Gokhan Ertug is Sasakawa Fellow and a PhD candidate in Organizational Behavior at INSEAD. His research interests include the affiliation basis of status, the effects of social networks on cooperation and competition, and the undesirable consequences of excessive trust in organizations.

Martin Gargiulo is an Associate Professor of Organizational Behavior at INSEAD in Singapore. He received his PhD in sociology from Columbia University. He has published his work in journals such as *Administrative Science Quarterly*, *Academy of Management Journal* and *American Journal of Sociology*. His research focuses on the effects of social networks on interpersonal and interorganizational cooperation, as well as the effects of this cooperation or lack thereof on individual and organizational performance.

Jared Harris is an Assistant Professor at the University of Virginia's Darden Graduate School of Business. His work on financial misrepresentation won the University of Notre Dame's 2005 Excellence in Ethics Dissertation Competition, and qualified him as a finalist for the 2005 INFORMS/Organization Science Dissertation Competition. While completing his studies at the University of Minnesota, Jared received doctoral fellowships from the Strategic Management Society, the Juran Center for Leadership in Quality, and the Business Roundtable Institute for Corporate Ethics.

Violet T. Ho is Assistant Professor at Nanyang Business School, Nanyang Technological University of Singapore. She received her PhD in Organizational Behavior and Theory from the Tepper School of Business at Carnegie Mellon University. Her research interests include social networks, psychological contracts and cognitive structures.

Andrew C. Inkpen is the J. Kenneth and Jeanette Seward Professor in Global Strategy at Thunderbird. He received his PhD from the Ivey School, University of Western Ontario. His research interests include the management of knowledge in strategic alliances, trust in strategic alliances, and learning in multinational organizations. His research has been published in a variety of journals, including *Academy of Management Review*, *California Management Review*, *Journal of International Business Studies*, *Journal of Management Studies*, *Organization Science* and *Strategic Management Journal*.

Martyna Janowicz is Research Fellow at the Department of Organization Studies at Tilburg University, The Netherlands. She obtained her PhD at the CentER for Economic Research and the Department of Organization and Strategy at Tilburg University. Her research focuses on interorganizational learning in the context of international strategic alliances, trust building and repair, as well as temporary organizations.

Roderick M. Kramer is the William R. Kimball Professor of Organizational Behavior at the Stanford Graduate School of Business, California. He is the author or co-author of over 95 scholarly articles and essays. His research has appeared in numerous journals and books, including *Administrative Science Quarterly*, *Academy of Management Journal*, *Annual Review of Psychology*, *Harvard Business Review*, *Journal of Personality and Social Psychology*, *Journal of Experimental Social Psychology* and *Journal of Conflict Resolution*. He is also the co-author or co-editor of ten books, including *Trust in Organizations: Frontiers of Theory and Research*, with Tom Tyler (Sage Publications, 1996), and *Trust and Distrust Within Organizational Boundaries*, with Karen S. Cook (Russell Sage Foundation, 2004). Formerly, he was an Associate Editor of *Administrative Science Quarterly*.

Nathalie Lazaric is a Senior Research fellow at CNRS (GREDEG, University Nice Sophia Antipolis). Her work focuses on learning in organizations, organizational routines and social dynamics in knowledge exchange processes. Among her publications are articles in *Industrial and Corporate Change*, *Journal of Evolutionary Economics* and *Research Policy*. Together with Edward Lorenz she edited *Trust and Economic Learning* (Edward Elgar, 1998).

Chris P. Long is Assistant Professor of Organizational Behavior at the Olin School of Business, Washington University in St Louis. His research examines how leaders integrate their efforts to promote control, trust and fairness within both traditional organizations and new organizational forms in order to accomplish organizational performance objectives (e.g., commitment, innovation, efficiency) and formulate effective responses to aspects of complex and dynamic business environments.

Edward Lorenz received his PhD in Economics from the University of Cambridge. He is currently Professor of Economics at the University of Nice Sophia Antipolis and

Assigned Professor at the University of Aalborg, Denmark. Also, he is Research Associate at the Centre for Employment Studies in Marne-la-Vallée. His research interests include the economics of innovation, knowledge management and organizational behaviour. His publications appeared in journals such as *Cambridge Journal of Economics, Industrial Relations* and *Regional Studies*.

Anoop Madhok is Professor of Strategy at the Schulich School of Business, York University, Toronto, and a Visiting Professor in the Department of Public Administration and Organization Science, Free University of Amsterdam. He obtained his PhD in 1993 from McGill University. He was formerly a Professor of Management at the David Eccles School of Business, University of Utah, Salt Lake City. His research interests span strategy and international management and include topics such as multinational firm strategy, foreign market entry, strategic alliances, trust and interfirm collaboration, and the theory and boundaries of the firm. His work has been published in the *Academy of Management Journal, Strategic Management Journal, Organization Science* and *Journal of International Business Studies*. He serves on the Editorial Review Boards of *Strategic Management Journal, Journal of International Business Studies* and *Journal of International Management*.

Bill McEvily is Associate Professor of Strategic Management at the Rotman School of Management, University of Toronto. He has published in journals such as *Administrative Science Quarterly, Management Science, Organization Science* and *Strategic Management Journal*. He also serves as a Senior Editor of *Organization Science*. His research interests include social networks and trust in and between organizations.

D. Harrison McKnight received his PhD in Management Information Systems from the University of Minnesota in 1997. He serves in The Eli Broad College of Business at Michigan State University. His research interests include trust-building within electronic commerce and organizational settings, and the retention and motivation of systems professionals. His work has appeared in such journals as the *Academy of Management Review, Information Systems Research, MIS Quarterly* and *International Journal of Electronic Commerce*. For ten years previous to pursuing an academic career, Harrison held financial and managerial positions in American Airlines' SABRE division.

Guido Möllering is a Research Fellow at the Max-Planck-Institute for the Study of Societies in Cologne. He holds a PhD in Management Studies from the University of Cambridge. His research is generally in the area of inter-organizational relationships and the constitution of markets with specific interests in trust and collective institutional entrepreneurship. He has published in journals such as *Organization Science* and *Sociology*, and is co-editor of a special issue of the *Journal of Managerial Psychology* on the micro-foundations of organizational trust. He is also the author of *Trust: Reason, Routine, Reflexivity* (Elsevier, 2006).

Niels Noorderhaven is Professor of International Management and Head of the Department of Organization and Strategy at Tilburg University, The Netherlands. He holds a PhD from the University of Groningen. His publications include articles in the

Academy of Management Journal, Organization Studies and *Organization Science*. His research focuses on (international) cooperation in business, with a special interest in issues of culture and trust.

Bart Nooteboom is Professor of Innovation Policy at Tilburg University, Netherlands. His research interests include: innovation, entrepreneurship, organizational learning, inter-firm collaboration and networks, and trust. He has published six books and 200 papers on these and related topics. He is a member of the Royal Netherlands Academy of Arts and Sciences and was member of a Dutch government committee on technology policy. He was awarded the Kapp prize for his work on organizational learning and the Gunnar Myrdal prize for his work on trust.

Carla Pavone is a PhD student in Strategic Management and Organization at the University of Minnesota. Her research interests include entrepreneurship and corporate venturing. Her first career was in magazine and book publishing. Her second career was in financial services, where she helped lead start-ups and turnarounds, as well as new product development and reengineering efforts. She has a BA in Biology from the University of Pennsylvania and an MBA in General Management from Harvard Business School.

Sim B. Sitkin is Professor of Management and Faculty Director of the Center of Leadership at the Fuqua School of Business at Duke University. His research focuses on leadership and control systems and their influence on how organizations and their members become more or less capable of change, innovation, trust and learning. He has authored/edited over 60 books, articles and chapters, including *The Legalistic Organization* (Sage, 1994).

Peter Smith Ring is Professor of Strategic Management at the College of Business Administration, Loyola Marymount University, California. His work has appeared in journals such as the *Strategic Management Journal, Academy of Management Review* and *Journal of Management Studies*. His research interests in addition to the role of trust in economic exchanges include: networks and strategic alliances, the processes of managing strategic alliances, strategies for managing competitive and political environments, and public sector–private sector collaboration.

Jörg Sydow is Professor of Management at the School of Business and Economics, Free University of Berlin. Previously he held a Chair for Planning and Organization at the University of Wuppertal, and Visiting Professorships at Bentley College and the Universities of Innsbruck, Vienna and Arizona. Currently he is an International Visiting Fellow of the Advanced Institute of Management Research (AIM), UK. He is founding co-editor of two leading German journals, *Managementforschung* and *Industrielle Beziehungen – The German Journal of Industrial Relations*. Also, he is a member of the Editorial Boards of leading journals, including *Organization Studies, Organization Science* and *The Scandinavian Journal of Management*.

Andrew H. Van de Ven is the Vernon H. Heath Professor of Organizational Innovation and Change in the Carlson School of Management, University of Minnesota. He received his PhD from the University of Wisconsin at Madison, and taught at Kent State University and the Wharton School of the University of Pennsylvania before his present appointment. He is co-author of *The Innovation Journey* (1999), *Organizational Change and Innovation Processes: Theory and Methods for Research* (2000), and the *Handbook of Organizational Change and Innovation* (2004), all by Oxford University Press. He also served as 2000–2001 President of the Academy of Management.

Roberto A. Weber is Associate Professor of Economics, and of Social and Decision Sciences at Carnegie Mellon University. His research areas include trust, fairness and altruism, and behavioural game theory and economics. He has published in journals such as *Organization Science* and *Management Science*.

Marc van Wegberg teaches at the University of Maastricht, Faculty of Economics and Business Administration, Department of Organization and Strategy. His publications include book chapters and articles in journals such as the *Journal of Economic Behavior and Organization* and *Technology Analysis and Strategic Management*.

Arjen van Witteloostuijn is Professor of International Economics and Business at the University of Groningen, Netherlands, and Professor of Strategy at the University of Durham, UK. He received his PhD in Economics from the University of Maastricht. He is member of the Editorial Boards of the *Academy of Management Journal, Industrial and Corporate Change, Organization Studies* and *Strategic Organization*. He has published widely in such journals as the *Academy of Management Review, Academy of Management Journal, American Sociological Review, Economica, Management Science* and *Strategic Management Journal*. His current research ranges from international trade theory and industrial organization to top management team leadership and personality psychology.

Akbar (Aks) Zaheer is Curtis L. Carlson Professor of Strategic Management and Organization and Director of the Strategic Management Research Center at the Carlson School of Management, University of Minnesota. He is Associate Editor of *Academy of Management Review*, and serves on the Editorial Board of *Strategic Management Journal*. He was a Guest Editor of the special issue of *Organization Science* on 'Trust within and Between Organizations', and is currently a Guest Editor for the *Academy of Management Review* special issue on 'Repairing Relationships'. He has published several papers in the area of trust, and also researches issues around networks, alliances, and mergers and acquisitions.

Introduction

Reinhard Bachmann and Akbar Zaheer

In recent times, research on trust in organizational and inter-organizational contexts has become a major field in the domain of management. While it remained a relatively narrow niche with only a few scholars interested in it until about the late 1980s, it has grown strongly to become a central issue now both in its own right and also as a theme that bundles and reflects many strands of current debates on the processes, structure, and performance of organizational and inter-organizational relationships. Numerous articles, as well as authored and edited books, on trust have appeared in the last 15 years or so, conferences and conference tracks have been organized, and a number of top journals of the field have published special issues in the area of trust. At the same time, many important but not necessarily convergent streams of trust research have developed among scholars both in Europe and in the USA. The rationale for this *Handbook* is to consolidate, take stock of and assess the current state of the field of trust research by bringing together contributions from some of the most prominent researchers in the field, from both sides of the Atlantic. In the rest of this introduction, we consider the reasons for the rise of trust as a research field, present some of our own thoughts and observations on the role and nature of trust in business relationships, say a few words about the motivation for the *Handbook* as well as the process we followed in inviting and editing the contributions, introduce and group the chapters of the *Handbook*, and conclude by identifying some key themes in trust research which run through the book.

The role of trust in business relations
There are at least two related questions that need to be addressed in order to fully understand the rise of trust as a burgeoning field of research: first, how and why has trust managed to become an established field in management research so quickly and forcefully; and second, why has it attained such a central position that today it can truly be seen as one of the core themes of organizational analysis and management as a whole?

The first of these two questions seems easier to answer than the second. However, it also has its tripwires as a number of interdependent factors that are difficult to disentangle play a role here. These include increased competition in global markets; the disintegration of production processes; the availability of advanced communication technologies and systems; and post-bureaucratic forms of work organization.

The advent of these factors have made today's world of business quite different from what it used to be even two decades ago. In the classic era of bureaucratic organization there was hardly any awareness of the problem of trust; it simply did not exist in any considerable proportion, in either the practitioner or the academic worlds. In the former, where rigid procedures existed for everything, job descriptions were narrow, the environment of the organization was stable, and interfirm contracts were limited in number and scope, neither individuals nor organizations really needed to bother with trust or the trustworthiness of employees or business partners. Monitoring behaviour and control of actions were effective and easy to exert under these conditions. Consequently, trust was of limited interest as it was neither a scarce resource nor needed in large quantity (Grey and Garsten, 2001). Thus it is not surprising that organization theorists like Max Weber had little to say about trust in the age of bureaucracy.

Today, much has changed since Weber's times and, despite some signs of rebureaucratization (Reed, 2005), modern organizations, their structures and their relationships are enormously different from what they were. In particular, the vast degree of uncertainty and the need for flexibility that characterizes relationships within and between firms is unprecedented in the history of modern organizations. This, in many ways, requires approaches that have little in common with management knowledge that was valid and applicable in the first three-quarters of the last century. Interestingly, both phenomena, the need for flexibility and the presence of uncertainty, are two sides of the same coin, as the former is a partial response to the latter. Flexibility seems both to allow and demand more cooperativeness in intra- and inter-organizational relations. In particular the automobile industry in the late 1970s illustrates this point nicely, at least for vertical relationships. At that time, Western firms realized that they had to become more flexible in their relationships with suppliers in order to match the competitiveness of Japanese manufacturers. In addition, increased global competition and the rising level of turbulence in organizational and inter-organizational relationships have made uncertainty an intrinsic feature of modern business. In this situation, where flexibility is required and uncertainty abounds, trust is needed more than ever. Little wonder that it has become one of the key issues in current management research.

The answer to the second of the two questions is closely linked to these observations. In the last two decades of the twentieth century, trust has arguably become one of the fundamental modes of coordinating organizational relationships (Bachmann, 2001; McEvily et al., 2003) or – to use Reed's (2001) words – 'the explanatory focus of organizational analysis'. Only power (or hierarchy) and monetary incentives (or the market) may be seen as equally basic coordination mechanisms in business relationships (Bradach and Eccles, 1989). While power is the prime coordination in hierarchical relationships and monetary incentives the central coordination mechanism in market-based relationships, trust is suggested to be characteristic of 'hybrid' forms of economic transactions. As these hybrid organizational forms – which include alliances, joint ventures, partnerships and the like – increase rapidly in number and strategic relevance in modern business systems, trust moves centre stage as a vital mechanism that ensures coordinated interaction in complex relational arrangements.

Very few early sociologists foresaw the need for trust in modern society. More than just 'a state of mind', as Simmel, virtually the only theorist of classical sociology who was interested in trust, suggested, this phenomenon has developed into a mechanism both crucial and at the same time deep-seated in our daily interactions. So much so that without it neither our highly differentiated modern societies would exist nor would advanced business systems be able to function and create the levels of individual and collective wealth that we are used to. More recently, systems theory (Luhmann, 1979; 1984) and structuration theory (Giddens, 1984) alike see the processes of societal and organizational modernization as those that *inevitably* lead to an increased need of trust. The more complex and dynamic social and economic relations and exchange arrangements are today, the more trust is needed as a lubricant to keep the motor running (Arrow, 1974).

In this context, Giddens (1990), for example, argues that modern societies are built on collective trust in the competence and goodwill of professional specialists. If, to refer to one of his examples, we did not trust the air traffic control systems, which normal airline passengers have little chance to understand themselves, we could not travel around the world as many of us do. Also, we would know a lot less about foreign cultures, have fewer business contacts and lose many opportunities and conveniences that make life as diverse and economically developed as it is in large parts of the world. In short, our standard of living would decrease sharply if we decided not to trust experts anymore.

In the context of business, specifically, trust plays an increasingly important role in facilitating contractual relations between business partners, not least where the products or services exchanged are difficult to describe *ex ante* or difficult to evaluate *ex post*. As is well known, contracts are hardly a remedy against opportunistic behaviour (Williamson, 1985) and thus do not make trust irrelevant. Not only are contracts always somewhat risky, in part because of the time gap between one side delivering and the other side fullfilling its promises (Macneil, 1980; Coleman, 1990), but with greater complexity and uncertainty contracts have *increasingly* become 'incomplete' in differentiated socioeconomic systems. In these circumstances, 'contract trust' (Sako, 1992), namely the trust that contractors will honour the terms of the contract, has gained increased relevance today.

From these brief observations and examples, it is apparent that trust is not only immensely important from a management practitioner point of view; it also has become a core issue of organization theory, management research, and the analysis of modern society as a whole. While in the 1980s risk was a central focus of social and organizational theory, and some scholars saw this category as the hallmark of that time, trust connects to and encompasses this concept. More than in a 'risk society' (Beck, 1986), we are living in a *trust society* where much of our well-being depends on the phenomena of trust and trustworthiness. As academics, it is our role to identify, draw attention to, better understand, theorize about and explain these phenomena. This *Handbook* is an effort to do precisely that, through a large number of diverse contributions to the study of trust.

Motivation for the *Handbook*

The invitation to the authors of the *Handbook*, all eminent trust researchers, was to reflect on their own seminal contribution to the field of trust. Researchers were asked to present their current thinking on trust in business relationships, or assess the impact their contributions had made to the field, on how their own thinking may have changed since they made their contributions, and on what enduring and new research directions they could identify which would move the field forward at this time.

One of the prime motivations for the *Handbook*, aside from our conclusion that it was time to take stock of and consolidate an increasingly important subject, was our observation that while the field of trust research is vibrant and thriving on both sides of the Atlantic, at times one gets the impression that researchers in America and Europe appear to be talking past each other. There appears to be relatively little cross-fertilization of ideas, or a cumulating research tradition that encompasses research from both Europe and America, as a casual perusal of the relative weight of citations in articles from the respective continents will make evident. This mutual exclusion occurs despite the commonality of the subject matter, and despite the fact that some of the classics that both sides draw on, such as Simmel, or Luhmann, are the same.

However, it also reflects somewhat different fundamental approaches to research. Europe-based researchers, as a broad generalization, tend to be more theory-driven, more wide-ranging in their treatment of trust, and more prone to making connections with classic theorists. North American scholars, on the other hand, tend to be more empirically focused, more specific in their approach, and more likely to reference current literature, especially if it is based on quantitative methodologies. Of course, there are notable exceptions on both sides, but as a generalization this holds true and, from our point of view, creates a sub-optimal situation for the field of trust research as a whole.

In order to draw together these divergent styles and trust research approaches, the editors (Reinhard and Aks), as a conscious policy, decided to invite the most prominent researchers in the field from both sides of the Atlantic to contribute to this *Handbook*. Each of the editors, being based respectively in Europe and the USA, thereafter undertook to manage the editorial process for contributions from the other continent – Reinhard handled the US-based contributions, and Aks the Europe-based ones. Moreover, each chapter was subject to friendly reviewing by a reviewer from the other side of the Atlantic.

The results of this elaborate exercise were, to our mind, deeply gratifying. Many authors received quite critical comments from the other continent. Often, the Europeans were told that their arguments were confusing and the question that they were tackling not clear-cut enough. In contrast, the Americans frequently had to read that their arguments were too narrowly based on just a few simple assumptions and insufficiently embedded in a wider theoretical context. The final versions of the chapters benefited considerably from this review process. Authors paid close and careful attention to the reviewers' comments and suggestions, and made significant, and sometimes major, modifications to their chapters.

Organization of the *Handbook*

We have organized the chapters of the *Handbook* by levels of analysis, as this seemed to us to be a powerful way to bring some order to the diverse field of trust research as reflected in the contributions that follow. Beginning from the micro level of the individual, to the level of the organization and the inter-organizational levels, to cross-level approaches, the level of the society and the economy, the chapters that follow cover them all (see Figure I.1).

Micro or individual level

The chapter by Dirks deals with the question of what it means when followers have or do not have trust in leaders. It refers to a number of empirical studies which have provided some insight into the nature of trust in leaders, in what factors are conducive or detrimental to developing trust in leaders, and in what can be done to repair trust in leaders where it has been damaged. In this context, the author of this chapter differentiates between a relationship-based and a character-based form of trust. Also, Dirks suggests that trust in supervisors and trust in senior management should be seen as two different issues. The empirical research that Dirks refers to provides evidence that these differences are important and that trust in leaders has individual-level effects and group-level effects. Leadership roles, Dirks argues towards the end of his chapter, may have inherent dilemmas with regard to building and damaging trust, and concludes that more investigation into how to repair trust in leader–follower relationships rates high on the research agenda.

Micro or individual level	Organization or inter-organization level	Cross-level approaches	Society and economy level
• Dirks • McKnight and Chervany • McEvily, Weber, Bicchieri and Ho • Kramer	• Long and Sitkin • Madhok • Bromiley and Harris • Van de Ven and Ring • Gargiulo and Ertug • Arena, Lazaric and Lorenz • van Witteloostuijn and van Wegberg • Deakin	• Currall and Inkpen • Nooteboom • Janowicz and Noorderhaven • McEvily and Zaheer	• Banerjee, Bowie and Pavone • Beckert • Casson and Della Giusta • Möllering • Sydow • Bachmann

Figure I.1   Organization of the Handbook's *chapters by level of analysis*

McKnight and Chervany's chapter is about the development of trust in early phases of relationships. In the first part of this contribution, the authors summarize the key features of the initial trust formation model which they had published, together with Cummings, in *Academy of Management Review* in 1998. In the second part, they review the literature that has been referring to and drawing on their model since. Useful applications, they found, appeared primarily in three areas: organization, e-commerce and virtual teams. Also, the discussion on several theoretical aspects of trust such as, for example, the interrelatedness of various trust types or the relationship between trust and distrust, are shown to have benefited from the authors' initial trust formation model. None the less a great deal more work, especially empirical testing of assumptions underlying the model, is necessary in future research.

McEvily, Weber, Bicchieri and Ho discuss the question of whether individual actors can actually trust collective entities or only individual members of groups. In doing so, they refer to Zaheer et al.'s work (1998), confirming the notion that 'interpersonal' and 'interorganizational' trust are different – albeit related – phenomena. The authors of this chapter report on the results of a laboratory experiment that they conducted in 2000/2001 with students from Carnegie Mellon and the University of Pittsburgh. In this 'trust game', which was played in two rounds, evidence was found that potential trustors use membership in a collectivity as a heuristic for determining the trustworthiness of potential trustees. Thus the authors conclude that it makes sense to differentiate between individuals and groups or organizations as the object of trust.

Kramer's chapter reconceptualizes trust as a decision dilemma. On the one hand, investing trust in a relationship promises benefits to the trustor but, on the other, the risk that trust may turn out to be misplaced can never be ruled out. As the aim of this contribution is to analyse how trust-related decisions are made, potential trustors' decisional and behavioural tendencies are examined and, Kramer suggests, this leads to the notion of the 'intuitive social auditor'. Although Kramer's social psychology perspective has a long history in laboratory research, he insists on the importance of studying social actors' expectations and interactions in real-world settings. In this vein, he describes his own empirical work in which he has applied 'autobiographical narratives and mental accounting' methods, as well as interview techniques, and found that trust can be understood as situated cognition where decisions are based on heuristics that allow social actors to free themselves from unmanageable complexity.

Organizational or inter-organizational level
Long and Sitkin analyse the relationship between task control and trust-building activities in their chapter. They suggest that it is appropriate to look at this relationship from a manager's point of view where the right balance between control and trust is an important facilitator of organizations' performance. Three different relationships are seen as possible and important: (a) the more control, the lower the level of trust can be maintained and vice versa (antithetical); (b) control and trust are independent of one another (orthogonal); and (c) control can foster trust and vice versa. Contrary to those views in the literature that assume that trust is merely a by-product in organizational relationships, Long and Sitkin insist that trust can be managed and that managers need to integrate their actions in promoting trust and control. Their chapter includes a model of action with regard to managers' control and trust-building activities within organizations.

The chapter by Madhok looks at the relationships between knowledge creation and knowledge transfers, trust, and monitoring and control costs that occur in firms. The author argues that firms need to strike the right balance between investing in monitoring potentially opportunistic behaviour and investing in the development of an atmosphere of trust. The latter, Madhok argues, is often more conducive to managing knowledge and value in the firm. The classic economic view which focuses on the opportunistic nature of employees and related incentive problems is seen as insufficient to understand the management of organizations. Finally, Madhok places emphasis on the management of knowledge flows in the value creation process and suggests that trust is a very important facilitator for the efficient coordination of resource knowledge.

The chapter by Bromiley and Harris, a wide-ranging critique of transaction cost economics (TCE) and its view of trust, suggests that trust and calculativeness are best understood as distinct concepts. The authors connect to Bromiley and Cummings (1995) and Cummings and Bromiley (1996) and find that, in a review of the literature citing these contributions, this work has been widely acknowledged by management researchers but largely ignored by TCE scholars. In the present chapter they explain why TCE 'assumes away' trust although the place for trust is obvious in the TCE framework. A key problem that they identify is that Williamson (1985; 1993) suggests an argument which is contradictory in itself. The notion of bounded rationality, for example, which is central within TCE, is not applied consistently in Williamson's work. TCE's assumption that trust has no explanatory power is shown to be an arbitrary one borne out by empirical studies that provide ample evidence that not only can the instrumental logic of business spill over to the social world of friends, family and leisure, as Williamson admits, but also the spill-over is a common phenomenon in the reverse direction. Although not claiming that the concept of calculative behaviour is useless, Bromiley and Harris insist that trust can more plausibly be the best explanation for certain types of behaviour in the world of business.

The chapter by Van de Ven and Ring reviews the literature that has referred to their much-cited articles published in 1992 (*Strategic Management Journal*) and 1994 (*Academy of Management Review*). These articles looked at antecedents and consequences of trust in interpersonal and inter-organizational relationships. The approach focused on trust as faith in the goodwill of others, as opposed to the notion of trust as a mechanism to provide predictability of actors' future behaviour. Within this perspective, Van de Ven and Ring discuss how trust may influence governance choices and how the process of trust can be conceptualized. Among other aspects of trust, these two issues were taken up by many scholars, both in theoretical and empirical work, and in many ways confirmed the value of their early articles. Towards the end of their chapter, the two authors reflect upon the trust research agenda for the future. Assuming that the general decline of trust in inter-personal and inter-organizational relations as well as in society will continue, Van de Ven and Ring suggest that the issue of how to repair trust and to practise forgiveness ranks high on the research agenda.

Gargiulo and Ertug 'seek to correct the optimistic bias that permeates the research on trust' by identifying negative outcomes of trust. They begin by reviewing the litera-ture on the benefits of trust, and show how the very same benefits in excess can have negative outcomes. In particular, they identify how trust lowers monitoring, produces greater commitment, and enhances the scale and scope of relationships. But those mechanisms may also lead to blind faith, complacency, and excess obligations from over-embeddedness. They end their wide-ranging review by presenting reasons for the creation of trust beyond the optimal threshold, and suggest directions for researching trust's downside.

Arena, Lazaric and Lorenz present a case study of the articulation and codification of knowledge by operators of a blast furnace in a steel plant which was threatened by massive layoffs and thereby faced the prospect of the extinction of a painstakingly devel-oped knowledge base. Traditionally, knowledge transfer had occurred through an appren-ticeship system and the plant decided to codify the tacit learning through an expert system. While trust might appear irrelevant in this case, in fact it was crucial because of three factors: the uncertain impact of knowledge codification on decision-making power; causal ambiguity; and knowledge obsolescence. In particular, the authors suggest that trust in management is necessary for the operators because the articulation and codifica-tion of knowledge represented a potential loss of power that emanated from the posses-sion of tacit knowledge in an organization. The chapter explores and identifies factors that helped the development of trust in this situation, primarily the formation of an 'epis-temic community'.

In 'Trust attitudes, network tightness and organizational survival' van Witteloostuijn and Wegberg examine the premise that trusting relationships, while beneficial, may lock the partners into inflexible positions, reducing their entrepreneurial ability to make new contacts. The authors draw on game theory, organization theory and network theories to develop a simulation model which shows that network tightness may be able to reduce the risk of opportunistic exploitation by spreading information about the trustworthiness of potential partners.

Deakin takes issue with two popular theses: one, the sociology-inspired view that parties to business transactions make little use of contract law, relying instead on infor-mal norms and trust; and two, the economics-inspired one that contract law directly influ-ences economic behaviour and outcomes, operating much as do surrogate prices. The author presents a unified framework drawing on research on conventions and norms. He argues that an exclusive focus on the extra-legal aspects of contracting misses the role that the legal system plays in the diffusion of contractual learning and the institutionalization of trust. Deakin outlines how the role of law and related public institutions promotes the growth of conventions which serve as coordination mechanisms in contracting practice and how the interplay between contract law and practice differs by institutional environment, using examples from Germany, Italy and Britain.

Cross-level approaches
Currall and Inkpen's chapter discerns three different levels at which trust can occur in an organizational context: trust between individuals, group-level trust, and trust at the organizational level. This contribution argues that trust is usually a multi-level phenomenon which makes it important to study trust not only at the focal level. For example, where trust at the group level is under review, Currall and Inkpen argue that the organizational as well as the individual level needs to be looked at in order to understand the complexity and the evolutionary nature of trust. The authors specifically refer to the literature on joint ventures to illustrate their argument. In the latter context, trust is also shown to sometimes be blocked and to not freely travel from one level to another.

In 'Forms, sources and processes of trust' Nooteboom posits that trust is a paradoxical concept that encompasses many dissimilar and sometimes conflicting dimensions. For example, one paradox is that trust can be based both on control (based on narrow self-interest) and can extend beyond control (beyond narrow self-interest). Other paradoxes include the complexity of trust: it is both a mental state and an action, both competence and intention-targeted, both emotionally and rationally based, and both positive and negative in its outcomes. Nooteboom clarifies and elaborates on these paradoxes and draws out the links between decision biases, heuristics and trust, and discusses the relationship between trust and contracts, and the limits of trust. He concludes by pulling some of his ideas together and applying them to a case study of trust in the Dutch police.

In 'Levels of inter-organizational trust' Janowicz and Noorderhaven tackle the issue of how organizations may be both the objects and the subjects of trust, and how trust may be appropriately conceptualized and measured as an organizational-level phenomenon. They suggest that it may be impractical to measure the trust held by all the members of an organization toward another organization since it is the boundary spanners that manage the relationship between the two organizations. At the same time, the trust held by top managers toward another firm may be different to that held by other members of the organization, and should be taken into account as strategic-level trust, which is independent of operational-level trust.

The chapter by McEvily and Zaheer looks at the literature that has discussed issues raised in an article published by Zaheer, McEvily and Perrone in *Organization Science* in 1998. That article dealt with the relationship between interpersonal trust, inter-organizational trust and performance. In this chapter, McEvily and Zaheer find that the core assumptions that they developed in their article have been elaborated on by numerous scholars. Two of their core assumptions, in particular, have received ample support in the literature: trust matters with regard to performance; and inter-organizational trust and interpersonal trust are related and affect performance differently. At the end of the chapter, the authors identify five top research questions, including whether trust lowers transaction costs or whether it indeed enhances transaction value, and the effects different forms of trust may exert on organizational performance.

Trust at the level of society and the economy

Banerjee, Bowie and Pavone look at the ethical dimension of trust. In their chapter, they discuss a variety of definitions of trust from the management and sociological literatures. What they find is that the acceptance of vulnerability by the trustor occurs in virtually all definitions of trust. Following from this observation, the authors argue that the normative dimension of the trust relationship originates in the assumption of the trustor that his or her vulnerability will not be exploited unfairly by the trustee. They show that the question of whether or not a trustee living up to the trustor's expectations is unethical can only be answered when the situational context of a specific trust relationship is considered. However, when circumstances change and this is beyond the control of the trustee, the disappointment of the trustor's expectations is not necessarily unethical.

Beckert argues that it is reductionist to view trust in markets as facilitated only by institutions, norms, long-term relations and calculation. Since market uncertainty persists despite these, it is important to consider the actions of the 'trust-taker' in persuading the 'trust-giver' to undertake the transaction. Drawing on signalling theory, Beckert posits that these actions are aimed at demonstrating the trust-taker's inherent trustworthiness with behaviours that signal the trust-taker's commitment, competence, integrity and so on, in a manner that would be costlier for an untrustworthy trust-taker.

Casson and Della Giusta adopt an economic approach to explaining the value and antecedents of trust in society and in business relations. They reason that from a neoclassical perspective trust is not only scarce itself but also valuable for efficient resource allocation. Trust is valuable because it allows transactions to occur at lower cost and because creating a reputation for trustworthy behaviour is beneficial. Incentives help generate trust in this setting. At the same time, trust also has an emotional and moral basis, and together the authors see trust as 'a belief that the other party will honour their obligations'. Obligations themselves are of different types and have certain characteristics that signify the depth of trust. Different kinds of moral authority and values are identified that are associated with trust.

Möllering explores, elaborates on and provides broad theoretical support for the notion that institutions matter for trust. While this by itself is not a new idea, the author presents a systematic treatment of how institutions can be seen as trustworthy and how individual actors both interpret and come to trust institutions. He presents a review and commentary on the nature and bases of institutional-based trust and develops his basic thesis by applying sociological concepts such as 'natural attitude' and 'institutional isomorphism' to the problem of institutional trust. Drawing widely on neo-institutionalist theories, theories of institutional isomorphism, of institutionalized rules, roles and routines, and Giddens's concept of 'active trust', Möllering echoes Simmel's contributions regarding the role of agency in the development and creation of trust, symbolized by the 'leap of faith' in trust.

Sydow's chapter takes Giddens's structuration lens to the question of trust, and presents a complex but appropriately socialized picture of the role of trust in inter-organizational contexts. The chapter focuses on the issue of how organizations can not only be trusted, but, as social systems, how they can also themselves actively trust. The author uses structuration theory to explain trust in inter-organizational relationships whereby the processual and embedded aspects of trust-building are emphasized. Trust is conceptualized 'as both an ingredient and an outcome of structuration processes'. Furthermore, trust in persons is distinguished from trust in systems, although they are inter-linked. Sydow also considers the role of knowledge, control and power as they relate to organizational trust; these are not simply substitutes for trust but are related to trust in complex and intriguing ways.

Bachmann, finally, sets up the problem of trust as one of coordinating the expectations of social actors, and reducing complexity and uncertainty. Trust, facilitated by institutional norms, converts the uncertainty into more acceptable risk. The role of institutional trust is highly salient, as it paved the way for economic modernization by creating 'mass-produced' trust, the costs of which were borne by the business system, not by individual businesspeople. Where the institutional environment is weak, interactional or personal trust has to step in, which is costly. Bachmann goes on to posit that power can be a combinable functional substitute for trust, and also has interactional and institutional variants. Depending on the institutional environment, he argues, trust and power tend to appear in different forms which relate to one another in different ways.

Themes in trust research – future perspectives

In addition to being conceptualized by levels of analysis, the chapters of this *Handbook* cover a variety of issues that the research on trust has identified as key to understanding this phenomenon and that point the way for future research. Six basic themes run through the contributions to this volume (see Figure I.2). The first concerns the antecedents and consequences of trust and the question of whether and how trust can be managed actively in an organizational context. The chapters by Dirks, McKnight and Chervany, as well as Van de Ven and Ring, relate to these questions. A second 'big issue' in trust research is the relationship between trust and concepts such as (tacit) knowledge, contracts, calculativeness and control. The chapters by Long and Sitkin, Madhok, by Arena, Lazaric and

Antecedents, consequences and management of trust	Trust, knowledge, contracts, calculativeness and control	Trust as a complex phenomenon, subjects and objects of trust
• Dirks • McKnight and Chervany • Van de Ven and Ring	• Long and Sitkin • Madhok • Arena, Lazaric and Lorenz • Bromiley and Harris • Deakin • Sydow	• McEvily, Weber, Bicchieri and Ho • Curall and Inkpen • Nooteboom • Janowicz and Noorderhaven • McEvily and Zaheer

Reintegrating trust into economic and social theory	Dark side of trust and ethical dimensions of trust	Methodological approaches to trust
• Beckert • Casson and Della Giusta • Möllering • Bachmann	• Gargiulo and Ertug • Banerjee, Bowie and Pavone	• Kramer • van Witteloostuijn and van Wegberg

Figure I.2   Organization of the Handbook's *chapters by thematic clusters*

Lorenz, and by Bromiley and Harris as well as Sydow focus on these issues. A third area that receives much attention refers to the insight that trust is a relatively complex phenomenon due the fact that it can occur at various levels of analysis (see the contributions by Currall and Inkpen as well as Nooteboom). Questions such as who can be considered a subject or an object of trust follow quite naturally and deserve to be investigated thoroughly (see the chapters by McEvily, Weber, Bicchieri and Ho, by Janowicz and Noorderhaven and by McEvily and Zaheer). Fourth, quite strong efforts are being undertaken in (re)integrating the concept of trust into basic economic (see the chapters by Beckert, and Casson and Della Giusta) and social theory (see the contributions by Möllering and by Bachmann). Fifth, slightly less represented by current research, but increasingly recognized, are areas such as those covered by Gargiulo and Ertug (the dark side of trust) and by Banerjee, Bowie and Pavone (the ethical dimension of trust). Finally, the question of what is an appropriate methodology to research trust is, either implicitly or explicitly, present in many contributions to the debate on trust. In this volume, the chapters by Kramer (autobiographical narratives and mental accounting) and by van Witteloostuijn and Wegberg (game theory) mark the two ends of the scale.

While far from suggesting that this set represents an exhaustive list of themes in trust research, we claim that, given the current state of the art, these are the areas about which we know the most but also about which we need to know much more. Future research on trust is most likely to deal with a number of blind spots on our current trust research map, or even revise the map altogether, but this, surely, seems better than moving into the wild without any map. This *Handbook* is meant to provide such a map that, in our view, no trust research adventurer should miss consulting.

Acknowledgments

We acknowledge with thanks helpful comments by Jared Harris on an earlier draft of this introduction.

References

Arrow, K.J. (1974), *The Limits of Organization*. New York: Norton.

Bachmann (2001), Trust, power and control in trans-organizational relations. *Organization Studies* **22** (2): 337–65.

Beck, U. (1986), *Risikogesellschaft. Auf dem Weg in eine andere Moderne [Risk Society. Towards a New Modernity]*. Frankfurt/M.: Suhrkamp.

Bradach, J. and R.G. Eccles (1989), Price, authority and trust: From ideal types to plural forms. *Annual Review of Sociology* **15**: 97–118.

Bromiley, P. and L.L. Cummings (1995), Transaction costs in organizations with trust. In: Bies, R., B.H. Sheppard and R.J. Lewicki (eds), *Research on Negotiation in Organizations*. Greenwich, CT: JAI Press, Vol. 5: 219–47.

Coleman, J. (1990), *Foundations of Social Theory*. Cambridge, MA: Harvard University Press.

Cummings, L.L. and Bromiley P. (1996), The Organizational Trust Inventory (OTI): Development and validation. In: R.M. Kramer and T.R. Tyler (eds), *Trust in Organizations: Frontiers of Theory and Research*. Thousand Oaks, CA: Sage.

Giddens, A. (1984), *The Constitution of Society*. Cambridge: Polity.

Giddens, A. (1990), *The Consequences of Modernity*. Stanford, CA: Stanford University Press.

Grey, C. and C. Garsten (2001), Trust, control and post-bureaucracy. *Organization Studies* **22** (2): 229–50.

Luhmann, N. (1979), *Trust and Power*. Chichester: Wiley.

Luhmann, N. (1984), *Soziale Systeme [Social Systems]*. Frankfurt/M.: Suhrkamp.

McEvily, B., V. Perrone and A. Zaheer (2003), Trust as an organizing principle. *Organization Science* **14**: 91–103.

Macneil, I.R. (1980), *The New Social Contract. An Inquiry into Modern Contractual Relations*. New Haven, CT: Yale University Press.

Reed, M. (2001), Organization, trust and control. A realist perspective. *Organization Studies* **22** (2): 201–28.

Reed, M. (2005), Beyond the iron cage? Bureaucracy and democracy in the knowledge economy and society. In: Paul Du Gay (ed.), *The Values of Bureaucracy*, Oxford: Oxford University Press: 115–40.

Ring, P.S. and A.H. Van de Ven (1992), Structuring cooperative relationships between organizations. *Strategic Management Journal* **13**: 483–98.

Ring, P. S. and A.H. Van de Ven (1994), Developmental processes in cooperative interorganizational relationships. *Academy of Management Review* **19**: 90–118.

Sako, M. (1992), *Prices, Quality and Trust. Inter-firm Relations in Britain and Japan*. Cambridge: Cambridge University Press.

Williamson, O.E. (1985), *The Economic Institutions of Capitalism*. New York: The Free Press.

Williamson, O.E. (1993), Calculativeness, trust and economic organization. *Journal of Law and Economics*, **36**: 453–86.

Zaheer, A., B. McEvily and V. Perrone (1998), Does trust matter? Exploring the effects of interorganizational and interpersonal trust on performance. *Organization Science* **9** (2): 141–59.

PART I

MICRO OR INDIVIDUAL LEVEL

1 Three fundamental questions regarding trust in leaders

Kurt T. Dirks

Leaders play a prominent role in organizations – particularly from the point of view of followers. The formal and informal power that leaders possess puts them in a position to significantly influence followers as they set the goals that individuals work toward, control resources they value, and make decisions that impact their compensation and careers. As a consequence, followers have significant interest in evaluating whether or not they can trust the leader. While the recognition of the centrality of trust in leaders has long been of concern to followers, only recently has it taken on a prominent role in organizational research.

This chapter examines three fundamental questions about trust in leaders: why is trust in leaders important? What factors build or undermine trust in leaders? What can leaders do to try to repair trust after it is damaged? The chapter attempts to summarize research on these three questions, including theoretical foundations and empirical evidence. It also raises some issues for future research on the three questions. The chapter is an attempt to summarize my own perspectives and research on these questions, but I also draw liberally from work of other scholars.

In this chapter, I conceptualize trust as a psychological state held by the follower involving confident positive expectations about the behavior and intentions of the leader, as they relate to the follower.

Theoretical perspectives

Over the past four decades, trust in one's leader(s) has been an important concept in multiple disciplines: organizational psychology, management, public administration, organizational communication, and education, among others. In research on the organizational behavior literature, for instance, trust has been identified as an important (although arguably under-recognized) part of numerous leadership theories. Transformational and charismatic leaders build trust in their followers (Kirkpatrick and Locke, 1996; Podsakoff et al., 1990). Trust is a crucial element of the consideration dimension of effective leader behavior (Fleishman and Harris, 1962) and leader–member exchange theory (Schriesheim et al., 1999). Other studies show that promoting trust can be important for leader effectiveness (Bass, 1990; Hogan et al., 1994). In addition to its role in leadership theories, trust has been linked to positive job attitudes, organizational justice, psychological contracts and effectiveness in terms of communication, organizational relationships and conflict management.

Although the vastness of this research base can be a potential strength for understanding trust, it can also present a challenge in terms of accessing and making sense of this body of research. In an attempt to integrate some of the research literature regarding the processes by which trust forms, and the nature of the construct itself, research to date can be viewed in terms of two qualitatively different theoretical perspectives of trust in leadership in the literature: a *relationship-based* perspective and a *character-based* perspective (Dirks and Ferrin, 2002). Distinguishing between these two perspectives is important because, as I explore further in this chapter, they have implications for how trust develops in the workplace, as well as the consequences of trust.

As the name denotes, the relationship-based perspective focuses on the nature of the leader–follower relationship and, more precisely, how the follower understands the nature of the relationship. For instance, some researchers describe trust in leadership as operating according to a social exchange process (e.g. Konovsky and Pugh, 1994; Whitener et al., 1998). Followers see their relationship with their leader as beyond the standard economic contract such that the parties operate on the basis of trust, goodwill and the perception of mutual obligations. The exchange denotes a high-quality relationship, and issues of care and consideration in the relationship are central. The form of exchange might be best be characterized as 'communal' in nature, whereby individuals provide benefits in response to the needs of the partner as opposed to the focus on what will be received (Clark and Mills, 1979; Fiske, 1992) – although most research has stripped away much of the effect. Researchers have used this perspective in describing how trust in leader–follower relationships elicits citizenship behavior (Konovsky and Pugh, 1994), on the operation of transformational leadership and trust (Pillai et al., 1999), and on the critical aspects of leader–member exchange relationships (e.g. Schriesheim et al., 1999).

The character-based perspective, in contrast, focuses on the perception of the leader's character and how it impacts a follower's vulnerability in a hierarchical relationship (e.g. Mayer et al., 1995). According to this perspective, trust-related concerns about a leader's character are important because the leader may have authority to make decisions that have a significant impact on a follower and the follower's ability to achieve his or her goals (e.g. promotions, pay, work assignments, layoffs). This perspective implies that followers make inferences about the leader's characteristics such as integrity, dependability, fairness and ability, and that these inferences have consequences for work behavior and attitudes. Drawing a parallel with the relationship-based perspective, the character-based perspective might include forms of exchange in which the focus is on what will be received in the exchange and the likelihood of receiving it (Clark and Mills, 1979; Fiske, 1992). Examples of research using this perspective include models of trust based on characteristics of the trustee (Mayer et al., 1995), research on perceptions of supervisor characteristics (e.g. Cunningham and MacGregor, 2000; Oldham, 1975) and research on some forms of leader behavior (Jones et al., 1975). In both of the two perspectives, trust is a belief or perception held by the follower; it is not a property of the relationship or the leader *per se*.

Whereas these two perspectives capture much of the existing research on trust in leaders, there is an additional perspective from the trust literature that warrants consideration. Researchers have discussed 'institutional' or 'system' perspectives on trust (e.g. Bachmann, 2001; Zucker, 1986). These researchers suggest that trust in the system in which an individual is embedded can serve as a powerful means of reducing perceived vulnerability. Thus, instead of drawing inferences about the leader's characteristics or the relationship, the individual holds perceptions about the institution or organization. The implication for the present topic is that system trust might increase the likelihood that individuals will follow the leader, be willing to invest energy in organizational goals, and so on. It might also play an important role when individuals have limited confidence in the specific leader *per se*. This perspective would provide a multi-level understanding of trust in leaders. The idea of system trust clearly deserves further consideration in research on the topic of trust in leaders.

Does trust in leadership matter?
Although some individuals may find it intuitively appealing to believe that trust in leaders is important for individuals, groups and organizations, social scientists have provided mixed views and evidence on this issue. For instance, scholarly views have ranged from trust as having little or no impact (Williamson, 1993) to trust being a concept of substantial importance (Golembiewski and McConkie, 1975) to organizational effectiveness. In this section, I examine some of the theory and evidence for the impact of trust through the lenses of two theoretical perspectives and discuss some unresolved questions.

Consequences of trust for individuals
The two theoretical perspectives outlined earlier describe two different mechanisms by which trust might affect behavior and performance. The relationship-based perspective is based on principles of social exchange and deals with employees' willingness to reciprocate care and consideration that a leader expresses in a relationship. That is, individuals who feel that their leader has, or will, demonstrate care and consideration tend to reciprocate this sentiment in the form of desirable behaviors. Konovsky and Pugh (1994) drew on this logic, suggesting that a social exchange relationship encourages individuals to spend more time on required tasks and be willing to engage in organizational citizenship behavior (i.e. going above and beyond the call of duty).

In contrast, the character-based perspective focuses on how perceptions of the leader's character impact a follower's vulnerability in a hierarchical relationship. Drawing on this idea, Mayer et al. (1995) provided a model proposing that when followers believe their leaders have integrity, capability or benevolence, they should be more comfortable engaging in behaviors that put them at risk (e.g. sharing sensitive information). For example, Mayer and Gavin (1999) suggested that when employees believe their leader cannot be trusted (e.g. because the leader is perceived not to have integrity), they will divert energy toward 'covering their back', which can detract from employees' work performance. Both theoretical perspectives suggest that trust may result in higher performance and citizenship behavior – but reach this end by distinct, and potentially complementary, routes.

Dirks and Ferrin (2002) conducted a meta-analysis that summarizes the research over the past four decades. They report that trust in leadership had a significant relationship with individual outcomes, including job performance ($r = 0.16$), organizational citizenship behavior (altruism, $r = 0.19$), turnover intentions ($r = -0.40$), job satisfaction ($r = 0.51$), organizational commitment ($r = 0.49$), and a commitment to the leader's decisions ($r = 0.24$). Data from the samples were drawn from a variety of contexts ranging from financial institutions, to manufacturing firms, to military units to public institutions. The effect sizes for behavioral and performance outcomes tend to be as high or greater than the effect sizes observed between similar criteria and other key attitudinal variables such as job satisfaction, organizational commitment, job involvement and procedural justice (for examples of similar meta-analytic reviews, see Brown, 1996; Colquitt et al., 2001; Mathieu and Zajac, 1990). Thus, one conclusion is that, compared to these other frequently studied variables, trust is as important, or more important, to the effective functioning of organizations.

Trust in different types of leadership referents   In summarizing this work, it is useful to consider different leadership referents. To this point, I (like much of the literature) have used the term 'trust in leader' without allowing for the variation in leadership roles. Researchers have given little attention to the question of when an organization should focus its efforts on establishing trust in supervisor–subordinate relationships versus on building trust in senior management. Although building trust in both relationships is likely to be important, limited resources may cause organizations to focus more efforts on some relationships than others.

Following social exchange principles, the relationship-based perspective implies that followers will reciprocate benefits received, and that individuals will target their efforts to reciprocate toward the source of the benefit received. For example, trust in a direct leader should be associated with reciprocation primarily aimed at that leader, as opposed to senior leadership (e.g. top management team). Likewise, efforts to reciprocate trust in senior leadership would be targeted toward senior management.

Research reviewed by Bass (1990) indicates that supervisors tend to perform activities such as managing performance and day-to-day activities on the job. In contrast, senior executives perform more strategic functions such as setting strategic direction, allocating resources to various projects and departments, communicating to employees the goals of the organization, and so on. Given the distinction in the roles of the different leadership referents, reciprocating trust in one's immediate leader may be related to job-related outcomes such as increasing job performance or engaging in citizenship behaviors. For instance, individuals might give extra time to fulfill supervisor requests, or may engage in helping behavior such as staying late to help a supervisor or co-worker due to a social exchange process involving a supervisor. In contrast, trust in senior leadership may involve reciprocating to that referent with high commitment to the organization and its mission.

Supporting these ideas, Dirks and Ferrin (2002) found that trust in a supervisor was more strongly related to job-level variables, whereas trust in senior leadership was more strongly related to organizational-level variables. As one example, they found that job performance related at a significantly higher level with trust in supervisor ($r = 0.17$) versus trust in senior management ($r = 0.00$). In contrast, organizational commitment was related at a significantly higher level with trust in senior leadership ($r = 0.57$) than with trust in a supervisor ($r = 0.44$). Further research is needed, however, as this research was not able to examine these differences within a single sample to separate the unique variance attributable to trust in each referent.

Limitations and future research   Although there has been considerable research on the relationship of trust and individual outcomes, the literature is limited on several important issues. First, almost all research to date has been based on cross-sectional designs where the direction of causality cannot be inferred. For instance, rather than trust impacting job performance, it is possible that for some employees, higher job performance inspires increased trust in one's leader. What are needed are experimental and longitudinal research designs that empirically test causality. Second, few or no studies have explored explicitly *why* trust is related to work outcomes. Empirical research is needed that explores the mediating processes by which trust predicts various individual attitudes and behavior. A corollary of this research question is how the two perspectives described above differ with respect to how trust relates to various attitudes and behaviors. For example, is trust arising from one perspective more significant and enduring than trust arising from the other perspective? What is the implication of establishing a high level of trust from the character perspective, but a low level in terms of the relational perspective? Third, research is also needed to explore more thoroughly the differences between the relational and character-based perspectives. As an initial step toward addressing this issue, the results from Dirks and Ferrin (2002) indicated that for some variables, such as job performance and altruism behavior, the relational model may be more predictive, while for other variables, such as job satisfaction and organizational commitment, the character model may be more predictive.

Consequences for groups and organizations
The research described above suggests that trust is associated with individual-level effects, although their magnitude might be small to moderate. If trust in leaders indeed has a small to moderate relationship with proximal outcomes such as individual performance, one might ask whether trust in leaders is associated with more distal 'bottom-line' benefits for groups and organizations. Three recent studies suggest that it is.

Trust in leadership is related to bottom-line outcomes for teams and work groups, as demonstrated in Dirks's (2000) study of National Collegiate Athletic Association (NCAA) basketball teams. Using survey data from players collected early in the season, and statistically adjusting for other potential determinants of team performance (i.e. player talent and tenure, coach experience and record, pre-season performance, performance in prior years, and trust between team members), trust in head coach (team leader) accounted for almost 7 percent of the variance in winning percentage. Illustrating the substance of the relationship, the team with the highest trust rating played for the national championship, while the team with the lowest trust score won approximately 10 percent of their remaining games (with the coach being fired at the end of the season). The variance explained by trust was nearly equivalent to that explained by team member ability. Moreover, in a context where one would expect trust in one's team mates to be highly crucial for success, trust in leadership proved to be a more important predictor of team performance than was trust in team mates.

The effect is not limited to teams or sports contexts. Davis et al. (2000) examined the relationship between trust in a business unit's general manager and organizational performance. They found that trust was significantly related to sales, profits and employee turnover in a small sample of restaurants. Simons and McLean Parks (2002) investigated whether a senior manager's 'behavioral integrity' created collective trust in the senior manager that, in turn, translated into higher performance. Using a sample of hotels, they reported that perceptions of behavioral integrity and trust in the senior manager were related to customer satisfaction and profitability. The model explained almost 13 percent of variance in profitability; trust appeared to play a major role in these effects.

In summary, all three studies demonstrate support for the conclusion that trust is related to 'bottom-line' effects in terms of group and organizational performance. What is interesting is the magnitude of the effect suggested by the studies – the effect is even stronger than might be expected based on the data from studies of trust at the individual level and its relationship with seemingly more proximal factors such as individual performance and organizational citizenship behavior. Understanding why this occurs, as well as when trust in leadership is related to group and organizational performance, requires additional theory and research.

As with research at the individual level of analysis, studies of trust at the group and organizational levels need to examine the direction of causality. The results from Dirks (2000) indicate that performance and trust are reciprocally related: past performance impacts trust which in turn impacts future performance. Second, research might also explore exactly how trust impacts group and organizational performance. We suggest that trust in leadership might impact group or organizational performance in two complementary ways. One way is via increasing individual-level outcomes such as individual performance and citizenship behavior. A second way is suggested by *post hoc* interviews from my study of basketball teams. In explaining why trust in a leader is important to team success, one coach offered the following analogy of a team of horses: 'In order to pull the wagon, all the horses have to be pulling in the same direction and cadence. Trust helps with that.' In making a similar point, one player gave the following illustration: 'once we developed trust in Coach ——, the progress we made increased tremendously because we were no longer asking questions or were apprehensive. Instead, we were buying in and believing that if we worked our hardest, we were going to get there.' These observations illustrate that trust in leadership allows the individuals in the team or organization to suspend their individual doubts and personal motives and direct their efforts toward a common team goal. In summary, trust in a leader has two complementary impacts: it first helps maximize individual efforts and performance and second harnesses or focuses those efforts toward a common goal or strategy. These ideas provide only a beginning to a complex issue that deserves further research. For example, it is possible that relational and character-based perspectives operate together in this process: the relational elements of trust may inspire individuals to be willing to go above and beyond requirements and the character-based factors such as perceived competence and integrity make individuals willing to take the risk of focusing these toward a common goal.

Last, research might explore the conditions under which trust in leadership is more or less important. Building on Martin Luther King's observation that 'the measure of a man is not where he stands in moments of comfort, but where he stands at times of challenge and controversy', from a follower's perspective, trust in a leader may be particularly important in times of challenge and adversity. *Post hoc* analysis of the data from the basketball study described above shows that, although trust in a leader may indeed be higher for teams that are winning than teams that are losing, the relationship between trust and performance is significantly greater when the team is doing poorly. Specifically, for teams that had been performing well or moderately well, there was little or no relationship between trust and performance. However, for teams that had been performing poorly, the relationship was positive and strong. One interpretation of these results is that trust in a leader may not be salient or may not be seen by employees as critical during times in which the environment is positive (the team is doing well). However, trust is highly relevant to employee performance when the environment is negative (e.g. recessive economy, organization in decline, little system trust). Researchers need to explore these and other conditions under which trust is more versus less related to performance.

The moderating role of trust
Much of the work on trust, including the work described above, models the effect of trust in a relatively straightforward manner: trust results in distinct (main) effects such as more positive attitudes, higher levels of cooperation (and other forms of workplace behavior),

and superior levels of performance. A handful of studies suggest that trust instead facilitates the effects of other determinants on desired outcomes. Hence, instead of proposing that trust directly results in desirable outcomes, this model suggests that trust provides the conditions under which certain outcomes, such as cooperation and higher performance, are likely to occur.

This idea was explored by Dirks and Ferrin (2001), who proposed that trust engenders two distinct processes through which it fosters or inhibits positive outcomes in the relationship. First, trust affects how one *assesses the future behavior of the leader*. In one of the earliest empirical studies of trust, Read (1962) found that as individuals' motivation to be promoted increased, they were less likely to share negative information about their work with their bosses. He also found that this relationship would be moderated by trust; that is, the tendency to withhold information was particularly acute when the subordinate did not trust the boss. Second, trust also affects how one *interprets the past (or present) actions of the leader*, and the motives underlying the actions. As an example, Robinson (1996) found that initial trust in an employer moderated the relationship between a psychological contract violation and subsequent trust in the employer. She argued that because of the tendency toward cognitive consistency, initial trust guides individuals to selectively perceive and interpret information about the violation in different ways. For example, an individual with high initial trust will tend to perceive the violation in ways consistent with that level of trust (e.g. as unintentional, a misunderstanding); through this process a high level of trust is preserved. Under low trust, the opposite was proposed to occur.

In sum, trust may often not operate as a direct causal force or elicit particular outcomes itself. Instead, trust moderates the effect of primary determinants (causal factors) on outcomes by affecting how one assesses the future behavior or interprets the past actions of another party. This perspective has seen limited use in the research on trust in leaders, despite its potential. Indeed, the papers reviewed by Dirks and Ferrin (2001) showed significant and consistent support for the ideas.

Factors that build or undermine trust in leaders
Given that trust in leaders does facilitate important outcomes for organizations, a key question is: what factors build or undermine trust? Intuitively, one would expect that one of the most important factors determining trust is the behavior of the leader. Scholars have seized on this idea and it has become a centerpiece for research directed at understanding the factors that determine trust. Attribution theory is well suited for this approach and has been used by several scholars. Attribution theory attempts to understand individuals' causal explanations for events and individuals' perceptions and judgments of others. Trust development can be viewed as an attributional process. For example, an individual may develop beliefs about another person's trustworthiness based on whether the person's behavior is judged to be caused by internal versus situational factors (e.g. Korsgaard et al., 2002). The theory is also helpful for understanding other factors that play into this process such as biases in trust development, including the correspondence bias, which is one of the most commonly documented attributional biases, and the effects of suspicion (Ferrin and Dirks, 2003).

Other theoretical frameworks in the literature rely on a similar logic. For example, exchange theory discussed how past behaviors in the relationship are used to diagnose trustworthiness in future exchanges (Blau, 1964; Konovsky and Pugh, 1994).

This framework is not inconsistent with attribution theory but instead tends to focus on the social, as opposed to the psychological, processes. Lewicki and Bunker (1996) developed a model that describes the process by which trust develops through interactions between two parties. All three of the perspectives place the responsibility for building and maintaining trust in the hands of the leader. Indeed, Whitener et al. assert that 'managers' actions and behaviors provide the foundation for trust and that it is actually management's responsibility to take the first step' (1998: 514).

Thus, the question is what types of behaviors should leaders engage in to build trust? Answering this question relies on recognizing what type of behaviors will be seen as signaling different bases of trustworthiness such as integrity, competence and benevolence (Mayer et al., 1995). Obviously, there are many behaviors that can signal these factors. Whitener et al. (1998) proposed five categories of behavior that impact trust, including behavioral consistency, behavioral integrity, participative decision-making, communication and demonstrating concern, although they did not align these with specific forms of trust.

The Dirks and Ferrin (2002) meta-analysis provides insight into which behaviors tend to be most highly correlated with trust. One set of variables that is most highly associated with trust is different forms of fairness. In particular, perceived fairness of procedures used to make decisions ($r = 0.61$) and interpersonal interactions in the decision process ($r = 0.65$) have particularly strong associations with trust. Their analysis also suggested that procedural fairness is more likely to be associated with character-based forms of trust than relationship-based. Other forms of behaviors that were strongly associated with trust, and which were related to Whitener et al.'s classification, were perceived organizational support ($r = 0.69$), participative decision-making ($r = 0.46$), and failure to meet expectations of subordinates ($r = -0.40$).

Clearly, trust is a function of more factors beyond the behaviors that the leaders engage in. Factors such as demographic differences, personality of leaders and subordinates, and structural factors, will also play a role and are worthy of understanding. It is my contention, however, that these factors tend to play a much smaller role in determining trust or that some of these factors will operate via their effect on behavior. For example, personality of leaders, demographic differences, or structural factors may influence leader behavior which in turn may impact trust (e.g. see Whitener et al., 1998). And efforts to make a difference in practice may be most effective by focusing on behaviors as the base.

The challenge of building and maintaining trust in leadership
As noted above, the ideas that behaviors serve as the basis for trust, and the behaviors that have been studied, are relatively intuitive and many leaders would instinctively agree. Hence, what may be more interesting and more puzzling than these factors is the apparent challenge associated with building or maintaining trust in the workplace. For example, a recent survey suggested that almost two-thirds of employees report having little or no trust for their employers (AFL–CIO, 2001). Another survey found that over 52 percent of employees don't trust the management of their organization and don't believe the information that they receive (Katcher, 2002).

From the leaders' perspective, we also suspect that many leaders who have developed high levels of trust may be achieving less trust than they would like. Anecdotal evidence describing this notion comes from the study of college basketball teams described earlier

(Dirks, 2000). After the research was completed, one of the coaches in the study telephoned the first author to inquire about the level of trust that his players had reported about him in the survey. The data showed that his ratings were quite high. Even though his trust rating was high compared to other teams in the study, he expressed surprise and disappointment in these results because he had expected it to be higher given his efforts: 'I don't understand. Why don't they trust me completely?' This coach had almost two decades of coaching experience, was the recipient of almost every major coaching award, and felt that he had the best interests of his players at heart and worked hard at establishing relationships with them. This anecdote is important in that it reveals that even this highly successful leader, largely trusted by his players, was challenged to achieve the level of trust he desired and expected.

What factors may account for the challenge that leaders face in building and maintaining trust? There are clearly numerous potential answers to this question. One might, for example, place the challenge within the leader. Some researchers have suggested that leaders are often selected on the basis of technical rather than interpersonal competencies (Hogan et al., 1994). Hence, this argument would suggest that many leaders do not always possess the competencies or motivation to build trust. The principles for building trust do not, on the surface, appear to be mysterious, so one reason for the challenge of building trust is that many leaders may prefer to focus their efforts on other goals.

The challenge of building and maintaining trust in the leadership role may also lie partly in the role itself, as opposed to the individuals in those roles. I feel that this represents one of the more interesting and plausible reasons. These reasons might be called 'trust dilemmas' because of the many tradeoffs involved in maintaining trust in multiple relationships.

As part of a larger research study in a financial services firm, Daniel Skarlicki and I conducted focus groups investigating the behaviors that build or break trust. As expected, many individuals mentioned the behaviors discussed earlier (e.g. fairness, behavioral integrity, etc.). An unanticipated and interesting theme regarding the implementation of these behaviors arose: roles in organizations, particularly leadership roles, put individuals in dilemmas which make it difficult to consistently engage in trust-building behaviors, and often encourage individuals to engage in trust-breaking behaviors. More specifically, these situations put leaders in a dilemma: they may have to simultaneously *meet the expectations of one party* and *violate the expectations of another*. For example, a leader might face demands to meet goals set by superiors (e.g. cut costs), and have made compensation promises to subordinates that conflict with those demands. As another example, leaders often feel the need to give special treatment to high-potential employees, while having expectations from other employees about treating all subordinates (even those with limited potential) as equals. Or, leaders must often try to manage the perceptions of diverse constituencies and in doing so represent themselves in inconsistent ways (Simons, 2002). Hence the leader faces a 'trust dilemma' in which individuals are forced to take an action that may sustain the trust of one party, but break the trust of another.

Several psychological factors associated with attribution processes grounded *in the perceivers* are also likely to accentuate the problem. First, leaders face a high level of scrutiny from followers because the latter are outcome-dependent on the former (Berscheid et al., 1976). As a consequence of the increased scrutiny, employees may be particularly likely to notice when managers do not fulfill expectations (Simons, 2002). Illustrating this idea by examining pairs of graduate students and their advisors, Kramer (1996) found that the former spent a substantial amount of their time observing the latter and ruminating about the behavior (they spent three to nine times more time than faculty in these activities!). In addition, students often drew very negative conclusions about faculty behaviors toward them, even when those behaviors had no intention behind them. In searching for signs of whether or not to trust a leader, individuals may find trust dilemmas particularly rich in information, given that these situations may be seen as revealing a leader's 'true' motives as they are put to the test under conflicting pressures.

A second factor involved in the perceptual process builds on a well-established finding from attribution research that indicates that individuals typically discount the extent to which situational factors are the cause of individual behavior, relative to dispositional factors (Fiske and Taylor, 1991). In other words, individuals may over-attribute the behavior to the leader's disposition – for example, his or her trustworthiness – as opposed to the dilemma the leader faces. When individuals have an unfulfilled expectation there may be an increased chance that they may search for the source of responsibility in the disposition of the person causing that negative outcome.

Third, trust may be more easily broken than built; a single incident of broken trust may create a significant drop in broken trust (e.g. Lewicki and Wiethoff, 2000). Hence, even if a party violates the expectations of followers in a single incident, that incident can create a significant drop in the level of trust and make followers more sensitive to future actions that may be interpreted as a violation. As noted above, trust dilemmas create the conditions under which a single violation is likely.

In summary, future research might explore the factors that challenge the difficulty in building trust. Exploring how trust in leaders is built and broken in situations involving 'trust dilemmas' may be an interesting direction to take. Research on these would involve identifying the characteristics of managers more or less likely to get into these dilemmas or who are more or less able to navigate them once they are in them.

Regarding the former, the literature on cognitive biases may highlight why some managers are more likely to get into such dilemmas. For example, managers may vary on an overconfidence bias that creates a propensity for them to overcommit to promises which will be difficult to fulfill.

Some managers might also simply be more skilled at navigating the trust dilemmas they face by managing impressions. As one example, some managers may be effective at making their trust-related behaviors visible to subordinates or be better at creating perceptions of sincerity (warranted or not) of the leader's gestures. This line of inquiry will have implications for managers who might not understand why, despite exhibiting the necessary behaviors, they might not be reaping the rewards of doing so.

When trust is damaged

At some point in their careers, many leaders are likely to damage trust in some relationships (or at least the employees perceive it to be damaged). Robinson and Rousseau (1994) discovered that 55 percent of their respondents reported that their employer had violated a psychological contract and that this violation significantly reduced trust. These issues have become particularly salient in recent years with publicity in the news media that is likely to make individuals more aware of violations or at least more vigilant.

While the attributional perspective described above is still a core theoretical basis of trust, there are at least two reasons why the process of repairing trust may be more difficult, and require different strategies, than building trust initially (Kim et al., 2004). One of the challenges of repairing trust is that the magnitude of the required increase in trust may actually be greater than in initial trust development, given that a violation causes trust to plunge below its initial level. A second challenge of repairing trust is that mistrusted parties must not only re-establish positive expectations, but also overcome negative expectations from events that may remain salient over time.

Despite the importance of addressing such issues, surprisingly few studies have directly examined how trust might be repaired. And much of the work that has been conducted has not focused on trust in leaders *per se*. This work does, however, provide relevant insights.

A significant amount of recent research has focused on how individuals verbally respond in the aftermath of a trust violation. This work is built on the notion that providing a verbal response is an important first step in stemming the damage and that this may shape how subsequent behaviors are interpreted. For example, trustworthy behavior is likely to be more effective following a verbal signal of redemption (e.g. apology), as the verbal signal provides the frame through which the behavior is interpreted.

One question in the literature relevant for trust in leaders has been the potential effects of offering an apology. Researchers have examined how apologizing for the transgression can have restorative effects (Bottom et al., 2002; Ohbuchi et al., 1989; Tomlinson et al., 2004) because it shows regret and perhaps repentance. However, other research observes that an apology may fail to ameliorate the negative consequences of an accusation because it involves an acknowledgment of guilt. Two studies of individuals in leadership roles support this idea. Sigal et al. (1988) asked participants to watch a videotape of a simulated debate in which one political candidate was accused of sexual or financial misconduct by the other. Sigal et al. found that the accused party received more votes and was considered to be more honest, ethical and trustworthy when that party denied culpability, rather than apologized, for the misconduct. Exploring the role of social accounts, Riordan et al. (1983) used fabricated reports of a fictitious senator having taken a bribe and found that subsequent character evaluations of the senator were less negative when the senator denied, rather than admitted, responsibility for the transgression.

Kim et al. (2004) tried to reconcile the conflicting findings about apologies versus denials and to provide a theoretical basis for understanding their effectiveness. These researchers based their work on a schematic model of dispositional attribution, which suggests that there may be some inherent differences in the way people assess positive versus negative information about competence versus integrity (Reeder and Brewer, 1979). In particular, this schematic model and supporting evidence indicate that although individuals tend to weigh positive information about competence more heavily than negative information about competence, they tend to weigh negative information about integrity more heavily than positive information about integrity.

People intuitively believe, for example, that those with high competence are capable of exhibiting many levels of performance, depending on their motivation and task demands, whereas those with low competence can only perform at levels that are commensurate with or lower than their competence level. As a result, a single success is typically considered to offer a reliable signal of competence, given the belief that those who are incompetent would not have been able to achieve that performance level. However, a single failure is generally discounted as a signal of incompetence, given that those who are competent or incompetent can each perform poorly in certain situations (e.g. when there is inadequate motivation or opportunity to perform well).

Along similar lines, people intuitively believe that those with high integrity would refrain from dishonest behavior regardless of the situation, whereas those with low integrity may exhibit either dishonest or honest behaviors depending on their specific incentives and opportunities. As a result, a single honest act is typically discounted as a signal of honesty, given that those who are honest or dishonest can each behave honestly in certain situations (e.g. when there are benefits to behaving honestly or sufficient surveillance to prevent dishonest acts). However, a single dishonest act is generally considered to offer a reliable signal of low integrity, given the belief that only persons of low integrity would behave dishonestly.

Kim et al. (2004) drew on these differences in the perceived diagnosticity of information to predict that the relative influence of an apology's signals of guilt and redemption, and hence the benefits of such a response for repairing trust, would depend on whether the violation concerns matters of competence or integrity. When the violation concerns matters of competence, the negative effect on trust from an apology's admission of guilt may be outweighed by its positive effects on trust from signaling the intent to prevent future violations, because people may be willing to believe that the incident was an anomaly and that the mistrusted party will demonstrate competence in the future (i.e. people would weigh positive information about competence more heavily than negative information about competence). However, when the violation concerns matters of integrity, confirming one's guilt with an apology should offer a reliable signal that one lacks integrity that would outweigh any positive effects on trust from the apology's signals of redemption, because people tend to believe that a lack of integrity would only be exhibited by those who do not possess it and this belief, once established, would be difficult to disconfirm (i.e. people would weigh negative information about integrity more heavily than positive information about integrity). These predictions were supported by two empirical studies (Kim et al., 2004).

This body of work represents only a beginning; there are clearly substantial opportunities for making contributions to better understanding how leaders can repair trust after it has been damaged. In terms of better understanding verbal responses, it would be useful to explore how apologies might be more effectively delivered. For example, how can a leader best signal that he or she will ensure that the same event does not happen again? Following Kim et al. (2004), how does the perceived nature of the violation impact what strategy is most effective?

At this point, little research has explored how to effectively follow up the verbal response with behavior to rebuild trust. Extending the logic of the theory used by Kim et al. (2004), rebuilding trust after integrity violations may take different forms or magnitudes of behaviors than would be the case with competence violations. What degree of positive displays of trustworthiness will it take to rebuild trust in integrity? What strategies are more effective for doing so?

Research might also explore how the strategies for repairing relationship-based trust, which has an affective basis, may differ from strategies for building character-based trust, which has a cognitive basis. Is forgiveness more forthcoming in the former or is it more difficult to obtain?

Conclusion

The intent of this chapter was to explore three fundamental questions regarding trust in leaders: why is trust in leaders important? What factors build or undermine trust in leaders? What can leaders do to try to repair trust after it is damaged? While I believe the issues raised in this chapter are important to developing our understanding of trust in leadership, it is clear that they are not exhaustive. Readers should recognize that many questions regarding trust in leadership have not been tested, and I hope this chapter will stimulate further thinking and research on trust in leadership. Leaders play a crucial role in management practice and in organizational research. The study of trust in leaders can advance both domains.

References

AFL–CIO (2001), *Workers' Rights in America: What employers think about their jobs and employers*. Peter D. Hart Associates.

Bachmann, R. (2001), Trust, power, and control in trans-organizational relations. *Organization Studies*, **22**, 337–65.

Bass, B.M. (1990), *Bass and Stogdill's Handbook of Leadership: Theory, research, and managerial applications* (3rd edn). New York: Free Press.

Berscheid, E., W. Graziano, T. Monson and M. Dermer (1976), Outcome dependency: Attention, attribution, and attraction. *Journal of Personality and Social Psychology*, **34**, 978–89.

Blau, P. (1964). *Exchange and Power in Social Life*. New York: Wiley.

Bottom, W.P., K. Gibson, S. Daniels and J.K. Murnighan (2002), When talk is not cheap: Substantive penance and expressions of intent in rebuilding cooperation. *Organization Science*, **13**, 497–513.

Brown, S. (1996), A meta-analysis and review of organizational research on job involvement. *Psychological Bulletin*, **120**, 235–55.

Clark, M. and J. Mills (1979), Interpersonal attraction in exchange and communal relationships. *Journal of Personality and Social Psychology*, **37**, 12–24.

Colquitt, J., E. Conlon, M. Wesson, C. Porter and K. Ng (2001), Justice at the millennium: A meta-analytic review of 25 years of organizational justice research. *Journal of Applied Psychology*, **86**, 425–45.

Cunningham, J.B. and J. MacGregor (2000), Trust and the design of work: Complementary constructs in satisfaction and performance. *Human Relations*, **53**, 1575–91.

Davis, J., D. Schoorman, R. Mayer and T.H. Tan. (2000), The trusted general manager and business unit performance: Empirical evidence of a competitive advantage. *Strategic Management Journal*, **21**, 563–76.

Dirks, K.T. (2000), Trust in leadership and team performance: Evidence from NCAA basketball. *Journal of Applied Psychology*, **85**, 1004–12.

Dirks, K.T. and D.L. Ferrin (2001), The role of trust in organizational settings. *Organization Science*, **12**, 450–67.

Dirks, K.T. and D.L. Ferrin (2002), Trust in leadership: Meta-analytic findings and implications for organizational research. *Journal of Applied Psychology*, **87**, 611–28.

Ferrin, D.L. and K.T. Dirks (2003), The use of rewards to increase and decrease trust: Mediating processes and differential effects. *Organization Science*, **14**, 18–31.

Fiske, A.P. (1992), The four elementary forms of sociality: Framework for a unified theory of social relations. *Psychological Bulletin*, **99**, 689–723.

Fiske, S. and S. Taylor (1991), *Social Cognition*, 2nd edn. New York: McGraw-Hill.

Fleishman, E. and E.F. Harris (1962), Patterns of leadership behavior related to employee grievances and turnover. *Personnel Psychology*, **15**, 43–56.

Golembiewski, R. and M. McConkie (1975), The centrality of interpersonal trust in group process. In C. Cooper (ed.), *Theories of Group Process*. New York: Wiley, pp. 131–85.

Hogan, R., G. Curphy and J. Hogan (1994), What we know about leadership: Effectiveness and personality. *American Psychologist*, **49**, 493–504.

Jones, A., L. James and J. Bruni (1975), Perceived leadership behavior and employee confidence in the leader as moderated by job involvement. *Journal of Applied Psychology*, **60**, 146–9.

Katcher, B. (2002), How to improve employee trust in management. *HR.com* [online serial].

Kim, P., D.L. Ferrin, C. Cooper and K.T. Dirks (2004), Removing the shadow of suspicion: The effects of apology versus denial for repairing competence- versus integrity-based trust violations, *Journal of Applied Psychology*, **89**, 104–18.

Kirkpatrick, S.A. and E.A. Locke (1996), Direct and indirect effects of three core charismatic leadership components on performance and attitudes. *Journal of Applied Psychology*, **81**, 36–51.

Konovsky, M. and D. Pugh (1994), Citizenship behavior and social exchange. *Academy of Management Journal*, **37**, 656–69.

Korsgaard, M.A., S. Brodt and E. Whitener (2002), Trust in the face of conflict: The role of managerial trustworthy behavior and organizational context. *Journal of Applied Psychology*, **87**, 312–19.

Kramer, R. (1996), Divergent realities and convergent disappointments in the hierarchic relation: Trust and the intuitive auditor at work. In R. Kramer and T. Tyler (eds), *Trust in Organizations: Frontiers of theory and research*. Thousand Oaks, CA: Sage, pp. 226–45.

Lewicki, R.J. and B.B. Bunker (1996), Developing and maintaining trust in work relationships. In R.M. Kramer and T.R. Tyler (eds), *Trust in Organizations: Frontiers of theory and research*. Thousand Oaks, CA: Sage, pp. 114–39.

Lewicki, R.J. and C. Wiethoff (2000), Trust, trust development, and trust repair. In M. Deutsch and P. Coleman (eds), *The Handbook of Conflict Resolution: Theory and practice*. San Francisco, CA: Jossey-Bass, pp. 86–107.

Mathieu, J. and D. Zajac (1990), A review and meta-analysis of the antecedents, correlates, and consequences of organizational commitment. *Psychological Bulletin*, **2**, 171–94.

Mayer, R. and M. Gavin (1999), Trust for management and performance: Who minds the shop while the employees watch the boss? Paper presented at the Annual Meeting of the Academy of Management, Chicago, IL.

Mayer, R.C., J.H. Davis and F.D. Schoorman (1995), An integrative model of organizational trust. *Academy of Management Review*, **20**, 709–34.

Ohbuchi, K., M. Kameda and N. Agarie (1989), Apology as aggression control: Its role in mediating appraisal of and response to harm. *Journal of Personality and Social Psychology*, **56**, 219–27.

Oldham, G.R. (1975), The impact of supervisory characteristics on goal acceptance. *Academy of Management Journal*, **18**, 461–75.

Pillai, R., C. Schriesheim and E. Williams (1999), Fairness perceptions and trust as mediators for transformational and transactional leadership: A two-sample study. *Journal of Management*, **6**, 897–933.

Podsakoff, P., S. MacKenzie, R. Moorman and R. Fetter (1990), Transformational leader behaviors and their effects on followers' trust in leader, satisfaction, and organizational citizenship behaviors. *Leadership Quarterly*, **1**, 107–42.

Read, W.H. (1962), Upward communication in industrial hierarchies. *Human Relations*, **15**, 3–15.

Reeder, G.D. and M.B. Brewer (1979), A schematic model of dispositional attribution in interpersonal perception. *Psychological Review*, **86**, 61–79.

Riordan, C.A., N.A. Marlin and R.T. Kellogg (1983), The effectiveness of accounts following transgression. *Social Psychology Quarterly*, **46**, 213–19.

Robinson, S. (1996), Trust and the breach of the psychological contract. *Administrative Science Quarterly*, **41**, 574–99.

Robinson, S.L. and D.M. Rousseau (1994), Violating the psychological contract: Not the exception but the norm. *Journal of Organizational Behavior*, **15**, 245–59.

Schriesheim, C., S. Castro and C. Cogliser (1999), Leader–member exchange (LMX) research: A comprehensive review of theory, measurement, and data-analytic procedures. *Leadership Quarterly*, **10**, 63–113.

Sigal, J., L. Hsu, S. Foodim and J. Betman (1988), Factors affecting perceptions of political candidates accused of sexual and financial misconduct. *Political Psychology*, **9**, 273–80.

Simons, T. (2002), Behavioral integrity – The perceived alignment between managers' words and deeds as a research focus. *Organization Science*, **13**, 18–35.

Simons, T. and J. McLean Parks (2002), Empty words: The impact of perceived managerial integrity on employees, customers and profits. Working paper.

Tomlinson, E.C., B.R. Dineen and R.J. Lewicki (2004), The road to reconciliation: Antecedents of victim willingness to reconcile following a broken promise. *Journal of Management*, **30**, 165–87.

Whitener, E., S. Brodt, M.A. Korsgaard and J. Werner (1998), Managers as initiators of trust: An exchange relationship for understanding managerial trustworthy behavior. *Academy of Management Journal*, **23**, 513–30.

Williamson, O. (1993), Calculativeness, trust and economic organization. *Journal of Law and Economics*, **36**, 453–86.

Zucker, L.G. (1986), Production of trust: Institutional sources of economic structure. In B. Staw and L.L. Cummings (eds), *Research in Organizational Behavior*, Greenwich, CT: JAI Press, pp. 53–111.

2   Reflections on an initial trust-building model
D. Harrison McKnight and Norman L. Chervany

Trust is important to organizations because it lubricates the relationships that form the interlocking components of coordination, which, like gears, turn the wheels of commerce. Trust becomes especially important during an organizational crisis (Mishra, 1996) or when supportive structures are inadequate. Thus it is vital to examine how trust forms in various work and commercial settings, because if one can understand the conditions, factors and processes determining this, one can thereby influence the coordinative consequents of trust.

One of many depictions of how trust forms is found in McKnight et al. (1998). Here trust is depicted as it forms in the initial phase of a relationship. The initial phase refers to when parties are unfamiliar with each other (Bigley and Pearce, 1998). By unfamiliar, we mean they have little solid, verifiable information about each other, and what they do know is not from first-hand, personal experience. This condition usually results from the newness of the relationship (that is, when parties first meet), but may also result from a combination of newness and relationship distance, because when parties are socially distant (for example, virtual team members or Internet transactional partners), they may not receive first-hand, verifiable information about the other for some time. This defini- tion of the initial phase means the initial phase stops after parties gain verifiable infor- mation by first-hand interactional or transactional experience with each other. Hence experience is not considered a factor of initial trust.

The import of initial trust-building
In part, initial trust formation is important because it is pervasive. Almost every rela- tionship begins with an initial phase. The initial phase can be characterized by uncertainty and doubt, in which parties feel around for the right level of trust to accord the other. Initial trust is also important because many critical tasks or transactions are done in the initial phase. These include brief negotiations, sales of various kinds (includ- ing e-commerce transactions), chance business meetings, temporary tasks (Meyerson et al., 1996), and brief team project or committee work. Bigley and Pearce (1998) provide examples of unfamiliar relationships that fall under the initial phase. During this phase, parties may extend or withdraw cooperation, and may do so willingly or unwillingly, with either confident and secure feelings or with tension, doubt and skepticism. In any case, the level of trust may impact their effectiveness, making it easy or difficult to accomplish the parties' interdependent tasks. Initial trust is therefore key to what the parties to the relationship can accomplish together.

Initial trust has further import because it excavates a cognitive/affective channel that often has lasting implications for the future mental model of the relationship. Relational schemas formed early are influential (Baldwin, 1992). For example, Berscheid and Graziano (1979) argue that the first part of a relationship is key because opinions and beliefs formed early tend to continue into the future, perpetuated by belief-maintaining mechanisms (see also Boon and Holmes, 1991). Social perception is a process strongly

affected by initial impressions (Darley and Fazio, 1980). Since trust is central to any relationship (Mishra, 1996), initial trust is a key harbinger of the future of the relationship.

This chapter briefly summarizes the McKnight et al. (1998) model and what makes it
unique. The features of the model include a time dimension boundary, an interrelated set
of trust constructs, trust-building factors and processes, and predictions regarding the
fragility and robustness of trust. Next, the impact of the article is traced, along with
empirical evidence regarding the model, based on the work of those who have cited it.
Finally, some research needs are outlined with respect to the model.

Original model – a summary

The initial trust formation model
The McKnight et al. (1998) model offers a set of factors and processes by which trust is
built initially, before parties have time to get to know each other via interaction or transactions (Figure 2.1). Two interpersonal trust concepts are predicted: trusting intention
(a secure, committed willingness to depend upon, or become vulnerable to, the other
party) and trusting beliefs (a secure conviction that the other party has favorable attributes, such as benevolence, integrity, competence and predictability). In this article, the
terms 'trust' or 'interpersonal trust' refer to a combination of trusting intention or trusting beliefs. Disposition to trust (assumptions that in general others are trustworthy –
Rotter, 1971) and institution-based trust (beliefs that the situation and/or structures make

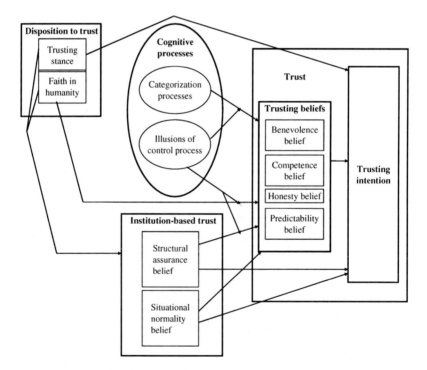

Figure 2.1   Initial trust-building model (McKnight et al., 1998)

the context conducive to trusting – Lane and Bachmann, 1996; Shapiro, 1987; Zucker, 1986) are the two factors proposed to influence interpersonal trust.

The article also posits that several cognitive processes impact initial trust: reputation inference, and two social categorization mechanisms – in-group categorization and stereotyping – and illusions of control. Reputation inference means one infers positive traits about the trustee based on second-hand information. In-group categorization refers to placing the trustee in the same grouping as oneself. Stereotyping means placing the trustee in a general grouping from which inferences can be made about trustee attributes. Reputation inference, in-group categorization and stereotyping have direct effects on initial trust. Moderating these effects (and others – Figure 2.1) are illusions of control. By token control efforts (Langer, 1975), one can become overconfident in one's assessment of the other through social categorization or reputation inference.

The article also posits factors affecting whether trusting intention will be robust or fragile over time. Trusting intention will be fragile when: (a) supported by few antecedents; (b) based primarily on assumptions; and (c) perceived situational risk is high. Trusting intention will be robust when: (a) supported by many antecedents; and (b) low risk or continued success encourage low attention to the trustee's behavior.

This model builds on the work of many trust researchers – too many to name. Most influential are the work of Holmes (1991) and associates (Holmes and Rempel, 1989; Rempel et al., 1985) regarding assumptions and attributions behind trust, Luhmann's (1979) integration of interpersonal and 'system' trust (similar to institution-based trust), Zucker's (1986) model of the tradeoffs among personal and structural trust types, and the integrative models or discussions of Barber (1983), Bromiley and Cummings (1995), Dobing (1993), Gabarro (1978), Gambetta (1988), Giffin (1967), Good (1988), Kramer (1994), Lewis and Weigert (1985a,b), an early version of Mishra (1996), Ring and Van de Ven (1994), and Sitkin and Roth (1993).

Unique features of the initial trust model

Temporal anchoring   The model has several unique features. We use the term unique loosely, recognizing that none of the model's individual features is genuinely unique. First, it is anchored to the initial relationship time period, but proposes, in a limited way, how trust might progress after the initial relationship period. Its temporal boundary implies that trust-building factors differ by relationship phase. That is, the factors and processes by which trust is built in the initial phase are not the same as those factors and processes by which trust is built in the ongoing relationship phases. Experience with the trustee that enables an interaction history is implied as the major factor of ongoing trust. The article begins by sharing anecdotal evidence that trust may develop quickly to a high level rather than growing incrementally and gradually over time. Then it proposes factors and processes enabling this to occur. The model was first conceived when the first author found evidence, in 1993, of high trust early in a relationship and reread the trust literature in an attempt to understand how this could be possible.

Typology of trust types   Second, the model is unique in that it includes several inter-related types of trust, including four trusting beliefs and two types of both disposition to trust and institution-based trust. Thus it offers a typology of nine distinct types of trust.

This is important because trust types have proliferated, making types of trust overlapping and hard to reconcile (Lewis and Weigert, 1985b; Shapiro, 1987). This means that one research finding is hard to compare with another because a glut of trust types exists without rules to translate one finding to another (McKnight and Chervany, 2001a; Rubin, 1988). The model offers this set of trust types in order to represent in a parsimonious manner a larger set of literature trust types.

Interrelated trust types   The model also depicts relationships among these trust types, something that Tiryakian (1968) says a good typology does. The model depicts the more generalized construct (disposition to trust) affecting the contextual construct (institution-based trust), which then affects the specific interpersonal trust constructs. Some unmediated effects of disposition to trust are also proposed. Many others have hypothesized different types of trust (Barber, 1983; Gabarro, 1978; Mayer et al., 1995; Mishra, 1996; Butler, 1991). This model is unique in terms of: (a) the number of types, (b) the broad, cross-disciplinary origin of the types, and (c) the manner in which the types interrelate.

Specific trust-building processes   Fourth, the model includes both cognitive processes and factors. This makes it hard to test in one empirical study, where mixing process and variance methods may be awkward. But it does provide several ways to test the model in separate modes. It is acceptable for researchers to create a larger theoretical model than can be tested in a given study (Sutton and Staw, 1995). The process aspects of trust development are interesting because they go beyond the normal variance theory approach that explains 'what leads to what' and posit positive mechanisms explaining how trust develops.

Fragility versus robustness of trust   Fifth, by specifying what might cause trust to be fragile or robust, the article juxtaposes two theoretical paths for the progression of trust. The fragile path says that initial trusting intention will take large swings (often downward) as the trustor takes into account new, less assumptional information about the trustee. The robust path says that trusting intention will stay firm, as belief confirmation mechanisms cause one to reinforce early impressions by ignoring or rationalizing contrary evidence about the trustee.

Impact of the article and its model
In order to assess the impact of the model, we looked at which articles had cited this article and what, if anything, those articles had said and done about it. Hence, this section catalogs the work of those citing McKnight et al. (1998).

Applications of the model have been found primarily in three domains: organizations, e-commerce and virtual teams. For example, Wells and Kipnis (2001) and Bell et al. (2002) suggest that the McKnight et al. (1998) model (hereafter termed MCC98) was an example of a trust-building model in the organizational domain. Tan and Thoen (2003) review how MCC98 introduces trust-building factors for initial relationships and how McKnight and Chervany (2001a) apply these in the e-commerce domain. Tan and Thoen and Jarvenpaa and Tractinsky (1999) argue that initial trust formation is especially applicable to e-commerce because in this domain, many of the partners have never dealt with each other before. In the virtual teams arena, Brown et al. (2004) apply dispositional aspects of MCC98 while Kasper-Fuehrer and Ashkanasy (2001) use MCC98 to argue that trust can exist in virtual teams. We now review more specific impacts of the article organized by the five unique features of the model explained above.

Temporal (initial phase) anchoring of the model
The nature of trust in its initial (versus ongoing) phase has drawn some discussion (Bhattacherjee, 2002; Tschannen-Moran and Hoy, 2000). Zaheer et al. (1999) used MCC98 as an example of the importance of the time dimension in organizational research, arguing that initial trust has different antecedents from later phase trust and that initial trust is fragile. Oliver and Montgomery (2001) use MCC98 to argue that the information needed for trust in the initial relationship is different from the information needed for trust in ongoing, interactive relationships. Gefen (2004) argues that disposition to trust is not needed in their model of ongoing, mature client trust in the software vendor because MCC98 argues that disposition will only be an effective predictor before parties interact. Siau and Shen (2003) argue that trust in mobile commerce vendors requires different antecedents in the ongoing phase from the initial trust phase. Williams (2001) cites MCC98 to argue that initial trust can develop without in-group similarity (that is, through institutional supports), complicating the relationship between trust and group membership over time. Crisp and Jarvenpaa (2000) use MCC98 to argue that trust can exist among virtual team members with no prior experience with each other. Cunningham and McGregor (2000) use MCC98 to argue against the leader–member exchange (LMX) assumptions that personal relationships develop over time. Both Crisp/Jarvenpaa and Cunningham/McGregor say that MCC98 challenges the view that trust can only develop as people interact over time. Kim et al. (2004) note both that MCC98 posits that initial trust may be high before interaction and explains the reasons why. Jackson (1999) cites MCC98 about how trust can be high initially and then may deteriorate over time. They point out that today's frequent organizational changes frequently bring about these novel and ambiguous initial trust situations. Droege et al. (2003) address the difference between initial trust and what they call gradual trust. They suggest that trust formed 'gradually invokes different cognitive processes than swift or initial trust ... Rather than placing emphasis on the safeguards of reputation, sanctions, formal roles, norms, and assumptions of trustworthiness, gradual trust is based on knowledge and past interaction' (2003: 51).

In terms of the MCC98 proposal that trust can begin at medium to high levels, rather than growing gradually, several papers have provided empirical evidence. In a three-phase virtual team exercise, Kanawattanachai and Yoo (2002) find mixed support for trust becoming high quickly versus the incremental trust development model (for example, Blau, 1964). They report that virtual team trust reached medium levels by T1. Low-performing teams' trust remained at this level at T2 and T3. High-performing teams' trust rose again at T2, but remained constant at T3. Jarvenpaa and Leidner (1998) find that in virtual teams, trust tends to stay at about the same level at T1 and T2. Crisp and Jarvenpaa (2000) hypothesize that trust in virtual teams from different countries will decrease over time because it is initially based on such weak supports as social categorization and stereotyping. They find that initial trust in the team was statistically the same level (3.9 on a 1–5 scale) three weeks before the exercise began and one week before the exercise began (after students were assigned to teams). Team trust dropped significantly to 3.7 on average at T2 (project midpoint), where it remained at T3 (after task completion). Some teams did increase trust levels over time, but the general trend was slightly downward, which they say supports the MCC98 initial trust thesis. Although the above represents a few empirical tests supporting the initial trust-building model, results are mixed and more research is needed.

Another way to see whether the initial trust-building model or the incremental interaction trust-building model predicts best is to see the extent to which familiarity with the trustee predicts trust in the trustee. A salient familiarity factor would favor the incremental model. Results here are mixed. Gefen (2000), Gefen et al. (2003b), and Bhattacherjee (2002) find familiarity with Amazon.com to be significantly related to trust in Amazon.com. On the other hand, Pavlou (2002) finds that familiarity did not predict trust in the E-bay environment. It is not clear from the Gefen and Bhattacherjee measures whether familiarity had to do with interaction with Amazon or hearing about Amazon second-hand.

Time boundary issue   MCC98 implies that the factors and processes proposed to develop initial trust are not effective after the initial phase. In this regard, we present two key research questions: (1) Do the same factors MCC98 proposes as antecedents to trust in the initial time frame continue to predict trust afterwards? (2) To what extent do quantity and quality of experience replace the MCC98 antecedents once the parties gain significant experience with each other? Gefen et al. (2003b) address item (1) in terms of the efficacy of disposition to trust. Note that both MCC98 and Mayer et al. (1995) propose that disposition to trust only predicts trust variables before parties have experience with each other. Gefen et al. compare the link between disposition to trust and consumer trust in the e-vendor (Amazon.com) among potential customers (those who have not yet purchased from Amazon) and repeat customers. They find the link to be significant among both customer types, though the link coefficient decreases significantly ($p<0.01$) from 0.45 ($p<0.01$) to 0.35 ($p<0.01$). Addressing the quantity aspect of (2), Gefen and associates propose that familiarity will become more important to trust among repeat customers than potential customers. They find that while the coefficients are nominally different (0.18 for repeat customers, 0.13 for potential customers), these differences are not significant.

McKnight and Chervany (2005) address the same questions using technical system troubleshooters reporting about their trust in the supervisor. Troubleshooters had worked with the supervisor for an average of 4.0 years and all had worked closely with the supervisor for more than six months, placing them beyond the initial phase. The trust construct portion of the MCC98 model is run, with variables representing dispositional and institutional trust, trusting beliefs and trusting intention. Addressing question (1), McKnight and Chervany (2005) find that in this ongoing trust phase: (a) disposition to trust predicts both structural assurance and trusting intention, but not trusting beliefs; (b) structural assurance predicts trusting beliefs but not trusting intention; and (c) both trusting beliefs predict trusting intention. Therefore, even after the initial relationship, these variables continue to operate as MCC98 propose except that the links from structural assurance to trusting intention and from disposition to trust to trusting beliefs become fully mediated. McKnight and Chervany (2005) address question (2) by adding one variable each for quality and quantity of experience, predicting that only quality of experience will matter. They find that: (a) quantity of experience does not predict trusting beliefs or trusting intention; (b) quality of experience predicts both trusting beliefs and trusting intentions, even in the presence of the experience variables; (c) structural assurance continues to predict trusting beliefs; (d) trusting beliefs continues to predict trusting intention; and (e) disposition to trust continues to predict trusting intention. Although these studies need to be replicated, they provide an early indication that the time boundary of the MCC98 model may not be as firm as originally proposed. More tests of the time boundary of the efficacy of the initial trust predictors should be done to see under what conditions the boundaries hold.

Typology of trust types
A number of studies comment on the MCC98 trust typology. Kim et al. (2004) support the idea that trust is multi-faceted. Following MCC98, some researchers have distinguished between trusting intentions and trusting beliefs (Boyd, 2003; Nicholson et al., 2001; Pavlou, 2003), and between institution-based trust and interpersonal trust (Jackson, 1999; Jarvenpaa and Tiller, 2001). Some either cite or use MCC98 for various trust definitions (George, 2002; Povey, 1999), including the distinction among four trusting beliefs – competence, benevolence, honesty and predictability (Boyd, 2003; Cunningham and MacGregor, 2000; Gallivan and Depledge, 2003; Grazioli and Jarvenpaa, 2003; Pavlou, 2003; Shankar et al., 2002) and the distinction among disposition to trust types – faith in humanity and trusting stance (Gefen et al., 2003b). Pennington et al. (2003, p. 199) follow and discuss the MCC98 typology: 'McKnight et al. (1998) develop a useful typology of trust . . . Collectively, these constructs provide a reasonable definition of the construct space for the trust variable. Consistent with this work, Castelfranchi and Falcone (1998) regard these perceptions of trust as a belief system of the truster regarding the trustee.' Pennington and associates conclude that more work is needed that uses such granular measures of trust. On the other hand, many examples exist of research that uses the term trust to describe what MCC98 would term either trusting beliefs or trusting intention. Thus a condition of homonymy is expected to continue into the future. Homonymy means one label is used to encompass more than one concept (Smith, 1990). However, the severity of trust homonymy is lessening over time.

In what they call a ' "grammar" of trust,' McKnight and Chervany (2001a: 42) expand the conceptual basis for the typology. They argue that trust is like a sentence, with a subject (trustor), verb (trust), and direct object (trustee). It is the direct object that determines many of the types of trust in use. If the direct object of trust is a person, the construct is interpersonal trust; if the object is an institution, the construct is institution-based trust; and if the object is general other people, the construct is disposition to trust. This assumes, of course, that the subject of trust is one person, but this could also be varied to produce different types or levels of trust.

Recent typology extensions   The typology of nine trust constructs in MCC98 has been expanded in several ways. First, building on McKnight and Chervany (1996), McKnight and Chervany (2001a) define trusting intention as two constructs: trusting intention – willingness to depend (willingness to be vulnerable to the other by depending on them); and trusting intention – subjective probability of depending (the extent to which one predicts that one will depend on the other party). The latter is a stronger or more risk-laden construct as it involves an implicit commitment to do something specific rather

Table 2.1   Trust constructs as combinations of conceptual types and trustee attributes

Referent characteristic	Dispositional	Structural/ institutional	Conceptual types			
			Belief	Attitude	Intention	Behavior
Competence	*	*	X	X		X
Benevolence	*	*	X	X	X	X
Integrity	*	*	X	X	X	X
Predictability			X	X		X
Other	X	X	X	X	X	X

Notes:
X denotes definitions already in existence in this conceptual region, per McKnight and Chervany (2001a).
* denotes cells filled by constructs measured in McKnight et al. (2002a).

Source: Adapted from McKnight and Chervany (2001a).

than a general willingness to depend. Second, they added a behavioral concept – trust-related behaviors. These behaviors were specified for the Internet environment as purchasing a product, cooperating with the vendor, and sharing personal information with the vendor. A large number of existing definitions of trust as a behavior fit this category (e.g. Baier, 1986; Bonoma, 1976; Dobing, 1993; Giffin, 1967; Riker, 1971; Zand, 1972 – see McKnight and Chervany, 1996 for more).

McKnight and Chervany (2001a) also outline a way to expand the types of trust in an organized way by matching each of the major trustee characteristics (competence, benevolence, integrity, predictability) with conceptual types (behavior, intention, belief, attitude, disposition, structural/institutional). Matching these types would potentially yield 24 (4 × 6) trust constructs (Table 2.1), or more, if additional trustee characteristics were used.

The McKnight and Chervany (2001a) Internet constructs and definitions are adapted to a more general trust research audience in McKnight and Chervany (2001b). Here, the same constructs are defined but for use in organizations rather than in e-commerce. They also outline additional trust-related behaviors for organizational use. In addition to cooperating and sharing information, their chapter (2001b) suggests these behaviors: entering an informal agreement, reducing the controls placed on another, allowing another to influence one, and granting another decision-making power. They argue that each of these behaviors makes one vulnerable to the other, matching the most basic definition of trust. The other contribution of McKnight and Chervany (2001b) is that it defines distrust constructs. Each trust concept is given a corresponding distrust concept definition, building on Lewicki et al.'s (1998) position that trust and distrust are separate concepts, not just two ends of the same continuum. McKnight and Chervany suggest that trust and distrust differ due to the intensity of the emotions each inheres. 'In terms of emotion . . . one might picture trust as the satisfied zoo elephant, calmly eating hay, while distrust is more like the raging wild bull elephant charging the tusk hunter who threatens the herd' (2001b: 42).

Concepts are only useful to the extent that they can be measured. McKnight et al. (2002a) measured most of the trust concepts defined above for e-commerce and performed tests of their psychometric properties. They were able to distinguish among 16 measured trust constructs: four for disposition to trust, five for institution-based trust, three for trusting beliefs, and four for trusting intentions. The disposition to trust and institution-based trust concepts included delineations that mirrored conceptually the benevolence, honesty and competence aspects of the three trusting beliefs. For example, the faith in humanity–benevolence measures tapped the idea that one assumes other people generally have one's interests at heart. This construct was distinct from the faith in humanity–integrity measures, which reflected the assumption that other people generally are honest. The trusting intentions include willingness to depend and three subjective probability of depending constructs: intention to follow the e-vendor's advice, to give the vendor personal information, and to purchase from the vendor.

McKnight et al. (2002b) measure these trust concepts: structural assurance of the Web, trusting beliefs, trusting intention–willingness to depend, trusting intention–follow vendor advice, trusting intention–share personal information with the vendor, and trusting intention–purchase from the site. They distinguish these concepts from each other empirically and from perceived vendor reputation, perceived site quality, and perceived Web risk. However, the three trusting beliefs they measure (benevolence, competence, integrity) were treated as one construct rather than being distinguished from each other. Bhattacherjee (2002) measured the same three trusting beliefs in Amazon.com with three items each and found they formed a second-order concept. On the other hand, Mayer and Davis (1999) found that the three trusting beliefs factored separately. This leaves outstanding the question of what circumstances cause trusting beliefs to merge or to be distinct (see Lewicki et al., 1998 for one theory). A number of researchers have measured two or more trust constructs in the same study, though their construct labels often differ from those of MCC98 (for example, Gefen et al., 2003a; Jarvenpaa et al., 2000; Pavlou and Gefen, 2004; Ridings et al., 2002).

Distrust and trust in technology extensions   McKnight et al. (2003–2004) empirically contrast disposition to trust–faith in humanity and disposition to distrust–suspicion of humanity. They measure both faith in humanity-general and suspicion of humanity-general and find these forms of dispositional trust and distrust to be distinct empirically, with a correlation of only −0.38. Following Lewicki et al.'s (1998) suggested tests, they find that dispositional trust and distrust are distinct in that they coexist and predict different dependent variables in the model. Indicative that the distrust side inheres more of the emotional, risk-laden aspect, suspicion of humanity-general correlates with perceived Web risk at +0.28, while faith in humanity-general correlates with perceived Web risk at only −0.09.

The MCC98 typology has recently been applied to trust in technology (as opposed to trust in people, teams or organizations). Trust in technology (Muir, 1994) is an important domain for trust because of the pervasiveness, power effects and frustrating potential of technology in organizations today (Zuboff, 1988). McKnight and Thatcher (2004) have proposed and measured eight constructs related to trust in technology: faith in general technology, trusting stance–general technology, situational normality–technology, structural assurance–technology, trusting intention–specific technology, and three trusting beliefs–specific technology: reliability, capability and helpfulness. With these constructs, the direct object of trust is a specific or general technology rather than a person. Because technologies are human artifacts that lack the same range of attributes as people (for example, no volition), these trusting beliefs differ conceptually from those involving people as trustees. However, they are similar to trusting beliefs in people in that they describe a person's perceptions about the characteristics of the trust object. Other expansions of the typology exist. For example, Galvin et al. (2001) conceptualized and measured trust in a team instead of in an individual. Team member trust in the team itself ratchets up a level from the individual-to-individual trust theorized in MCC98.

Proliferation versus consensus regarding institution-based trust types   Whereas a solid consensus is forming on the major types of trusting beliefs, less consensus exists on the types of institution-based trust. While several have cited or used the MCC98 delineation into structural assurance and situational normality (Boyd, 2003; Gefen et al., 2003a; Pennington et al., 2003; Tschannen-Moran and Hoy, 2000), others are using more specific aspects of institution-based trust, such as the perceived effectiveness of escrow services, credit card guarantees, or online feedback mechanisms (Pavlou, 2002; Pavlou and Gefen, 2004). What needs resolution is whether the latter are subsets (subtypes) or antecedents of institution-based trust. A suggestion: if, as in MCC98, structural assurance and situational normality are defined as beliefs that the context contains supportive structures and properly ordered situations, then the above online mechanisms should be viewed as antecedents of these institution-based trust concepts.

Many researchers reference the sociological roots of the situational normality and structural normality concepts (such as Schutz, Simmel, Garfinkel, Luhmann and Zucker) rather than adopting the two MCC98 institutional constructs. This makes for an excellent discussion grounded in rich sociological heritage (for example, see Möllering, Chapter 20 in this volume). It also provides some flexibility in the use of structural or situational constructs that may or may not 'fit' the specific MCC98 definitions (Child and Möllering, 2003; Pavlou and Gefen, 2004). On the other hand, the use of these two specific constructs can be helpful because they delineate the structural assurance aspect of institution-based trust, which is based on trust in supportive institutions such as law and licensing (Shapiro, 1987; Zucker, 1986), from the situational normality aspect, which is based more on phenomenology's 'natural attitude' (Schutz, 1967: 98), constitutive expectancies (Garfinkel, 1963), expected role performance (Baier, 1986; Barber, 1983), and contextual familiarity (Schutz, 1964). The common theme among these latter foundational concepts emerges from situational normality's emphasis on perceptions that the context is favorable, normal, or well ordered, in terms of how the world works, what the binding rules are, what common set of role expectations exist, or some level of familiarity with how things will operate. Thus situational normality is defined broadly enough to encompass several types of phenomenological concepts that differ only in terms of the subject of what is normal or well ordered, not so much in terms of the kind of normality or ordering (see Möllering, this volume). Similarly, structural assurance may be thought of as a generalized comforting belief that reflects the effects of many types of mechanisms that support confidence in contextual actors because they provide safety nets or prevent or redress losses due to opportunism. Our constructs are therefore super-types that encompass more detailed institution-based trust subtypes.

Likewise, structural assurance may be thought of as separate from, but related to, calculus-based trust. Calculus-based trust means one projects that the other party has no incentive to act opportunistically and therefore will not. Structural assurance means one believes structures are in place to support the legal or other contextual sanctions that would enable calculus-based trust to form. Therefore structural assurance may be considered an antecedent of calculus-based trust. That is, mental trust calculations are usually based on institutional structures (often incentives) in the context that lead one to believe that the trustee will or will not behave in a certain way.

A number of studies are following the lead of MCC98 to treat trust as a set of granular, related constructs. Overall, the trust constructs have been expanded to accommodate both trust and distrust, for people and technology. The more the MCC98 terms are used, the more trust types will be researched in an synonymous, instead of homonymous, manner, such that meta-analyses can be done across disciplines. Currently, almost no such trust research meta-analyses exist, perhaps because trust definitions have not been comparable across studies and disciplines (McKnight and Chervany, 2001a).

Interrelationships among the trust types

Trusting beliefs to trusting intentions   Several researchers have proposed or discussed links from trusting beliefs to trusting intentions (Kim et al., 2004; Pennington et al., 2003; Stewart, 2003). Several tests of this link have been performed. Ridings et al. (2002) find that trusting beliefs–ability leads to the intention to share information (beta = 0.15 [p < 0.01]) and that trusting belief–benevolence/integrity predicts intention to share information (beta = 0.29 [p < 0.01]). Jarvenpaa et al. (1998) find ability, integrity and benevolence beliefs to be factors of trust (defined like a trusting intention) in virtual teams, though ability becomes non-significant at T2 and benevolence is non-significant at T1. Pavlou (2003) finds that trust in a Web vendor predicts intention to transact with the vendor (beta = 0.35 [p < 0.01]). Pavlou and Gefen (2004) find that trusting beliefs in Amazon's online auction community of sellers is a significant factor for trusting intentions to transact. Galvin et al. (2001) find that trusting beliefs in the team predicts trusting intentions regarding the team in four of four times tested. McKnight and Chervany (2005) find that trusting beliefs–competence and –benevolence in the supervisor are predictors of trusting intention in the supervisor. McKnight et al. (2002b) find trusting beliefs in the Web vendor predicts four trusting intentions in the Web vendor: willingness to depend (beta = 0.60 [p < 0.01]), willingness to follow vendor advice (beta = 0.27 [p < 0.01]), willingness to share personal information (beta = 0.30 [p < 0.01]), and willingness to purchase at the site (beta = 0.13 [p < 0.01]). McKnight et al. (2002a) find that a second-order combination of three trusting beliefs (benevolence, competence, integrity) predicts a second-order combination of trusting intentions (willingness to depend, follow advice, give information and make purchases).

Institution-based trust links to trusting beliefs or trusting intentions   The social context, including institutional safety sources, is critical to understanding the development of interpersonal trust. Several have proposed or acknowledged that institution-based trust (also called system trust, based on Luhmann, 1979) influences or relates to trusting beliefs or intentions (Tan and Thoen, 2003; Tschannen-Moran and Hoy, 2000). Empirical work supports this theme. Child and Möllering (2003) find that Hong Kong manager confidence in the Chinese institutional context supports trust in a group working within that context. Specifically, they find that three aspects of the institutional context build trust in the local staff: confidence in the Chinese legal system, lack of arbitrariness of Chinese officials, and the availability of Chinese human resources. Together, these three contextual variables explain 27 percent of the variance in trust. Pennington et al. (2003) find system trust to be a strong predictor of perceived trust in the Internet vendor. McKnight et al. (2002b) find small but significant links from structural assurance to trusting beliefs and trusting intention–willingness to depend in a Web vendor. On the other hand, McKnight et al. (2002a) find no significant link between a second-order institution-based construct (combining situational normality and structural assurance of the Web) and second-order trusting beliefs and intentions in a specific Web vendor.

In traditional organizational research, few besides Lane and Bachmann (1996) and Child and Möllering (2003) have linked these concepts as yet, with these exceptions: Nyhan (1999) finds what he calls systems trust to be correlated at 0.69 with supervisory trust. McKnight and Chervany (2005) find structural assurance–fairness to predict trusting beliefs–competence and –benevolence in the supervisor at beta = 0.27 and 0.41 (both p<0.01), respectively. Galvin et al. (2001) find both situational normality and structural assurance to predict (8 of 12 times) a second-order concept called trusting beliefs in the team.

Pavlou and Gefen (2004) find that three institution-based trust structures affect trust in the community of Amazon auction sellers: perceived effectiveness of feedback mechanism, perceived effectiveness of escrow services, and trust in the intermediary. Pavlou (2002) finds that three forms of institution-based trust affect trust in eBay sellers (perceived monitoring, perceived feedback, cooperative norms), while two do not (perceived accreditation, perceived legal bonds). He argues that the significant links help establish and clarify the link from institution-based trust to organizational trust. This link

> has been traditionally viewed as a substitution or complementary relation . . . Sitkin and Roth (1993) argue that 'legalistic remedies have been described as weak, impersonal substitutes for trust'. Tan and Thoen (2001) posit . . . that trust in a given transaction is the sum of party (interpersonal) and control (institution-based) trust. However, McKnight et al. (1998) argue for a sequential relationship where institution-based trust leads to party trust . . . This study empirically corroborates the latter view . . . (Pavlou, 2002: 234)

Antecedents of institution-based trust   Little work has been done on the antecedents of institution-based trust. Tschannen-Moran and Hoy (2000: 560) say institution-based trust is built by 'formal structures . . . such as having a license or certification . . . or mechanisms such as guarantees, insurance, or contracts'. Tan and Thoen (2003) suggest that contracts create structural assurance. Boyd (2003) says offline firms should take advantage of offline strength to build situational normality. Pennington et al. (2003) test three antecedents of system trust. Vendor guarantees predicted system trust, but customer ratings and third-party assurance seals did not. This study needs to be replicated to understand the 'why' behind the finding.

Several studies have confirmed disposition to trust as an antecedent of institution-based trust. Kaplan and Nieschwietz (2003) find that disposition to trust is a significant factor (p = 0.002) of assurance beliefs, which is similar to structural assurance. McKnight et al. (2002a) find that a second-order disposition to trust concept predicts a second-order institution-based trust concept at beta = 0.52 [p<0.01]. Galvin et al. (2001) find that disposition to trust predicts situational normality and structural assurance 10 out of 12 times tested. McKnight et al. (2004b) find that three types of disposition to trust (faith in humanity-general, faith in humanity-professionals, and trusting stance) predict either situational normality or structural assurance in five out of six tests.

Other model links from disposition to trust   Jarvenpaa et al. (1998) find that propensity to trust (a.k.a. disposition to trust) is a significant factor ($p<0.05$) of trusting intention at both T1 and T2 for virtual teams. Gefen (2000) finds that disposition to trust affects subjects' trust in the vendor (Amazon.com) more (beta = 0.53 [$p<0.01$]) than does familiarity with the vendor (beta = 0.17 [$p<0.05$]), showing that disposition predicts trust well when little interaction has taken place. Kaplan and Nieschwietz (2003) find that disposition to trust is a significant factor ($p = 0.012$) of trusting beliefs in a Web company, but is not a factor of trusting intentions to purchase. Ridings et al. (2002) find that disposition to trust predicts trust in the members of the virtual communities' ability (beta = 0.15 [$p < 0.01$]) and benevolence/integrity (beta = 0.18 [$p<0.00$]). McKnight et al. (2002a) find that disposition to trust predicts trusting beliefs but not trusting intentions. McKnight et al. (2004a) find that disposition to trust was a significant predictor of trusting beliefs and trusting intentions in the Web vendor at two early phases. On the other hand, Koufaris and Hampton-Sosa (2004) find that customer disposition to trust does not affect initial trust in an online company.

One gap in this literature is that very little research has tested all or even most of the trust concept linkages that MCC98 proposes (Figure 2.1). Here are some exceptions. McKnight et al. (2002a) test links between dispositional trust, insititution-based trust, trusting beliefs, and trusting intentions at a second-order construct level and provide fit statistics for the model. Pavlou and Gefen (2004) test links from dispositional trust and institutional trust to trusting beliefs, but do not link dispositional and institutional trust. Galvin et al. (2001) test the full set of constructs, as do McKnight and Chervany (2005). Knowing how all the constructs fit together is an important step towards understanding the complexities that enable effective interventions for practice.

Specific processes by which trust develops

Reputation inference process   MCC98 posit that reputation inference builds trust in the initial relationship. Reputation has been proposed and tested as a trust antecedent by several researchers. Tschannen-Moran and Hoy (2000) use MCC98 to argue that reputation makes a negative event less likely to reduce a high trust level. Klaas (2003) suggests that initial skepticism can block the development of relational trust, but third-party reputation information can help. Pavlou (2003) finds that Web vendor reputation predicts trust in the Web vendor (beta = 0.30 [$p<0.01$]). Jarvenpaa et al. (2000) find perceived reputation to predict trust in the Web store. McKnight et al. (2002b) find perceived Web vendor reputation to predict trusting beliefs (beta = 0.39 [$p<0.01$]) and trusting intention–willingness to depend (beta = 0.41 [$p<0.01$]). The above studies treat reputation as a measured perception variable. McKnight et al. (2004a) create a reputation advertising treatment and find that it too is a significant predictor of trusting beliefs and trusting intentions in the Web vendor at two early phases (betas = 0.13 [$p<0.05$], 0.14 [$p<0.05$], 0.17 [$p<0.01$], 0.12 [$p<0.05$]). Using game theory, Ba et al. (2003) explain how reputation awarded through trusted third parties is like taking a hostage – ensuring that participants in an online market will be honest. Ba (2001) develops these ideas for online communities as well. However, Ba et al. (2003) also point out the limitations of online marketplaces for enforcing honesty, such as the fact that players can move from one online marketplace to another under different names. Reputation is well entrenched as a trust factor.

Social categorization process   In this area, Leanna and Van Buren (1999) say that social capital (including trust) is built through shared values, presumably because of unit grouping categorization. Nicholson et al. (2001) suggest that similarity leads to trust. Duffy and Ferrier (2003: 220) cite MCC98 to argue that 'those who are "grouped together" (for example, race or gender) tend to perceive themselves in a common "positive light"'. Jarvenpaa and Leidner (1998) discuss how in-group categorization can take place swiftly in virtual work teams. After finding that site quality perceptions had a large effect on trusting beliefs, McKnight et al. (2002b) explain this effect as similar to the what-is-beautiful-is-good effect Dion et al. (1972) found among dating partners – that, in the case of the Web site, first impressions on seeing the site cement either bad or good perceptions of the site and therefore trusting beliefs in the site vendor. This means subjects made inferences that led to placement of the site/vendor into general good or bad categories depending on first impressions of site quality. Similar inferences are made, according to Jarvenpaa et al. (2000: 48), based on the size of the vendor, which implies the seller 'can be trusted . . . [it] signals that the firm should have the necessary expertise and resources for support systems such as customer and technical services . . . [which] encourages trust . . .' In organization research, Child and Möllering (2003) found that similarity had no direct effect on Hong Kong manager trust in the mainland Chinese staff. However, similarity did increase the influence of trust-building managerial actions on trust in the mainland staff. In e-commerce research, Gefen (2004) found shared cultural characteristics to be a factor of client trust in the vendor (beta $= 0.15$ [p < 0.05]).

Also, some work has been done on the transfer of trust, a form of in-group social categorization. Transfer of trust occurs cognitively as a consumer associates an unknown Web site with a known, trusted Web site (Stewart, 2003). Stewart explains that this occurs due to perceptions that the Web sites are similar and that they interact, which implies that the trusted Web site legitimates the unknown site. Stewart also finds that trusting intention (that is, intention to buy) transfers from traditional to Web-based shopping channels as consumers see evidence that the Web store has an offline retail presence, a helpful way to contextualize trust-building.

Although two articles cite MCC98 regarding the moderating effects of illusions and assumptions (Kim et al., 2004; Tschannen-Moran and Hoy, 2000), no empirical work on this has been done to our knowledge. Overall, it appears that much more work needs to be done on both social categorization and illusion.

Juxtaposing the fragility and robustness of trust
Kim et al. (2004) and Boyd (2003) cite MCC98 to support the argument that initial trust is fragile because of the assumption-laden nature of its bases. Little work has been done to test the specific MCC98 arguments for trust fragility or robustness. Oliver and Montgomery (2001) cite MCC98 for having explored the process of trust dynamics. They expand on existing work to create a more complete cybernetic model of how trust progresses over time. The model suggests that trust is enhanced when information about the

trustee is congruent with the trustor's cognitive map of trustworthiness; otherwise, trust may erode unless the trustee provides remedial feedback.

Zaheer et al. (1999) cite MCC98 to suggest that initial trust is by nature fragile. Droege et al. (2003: 51) argue that initial trust is fragile because it 'is a function of conditions – reputations, sanctions, roles, norms, and assumptions – extrinsic to the [trustee]'. Citing Robinson (1996), they suggest that initial trust is fragile in that small violations early in the relationship result in a predisposition to see the trustee as not trustworthy in the future. Trust that develops gradually, on the other hand, is resilient because it is based on affect toward the individual that develops over an interaction cycle, such that small trust breaches are ignored. Child and Möllering (2003) suggest that in places like China, where trust-supporting institutions are still in development, trust built through personal communication is fragile because it is entirely dependent upon the trustor making a leap of faith without structural safety nets.

Almost no empirical work has tested whether initial trust is fragile or robust. This kind of testing would be very helpful. For example, Kim et al. (2004) suggest that because trust is often elevated at first, this provides a platform for it to become even higher through experience. This is possible, of course. But what is also possible is that trust levels could decrease from their initial levels, especially if elevated because of assumptions or inferences that create hard-to-fulfill expectations. It seems critical to explore what circumstances make these upward and downward possibilities more likely. In this way, practical interventions can be recommended.

Some empirical work has been done. The earlier reported work of Jarvenpaa and Leidner (1998) and Crisp and Jarvenpaa (2000) addresses the movement of trust over time, which relates to fragility/robustness. Another paper addressing this topic is Wilson et al. (2000). They measure team member trust (cognitive and affective) at three time periods with different combinations of electronic and face-to-face teams. When groups start in face-to-face (F2F) mode, their trust levels stay about the same. When groups start in electronic mode, their trust levels tend to be lower than F2F groups at T1 and then to increase to F2F group trust levels, increasing at either T2 or T3 or both. Rocco (1998) finds via an experiment that in electronically mediated team communication, trust breaks down, but that it can be restored through face-to-face communication that allows collaborative norms to be established. Rocco also finds that an initial face-to-face session helps establish enough initial trust to have a good experience. More work like the above examples should be done in order to understand what causes trust to change over time.

Ongoing research puzzles and possibilities

Time and fragility

The time issue still looms as one of the biggest unexplored aspects of trust empirical work. Although many theorize about trust fragility (for example, Child and Möllering, 2003; Ring, 1996), very little trust work has been done in a longitudinal way, and even less has been done on trust using process theory methods instead of variance theory methods (Mohr, 1982). This could be done at the organization level, using techniques developed by Van de Ven and Poole (1990). It could also be traced at an individual trustor level, using protocol analysis (Xiao and Benbasat, 2003) or process sequence analysis (Sabherwal and Robey, 1993). For example, cognition about trust is proposed to involve attentional and attributional processing (Holmes, 1991). Hence, researchers should test the extent to which people notice trust-related events and make attributions about them. Unless such methods are used, little will be determined about how trust unfolds over time. Therefore, the questions of fragility/robustness and trust progression will largely go unanswered. Also, the questions raised earlier about how the factors of initial trust work over time need to be addressed. This call for work on process theory of how trust develops over time is similar to Child and Möllering's (2003) call to pursue active trust.

Social, rumor and technology effects on trust development
One of the more neglected research areas is the impact of social issues on the movement of trust over time. Rumors have been shown to affect trust (Burt and Knez, 1996). But the effects are complicated. For example, rumors had very different effects experimentally on different agent types (forgiving versus reactive) in the Prietula and Carley (2001) study. It is also possible that individual traits enter the equation, in that negative rumors may be believed more by those with low disposition to trust. More work should be done to understand the combined impacts of individual disposition to trust and institution-based trust on the effects of rumors.

Social contact with those one meets initially can build or solidify trust. In Internet or virtual environments, distance may prohibit such interaction. But can video conferencing or instant messaging 'chats' compensate for lack of face-to-face interaction (Rosenbloom, 2000)? Under what conditions? Which type of proxy contact works best? This needs to be researched.

Trust factors: a complex, interconnected network
The trust typology increases the complexity of the issue of whom we trust. For example, in trusting e-commerce sites, are you trusting the site itself, its information, its designers, or the designers' employers (Rosenbloom, 2000)? And which of these objects of trust matters the most to success in electronic vending? The interrelatedness of the trust types introduces the question of whether we are measuring the right one. For example, America is finding out through recent corporate meltdowns that confidence in the stock market and a particular stock is founded on trust in a behind-the-scenes network of interrelated players that include the company's board and management, its internal and external auditors, the SEC (Securities and Exchange Commission) and other enforcement officials, industry-specific regulators, and the stock brokerage units. Each of these building blocks of investor trust is typically taken for granted until it shows signs of weakness. But as in a house of cards, each structural support may represent a key building block on which others depend. If any block fails in its fiduciary duty in a way that casts aspersions on the overall market institution, the stock market can, like a house of cards, collapse. Similarly in organizations, based on the initial trust model, the overall object of trust may involve a complex, interrelated network of general others, protective procedures, a given situation, individuals, teams, support groups, various levels of supervisors/managers, boundary spanners and respective vendors, all interacting and interactive. Knowing which component affects which other components has not been researched to any great extent.

Interest in trust or in one of the supports behind trust can shift in an ironic manner. Like water, the need for trust is not noticed until it becomes scarce in an environment. For example, trust research burgeoned in the e-commerce domain simply because the absence of trust-supporting structures was felt. This idea applies to the strength of different antecedents of trust. The greater the need, or lack of, the trust antecedent, the greater its significance in predicting trust. As an example, Child and Möllering's (2003) study of a Hong Kong manager trust found that because of the dearth of institutional supports in China, the contextual confidence variables were more powerful predictors of trust in their mainland China staff than were specific managerial actions to build trust, such as establishing personal rapport and recruiting locally. Similarly, in e-commerce, disposition to trust became a key antecedent to consumer trust in the e-vendor because of the perceived lack of institutional supports of, and experience with, the Internet. This exposes a lack of robust theory on how the network of trust factors can shift.

The nomological network within which the MCC98 constructs operate is beginning to be defined. Here are a few more examples. Jarvenpaa et al. (2000) relate trusting intention in the Web store to both perceived risk of the transaction and attitude toward the Web store. More work relating trust and distrust to risk is needed. Gefen et al. (2003a) and Pavlou (2003) relate trusting beliefs and trusting intentions to perceived usefulness and perceived ease of use constructs from the Technology Acceptance Model (TAM). McKnight et al. (2002a, b) relate the trust constructs to personal innovativeness, site quality, Web experience and Web risk. These extensions are important in terms of seeing how trust constructs work among other useful constructs. Obviously, much more could be done.

A few have researched the complex interplay between Zucker's (1986) process-based (personal interaction-based), social characteristics similarity-based, and institution-based trust factors (Gefen, 2004; Lane and Bachmann, 1996). Zucker argued that institution-based trust-building factors substituted for the other two types in America over time. The latter two are found in the MCC98 model in terms of in-group categorization and structural assurance. Lane and Bachmann (1996) found all three factors at work among British and German buyer and supplier firms, as did Gefen (2004) in customers of enterprise software packages. Gefen found process-based to be the strongest of the three factors. This is an area needing much more research to bring forward contextual reasons for the salience of one trust factor over another.

Distrust versus trust
The distrust area needs much more work. Something is known about the impact of disposition to distrust, but not much else is known. This is important to pursue, for example, because McKnight et al. (2003–2004) find dispositional distrust to predict different constructs than does dispositional trust, and because Xiao and Benbasat (2003) find that customers formed both trust and distrust as they interacted experimentally with an online recommendation agent. It is not known whether distrusting beliefs influence trusting intentions or whether they just influence distrusting intentions. It is not known what institution-based distrust influences or how its effects differ from the effects of risk constructs. Researchers should also see which has a greater effect on key outcomes over time – trust or distrust variables. Very little is known in this regard.

Methods and measurement
As MCC98 challenged, researchers should examine different combinations of research methods in order to capture more fully the nuances of the trust phenomenon. For example, the effects of dispositional and institution-based trust on the actors in

a trust-related situation have been examined in a questionnaire methods venue, but not in an experimental one. Rather than trying to manipulate these, why not measure them while manipulating other variables, in order to see whether they have an impact on whatever is of interest in the experiment? This would answer the call of Kee and Knox (1970) to try to understand the mental states of those being studied in the laboratory instead of merely examining the resultant experimental behaviors.

Gambetta (1988) asked a question that focuses on an ongoing trust issue: can we trust trust? Likewise, Tan and Thoen (2003) suggest that you have to determine the trust or confidence you have in a structural assurance in order to determine how much it will affect trust. This second-order issue needs to be addressed both conceptually and through proper measurement. Conceptually, work should be done to better link trust and feelings of confidence or security in that trust. Our definitions of trusting intentions and trusting beliefs above constitute a start. Following Povey (1999), we suggest that the trust level could also be measured in two steps: the raw scale score (for example, on a 1–5 Likert scale), and confidence in that score (a second scale). This would provide a way to assess the strength or hardness of the trust expressed, which is currently lacking. An interim step would be to build into the items words that convey how strong one feels about the trusting belief or intention, as Rempel et al. (1985) did.

Applying the model to distant relationships
Initial trust arises due to the newness of the relationship – but the same principles may apply when the social distance of the relationship is great (Shamir, 1995). That is, initial trust appears most applicable in what might be called 'distant relationships'. Perhaps one reason initial trust principles work for e-commerce and virtual teams is because of the social distance between players. Similarly, employee trust in senior management, since it is more socially distant due to lack of interaction, may be another fruitful field for applying initial trust. Another socially distant venue might be public trust in politicians, government (Nye et al., 1997), or other public officials or bodies (for example, the IRS – Internal Revenue Service) with whom most people never interact in person. Cultural differences between countries also create a kind of social and ideological distance, providing yet another fruitful domain for exploring the efficacy of initial trust-building principles. Very little cultural differences work has been done regarding initial trust-building.

Conclusion: the progression of initial trust research
Overall, the research trajectory based on MCC98 is moving forward. Empirical evidence continues to mount that trust often begins at a medium or high level, calling into question models of gradual or incremental trust progression. The specific trust types proposed in the original model are being validated through a number of measurements. Orderly extensions to the typology have been made, in terms of new trust constructs, corresponding distrust constructs, and constructs representing trust in technology. More researchers are using common trust terminology, making comparisons among studies more feasible than before. The links among the factors in the model are being tested (and largely confirmed) in both organizational and e-commerce domains, and the position of trust variables in wider nomological networks is being charted.

As explained in more detail above, many empirical and certain theoretical gaps remain, and much additional reesarch is required to understand the developmental nature and progression of initial trust. Four particular domains that need much more research are: the fragility and robustness of trust, the key interplay between trust and risk, the tradeoffs among competing trust factors across conditions and time, and how and why trust and distrust progress from one level to another as parties interact over time.

Acknowledgments

This chapter has benefited from the insightful comments of the editors and Guido Möllering. We appreciate the timely aid of Roger Stace in enabling us to prepare this chapter. Special thanks to Sim Sitkin, special issue editor of the original article. We also honor the memory of the late Larry Cummings, co-author and colleague.

References

Ba, S. (2001), 'Establishing online trust through a community responsibility system', *Decision Support Systems*, **31**, 323–36.
Ba, S., A.B. Whinston and H. Zhang (2003), 'Building trust in online auction markets through an economic incentive mechanism', *Decision Support Systems*, **35**(3), 273–86.
Baier, A. (1986), 'Trust and antitrust', *Ethics*, **96**(2), 231–60.
Baldwin, M.W. (1992), 'Relational schemas and the processing of social information', *Psychological Bulletin*, **112**, 461–84.
Barber, B. (1983), *The Logic and Limits of Trust*. New Brunswick, NJ: Rutgers University Press.
Bell, G.G., R.J. Oppenheimer and A. Bastien (2002), 'Trust deterioration in an international buyer–supplier relationship', *Journal of Business Ethics*, **36**, 65–78.
Berscheid, E. and W. Graziano (1979), 'The initiation of social relationships and interpersonal attraction', in R.L. Burgess and T.L. Huston (eds), *Social Exchange in Developing Relationships*, New York: Academic Press, 31–60.
Bhattacherjee, A. (2002), 'Individual trust in online firms: Scale development and initial test', *Journal of Management Information Systems*, **19**(1), 211–42.
Bigley, G.A. and J.L. Pearce (1998), 'Straining for shared meaning in organization science: Problems of trust and distrust', *Academy of Management Review*, **23**(3), 405–21.
Blau, P.M. (1964), *Exchange and Power in Social Life*. New York: John Wiley & Sons.
Bonoma, T.V. (1976), 'Conflict, cooperation, and trust in three power systems', *Behavioral Science*, **21**(6), 499–514.
Boon, S.D. and J.G. Holmes (1991), 'The dynamics of interpersonal trust: Resolving uncertainty in the face of risk', in R.A. Hinde and J. Groebel (eds), *Cooperation and Prosocial Behavior*, Cambridge, UK: Cambridge University Press, 190–211.
Boyd, J. (2003), 'The rhetorical construction of trust online', *Communication Theory*, **13**(4), 392–410.
Bromiley, P. and L.L. Cummings (1995), 'Transactions costs in organizations with trust', in Bies, R., R. Lewicki and B. Sheppard (eds), *Research on Negotiation in Organizations*, Greenwich, CT: JAI Press, 5, 219–47.
Brown, H.G., M.S. Poole and T.L. Rogers (2004), 'Interpersonal traits, complementarity, and trust in virtual collaboration', *Journal of Management Information Systems*, **20**(4), 115–37.
Burt, R.S. and M. Knez (1996), 'Trust and third-party gossip', in R.M. Kramer and T.R. Tyler (eds), *Trust in Organizations: Frontiers of Theory and Research*, Thousand Oaks, CA: Sage, 68–89.
Butler, J.K. (1991), 'Toward understanding and measuring conditions of trust: Evolution of a conditions of trust inventory', *Journal of Management*, **17**, 643–63.
Castelfranchi, C. and R. Falcone (1998), 'Social trust: Cognitive anatomy, social importance, qualification and dynamics', paper presented at the Workshop on Deception, Fraud and Trust in Agent Societies. Minneapolis, May.
Child, J. and G. Möllering (2003), 'Contextual confidence and active trust development in the Chinese business environment', *Organization Science*, **14**(1), 69–80.
Crisp, B. and S. Jarvenpaa (2000), 'Trust over time in global virtual teams', Working paper, University of Texas at Austin, 20 July.
Cunningham, J.B. and J. MacGregor (2000), 'Trust and the design of work: Complementary constructs in satisfaction and performance', *Human Relations*, **53**(12), 1575–91.
Darley, J.M. and R.H. Fazio (1980), 'Expectancy confirmation processes arising in the social interaction sequence', *American Psychologist*, **35**, 867–81.
Dion, K.K., E. Berscheid and E. Walster (1972), 'What is beautiful is good', *Journal of Personality and Social Psychology*, **24**, 285–90.

Dobing, B. (1993), 'Building trust in user-analyst relationships', unpublished doctoral dissertation, Carlson School of Management, University of Minnesota.

Droege, S.B., J.R. Anderson and M. Bowler (2003), 'Trust and organizational information flow', *Journal of Business and Management*, **9**(1), 45–59.

Duffy, M.K. and W.J. Ferrier (2003), 'Birds of a feather . . .? How supervisor–subordinate dissimilarity moderates the influence of supervisor behaviors on workplace attitudes', *Group & Organization Management*, **28**(2), 217–48.

Gabarro, J.J. (1978), 'The development of trust, influence, and expectations', in A.G. Athos and J.J. Gabarro (eds), *Interpersonal Behavior: Communication and understanding in relationships*, Englewood Cliffs, NJ: Prentice-Hall, 290–303.

Gallivan, M.J. and G. Depledge (2003), 'Trust, control and the role of interorganizational systems in electronic partnerships', *Information Systems Journal*, **13**, 159–90.

Galvin, J.E., D.H. McKnight and M.K. Ahuja (2001), 'Innocent until proven guilty: A study of antecedents to project team members' trust and cooperation', in *Trust in an Organizational Context*, Organization Science – SDA Bocconi conference proceedings, Moltrasio, Como, Italy, III, 2–34.

Gambetta, D. (1988), 'Can we trust trust?' in D. Gambetta (ed.), *Trust: Making and Breaking Cooperative Relations*, New York: Blackwell, 213–37.

Garfinkel, H. (1963), 'A conception of, and experiments with, "trust" as a condition of stable concerted actions', in O.J. Harvey (ed.), *Motivation and Social Interaction*, New York: Ronald Press, pp. 187–238.

Gefen, D. (2000), 'E-Commerce: The role of familiarity and trust', *Omega: The International Journal of Management Science*, **28**, 725–37.

Gefen, D. (2004), 'What makes an ERP implementation relationship worthwhile: Linking trust mechanisms and ERP usefulness', *Journal of Management Information Systems*, **21**(1), 275–301.

Gefen, D., E. Karahanna and D.W. Straub (2003a), 'Trust and TAM in online shopping: An integrated model', *MIS Quarterly*, **27**(1), 51–90.

Gefen, D., E. Karahanna and D.W. Straub (2003b), 'Inexperience and experience with online stores: The importance of TAM and trust', *IEEE Transactions on Engineering Management*, **50**(3), 307–21.

George, J.F. (2002), 'Influences on the intent to make Internet purchases', *Internet Research: Electronic Networking Applications and Policy*, **12**(2), 165–80.

Giffin, K. (1967), 'The contribution of studies of source credibility to a theory of interpersonal trust in the communication process', *Psychological Bulletin*, **68**(2), 104–20.

Good, D. (1988), 'Individuals, interpersonal relations, and trust', in D. Gambetta (ed.), *Trust: Making and Breaking Cooperative Relations*, New York: Blackwell, 31–48.

Grazioli, S. and S. Jarvenpaa (2003), 'Consumer and business deception on the Internet: Content analysis of documentary evidence', *International Journal of Electronic Commerce*, **7**(4), 93–118.

Holmes, J.G. (1991), 'Trust and the appraisal process in close relationships', in W.H. Jones and D. Perlman (eds), *Advances in Personal Relationships*, London: Jessica Kingsley, 2, 57–104.

Holmes, J.G. and J.K. Rempel (1989), 'Trust in close relationships', in C. Hendrick (ed.), *Close Relationships: Review of Personality and Social Psychology*, **10**, 187–220.

Jackson, P.J. (1999), 'Organizational change and virtual teams: strategic and operational integration', *Information Systems Journal*, **9**, 313–32.

Jarvenpaa, S.L. and D.E. Leidner (1998), 'Communication and trust in global virtual teams', *Journal of Computer-Mediated Communication*, **3**(4), http://www.ascusc.org/jcmc/vol3/issue4/jarvenpaa.html, accessed 6 September 2004.

Jarvenpaa, S.L. and E.H. Tiller (2001), 'Customer trust in virtual environments: A managerial perspective', *Boston University Law Review*, **81**, 665–86.

Jarvenpaa, S.L. and N. Tractinsky (1999), 'Consumer trust in an Internet store: A cross-cultural validation', *Journal of Computer-Mediated Communication*, **5**(2), http://www.ascusc.org/jcmc/vol5/issue2/jarvenpaa.html, accessed 6 September 2004.

Jarvenpaa, S.L., K. Knoll and D.E. Leidner (1998), 'Is anybody out there? Antecedents of trust in global virtual teams', *Journal of Management Information Systems*, **14**(4), 29–64.

Jarvenpaa, S.L., N. Tractinsky and M. Vitale (2000), 'Consumer trust in an Internet store', *Information Technology and Management*, **1**, 45–71.

Kanawattanachai, P. and Y. Yoo (2002), 'Dynamic nature of trust in virtual teams', *Journal of Strategic Information Systems*, **11**(3–4), 187–213.

Kaplan, S.E. and R.J. Nieschwietz (2003), 'An examination of the effects of WebTrust and company type on consumers' purchase intentions', *International Journal of Auditing*, **7**, 155–68.

Kasper-Fuehrer, E.C. and N.M. Ashkanasy (2001), 'Communicating trustworthiness and building trust in interorganizational virtual organizations', *Journal of Management*, **27**, 235–54.

Kee, H.W. and R.E. Knox (1970), 'Conceptual and Methodological Considerations in the Study of Trust and Suspicion', *Journal of Conflict Resolution*, **14**, 357–66.

Kim, P.H., D.L. Ferrin, C.D. Cooper and K. Dirks (2004), 'Removing the shadow of suspicion: The effects of apology versus denial for repairing competence- versus integrity-based trust violations', *Journal of Applied Psychology*, **89**(1), 104–18.

Klaas, B.S. (2003), 'Professional employer organizations and their role in small and medium enterprises: The impact of HR outsourcing', *Entrepreneurship Theory and Practice*, Fall, 43–61.

Koufaris, M. and W. Hampton-Sosa (2004), 'The development of initial trust in an online company by new customers', *Information and Management*, **41**(3), 377–97.

Kramer, R.M. (1994), 'The sinister attribution error', *Motivation and Emotion*, **18**, 199–231.

Lane, C. and R. Bachmann (1996), 'The social constitution of trust: Supplier relations in Britain and Germany', *Organization Studies*, **17**(3), 365–95.

Langer, E.J. (1975), 'The illusion of control', *Journal of Personality and Social Psychology*, **32**, 311–28.

Leanna, C.R. and H.J. Van Buren (1999), 'Organizational social capital and employment practices', *Academy of Management Review*, **24**(3), 538–55.

Lewicki, R.J., D.J. McAllister and R.J. Bies (1998), 'Trust and distrust: New relationships and realities', *Academy of Management Review*, **23**(3), 438–58.

Lewis, J.D. and A.J. Weigert (1985a), 'Trust as a social reality', *Social Forces*, **63**(4), 967–85.

Lewis, J.D. and A.J. Weigert (1985b), 'Social atomism, holism, and trust', *The Sociological Quarterly*, **216**(4), 455–71.

Luhmann, N. (1979), *Trust and Power*, New York: Wiley.

Mayer, R.C. and J.H. Davis (1999), 'The effect of the performance appraisal system on trust for management: A field quasi-experiment', *Journal of Applied Psychology*, **84**, 123–36.

Mayer, R.C., J.H. Davis and F.D. Schoorman (1995), 'An integrative model of organizational trust', *Academy of Management Review*, **20**, 709–34.

McKnight, D.H. and N.L. Chervany (1996), 'The meanings of trust', *University of Minnesota MIS Research Center Working Paper series*, WP 96–04, http://misrc.umn.edu/wpaper/WorkingPapers/9604.pdf

McKnight, D.H. and N.L. Chervany (2001a), 'What trust means in e-commerce customer relationships: An interdisciplinary conceptual typology', *International Journal of Electronic Commerce*, **6**(2), 35–59.

McKnight, D.H. and N.L. Chervany (2001b), 'Trust and distrust definitions: One bite at a time', in R. Falcone, M. Singh and Y.H. Tan (eds), *Trust in Cyber-Societies: Integrating the Human and Artificial Perspectives*, Berlin: Springer, 27–54.

McKnight, D.H. and N.L. Chervany (2005), 'What builds system troubleshooter trust the best – Experiential or non-experiential factors?' Forthcoming, *Information Resources Management Journal*.

McKnight, D.H. and J.B. Thatcher (2004), 'Trust in technology: Development of a set of constructs and measures', Working paper, Michigan State University.

McKnight, D.H., V. Choudhury and C.J. Kacmar (2002a), 'Developing and validating trust measures for e-commerce: An integrative typology', *Information Systems Research*, **13**(3), 334–59.

McKnight, D.H., V. Choudhury and C.J. Kacmar (2002b), 'The impact of initial consumer trust on intentions to transact with a Web site: A trust building model', *Journal of Strategic Information Systems*, **11**(3–4), 297–323.

McKnight, D.H., L.L. Cummings and N.L. Chervany (1998), 'Initial trust formation in new organizational relationships', *Academy of Management Review*, **23**, 1–18.

McKnight, D.H., C.J. Kacmar and V. Choudhury (2003–2004), 'Dispositional trust and distrust distinctions in predicting high- and low-risk Internet expert advice site perceptions', *e-Service Journal*, **3**(2), 35–58.

McKnight, D.H., C.J. Kacmar and V. Choudhury (2004a), 'Shifting factors and the ineffectiveness of third party assurance seals: A two-stage model of initial trust in an e-vendor,' *Electronic Markets*, **14**(3), 252–66.

McKnight, D.H., C.J. Kacmar and V. Choudhury (2004b), 'Do individual differences matter to safety/security beliefs about the Web? The varied effects of personal innovativeness and dispositional trust/distrust', Working paper, Michigan State University.

Meyerson, D., K.E. Weick and R.M. Kramer (1996), 'Swift trust and temporary groups', in R.M. Kramer and T.R. Tyler (eds), *Trust in Organizations: Frontiers of Theory and Research*, Thousand Oaks, CA: Sage, 166–95.

Mishra, A.K. (1996), 'Organizational responses to crisis: The centrality of trust', in R.M. Kramer and T.R. Tyler (eds), *Trust in Organizations: Frontiers of Theory and Research*, Thousand Oaks, CA: Sage, 261–87.

Mohr, L.B. (1982), *Explaining Organizational Behavior*, San Francisco, CA: Jossey-Bass.

Muir, B.M. (1994), 'Trust in automation: Part I. Theoretical issues in the study of trust and human intervention in automated systems', *Ergonomics*, **37**(11), 1905–22.

Nicholson, C.Y., L.D. Compeau and R. Sethi (2001), 'The role of interpersonal liking in building trust in long-term channel relationships', *Academy of Marketing Science Journal*, **29**(1), 3–15.

Nye, J.S., Jr, P.D. Zelikow and D.C. King (1997), *Why People Don't Trust Government*, Cambridge, MA: Harvard University Press.

Nyhan, R.C. (1999), 'Increasing affective organizational commitment in public organizations', *Review of Public Personnel Administration*, **19**(3), 58–70.

Oliver, A.L. and K. Montgomery (2001), 'A system cybernetic approach to the dynamics of individual- and organizational-level trust', *Human Relations*, **54**(8), 1045–63.

Pavlou, P.A. (2002), 'Institution-based trust in interorganizational exchange relationships: The role of online B2B marketplaces on trust formation', *Journal of Strategic Information Systems*, **11**(3–4), 215–43.

Pavlou, P.A. (2003), 'Consumer acceptance of electronic commerce: Integrating trust and risk with the Technology Acceptance Model', *International Journal of Electronic Commerce*, **7**(3), 101–34.

Pavlou, P.A. and D. Gefen (2004), 'Building effective online marketplaces with institution-based trust', *Information Systems Research*, **15**(1), 37–59.

Pennington, R., H.D. Wilcox and V. Grover (2003), 'The role of system trust in business-to-consumer transactions', *Journal of Management Information Systems*, **20**(3), 197–226.

Povey, D. (1999), 'Developing electronic trust policies using a risk management model', in R. Baumgart (ed.), *Proceedings of CQRE[Secure] Congress*, 1–16.

Prietula, M.J. and K.M. Carley (2001), 'Boundedly rational and emotional agents: Cooperation, trust and rumor', in C. Castelfranchi and Y. Tan (eds), *Trust in Virtual Societies*, Dordrecht: Kluwer Academic Publishers, 169–93.

Rempel, J.K., J.G. Holmes and M.P. Zanna (1985), 'Trust in close relationships', *Journal of Personality and Social Psychology*, **49**, 95–112.

Ridings, C.M., D. Gefen and B. Arinze (2002), 'Some antecedents and effects of trust in virtual communities', *Journal of Strategic Information Systems*, **11**(3–4), 271–95.

Riker, W.H. (1971), 'The nature of trust', in J.T. Tedeschi (ed.) *Perspectives on Social Power*, Chicago: Aldine Publishing, pp. 63–81.

Ring, P.S. (1996), 'Fragile and resilient trust and their roles in economic exchange', *Business & Society*, **35**(2), 148–75.

Ring, P.S. and A.H. Van de Ven (1994), 'Developmental processes of cooperative interorganizational relationships', *Academy of Management Review*, **19**, 90–118.

Robinson, S.L. (1996), 'Trust and breach of the psychological contract', *Administrative Science Quarterly*, **41**, 574–99.

Rocco, E. (1998), 'Trust breaks down in electronic contexts but can be repaired by some initial face-to-face contact', in *Proceedings of CHI'98*, 496–502.

Rosenbloom, A. (2000), 'Trusting Technology', *Communications of the ACM*, **43**(12), 31–2.

Rotter, J.B. (1971), 'Generalized expectancies for interpersonal trust', *American Psychologist*, **26**, 443–52.

Rubin, Z. (1988), 'Preface', in R.J. Sternberg and M.L. Barnes (eds), *The Psychology of Love*. New Haven, CT: Yale University Press, vii–xii.

Sabherwal, R. and D. Robey (1993), 'An empirical taxonomy of implementation processes based on sequences of events in information systems development', *Organization Science*, **4**(4), 548–76.

Schutz, A. (1964), *Studies in Social Theory: Collected Papers II*, The Hague: Nijhoff.

Schutz, A. (1967), *The Phenomenology of the Social World*, trans. G. Walsh and F. Lehnart, Evanston, IL: Northwestern University.

Shamir, B.M. (1995), 'Social distance and charisma: Theoretical notes and an exploratory study', *Leadership Quarterly*, **6**, 19–47.

Shankar, V., G.L. Urban and F. Sultan (2002), 'Online trust: A stakeholder perspective, concepts, implications, and future directions', *Journal of Strategic Information Systems*, **11**(3–4), 325–44.

Shapiro, S.P. (1987), 'The social control of impersonal trust', *American Journal of Sociology*, **93**(3), 623–58.

Siau, K. and Z. Shen (2003), 'Building customer trust in mobile commerce', *Communications of the ACM*, **46**(4), 91–4.

Sitkin, S.B. and N.L. Roth (1993), 'Explaining the limited effectiveness of legalistic remedies for trust/distrust', *Organization Science*, **4**, 367–92.

Smith, G.F. (1990), 'The method of conceptual analysis: Applications in the management and organization sciences', unpublished working paper, University of Minnesota.

Stewart, K.J. (2003), 'Trust transfer on the World Wide Web', *Organization Science*, **14**, 5–17.

Sutton, R.I. and B.M. Staw (1995), 'What theory is not', *Administrative Science Quarterly*, **40**, 371–84.

Tan, Y. and W. Thoen (2001), 'Toward a generic model of trust for electronic commerce', *International Journal of Electronic Commerce*, **5**(2), 61–74.

Tan, Y. and W. Thoen (2003), 'Electronic contract drafting based on risk and trust assessment', *International Journal of Electronic Commerce*, **7**(4), 55–71.

Tiryakian, E.A. (1968), 'Typologies', in D.L. Sills (ed.), *International Encyclopedia of the Social Sciences*, New York: The Macmillan Company and The Free Press, 16, 177–86.

Tschannen-Moran, M. and W.K. Hoy (2000), 'A multidisciplinary analysis of the nature, meaning, and measurement of trust', *Review of Educational Research*, **70**(4), 547–93.

Van de Ven, A.H. and M.S. Poole (1990), 'Methods for studying innovation development in the Minnesota innovation research program', *Organization Science*, **1**(3), 313–35.

Wells, C.V. and D. Kipnis (2001), 'Trust, dependency, and control in the contemporary organization', *Journal of Business and Psychology*, **15**(4), 593–603.

Williams, M. (2001), 'In whom we trust: Group membership as an effective context for trust development', *Academy of Management Review*, **26**(3), 377–96.

Wilson, J.M., S.G. Strauss and W. McEvily (2000), 'All in due time: The development of trust in electronic and face-to-face groups', Working paper, Carnegie Mellon University.

Xiao, S. and I. Benbasat (2003), 'The formation of trust and distrust in recommendation agents in repeated interactions: A process-tracing analysis', in N. Sadeh (ed.), *Fifth International Conference on Electronic Commerce*, Pittsburth, PA: ACM, 287–93.

Zaheer, S., S. Albert and A. Zaheer (1999), 'Time scales and organizational theory', *Academy of Management Review*, **24**(4), 725–41.

Zand, D.E. (1972), 'Trust and managerial problem solving', *Administrative Science Quarterly*, **17**, 229–39.

Zuboff, S. (1988), *In the Age of the Smart Machine*, New York: Basic Books.

Zucker, L.G. (1986), 'Production of trust: Institutional sources of economic structure, 1840–1920', in B.M. Staw and L.L. Cummings (eds), *Research in Organizational Behavior*, Greenwich, CT: JAI Press, Vol. **8**, 53–111.

3   Can groups be trusted? An experimental study of trust in collective entities

Bill McEvily, Roberto A. Weber, Cristina Bicchieri and Violet T. Ho

Introduction

Trust is the topic of a considerable amount of recent research in the social sciences. This trend is particularly noteworthy in the economics, organizational and strategy literatures, where trust is considered extremely important for many kinds of interaction. For instance, several economists argue that trust is an essential 'lubricant' without which even the simplest forms of economic exchange can not occur (Arrow 1974).[1] Trust increases the efficiency of exchange by reducing the expectation of opportunistic behavior and consequently lowering associated transaction costs (Bromiley and Cummings 1995; John 1984; McEvily and Zaheer, chapter 16, this volume). Strategy researchers suggest that trust is a strategic resource that has the potential to provide a source of sustained competitive advantage (Barney and Hansen 1995), while other organizational researchers conceptualize trust as a governance form that provides a framework to guide and direct the organization and coordination of economic activity (Bradach and Eccles 1989; McEvily et al. 2003; Powell 1990).

Incorporating the concept of trust into economic, strategic and organizational theories clearly holds the potential of producing far-reaching implications for our understanding of exchange, competition and behavior in economic and organizational settings. By focusing on the motives and intentions of economic actors, this line of research promises to explicitly investigate and sharpen the core assumptions upon which theory is based. At the same time, however, integrating the concept of trust into existing theory poses a number of challenges. Chief among these is the question of how to extend – or whether it is reasonable to extend – an individual-level construct such as trust to more aggregate levels of analysis.

To a large extent placing trust in individuals and placing trust in collective entities (e.g. groups, organizations, industries, institutions, etc.) are used interchangeably in the literature and without specific consideration for whether differences in the object of trust are meaningful or appropriate. For example, transaction costs economics proposes that 'human agents are given to opportunism' (Williamson 1985, p. 64), but that *firms* must safeguard their transactions against the threat of such untrustworthy behavior. As a result there is ambiguity about the object of trust that is most relevant to minimizing transaction costs of exchange – the individual agent or the partner organization. This raises several questions. First and foremost, does trust exist at different levels of analysis (individual versus collective)? If so, is trust across levels related and does trust at one level influence trust at another? For instance, if one trusts the individual agent with whom one deals, then is one necessarily more inclined to trust that person's organization? Or is it even possible to trust a collective entity, independent of the trust one has for its individual members? And, perhaps most importantly, does trust at different levels of analysis affect economic behaviors in different ways?

Surprisingly, these fundamental questions have received relatively little research attention despite the widespread application of trust to economic and organizational relationships involving collective entities. A related stream of research in sociology focuses on 'system' (Luhmann 1979; Giddens 1990) and 'institutional-based' (Zucker 1986) trust. These forms of trust refer to abstract structures that shape expectations through generalized rules of behavior. System and institutional-based trust create commonly accepted background assumptions, and thereby lower the inherent risk of trusting a counterpart (Bachmann 2001; 2003). Similar to our notion of trust in collective entities, system and institutional-based trust are 'impersonal' forms of trust that are not based on familiarity with a specific individual. At the same time, our view of trust in a collective entity presupposes that the individual is involved in a direct relationship (economic exchange in this study) with the collective entity, whereas system and institutional-based trust primarily refer to the economic framework within which the relationship is embedded. For instance, in the context of buyer–supplier interfirm exchanges, trust in a collective entity would be a purchasing manager's trust in the buyer organization while system and institutional-based trust would focus on, for example, the legal system of contract enforcement, regulatory agencies, third-party brokers, etc.

Although the work on system and institutional-based trust is conceptually related to our focus on trust in a collective entity, there is virtually no empirical work validating the existence of trust in collective entities. A notable exception is a study by Zaheer et al. (1998) that explores, using survey responses of boundary-spanning agents in buyer–supplier interfirm exchanges, the relationship between trust in a specific individual dealt with and trust in that individual's organization, referred to as interpersonal and inter-organizational trust respectively. Zaheer et al. (1998) find that interpersonal and inter-organizational trust are related, but distinct; economic agents discriminate between the two types of trust, but also view trust at different levels of analysis as strongly related. Although their study provides evidence consistent with the concept of trust in a collective entity, it does not definitively rule out the possibility that trust in a collective entity (i.e. inter-organizational trust) is merely an artifact of trust in the individual members of the collective entity (i.e. interpersonal trust). In particular, it may be the case that trust in a collective entity is simply a function of trust in its individual members. If so, trust in a collective entity is reducible to trust in individuals and does not exist as a separate concept. This suggests that validating the existence of trust in a collective entity requires evidence that is not specifically tied to trust in individuals and raises the question of whether there is some aspect of trust in a collective entity that exists apart from trust in the members of a collective entity.

The purpose of this chapter is to explore the relationship between trust in individuals and trust in collective entities, and the relationship of these two types of trust to economic behavior. We argue that trust can be meaningfully applied to economic transactions involving both individual and collective entities, and that trust at these two levels is related. We propose that economic actors form perceptions about the trustworthiness of collective entities based on exchanges conducted with individual members of the collectivity. This trust in the collective then becomes transferable to other individuals within the collectivity and serves as a proxy for individual trust where detailed knowledge of individual members of the collectivity is limited or absent (McEvily et al. 2003; Stewart 2003). This is true even when there is no reason to believe that these other individuals are likely to exhibit similar trust-related properties. Thus trust in the collective entity is used as a heuristic for trust in individuals and is extended to transactions with other members of the collectivity, even those that are unknown and about which there is little or no information for determining trustworthiness. In this way, membership in a collectivity or group can be taken to signal trustworthiness (Kramer et al. 1996), without each member having to exhibit his or her trustworthiness directly to all other parties in an economic exchange.

Based on the above ideas, we address the following research question: *Is an individual's perception of a counterpart's trustworthiness affected by the counterpart's membership in a group and by the past actions of others in that group, even in a situation where membership in the group conveys no meaningful information about trustworthiness?*

To explore this question we conducted a laboratory experiment where the outcomes of economic exchanges were influenced by the degree to which subjects trusted their counterparts and the extent to which those counterparts actually upheld the trust that was placed in them. Our research builds on previous experiments using the 'trust' (or 'investment') game (e.g. Berg et al. 1995). We extend this paradigm by including a treatment in which we embed exchange within the context of minimally defined collective entities. In this treatment, transactions among individual economic actors are no longer isolated events, but rather are linked through individuals' membership in collective entities.

Conceptualizing trust in a collective entity

Trust is an inherently complex concept (Corazzini 1977) that has been studied from a number of different disciplinary perspectives. As a result, a wide variety of definitions exist. Despite the heterogeneity in conceptualizations, there are a number of common elements unifying the many different usages of trust. In particular, there is widespread agreement that *trust is the willingness to be vulnerable based on the positive expectation of the intentions or behavior of others* (Mayer et al. 1995; Rousseau et al. 1998). Moreover, for trust to arise, interdependence and uncertainty are necessary conditions. Interdependence means that the interest of one party cannot be fulfilled without reliance on another party. Uncertainty means that the possibility of experiencing negative outcomes by relying on another party requires taking a 'leap of faith' (Lewis and Weigert 1985). If another's intentions could be ascertained with complete certainty, trust would not be needed. Accordingly, trust is the choice to make oneself vulnerable under the conditions of interdependence and uncertainty.

Consistent with the broader literature on trust we refer to the extent to which one individual trusts another individual with whom she deals as *trust in an individual*. The degree to which a sales representative trusts the specific purchasing manager with whom she deals is an example of trust in an individual. In contrast, *trust in a collective entity* represents the extent of trust that an individual places in a collectivity with which she deals. Trust in a collective entity exists between an individual on the one hand and a collection of individuals on the other. A sales representative's trust for the buyer organization that she transacts with is an example of trust in a collective entity. The distinction between trust in an individual and trust in a collective entity is based on the object of trust. Whereas the source of trust resides in individuals for both, the object of trust differs. Rather than being directed at a specific individual, the referent of trust in a collective entity is an aggregate social system comprising a number of individuals. The placing of trust in a collective entity, rather than a specific individual, is consistent with definitions of trust that emphasize 'confidence in or reliance on some quality or attribute of a *person or thing*' (*Oxford English Dictionary*, emphasis added).[2]

While the conceptual distinction between trust in an individual and trust in a collective entity is fairly well established, empirical evidence substantiating the distinction is largely absent. As noted previously, in order to distinguish the two forms of trust it is important to separate the trust an individual places in a collective entity from the trust that an individual places in individual members of the collective entity. For instance, an individual may claim to trust a certain organization, but may only be referring to the trustworthiness of specific individuals in the organization or of the general population from which the organization draws its membership. Similarly, one may generally believe that people are trustworthy, and therefore most organizations comprising ordinary people are also trustworthy. Or, one may feel that a group is trustworthy because of familiarity with all of the members of the group and their trustworthiness. We argue that these are not instances of trust in a collective entity, since there is no separate attribution of trustworthiness to the organization as an entity in itself. Instead, we suggest that trust in a collective entity can be more cleanly distinguished from trust in individuals by studying a behavioral manifestation of trust that is clearly separable across, and distinctly attributable to, the two types of trust.

To disentangle trust in individuals and trust in collective entities, we designed a laboratory experiment that allowed us to directly explore the possibility that trust may exist for groups, independent of the trust for the individuals in those groups. In the experiments, we created a very basic form of collective using a variant of the well-known 'minimal group paradigm' (Tajfel et al. 1971). Research on minimal groups shows that there is a discontinuity between individual and group behavior: people tend to behave differently when confronting another individual or a group, or when they themselves act as group members. What is even more striking is that this discontinuity occurs even when the group is created on the basis of an inconsequential criterion, and group membership is anonymous. We thus expected to find a difference in behavior when subjects were faced with 'unlabeled' individuals as opposed to members of a designated group. In the absence of previous interactions with a specific member of a group, we were interested in exploring whether an initial experience with an anonymous member of the same group translates into a stereotypical judgment of the whole group, on some chosen dimension.

In particular, we explored the extent to which subjects were likely to exhibit trust in another subject based on experience with a previous member of that subject's group. Specifically, participants in our experiment played the trust game twice. Our focus is on how the actions of the first counterpart affected decisions when playing the game with the second counterpart. We are especially interested in whether membership of the two counterparts in the same 'minimal group' makes this effect stronger. We find a modest effect, in both magnitude and significance. However, the presence of a positive result is compelling, even given the modest significance, since we used the weakest possible form of group identity in our experiments. More generally, the finding is important because it provides a clear and carefully controlled demonstration that lends support to the existence of trust in collective entities.

The trust game
As its name suggests, the trust game creates a situation where one player must decide whether to trust another, and this other must then decide whether to honor or abuse this trust. Specifically, Player 1 is given some initial wealth allocation of which she must decide how much to 'trust' to Player 2. Player 2 can be thought of as an agent of Player 1 who has the ability to turn this trusted amount into an even greater sum. Therefore, the amount received by Player 2 is some multiple of the amount trusted to Player 2 by Player 1. After receiving this amount, Player 2 must decide how much, if any, of the total amount received to return to Player 1.

This game models several situations in which the attractiveness to one party of a welfare-increasing investment hinges on the trustworthiness of another. For instance, consider a situation where the owner of a small firm has to decide how much training to provide an employee. This training is costly for the owner of the firm, but can yield greater profits for both the employee and the firm, provided the employee remains with the firm after the training. Once the owner decides how much to commit to training and the training actually takes place, the employee then decides how long to remain with the firm. Assuming that the employee can realize greater profit by leaving to go to another firm once the training is received, the problem is exactly the one modeled by the trust game. Player 1 (the owner) decides how much of some allocation to commit to Player 2 (the employee), who then decides whether to honor this trust (remain with the firm, in which case both employee and owner receive a better payoff than if there had been no training) or abuse this trust (leave the firm immediately after training, yielding the highest payoff to the employee but the lowest to the owner).

The game can also be described formally. In the continuous version of the game, Player 1 is given some amount $W>0$, which she can divide between one amount she keeps for herself and one she trusts to Player 2. Label the amount she trusts to Player 2 as x, with $0 \leq x \leq W$. The amount x is then multiplied by a constant, $r>1$, so that the second player receives the greater amount rx. Player 2 must then decide what proportion, k, of rx to return to Player 1, keeping the rest, $(1-k)rx$, for himself. Assuming that Player 2 also receives some fixed sum c (which might be zero), the following are the payoffs for the game:

$$\text{Payoff to Player 1:} \quad \pi_1 = (W-x) + xrk = W + (kr-1)x$$
$$\text{Payoff to Player 2:} \quad \pi_2 = c + (1-k)rx$$

Player 2 moves second and the choice of k does not affect x, which has already been determined. Therefore, as long as Player 2 is maximizing his monetary payoff, he will select k equal to zero and keep the entire amount rx. Knowing this, Player 1 should always keep the entire amount W and set x equal to zero. Thus, in the unique subgame-perfect Nash equilibrium to the game, $x = k = 0$, $\pi_1 = W$, and $\pi_2 = c$.

The game is interesting, however, because trust on the part of Player 1 can lead to an outcome that Pareto-dominates (i.e. is more efficient than) this equilibrium. This is true for any outcome in which x is greater than zero and kr is greater than one, meaning that Player 1 invests a positive amount and receives more than that amount back from Player 2.

Several laboratory experiments studied the trust game. In the first example of such a study, Berg et al. (1995) used the trust game to determine whether or not trusting behavior can be found when social enforcement is not possible. In their experiments subjects played the game in an environment where the usual self-interested motivations assumed by economists to lead to trusting behavior were eliminated. Subjects played the game only once and under complete (double-blind) anonymity. In spite of this anonymity and lack of repetition, only two of the 32 subjects in the role of Player 1 sent $0. On the other hand, five subjects sent the entire amount of $10. The average amount sent was $5.16 and the average amount returned was $4.66, indicating that sending money led to slight losses on average for Player 1.[3]

Taken together, the experiments by Berg et al. and others using different variations of the trust game – with varying payoffs and parameters – show some consistent results, even across cultures (e.g. Van Huyck et al. 1995; Güth et al. 1997; Snijders and Keren 1998; Buchan et al. in press; Ashraf et al. 2005). First, the subgame-perfect equilibrium prediction is rarely observed. Most subjects in the role of Player 1 send a positive amount to Player 2. On the other hand, most subjects who sent money as Player 1 did not send the full amount W. A second main finding is that while many subjects in the role of Player 2 returned a positive amount to Player 1, the returns tended to be slightly less than the original investment on average. Therefore, while subjects in general exhibited trusting behavior, this trust was often repaid, but usually not sufficiently to prevent it from being costly. Consequently, in our experiments, which use a variation of the trust game, we expect a significant amount of trusting behavior. However, our attention is primarily on whether trusting behavior is influenced by past experience with counterparts who belong to the same group.

One previous study explored the connection between group boundaries and trust, although with an entirely different focus than ours. Buchan et al. (2002) used random assignment to divide subjects into two groups (Proposers and Responders) and then used the trust game to measure the extent to which subjects in the first group exhibited trust for subjects in the second group. The treatment variable was the nature of the relationship between Proposers and Responders. In a Direct condition, a Proposer sent money to a Responder who then sent money back to the same Proposer. In a Group condition, Proposer A sent money to Responder A while Proposer B sent money to Responder B, and Responder A then sent money back to Proposer B while Responder B sent money back to Proposer A. In this condition, reciprocity was indirect, but two Proposers and two Responders were mutually linked by their actions. Finally, in a Society condition, Proposer A sent money to Responder B, who sent money back to a randomly selected Proposer C. In this condition, reciprocity was indirect and links between Proposers and Responders were much more distant than in the Group condition. The results in all three conditions revealed significant amounts of trust and reciprocation, though both of these decreased as the interaction between Proposers and Responders became less direct. Buchan et al.'s experiments demonstrate that trust exists even when it involves indirect reciprocation between members of randomly determined groups, but that this trust (measured by the amount sent by Proposers) is less the more indirect the relationship.

The study by Buchan et al. is relevant for our experiment since it shows that subjects exhibit trusting behavior even when the object of this trust is not directly responsible for reciprocating it. One interpretation of their results is that, even with groups determined by an entirely random process, subjects are willing to trust counterparts when someone else in this counterpart's group must reciprocate this trust. In this case the object of trust seems to be the group rather than a specific individual.[4] While the experiments do not constitute a direct test of trust in a collective entity, the results are consistent with the notion that subjects can trust a group rather than an individual.

Our experiments differ from those of Buchan et al. in that we *directly* explore trust in a collective entity. In particular, we focus on whether a subject's past history of dealing with one member of a group influences that subject's propensity to trust another member of the same group, beyond the information that such history provides about the trustworthiness of the second individual.

Experimental design

Our experiment tests whether subjects assigned minimal group labels use these labels to draw inferences about the trustworthiness of other individuals. In our experiment, subjects play the trust game twice against two subjects randomly selected from the population of other participants. Our treatment variable is the relationship between these two other subjects. In the Control condition, they are simply referred to as two other subjects of the opposite role (Player 1 or Player 2), which was randomly determined at the beginning of the experiment. In the Group condition, these two other subjects are members of the same 'minimal group' that was determined by responses to an unrelated question. We are particularly interested in how subjects respond to the outcome of the first game, when playing the second game. Our hypothesis is that subjects in the Group condition will be more influenced by what their first counterpart did than those in the Control. Therefore, our experiment is primarily intended to test whether perceptions of trustworthiness are transferred more readily across individuals who are in the same group than across individuals with no such group label.

Subjects in our experiment played two rounds of the following discrete version of the trust game:

- Player 1 was given an allocation of $4 at the beginning of the game.
- Player 1 then chose an amount to send to Player 2. This amount was $0, $2 or $4.
- Player 2 received an amount equal to four times the amount sent by Player 1.
- Player 2 then decided whether to return to Player 1 either $0 or half of the amount received.

Note that this is the same as the trust game discussed in the previous section, with $W = 4, $x \in \{\$0, \$2, \$4\}$, $r = 4$, $c = \$0$, and $k \in \{0, \frac{1}{2}\}$. Therefore, the payoffs to Player 1 and Player 2, respectively, were:

$$
\begin{aligned}
\pi_1 &= 4 + (4k - 1)x \\
\pi_2 &= (1 - k)\, 4x.
\end{aligned}
$$

As in other versions of the trust game, the unique subgame-perfect Nash equilibrium is for Player 1 to send $0 and for Player 2 to return $0 for any amount received, leaving Player 1 with $4 and Player 2 with $0. However, this equilibrium outcome is Pareto-dominated by the outcome in which Player 1 sends $4 and Player 2 returns half, leaving both players with $8.

Each of the sessions in our experiment consisted of 10–20 subjects recruited from a distribution list of students at Carnegie Mellon and the University of Pittsburgh. At the beginning of the session, subjects were divided into two groups (explained in more detail below). Each subject then played the game twice, in the same role, with two randomly selected subjects from the other group. Subjects did not know the identity of the other subjects with whom they were playing the game.

In each play of the game, actions were made and recorded using a choice sheet. At the beginning of the game, Player 1 circled on the choice sheet how much he or she wanted to send to Player 2. The sheet was then collected, the choice recorded, and the sheet was given to a Player 2. This Player 2 then circled his or her choice of how much to send back to Player 1.[5] The sheets were then collected, the choices recorded, and the sheet was given back to Player 1 who could observe the outcome of the game. Players also had record sheets on which they recorded what happened in each of the two games.

The only difference between the two treatments was in how the groups were determined and in the labels used to refer to the two roles.

- In the Control condition, subjects were randomly assigned participant numbers at the beginning of the experiment. They were then told that odd participant numbers corresponded to the role of Player 1 and that even participant numbers corresponded to the role of Player 2. Subsequently, the two roles were referred to as 'Player 1' and 'Player 2'.
- In the Group condition, subjects were also randomly assigned participant numbers, but these were not used to determine the roles. Instead, subjects were asked to make a guess about the number of days it would rain the following year in San Francisco. A median split of these guesses was then used to divide the subjects into two groups: High Guessers and Low Guessers. High Guessers played the role of Player 1, while Low Guessers played the role of Player 2. Subsequently, all reference to the two roles was made using the terms 'High Guessers' and 'Low Guessers'.

Note that this is a very weak group manipulation. In one condition, the roles are simply determined by a guess about something unrelated to the game. There was no other difference between the two treatments. In both treatments, subjects who were in the role of Player 1 were seated on one side of the room while subjects in the role of Player 2 were seated on the other. Subjects were visible to each other during the experiment, but did not know with whom they were matched.[6] At the end of the experiment, subjects completed a questionnaire measuring their general propensity to trust (Rotter, 1967).

We conducted 12 sessions (six in the Control condition and six in the Group condition), using a total of 174 Carnegie Mellon and University of Pittsburgh graduate and undergraduate students (80 in Control and 94 in Group). Subjects were recruited from a large pool of potentially interested participants via an e-mail announcement that provided little information on the details of the experiment. The sessions were conducted between September 2000 and May 2001.

Results

Our main hypothesis is that the interaction between experience (what happens in the first round) and experimental treatment affects the amount sent in the second round by Player 1. Specifically, the presence of trust in a collective entity implies that subjects in the Group condition will be more influenced by experience than subjects in the Control. We begin our analysis by exploring the aggregate data for other patterns of behavior related to the group manipulation.[7]

Aggregate behavior

Table 3.1 presents the total amounts sent by subjects in the role of Player 1 by condition. The aggregate choices by subjects do not differ greatly by condition. There are slightly more Player 1s who sent $4 in the Control (60 percent) than in the Group condition (48 percent), but this difference is not significant. Moreover, almost twice as many subjects in the Group condition (32 percent) than in the Control (18 percent) initially sent $2. In fact, while about 80 percent of subjects in the role of Player 1 in both conditions sent some amount of money in the first round, a larger proportion *of those sending some money* sent $4 in the Control condition (25 of 32, 78 percent) than in the Group condition (22 of 37, 59 percent). This difference in amount sent among those who sent money is marginally significant in a Fisher Exact test (p = 0.08). However, this pattern is reversed – but is not significant – when we look at the choices in Round 2. Specifically, in the second round we see that a smaller proportion *of those sending some money* sent $4 in the Control condition (23 of 29, 79 percent) than in the Group condition (23 of 28, 82 percent).[8] Note also that in both treatments the frequency of players sending $0 increased between Rounds 1 and 2, and that this increase was greater in the Group condition (from 21 to 40 percent) than in the Control condition (from 20 to 28 percent). Overall, among subjects in the role of Player 1, there are slight differences in behavior between the two conditions when looking at the aggregate data. In particular, of those sending some money, the distributions of amounts sent differ between the treatment and control conditions.

Table 3.2 reports the behavior of subjects in the role of Player 2 by condition and round. Each entry in the table gives – for each possible amount sent – what proportion of Player 2s returned one-half of the amount received, resulting in an improvement for Player 1 over the initial allocation. The remaining subjects all returned $0, resulting in a

Table 3.1   Frequencies of amounts sent by Player 1

Condition	Amount sent	Round 1	Round 2	Total
Control	$0	8 (20%)	11 (28%)	19 (24%)
	$2	7 (18%)	6 (15%)	13 (16%)
	$4	25 (63%)	23 (58%)	48 (60%)
Group	$0	10 (21%)	19 (40%)	29 (31%)
	$2	15 (32%)	5 (11%)	20 (21%)
	$4	22 (47%)	23 (49%)	45 (48%)

Table 3.2   Percentage of Player 2s returning half by offer

Condition	Amount sent	Round 1	Round 2	Total
Control	$2	4/7 (57%)	1/6 (17%)	5/13 (38%)
	$4	13/25 (52%)	12/23 (52%)	25/48 (52%)
	Total	17/32 (53%)	13/29 (45%)	30/61 (49%)
Group	$2	3/15 (20%)	3/5 (60%)	6/20 (30%)
	$4	11/22 (50%)	12/23 (52%)	23/45 (51%)
	Total	14/37 (38%)	15/28 (54%)	29/65 (45%)

loss for Player 1. Cases where Player 2 received $0 meant there was no subsequent choice and are therefore not included in the table.

Again, when we look at the aggregate data we see small differences between the two treatments. Note first that in Round 1, the number of subjects who returned half is greater in the Control (53 percent) than in the Group condition (38 percent), but this difference is not significant. This difference is largest for subjects who were sent $2. In the Control condition, 4 of 7 (57 percent) such subjects returned one-half; in the Group condition, only 3 of 15 (20 percent) such subjects did so. This difference, however, is not significant in a Fisher Exact test ($p = 0.11$). When pooling across rounds and amounts sent, we see that Player 2s in the Control condition were only very slightly more likely to return half (49 percent) than those in the Group condition (45 percent).

Individual behavior and trust in a collective entity
When a subject in the role of Player 1 sends either $2 or $4 to a Player 2, the outcome is one of two possibilities: either half the multiplied amount is returned or nothing is returned. In one case, Player 1 is better off – relative to the initial allocation – for having sent an amount greater than $0, and in the other Player 1 is worse off. Therefore, we can think of these as situations where initial trust in Round 1 is either 'honored' or 'abused'. The main aim of this chapter is to explore what happens in Round 2 when trust is either honored or abused in Round 1 and, in particular, whether subjects in the Group condition are more affected by these events than those in the Control sessions. Such behavior is directly relevant for testing our main prediction that trust in a collective entity is separable from trust in the individual members of that collectivity. The results in Tables 3.1 and 3.2, however, do not allow us to test this hypothesis because the results are presented at an aggregate level across rounds. Instead it is necessary to examining subjects' experiences across rounds and within conditions, which is how the data are organized in Table 3.3.

Table 3.3   Choices in Round 2 by Player 1 contingent on outcomes in Round 1

Sent in Round 1	Returned in Round 1	Trust honored or abused	Sent in Round 2	Control	Group
$0	N/A	No information	$0	5 (13%)	7 (15%)
			$2	3 (8%)	1 (2%)
			$4	0 (0%)	2 (4%)
$2	$0/$8	Trust abused	$0	3 (8%)	8 (17%)
			$2	0 (0%)	2 (4%)
			$4	0 (0%)	2 (4%)
$2	$4/$8	Trust honored	$0	0 (0%)	0 (0%)
			$2	1 (3%)	0 (0%)
			$4	3 (8%)	3 (6%)
$4	$0/$16	Trust abused	$0	3 (8%)	4 (9%)
			$2	0 (0%)	2 (4%)
			$4	9 (23%)	5 (11%)
$4	$8/$16	Trust honored	$0	0 (0%)	0 (0%)
			$2	2 (5%)	0 (0%)
			$4	11 (28%)	11 (23%)
Total				40	40

Table 3.3 presents, for all possible outcomes of Round 1, the subsequent Round 2 choices of subjects in the role of Player 1 in each condition. The first two columns in the table present the possible outcomes in the first round. The next column classifies these outcomes into three possible categories from Player 1's point of view: no information (if $0 was sent and no action of Player 2 was observed), trust abused (if either $2 or $4 was sent and $0 was returned), and trust honored (if either $2 or $4 was sent and one-half of the multiplied amount was returned). The fourth column presents the possible amounts sent in Round 2 by a Player 1, and the last two columns give the number of subjects in each condition who sent that amount after observing the outcome described in the first three columns.

The results in the table reveal greater sensitivity to prior outcomes in the Group condition than in the Control condition. For instance, of those subjects in the role of Player 1 who sent $4 in Round 1 and received back $0 (i.e. trust was abused), 9 of 12 subjects (75 percent) in the Control condition again sent $4. In the Group treatment, however, only 5 of 11 such subjects (45 percent) again sent $4. Similarly, of the subjects who sent $4 in Round 1 and received $8 back (i.e. trust was honored), all of the 11 subjects in the Group condition again sent $4, but a smaller fraction (9 of 11; 85 percent) did so in the Control group. However, neither of these differences alone is significant in a Fisher Exact test. Still, these results suggest a greater sensitivity to first-round results on the part of subjects in the Group condition than the Control condition.

A direct test of our hypothesis involves looking at how subjects in the role of Player 1 react when their initial trust is either abused or honored. To demonstrate the existence of trust in a collective entity, we need to show that subjects in the Group condition whose trust is abused (honored) in Round 1 are likely to send less (more) in Round 2 than subjects in the Control condition whose trust is abused (honored). Table 3.4 presents the relevant results. Specifically, the Round 2 choices of subjects in the role of Player 1 are given, by condition and outcome in Round 1. Using Table 3.4, we can see whether behavior in the two conditions differs in the way we predicted, and in a way consistent with subjects

Table 3.4   Choices of Player 1 in Round 2 by Round 1 outcomes and condition

Amount sent in Round 2	Trust honored in Round 1		
	Control	Group	Total
$0	0 (0%)	0 (0%)	0
$2	3 (18%)	0 (0%)	3
$4	14 (82%)	14 (100%)	28
Total	17	14	31

Amount sent in Round 2	Trust abused in Round 1		
	Control	Group	Total
$0	6 (40%)	12 (52%)	18
$2	0 (0%)	4 (17%)	4
$4	9 (60%)	7 (30%)	16
Total	15	23	38

displaying trust in a collective entity, even with the minimal form of groups created in our experiments.

As the top part of Table 3.4 indicates, in the Group condition, all 14 subjects (100 percent) whose trust was honored subsequently sent $4, while in the Control 14 of 17 subjects (82 percent) did so and the other 3 only sent $2 (18 percent). While the direction of this difference – that subjects in the Group condition whose trust is honored are slightly more likely to send $4 in the next round – is consistent with our hypothesis, deviations by three subjects is insufficient to produce a significant difference.

Additional, and more compelling, direct support for our hypothesis can be found in the bottom part of Table 3.4. Here, we explore the behavior of subjects in the role of Player 1 who had their trust abused in the first round (they sent some amount of money and received $0 in return). There is a clear difference in the pattern of choices between the two conditions. In the Control, a majority of subjects (60 percent) whose trust was abused still sent $4 in the next round. In the Group condition, however, only 30 percent of such subjects did so, and a majority of subjects (52 percent) sent $0. The difference between the distributions of actions in the two conditions is significant at the $p < 0.1$ level in a chi-square test ($\chi^2(2) = 4.78$).[9] Therefore, we see a significant difference in behavior consistent with our hypothesis of trust in a collective entity: subjects in the Group condition whose trust is abused in Round 1 were significantly more likely to react negatively in Round 2 than those in the Control.[10]

We can also explore our hypothesis using regression analysis to determine the effect of first-round experience on behavior in the second round. Specifically, we used ordered logit estimation to explore how the amount sent in Round 2 is affected by the experimental treatment variable, Round 1 history, and an interaction between treatment and history.[11] The results of this estimation are reported in Table 3.5.[12] The first three independent

Table 3.5   Ordered logit regression of amount sent in Round 2

Dependent variable: amount sent in Round 2	(1)	(2)	(3)	(4)[a]	(5)[a]
Trust abused (Rd 1)		−2.670***	−2.599***	−1.518**	−1.150*
		(0.696)	(0.729)	(0.827)	(0.884)
Group condition		−0.286	−0.315	0.955	1.055
		(0.576)	(0.598)	(1.211)	(1.221)
Trust abused x Group				−1.901*	−2.206*
				(1.385)	(1.422)
Dispositional trust	0.644*		0.154		0.419
	(0.395)		(0.579)		(0.565)
Gender (Male = 1)	−0.533		−0.141		−0.594
	(0.432)		(0.630)		(0.624)
Obs	87	69	69	69	69
Log likelihood	−81.76	−48.88	−48.83	−50.55	−49.89
Pseudo R-squared	0.027	0.185	0.186	0.182	0.192

Notes:
Standard errors are in parentheses.
[a] Value of one observation of dependent variable changed (see note 12).
* $p < 0.1$; ** $p < 0.05$; *** $p < 0.01$; all one-tailed.

variables are binary variables indicating whether trust was abused in Round 1, whether the subject was in the Group condition, and the interaction between the two. To test robustness, we also include a gender dummy variable and a construct from questionnaire responses measuring an individual's general propensity to trust.

As the results indicate, if trust was abused, subjects sent significantly less than if it was not. However, the negative effect of trust being abused on amount sent in the subsequent round is even stronger for subjects in the Group condition (at least twice as big). The coefficient on the interaction term ($p < 0.09$ in model 4 and $p < 0.06$ in model 5, one-tailed) is statistically significant providing further support for our hypothesis.

Conclusion

The above experiment and analysis reveal evidence of trust in a collective entity. Subjects in the Group condition show a greater reaction to previous experience, particularly when this experience is negative. While the effect is not small, it is only weakly statistically significant. This is probably due to several features of our research design. First, even though we used 174 subjects in the experiments, the analysis focuses on only those subjects in the role of Player 1, reducing our sample size by one-half. The sample size is further reduced since we are interested in those subjects who had either a positive or negative experience in the first round, eliminating those who sent $0 in the first round. While using deception would have allowed us to collect much more data, we felt that it was important to rely on a situation where subjects were actually matched with two other people in the room and this was transparent.

A second reason for not observing a larger effect may have to do with the subtlety of our Group treatment. In our experiment, trust in a collective entity is based solely on an individual's limited experience with members of a nominal group. By contrast, in an organizational context individuals typically have repeated experience with long-standing groups that strongly influence their members' lives. In such circumstances, it is reasonable to expect uniformity in behavior by group members. In our experiments, however, the 'group' was randomly determined by a median split of individuals' responses to an irrelevant and trivial guess. Therefore, it is striking that we observed *any* effect with such a slight group identity manipulation and we would expect an even larger effect in situations where the group or organizational identity is stronger.

The results are even more compelling when one considers that our group identity manipulation also likely created an 'out-group' bias, which would clearly work against our hypothesis. Individuals tend to view out-groups as less cooperative, honest, and trustworthy, and tend to expect less positive behavior from out-group members (Brewer 1979). Consequently, subjects interacting with counterparts categorized as members of an out-group would be biased toward viewing their counterparts as untrustworthy. Therefore, we expect that having subjects in the Group condition interact with two members of the same group – without it being a counterpart to their own group – might produce more striking results.

These limitations notwithstanding, we believe that this study makes a number of important contributions to research on trust in the economics, strategy and organizational literatures. Most importantly, the results of our experiment reinforce, and validate in a more carefully controlled setting, the finding by Zaheer et al. (1998) that trust in individuals and trust in collective entities are related but distinct. This suggests not only that it is meaningful to conceptualize the placing of trust in a collective entity, but also that such trust may influence economic activity over and above individual trust. Consequently, it is important to carefully consider which level of analysis is most relevant when theorizing about the role of trust in the organization and coordination of economic activity. Further, recognizing that trust in a collective entity has a basis in group identification (Kramer et al. 1996) is essential.

We also go beyond earlier empirical research on trust in collective entities by highlighting trust transfer as an underlying causal mechanism that links trust in individuals and trust in collective entities. The evidence reported here is consistent with the idea that individuals use membership in a collectivity as a heuristic for determining the trustworthiness of members with whom they have no prior knowledge of or experience. This finding is striking because it suggests that the effects of an initial experience with a given representative of a collectivity extend beyond that relationship to interactions with other members of the collectivity. New relationships and interactions with previously unknown members of a collectivity do not start from a clean slate, but are construed through the lens of shared group identity with those with whom one has prior experience.

This study also makes a valuable empirical contribution by extending the trust game research paradigm. By embedding exchange relationships within the context of collective entities we are able to broaden the application of the trust game to a wider and more diverse set of phenomena that are more closely related to actual economic organizations and activities (cf. Buchan et al. 2002). Future research can draw on the research design developed here to address other questions involving trust in collective entities.

While this study advances our understanding of the relationship between trust in individuals and trust in collective entities, it also raises a number of important questions for future research. In particular, understanding the conditions that accelerate, alter or prevent the process through which trust transfers between individuals and collectivities represents a fruitful area of inquiry. For instance, in an organizational context, do certain structures, processes or incentives fundamentally alter the degree to which individuals rely on group identity as a heuristic for formulating initial trust impressions? A related and equally important question would be ascertaining the conditions under which group identity represents a useful and efficient heuristic versus an erroneous and costly bias. To the extent that these different circumstances can be identified, we would also want to gain insight into whether group identity as a basis for trust can be actively managed, produced or discouraged.

In sum, this research supports the idea that trust in a collective entity is related to, but distinct from, trust in the individual members of that collectivity. The findings are consistent with the view that economic actors develop perceptions about the trustworthiness of collective entities based on exchanges conducted with individual members of the collectivity. This trust in the collective entity then serves as a heuristic for trust in individuals where prior history or knowledge of members of the collectivity is limited or absent.

Acknowledgements
We would like to thank Robin Dawes and participants in the Organizational Behavior and Theory seminar series at Carnegie Mellon University and at the 2003 Economic Science Association meetings for useful comments on earlier versions of this chapter.

Notes

1. For similar arguments in sociology see Granovetter (1985) and Macauley (1963).
2. While we acknowledge differences in the object of trust, we do not consider differences in the origin of trust. Specifically, collective entities placing trust in (e.g. groups or organizations trusting) individuals or other collective entities is beyond the scope of this chapter (for a thoughtful discussion of this issue see research by Currall and Inkpen Chapter 13 this volume; 2002).
3. However, the average returns for sending $5 and $10 were $7.17 and $10.20, respectively. Berg et al. argue that the higher returns for these two amounts may reflect social norms concerning behavior towards players who sent half or the entire possible amount.
4. A plausible interpretation of this 'group effect' is that trusting behavior is normative, in the sense that it is part of a script that is primed by the experimental situation. If trusting behavior is primed, it will be rather insensitive to the object of trust, be it a specific person of a group member.
5. In the event that Player 1 had sent $0, Player 2 did not need to make a choice, but we still required them to circle 'no choice' on the sheet so it would not be apparent who had received $0 from their failure to circle something on the sheet.
6. Since we recruited from two large universities (total student populations 8000 and 16 000) and from a large list of potential subjects, most participants did not know each other. Among the few that appeared to recognize someone in the room, it was very unlikely that they would be matched with the person they knew.
7. The gender composition did not differ significantly between the Control (30 percent female) and Group (39 percent female) conditions. Moreover, there are no gender differences in how much the first player sent to the second player in Round 1. Therefore, we omit further analysis of gender.
8. The change is brought about by an increase in the Group condition of the proportion of those sending money that send $4. In the Control condition the proportion of those sending money that send $4 remains roughly the same.
9. We can also use Goodman's (1964) test of 2 x 2 x 2 contingency tables to look for our hypothesized relationship between amount sent in Round 2, history and condition. Looking only at decisions to send $4 versus a smaller amount in the second round (which is natural given the near 50–50 split of first-round choices using such categories), we find that we can reject the null hypothesis at $p < 0.1$. This is even though we change one value of 0 to 1 in order to perform this test, making the test more conservative.
10. Our results suggest an apparent asymmetry in that they are stronger when trust is abused than when it is honored, indicating that individuals may react to collective entities more strongly when a member violates their trust. However, there are at least two other possible explanations for such an asymmetry. First, almost everyone who trusts in the first round and has their trust honored, trusts again in the second round. Therefore, while there may be a difference in the propensity to trust in Round 2 between subjects in the Group and Control conditions, we might not observe it in these data due to such a 'ceiling effect'. Second, work on loss aversion (e.g. Kahneman and Tversky, 1979) indicates that outcomes that fall below a reference level carry more weight than those that exceed it. Following from this, one might expect that having trust abused (and ending up with a 'loss') might have a stronger effect than having it honored (and ending up with a 'gain').
11. The results are substantively unchanged if we use ordinary least squares instead of ordered logit.
12. All 14 subjects in the Group treatment who had trust honored in Round 1 sent $4 in Round 2 (see Table 3.4). Therefore, behavior in this cell is perfectly identified in the second regression in Table 3.5. Consequently, we changed one such observation to $2 in order to conduct the estimations for the fourth and fifth models in Table 3.5. This change works against our hypothesis, making the results more conservative. The results for the fourth model are exactly the same for any of the 14 values we could change. In column 5, we report the results of the regression using the change that produced the best fit (highest log-likelihood). However, the substantive results are unchanged for any of the 14 possible changes (i.e. the coefficients for the first and third independent variables are always significant at $p < 0.1$, while the coefficients for the other three independent variables are never statistically significant).

References

Arrow, K. (1974), *The Limits of Organization*, New York: Norton.
Ashraf, N., I. Bohnet and N. Piankov (2005), 'Measuring trust and trustworthiness', working paper.
Bachmann, R. (2001), 'Trust, power and control in trans-organizational relations', *Organization Studies*, **22**, 337–65.
Bachmann, R. (2003), 'The coordination of relations across organizational boundaries', *International Studies of Management & Organization*, **33**, 7–21.
Barney, J.B. and M.H. Hansen (1995), 'Trustworthiness as a source of competitive advantage', *Strategic Management Journal*, **15** (special issue), 175–90.
Berg, J., J. Dickhaut and K. McCabe (1995), 'Trust, reciprocity, and social history', *Games and Economic Behavior*, **10**, 122–42.

Bradach, J.L. and R.G. Eccles (1989), 'Price, authority, and trust: From ideal types to plural forms', *Annual Review of Sociology*, **15**, 97–118.

Brewer, M.B. (1979), 'In-group bias in the minimal intergroup situation: A cognitive-motivational analysis', *Psychological Bulletin*, **86**, 307–24.

Bromiley, P. and L.L. Cummings (1995), 'Transaction costs in organizations with trust', in R. Bies, B. Sheppard and R. Lewicki (eds), *Research on Negotiation in Organizations*, Greenwich, CT: JAI Press.

Buchan, N., R. Croson and R. Dawes (2002), 'Swift neighbors and persistent strangers: A cross-cultural investigation of trust and reciprocity in social exchange', *American Journal of Sociology*, **108**(1), 168–206.

Buchan, N., R. Croson and E. Johnson (in press), 'Trust and reciprocity: An international experiment', *Journal of Economic Behavior and Organization*.

Corazzini, R. (1977), 'Trust as a complex multi-dimensional construct', *Psychological Reports*, **40**, 75–80.

Currall, S.C. and A.C. Inkpen (2002), 'A multilevel approach to trust in joint ventures', *Journal of International Business Research*, **33**(3), 479–95.

Giddens, A. (1990), *The Consequences of Modernity*, Stanford, CA: Stanford University Press.

Goodman, Leo A. (1964), 'Simple methods for analyzing three-factor interaction in contingency tables', *Journal of the American Statistical Association*, **59**, p. 405.

Granovetter, M. (1985), 'Economic action and social structure: The problem of embeddedness', *American Journal of Sociology*, **91**(3), 481–510.

Güth, W., P. Ockenfels and M. Wendel (1997), 'Cooperation based on trust: An experimental investigation', *Journal of Economic Psychology*, **18**, 15–43.

John, G. (1984), 'An empirical investigation of some antecedents of opportunism in a marketing channel', *Journal of Marketing Research*, **21**, 278–89.

Kahneman, D. and A. Tversky (1979), 'Prospect theory: An analysis of decisions under risk', *Econometrica*, **47**, 313–27.

Kramer, R.M., M.B. Brewer and B.A. Hanna (1996), 'Collective trust and collective action: The decision to trust as a social decision', in R.M. Kramer and T.R. Tyler (eds), *Trust in Organizations: Frontiers of Theory and Research*, Thousand Oaks, CA: Sage.

Lewis, J.D. and A.J. Weigert (1985), 'Trust as social reality', *Social Forces*, **63**(4), 967–85.

Luhmann, N. (1979), *Trust and Power*, Chichester: Wiley.

Macauley, S. (1963), 'Non-contractual relations in business', *American Sociological Review*, **28**, 55–67.

Mayer, R.C., J.H. Davis and F.D. Schoorman (1995), 'An integrative model of organizational trust', *Academy of Management Review*, **20**, 709–34.

McEvily, B., V. Perrone and A. Zaheer (2003), 'Trust as an organizing principle', *Organization Science*, **14**, 91–103.

Powell, W.W. (1990), 'Neither market nor hierarchy: Network forms of organization', in L.L. Cummings and B. Staw (eds), *Research in Organizational Behavior*, Greenwich, CT: JAI Press, vol. **12**, 295–336.

Rotter, J.B. (1967), 'A new scale for the measurement of interpersonal trust', *Journal of Personality*, **35**, 651–65.

Rousseau, D.M., S.B. Sitkin, R.S. Burt and C. Camerer (1998), 'Not so different after all: A cross-discipline view of trust', *Academy of Management Review*, **23**, 292–404.

Snijders, C. and G. Keren (1998), 'Determinants of trust', in D.V. Budescu, I. Erev and R. Zwick (eds), *Games and Human Behavior: Essays in Honor of Amnon Rapoport*, Mahwah, NJ: Lawrence Erlbaum.

Stewart, K.J. (2003), 'Trust transfer on the world wide web', *Organization Science*, **14**, 5–17.

Tajfel, H., M. Billig, R.P. Bundy and C. Flament (1971), 'Social categorization and intergroup behavior', *Journal of Experimental Social Psychology*, **1**, 149–77.

Van Huyck, J.B., R.C. Battalio and M.F. Walters (1995), 'Commitment versus discretion in the peasant-dictator game', *Games and Economic Behavior*, **10**, 143–70.

Williamson, O.E. (1985), *The Economic Institutions of Capitalism*, New York: The Free Press.

Zaheer, A., B. McEvily and V. Perrone (1998), 'Does trust matter? Exploring the effects of interorganizational and interpersonal trust on performance', *Organization Science*, **9**(2), 141–59.

Zucker, L.G. (1986), 'Production of trust: Institutional sources of economic structure', in L.L. Cummings and B.M. Staw (eds), *Research in Organizational Behavior*, Greenwich, CT: JAI Press, vol. **8**, 53–111.

4 Trust as situated cognition: an ecological perspective on trust decisions

Roderick M. Kramer

> To serve human action in adaptive ways, our cognitive processes are responsive to the environment in which we pursue our goals. This responsiveness ranges from higher accessibility of knowledge relevant to a given situation . . . to the choice of processing strategies that meet situational requirements.
>
> Schwarz (2002, p. 146)

The benefits of trust have been amply established by many empirical studies, ranging from experimental investigations in laboratory settings (Ostrom and Walker, 2003) to explorations of trust in real-world social and organizational settings (Fukuyama, 1995; Kramer and Cook, 2004; Lane and Bachmann, 1998; Sztompka, 1999). Obtaining those benefits, however, is often more problematic (Brothers, 1995; Janoff-Bulman, 1992; Kanter and Mirvis, 1989; Seligman, 1997). One of the problems is that the anticipated gains from trust materialize only when we happen to be dealing with a trustworthy other (e.g. someone willing to reciprocate our own trusting behavior). Misplaced trust – engaging in trusting behavior with individuals who exploit that trust – can be enormously costly. Such trust mistakes are costly, moreover, not only in terms of their immediate, short-term consequences (e.g. rewards foregone and opportunities lost), but also their long-term effects (e.g. our diminished willingness to trust again). Accordingly, it makes sense for us to trust, but only when that trust is likely to be honored by others.

From a judgment and decision-making perspective, therefore, among the fundamental questions we confront in our lives are such questions as 'Whom we can trust?' 'How much?' and 'Under what circumstances?' As easily as they may be posed, such questions constitute vexing judgmental challenges for decision-makers. Such questions direct our attention to the thorny problem of *discrimination* – harvesting the benefits of trust clearly hinges, at least in part, on our ability to accurately detect trustworthiness in others (Bacharach and Gambetta, 2001; Hardin, 2002; Yamagishi, 2001).

The difficulty of this judgmental task is amplified, of course, by the problem of *social uncertainty* (Bachmann, 2001; Gambetta, 1988): we can never know for certain the intentions or motives that animate another's actions or inactions, as Monica Lewinsky only belatedly and regretfully discovered in her friendship with Linda Tripp. The decisions we make with respect to trusting (or distrusting) others, therefore, are both consequential and problematic, giving rise to the familiar *trust dilemma*. In a trust dilemma, decision-makers hope to reap some perceived benefit from engaging in trusting behavior with another person. Pursuit of that opportunity, however, exposes them to the prospect that their trust might be exploited or betrayed. This conjunction of opportunity and vulnerability is, of course, the *sine qua non* of a trust dilemma (Heimer, 2001; Messick and Kramer, 2001). Because of our dependence on, and interdependence with, other people, trust dilemmas are an inescapable feature of social and organizational life. (Note: Not all situations involving trust constitute decision dilemmas, however. If we feel we have adequate grounds for trusting others – as in accounts of encapsulated trust (Hardin, 2001) – there may be no psychological dilemma at all. Similarly, if we feel we have adequate grounds for distrust, there may be no decision dilemma involved in our choice. In this chapter, however, I am interested in those situations where the tension between trusting and distrusting choice is psychologically salient to decision-makers.)

In this chapter, I explore some of the antecedents of trust decisions in such dilemmas. In particular, I present a framework that I characterize as the *intuitive social auditor model*. According to this model, decision-makers in trust dilemma situations employ a variety of cognitive and behavioral rules that guide their trust-related judgment and choice. In aggregate, such rules constitute a 'rule system' that embodies a social perceiver's 'street-level epistemology' (Hardin, 2002, p. 115) regarding their trust-related decisions. The psychological and behavioral 'rule systems' of the intuitive social auditor are construed as *intendedly* adaptive orientations that decision-makers adopt when responding to the uncertainty intrinsic to trust dilemmas. Even though trust errors do occur on occasion (e.g. people sometimes trust too little or too much in their dealings with specific others), these errors are assumed to be unintended and unforeseen.

Unpacking the decision to trust

One way of thinking about the advantages of trust – or, more precisely, the benefits associated with our willingness to engage in trusting behavior when interacting with individuals about whom we harbor some uncertainty – is in terms of its potential for increasing individual's social or political capital (Burt, 2003). In other words, trust is presumably a valuable resource for individuals because it facilitates the attainment of desired outcomes (valuable resources, useful or pleasurable relationships, etc.). Thus we may disclose information of a personal and sensitive nature to other people in the hope of eliciting comparable disclosures from them in return. Such reciprocal self-disclosures are one way of building intimate relationships in which 'thick' trust can flourish (Lindskold, 1978). The extent to which our individual trust decisions actually add to our stock of social capital, however, is clearly contingent on making judicious decisions regarding whom to trust, how much, and under what circumstances. Wise or prudent trust decisions enhance our reservoir of individual social capital; conversely, poor decisions deplete it.

The wisdom of our decisions to trust, therefore, depends clearly on the actual trustworthiness of the prospective trustees with whom we interact (Hardin, 2002). More precisely, optimal trust can be construed in terms of a 'good fit' or correlation between our decisions to trust others and their actual trustworthiness. Too much trust extended uncritically or indiscriminately can be costly – even fatal. On the other hand, too little trust in others can be inefficient and wasteful in terms of beneficial social opportunities and material gains foregone.

Unfortunately, there is often considerable uncertainty regarding the level of trustworthiness among those with whom we must interact in social groups or organizations. For many reasons, we must engage in interactions with others not knowing fully how trustworthy or untrustworthy they are. At a psychological level, therefore, trust dilemmas are animated by this fundamental uncertainty regarding the trustworthiness of the other decision-maker(s) on whom we are dependent. Social uncertainty of this sort is indeed intrinsic to the problem of trust. As Gambetta (1988) aptly observed in an early and influential treatment of this problem, 'The condition of ignorance or uncertainty about other people's behavior is central to the notion of trust. It is related to the limits of our capacity ever to achieve a full knowledge of others, their motives, and their responses to endogenous as well as exogenous changes' (p. 218).

Given such uncertainty, an interesting question arises with respect to the decision to trust: on what basis do people decide whom to trust, how much, and under what circumstances? In the next section, I offer one perspective on how decision-makers approach these fundamental questions.

Coping with social uncertainty: the intuitive social auditor model
How do decision-makers in trust dilemma situations cope with the problem of social uncertainty? How do they decide, for example, how much trust or distrust is appropriate when dealing with other social actors about whom they possess imperfect and incomplete social information? I approach this question from the perspective of recent cognitive theory and research on social judgment and choice. I characterize this perspective as the 'intuitive social auditor model'. A central feature of this model is its emphasis on the role cognitive and behavioral rules play in trust-related judgment and decision-making.

In almost every important domain of social and organizational life, there is good evidence that people rely on various kinds of cognitive and behavioral 'rule systems' to help them assess problems and make decisions. As suggested earlier, by a 'rule system' I mean simply some set of implicit or explicit prescriptions for dealing with commonly encountered problems in those domains. We know from studies of expertise in various domains, for example, that experts typically possess fairly elaborate rule systems for evaluating and acting in situations common to those domains. Thus chess players have rules for dealing with end games, and mushroom collectors have rules for selecting and preparing mushrooms that are safe for human consumption (Fine and Holyfield, 1996). Indeed, rule systems of this sort are such a pervasive feature of social and organizational life that March et al. (2000) have aptly noted that rules 'are a basic reality of individual and social life; individual and collective actions are organized by rules, and social relations are regulated by rules' (p. 5).

But how do cognitive rule systems function in the context of trust dilemma situations? Can we bring further organization to our understanding of the sort of cognitive rules that help us cope with the kinds of social uncertainty we encounter in such situations? The intuitive social auditor model is intended to address such questions by offering a descriptive platform for thinking about how people think and act 'in the shadow of doubt' regarding others' trustworthiness. The phrase 'social auditor' is intended to direct attention to a basic – albeit admittedly quite simple and *prima facie* obvious – feature of social perception in trust dilemmas: people in such situations tend to pay attention to what's going on, especially if the perceived stakes are high enough and/or uncertainty regarding the other's trustworthiness is sufficiently strong. For example, in an extremely important negotiation, we are likely to remain fairly vigilant with respect to any evidence that the other party is untrustworthy. The word 'intuitive' reflects our understanding of the fact that people often rely on a variety of more or less explicitly articulated rules governing such vigilance. People often operate, in other words, as intuitive scientists who try to understand the patterns of causal relation governing their social transactions. Thus individuals' cognitive and behavioral rules reflect both their implicit and explicit theories about people and situations (Ross, 1977).

According to the intuitive social auditor model, it is assumed that individuals possess various kinds of cognitive and behavioral rules to use when trying to (1) make sense of a given trust dilemma situation and (2) decide how to act on the basis of the interpretation they form of the situation.[1] The primary cognitive rules of the intuitive social auditor include both *orienting* and *interpretation* rules. Orienting rules help us categorize or code a given trust dilemma prior to our actions. Orienting rules thus encompass such things as the various expectations we bring to bear on sizing up a situation. As sensemaking devices, orienting rules also guide and direct our attention in that they implicitly or explicitly prescribe the sort of further evidence we should look for when trying to assess another decision-maker's trustworthiness. Orienting rules are thus prospective sensemaking devices (in contrast to interpretation rules, which constitute retrospective sensemaking devices).

If orienting rules guide our expectations and assessments of trust dilemma situations, our behavioral responses to trust dilemmas reflect the various *action rules* we use when responding to them. Action rules represent decision-makers' beliefs about what sort of conduct is prudent and should be employed in a trust dilemma situation. Action rules can serve various instrumental goals. They can be intended, for instance, to elicit trustworthiness from others. Alternatively, they can be intended to reassure others of our own trustworthiness. Yet again, they can also be used to deter exploitative behavior from predatory others. Rules such as Tit-for-Tat, for example, operate on the assumption that trust-building proceeds by demonstrating the willingness to trust initially, and also the willingness to reciprocate others' trustworthiness (Kramer et al., 2001; Lindskold, 1978; Pilisuk and Skolnick, 1968).

According to the intuitive social auditor model, decision-makers also monitor the consequences of rule use through the use of interpretative cognitive rules. In other words, they pay attention to what happens after they have employed a given behavioral rule when interacting with a specific other. During this post-decision 'auditing' process, they attempt to discern, for example, whether the amount of trust they have displayed toward the other seems prudent or imprudent. Was too much trust afforded or too little? The interpretation rules of the post-behavior auditing phase thus help us evaluate situations after we have taken action. Interpretation rules are retrospective sensemaking devices in this sense. They are used to help us answer such questions as, 'Was I right in thinking this person was trustworthy? Did I get the payoff or outcome I expected?' Interpretation rules are used, in a sense, to decode and categorize behavioral evidence viewed as diagnostic of others' trustworthiness or lack of trustworthiness.

On the basis of the inferences and conclusions they reach, decision-makers in a trust dilemma situation are likely to change their subsequent behavior when interacting further with the individual. The results of the post-decision auditing process then are assumed to inform (i.e. validate or invalidate) one's mental model of the dilemma, resulting in possible modification of the rule system invoked, and possibly resulting in a change in future rule use. The model thus posits a cyclic, adaptive learning system of the sort described by March and his colleagues (March, 1994; March et al., 2000).

In concert, these cognitive and behavioral rules provide the intuitive social auditor with a basis for anticipation, action and reflection in trust dilemma situations. They are intendedly adaptive cognitive and behavioral orientations in the specific sense that decision-makers, in using them, believe such rules will help them (1) reap the benefits of trust expected when one is dealing with a trustworthy other and (2) minimize the costs of misplaced trust when one is interacting with an untrustworthy other. In the ideal, a perfect auditing and action system would produce optimal trust decisions.

As the intuitive social auditor model indicates, there are at least two broad approaches decision-makers can take for coping with social uncertainty. One approach is to aim for better discrimination. In particular, if we can more accurately discriminate between trustworthy and untrustworthy social actors, we can selectively engage in productive transactions with those who will reciprocate our trust and eschew or shun those who will not. Recognizing its importance, there has been considerable interest in the efficacy of discrimination or selective play as a strategy for improving the yield from one's trust-related transactions (see, e.g., Bacharach and Gambetta, 2001; Yamagishi, 2001).

A second approach for dealing with social uncertainty is to engage in behaviors ourselves that are aimed at eliciting trustworthy behavior from others, regardless of *their* prior intentions or motives. Individuals can use their own behavior, for example, to encourage and reward others' trustworthy behavior. They can also use their own behaviors to signal their unwillingness to be exploited. When individuals clearly communicate their willingness to trust others, along with their unwillingness to be exploited, they in effect reduce others' social uncertainty (i.e. their uncertainty about us). They thus help others solve *their* trust dilemma when dealing with us – an important route to trust-building. The aim of this second approach is, of course, in a sense to 'educate' the other about us, and to shape his or her trust-related behavior in a direction we desire. There has been considerable interest in this approach as well (e.g. Axelrod, 1984; Axelrod and Cohen, 1999; Bendor et al., 1991; Lindskold, 1978; Wu and Axelrod, 1997).

The two approaches are not mutually exclusive, of course. Clearly, social actors are better off if they can *both* more clearly identify mutually productive social relationships *and* if they are skillful at managing those relationships. In fact, they can be viewed as highly complementary social competencies. In concert, the two approaches amount to deciding on the specific 'mix' of cognitive decision rules we can use to *identify* trustworthy others and the best behavioral decisions rules we should use to *elicit* trustworthy behavior from them. The intuitive social auditor model can be construed, therefore, as a descriptive model of how social actors think and act in trust dilemma situations. As such, it is but one particular example of a large class of experiential learning and sensemaking models found in the social science literature. Thus formulated, the framework embodies many of the essential elements found, for instance, in March's experiential learning model (e.g. March, 1994) as well as Weick's sensemaking framework (Weick, 1995).

From a pragmatic perspective, one utility of such models is that they direct a theorist's attention to points of special interest in the sensemaking and learning process. For example, in the case of trust-related judgments and decisions, we might wonder what specific rules guide choices in particular trust dilemma situations. In other words, what are the actual, explicit cognitive rules that guide a given decision-maker's *a priori* expectations regarding others' trust-related behavior? Further, what cognitive rules govern their interpretation of feedback they receive about others' trust-related behaviors?

Attempts to answer such questions remind us of the many ways in which cognition is adaptive to the particular situations in which it occurs. As Salancik and Pfeffer (1978) once suggested in this regard, 'one can learn most about individual behavior by studying the informational and social environment within which that behavior occurs and to which it adapts' (p. 226). The situated-cognitions perspective assumes, under ideal conditions, an intimate 'fit' between cognition and context (see Schwarz, 2002 for an excellent treatment). From this perspective, the heuristic value of the framework is that it helps organize a program of empirical research centered around filling in the missing gaps in our understanding of the processes linked to sensemaking, learning and action in trust dilemma situations.

In sum, the framework presented depicts one model of how social perceivers might process trust-related information and how, in turn, they might act on that information. A major presumption of the model, of course, is that cognitive and behavioral rules inform judgment and guide decision-making in trust dilemma situations. Accordingly, discovering those specific rules and documenting how they function constitutes a sensible aim of any research agenda driven by such a perspective. In the next section, therefore, I turn attention to some methodological implications of the intuitive social auditor framework.

Methods for studying the trust rules of the intuitive social auditor
Before describing the individual methods and results of two representative studies, a few general remarks might be in order regarding methodological implications of the intuitive auditor/situated cognition perspective.[2] A central value guiding this research is the need to remain true to trust-related cognitions and choices as they occur in natural organizational environments and social ecologies. There is a long tradition in social psychological research of using laboratory experiments to test hypotheses about trust. Such experiments have yielded important insights and, when designed and executed carefully, have the advantage of high internal validity. However, they also suffer from well-known limitations. For example, the criteria for making judgments and the choices available to experimental participants are sharply constrained: participants are typically presented with abstract information regarding a stylized trust dilemma (e.g. a simple trust game with binary choices). Moreover, they are presented typically with minimal social information (the 'other' is often not even physically present, but presumably located at another computer terminal somewhere in the lab; and sometimes this supposed 'other' is actually just a pre-programmed computer strategy).

Although appreciating the value of such experiments, I have tried in my recent research to probe people's idiographic cognitions about trust. Using methods that capture real-world thought processes of real-world individuals in natural contexts allows researchers to explore the way people actually do (and don't) think about trust.[3] The aim of such research, therefore, is twofold. The first aim is to produce rich and faithful accounts of trust. The second is to elucidate some of the psychological and social processes that drive trust-related social information processing.

This situated-cognitions or ecological orientation towards trust decisions has other methodological implications. In particular, it suggests the utility of using methods that elicit 'online' thought processes and judgmental heuristics that social decision–makers use in real-world domains. One advantage of these fairly direct, naturalistic approaches is that they enable us to learn something about how people confronting various real-world trust dilemmas actually think. In contrast with survey methods, where researchers determine in advance the universe of questions (and also how those questions are framed and anchored), researchers using more open-ended, elicitative approaches let their respondents define for themselves the content and range of variables they consider valid, appropriate or diagnostic (see also Clases et al., 2003 for an interesting approach using Kelly's repertory grid methodology). For example, we can learn something about the kinds of social/behavioral cues people look for and consider diagnostic when trying to assess others' trustworthiness in such contexts. Similarly, we can learn something about the behavioral rules they believe will work well or poorly in a given trust dilemma situation. We can also learn something about what they think other people are likely to do or not do in that situation (i.e. the common interpretation and action rules they expect others to use). Thus such methods have the advantage of being inductive, thereby minimizing researcher assumptions regarding these important questions.

In the following sections, I describe two studies using two different naturalistic methods of this sort and summarize some of the findings they yield. To place these studies in their proper context, let me preface the discussion by noting that both studies focus on problems of trust and distrust that arise in hierarchical relationships. Hierarchical relationships are characterized by asymmetries in power-dependence relations among the interdependent parties. As has been appreciated almost since the inception of organizational theory, hierarchical relationships are among the most important and prevalent form of social and organizational relation. As a form of ordering and organizing social relationships, the virtues of hierarchy are numerous and long noted (Leavitt, 2004; March and Simon, 1958). As with most virtues, however, hierarchy enjoys its share of problems, the catalog of which varies depending on where in the hierarchical relationship one happens to be situated (Kanter, 1977; Leavitt, 2004). From the standpoint of those in a position of greater dependence and lower power, concerns about the motives, intentions and concealed actions of those decision-makers who control their fate are likely to be consequential. For individuals in a position of higher power and less dependence, in contrast, monitoring such matters as the commitment, compliance, deference and trustworthiness of those below them is critical as well (Miller, 1992). Because of the asymmetries in power-dependence inherent in hierarchical relationships, the 'content' of trust-related judgments and decisions might be expected to vary as a function of one's location in the relationship. Relatedly, one might expect the features of the situation or context itself to be quite consequential. For example, the concerns that govern trust relations between an airline pilot and air traffic controllers are likely to be different from those that characterize doctors and their patients. Accordingly, the hierarchical context seems particularly fertile ground for studying the deliberations of our intuitive social auditor.

Study 1: Autobiographical narratives and mental accounting in the social auditing process
As noted earlier, many models of trust development emphasize the important role reciprocity plays in the trust-building process (Lindskold, 1978; Pilisuk and Skolnick, 1968). According to such models, trust builds incrementally when others affirm or reciprocate our trusting initiatives. Conversely, when others fail to reciprocate those initiatives, trust weakens or decays. Along such lines, Boyle and Bonacich (1970) argued and showed in an experimental setting that individuals' beliefs and expectations about others' trustworthy behavior tend to change 'in the direction of experience and to a degree proportional to the difference between this experience and the initial expectations applied to it' (p. 130).

As important as these experimental studies are in suggesting that a history of reciprocity is helpful in calibrating others' trustworthiness, they suffer from an important limitation. In particular, they don't tell us much about what people really pay attention to in real-world trust dilemma situations when trying to gauge other's trustworthiness. In this respect, they provide little insight into the deliberations of the intuitive social auditor. For example, in the confines of the experimental laboratory, both expectations regarding others' reciprocity and feedback pertaining to the confirmation or violation of those expectations tend to be explicitly specified and therefore rendered completely unambiguous. Experimental participants' expectations are crisply defined because they know precisely what constitutes trustworthy behavior from the other. After all, the parameters of such behavior have been fully defined *ex ante* by the experimenter (e.g. others can make either one of two choices in a binary-choice trust dilemma game). Similarly, the experimental participants learn with complete certainty how trustworthy the other has been (i.e. the other either did or did not choose the cooperative response). In real-world trust dilemmas, of course, assessing or auditing reciprocity is apt to be a much messier judgmental process. The accuracy of interpretations regarding others' behavior is likely to be impaired or clouded by misperception, self-serving cognitive biases and imperfections in memory. For example, consider the prospects for misunderstanding to develop even between two academic trust theorists: one professor may feel she really went out of her way to help a colleague improve a manuscript he sent her for comments, whereas she believes he offered her, in return, only perfunctory and fairly obvious comments. He, in turn, may remember the situation quite differently: he may feel she was very *slow* in responding to his request for comments, and when they finally arrived, there were far too many suggestions, many of which he found nit-picky and not welcome. In contrast, he regarded his responses to her manuscript as crisp, cogent and very timely. Thus both parties feel slighted in the exchange because both are using different metrics for evaluating what constitutes a trustworthy performance. The development of trust thus falters in this case. It is important to emphasize here that both decision-makers are justified in feeling disappointed.

As this example illustrates, it is important to know more about what individuals in real-world trust dilemma situations pay attention to when trying to calibrate others' trustworthiness. One methodology that is appropriate and useful in this regard is the *autobiographical narrative method* described by Baumeister et al. (1990). Autobiographical narratives are generated by asking individuals to recall and describe significant events in their lives. These accounts can then be content-analyzed in terms of dimensions of theoretical interest to the researcher. For example, using this method Baumeister et al. (1990) explored symmetries and asymmetries in perpetrators' and victims' accounts of past aggressive acts. As other studies using this methodology have demonstrated, autobiographical accounts can provide richly detailed and textured data regarding how individuals construe past experiences in their lives. Such data, in turn, can be used to extract the the significant codified 'lessons' (rules or generalizations) people extract from those experiences (see Baumeister et al. 1990).

Using this approach, one study examined how university professors and their graduate students construe reciprocal trust and trustworthiness in their relationship (Kramer, 1996). Reciprocal trust is important in professor–student relationships for several reasons. First, from the professor's standpoint, trust is important because professors depend on students to collect research data and analyze those data in order to test their research hypotheses. Not only does the whole scientific enterprise depend on the integrity of that data collection and analysis process, but a professor's status and reputation depend on such integrity as well. Thus professors must trust their students to execute the work in a competent and conscientious fashion. Although some oversight and monitoring is possible, it is difficult for professors in busy labs to supervise every data point. Thus professors are both dependent and vulnerable on their students, and to some degree always uncertain about the students' trustworthiness.

The graduate students in such relationships, in turn, depend on professors to mentor them and protect their professional well-being. This includes the willingness to invest the time and resources in helping them learn to do top-tier research, get published, and advance their interests in the department and their field. In short, students are also dependent on their faculty; they are vulnerable should their faculty members' generosity, priorities or loyalties shift. And they too are fundamentally uncertain about the professors' ongoing trustworthiness: things can change.

To conceptualize how professors and students might 'audit' trust-related transactions in this relationship, I drew on research on mental accounting. Mental accounting is an interesting cognitive phenomenon. There is considerable evidence that people tend to organize information about their economic and social transactions in terms of cognitive 'mental accounts' and that these mental accounts can, in turn, influence their subsequent judgments and preferences (Kahneman and Tversky, 1984; Kramer et al. 1990). Based on this research, I assumed that individuals in relationships involving mutual trust would possess 'mental accounts' they use when trying to store trust-related information. In other words, they would pay attention to the other's behavior and code instances of trust-affirming versus trust-violating behavior. This coded information, in turn, would be used to form impressions or judgments regarding the other's trustworthiness, reliability and so on. In particular, I hypothesized that both parties to the role would be vigilant about assessing the others' trustworthiness and that this vigilance would lead them to notice and remember trust-related actions. I further hypothesized that because of their comparatively greater dependence and vulnerability, graduate students (who occupy the low power-status role in this dyad) would be comparatively more attentive to trust-related information. They would also tend to ruminate more about such information (i.e. not only would they pay more attention to their professor's behaviors, but they would also ruminate about its significance or meaning for the relationship). These differences would be reflected, in turn, in the cognitive complexity or elaborateness of their mental accounting systems, with students possessing more differentiated 'fine-grained' mental accounting systems. Content analysis of the autobiographical narratives bore out this expectation.

Based on previous research on positive illusions (Taylor, 1991) and self-serving biases (Messick et al., 1985), I also expected to see some evidence of self-serving construal of the history of trust-related exchanges in these relationships. Consistent with these ideas, I found several notable patterns in the number of trust-increasing behaviors that self and other had done, such that both students and faculty recalled more things they had done to increase trust in the relationship. However, they recalled more things the other party had done that had adversely impacted the trust-building process.

Another interesting difference that emerged was in the content of the mental accounts. I had argued that, all else equal, faculty would tend to define student trustworthiness in terms of task-related or fiduciary considerations. After all, what professors really care about primarily is getting their research done (getting published, getting tenure and so on). Therefore for them the issue of trust is construed largely in terms of student's task-related behaviors, such as their competence and their reliability at executing research. For graduate students, in contrast, the picture is a bit more complicated. Obviously, students care about a professor's technical competence and reliability (they also want to get published and graduate!). However, they also care about social considerations, such as the professor's feelings towards them and interests in their welfare. They care, for example, that their professors like them, care about them, and intend to support them. Thus motives and intentions matter as well. Using this line of reasoning, I expected that relational considerations would tend to loom larger in how trustworthiness was defined by students. Consistent with this theoretical expectation, I found that faculty recalled significantly more things their students had done and not done that affected their joint work. In sharp contrast, trustworthiness of students was largely 'operationalized' by faculty in terms of competence-related concerns (e.g. compliance, reliability, dutifulness, etc.). The mental accounts of students, in contrast, revealed much more attentiveness to relational data, including how well students were treated as persons.

Although this is only a partial summary of some of the findings from this study, I hope it serves to illustrate how the autobiographical narrative method can be used to uncover the cognitive structures and content of trust rules (in this case the cognitive rules students and professors use to track trust-related exchanges in their relationship).

In a second study, a different approach was taken to uncovering some of the cognitive structure and content of the intuitive social auditor's work.

Study 2: Cue-based cognition and the decision to trust: insights from patient–physician focus groups and interviews

A large body of social cognitive theory and research indicates how readily people draw inferences regarding trust-related attributes such as others' cooperativeness, honesty, credibility, likability, fairness and intelligence from even very minimal social cues (see, e.g. Zebrowitz, 1997). Drawing on this previous theory and research, Cook et al. (2004) explored the perceived determinants of trust and trustworthiness within the context of physician–patient relationships.

Certainly, there are few relationships where concerns about trust loom larger and decisions are more consequential than in the relationship between patients and their physicians (Barber, 1983). Patients' emotional and physical well-being, even their very lives, are often quite literally in the hands of their physicians. Although the opposite relationship is much less studied, physicians often care a great deal about the trustworthiness of their patients. Their professional standpoint and emotional well-being also depend on the quality of their relationships with their patients. They depend on their patients, for example, to be honest about revealing relevant information to their successful treatment (e.g. to accurately report their true level of compliance). They also depend on their patients not to harm them through law suits should things turn out less than perfectly. Despite recognition of the importance of this relationship, many fundamental questions regarding the antecedents and consequences of reciprocal trust in such relationships remain unanswered (see, e.g. Pearson and Raek, 2000).

In pursuing answers to such questions, we used focus groups and semi-structured interviews to explore the cognitive and behavioral rule systems that decision-makers employ in real-world trust dilemmas to ask people directly about the kinds of social cues they pay attention to when trying to assess others' trustworthiness (see, e.g., Henslin's 1968 creative study of trust decisions among cab drivers and their passengers). Formal theory pertaining to this issue is still in its infancy, although important conceptual inroads have been laid by Bacharach and Gambetta (2001), who note that 'There are many possible properties . . . that can make a trustee trustworthy' (p. 153). They characterize these as *trust-warranting properties* (p. 153). Guided by such assumptions, Cook et al. (2004) explored both physicians' and patients' intuitive theories regarding trust-warranting properties in their doctor–patient relationships.

There are several findings that illustrate the kinds of category-based information individuals in such relationships attend to when forming impressions of others' trustworthiness. Among the larger categories of cues that both patients and physicians emphasized are behavioral (verbal and nonverbal) cues construed as diagnostic of caring, concern and empathy. For example, one patient observed generally, 'I think it [trust] also depends on the doctor . . . on the way they [*sic*] treat you . . . are they looking at you when they examine you and how they treat you as a person, not only as a patient' (Patient 38, quoted in Cook et al., 2004, p. 71). Numerous patients cited the diagnostic importance of seemingly very small behaviors and gestures, such as eye contact during an examination. One patient put it this way: 'I think eye contact is one of the most important things when you're talking to a doctor so that you don't feel like they are ignoring you' (Patient 38, p. 71). Another elaborated: 'When she [my physician] is done, she puts her pen down, and she will make eye contact with me immediately after she's done writing. Her eye contact starts when she enters the room' (Patient 36, p. 71).

There was also considerable evidence that cues construed as diagnostic of physician competence were salient to patients. As Brockner and Siegel (1996) noted, judgments about trustworthiness reflect not only attributions regarding benign intentions with respect to being trustworthy, but also competence at being trustworthy. In other words, in order for someone on whom we are dependent to be judged trustworthy, we not only need to know they have our interests at heart (i.e. that their motives and intentions are benevolent), but also that they are competent to act on and successfully execute those benign intentions and motives. Consistent with this contention, we found patients attached considerable importance to the apparent knowledge and competence of their physicians. As one patient put it, 'He's pretty confident about his decisions. So that kind of helps. He seems to know what he's talking about. I'm not a doctor, so I couldn't tell you if what he's telling me is right, but it sounded pretty good' (Patient 37, quoted in Cook et al., 2004, p. 75).

In addition to discovering that patients and physicians had many beliefs regarding the perceived determinants of trust and trustworthiness in their relationships, we also identified a variety of cues that contributed to distrust in such relationships. Some of the cues were subtle nonverbal behaviors that physicians may not even have intended or noticed, but that were afforded considerable importance to patients. One patient described how she was lying on the table, wearing only a paper hospital gown, awaiting her first visit from her surgeon. 'So, when I was on the table . . . feeling pretty vulnerable, he comes in, mumbles something . . . and stood at the foot of my bed, with his arms crossed . . .You know, you belong at my bedside, not the foot of my bed. Uncross your arms; get your hands out of your pockets . . . and look me in the eye. . . .as soon as he walked in the door and stopped at the foot of my bed, that set the tone' (Patient 36, quoted in Cook et al., 2004, p. 77).

Patients and physicians both drew attention to the deleterious impact of perceived unavailability or time-urgency on trust. One patient described her physician as 'Very sterile, very – no smile, no sense of humor, just quick, quick, let's get the job done' (Patient

21, quoted in Cook et al., 2004, p. 77). Relatedly, the tendency for busy physicians to give incomplete or hurried explanations, and to make patients feel as if they aren't respected, was felt to undermine trust. One patient complained, for example, that 'I get very frustrated because so many doctors take an authoritative position . . . I'm going to tell you what to do, I don't have to explain it, I don't have to pay any attention to your knowledge or your awareness' (Patient, 22, p. 79).

One of the more important and novel findings that emerged from this study was the extent to which patients' and physicians' judgments about trust and trustworthiness were influenced by contextual factors outside interpersonal transactions within the actual relationship. By contextual factors in this instance, I mean the specific institutional arrangements associated with the managed care settings in which these physicians worked. In sharp contrast to the old-fashioned image of the heroic family physician attending the loyal patient, the physician–patient transactions in our study were embedded in a managed care setting in which often teams of physicians shared responsibilities for patients, physicians' care decisions were constrained by institutional rules and regulations, and patients' stereotypes about the managed care setting all directly impacted perceptions of trust and trustworthiness in their relationships. Often in past research on reciprocal trust between patients and physicians, the two parties were considered part of an enclosed, isolated social system (e.g. doctors and patients treated purely as an interpersonal unit independent of context).

In the present study, we found that the managed care setting cast a rather large and ominous shadow over trust in the doctor–patient relationship in several ways. First, the time constraints imposed by the managed care system were generally seen as adversely impacting the quality of reciprocal trust between doctors and their patients. This cut both ways. As one physician put it, 'And there are time constraints in the sense that if I spend longer than that [the allotted 15 minutes recommended] with a patient, then I'm getting later and later, and I know I'm going to keep other patients waiting . . . So it's a constant tension between trying to respond to the needs that people have and give as much time as necessary but knowing . . . that it's going to affect everything that happens for the rest of the day' (Physician 5, quoted in Cook et al., 2004, p. 84).

This same physician was acutely aware of the erosion of trust associated with the constant and unrelenting pressures to juggle the clock for the sake of efficiency and profitability. 'I often feel like I'm spending a lot of saved-up goodwill with my patients. Making little withdrawals and spending it . . . but it's as if we're gradually depleting it and I'm not so sure how long that could go on without them saying . . . "You're not the same physician I used to know." ' (p. 84).

A second way in which context affects the decision to trust in this setting concerns the perceived lack of continuity and fragmentation of care. Patients assume, based on their previous experience, that physician mobility and turnover are likely to be high. Thus they are less likely to make the same level of investment and commitment to the relationship, because they believe it will be short-lived. Physicians recognize the same reality. Additionally, in managed care settings, physicians are more likely to be part of a multidisciplinary team, resulting in diffusion of responsibility as care is parceled out to multiple physicians treating the patient at different times, depending on schedule, availability and need. Finally, we found that perceived economic realities of the managed care environment cast a shadow over the relationship as well. In particular, physicians and patients both expressed concerns about the *perception* (even if not the reality) that insurance and other economic considerations were driving physician recommendations and decisions.

To summarize, this second study suggests the cognitive complexity of social perceivers' judgments about trust and trustworthiness in their interpersonal relationships embedded in real-world contexts where trust is problematic and consequential. It also illustrates how stereotypes or beliefs about a context can color such judgments independent of the actual behavior of the interactors. One implication of this latter finding is that both patients and physicians might facilitate the trust-building process and strengthen the resiliency of mutual trust by explicitly drawing attention to, and discussing, such factors. Moreover, both might take pains to engage in behaviors that violate such negative expectations. Indeed, we found that some physicians built trust by 'hanging a lantern' on the problems created by managed care settings. For example, they emphasized that they only prescribed drugs they *personally* knew about and in which they believed, and that they would take the time needed to deliver high-quality care. The ability to identify and respond effectively to such implicit beliefs is part of the 'social intelligence' (Yamagishi, 2001) of the intuitive social auditor.

Implications and conclusions

Conceptualizing individuals' trust-related judgments and decisions as rule-based forms of situated cognition and action locates such choices within a much larger class of decisions that have been extensively studied by behavioral decision theorists. This prior research takes as a starting point the recognition that humans are imperfect information processors who must often act before all of the facts are known. This idea was first systematized, of course, in the notion of satisficing (March and Simon, 1958; Simon, 1957), and was originally offered to supplant a view of human decision-making that presumed thoroughness of information search and rationality of choice. This alternative imagery stressed the idea that complete or comprehensive rationality may be unreachable because information search tends to be flawed, biased, or even curtailed by human proclivities toward effort aversion. Thus, rather than consistently finding the best alternative available, this research showed that people often seek and are satisfied with acceptable alternatives. They sometimes aim only to do 'well enough', rather than to pursue what is optimal (see Bachmann, 2001 for an application to trust theory).

This core intuition regarding the utility of satisficing led to the subsequent identification of numerous *heuristics* – simple judgment and decision rules – that could replace and approximate normatively optimal rules. Polya (1945), for example, argued for the value of heuristic reasoning, positing that 'We may need the provisional before we attain the final' (p. 112). As did other decision theorists subsequently, Polya viewed heuristic reasoning from a functionalist perspective: the use of such heuristics could lead to the generation of plausible hypotheses, sensible hunches and reasonable approaches. Heuristic reasoning, he went on to propose, is like the scaffolding needed to erect a building.

After enjoying a period of considerable vogue, stimulated largely by the pioneering work of Kahneman and Tversky (1982), the study of heuristic reasoning came under some attack. A number of decision theorists, including most notably Hogarth (1981) and von Winterfeld and Edwards (1986), suggested that the contemporary focus on the weaknesses of human cognition misrepresents reality and constitutes 'a message of despair' (von Winterfeld and Edwards, 1986, p. 531). To be sure, the predominant emphasis of experimental research for several decades did seem to be the documentation of judgmental and decisional shortcomings of the intuitive statistician (Dawes, 2001; Gilovich, 1991). Recently, however, a variety of studies have undertaken the task of rehabilitating the notion of heuristic information processing (e.g. Allison and Messick, 1990). Of particular note, there has been a movement away from thinking that heuristics are sources of biased or flawed cognition, and toward thinking of heuristics as adaptive cognitions (Gigerenzer, 2000; Gigerenzer and Todd, 1999). These studies, and many others, converge on the proposition that, in contrast to the view that the use of heuristics leads to poor performance, in some contexts even very simple decision heuristics can produce highly efficient and satisfactory results for a variety of important information-processing tasks.

In support of this new look (or, perhaps more accurately, second look) at heuristic modes of judgment and choice, there has been a recent surge of empirical work using agent modeling (e.g. Axelrod and Cohen, 1999; Falcone et al., 2001). Research in this vein has shown how various kinds of social decision heuristics can facilitate cooperation and trust-related behavior, especially under conditions of varying levels of social uncertainty (Axelrod, 1984; Bendor et al., 1991; Kollock, 1993). From the perspective of such work, rule-based modes of judgment and decision-making may be quick and dirty. They may even reflect hastily assembled expectations and incomplete appraisal.

However, this does not necessarily imply they are either superficial or irrational in their consequences. In fact, quick and shallow decisions of even the heuristic sort may be something human beings have evolved to do rather well – out of necessity. As Hertwig et al. (1999) noted in this regard, 'For many evolutionarily important tasks, from choosing where to forage to deciding whether to fight, adaptive behavior hinges partly on organisms' ability to estimate quantities. Such decisions often have to be made quickly and on the basis of incomplete information' (p. 234). From the standpoint of this new stream of research, there may be more depth in shallowness than initially meets the eye. This is very much in the spirit of a situated-cognitions perspective, of course.

Along such lines, an ecological analysis of the merits of rule-based trust decisions, as conceptualized in this chapter and as applied to trust dilemmas, helps us understand a very obvious feature of social and organizational life: that is, that people actually do trust others a fair bit. Indeed, as the philosopher Hollis (1999) observed, 'Everyday life is a catalogue of success in the exercise of trust' (p. 1). Given the obvious risks of engaging in many forms of trusting behavior (risks that are much discussed by rational choice theorists), it nonetheless remains striking the extent to which people are often willing to engage in trusting behavior when interacting with other people about whom they know relatively little. On a day-to-day basis, trust behavior is readily apparent throughout most social systems and organizations. People often exchange personal information and rely on others to carry out tasks even when they don't know much about their character, competence, diligence or motivation. People seem quite willing to trust others even on the basis of scant information or when they have only the thinnest grounds for positive expectations. The intuitive social auditor framework helps us understand some of the cognitive and behavioral antecedents of such trust.

Acknowledgments
The preparation of this research was supported by a GSB Faculty Fellowship and the William R. Kimball family. I gratefully acknowledge helpful discussions with Karen

Cook, J. Richard Hackman, Russell Hardin, David Messick and Nancy Katz in the development of these ideas. I also am very appreciative to Reinhard Bachmann for his detailed and constructive editorial comments.

Notes

1. Although space limitations preclude a complete discussion of these interpretation rules, they include and reflect, presumably, the various cognitive knowledge structures, including social category information, that people use to navigate through trust dilemmas. People's mental models include their *social representations*, which encompass everything they believe about other people, including all of their trust-related beliefs and expectations, their *self representations* (e.g. their beliefs about their own sophistication and competence at judging others' trustworthiness), and their *situational taxonomies* (e.g. their beliefs about the various kinds of social situations they are likely to encounter in their social lives). These mental models are used to help people interpret the trust dilemmas they confront. On the basis of these interpretations, they make choices.
2. In a recent chapter (Kramer et al., 2001), Bendor, Wei and I focused in some detail on explicating the efficacy of different behavioral rules for responding to trust dilemmas. In this chapter, accordingly, I shift attention to the issue of the kinds of sensemaking or interpretation rules individuals use.
3. For another novel methodological approach using Kelley's repertory grid methodology to studying trust-related cognition, see Clases et al. (2003).

References

Allison, S. and Messick, D. (1990). Social decision heuristics in the use of share resources. *Journal of Behavioral Decision Making*, **3**, 195–204.

Axelrod, R. (1984). *The Evolution of Cooperation*. New York: Basic Books.

Axelrod, R. and Cohen, M.D. (1999). *Harnessing Complexity: Organizational implications of a scientific frontier*. New York: Free Press.

Bacharach, M. and Gambetta, D. (2001). Trust in signs. In K.S. Cook (ed.), *Trust in Society*, pp. 148–84. New York: Russell Sage Foundation.

Bachmann, R. (2001). Trust, power, and control in trans-organizational relations. *Organization Studies*, **22**, 337–65.

Barber, B. (1983). *The Logic and Limits of Trust*. New Brunswick, NJ: Rutgers University Press.

Baumeister, R.F., Stillwell, A. and Wortman, S.R. (1990). Victim and perpetrator accounts of interpersonal conflict. *Journal of Personality and Social Psychology*, **59**, 995–1005.

Bendor, J., Kramer, R.M. and Stout, S. (1991). When in doubt: Cooperation in the noisy prisoner's dilemma. *Journal of Conflict Resolution*, **35**, 691–719.

Boyle, R. and Bonacich, P. (1970). The development of trust and mistrust in mixed-motive games. *Sociometry*, **33**, 123–39.

Brockner, J. and Siegel, P. (1996). Understanding the interaction between procedural justice and distributive justice: The role of trust. In R.M. Kramer and T. Tyler (eds), *Trust in Organizations: Frontiers of theory and research*, pp. 390–413. Thousand Oaks, CA: Sage.

Brothers, D. (1995). *Falling Backwards: An exploration of trust and self-experience*. New York: Norton.

Burt, R.S. (2003). *Trust, Reputation, and Competitive advantage*. Oxford: Oxford University Press.

Clases, C., Bachmann, R. and Wehner, T. (2003). Studying trust in virtual organizations. *International Studies of Management and Organization*, **33**, 7–27.

Cook, K.S., Kramer, R.M., Thom, D.H., Stepanikova, I., Mollborn, S.B. and Cooper, R.M. (2004). Trust and distrust in patient–physician relationships: Perceived determinants of high- and low-trust relationships in managed care settings. In R.M. Kramer and K.S. Cook (eds), *Trust and Distrust in Organizations: Dilemmas and approaches*, pp. 65–98. New York: Russell Sage Foundation.

Dawes, R.M. (2001). *Everyday Irrationality: How pseudo-scientists, lunatics, and the rest of us systematically fail to think rationally*. Boulder, CO: Westview.

Falcone, R., Singh, M. and Tan, Y.H. (2001). *Trust in Cyber-societies: Integrating the human and artificial perspectives*. New York: Springer-Verlag.

Fine, G. and Holyfield, L. (1996). Secrecy, trust, and dangerous leisure: Generating group cohesion in voluntary organizations. *Social Psychology Quarterly*, **59**, 22–38.

Fukuyama, F. (1995). *Trust: The social virtues and the creation of prosperity*. New York: Free Press.

Gambetta, D. (1988). Can we trust trust? In D. Gambetta (ed.), *Trust: Making and breaking cooperative relationships*, pp. 213–37. Cambridge, MA: Basil Blackwell.

Gigerenzer, G. (2000). *Adaptive Thinking: Rationality in the real world*. Oxford: Oxford University Press.

Gigerenzer, G. and Todd, P.M. (1999). *Simple Heuristics That Make Us Smart*. Oxford: Oxford University Press.

Gilovich, T. (1991). *How We Know What Isn't So: The fallibility of human reason in everyday life*. New York: Free Press.

Hardin, R. (2001). Conceptions and explanations of trust. In. K.S. Cook (ed.), *Trust in Society*, pp. 3–39. New York: Russell Sage Foundation.

Hardin, R. (2002). *Trust and Trustworthiness*. New York: Russell Sage Foundation.

Heimer, C.A. (2001). Solving the problem of trust. In K.S. Cook (ed.), *Trust in Society*, pp. 40–88. New York: Russell Sage Foundation.

Henslin, J.M. (1968). Trust and the cab driver. In M. Truzzi (ed.), *Sociology and Everyday Life*, pp. 138–58. Englewood Cliffs, NJ: Prentice-Hall.

Hertwig, R., Hoffrage, U. and Martignon, L. (1999). Quick estimation: Letting the environment do the work. In G. Gigerenzer, P.M. Todd and the ABC Research Group (eds). *Simple Heuristics That Make Us Smart*, pp. 191–208. New York: Oxford University Press.

Hogarth, R.M. (1981). Beyond discrete biases: Functional and dysfunctional aspects of judgmental heuristics. *Psychological Bulletin*, **90**, 197–217.

Hollis, M. (1999). *Trust within Reason*. Cambridge, UK: Cambridge University Press.

Janoff-Bulman, R. (1992). *Shattered Assumptions: Towards a new psychology of trauma*. New York: Free Press.

Kahneman, D. and Tversky, A. (1982). *Judgment under Uncertainty: Heuristics and biases*. Cambridge, UK: Cambridge University Press.

Kanter, R. (1977). *Men and Women of the Corporation*. New York: Basic Books.

Kanter, D.L. and Mirvis, P.H. (1989). *The Cynical Americans: Living and working in an age of discontent and disillusion*. San Francisco, CA: Jossey-Bass.

Kollock, P. (1993). An eye for an eye leaves everyone blind: Cooperation and accounting systems. *American Sociological Review*, **100**, 313–43.

Kramer, R.M. (1996). Divergent realities and convergent disappointments in the hierarchic relation: The intuitive auditor at work. In R.M. Kramer and T.R. Tyler (eds), *Trust in Organizations: Frontiers of theory and research*. Thousand Oaks, CA: Sage.

Kramer, R.M. and Cook, K.S. (2004). *Trust and Distrust in Organizations: Approaches and dilemmas*. New York: Russell Sage Foundation.

Kramer, R., Meyerson, D. and Davis, G. (1990). How much is enough? Psychological components of 'guns versus butter' decisions in a security dilemma. *Journal of Personality and Social Psychology*, **58**, 984–93.

Kramer, R.M., Wei, J. and Bendor, J. (2001). Golden rules and leaden worlds: Exploring the limitations of tit-for-tat as a social decision rule. In J. Darley, D.M. Messick and T. Tyler (eds), *Social Influence and Ethics*, pp. 177–99. Mahwah, NJ: Erlbaum.

Lane, C. and Bachmann, R. (1998). *Trust Within and Between Organizations: Conceptual issues and empirical applications*. New York: Oxford University Press.

Leavitt, H.J. (2004). *Top Down: Why hierarchies are here to stay and how to manage them more effectively*. Boston, MA: Harvard Business School Press.

Lindskold, S. (1978). Trust development, the GRIT proposal, and the effects of conciliatory acts on conflict and cooperation. *Psychological Bulletin*, **85**, 772–93.

March, J.G. (1994). *A Primer on Decision Making*. New York: Free Press.

March, J.G. and Simon, H.A. (1958). *Organizations*. New York: John Wiley.

March, J.G., Schulz, M and Zhou, X. (2000). *The Dynamics of Rules: Changes in Written Organizational Codes*. Stanford, CA: Stanford University Press.

Messick, D.M. and Kramer, R.M. (2001). Trust as a form of shallow morality. In K.S. Cook (ed.), *Trust in Society*, pp. 89–118. New York: Russell Sage Foundation.

Messick, D.M., Bloom, S., Boldizer, J.P. and Samuelson, C.D. (1985). Why we are fairer than others. *Journal of Experimental Social Psychology*, **21**, 480–500.

Miller, G.J. (1992). *Managerial Dilemmas: The political economy of hierarchies*. New York: Cambridge University Press.

Ostrom, E. and Walker, J. (2003). *Trust and Reciprocity: Interdisciplinary lessons*. Oxford: Oxford University Press.

Pearson, S.D. and Raek, L.H. (2000). Patient's trust in physicians: Many theories, few measures, and little data. *Journal of General Medicine*, **15**, 509–13.

Pilisuk, M. and Skolnick, P. (1968). Inducing trust: A test of the Osgood proposal. *Journal of Personality and Social Psychology*, **8**, 121–33.

Polya, G. (1945). *How to Solve It*. Princeton, NJ: Princeton University Press.

Ross, L. (1977). The intuitive psychologist and his shortcomings. In L. Berkowitz (ed.). *Advances in Experimental Social Psychology*, Vol. 10. New York: Academic Press, pp. 131–48.

Salancik, G.R. and J. Pfeffer (1978). A social information processing approach to job attitudes and task design. *Administrative Science Quarterly*, **22**, 224–33.

Schwarz, N. (2002). Situated cognition and the wisdom in feelings. In L.F. Barrett and Peter Salovey (eds), *The Wisdom in Feeling: Psychological processes in emotional intelligence*, pp. 144–66. New York: Guilford.

Seligman, A.B. (1997). *The Problem of Trust*. New Haven, CT: Princeton University Press.

Simon, H.A. (1957). *Models of Man*. New York: Wiley.

Sztompka, P. (1999). *Trust: A sociological theory*. Cambridge, UK: Cambridge University Press.

Taylor, S.E. (1991). *Positive Illusions*. New York: Basic Books.

von Winterfeld, D. and Edwards, W. (1986). *Decision Analysis and Behavioral Research*. Cambridge, UK: Cambridge University Press.

Weick, K.E. (1995). *Sensemaking in Organizations*. Thousand Oaks, CA: Sage.

Wu, J. and Axelrod, R. (1997). Coping with noise: How to cope with noise in the iterated prisoner's dilemma. In R. Axelrod (ed.), *The Complexities of Cooperation*. Princeton, NJ: Princeton University Press, pp. 30–39.

Yamagishi, T. (2001). Trust as a form of social intelligence. In K.S. Cook (ed.), *Trust in society*, pp. 121–47. New York: Russell Sage Foundation.

Zebrowitz, L.A. (1997). *Reading Faces: Window to the soul?* Boulder, CO: Westview Press.

PART II

ORGANIZATIONAL OR INTER-ORGANIZATIONAL LEVEL

5 Trust in the balance: how managers integrate trust-building and task control

Chris P. Long and Sim B. Sitkin

Introduction

Researchers have shown that managers' efforts to build trust comprise key mechanisms for enhancing organizational effectiveness (Barney and Hansen, 1994). Managers who promote organizational trust increase levels of voluntary subordinate compliance, augment subordinate commitment to organizational goals and enhance the willingness of employees to exhibit extra-role behaviors (Barney and Hansen, 1994; Dirks and Ferrin, 2001). As a result, managers who build trust often reduce the time and effort they must take to measure and monitor the work of their employees while enhancing the quality of their subordinates' contributions and their capacity to achieve organizational objectives (Frank, 1988; Hosmer, 1995; Jones, 1995).

The growing amount of research that has shown how managers' efforts to build organizational and managerial trust are key to organizational effectiveness (Barney and Hansen, 1994) has primarily examined subordinates' evaluations of managerial activities. While scholars have utilized this perspective to identify various forms of trust and classify their antecedents, trust scholars have generally not directly examined managers' decisions and actions and thus have not, as yet, developed a clear understanding of the factors that influence managers to act (or not to act) to promote (or fail to promote) organizational trust.

We contend, however, that it is important for scholars to develop an understanding of managerial actions since employees may not be able to discern all of the elements that their managers balance in trying to achieve broad organizational outcomes. Several perspectives emerging from the organizational literature provide a basis for this assertion and suggest that managers integrate and balance their attempts to promote organizational trust with their efforts to apply organizational controls. For example, Bradach and Eccles (1989), who view trust as a form of control, argue that managers direct subordinates by combining market-based, hierarchy-based and trust-based control mechanisms. Das and Teng (2001), in examining strategic alliances, argue that both trust and control are essential to promoting cooperation between alliance partners. Long et al. (2003) suggest that managers coordinate their efforts to promote trust with their organizational control activities in order to respond to intra-organizational conflicts.

While research-based and practice-based accounts of managerial actions suggest that managers attempt to calibrate their efforts to simultaneously promote trust and control (Nooteboom, 2002; Kim and Mauborgne, 1997), scholars have not yet developed an overarching framework for understanding the determinants of these joint actions.

In this chapter, we draw on the concepts of *balance* and of *balancing processes* to assist us in understanding how managers integrate their trust-based and control-based actions in ways they deem appropriate for situational conditions (Sutcliffe et al., 2000; Cardinal et al., 2004). To examine the role of balancing processes in managerial trust-control actions, we first identify key trust and control concepts. We then use alternative notions of balancing processes conceptualized by Sutcliffe and colleagues (2000) to outline the various ways in which managers combine and integrate their trust and control efforts. Thereafter, we propose a theoretical model outlining key factors that affect the particular types of trust-control balance that managers attempt to obtain. Our investigation concludes with a discussion of how the constructs we outline in this chapter extend organizational trust and organizational control research as well as work on the integration of these activities.

The need for conceptual clarity
Although relationships between trust and control may be key to promoting organizational effectiveness, Das and Teng (1998) argue that the current state of the literature is 'unclear and inconclusive about the relationships between trust and control'. We contend that much of this confusion results from the fact that scholars have generally conceptualized trust between exchange partners as being a by-product and often 'the unintended by-product of otherwise intended action' (Sydow, 1998: 54). This general proposition, when combined with the observations of trust scholars that 'opportunities to produce trust tend to be overestimated' by trustees (Nooteboom, 2003: 85) explains the dearth of research on how and why trustees (i.e. managers) work to promote (i.e. or not to promote) various forms of subordinate trust.

While research on the role of trust in organizations has greatly expanded in recent years (for a review see Dirks and Ferrin, 2001), scholars have focused most of their attention on the role of trustors in exchange relationships. This has generally left researchers to infer and indirectly glean information regarding the role of trustees from this work. We contend, however, that situations as seen by trustees are important elements to directly address because trustees often experience their relationships very differently from their trustors (Nooteboom, 2002). For example, a trustee's perspective on how trust and control can be employed in a particular relationship can be significantly affected by the power they perceive themselves to have (Hardy et al., 1998). Numerous other individual and relational factors can impact trustees' actions by directly and differentially (i.e. from trustors) affecting their perspectives on vulnerability, risk and the role of trust in their relationships.

Those researchers who have focused more directly on trustees' actions generally contend that while trustees 'can take into account how decisions, forms of contracting, monitoring, communication events, procedures and forms of punishment and reward can affect the development of trust', 'trust or trustworthiness is not something one can install or inject' (Nooteboom, 2003: 85). As a result, this research suggests that, at their most active, managers may maintain a posture of 'trust-sensitive management' to cultivate subordinate trust in themselves or their organization and attempt to influence trust development only indirectly, by identifying and placing themselves in situations (e.g. organizational cultures, inter-organizational networks) conducive to the development of trust (Sydow, 1998). Whitener et al.'s (1998) theory on trustworthiness is particularly noteworthy here in that they outline several key individual, relational and organizational factors that affect an individual's tendency to act in ways that may be viewed by others as trustworthy.

A focus on managers as organizational trustees
Although limited, prior research provides a basis for specifically evaluating the decisions and actions of trustees. We contend, however, that much can be gained by utilizing a more active perspective on the role of trustees and directly examining the roles they play in their social relationships. Thus we focus our investigation here on the experience of managers as organizational trustees to reflect that managers often take a very active role in developing and integrating their efforts to promote and direct the development of trust and control in their organizations. In general, we contend that managers take actions to concurrently promote levels of trust and control that they believe are appropriate for the task and relational contexts within which they operate. In addition, we argue that managers combine their trust-based and control-based efforts in order to promote the achievement of organizational goals and the development of positive superior–subordinate relations.

In the sections that follow, we build on previous work regarding trust and trustworthiness to examine how managers integrate their actions in promoting trust and control. We first outline key trust and control concepts. Then we examine how managers use various types of balancing processes to affect subordinate task performance and superior–subordinate relationship quality.

Identifying key trust and control concepts
In developing our perspective on managerial action, we acknowledge that previous scholars have introduced frameworks that employ various trust and control constructs (Mayer et al., 1995; Nooteboom, 2002; Cardinal et al., 2004). Because we focus on the individual manager as trustee in this chapter, we employ constructs of trust and control that research suggests are potentially relevant to individual trustees (Mayer and Davis, 1999; Dirks and Ferrin, 2002). We describe these constructs below and, thereafter, use them to examine how managers integrate their activities in ways that balance their trust-building and task control efforts.

Organizational trust
Trust generally is defined as 'a psychological state comprising the intention to accept vulnerability based upon positive expectations of the intentions or behavior of another' (Rousseau et al., 1998: 395). Using studies that focus primarily on the effects of trust on trustors' attitudes and actions, researchers have catalogued both the positive aspects of organizational trust and the various forms of trust that exist in organizations. For example, in their review of the trust literature, Ferrin and Dirks (2002) outline how trust in leader–follower relationships can both directly and indirectly lead to the development of positive trustor attitudes, a range of positive organizational behaviors (e.g. organizational citizenship behaviors) and more positive social exchange outcomes.

The constructs we utilize here outline the actions managers take to promote organizational trust. Long et al. (2003) describe these efforts as trust-building activities which they define as 'mechanisms that individuals use to assure others of their capabilities, their interest in accommodating others' needs and their willingness to fulfill promises made to others' (p. 13). They suggest that managers use trust-building activities to promote positive subordinate evaluations along the trust dimensions described by Mayer et al. (1995) and examined empirically by Mayer and Davis (1999): their *ability* on various performance dimensions, their *benevolence* or interest in accommodating a trustor's specific needs and their *integrity* or their willingness to fulfill promises and obligations made to trustors.

According to their particular situation, Long et al. (2003) suggest that managers take actions that promote various forms of subordinate trust. Building from the work of Rousseau et al. (1998) and Nooteboom (2002), we also argue that, through trust-building efforts, managers may attempt to promote trust in themselves (i.e. as an individual) or in the institutions they represent (i.e. institutional trust). Managers' trust-building efforts fall into two general categories. The first category describes the attempts of managers to promote calculative trust (also called cognitive trust or knowledge-based trust). Here, managers attempt to promote an understanding that their intentions and actions will benefit others in calculable ways (Williamson, 1993; Lewicki and Bunker, 1996). The second category describes managers' efforts to promote relational trust (also called affective or value-based trust). When promoting this form of trust, managers express interpersonal care and concern for their subordinates while they attempt to establish value congruencies that assure their subordinates that their manager (or their organization) shares their interests and motivations (Sitkin and Roth, 1993).

We contend that trust-building is not a cost-free exercise and what costs are involved will vary with contextual conditions (Creed and Miles, 1996). As a result, if the value added by increased trust is not carefully weighed against the costs of building increased trust, attempts to develop a level of trust deeper than an organizational context requires may waste valuable organizational resources. On the other hand, managers who promote a level of trust that is too shallow for a particular organizational context may lead managers to neglect opportunities to build cooperative relationships and, thereby, substantially miss value-enhancing opportunities afforded through the promotion of high levels of organizational trust (Bromiley and Cummings, 1996; Wicks et al., 1999).

Task control defined
Organizational controls comprise one contextual element that both affects and is affected by superior–subordinate trust (Sitkin, 1995; Sitkin and Stickel, 1996; Long, 2002; Long et al., 2003). Scholars have traditionally adopted a broad definition and suggested that organizational controls include essentially any mechanism that managers use to ensure that an organization's 'sub-units act in a coordinated and cooperative fashion, so that resources will be obtained and optimally allocated in order to achieve the organization's goals' (Lebas and Weigenstein, 1986: 259).

Building from these broad conceptualizations of control, discussions of relationships between trust and control have varied greatly in their explanatory focus. Because in this chapter we specifically focus on examining the ways that managers balance their interpersonal trust-building and control-based efforts, we focus our explanations on *task controls* which describe the range of *formal* (i.e. written contracts, monetary incentives and surveillance) and *informal* (i.e. values, norms and beliefs) mechanisms that managers use to direct subordinates toward the efficient and effective completion of organizational tasks (Ouchi, 1977; Mintzberg, 1979; Roth et al., 1994; Cardinal et al., 2003). We use various forms of task controls in our discussion here because they describe distinct categories of control mechanisms over which managers generally hold a reasonable amount of discretion regarding their application (Long, 2002).

In addition, while a manager's use of controls may lead to the development of subordinate trust, we contend that managers tailor their organizational control applications to direct subordinate task activities at various points of the production process (Merchant, 1985; Snell, 1992; Cardinal, 2001; Long et al., 2002; Cardinal et al., 2004). Managers specifically utilize *input controls* such as training and socialization to guide the selection and preparation of human and material production resources (Arvey, 1979; Van Maanen and Schein, 1979; Wanous, 1980). Managers apply *process controls* on subordinates performing organizational tasks to ensure that they employ prescribed task production methods. Finally, managers use *output controls* and measure the outputs employees produce against established metrics to ensure that prescribed performance standards are met (Ouchi, 1977, 1979; Mintzberg, 1979).

Trust–control relationships
While research suggests that both trust and control affect subordinate task performance and the quality of superior–subordinate relationships, Das and Teng (1998) observe that there exists 'little consensus regarding the relationship between trust and control' (p. 495). Concurring with this observation, Bachmann (2001a) states that 'there are numerous examples in the literature where control chases out trust and situations in which trust seems to remove the necessity for control, there are equally as many examples of trust and control being complementary, or going hand in hand' (p. v). Pennings and Woiceshyn (1987) and Bradach and Eccles (1989), for example, view trust as a form of control. Other scholars (e.g. Sitkin and Roth, 1993; Leifer and Mills, 1996) have focused on trust and control as substitutes and suggest that they are negatively related. Still others (i.e. Sitkin, 1995; Poppo and Zenger, 2002) suggest that trust and control 'jointly and independently' (Das and Teng, 1998: 496) affect actions within and between organizations.

The key implication when combining these perspectives is that trust and control are related and that managers should consider trust and control jointly if they wish to optimize organizational effectiveness. This observation suggests that we must go beyond past work that looked at the effects of managerial actions and begin to theorize about how managers can (and perhaps do) actively balance various mixes of trust and control in their organization.

The necessity of developing this managerial-based perspective is further emphasized when one considers two additional observations regarding the management of trust–control relations. First, while appearing static for periods of time, the particular mix of trust and control in a relationship or organization is constantly in flux (Nooteboom, 2002). Second, to address the dynamic nature of relational and institutional arrangements, managers must balance the mix of trust and control in their organization if they are to achieve organizational goals and cultivate positive social relationships (Bachmann, 2001a).

In conceptualizing the balance between task controls and trust-building efforts that managers attempt to obtain, we draw from the definition proposed by Sutcliffe et al. (2000) in their examination of organizational exploration and exploitation activities. We use their definition of balance here to argue that managers achieve a trust–control balance when they obtain 'a state where their superior–subordinate relations exhibit a harmonious' integration of trust-building and task control activities. Using this conceptualization of balance, we propose that the level of harmony achieved between a configuration of task control and trust-building activities is partially determined by the context within which that integration occurs (Cardinal et al., 2004).

We distinguish three types of balancing processes that managers utilize to achieve a balance between trust-building and task control activities (Sutcliffe et al., 2000). Sutcliffe et al. (2000) outline these process categories. They discuss how a manager's attention to various activities can be negatively related and result in *antithetical* balancing processes. To explain 'antithetical', they describe a situation where as one chooses more of one option, one necessarily must choose less of other options. In addition, they also describe how decision options about these types of activities can be unrelated and result in *orthogonal* balancing processes. Here the choices one makes regarding how much to engage in each of two or more action options is completely independent of what is decided concerning other potential options. Lastly, they describe how activities can be positively related and focus managers towards *synergistic* balancing processes. In this situation, adopting one action option makes it easier and/or more effective to also pursue specific, additional action options.

Sutcliffe et al.'s (2000) conceptualizations of balancing processes are particularly applicable here because we suggest that managerial trust and control actions have a far greater range of potential configurations than past work on trust and control has systematically considered. Thus the antithetical, orthogonal and synergistic balancing processes we utilize here provide scholars with a systematic way of organizing the variety of trust–control relationships that are described in the scholarly literature and observed in organizational life. Similar to the ways that managers balance various forms of controls (Cardinal et al., 2004), we argue that managers will use a particular type of balancing process to integrate trust-building and task control activities in ways that align with changing organizational and relational contexts.

While consistent with previous work, we further contend that the balancing processes we utilize here refine and extend previous propositions that describe how trust and control in organizations can serve as operational substitutes or complements (Bachmann, 2001a; Nooteboom, 2002; Lazzarini et al., 2004). For example, while managers who utilize antithetical balancing processes may view trust and control as substitutes, antithetical balancing processes may also be used by managers who employ increasing amounts of control in organizations that no longer can sustain high levels of trust. Here trust and control would not be substitutes because control represents a clearly superior activity. Similarly, managers who engage in synergistic balancing processes may view trust and control as complements. However, our concept of synergistic balancing processes not only describes managers' attempts to find activities that can coexist, but their efforts to significantly enhance levels of particular types of trust and control through the use of mutually reinforcing combinations of trust-building and task control activities.

Below, we describe in more detail the three types of balancing process that managers use to integrate their trust-building and task control activities. We begin by describing antithetical balancing processes. Thereafter, we discuss orthogonal and synergistic balancing processes. Table 5.1 outlines the elements and key considerations inherent in each balancing process.

As we note in Table 5.1, each type of balancing process can be distinguished by the general balancing mechanisms they employ, the intermediate outcomes they are intended to produce and the implementation challenge they present to managers. We contend that

Table 5.1 Forms of balancing processes for trust-building/task control relationships in organizations

	Relationship between trust-building and task control		
	Antithetical	Orthogonal	Synergistic
Description of balancing process	A manager implements a type of trust-building or task control activity and reduces their focus on alternate activities	A manager implements a combination of multiple, unrelated trust-building and task control activities	A manager implements combinations of multiple, mutually reinforcing trust-building and task control activities
Desired outcome	Management of subordinates using a singular form of trust or singular form of task control	Management of subordinates using combinations of multiple, unrelated trust-building and task control activities	Management of subordinates using combinations of multiple, mutually reinforcing trust-building and task control activities
Managerial challenge	Effective implementation of the single most appropriate managerial trust-building and/or task control activity	Ongoing maintenance of multiple, sometimes contradictory, trust-building and task control activities	Identification and maintenance of synergies between multiple trust-building and task control activities

Source: Adapted from Sutcliffe et al. (2000).

through ongoing attempts to balance their trust-building and task control activities, managers work to smoothly align and re-align combinations of activities in order to achieve isomorphism with the task and relational demands they encounter (Cardinal et al., 2004). In addition, we argue that managers attempt to promote an appropriate balance between task control and trust-building activities in order to achieve both high levels of subordinate task performance and to maintain appropriate superior–subordinate relationships.

Antithetical balancing processes on trust-building and task control

Antithetical notions of balance describe the negative effects that trust-building efforts can have on efforts to promote control and the negative effects that task control efforts can have on efforts to build trust. Here trust-building and task control activities are applied in a zero-sum world, where an emphasis on task controls compromises the emphasis managers place on trust-building and vice versa. Below, we use these antithetical notions of balance to describe situations where an emphasis on task controls can reduce the ability and willingness of managers to build particular forms of trust. We also describe how an emphasis on trust-building often reduces the ability and willingness of managers to implement forms of control.

Managers often initiate antithetical balancing processes in order to ensure that they do not promote activities which compromise the successful realization of a task or a relational priority which is central to their primary organizing preference. Effectively promoting positive perceptions of trust and control takes time and, as a result, we contend that managers will often shy away from implementing initiatives that appear more costly and risky than mechanisms which align with and support their primary organizing philosophy (McEvily et al., 2003).

Several researchers suggest that an antithetical relationship exists between formal task controls and relational trust (Powell, 1996; Wicks et al., 1999). For example, Das and Teng (1998) and Inkpen and Currall (2004) argue that, when a strategic alliance partner chooses to use formal control mechanisms in the execution of a strategic alliance agreement, that choice will compromise the development of relational trust between the alliance partners. Conversely, McEvily et al. (2003) argue that managers who have adopted a philosophy of organizing around relational trust considerations will tend to avoid efforts to implement formal control mechanisms.

Sitkin and Bies (1994) describe how antithetical balancing processes lead many organizations to adopt legalization practices composed primarily of formal controls while retarding the development of relational trust in those organizations. When managers believe that formal controls are effective in addressing their reliability-based concerns about subordinates, those managers may begin to increasingly rely on legalistic control mechanisms in order to promote efficiency. However, if managers increasingly rely on formal control mechanisms, value incongruencies between superiors and subordinates may increase, because 'while legalistic mechanisms are often effective in ameliorating context-specific reliability problems, they are less effective in dealing with generalized value incongruence' (Sitkin and Roth, 1993: 373). This, in turn, can lead to a cycle where managers attempt to solve their trust problems with subordinates using greater amounts of controls. In furthering this cycle, subordinates may react negatively to increasing controls with actions that diminish their perceived trustworthiness (Fox, 1974; Sitkin and Stickel, 1996).

While antithetical balancing processes often describe how managers change the overall emphasis they place on trust or control within their organization, they may also describe the emphasis managers place on particular types of task control activities (i.e. over other types of control) or on particular types of trust-building activities (i.e. over other types of trust-building activities). For example, Cardinal et al. (2004) describe how a local moving company's managers, over a ten-year period, focused first on implementing primarily informal task controls (i.e. neglecting formal task controls), then switched and focused almost exclusively on implementing formal task controls (i.e. neglecting informal task controls).

Regarding a focus on specific forms of trust, Sheppard and Sherman (1998) describe how relationships between individuals within organizations characterized by deep interdependence are 'predicated on the assumption that the trustee has internalized the trustor's preferences and ways of viewing the world' (p. 430). Using their perspective, one can easily envision how individuals in these contexts who seek to maintain high levels of relational trust would be very reluctant to engage in trust-building activities that promote conscious calculations of trust and trustworthiness.

Orthogonal balancing processes on trust-building and task control

Orthogonal balancing processes describe situations in which managers do not attempt to align their trust-building and task control efforts. Acting on the presumption (correct or not) that how they do at trust-building will not help or hinder their control efforts (and vice versa), managers may independently consider their efforts to gain their subordinates' trust and their attempts to implement organizational task controls. Below, we describe some characteristics and examples of orthogonal balancing processes.

Managers may use orthogonal balancing processes when they have little discretion over the task controls that affect their subordinates' work efforts. For example, a sales manager, whose sales associates are motivated primarily by company-wide incentive policies, may not integrate the forms of subordinate trust they attempt to develop and the types of task controls they apply. Here, organizational performance incentives are clear and unquestioned. Consequently, the level of trust that subordinates have in their manager may only minimally affect the ability and willingness of those sales associates to achieve the organization's sales targets. As a result, managers in this context may promote forms and levels of trust without consideration for the effects that that trust may have on the tasks that subordinates pursue.

Managers may also use orthogonal balancing processes when the trust that subordinates have in their manager will not affect their implementation of task controls. An example of this might be found in military contexts where stories are common of non-commissioned officers (NCOs) who develop strong relational bonds with their subordinates despite the fact that they may have to repeatedly order those soldiers into highly risky situations (i.e. compromise calculative trust). Under these circumstances, front-line soldiers understand that their NCOs are given little discretion over the orders they are charged to implement and, as a result, the level of trust that a particular NCO will gain from their subordinates will not necessarily affect the controls they utilize to enable the soldiers under their command to successfully execute those orders. The NCOs in these situations may then implement their orders (i.e. implement task controls) with little direct consideration for the effects that their actions will have on the maintenance, dissolution or augmentation of the levels of trust their subordinates have in them.

Synergistic balancing processes on trust-building and task control

Synergistic balancing processes describe situations where managers attempt to implement both trust-building and task control mechanisms so that these activities are 'mutually reinforcing in that each process facilitates and contributes to the effectiveness of the other' (Sutcliffe et al., 2000: 326). In attempting to implement a synergistic balance of trust-building and task controls, managers work to promote particular forms of task controls and promote particular forms of subordinate trust because the level of trust that managers promote reinforces the controls they apply. Similarly, the controls managers implement enhance the forms and levels of superior–subordinate trust that those managers seek to maintain.

In some cases, managers may use synergistic balancing processes to reinforce the strengths of particular types of task controls or particular forms of trust. For example, a manager in a market organization that relies almost exclusively on monetary incentives to motivate workers may make extra efforts to maintain and enhance the calculative trust that subordinates have in them. By focusing specifically on calculative trust, these managers attempt to motivate their subordinates to pursue lofty sales goals in the confidence that they will be handsomely rewarded for their extra efforts. In another example, Sitkin (1995) suggests that legalistic control mechanisms can increase the calculative and institutional trust that subordinates have in their managers because those mechanisms, by placing constraints on a manager's actions, help to ensure that managers will protect their subordinates' interests.

Inkpen and Currall (2004) outline how a synergistic focus on formal and informal output controls and relational trust between alliance partners can enhance the effectiveness of monetary incentives in facilitating the continued development of the alliance. The development of relational trust between alliance partners mitigates the potential for either partner to become greedy, focus only on their instrumental interests and pursue opportunistic objectives. The development of relational bonds supplements the motivational impact of existing monetary incentives by increasing the commitment of each partner to the alliance and stimulating each to work hard not only for their own interest, but for the interest of the associate with whom they share important values.

Factors affecting the trust–control balance

Because superior–subordinate relations are dynamic, the achievement of balance between task control and trust-building activities is a moving target which changes as organizational task and relational conditions change. In attempting to maintain an appropriate trust–control balance, we argue that managers alter the emphasis they independently place on task control and trust-building efforts and the ways in which they integrate these activities (Sutcliffe et al., 2000; Cardinal et al., 2004). We contend that managers do this in order to identify configurations of controls that allow them to efficiently and effectively direct subordinate task efforts while simultaneously promoting levels of subordinate trust that are appropriate based on situational constraints.

Figure 5.1 depicts our effort to explain the general process by which managers balance their trust-building and task control efforts. In this model, we identify key features of the manager's task and relational environments that affect their actions. Below, we describe how these features affect managerial trust-related and control-related decisions.

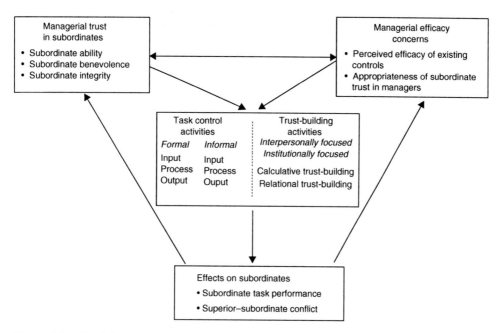

Figure 5.1   Model of managerial task control and trust-building activities

In Figure 5.1 we attempt to clarify several key trust–control relationships that are salient to managers and affect their actions. While previous research has identified trust and control as important in superior–subordinate exchanges, we contend that most of this work has been conducted on *post-hoc* evaluations and has often not identified the specific trust-based and control-based antecedents and products experienced by exchange participants. In contrast, our model attempts to clarify how various trust-based and control-based elements are determined, integrated and actuated in the ongoing development of managerial attention and action.

The cyclical nature of the ongoing processes that we depict in Figure 5.1 reflects the dynamic nature of organizational trust and control development (Peterson and Behfar, 2003; Inkpen and Currall, 2004). We begin by explaining that the trust-building and task control activities that managers undertake affect subordinate task performance and the quality of superior–subordinate relationships. In turn, managers use their evaluations of subordinate task performance and of superior–subordinate conflicts to assess both the efficacy of the task controls they utilize and the appropriateness of both the level and type of trust that their subordinates maintain in them or their organization. We contend, however, that these self-reflections remain separate from the determinations managers make about their subordinates' trustworthiness (i.e. their subordinates' ability, benevolence and integrity). To evaluate both their perceived trustworthiness and the trustworthiness of their subordinates, managers examine different elements of subordinate task performance and their superior– subordinate relationships. However, both categories of evaluations combine to affect the combinations of task controls and trust-building activities that managers undertake.

Effects of task control and trust-building on subordinate performance

Whereas organizational control theorists (e.g. Ouchi, 1980; Bradach and Eccles, 1989) have focused primarily on the effects of task control on task performance, trust researchers (Dirks and Ferrin, 2001) have examined primarily how the tendency for managers to promote (or not promote) trust affects the quality of superior–subordinate relationships. More recent work, however, has argued that it is the interaction of forms of trust and control – rather than either in isolation – that is key to obtaining *both* performance and relationship effects (Bachmann, 2001b; Nooteboom, 2002). If managers identify and implement appropriate forms of trust *and* control, research suggests they can reduce their monitoring costs, promote positive superior–subordinate relations and provide their organizations with competitive advantage (e.g. Barney and Hesterly, 1994; Wicks et al., 1999).

Performance, relationships and efficacy concerns

While recent research has begun to acknowledge the importance of trust and control in facilitating both subordinate task performance and superior–subordinate relationship quality, analyses of how these factors affect future managerial actions is less well understood. We propose that by observing their subordinates' performance and observing the quality of their superior–subordinate relationships, managers obtain important information that they use in crafting their ongoing managerial approach. In particular, these observations provide managers with important signals about both the efficacy of the controls that they utilize and the appropriateness of the trust that they have developed with subordinates.

Drawing on research on the cybernetic nature of organizational control systems (Green and Welsh, 1985; Flamholtz et al., 1985), we contend that managers may glean information about the effectiveness of their controls directly from observations of subordinate task performance. Here the failure of subordinates to adequately perform tasks may signal to managers that their employees are inadequately trained (i.e. input controls are sub-optimal), directed (i.e. process controls are sub-optimal) or motivated (i.e. output controls are sub-optimal) to perform tasks in desired ways.

While providing managers with information about the efficacy of the controls they utilize, we also argue that evaluations of subordinates' task performance give managers information that they use in evaluating the appropriateness of their superior–subordinate relationships. For example, subordinates who fail to improve their performance in response to increasing incentives may signal to their managers that they lack calculative trust and do not believe that their efforts will be properly rewarded by that manager or their organization. Alternatively, a sudden decrease in performance in a clan-based, informally focused organization may signal to managers that the relational trust that previously motivated work may be compromised (Wilkins and Ouchi, 1983).

Superior–subordinate conflicts provide additional, important signals to managers regarding the existence or absence of control-based and trust-based problems. We contend that managers also use this information in planning future actions. Consistent with the proposition posed in Figure 5.1, Edwards (1979: 16) argues that superior–subordinate conflicts stimulate managers to organize their work environments in ways that enable them to contain real and potential superior–subordinate conflicts. Sullivan et al. (1990: 336), suggest that the information that managers glean from conflicts is so important 'that the nature and amount of resistance that a manager expects from a subordinate' constitutes a major factor that influences subsequent managerial actions.

We also argue that managers' evaluations of superior–subordinate conflicts provide them with additional information about whether the controls they have utilized are appropriate for a given context. As both Levinthal (1988) and Eisenhardt (1989) point out, appropriate managerial applications of organizational controls align the goals of superiors and subordinates in ways that minimize conflicts. By implication, the existence and persistence of superior–subordinate disagreements may then provide managers with evidence that the task controls they have in place are less than optimal.

Superior–subordinate conflicts may also provide managers with evidence that the level of trust a subordinate has in them is inappropriate. Ouchi (1980), for example, argues that superior–subordinate conflicts signal to managers that their relationships with subordinates may suffer from a 'lack of trust' (130). In extending this perspective, Long et al. (2003) argue that the presence of various types of manager–employee conflicts (goal, task, personal) present managers with strong evidence that subordinates may not trust them or their organization.

Performance, relationships and trust in subordinates

While providing a basis for self-reflection, observations of subordinates' task performance and of superior–subordinate conflicts also give managers key information about the trustworthiness of subordinates. In particular, we argue that by observing these elements, managers develop assessments of their subordinates' ability, benevolence and integrity and overall evaluations of their subordinates' trustworthiness (Mayer et al., 1995).

According to Ferrin and Dirks (2002), attributional processes represent key factors in trust development. Building from this premise, we argue that managers use subordinate task performance as a guide to assessing their subordinates' trustworthiness. Put simply, the words and actions that subordinates display while performing their tasks allow managers to gauge their ability, benevolence and integrity. For example, the failure or success of subordinates on tasks provides managers with information about the ability of subordinates along various performance dimensions. The efforts that subordinates put into their work gives managers information about the benevolence of their subordinates and, specifically, their willingness to support their managers' interests. Lastly, by observing subordinates' task performance, managers can assess the willingness of subordinates to act with integrity and fulfill their promises and obligations to their organization.

The level of conflict that managers experience with their subordinates also affects their perceptions of subordinate trust. Interpersonal conflicts may signal to managers that misalignments exist between managers and employees regarding task preferences, goals or values (Sitkin and Bies, 1993). As a result, we argue that managers should monitor their conflicts with subordinates to gauge the risk of subordinate opportunism (Williamson, 1975; 1993), the extent to which superior–subordinate interests are aligned and how advisable it would be to trust their subordinates in particular ways.

Mutual adjustment in expectations of managerial efficacy and subordinate trust

We argue that, while separate, managers' evaluations of their own actions and of their subordinates' trustworthiness are not mutually exclusive. Instead, managers' evaluations of the efficacy of their actions affect the evaluations they make about their subordinates' trustworthiness. In addition, their evaluations of subordinates' trustworthiness affect the evaluations managers make regarding the efficacy of their own actions.

We contend that managers should evaluate their own managerial efficacy, in part using evaluations of their subordinates' trustworthiness. Over time, these evaluations lead managers to adjust their expectations regarding the efficacy of the controls they employ and their ability to cultivate various forms of subordinate trust. For example, if managers have little trust in subordinates to begin with, they may have little initial faith in the efficacy of their task control and trust-building choices to produce positive effects on subordinate task performance and superior–subordinate conflict. On the other hand, if they trust employees a great deal, that trust may raise their expectations regarding the potential efficacy of the task controls they apply and their ability to develop effective superior–subordinate relationships.

We also argue that the efforts managers make to implement effective controls and to build trust can affect the level of trust they have in their subordinates. For example, a manager may tend to trust subordinates who perform well despite being under-rewarded and under-appreciated by that manager's organization. Conversely, managers whose subordinates perform poorly despite having their specific needs attended to may maintain an overall lower level of trust in their subordinates.

Effects of control efficacy and managerial trustworthiness on managerial action

We argue that managers should use these evaluations of themselves and their subordinates to chart their future task control and trust-building actions. For example, building from the work of control theorists who use a cybernetic perspective to examine the development of control systems, we argue that managers will adjust the configurations of task controls they employ based on the perceived effectiveness of task controls in producing expected results (Green and Welsh, 1985; Flamholtz et al., 1985). Put simply, if a particular configuration of task controls is perceived as effective, it will probably be maintained. If it is perceived as ineffective, it will be changed.

The trust that exchange partners have in each other comprises another factor affecting the control choices those partners make going forward, whether those partners are in an alliance (Inkpen and Currall, 2004) or in a hierarchy. For example, within a hierarchy Sitkin (1995) contends that managers may adjust the types of task controls they apply in order to augment or, in some cases, even reduce the level of certain types of superior–subordinate trust.

Although it has not been explicitly included in past models of managerial action, it seems intuitive that the decisions managers make about the forms and levels of trust they build may also be affected by the perceived efficacy of the task controls they employ. For example, managers working in highly formal (i.e. legalistic) environments may attempt to bolster the efficacy of the rules and procedures they employ by focusing primarily on building subordinate levels of trust in them or the organization they represent (Zucker, 1986). In doing so, managers attempt to lower perceived risks for subordinates of adhering to managerial directives, thereby facilitating subordinate participation in the pursuit of organizational objectives (Sitkin, 1995).

We also contend that managers chart their future trust-building activities based on an evaluation of subordinate trust. For example, if managers believe that the affective trust subordinates have in them is lacking, they may make extra efforts to increase the level of subordinate identity with the organization and will undertake efforts to promote superior–subordinate value congruence (Sitkin and Roth, 1993; Lewicki and Bunker, 1996; Stickel, 1999). Alternatively, if managers judge subordinates' calculative or institutional trust in them as too low, they may take actions to ensure that they and the institution they represent can be trusted to protect and further subordinates' instrumental interests (Zucker, 1986; Sitkin, 1995).

Effects of subordinate trustworthiness on managerial action

Managers' actions (both trust-building and task control) are not only influenced by their sense of how much their subordinates trust them, but by the trust that that manager has in their subordinates. Spreitzer and Mishra (1999), for example, argue that a manager's use of top–down (versus participatory) decision-making processes is determined, in part, by the level of trust that that manager has in their subordinates. Sitkin and Roth (1993) recount a similar situation when they observe how managers who maintain low levels of trust in HIV-infected employees rely increasingly on highly formal (i.e. legalistic) control mechanisms to direct those employees.

Several authors have described how the trust that a manager has in their subordinates can affect the efforts that manager makes towards promoting trust. For example, the work of Malhotra and Murnighan (2002) suggests that the trust individuals have in their exchange partners affects their subsequent efforts to build trusting relationships. As Leader–Member Exchange (LMX) research also suggests (e.g. Schriesheim et al., 1999), the trust that leaders have in their subordinates may affect the quality of social exchanges that managers attempt to produce.

Discussion

This chapter refines and extends ideas about relationships between trust and control in three ways. First, we outline the state of the trust and control literature and make a case for examining managerial actions. Second, we describe three different balancing processes that managers use to integrate their trust-building and task control activities. Third, we present a model of managerial action that outlines the general processes by which managers take trust-building and task control actions. In this concluding section, we examine some key parts of our general perspective and of the model we propose. In addition, we outline how the concepts and the relationships between trust and control that we present in this chapter broaden traditional perspectives of managerial attention and managerial action and contribute to research in several domains.

A managerial perspective on trust and control

Our understanding of the positive role of trust in organizations has been developed primarily through subordinate evaluations of managerial initiatives. This, in addition to perspectives that adopt a very limited role for managers in trust development (Sydow, 1998; Nooteboom, 2003), has left scholars to indirectly infer how and why managers might promote organizational trust.

By suggesting that managers actively concern themselves with promoting organizational trust, the view that we present in this chapter differs significantly from previous trust research (Sydow, 1998). Using this perspective, we focus on examining how managers combine their efforts to build trust with their efforts to apply organizational controls. We describe task control and trust-building as key managerial activities and theorize how task and relational contingencies affect the configurations of these activities that managers promote. Furthermore, we suggest that managers will promote combinations of trust-building and task control activities that are appropriate for the task and relational contexts they encounter, thereby helping to ensure that organizational goals are accomplished and that positive superior–subordinate relationships are developed and maintained.

The perspective we present in this chapter also expands approaches to organizational control research that has focused primarily on how aspects of organizational tasks affect the control-based actions managers take (e.g. Ouchi, 1979; 1980; Eisenhardt, 1989). Specifically, our theory describes how both task and relational elements affect managers' applications of task controls. Consequently, our theory generally supports those who advocate a broader perspective on organizational control research which examines how managers concurrently apply multiple forms of controls and influence strategies while responding to task and relational contingencies (Sitkin et al., 1994; Sitkin, 1995; Long et al., 2002; Cardinal et al., 2004).

We utilize conceptual differentiations between trust and control concepts because we contend that trust-building and task control actions comprise distinct managerial activities. While this viewpoint needs to be subjected to future empirical research, we argue that managers' motivations for using trust-building and task control activities differ and that managers combine various trust-building and task control activities in response to their evaluations of particular task and relational factors in their managerial environments.

The three balancing processes (antithetical, orthogonal and synergistic) that we describe represent distinct ways that managers attempt to integrate their task control and trust-building activities. We contend that conceptualizing managerial trust control actions as balancing processes significantly refines and extends previous conceptualizations of trust control relationships (Das and Teng, 1998). While prior work has suggested that trust can exist as a form of control (Pennings and Woiceshyn, 1987; Bradach and Eccles, 1989), as a complement to control (Sitkin, 1995) and as a substitute for control (Das and Teng, 1998), little work has examined how managers make these determinations and act on these evaluations. By utilizing an understanding of the various forms of balancing processes we describe in this chapter, researchers may begin to develop a clearer understanding of how managers promote their organizational philosophy while they respond to key situational factors (McEvily et al., 2003).

The model we propose here identifies key antecedents and outcomes of trust and control in superior–subordinate relationships. Because we are focused on understanding the processes through which trust is built and control is utilized by managers, we take pains in our theory to differentiate how a manager's understanding of their subordinates' trust in them, the trust they have in their subordinates and the efficacy of the controls they utilize affect their trust-building and task control activities. In addition, the cyclical nature of the model we present outlines the dynamism of superior–subordinate relations, of managers' evaluations and of the responses to those evaluations they make.

Directions for future research

Future research on managers' attempts to balance control and trust in organizations needs to incorporate three general issues. First, scholars should examine the composition of various combinations of trust-building and task control activities. Second, scholars need to develop a much clearer understanding of what leads managers to promote various forms of trust and control both jointly and independently. Third, researchers need to focus more effort on understanding how various combinations of task control and trust-building activities affect subordinate performance, superior–subordinate relationship quality and subsequent managerial evaluations and actions.

Future research should begin by examining how managers conceptualize trust-building and task controls. From established research on trust, we have conceptualized clear distinctions between various forms of trust-building and between trust-building and task control activities. Scholars, however, need to investigate whether managers indeed utilize the clear conceptual distinctions we outline here. Managers may not, for example, distinguish between attempts to develop affective trust and informal types of input control, which are hallmarks of deep socialization (Van Maanen and Schein, 1979), or between promoting structurally similar calculative trust-building and formal output (i.e. market-type) controls. To further evaluate these relationships, we suggest that research should utilize an understanding of balancing processes to evaluate how managers combine their trust-building and task control actions.

Future research should also examine why managers use combinations of trust-building and task control activities. This research should evaluate the goals managers seek to obtain and the response they exhibit towards a potentially wide array of important individual, relational and organizational factors. We anticipate that, through this work, we will significantly broaden our understanding regarding the roles of trust and control in the workplace.

References

Arvey, R.D. (1979), *Fairness in Selecting Employees*, Reading, MA: Addison-Wesley.
Bachmann, R. (2001a), 'Trust and control in organizational relations', *Organization Studies*, **22**, v–viii.
Bachmann, R. (2001b), 'Trust, power and control in trans-organizational relations', *Organization Studies*, **22**, 337–65.
Barney, J.B. and M.H. Hansen (1994), 'Trustworthiness as a source of competitive advantage', *Strategic Management Journal*, **15**, 175–90.
Barney, J.B. and W. Hesterly (1994), 'Organizational economics: Understanding the relationship between organizations and economic analysis', in S.R. Clegg, C. Hardy and W.R. Nord (eds), *Handbook of Organization Studies*, Thousand Oaks, CA: Sage, pp. 115–47.
Bradach, J.L. and R. Eccles (1989), 'Price, authority and trust: From ideal types to plural forms', *Annual Review of Sociology*, **15**, 97–118.
Bromiley, P. and L.L. Cummings (1996), 'Transactions costs in organizations with trust', in R. Bies, B. Sheppard and R. Lewicki (eds), *Research on Negotiations in Organizations*, Greenwich, CT: JAI Press, pp. 219–47.
Cardinal, L.B. (2001), 'Technological innovation in the pharmaceutical industry: Managing research and development using input, behavior and output controls', *Organization Science*, **12**, 19–36.
Cardinal, L.B., S.B. Sitkin and C.P. Long (2003), 'Toward a theory of the creation and development of organizational control: A configurational approach', Paper presented at the Annual Meeting of the Academy of Management, Seattle, WA.
Cardinal, L.B., S.B. Sitkin and C.P. Long (2004), 'Balancing and rebalancing in the creation and evolution of organizational control', *Organization Science*, **15**, 411–31.
Creed, W.E. and R.E. Miles (1996), 'Trust in organizations: A conceptual framework linking organizational forms, managerial philosophies and the opportunity costs of control', in R.M. Kramer and T.R. Tyler (eds), *Trust in Organizations: Frontiers of Theory and Research*, Thousand Oaks, CA: Sage, pp. 16–38.

Das, T.K. and B.-S. Teng (1998), 'Between trust and control: developing confidence in partner cooperation in alliances', *Academy of Management Review*, **23**, 491–512.

Das, T.K. and B.-S. Teng (2001), 'Trust, control and risk in strategic alliances: An integrated framework', *Organization Studies*, **22**, 251–84.

Dirks, K. and D. Ferrin (2001), 'The role of trust in organizational settings', *Organization Science*, **12**, 450–67.

Dirks, K. and D. Ferrin (2002), 'Trust in leadership: Meta-analytic findings and implications for research and practice', *Journal of Applied Psychology*, **87**, 611–28.

Edwards, R. (1979), *Contested Terrain: The Transformation of the Workplace in the Twentieth Century*, New York: Basic Books.

Eisenhardt, K.M. (1989), 'Agency theory: An assessment and review', *Academy of Management Review*, **31**, 57–74.

Ferrin, D. and K. Dirks (2002), 'The use of rewards to increase and decrease trust: mediating processes and differential effects', *Organization Science*, **14**, 18–31.

Flamholtz, E.G., T.K. Das and A.S. Tsui (1985), 'Toward an integrative framework of organizational control', *Accounting Organizations and Society*, **10**, 35–50.

Fox, A. (1974), *Beyond Contract: Work, Power and Trust Relations*, London: Faber.

Frank, R.H. (1988), *Passions with Reason: The Strategic Role of Emotions*, New York: Norton.

Green, S.A. and M.A. Welsh (1985), 'Cybernetics and dependence: Reframing the control concept', *Academy of Management Review*, **13**, 287–301.

Hardy, C., N. Phillips and T. Lawrence (1998), Distinguishing trust and power in interorganizational relations: Forms and facades of trust', in C. Lane and R. Bachmann (eds), *Trust Within and Between Organizations: Conceptual Issues and Empirical Applications*, Oxford: Oxford University Press, pp. 64–87.

Hosmer, L.T. (1995), 'Trust: the connecting link between organizational theory and philosophical ethics', *Academy of Management Review*, **20**, 379–403.

Inkpen, A.C. and S.C. Currall (2004), 'The coevolution of trust, control and learning in joint ventures', *Organization Science*, **15**, 586–600.

Jones, T.M. (1995), 'Instrumental stakeholder theory: a synthesis of ethics and economics', *Academy of Management Review*, **20**, 404–37.

Kim, W.C. and R.A. Mauborgne (1997), 'Fair process: Managing in the knowledge economy', *Sloan Management Review*, **38**, 65–75.

Lazzarini, S.G., G.J. Miller and T.R. Zenger (2004), 'Order with some law: Complementarity versus substitution of formal and informal arrangements', *The Journal of Law, Economics, & Organization*, **20**, 261–98.

Lebas, M. and J. Weigenstein (1986), 'Management control: The roles of rules, markets and culture', *Journal of Management Studies*, **23**, 259–72.

Leifer, R. and P.K. Mills (1996), 'An information processing approach for deciding upon control strategies and reducing control loss in emerging organizations', *Journal of Management*, **22**, 113–37.

Levinthal, D. (1988), 'A survey of agency models of organizations', *Journal of Economic Behavior and Organizations*, **9**, 153–85.

Lewicki, R.J. and B.B. Bunker (1996), 'Developing and maintaining trust in work relationships', in R.M. Kramer and T.R. Tyler (eds), *Trust in Organizations: Frontiers of Theory and Research*, Thousand Oaks, CA: Sage, pp. 114–39.

Long, C.P. (2002), 'Balancing organizational controls with trust-building and fairness-building initiatives', Unpublished doctoral dissertation, Duke University.

Long, C.P., R.M. Burton and L.B. Cardinal (2002), 'Three controls are better than one: A simulation model of complex control systems', *Computational and Mathematical Organization Theory*, **8**, 197–220.

Long, C.P., S.B. Sitkin and L.B. Cardinal (2003), 'Managerial use of trust-building, fairness-building and organizational controls to manage organizational conflicts', paper presented at the International Association of Conflict Management Conference, Melbourne, Australia.

Malhotra, D. and K. Murnighan (2002), 'The effects of contracts on interpersonal trust', *Administrative Science Quarterly*, **47**, 534–59.

Mayer, R.C. and J.H. Davis (1999), 'The effect of the performance appraisal system on trust for management: a field quasi-experiment', *Journal of Applied Psychology*, **84**, 123–36.

Mayer, R.C., J.H. Davis and D. Schoorman (1995), 'An integrative model of organizational trust', *Academy of Management Review*, **20**, 709–34.

McEvily, B., V. Perrone and A. Zaheer (2003), 'Trust as an organizing principle', *Organization Science*, **14**, 91–103.

Merchant, K.A. (1985), *Control in Business Organizations*, Marshfield, MA: Pitman Publishing.

Mintzberg, H. (1979), *The Structuring of Organizations*, Englewood Cliffs, NJ: Prentice-Hall.

Nooteboom, B. (2002), *Trust: Forms, Foundations, Functions, Failures and Figures*, Cheltenham, UK and Northampton, MA, USA: Edward Elgar Publishing.

Nooteboom, B. (2003), 'The trust process', in B. Nooteboom and F. Six (eds), *The Trust Process in*

Organizations: Empirical Studies of the Determinants and the Process of Trust Development, Cheltenham, UK and Northampton, MA, USA: Edward Elgar Publishing, pp. 16–36.

Ouchi, W.G. (1977), 'The relationship between organizational structure and organizational control', *Administrative Science Quarterly*, **22**, 95–113.

Ouchi, W.G. (1979), 'A conceptual framework for the design of organizational control mechanisms', *Management Science*, **25**, 833–48.

Ouchi, W.G. (1980), 'Markets, bureaucracies and clans', *Administrative Science Quarterly*, **25**, 129–41.

Pennings, J. and J. Woiceshyn (1987), 'A typology of organizational control and its metaphors', in N. Ditomaso and S.B. Bacharach (eds), *Research in the Sociology of Organizations*, Greenwich, CT: JAI Press, pp. 73–104.

Peterson, R. and K.J. Behfar (2003), 'The dynamic relationship between performance feedback, trust and conflict in groups: A longitudinal study', *Organizational Behavior and Human Decision Processes*, **92**, 102–12.

Poppo, L. and T. Zenger (2002), 'Do formal contracts and relational governance function as substitutes or complements?', *Strategic Management Journal*, **23**, 707–25.

Powell, W.W. (1996), 'Trust-based forms of governance', in R.M. Kramer and T.R. Tyler (eds), *Trust in Organizations: Frontiers of Theory and Research*, Thousand Oaks, CA: Sage, pp. 51–67.

Roth, N.L., S.B. Sitkin and A. House (1994), 'Stigma as a determinant of legalization', in S.B. Sitkin and R.J Bies (eds), *The Legalistic Organization*, Thousand Oaks, CA: Sage, pp. 137–68.

Rousseau, D.M., S.B. Sitkin, R.S. Burt and C. Camerer (1998), 'Not so different after all: A cross-discipline view of trust', *The Academy of Management Review*, **23**, 393–404.

Schriesheim, D., S. Castro and C. Cogliser (1999), 'Leader–member exchange (LMX) research: A comprehensive review of theory, measurement and data analytic procedures', *Leadership Quarterly*, **10**, 63–113.

Sheppard, B.H. and D.M. Sherman (1998), 'The grammars of trust: A model and general implications', *Academy of Management Review*, **23**, 422–37.

Sitkin, S.B. (1995), 'On the positive effect of legalization on trust', in R.J. Bies, R.J. Lewicki and B.H. Sheppard (eds), *Research on Negotiations in Organizations*, Greenwich, CT: JAI Press, pp. 185–217.

Sitkin, S.B. and R.J. Bies (1993), 'Social accounts in conflict situations: Using explanations to manage conflict', *Human Relations*, **46**, 349–70.

Sitkin, S.B. and R.J. Bies (1994), 'The legalization of organizations: A multi-theoretical perspective', in S.B. Sitkin and R.J. Bies (eds), *The Legalistic Organization*, Thousand Oaks, CA: Sage, pp. 19–49.

Sitkin, S.B. and N.L. Roth (1993), 'Explaining the limited effectiveness of legalistic remedies for trust/distrust', *Organization Science*, **4**, 367–92.

Sitkin, S.B. and D. Stickel (1996), 'The road to hell: The dynamics of distrust in an era of quality', in R.M. Kramer and T.R. Tyler (eds), *Trust in Organizations. Frontiers in Theory and Research*, Thousand Oaks, CA: Sage, pp. 196–215.

Sitkin, S.B., K.M. Sutcliffe and R.G. Schroeder (1994), 'Distinguishing control from learning in total quality management: A contingency perspective', *Academy of Management Journal*, **19**, 537–64.

Snell, S.A. (1992), 'Control theory in strategic human resource management: The mediating effect of administrative information', *Academy of Management Journal*, **35**, 292–327.

Spreitzer, G.M. and A.K. Mishra (1999), 'Giving up control without losing control: Trust and its substitutes' effects on managers involving employees in decision making', *Group and Organization Management*, **24**, 155–87.

Stickel, D. (1999), 'Building trust in the face of hostility', unpublished doctoral dissertation, Duke University.

Sullivan, J.J., T.L. Albrecht and S. Taylor (1990), 'Process, organizational, relational and personal determinants of managerial compliance-gaining communication strategies', *The Journal of Business Communication*, **27**, 331–55.

Sutcliffe, K.M., S.B. Sitkin and L.D. Browning (2000), 'Tailoring process management to situational requirements: beyond the control and exploration dichotomy', in R. Cole and W.R. Scott (eds), *The Quality Movement and Organizational Theory*, Thousand Oaks, CA: Sage, pp. 315–30.

Sydow, J. (1998), 'Understanding the constitution of interorganizational trust', in C. Lane and R. Bachmann (eds), *Trust Within and Between Organizations: Conceptual Issues and Empirical Applications*, Oxford: Oxford University Press, pp. 31–63.

Van Maanen, J. and E.H. Schein (1979), 'Toward a theory of organizational socialization', in B.W. Staw and L.L. Cummings (eds), *Research in Organizational Behavior*, Greenwich, CT: JAI Press, pp. 209–64.

Wanous, J.P. (1980), *Organizational Entry: Recruitment, Selection and Socialization of Newcomers*, Reading, MA: Addison-Wesley.

Whitener, E.M., S.E. Brodt, M.A. Korsgaard and J.A. Werner (1998), 'Managers as initiators of trust: An exchange relationship framework for understanding managerial trustworthy behavior', *Academy of Management Review*, **23**, 513–30.

Wicks, A.C., S.L. Berman and T.M. Jones (1999), 'The structure of optimal trust: Moral and strategic implications', *Academy of Management Review*, **24**, 99–116.

Wilkins, A.L. and W.G. Ouchi (1983), 'Efficient cultures: Exploring the relationship between culture and organizational performance', *Administrative Science Quarterly*, **28**, 468–81.

Williamson, O.E. (1975), *Markets and Hierarchies*, New York: Free Press.

Williamson, O.E. (1993), 'Calculativeness, trust and economic organization', *Journal of Law and Economics*, **30**, 131–45.

Zucker, L.G. (1986), 'Production of trust: Institutional sources of economic structure. 1840–1920', in B.M. Staw and L.L. Cummings (eds), *Research in Organizational Behavior*, Greenwich, CT: JAI Press, pp. 53–111.

6 Opportunism, trust and knowledge: the management of firm value and the value of firm management

Anoop Madhok

1. Introduction

In their analysis of firms, economic scholars interested in the theory of the firm have been concerned primarily with costs. Even for economists of organization (e.g. Coase 1937; Williamson 1985; Alchian and Demsetz 1972) who depart from the assumptions of neo-classical theory and are more interested in the nature of the firm itself, rather than the representation of the firm as a production function, the central issue is still costs (for instance transaction costs, agency costs, contracting costs), all such costs stemming in one way or another from the supposed self-interested nature of the human condition. This concern with costs has prompted prominent scholars such as Rumelt et al. (1994: 41) to remark:

> There are several concerns about the role of senior management . . . Why are they needed and what do they do? All theory available suggests that they add costs without corresponding value. Yet they persist, and though we know much about their activities, which are typically strategic in character, we do not know much about the value they create.

The concern expressed in the quote above calls attention to two key issues. First, much of earlier theory seeking to understand the behavior of firms and the role of management has tended to restrictively focus on the cost dimension. Second, and as a consequence of the first, although the value-creating role of managers is of immense strategic importance, this dimension of value has been relatively neglected, value being generally understood as the overall capacity of the firm to earn economic rents through the creation and exploitation of competitive advantage (Priem and Butler 2000; Madhok 1997).

I have repeatedly been expounding upon the distinction between cost and value in many of my earlier works (Madhok 1996a, 1996b, 1997, 1998, 2000a, 2000b, 2002; Madhok and Tallman 1998), especially with respect to the management of interfirm relations. Others (e.g. Dyer 1997; Zajac and Olsen 1993) have made a similar distinction and have likewise argued that too much of a focus on costs and cost minimization may end up sacrificing some of the value that can be created through nurturing the relationship and investing in it as a potentially productive and value-bearing asset. Trust is central to such relationships and management has an important role in engendering such trust (Doz 1996).

The crux of the value argument above, made with respect to interfirm relations by so many scholars, has equal importance and applicability to organization and management of the firm, especially regarding governance within the hierarchy. Interestingly, in contrast to the theory of the firm, many of the classic scholars of organization and management of the firm, both economists (e.g. Penrose 1959) and managers (e.g. Barnard 1938 and Fayol 1949) alike, have paid more attention to the role played and value provided by management. Edith Penrose (1959) noted that the growth and direction of the firm is the result of management perceiving and seizing productive opportunities. To Barnard, the primary function of the executive is to maintain a system of *cooperative* effort in the pursuit of productive opportunities. In emphasizing the coordinating role of management, he states that 'the securing of the appropriate combinations of the elements of the organization to produce utilities is the basis for the endurance of *cooperative* systems' (1938: 256; emphasis added). Likewise, Fayol also emphasizes management's coordinative role, arguing that management can act as a powerful stimulant by allowing and encouraging employees to exercise initiative, thus tapping into a substantial reservoir of human potential.

Noticeably, however, work on the theory of the firm has tended to develop quite separately from theoretical work on *management* of the firm. This is not surprising since they basically address two different questions respectively: why firms exist and how to manage firms for competitive advantage. With respect to the latter, it is being ever more forcefully argued today that the single most fundamental task for management has become the efficient and effective acquisition, leveraging and deployment of knowledge in the search for competitive advantage (Teece 1998; Hedlund 1994). This is so because, unlike most assets, knowledge has the potential to be the source of extraordinary returns. Against such a backdrop, practices that may have been appropriate in an earlier period may well be increasingly ill suited and less valuable in today's economy. With knowledge being dispersed throughout the firm at all levels, traditional bureaucratic and hierarchical methods fail to motivate, and often end up short-circuiting the process of tapping, leveraging and unleashing the hidden potential inherent in the knowledge base of the firm (Pfeffer 1994, 1997; Ghoshal and Moran 1996).

Knowledge-based arguments envision the firm as a bundle of knowledge (Winter 1988) and highlight the importance of such knowledge in producing the inherent value of the firm. With knowledge being so central, one concern expressed about economic theories of the firm and organization such as transaction cost or agency theory has been that, by being so preoccupied with economizing on costs, especially those associated with safeguarding against potential opportunism, and by not adequately accounting for how knowledge is managed, the theory becomes a rather tenuous explanator of the link between organization and competitive advantage (Liebeskind 1996).

In this chapter I argue that, to fully unlock the latent rent-earning potential that underlies firms' economic activities and that is tied to the management of knowledge, the firm and its management[1] have to be appreciative of trust, characterized by the quality of relations within the firm, since trust relations enable firms to better secure the cooperative efforts of individuals. Although work has been done on opportunism and trust, including some of my earlier (Madhok 1995a, 1995b) and more recent (Madhok 2000a, 2000b, 2002; Carson et al. 2003) work, it has been more in the context of interfirm relationships. Moreover, the link to managing knowledge within the firm has not been clearly or sufficiently articulated. By articulating the link between motivation and cognition, I also elaborate on the moderating role of trust between managerial effort and knowledge outcomes.

The chapter is organized as follows. The next section elaborates on aspects of trust, opportunism and knowledge. The following section discusses two kinds of costs, one associated with managing opportunism and the other associated with coordinating knowledge. This provides the raw material for the subsequent arguments. In section 4, I shift the focal lens to the firm as a value manager, where I argue that the allocation of resources between these two kinds of expenditures is fundamental to the management of the firm and the value creation process. A firm's choices in this regard in a sense reflect what I refer to as its 'organizing technology'. Section 5 discusses some of the implications of the arguments for our understanding of the behavior and organization of firms and the role of management.[2]

2. Opportunism, trust and the management of knowledge

Dahlman (1979) argues that all transaction costs are ultimately information costs associated with lack of information and bounded rationality. On a somewhat related note, Demsetz (1988) contends that information costs are an intrinsic component of transaction costs, but in a more fundamental way than theories such as transaction costs or agency theory contemplate. In this regard, Ouchi's (1980) approach to transaction costs is informative. Conceptualizing trust in terms of perceived equity, Ouchi argues that the need to create a perception of equity is what results in transaction costs, these being defined more broadly than in Williamson (1985) as 'any activity which is engaged in to satisfy each party to an exchange that the value given and received is in accordance with expectations' (1985: 130).

In order to elucidate my argument, it is useful to view relationships as having a structural and a social dimension. The structural component refers more to the organization design aspects whereas the social component refers to the intrinsic quality of the relationship itself. With respect to the latter, trust creates a common interest and shared expectations which then facilitate the tolerance of both partial goal conflict and temporary periods of inequity within the relationship (Wilkins and Ouchi 1983). Since greater trust widens the 'band of tolerance' for periodic inequitable interaction, it provides a desirable flexibility within a relationship. Moreover, by inducing desirable behavior, trust reduces the need for monitoring (Ouchi 1980; Dyer 1997) and promotes knowledge exchange (Ring and Van de Ven 1992), which becomes particularly important in situations of uncertainty. Thus trust has efficiency implications, with a regime of trust facilitating coordination as a result of a mutual orientation (Blau 1964; Ouchi 1980). As Jarillo (1990) emphasized, trust more than anything else is what is critical for sustaining a relationship.

Although critics of opportunism (e.g. Perrow 1986) argue that approaching relationships based on mitigating the threat of opportunism is clearly counterproductive, equally one cannot wish it away by simply claiming that relations are based on trust. The undeniable fact of the matter is that firms must confront the potential for opportunism as an inescapable reality. A more realistic middle ground is offered by authors such as Ghoshal and Moran (1996) and Noorderhaven (1996), who contend that economic actors at their core are characterized by the potential for both opportunistic (i.e. narrowly self-interested) and trusting (i.e. mutually oriented) behavior and are not predisposed towards one or the other. Rather, it is managerial action and the context surrounding such action which results in one or the other becoming operationally dominant.

Put differently, rather than an assumption as in the case of transaction cost theory, opportunism is a variable that can be managed (Ghoshal and Moran 1996; Jones 2001). Treating it as such, rather than approaching it as a given due to the potential for its occurrence, provides greater degrees of freedom to managers and enables them to approach the transaction in a more entrepreneurial manner, instead of being 'shackled' by the purported tension between opportunism and bounded rationality (Williamson 1985).

Therefore, for instance, in a situation where the bounded rationality of economic actors results in information and knowledge asymmetries, instead of the solution to possible opportunism being greater protection through more careful contracting, monitoring and other forms of safeguards, an alternate solution would be to reduce the extent of such asymmetries through a more mutual stance characterized by a greater sharing of information. This can potentially both lower the scope for opportunism, since information asymmetries are reduced, as well as facilitate the attainment of synergistic value by better coordinating and combining complementary knowledge streams.

Stated differently, in a situation characterized by information asymmetries, there are two approaches. One would be to become more knowledgeable by purchasing information, for example better Information Systems (IS), reporting systems, monitoring systems and so on, which reduces the probability of opportunistic behavior as well as the probability of early detection (Eisenhardt 1985). The other approach would be to instill an atmosphere of trust within the relationship, in which case information and knowledge would be more willingly and openly shared without a corresponding fear of self-serving behavior.

The above distinction has relevance when it comes to the nature and pattern of knowledge flows within the firm. As noted, when coordinating knowledge across actors, the quality of the relationship matters. That is, the nature and pattern of flows would not be the same in the absence of trusting relations as in its presence. In his study, for instance, Szulanski (1996) found that an arduous relationship between sender and recipient was a principal factor hindering knowledge flows within firms. Similarly, due to the lack of a mutual orientation, an arduous relationship between two actors can result in a unit being less willing to transmit knowledge (for reasons such as preserving power) or to seek or accept it (for reasons such as the not-invented-here syndrome or not wanting to acknowledge dependence).

Although a particular dyad or set of actors may exhibit trust or lack of trust, the generalized set of relations characterizing a particular entity would be reflected in its 'atmosphere' or culture (Ouchi 1980; Wilkins and Ouchi 1983). From the above, a more trustful atmosphere would tend to be more conducive to management's initiatives to coordinate and manage knowledge flows within the firm. Without relations of trust, attempts by firms' managers to coordinate and manage knowledge flows within and across firm units may confront greater difficulties and face more resistance. On the other hand, where there is trust, coordination efforts may be viewed as enabling.

3. Two kinds of costs
The distinction above, and the two corresponding approaches, can roughly be associated with two types of costs, one associated with management of opportunism and the other with coordinating knowledge flows. In contrast to the former, the latter is not so concerned with the potential for opportunism. For reasons of expositional convenience, I refer to these as Type A and Type B costs. They are the focus of this section, which provides the raw material for the subsequent arguments.

Type A costs: management costs related to opportunism
This set of arguments rests on the dual assumptions of opportunism and bounded rationality (Williamson 1985; Alchian and Demsetz 1972; Hennart 1993). The assumption of bounded rationality gives rise to a situation of incomplete and asymmetric information

which, in the light of the assumption of potential opportunism, renders the firm vulnerable to self-interested behavior on the part of economic actors, be they individuals, organizational subunits or other entities. Absent opportunism, information asymmetry ceases to be a problem since actors would, without reservation, be willing to honestly and voluntarily share relevant information as it becomes available and as the need arises. The presence of opportunism creates complications. For example, an actor may knowingly misrepresent his capabilities and it may be too difficult and costly to verify the accuracy of his claims. This is an information asymmetry problem. Or, even if competent, the other actor may consciously withhold, for self-interested reasons, the anticipated level and quality of resource commitments.

From the received argument, the firm is a means of governing economic activity hierarchically through direction or, in a stronger form, fiat. The main drawback associated with organizing an activity in-house lies in the lack of high-powered incentives since the link between outcomes and behavior is attenuated. Under the assumption of self-interested behavior, this provides an opportunity for shirking and free-riding by employees. For example, the incentive to expend maximal effort, to maintain equipment in top working condition or to remain at the cutting edge of knowledge is dulled. These are the 'unavoidable side effects' of organizing within the firm (Williamson 1985: 138). In order to protect against such behavior, firms need to devise elaborate rules for behavior or detailed specifications for output (Ouchi 1979; Eisenhardt 1989). However, not everything can be clearly delineated and specified and, in the case of joint team production, it is difficult if not impossible to individually calibrate efforts and rewards (Alchian and Demsetz 1972; Teece and Pisano 1994). In such situations, in order to contain the tendency towards self-interested suboptimization, individual (or subunit) behavior needs to be closely monitored. All this leads to increased management costs in house.

Type B costs: management costs associated with knowledge coordination
Information costs are clearly central to the above argument, yet as pointed out subsequently by others (Demsetz 1988; Jacobides and Croson 2001), the centrality of information is even more fundamental than these theories posit since there are information costs that firms incur which have little to do with opportunism. The two kinds of issues – opportunism-dependent and opportunism-independent (or Type A and Type B) respectively – need to be separated out (Dietrich 1996; Conner and Prahalad 1996) if we want to deepen our understanding of how firms function.

The Type B argument rests on the incremental and path-dependent nature of knowledge development. A firm is not a homogeneous entity but comprises a number of economic units – functional, divisional, product, geographical – interacting with one another in varying degrees. These various units undergo partially similar and partially unique experiences, which then influences the stock of skills and knowledge in their possession (Nelson and Winter 1982). Moreover, cumulativeness and path-dependence also limits the capacity to process divergent information and augments the cost of doing so. As a result of differences in their respective knowledge bases, different parts of a firm tend to perceive, evaluate and act on different things, and even on the same thing differently. This poses considerable difficulties and challenges when they interact with one another, since the disparate cognitions can give rise to misinterpretations, inability to process and absorb knowledge, and more generally act as a 'drag' in arriving at a common understanding.

These difficulties are present, and can be costly to overcome, even if there is full intent to cooperate. However, as I will argue, trust relations are central to how such difficulties could be overcome.

In essence, such Type B costs occur as a result of 'natural' friction stemming from differences in knowledge base due to bounded rationality. As mentioned, when confronted by bounded rationality and information asymmetries, the management of a firm has two alternatives. On the one hand, it can seek to protect against potential opportunism, for instance through contractual safeguards enumerating more detailed behavioral and output specifications. On the other hand, it can aim to bring about greater cognitive alignment (i.e. reduce cognitive differences) so as to 'lubricate' the coordinating interface and increase actors' receptivity toward one another. Bridging such differences involves efforts and costs dedicated towards persuading, negotiating and in general 'educating' one another in order to bring about greater cognitive convergence and to attenuate conflict. Studies on trust show that the effort to resolve such issues would only be undertaken more fully and readily if the relevant actors were deemed to be trustworthy (Deakin and Wilkinson 1998). Moreover, given that a relationship characterized by trust increases the partners' willingness to give and to receive, this enhances their absorptive capacity.

4.   The firm as value manager

A more discriminating approach towards the nature of costs incurred by firms expands the lens through which to understand issues pertinent to the organization and behavior of firms and the role of management.[3] As creator and manager of value, the firm has to pay close attention to the management of knowledge that is the basis of such value. This encompasses both its exploration and its exploitation activities (March 1991).

From the knowledge-based perspective, firms provide a distinctive and shared organizational context that enables the alignment of skills and knowledge so as to facilitate productive activity (Grant 1996; Ghoshal and Moran 1996; Madhok 1996a). In this regard, the low-powered incentives within firm organization, which have been argued to be a disadvantage relative to markets (Williamson 1985), can actually be a source of competitive advantage in that they enable team production through the coordination and integration of the cooperative efforts of individuals and subunits (Teece and Pisano 1994; Rumelt 1995). Different parts of the firm potentially offer a complementary knowledge base and a greater variety of routines to one another. Jointly, they potentially enable learning about new technologies and new ways of creating value through a process of novel combinations and interpretations that often are an essential aspect of the knowledge development and value creation process.

The challenge for management is to realize the underlying value potential, with trust relations being central to doing so. In this regard, value has broadly speaking both a static and a dynamic aspect. With respect to the former, the main concern is with efficient implementation or execution where parameters are known or given and there are few uncertainties. With respect to the latter, the full value is not known and, arguably, cannot be known fully in advance. It emphasizes the need for more entrepreneurial behavior within the firm, especially in situations where there are no meaningful output criteria or behavioral rules, for example product design and development, planning an ad campaign, and so on, and where one depends on the initiative and enthusiasm of knowledge workers. To a significant extent, this is where trust relations become particularly relevant, since the value generated and realized depends on the conduct and the pattern of interaction among the economic actors concerned.

Attention to the dynamic aspect of value, in order to create and more fully attain the latent potential, places a premium on what may be termed a firm's 'organizing technology'. A firm's organizing technology is critical to the successful functioning of the firm and has a strong bearing upon the allocation and misallocation of resources. I elaborate on this point in the section below.

Resource allocation and the firm's 'organizing technology': the Type A : Type B ratio

Hypothetically speaking, even if two competitors possessed the necessary 'hard' technology for producing a particular good or service, there could still be differences in productivity between the firms as a result of differences in the knowledge, expertise and skills in executing this technology and bringing the product to the market. The argument places a premium on the organizing technology of firms in terms of their ability to marshal and manage the skills and knowledge necessary to be at the competitive forefront. With respect to organizing technology, note that in the opportunism-dependent (Type A) argument on managing costs, for the detection of any deviation from the way the task should (optimally) be performed, the firm (monitor) must be fully knowledgeable about the details of the task being supervised. In reality, of course, this is not so in most cases, and especially not so in knowledge-intensive settings (Osterloh and Frey 2000). First, in order to fully specify behavior and detect shirking, a monitor/manager would need to fully master the task, which is both costly and inefficient if the monitor/manager is not a specialist in that task (Demsetz 1988; Grant 1996). Second, there is often a dynamic element to team production in that team members, through interaction and experience, learn how best to pool their skills and coordinate their efforts in a manner that best utilizes individual efforts, expertise and proclivity. Not all of this can be fully specified in advance or directed in detail since some of it emerges as tacit understandings over time.

Now, the team does not operate in a vacuum but is part of a larger entity, the firm, which can be envisioned as a collectivity of different kinds of units linked together in varying degrees in (it is hoped) a coherent manner through various routines. Normally, the output of team members does not possess a self-standing value in and of itself but is part of a broader institutional context. This value is created and realized through unique association with skills and knowledge resident in other parts of the firm. In this regard, being at the crossroads of information and communication channels and flows in various directions – vertical, lateral and diagonal, the manager plays a critical coordinating role in the knowledge development and deployment process. In fact, the proper management of knowledge capital may be the single most value-adding role of managers.

To do this effectively, of course, the manager has to simultaneously be an active 'hunter, gatherer, communicator and coordinator' of knowledge, in effect an enabler and catalyst. This requires the manager (a) to become more knowledgeable and informed about the activities of the focal unit in order to understand and appreciate its needs and contributions, (b) to, in a general sense, become both more knowledgeable and globally informed about the multifarious kinds of activities being performed within the various parts of the organization, and outside, and (c) to harness, leverage and channel the more pertinent information and knowledge to the relevant units and subunits in a productive manner through guidance and supervision.

Management costs, therefore, broadly comprise two components – one has to do with management through monitoring and the other has to do with management through coordinating and facilitating knowledge flows. Strictly from the Type A perspective, when outputs or task rules cannot be easily specified and efforts and rewards cannot be fully calibrated, which is often the case in knowledge-intensive activities, a firm (manager) is compelled to incur management costs dedicated to monitoring employee behavior in order to safeguard against the exacerbated potential for self-serving behavior (Ouchi 1979, Eisenhardt 1985). However, what if the failure to perform may be not for self-interested reasons but, rather, due to cognitive limitations of a genuine nature to do with bounded rationality, which results in different understandings, different interpretations of internal and external developments and the like? To an extent, such differences are to be expected where different actors within an organization are differentially exposed to ongoing developments. Under such a scenario, one could argue that the same amount of managerial effort could alternately be applied towards activities of the teaching, learning, guiding and catalyzing kind mentioned above, so that each other's needs and capabilities are better understood and appreciated and brought more into alignment with one another.

From the illustration above, management plays a dual function in guarding against dissipation of the rent stream, both checking opportunistic behavior and coordinating knowledge flows. In either case, firms would incur managing costs, though of a different nature. However, where one is in a safeguarding mode through monitoring, the additional costs associated with activities of a more cognitive nature would be comparatively small since it is the incremental costs that matter and a certain level of costs (such as the manager's salary) was being incurred anyway. The same is true for the reverse case, that is, where the primary function is a coordinating one and any additional costs associated with monitoring would only be incremental. Note that this does not mean that firms do not or should not expend on monitoring since in principle both kinds of expenditures could be high, but does suggest that a shift in relative emphasis, in terms of resource allocation – financial, temporal, managerial – between the two types of activities, could well be a fruitful endeavor. Instead of just adhering to behavior or output rules and specification, managers could work more closely with their subordinates (and relevant others) to nurture their capabilities and their absorptive capacity. Instead of deviations from procedure being approached as something undesirable, they could be treated as an opportunity for learning. In a situation of weak compliance, a manager could seek to understand what factors might be hindering better compliance. Instead of an incomplete contract being viewed negatively, it could be viewed as providing flexibility in the face of changing circumstances. Of course, all this would be facilitated where the firm is generally characterized by a culture of trust.

In effect, then, the allocation of effort between these two kinds of purposes – safeguarding (Type A) and guiding/learning (Type B) – both reflects and influences the quality of the relationship among the internal constituents, that is, the level of trust prevalent in the firm, and shapes the endogenous institutional context within which productive activity is organized. Moreover, to the extent that activities of a teaching and learning nature enable firms to more fully harness their underlying productive potential, such a reallocation is conducive to the creation and realization of value. This is especially the case in situations involving innovation since often behavior cannot be easily specified up front, outcomes are more probabilistic in nature than in more mature situations, and value cannot be fully known *ex ante*.

It is also worth noting the potential for interdependence between the two types of expenditures. For instance, more willing information-sharing and the expending of resources on trying to reduce cognitive disparities and misunderstandings can make a manager more knowledgeable about the relevant task, thus reducing information asymmetries and the perceived need to incur monitoring costs (Ring and Van de Ven 1992). By the same token, by monitoring a particular individual or unit behavior closely for signs of self-serving behavior, a manager may gain better insights into its capabilities.

The above argument is central to issues of organization design. Very often, organizing technology may be more than strict monitoring or coaching and guiding. Increasingly, in the 'new' forms of organization design we see a teamwork setting fulfilling both purposes. As mentioned, in such settings, managers may frequently lack the expertise to actually and meaningfully monitor or specifically guide the people concerned, who may be experts in the task. Under a regime of trust, front-line people can be empowered, and thus become motivated and can let their creative juices flow, and at the same time team members monitor each other. Such self-managing teams are currently at the forefront of (in-house) organizing technology.

Trust as a moderating variable
As mentioned earlier, value has both a static (i.e. a short-term) and a dynamic (i.e. a more long-term) aspect. With respect to the former, with the main concern of management being efficient execution and largely characterized by known parameters and few uncertainties in attaining the anticipated level of value, that is, a high level of measurability, management can simply monitor employee behavior. With respect to the latter, where the full value is not known and characterized by greater uncertainty, the main challenge for management is to build a shared perspective and common purpose among employees (Ouchi 1980; Ghoshal and Moran 1996), which in turn enables more effective coordination of knowledge flows within the firm.

Ideally speaking, the efforts of the executive – broadly, authority (or Type A-oriented) and discretion (or Type B-oriented) – should align with the situation towards which they are directed. Of course, the same activity could contain elements of monitoring and knowledge management. How does one classify such activities? This is where trust plays an important moderating role between managerial effort and outcome. If, as Bartlett and Ghoshal (1993: 45) put it, human beings are capable of both initiative and shirking, given to both collaboration and opportunism, and constrained by inertia but also capable of learning, then the actual response to managers' initiatives depends on the prevailing level of trust. For instance, whereas managerial oversight will be viewed with skepticism in a less trusting atmosphere, it may be accepted more open-mindedly in a more trusting one. Moreover, where the bedrock of trust has been solidified through past action, even the more monitoring type of behavior could well be viewed as appropriate for the purpose, rather than push the firm into a downward spiral (Ghoshal and Moran 1996).

This is where economic theories of the firm such as agency theory and transaction cost theory fall short. They assume opportunism to be a trait or disposition, one that is then treated as a given and held constant, and tend to place motivation and cognition in different silos for analytical convenience, thus overlooking the interaction between the two (Jones 2001; Foss 2003). Moreover, since transaction and agency costs are viewed as determined by exogenous characteristics, this denies the endogeneity that arises from the interaction between persons and situations (Jones 2001). Yet, as March (1994) emphasizes, such interaction is warranted since people tend to act according to what they know or consider to be appropriate, where how a person frames a situation influences both what motivates the person (broadly, external or internal) as well as the intensity of motivation.

Economic arguments must more explicitly recognize the interaction of motivation and cognition and the role of trust in this regard. Trust impacts the tension between authority and discretion in an important way. A greater level of trust can both enhance the employee's discretion in the value creation process as well as reduce the necessity of executing authority (i.e. Type A costs). When trust exists, employees are more likely to consider what is an appropriate action from the firm's perspective and be stimulated by both internal and external motivations to carry it out. On the contrary, if the trust level between the employee and the employer is low, employees are more likely to consider behavior that is more appropriate for their own interests, and thus the firm needs to use fiat, monitor and sanction to 'motivate' employees.

In contrast to the theory of the firm, arguments such as transaction cost analysis, which is essentially applied at the institutional level (i.e. market versus firm) and is more concerned with the *emergence* of the firm, the recent interest in the knowledge-based view is more concerned with the *management* of the firm and firm knowledge in the search for greater value. The argument more explicitly recognizes the interaction between motivation and cognition. An important reason to study knowledge management within the firm is the coexistence of initiative and shirking and the mixture of learning and inertia in the individual employee's behavior (Bartlett and Ghoshal 1993). Certainly, if there were no initiative, creativity, learning and collaboration factors in individual employees' behavior, then we would not need to study why a firm needs to incur Type B management costs (where trust matters for the creation and realization of value).

To conclude this section and to underscore the key point, approaches that consider costs too narrowly fail to appreciate and unlock the latent potential that underlies firms' economic activities. If one approaches transaction costs more broadly to incorporate Ouchi's (1980) perspective of costs associated with creating trust, then there is an incentive to incur expenditures dedicated specifically towards the quality of relations within a firm, since this potentially translates into improved knowledge management processes. In this sense, rather than a cost, such trust-building expenditures can be considered as an investment in future value. An overemphasis on opportunism-related Type A costs, by ignoring the knowledge-related costs and benefits associated with Type B, can often end up being myopic (Ghoshal and Moran 1996). It can impede the development and leveraging of knowledge throughout the relevant parts of the organization, which has negative implications in terms of value and, ultimately, competitive advantage.[4]

5. Discussion and implications

The basic argument of this chapter has important implications for competitive advantage. The crux of the argument is that within the firm similar organizational mechanisms, expressed through various firm initiatives and routines, can be applied towards different ends. The significance and value of various firm mechanisms is that they behave as responses to both incentive problems and coordination problems (Gulati and Singh 1998).

That is, they play a dual function in maintaining a firm's rent stream, both checking appropriative behavior as well as coordinating resource flows. In either case, the firm incurs costs, but the outcome may differ depending on how these mechanisms are applied. In other words, how the management of a firm chooses to utilize and apply the mechanisms at its disposal can cause interfirm performance differences.

In their article, Rumelt et al. (1991: 19) state that 'strategic management is about coordination and resource allocation *inside the firm*'. From the standpoint of this chapter, the organizing technology of a firm in a sense reflects the resource allocation between the two types of expenditures that firms ordinarily incur in the production process. A firm's stance towards this allocation is key to understanding the role of management in the value creation process, and reflects the ability to manage knowledge productively within the firm. The core argument of the chapter has important implications for our understanding of the behavior and organization of firms and the role of management.

Implications with respect to the firm as knowledge manager
In sentiment, the basic thrust of the chapter is clearly sympathetic to Hayek's (1945: 520–21) central argument that instead of the economic problem being 'merely a problem of how to allocate given resources . . . it is rather a problem of how to secure the best use of resources known to any of the members of society . . . Or, to put it briefly, it is a problem of the utilization of knowledge not given to anyone in its totality.' This is Hayek's well-known theme of dispersed knowledge. From the perspective of the firm as a repository and manager of knowledge (Kogut and Zander 1992; Demsetz 1988), the firm becomes 'a locus of innovative and entrepreneurial activity' and a 'unit of knowledge accumulation' rather than merely an efficient governance structure. In this regard, Cyert and Kumar (1996) assert that the organizing structure of the firm needs to be more dynamic under more turbulent circumstances since information search and knowledge acquisition acquire relative importance to more static internal adaptation.

I would contend that, under a regime of trust, the management of a firm is better able to cope with fast-changing environments. Trust enables smoother and more textured information flows within the firm, which can result in more dynamic and cohesive combinations of knowledge sets and thus has implications for competitive advantage. Basically, the organization, behavior and performance of firms driven by knowledge-based reasons of enhancing competitive advantage can be expected to be different from those where the dominant orientation is governance efficiency and the control of organized effort. The latter is less entrepreneurial in nature and, while it may enable cost improvements, would be challenged in stimulating the creation of new knowledge (Adler 2000). While managers could function in a more limited fashion where the emphasis is on controlling organized effort (Alchian and Demsetz 1972), an equally important role of managers in today's economy is as orchestrator of knowledge flows, one who enables and facilitates flows of knowledge in a coordinated way in order to generate surplus value through the cooperative efforts of individuals and teams. Such skills as applied to the productive task can become an important contributor to competitive advantage. Trust relations become important in this regard.

By placing the focal lens on the firm as a knowledge-managing entity, one which seeks to earn rents through the knowledge management process rather than through mere contractual efficiency, the relative emphasis shifts from containing opportun*ism* to more entrepreneurial opportun*ity*-seeking, which in turn provides more tools in the hands of a manager to add value to an activity. This shift in orientation has important implications for the manner in which relationships within firms are managed.

Implications with respect to opportunism
From the perspective of this chapter, governance and management mechanisms play the role not only of constraining unproductive rent-seeking behavior but also create possibilities for productive rent-seeking behavior in the first place. Earlier, a distinction was made between the static and more dynamic aspects of value, where the dynamic component was partially and continually created by the participants through the quality and process of ongoing interaction. Arguably, then, with the pattern of resource allocation being a strategic choice, to the extent that an emphasis on building trust relations, characterized by greater teaching-/learning-related (Type B) expenditures relative to Type A ones, opens up future possibilities which may not have occurred in the absence of such expenditures, this becomes conducive to the pursuit of value since it enables a fuller attainment of the latent value potential.

The distinction between the two aspects of value has significant implications with respect to resource allocation. For instance, if the real problem confronted by a firm and its management is Type B, in terms of the need for coaching, guiding, enabling and catalyzing, and so on, but the firm misreads it and accordingly resorts to problem-solving tools of an opportunism-related nature, this essentially amounts to a misallocation of resources that may ultimately destroy potential value. Basically, problem misspecification results in mistreatment, along with the accompanying detrimental consequences.

Expressed differently, a simplistic approach towards costs might fail to distinguish between problems that manifest the same level of costs but are qualitatively of a very different nature (Szulanski 1996). To draw upon a statistical analogy, from the Type A perspective, the critical decision rule would effectively read as something similar to the following:

> If the behavior of an economic actor deviates from (contractual) obligations, conclude (H_0) that the actor is in all likelihood being opportunistic.

From a statistical standpoint, rejecting the null hypothesis when true amounts to alpha risk, also known statistically as a Type I error. In such a case, a firm renders itself vulnerable to opportunistic behavior. On the other hand, beta risk, also known statistically as a Type II error, denotes the failure to reject the null hypothesis when false. That is, even when there is no opportunistic intent, you conclude that it is indeed so.

Note that theories which rest on opportunism-dependent arguments, such as transaction costs and agency theory, do not claim that all actors behave opportunistically always, but that some of them do so some of the time. It is a probabilistic argument. Yet the difficulty of identifying and filtering out such behavior makes it less costly (more convenient?) to assume potential opportunism. In this respect, Kogut and Zander (1992) fault such theories for being overdetermined due to the assumption of potential opportunism. Along similar lines, Ghoshal and Moran (1996) emphasize in their thought-provoking critique of TC economics that fuller creation and attainment of value also requires that actors behave entrepreneurially and imaginatively and accordingly take novel and innovative actions as unanticipated opportunities unfold. In this context, they conspicu-ously contend that 'because opportunism is difficult to distinguish *ex ante* from partner-ship, in an effort to control the former, they will destroy the latter' (1996: 38). This is a noteworthy point. In the light of our statistical analogy, what this amounts to is that not only is TC theory incapable of distinguishing between value (mis)appropriation and (potentially) value-creating behavior but, being 'shackled' by its assumption of oppor-tunism, it tends to be overly conservative and is therefore prone to making Type II errors. Here, opportunism concerns drive out entrepreneurial ones, possibly because they are of a 'harder' and more clearly defined nature.

Of course, this does not mean to suggest that opportunism cannot occur and that firms should not invest in protection mechanisms. Clearly, the risk of opportunistic behavior (alpha risk) is ever present and firms must have recourse to safeguards. Yet the logical corollary to some actors being opportunistic some of the time is that most actors do not act opportunistically most of the time, that is, they are trustworthy. Therefore, overem-phasis on alpha risk may result in sacrificing the benefits associated with cooperative behavior, which may collectively offset any alpha-risk-related losses. The more important point is that investing in protective mechanisms may not be sufficient in and of itself to fully realize the value potential underlying a transaction and may even destroy value. The search for value may necessitate some tradeoffs against opportunism-related concerns (i.e. a tradeoff between alpha risk and beta risk), especially in situations where knowledge-related gains, such as technological capabilities or understanding of rapidly changing markets, are particularly critical for future rents.

To enunciate the point, the primary role of firms is to provide an institutional setting to solve the challenge of pluralistic knowledge generation and simultaneous coordination across its various activities rather than to check opportunistic behavior. As Loasby (1998: 7) states, while opportunism is significant, 'the problems and opportunities of developing and coordinating knowledge deserve priority'. What this suggests is not that opportunism is not important but that it may be *relatively* less important. In spite of the (occasional) acts of opportunism, building trust relations may have a greater general payoff. Jones (2001) makes a noteworthy point in contending that perhaps it would be better to start off with assuming trust (rather than opportunism) unless proved otherwise.

Implications with respect to organization design
The argument in this chapter has important implications for organization design. To quote Hayek (1945: 83): 'The economic problem of society is mainly one of rapid adapt-ation to changes in the particular circumstances of time and place. Therefore ultimate decisions must be left to the people who are most familiar with these circumstances.' What this translates into at the firm level is the importance of a balance between decentraliza-tion, in order to enable localized learning and knowledge generation, and some form of centralization or hierarchical coordination, in order to leverage the localized learning firm-wide and thus provide the firm with both the benefit of such diverse knowledge and, ultimately, its overall coherence.

How to manage this balance becomes the central organizational challenge. Hierarchical coordination is not just about authority and contractual incentives but also about learn-ing (Foss 1996), which then highlights the interaction between motivation and cognition. While organization design choices, whether internal or external, may be explained by TC theory, yet 'it may be more informative to focus on the additional value that can be created within an administrative framework which facilitates interaction and thereby creates opportunities' (Loasby 1996: 47; Madhok 2002). Accordingly, the main problem to overcome is often a coordinative one of making individual efforts, localized activities, learning processes, strategies and, more generally, distributed knowledge mesh, 'rather than the logically secondary problem of, for example, controlling and influencing the level of effort once everything is in place' (Foss 1997: 189). This is the principal responsibility of organization design. Managing motivation is also an important issue in this regard, especially where tacit knowledge is involved, since intrinsic motivation is more critical here than external motivation, and misapplication of external incentive mechanisms risks a 'crowding out' of the former (Osterloh and Frey 2000). Once again, trust relations play an important role in instilling such instrinsic motivation.

6.   Conclusion

Knowledge capital is increasingly the most critical resource in the possession of a firm. One key argument of this chapter was that the nature of the expenditures incurred by a firm, as applied to a particular set of activities, is an important criterion for the successful generation and extraction of the value potential that resides in its knowledge base. In line with this, the firm was addressed in two different ways: as a more controlling and policing entity and as a more coordinating and learning entity characterized by greater trust relations. As a manager of value, the firm can be conceived more broadly as a knowledge-managing entity, a composite comprising the two roles, with the relative weights shifting depending on circumstances. This more complex portrait appears to be a more appropriate representation of the modern firm, one that is better viewed as a coordinator of value-adding activity. As a coordinator of value-adding activity, the strategy and organization of the firm today has more to do with how a firm's resources, capabilities, competencies and knowledge can best be developed, coordinated and deployed in order to create and realize value. Trust relations are crucial to this process.

To conclude, the argument in the chapter has important implications with respect to the behavior and organization of firms and to organization design, and raises some challenging questions for research. How do managers make such allocative choices regarding the two types of expenditures? When and under what circumstances would such expenditures be justified? What are the tradeoffs involved and how are they made? How do these tradeoffs relate to the management of alpha and beta risk? How are these reflected in design choices? The issue is not about one or the other – efficient and effective governance – but a judicious combination of the two.

Notes

1.   I use the term management both in the subject sense, i.e. pertaining to managers, as well as the verb sense, i.e. the act of managing. The particular context should make the usage apparent.
2.   I would like to make clear at the outset that while I acknowledge the concerns associated with opportunism in this section, I downplay these in order to concentrate on my core point.
3.   The broad distinction being made is similar to Milgrom and Roberts's (1992) distinction between motivation-based and coordination-based costs, the former stemming from the potential for opportunism and the latter stemming from the costs of information transmission. However, my emphasis with respect to the latter differs in that, as should become apparent, I approach it in a more dynamic manner in line with the active creation of value. Also, I am more specifically interested in the allocation of expenditures between the two types and the implications thereof.

4. It is worth mentioning in this regard that often there are situations where Type B expenditures would be unnecessarily costly, especially in the more simple situations where a Type A approach would be sufficient for the purpose.

References

Adler, P.S. (2000). Market, hierarchy and trust: The knowledge economy and the future of capitalism. *Organization Science*, **12**, 215–34.

Alchian, A.A. and H. Demsetz (1972). Production, information costs, and economic organization. *American Economic Review*, **62**, 777–95.

Barnard, C.I. (1938). *The Functions of the Executive*. Cambridge, MA: Harvard University Press.

Barney J. (1991). Firm resources and sustained competitive advantage. *Journal of Management*, **17** (1), 11–120.

Bartlett, C.A. and B. Ghoshal (1993). Beyond the M-form: Toward a managerial theory of the firm. *Strategic Management Journal*, **14** (special issue), 23–46.

Blau, P.M. (1964). *Exchange and Power in Social Life*. New York: Wiley.

Carson, S., A. Madhok, R. Varman and G. John (2003). Information processing moderators of the effectiveness of trust-based governance in inter-firm R&D collaboration. *Organization Science*, **14**, 45–56.

Coase, R.E. (1937). The nature of the firm. *Economica*, **4**, 386–405.

Conner, K.R. and C.K. Prahalad (1996). A resource-based theory of the firm: Knowledge versus opportunism. *Organization Science*, **7** (5), 477–501.

Cyert, R.M. and P. Kumar (1996). Economizing by firms through learning and adaptation. *Journal of Economic Behavior and Organization*, **29**, 211–31.

Dahlman, C. (1979). The problem of externality. *Journal of Law and Economics*, **21**, 141–62.

Deakin, S. and F. Wilkinson (1998). Contract law and the economics of interorganizational trust. In C. Lane and R. Bachmann (eds), *Trust Within and Between Organizations*. Oxford: Oxford University Press, 146–72.

Demsetz, H. (1988). The theory of the firm revisited. *Journal of Law, Economics and Organization*, **4** (1), 141–61.

Dietrich, M. (1996). Opportunism, learning and organizational evolution. In J. Groenewegen (ed.), *Transaction Cost Economics and Beyond*, Boston: Kluwer, 225–48.

Doz, Y.L. (1996). The evolution of cooperation in strategic alliances: Initial conditions or learning processes. *Strategic Management Journal*, **17** (special issue), 55–84.

Dyer, J.H. (1997). Effective interfirm collaboration: How transactors minimize transaction costs and maximize transaction value. *Strategic Management Journal*, **18**, 535–56.

Eisenhardt, K.M. (1985). Control: Organizational and economic approaches, *Management Science*, **31**, 134–49.

Eisenhardt, K.M. (1989). Agency theory: An assessment and review. *Academy of Management Review*, **14**, 57–74.

Fayol, H. (1949). *General and Industrial Management*. London: Pitman.

Foss, N.J. (1996). The 'alternative' theories of Knight and Coase, and the modern theory of the firm, *Journal of the History of Economic Thought*, **18**, 76–95.

Foss, N.J. (1997). Austrian insights and the theory of the firm. *Advances in Austrian Economics*, JAI Press, vol 4, 173–96.

Foss, N.J. (2003). Cognition and motivation in the theory of the firm: Interaction or 'Never the Twain Shall Meet'? Copenhagen Business School, Center for Knowledge and Governance working paper no. 2003–12.

Ghoshal, S. and P. Moran (1996). Bad for practice: A critique of transaction cost theory. *Academy of Management Review*, **21** (1), 13–47.

Grant, R. (1996), Toward a Knowledge-Based Theory of the Firm. *Strategic Management Journal*, **17** (special issue), 109–22.

Gulati, R. and H. Singh (1998). The architecture of cooperation: Managing coordination costs and appropriation concerns in strategic alliances, *Administrative Science Quarterly*, **43**, 781–814.

Hayek, F. (1945). The use of knowledge in society. *American Economic Review*, **35**, 519–30.

Hedlund, G. (1994). A model of knowledge management and the N-form corporation. *Strategic Management Journal*, **15** (special issue), 73–90.

Hennart, J.F. (1993). Explaining the swollen middle: Why most transactions are a mix of 'market' and 'hierarchy'. *Organization Science*, **4**, 529–47.

Jacobides, M. and D. Croson (2001). Information policy: Shaping the value of agency relationships. *Academy of Management Review*, **26**, 202–23.

Jarillo, J.C. (1990). Comments on 'transaction costs and networks'. *Strategic Management Journal*, **11**, 497–9.

Jones, G.R. (2001). Towards a positive interpretation of transaction cost theory: The central roles of entrepreneurship and trust. In M.A. Hitt, R.E. Freeman and J.S. Harrison (eds), *Handbook of Strategic Management*, Oxford: Blackwell, 208–28.

Kogut, B. and U. Zander (1992). Knowledge of the firm, combinative capabilities, and the replication of technology. *Organizational Science*, **3** (3), 383–97.

Liebeskind, J. (1996). Knowledge, strategy, and the theory of the firm. *Strategic Management Journal*, **17** (special issue), 93–107.

Loasby, B. (1996). The organization of industry. In N.J. Foss and C. Knudsen (eds), *Towards a Competence Theory of the Firm*, London: Routledge, 38–53.

Loasby, B. (1998). Decision premises and economic organization. Paper presented at the DRUID conference on Competences, Governance and Entrepreneurship, Denmark, 9–11 June.

Madhok, A. (1995a). Opportunism and trust in joint venture relationships: An exploratory study and a model. *Scandinavian Journal of Management*, **11**, 57–74.

Madhok, A. (1995b). Revisiting multinational firms' tolerance for joint ventures: A trust-based approach. *Journal of International Business Studies*, **26**, 117–38.

Madhok, A. (1996a). The organization of economic activity: Transaction costs, firm capabilities and the nature of governance. *Organization Science*, **7** (5), 577–90.

Madhok, A. (1996b). Knowhow-, experience- and competition-related consideration in foreign market entry: An exploratory investigation. *International Business Review*, **5** (4), 339–66.

Madhok, A. (1997). Cost, value and foreign market entry mode: The transaction and the firm. *Strategic Management Journal*, **18**, 39–62.

Madhok, A. (1998). The nature of multinational firm boundaries: Transaction costs, firm capabilities and foreign market entry mode. *International Business Review*, **7** (3), 259–90.

Madhok, A. (2000a). Interfirm collaboration: Contractual and competence-based perspectives. In N. Foss and V. Mahnke (eds), *Governance, Competence and Entrepreneurship*, Oxford: Oxford University Press, 276–303.

Madhok, A. (2000b). Transaction (in)efficiency, value (in)efficiency and interfirm collaboration. In D.O. Faulkner and M. de Rond (eds), *Cooperative Strategies: Economic, Organizational and Business Issues*, Oxford: Oxford University Press, 74–95.

Madhok, A. (2002). Re-assessing the fundamentals and beyond: Ronald Coase, The transaction cost and resource-based theories of the firm and the institutional structure of production. *Strategic Management Journal*, **23**, 535–50.

Madhok, A. and S.B. Tallman (1998). Resources, transactions and rents: Managing value through interfirm collaborative relationships. *Organization Science*, **9**, 326–39.

March, J.G. (1991). Exploration and exploitation in organizational learning. *Organization Science*, **2**, 71–87.

March, J.G. (1994). *A Primer on Decision Making: How Decisions Happen*. New York: Macmillan.

Milgrom P. and J. Roberts (1992). *Economics, Organization and Management*. Englewood Cliffs, NJ: Prentice-Hall.

Nelson, R. and S. Winter (1982), *An Evolutionary Theory Of Economic Change*, Cambridge, MA: Harvard University Press.

Noorderhaven, N.G. (1996). Opportunism and trust in transaction cost economics. In J. Groenewegen (ed.), *Transaction Cost Economics and Beyond*, Boston: Kluwer, 105–28.

Osterloh, M. and B. Frey (2000). Motivation, knowledge transfer and organizational form. *Organization Science*, **11**, 538–50.

Ouchi, W.G. (1979). A conceptual framework for the design of organizational control mechanisms. *Management Science*, **25**, 833–48.

Ouchi, W.G. (1980). Markets, bureaucracies, and clans. *Administrative Science Quarterly*, **25**, 129–41.

Penrose, E. (1959). *The Theory of the Growth of the Firm*. London: Basil Blackwell.

Perrow, C. (1986). Economic theories of organization. *Theory and Society*, **15**, 11–45.

Pfeffer, J. (1994). *Competitive Advantage through People*, Boston, MA: HBS Press.

Pfeffer, J. (1997). *The Human Equation*, Boston, MA: HBS Press.

Priem, R.L. and J.E. Butler (2000). Is the resource-based 'view' a useful perspective for strategic management research? *Academy of Management Review*, **26**, 22–40.

Ring, P.S. and Van de Ven, A.H. (1992). Structuring cooperative relationships between organizations. *Strategic Management Journal*, **13**, 483–92.

Romme, A.G.L. (1996). A note on the hierarchy–team debate. *Strategic Management Journal*, **17**, 411–17.

Rumelt, R.P. (1995). Inertia and transformation. In C. Montgomery (ed.), *Resource-based and Evolutionary Theories of the Firm: Towards a Synthesis*, Boston: Kluwer, 101–32.

Rumelt, R., D.E. Schendel and D.J. Teece (1991). Strategic management and economics. *Strategic Management Journal*, **12** (special issue), 5–30.

Rumelt, R.P., D.E. Schendel and D.J. Teece (eds) (1994). *Fundamental Issues in Strategy*, Boston MA: HBS Press.

Szulanski, J. (1996). Exploring internal stickiness: Impediments to the transfer of best practice within the firm. *Strategic Management Journal*, **17** (special issue), 27–44.

Teece, D.J. (1998). Capturing value from knowledge assets: The new economy, markets for knowhow, and intangible assets. *California Management Review*, **49**, 55–79.

Teece, D.J. and G. Pisano (1994). The dynamic capabilities of firms: An introduction. *Journal of Economic Behavior and Organization*, **3**, 537–56.

Wilkins, A.L. and W. Ouchi (1983). Efficient cultures: Exploring the relationship between culture and organizational performance. *Administrative Science Quarterly*, **28**, 468–81.

Williamson, O.E. (1985). *The Economic Institutions of Capitalism*, New York: Free Press.

Winter, S. (1988). On Coase, competence and the corporation. *Journal of Law, Economics and Organization*, **4**, 163–80.

Zajac, E.J. and C.P. Olsen (1993). From transaction cost to transaction value analysis: Implications for the study of interorganizational strategies. *Journal of Management Studies*, **30**, 131–45.

7 Trust, transaction cost economics, and mechanisms
Philip Bromiley and Jared Harris

Introduction

Organizational scholars increasingly recognize trust as an important factor in intra- and inter-organizational relations, significantly influencing everything from the behavior of teams to the performance of strategic alliances and supply chains.

Ten years have passed since the publication of two early articles on organizational trust: Bromiley and Cummings (1995) and Cummings and Bromiley (1996). In reflecting on the scholarly impact of these papers – and what such an impact might mean for future work in organizational trust – we discuss the concept of trust, briefly revisit the papers, consider the different ways in which the research has been used, and offer thoughts on the relevance of trust to organizational research.

Bromiley and Cummings suggest that the inclusion of trust would expand and extend the research framework of transaction cost economics (TCE). Yet this call for TCE research to include the concept of trust has been largely ignored. Why? We summarize and analyze the apparent justifications for omitting or ignoring trust, leading to a critical examination of several theoretical aspects of TCE. We distinguish between TCE's calculativeness, based on assuming others are self-interest-seeking with guile, and trust, which we define as beliefs or actions not determined by such calculativeness.

Defining trust

All research on organizational trust faces the question of how to define trust. What do scholars mean when they use the term trust? Trust's many meanings in common usage have complicated the scholarly discussion. These alternative meanings make it difficult to clearly and rigorously define a scholarly construct. Trust researchers have responded to this complexity by defining trust in differing ways or by sub-dividing trust into a multiplicity of sub-constructs that attend to the different meanings that trust has for people and for organizations.

Therefore, scholars conceive of intra- and inter-organizational trust in many ways. Some define trust as intended or potential behavior. For example, Gambetta (1988, p. 217) defines trust as an assessment of another's likely behavior based on its influence on the probability of our choice of future actions:

> When we say that we trust someone or that someone is trustworthy, we implicitly mean that the probability that he will perform an action that is beneficial or at least not detrimental to us is high enough for us to consider engaging in some form of cooperation with him.

In contrast, some see trust primarily as a dispositional capacity of the trustor (Dasgupta, 1988; Hardin, 1993); or as being reciprocal or relational in nature (Hardin, 1991; Zaheer and Venkatraman, 1995).

The target of trust has also been discussed: scholars have defined trust based on where the trust is directed or in whom or what it is placed. For example, Ben-Ner and Putterman

(2001) separate trust into its self-regarding, other-regarding and process-regarding aspects. Trust has been connected to conceptions of morality (Baier, 1986), satisfaction with another's fairness (Ring and Van de Ven, 1994), or as a derivation of institutional (Shapiro, 1987) and cultural (Lane and Bachmann, 1996) influences. All of these conceptions capture important elements of trust.

In attempting to extend TCE, Bromiley and Cummings (1995) developed a trust construct addressing critical issues in TCE, defining trust as the answer to three questions. First, do you believe the other agent is honest in negotiations? Second, do you believe the other agent will make a good-faith effort to behave in accordance with its commitments? Third, do you believe the other agent will not take undue advantage of you should the opportunity become available? The answers to these questions comprise beliefs about the trustee's honesty, keeping of commitments, and forbearance in exploiting unanticipated advantages.

However, Bromiley and Cummings's (1995) trust construct allows for both calculative and non-calculative components. In their terminology, we could trust someone because we knew it was in that person's self-interest to keep commitments to us. We might trust bank tellers because we believe they operate in a system that makes their cheating us unlikely. At the same time, their definition also allowed trust to rest on non-calculative assessments. While useful in identifying three different components of trust, Bromiley and Cummings's (1995) trust definition does not discriminate trust from calculativeness, making it hard to use in an ongoing scholarly debate aimed at differentiating the two.

Williamson (1993b, pp. 458–9) suggests calculativeness is 'pervasive', and that calculative behavior which incorporates the TCE assumption of others' opportunistic 'self-interest seeking with guile' allows for 'superior deals to be made'. This analysis of self-interest assumes that everyone attempts to increase a utility function that reflects monetary returns.[1] Therefore we view economic calculativeness, for purposes of TCE, as an analytical process that assumes opportunism (self-interest seeking with guile) on the part of other actors.

To clarify the discussion, we revise Bromiley and Cummings's original definition of trust by restricting trust to beliefs that do not derive from a calculation that assumes the other's opportunism. Beliefs about another's likely behavior can derive from (i) a calculation of the actions most in the other's interests assuming opportunism, or (ii) a variety of other factors, including analysis that makes different assumptions or includes non-analytical beliefs about the other. A person's behavior toward another could reflect either trusting or calculative beliefs, or both. This means that trust and calculativeness are not necessarily mutually exclusive; rather, we argue simply that they are qualitatively different constructs and each is potentially influential in distinct ways.

Consequently, we define trust as one's *non-calculative* belief in another's honesty in negotiations, good-faith efforts to keep commitments, and forbearance from opportunism.

Background: trust and transaction costs

Bromiley and Cummings (1995) claim that trust reduces transaction costs. This assumes, contra Williamson (1985), that others can assess – to some extent – the degree to which an individual or an organization can be trusted. Whereas Williamson (1975) suggests that organizations must act as if individuals cannot be trusted, Bromiley and Cummings assume that varying degrees of trust exist and can be estimated, subject to some level of error. Employing this modified assumption, the authors invoke the basic logic of transaction cost economics to form a theoretical framework connecting transaction costs and trust.[2] By treating trust as a variable rather than an 'all-or-nothing' constant set at zero, they claimed to extend the TCE framework. If agents can assess approximately how trustworthy others are, then the optimal governance structure should vary depending on these assessments. Economic actors should build less costly control systems for relatively trustworthy people than for less trustworthy people. Accordingly, Bromiley and Cummings (1995) predict that, all else constant, trust will influence organizational behavior and performance.

Subsequently, Cummings and Bromiley (1996) developed and validated the Organizational Trust Inventory (OTI), an instrument for measuring trust within and between organizations. The authors formulate and test the instrument based on their explicit, three-pronged definition of trust, clarifying exactly what they mean by 'trust' and how it influences organizations. The authors' data analysis confirms that these three distinct aspects of trust can be captured and measured.

These two articles have appreciably influenced research in the area of intra- and inter-organizational relations. Scholars have drawn on the two papers in a variety of ways, and at least 66 citations have been recorded in publications such as *Organization Science, Academy of Management Journal, Academy of Management Review, Business Ethics Quarterly, Journal of International Business Studies, Strategic Management Journal* and others (see Table 7.1 for a summary of the citing articles). Among the citing articles, theoretical pieces outnumber empirical studies nearly two to one; indeed, only three studies actually employ all or modified portions of the OTI instrument itself (Ferrin and Dirks, 2003; Kostova and Roth, 2002; Saparito et al., 2004). The other empirical pieces primarily draw on Bromiley and Cummings's definition of trust (e.g. Jarvenpaa and Leidner, 1999; Zaheer et al., 1998), which is also the primary use of their research in the theoretical articles (e.g. Hosmer, 1995; McKnight et al., 1998). Articles citing Bromiley and Cummings's construct definition use it in various ways: some adopt the multifaceted definition of trust – generally referring to the three-pronged definition as a belief in another's reliability, predictability and fairness (e.g. Zaheer et al., 1998) – while others make only passing reference to the work in their literature review. The articles cover a variety of contexts, including e-commerce (McKnight and Chervany, 2001), strategic alliances (Das and Teng, 1998; Ring and Van de Ven, 1992), international joint ventures (Currall and Inkpen, 2002), corporate law (Mitchell, 1999), and human resource management (Whitener, 1997).

The most curious and interesting finding in Table 7.1 is that, while Bromiley and Cummings extended TCE and the work is widely cited, it has had little or no influence on TCE research itself. The vast majority of the citing articles appear in management journals and only a few even mention transaction costs. Only six of the articles even employ a TCE theoretical framework (e.g. Sutcliffe and Zaheer, 1998; Young-Ybarra and Wiersema, 1999) – and these primarily reference the trust definition without explicitly testing trust as a mechanism. Among the research drawing on the work of Bromiley and Cummings, one theoretical paper (Noorderhaven, 1996) explicitly argues for introducing trust into TCE, and only one case-study-based article (Ring, 1997) actually attempts to test basic TCE assumptions versus trust mechanisms.

Nooteboom (1996) models the distinct roles of both trust and opportunism in influencing interfirm relations. This has been shown empirically by demonstrating that

Table 7.1   *Scholarly research drawing on Bromiley and Cummings (1995) and*
               Cummings and Bromiley (1996)

	Author(s) and year	Journal or other location
1.	Husted and Folger (2005)	*Organization Science*
2.	Saparito et al. (2004)	*Academy of Management Journal*
3.	Bussing and Moranz (2003)	*Zeitschrift für Arbeitswissenschaft*
4.	Ferrin and Dirks (2003)	*Organization Science*
5.	McEvily et al. (2003)	*Organization Science*
6.	Olson and Olson (2003)	*Economics of Innovation & New Technology*
7.	Perrone et al. (2003)	*Organization Science*
8.	Pizanti and Lerner (2003)	*International Small Business Journal*
9.	Currall and Inkpen (2002)	*Journal of International Business Studies*
10.	Jutla et al. (2002)	*Internet Research – Electronic Networking Applications & Policy*
11.	Kostova and Roth (2002)	*Academy of Management Journal*
12.	McKnight et al. (2002)	*Information Systems Research*
13.	Pavlou (2002)	*Journal of Strategic Information Systems*
14.	Zaheer et al. (2002)	Chapter in Contractor and Lorange (eds), *Cooperative Strategies and Alliances*
15.	Adler (2001)	*Organization Science*
16.	Brinkman and Seifert (2001)	*Zeitschrift für Soziologie*
17.	McKnight and Chervany (2001)	*International Journal of Electronic Commerce*
18.	Möllering (2001)	*Sociology*
19.	Currall and Inkpen (2000)	Chapter in Faulkner and DeRonde (eds), *Cooperative Strategy*
20.	Gottschalk (2000)	*International Review of Law, Computers & Technology*
21.	Lazar (2000)	*Journal of Management in Engineering*
22.	Olson and Olson (2000)	*Human–Computer Interaction*
23.	Blois (1999)	*Journal of Management Studies*
24.	Bowie (1999)	Book, *Business Ethics: A Kantian Perspective*
25.	Bussing and Broome (1999)	*Zeitschrift für Arbeitswissenschaft*
26.	Dirks (1999)	*Journal of Applied Psychology*
27.	Jarvenpaa and Leidner (1999)	*Organization Science*
28.	Kostova (1999)	*Academy of Management Review*
29.	Kramer (1999)	*Annual Review of Psychology*
30.	Leana (1999)	*Academy of Management Review*
31.	Mitchell (1999)	*The Journal of Corporation Law*
32.	Young-Ybarra and Wiersema (1999)	*Organization Science*
33.	Bigley and Pearce (1998)	*Academy of Management Review*
34.	Darley (1998)	*Business Ethics Quarterly*
35.	Das and Teng (1998)	*Academy of Management Review*
36.	Dean et al. (1998)	*Academy of Management Review*
37.	Hagen and Choe (1998)	*Academy of Management Review*
38.	Jarvenpaa et al. (1998)	*Journal of Management Information Systems*
39.	Jones and Bowie (1998)	*Business Ethics Quarterly*
40.	McKnight et al. (1998)	*Academy of Management Review*
41.	Monge et al. (1998)	*Organization Science*

Table 7.1   (continued)

	Author(s) and year	Journal or other location
42.	Sako (1998)	Chapter in Lane and Bachmann (eds), *Trust Within and Between Organizations*
43.	Sheppard and Sherman (1998)	*Academy of Management Review*
44.	Sutcliffe and Zaheer (1998)	*Strategic Management Journal*
45.	Whitener et al. (1998)	*Academy of Management Review*
46.	Zaheer et al. (1998)	*Organization Science*
47.	Bowie (1997)	*Philosophical Studies*
48.	Lazar (1997)	*Journal of Management in Engineering*
49.	Leeuw (1997)	*Rationality and Society*
50.	Ring (1997)	*Journal of Management Studies*
51.	Whitener (1997)	*Human Resource Management Review*
52.	Creed and Miles (1996)	Chapter in Kramer and Tyler (eds), *Trust in Organizations*
53.	Kipnis (1996)	Chapter in Kramer and Tyler (eds), *Trust in Organizations*
54.	Mishra (1996)	Chapter in Kramer and Tyler (eds), *Trust in Organizations*
55.	Noorderhaven (1996)	Chapter in Groenewegen (ed.), *Transaction Cost Economics and Beyond*
56.	Ring (1996)	*Business & Society*
57.	Sheppard and Tuchinsky (1996)	*Research in Organizational Behavior*
58.	Currall and Judge (1995)	*Organizational Behavior and Human Decision Processes*
59.	Hosmer (1995)	*Academy of Management Review*
60.	Zaheer and Venkatraman (1995)	*Strategic Management Journal*
61.	Anderson et al. (1994)	*Academy of Management Review*
62.	Hudson et al. (1994)	*Entrepreneurship: Theory and Practice*
63.	Ring and Van de Ven (1994)	*Academy of Management Review*
64.	Zaheer and Venkatraman (1994)	*Management Science*
65.	Parkhe (1993)	*Organization Science*
66.	Ring and Van de Ven (1992)	*Strategic Management Journal*

trust – as distinct from calculativeness – has an effect on perceived dependence (Berger et al., 1995; Nooteboom et al., 1997). Some recent studies (Jap and Anderson, 2003; Lui and Ngo, 2004; Saparito et al., 2004) also empirically demonstrate that trust does not have to be calculative – and, therefore, that calculativeness and trust differ – yet the concept of trust has not been embraced by TCE researchers. Thus, Bromiley and Cummings's research has influenced the theoretical development of trust as a construct within the management literature, but has had no appreciable influence on TCE theory. Why?

Led by Williamson's writings, TCE scholars have offered three justifications for ignoring trust. First, they argue that individuals and organizations cannot discern the trustworthiness of other actors *ex ante* and so must act as if others cannot be trusted. Second, they argue that trust *per se* does not manifest itself in economic exchanges; rather, economic actors are always calculative whereas trust is reserved for very special social relations. Third, they assert that trust does not add any explanatory power to organizational research. We consider each of these justifications in turn, arguing that they are not only inconsistent and incorrect, but also inadequate reasons to ignore the intra- and inter-organizational implications of trust.

Trust: assumed away

TCE rests on three assumptions: bounded rationality, opportunism and asset specificity (Williamson, 1975, 1985). Due to bounded rationality, firms cannot forecast perfectly, nor can they write complete contracts. Opportunism means individuals and firms may lie to advance themselves, behavior termed 'self-interest seeking with guile' (Williamson, 1985, p. 30). Asset specificity means that investments can create positive returns in a given transaction but have less value outside that transaction. Efficient operation of a given transaction may require investments that have little value outside that relation, but the assumptions dictate that the parties cannot trust one another, nor can they write a perfect contract. Thus, for transactions with high asset specificity, bringing both parties to the transaction into the same hierarchy may offer greater efficiency than a comparable market transaction. The benefits of hierarchical organization may increase with the level of uncertainty.

Williamson's opportunism assumption eliminates trust. Specifically, he assumes that trustworthiness cannot be discerned, requiring economic actors to treat all others as opportunists:

> I do not insist that every individual is continuously or even largely given to opportunism. To the contrary, I merely assume that some individuals are opportunistic some of the time and that differential trustworthiness is rarely transparent *ex ante*. As a consequence, *ex ante* screening efforts are made and *ex post* safeguards are created. (1985, p. 64)

While Williamson refers to screening, he almost exclusively emphasizes the creation of safeguards through internalization and similar factors. That is, he mentions screening, but then proceeds as if it were impossible. If screening were taken seriously, TCE would need to address appropriate responses to differential levels of trustworthiness.

Williamson further notes that the difficulty of determining trustworthiness implies that forms of economic organization that assume high levels of trust and good intention are 'fragile'; that is, unscreened opportunists can enter and take advantage of the organization. Therefore viable cooperatives must take care whom they admit and must otherwise defend themselves against free-riders or other individuals who might exploit them.

In responding to criticisms of the opportunism assumption (e.g. Ghoshal and Moran, 1996), Williamson acknowledges that opportunism may be infrequent:

> My insistence that opportunism be accorded co-equal status with bounded rationality does not imply that I believe that most economic agents are engaged in opportunistic practices most of the time. Rather, most economic agents are engaged in business-as-usual, with little or no thought to opportunism, most of the time. (1993c, p. 98)

However, Williamson also deviates from this position. For example, shortly after the passage above, Williamson instead asserts that opportunistic behavior is pervasive, rather than rare:

> Opportunism is a less technical term than adverse selection and moral hazard. It suggests, correctly, that the troublesome behavior in question is not an arcane economic condition but is familiar and pervasive. (Ibid., p. 101)

These types of contradictions make it difficult to specify Williamson's position precisely; regardless, the frequency of opportunism is a peripheral issue. The ability to estimate trustworthiness matters more, since that ability lets agents modify their behavior based on the perceived trustworthiness of their exchange partners. At the core of the theory, Williamson assumes no one can tell whether others are trustworthy. Unable to discern another's level of honesty, agents must always assume the worst.

Why does TCE assume that agents cannot detect trustworthiness? It is more plausible – and certainly more consistent with TCE's bounded rationality assumption – to assume that, although individuals cannot perfectly recognize or predict trustworthiness, they can identify it to some extent, some of the time. Just as optimal insurance expenditures depend on the probability of an accident, optimal control systems depend on the probability of cheating. Yet, once again, the TCE reasoning is unclear; often Williamson implies that agents cannot detect trustworthiness, but also suggests that differential trustworthiness may be detectable, but only at great cost:

> Thus, if agents, though boundedly rational, were fully trustworthy, comprehensive contracting would still be feasible . . . Such devices will not work, however, if some economic actors (either principals or agents) are dishonest (or, more generally, disguise attributes or preferences, distort data, obfuscate issues, and otherwise confuse transactions), and it is very costly to distinguish opportunistic from nonopportunistic types *ex ante*. (1981, p. 554)

By assuming a high cost to detect trustworthiness, Williamson attempts to avoid explicitly acknowledging a more nuanced position on the detection of opportunism. Such a nuanced position formed the basis of Bromiley and Cummings (1995); they argued that scholars should treat the detection of opportunism as a continuous variable subject to empirical testing, rather than as a theoretical constant that assumes away the variation. Bromiley and Cummings (1995) argue – and Frank (1988) demonstrates – that individuals can judge the trustworthiness of others, *ex ante*, with a certain amount of reliability and without great cost.

Furthermore, Williamson's own discussion of reputation deviates from his strict opportunism assumption. In his response to Ghoshal and Moran (1996), for example, Williamson (1996) relates the metaphor of a hiker who, when traveling in a dangerous wilderness, will choose traveling companions with a reputation for cooperative behavior over those with bad or unknown reputations. This clearly deviates from the TCE assumption that all actors should treat others with equal suspicion as a safeguard against possible opportunists.

In his eagerness to avoid the term trust, Williamson offers another example of reputation-based integrity, wherein a Norwegian ship owner needs to pay for something immediately and calls his London banker who guarantees the payment: 'I would argue that the London banker's deep knowledge of the personal integrity of the Norwegian shipowner merely permitted him to improve his estimate of integrity' (1993b, p. 470). Here, Williamson clearly recognizes both that people differ in their willingness to be opportunistic, and that such differences can be apparent and discernible. Williamson's analysis implies that the London banker would behave differently depending on which client had called, even if the substantive facts of the described situation were similar.

TCE advocates might justify trust-like behavior by arguing that the individual being trusted has a valuable reputation for honesty. Since deception would damage such a reputation (and one assumes that damage would cost more than the benefits of cheating in this one transaction), one can count on the individual's word. However, neither Williamson's hiker nor banker examples fit this case. Consider the hiking example: if calculation rules supreme, even those with good reputations would behave badly if they knew their misdeeds would not influence their reputations – if they could be sure you would not return to tell on them.

In the banker example, Williamson emphasizes deep knowledge of personal integrity, which clearly indicates integrity as a personal trait, not good behavior to protect a reputation. Williamson's use of the term integrity implies being trustworthy, a meaning consistent with common usage. For example, the Funk and Wagnalls *Standard College Dictionary* (1963) begins its definition of integrity with '1. Uprightness of character; probity; honesty.' Thus integrity includes even more than honesty; it implies honesty and probity. By definition, integrity implies trustworthiness, not opportunism and guile. If we assume individuals differ in integrity, we can easily define and justify a common concept of trust as a perception of the integrity or honesty of the other actor. Williamson's use of 'integrity' instead of 'trust' seems like an attempt to invoke the concept of trust while assiduously avoiding the use of the word.

In sum, Williamson's work evidences difficulty in consistently defining and applying the TCE assumption of opportunism. Trust is sometimes invoked indirectly. TCE arguments sometimes invoke concepts that appear as trust, only stopping short of using the word. Yet instead of empirically addressing the issue of whether individuals can judge if others merit trust, TCE simply assumes it away. If, as Williamson (1996, p. 50) suggests, 'a more veridical and predictive theory of economic organization will recognize that the propensity for opportunism varies among individuals and between cultures', TCE continues to miss the opportunity to extend itself and become the type of predictive theory he describes. Recognizing the variability of opportunism, and studying trust creation, detection, and the implications for governance choice, would significantly refine and extend the research agenda of TCE.

Trust: not 'permitted' in business

The second justification for ignoring trust in TCE work simply asserts that trust *per se* has no place in economic exchanges. Williamson asserts that economic actors are strictly calculative, and trust is reserved for special social relations that lie outside of business dealings. Williamson says:

> it is redundant at best and can be misleading to use the term 'trust' to describe commercial exchange for which cost-effective safeguards have been devised in support of more efficient exchange. Calculative trust is a contradiction in terms. (1993b, p. 463)

> Wherein is trust implied if parties to an exchange are farsighted and reflect the relevant hazards in the terms of the exchange? Indeed, I maintain that trust is irrelevant to commercial exchange and that reference to trust in this connection promotes confusion. (Ibid., p. 469)

Williamson maintains that what might be called 'trust' in the setting of economic exchange is merely the cost–benefit analysis of risk. Real trust, then, is reserved for social relations that are 'nearly non-calculative'; Williamson claims such trust is impossible in economic relations.[3] Trust, therefore, 'should be concentrated on those personal relations in which it really matters' (ibid., p. 483). He argues:

> Personal trust is therefore characterized by (1) the absence of monitoring, (2) favorable or forgiving predilections, and (3) discreteness. Such relations are clearly very special . . . trust, if it obtains at all, is reserved for very special relations between family, friends, and lovers. Such trust is also the stuff of which tragedy is made. (Ibid., p. 484)

> Personal trust is made nearly non-calculative by switching out of a regime in which the marginal calculus applies into one of a discrete structural kind. That often requires added effort and is warranted only for very special personal relations that would be seriously degraded if a calculative orientation were 'permitted'. Commercial relations do not qualify. (Ibid., p. 486)

This argument is hard to reconcile in a theory that subscribes to bounded rationality. It assumes that – in contrast to their social behaviors – actors in the economic arena make only unbiased, quasi-rational calculations. Boundedly rational agents' analyses of commercial matters should include individual biases, including heterogeneous tendencies to trust or to cheat. Williamson assumes employees can check trust at the corporation door, since it is not 'permitted' in the realm of business. This prescribed banishment of trust from economic exchange seems arbitrary and normative.

In discussing other research opportunities, Williamson notes that the issues of 'dignitary values and trust' are better attacked by lawyers and organization theorists than by most economists. He notes that the completely instrumental approach of the economists (where people have no inherent value and are seen merely as things to use) is not an accurate description of most humans, and he points out that 'thinking about economic organization exclusively in an instrumentalist way can spill over into a treatment of individuals as instruments. Such excesses of instrumentalism have to be checked' (1985, p. 405). Williamson offers no suggestions on how to deal with this problem.[4] This also sets up an odd contrast by arguing that the world of economics can spill over into personal matters – with potentially detrimental effects – yet still assumes that social perspectives on trust cannot spill over into the business world.

Williamson (1993b) argues that the institutional environment only impacts the cost–benefit analysis of economic opportunism; economic actors have relations embedded in networks such that reputation effects reduce opportunism. This reduction in opportunism, however, comes solely from a calculative analysis rather than being a product of institutionalized trust. Williamson analyzes societal culture as just another kind of institutional process, an institutional environment within which firms make solely calculative assessments.

This offers an interesting opportunity to examine norms versus calculation. If calculation drives behavior, firms moving from one cultural environment to another should immediately adopt the new culture. For instance, if cultures differ in social norms regarding opportunistic behavior (e.g. misrepresentation), then a relocating or expanding company should immediately adopt the new norms. However, if social effects matter, we would expect cultural effects to linger. For example, someone moving from a culture with strong norms against misrepresentation to a culture without such norms would still tend to avoid misrepresentation, at least initially, due to resilient social effects. TCE assumptions predict immediate adoption of norms that increase profitability.

Yet Williamson at times appears to assume social norms can influence economic behavior directly, despite his generally strong assertions to the contrary. For example, he suggests that heterogeneity in opportunistic behavior may itself derive from differences in underlying social values, citing the fact that 'opportunism does not continuously intrude' as evidence that 'many economic agents are well-socialized' (1993c, p. 98).

This is problematic. Williamson describes agents who can employ personal trust and trustworthiness in social relations, yet cannot introduce these non-calculative elements to their economic activities. At the same time, he allows the idea of some economic agents being 'well socialized', implying a non-calculative effect on economic behavior, contradicting the asserted separation between economic and social matters. These arguments start to look like acrobatic contortions, intended to preclude the conceptual acknowledgement of trust at all costs; the assumptions employed to justify ignoring trust appear ancillary and *ad hoc*. Recall the first type of justification previously discussed: although opportunism may vary, one assumes individuals cannot discern it *ex ante*. The second justification allows trustworthiness in personal matters but assumes it out of economic affairs. TCE's economic actors can therefore vary in their undetectable opportunism, but by assumption must always be calculative – an implausible juxtaposition.

Husted and Folger (2005) make a compelling case that institutional norms involving justice and fairness fundamentally impact economic transactions. Furthermore, assuming that trust has no place in economics yet exists in social relations contradicts even casual observation. Various collectives have different norms about opportunistic behavior. Indeed, many groups define inappropriate opportunistic behavior quite differently depending on the object or target of the behavior. Members of a particular social group may have no qualms about persecuting individuals who are not members of the group, whereas they may view the same actions as inappropriate if directed at other group members. On the economic side, a community may happily exploit tourists while following strong norms against cheating one another. Some opportunists may even attempt to take advantage of most people, but not their friends. Specific examples are innumerable but the case is general – social and economic actors make differential judgments about trustworthiness. Most people would more willingly lend money to nuns than to convicted felons.

Trust: no explanatory power

The third justification for ignoring trust in TCE argues that trust does not add any explanatory power. Notwithstanding scholarly work that demonstrates the positive effect of trust on both macroeconomic development (Fukuyama, 1995; Zak and Knack, 2001) and organization-level strategic performance (Dyer and Chu, 2003; Sako, 1998; Zaheer et al., 1998), TCE theorists assume that trust cannot improve explanation at all in economic matters.

Defenses of this position follow a standard pattern. The author first poses a particular example that appears to imply that trust matters. The author then makes *ad hoc* assumptions to justify the example within the calculative TCE perspective. The author seldom if ever tests the assumptions. TCE apologists then argue that opportunistic calculative behavior explains the phenomenon, which makes including trust in the analysis unnecessary.

This line of defense reveals a bias: it assumes that theoretical explanations of a given behavior based on TCE are inherently *superior* to explanations of the same behavior based on trust. Thus, if calculative explanations explain the same phenomenon as trust-based explanations, the calculative explanation is automatically better – ostensibly because it offers a more rigorous underpinning. However, such analyses seldom if ever rigorously test the alternative explanations.

Williamson (1993b) asserts that calculative explanations of behavior are inherently better than non-calculative alternatives, taking numerous examples of trust-like behavior and offering calculative explanations for the behaviors. For example, in discussing a farmer lending equipment to a new neighbor, he says:

> If almost-automatic and unpriced assistance is the most efficient response, provided that the practice in question is supported by sanctions and is ultimately made contingent on reciprocity, then calculativeness obtains and appeal to trust adds nothing. (1993b, p. 471)

For TCE, explaining something as a result of a quasi-rational calculation is clearly preferred to explaining it as a result of other factors such as trust.

Williamson ignores both the *correctness of the assumptions* and the *correctness of the mechanism* in judging explanations. He arbitrarily assumes that 'the practice in question is supported by sanctions and is ultimately made contingent on reciprocity', without evidence. Whether such facts hold is critical; with arbitrary factual assumptions, many different theories can offer *post hoc* justification for almost any observation. Williamson's position also ignores whether the mechanism he offers actually operates in the situation in question. When scholars offer an explanation, they implicitly claim that the mechanisms of the explanation hold in the situation.

The correct mechanism matters. While two mechanisms may appear to make the same prediction with respect to a particular example, predictive differences often lie just beneath the surface explanation. For example, Williamson's calculative explanation for lending farm equipment implies that the farmer takes the availability of sanctions into account, refusing to lend whenever such protections do not exist. In contrast, a norm-based explanation suggests an initial following of the norm (lending), followed by a cessation of following the norm if the other does not also follow the norms (reciprocity). Norm-based explanations might also suggest that violation of other norms (even while complying with lending norms) might result in cessation of cooperation.

Some who question Williamson's ideas agree with him in preferring calculative explanations above those involving trust. For example, Craswell (1993, p. 493) criticizes pieces of Williamson's arguments, but supports without question the inherent superiority of calculative explanations to other types of explanations:

> On closer examination, however, Williamson finds that almost all of these choices are in fact consistent with the actor's calculated interests (when those interests are comprehensively understood) and that these choices can therefore be explained without having to posit any noncalculative forces.

This suggests that the key to uncovering the underlying – and supposedly superior – calculative explanation for economic behavior comes from 'comprehensively understanding' the true interests of the economic actor. Yet Craswell and other proponents of this view offer no hint that they might validate or test their assumptions about those interests; Craswell merely asserts that an absence of a calculative explanation indicates a lack of understanding.

Although Williamson (1993a) goes so far as to label trust a tautology, it appears that the reverse may in fact be more likely: TCE scholars can generate assumptions to justify almost any behavior as calculative – making such frameworks true by definition. As Sen says, the self-interested egoist model can fit almost any observed behavior because 'It is possible to define a person's interests in such a way that no matter what he does he can be seen to be furthering his own interests in every isolated act of choice' (1977, p. 322).

Therefore TCE shares a major problem with other rational or quasi-rational models – the results rest on largely untested factual assumptions. With such untested arbitrary assumptions, the calculative analysis can *post hoc* describe almost any behavior. This directly reverses the traditional view of how theory relates to empirical work. Instead of striving for correct assumptions in tandem with theory to develop testable predictions, here scholars select assumptions to fit the previously determined outcomes.

Additionally, in debating the relative merits of trust as a theoretical component of economic choice, proponents of the calculative view often depict trust as a straw man. Some TCE advocates imply the sociological view that includes trust may be cheery and flattering, but is too sanguine and non-descriptive. Along these lines, Williamson suggests that 'the object is not to describe human actors in a user-friendly way but to understand complex economic organization' (1993c, p. 99). In contrast, the assumption of unbridled opportunism is described as a reasonable and wise defense mechanism, an alternative to the weak myopia of trust and altruism:

> Whereas myopic parties must rely on altruism when a bad state realization occurs, lest one party take advantage of the other, farsighted parties who take hazard-mitigating actions in advance are less subject to the same vicissitudes. (Williamson, 1996, p. 54)

Such an argument paints trust as blind altruism and weakness, and calculative opportunism as wise, strategic thinking.

This misrepresentation of the positions of trust researchers includes claiming that trust scholars naïvely assume that everyone is trustworthy all the time. Trust critics offer a caricature of the arguments of trust advocates by claiming such advocates reject the very idea of calculation. For example, Williamson (1993c, p. 97) states that because 'opportunism corresponds to the frailty of motive "which requires a certain degree of circumspection distrust"', many 'interesting problems of economic organization are missed or misconstrued if opportunism is ignored or suppressed'.

Here, Williamson defends the complete opportunism assumption by pretending that trust advocates argue for the ignoring or suppressing of opportunism altogether. As far as we know, no trust researcher has suggested the possibility of zero opportunism. Rather, trust scholars merely question the need to view all economic actors as completely opportunistic, suggesting that a discernible variance in trustworthiness will matter to economic actors and organizations.

The contention that trust has little explanatory power is therefore premature and unfounded, because – like the other justifications for ignoring trust – it comes via the use of *ad hoc* assumptions rather than empirical inquiry. This raises legitimate questions about the other assumptions employed by TCE, including the assumption of bounded rationality.

TCE's inadequate use of bounded rationality

Bounded rationality implies that choices deviate from rationally calculative behavior. People often have limited information, and they cannot process the information they do have in a way that would allow them to make what traditional economists refer to as rational choices. Williamson (1985) explicitly accepts this description of individuals and positions it as fundamental to TCE theory.

However, TCE frequently lapses from this assumption, most commonly when discussing governance mechanisms. TCE analyzes commercial exchanges among boundedly rational individuals under the assumption that they can optimally calculate appropriate governance mechanisms, but in all other respects they are limited by bounded rationality. Therefore the rational choice of governance structure in TCE ignores the two *primary* ways by which boundedly rational individuals make decisions: satisficing and routines (March, 1994).

Satisficing (March and Simon, 1958; Simon, 1997) means that individuals and organizations look for solutions that are good enough: outcomes that exceed their aspiration levels as formed by historical experience and social comparison. With respect to transaction costs, satisficing implies that organizations and even entire business systems may never consistently make optimal choices.

For example, we would expect that firms in an industry in which all firms make reasonable profits would be slow to take risks in trying out potentially better organizational structures. Thus we expect industries with the greatest problems of vertical integration and with profitability difficulties to most quickly adopt a multidivisional (M form) structure. We would also expect to see sequential adoption. A poorly performing firm will try out something new; if it works, others learn from the adopters and move to the new structure. This kind of sequential learning, while completely consistent and a very standard component of bounded rationality analyses, has been ruled out of TCE by the assumption that firms can calculate and understand optimal governance procedures. Armour and Teece's (1978) study of the multidivisional hypothesis in oil companies found sequential adoption, not quick moves to the optimal structure.

In addition to satisficing, boundedly rational agents make decisions by routines (Cyert and March, 1963; Nelson and Winter, 1982). Indeed, organizations cannot function without routines. Trust – a belief about others' honesty, commitment-keeping, and forbearance from opportunism – may appear as a routine or 'rule of appropriate behavior' (March and Olsen, 1989, p. 27). This does not imply that trust is a routine, but rather that individuals may have routinized ways of exhibiting trust or trustworthiness.

For example, individuals may, based on generalized reputations, assume that certain types of individuals (e.g. police officers, ministers, etc.) are honest without specifically investigating the honesty of a *particular* individual. We stereotype to simplify our lives; this gives us general rules. Thus we may routinely trust certain people in certain situations based on routines or norms, rather than calculation.

Consider again the example where a farmer might offer to loan some equipment to another farmer who has just bought a property nearby. Williamson (1993b) explains the behavior as a calculative analysis, based on the positive expectation that such a neighbor will return the favor at some future date. Such an act resembles an investment in a future benefit. However, in many cases is it not simply an example of a trusting norm or routine? In other words, until someone demonstrates they will not behave appropriately, the resident farmer may see loaning equipment to neighbors in need as appropriate behavior. He would feel that he had behaved inappropriately if he did not make that offer.

In short, part of the perceived need for TCE to reject trust comes from the inconsistent use of bounded-rationality assumptions in the theory. True bounded rationality implies satisficing and using routines or norms to direct behavior. Both decision processes can lead to trust mattering. Bounded-rationality assumptions rule out the calculative, quasi-rational model of behavior framed by TCE to reject trust.

Despite these arguments, the TCE advocate (e.g. Craswell, 1993) might still reply that it does not matter, so long as the model predicts the behavior correctly. Let us consider this argument.

Empirical testing, calculativeness and trust
Much of the previous discussion comes back to problems in taking seriously the mechanisms proposed by a theory. Explanations involve preconditions and mechanisms; the mechanisms interact with the preconditions to generate predictions or explanations. The explanation inherently includes both the preconditions and the mechanisms. Good testing of an explanation thus involves testing both the preconditions and the mechanisms.

Following Friedman (1953), some scholars argue that it does not matter if their models make implausible assumptions; all that matters is that the model predicts well. This is both philosophically and scientifically incorrect. If we want to explain behavior, the scientific test of our explanation should attempt to verify whether the explanation matches reality. In everyday life, we would automatically reject explanations of behaviors based on assumptions we know to be incorrect or implausible.[5]

Good explanations offer a mechanism by which something actually occurs. One could attempt to invent an explanation based on calculative interests regarding nutrition, but if an Orthodox Jew or a devout Muslim refuses to eat pork for religious reasons, we should not imagine that the appropriate explanation has anything to do with the health benefits or detriments of pork or an analysis of such. Such a believer follows the dietary restrictions even when they do not positively influence health. A health-based explanation might explain historical evolution of religious practices, but cannot explain the current believer's behavior.

Care about mechanisms means that a theory's merit does not solely depend on its predictive power in one single dimension. Some have argued that prediction is the test of a theory, but philosophers of science have come to reject this naïve positivist approach, since it does not require any meaningful belief in the mechanism's underlying explanation. Furthermore, it does not even require what we would normally call an explanation. If we know that things do not or cannot occur the way that the so-called explanation says they do, then we must consider such an explanation inadequate.

Social science is not simply *post hoc* fitting some data, or even prediction of variables; rather, we wish to explain the mechanism by which something occurs. Whether the farmer is being calculative or simply following norms matters; the underlying mechanism differs. As scholars we want to *explain* things, which means that the causal mechanism we assert matches the causal mechanism in the field. As such, it matters whether people behave in a given way because 'it is the appropriate way to behave in our community' or whether they do so because they calculate that it pays off.

Understanding the mechanism can improve prediction. For example, understanding the underlying mechanism may dramatically influence the predicted effect of a change of circumstances. TCE analyses that explain someone acting honestly as the result of calculation must also predict that the individual will act dishonestly as soon as the situation changes to make such behavior profitable. On the other hand, if we explain honest behavior based on compliance with norms, we would predict continued honesty even if dishonesty became profitable, at least until the temptation became too great. Good prediction requires an understanding of the correct mechanism.

The TCE arguments also assume a causal direction without evidence. For example, Williamson (1993b, p. 479) argues that corporate culture simply folds into calculativeness by claiming that corporate culture influences performance outcomes. However, just because something influences performance does not mean that its influence on performance *explains* that thing's existence. Having a very large, quick child positively influences the chances that that child becomes a good basketball player; however, it does not normally explain the given child's size. Without additional evidence, just because Z is desirable and X leads to Z, we cannot conclude X was chosen to increase Z. While Williamson (Williamson, 1996, p. 55) claims TCE is an 'empirical success story', few of the empirical studies make any effort to test the underlying causal mechanisms. That the aggregate predictions of TCE fit the data does not differentiate between TCE and other explanations, including trust, nor does it justify the claim that these other explanations are eclipsed or subsumed by calculativeness.

Indeed, recent work in trust has begun to model and test how calculativeness differs from trust. For example, Saparito et al. (2004) distinguish between goodwill-oriented 'relational trust' and calculativeness, finding that relational trust mediates the relations between supplier firm customer service and customer firm loyalty, even after controlling for calculative factors. Thus trust can influence inter-organizational relations over and above instrumental motivations; such trust influences outcomes and changes the structure of the inter-organizational relation. Other research (e.g. Jap and Anderson, 2003) demonstrates that opportunism and trust differ empirically (but correlate -0.54) and interact in influencing performance and other outcomes. Trust can help minimize the negative effects of opportunism (Saparito et al., 2004).

Lui and Ngo (2004) divide trust into 'goodwill trust' and 'competence trust'. These authors conceive of both types of trust in terms of risk assessment; goodwill trust associates with aspects of the relation itself, whereas competence trust estimates another's transactional reliability. Their results indicate that the two types of trust moderate the relations between contractual safeguards and firm performance in different ways; goodwill trust serves as a substitute for contractual safeguards, whereas the more calculative assessment of the other party's competence functions as a complement to contracting.

These examples of recent scholarly work in organizational trust demonstrate that trust means something more than just calculativeness. Bearing this in mind, and contrary to the previously described TCE justifications for ignoring trust, we argue that trust has a meaningful place in explaining behavior, over and above calculativeness. Unlike Williamson's arguments for calculativeness that attempt to debunk trust, our argument in favor of acknowledging trust does not claim that calculativeness does not exist, but simply that the two concepts are distinct and both useful in explaining behavior. As such, we argue that trust is one's *non-calculative* belief in another's reliability, predictability and fairness.

Certainly, calculativeness explains some behaviors. Sometimes, we rely on someone's behavior strictly due to calculation – at times even assuming the person is opportunistic. Such reliance does not require trust. For example, we do not necessarily trust some of the organizations and individuals we deal with if we believe the system they operate under makes it hard for them to cheat us, and this may explain a certain amount of our behavior.

However, research on intra- and inter-organizational trust demonstrates behaviors and outcomes where non-calculative trust adds to the explanation offered by calculativeness. Many scholars have argued that trust is not simply encompassed by calculativeness (Granovetter, 1985; Kramer and Tyler, 1996; Nooteboom et al., 1997). Intuition and common experience reinforce this notion; colloquial usage typically attaches different meanings to the two ideas. We support both the common intuition and the scholarly view that trust – in addition to (and distinct from) calculativeness – meaningfully describes beliefs and behavior within and between organizations, influencing organizational outcomes.

Conclusions

Trust exists, not only in special interpersonal, social relations, but also in business arrangements and economic transactions. In cases where trust and calculativeness make some similar predictions, scholars need to empirically compare the two mechanisms. In other cases, trust can add explanatory power to certain individual and organizational actions that calculativeness alone cannot adequately explain. Indeed, Sen (1970; 1977) argues that our economic system would collapse and organizations could not viably exist in the absence of trust. Annette Baier eloquently refers to trust's prevalence and importance:

> The starry heavens above and the moral law within had better be about the only things that matter to me, if there is no one I can trust in any way. (1986, p. 231)

> We inhabit a climate of trust as we inhabit an atmosphere and notice it as we notice air, only when it becomes scarce or polluted. (Ibid., p. 234)

We suggest that the pervasiveness of trust she refers to exists in the world of commerce and economic organization, substantially influences organizational action, and – specifically – can have a profound influence on economic transaction costs.

Acknowledgement

We express thanks to Mark Casson, David Souder, conference participants and three anonymous reviewers from the 2005 Academy of Management annual meeting, and the editors for helpful review comments.

Notes

1. Allowing non-monetary factors in the utility function would vitiate most of the TCE analyses. The assumption of strictly monetary objectives simplifies the analysis greatly. However, if we allowed individuals to have non-monetary objectives, then we could have individuals who greatly value telling the truth. This violates the 'self-interest seeking with guile' assumption. The expression 'self interest seeking with guile' is used to refer to individuals who define self-interest largely in monetary terms, place no weight on moral values, and think strategically.

2.   Several other authors (for example Jones, 2001 and Chiles and McMackin, 1996), using slightly different frameworks, have also called for the integration of trust and TCE.
3.   Curiously, Williamson allows that even 'nearly noncalculative' relations can be intendedly so, and therefore, calculative (Williamson, 1993b, pp. 481–2).
4.   This has interesting implications for management education. Williamson states that the principles that *theoretically* govern behavior in the TCE framework are antithetical to healthy or desirable *actual* human interaction. What does this mean for our teaching practices? Instructing students in theories that assume everyone is wholly opportunistic and self-interest-seeking could have serious implications. If educators teach students that unbridled opportunism motivates all decisions, business schools may contribute to establishing this kind of behavior as a norm. If so, we should not be surprised if the students then follow such norms. Ghoshal and Moran (1996) allude to this possibility with specific reference to TCE, and research indicates that the likelihood of people making selfish choices increases with their exposure to economic assumptions (Frank, 2004; Frank et al., 1993; see also Ghoshal, 2005 and Ferraro et al., 2005).
5.   See Bromiley (2004) for additional, detailed discussion of these issues.

References

Adler, P.S. 2001. Market, hierarchy, and trust: The knowledge economy and the future of Capitalism. *Organization Science*, **12**(2): 215–34.

Anderson, J.C., Rungtusanatham, M., and Schroeder, R.G. 1994. A theory of quality management underlying the Deming Management method. *Academy of Management Review*, **19**(3): 472–509.

Armour, H.O. and Teece, D.J. 1978. Organizational structure and economic performance: A test of the multi-divisional hypothesis. *Bell Journal of Economics*, **9**: 106–22.

Baier, A. 1986. Trust and antitrust. *Ethics*, **96**(2): 231–60.

Ben-Ner, A. and Putterman, L. 2001. Trusting and trustworthiness. *Boston University Law Review*, **81**(3): 523–51.

Berger, H., Noorderhaven, N.G. and Nooteboom, B. 1995. Determinants of supplier dependence: An empirical study. In J. Groenewegen, C. Pitelis and S.-E. Sjostrand (eds), *On Economic Institutions: Theory and Applications*, 95–212. Aldershot, UK and Brookfield, VT: Edward Elgar.

Bigley, G.A. and Pearce, J.L. 1998. Straining for shared meaning in organization science: Problems of trust and distrust. *Academy of Management Review*, **23**(3): 405–21.

Blois, K.J. 1999. Trust in business to business relationships: An evaluation of its status. *Journal of Management Studies*, **36**(2): 197–216.

Bowie, N.E. 1997. The role of philosophy in public policy – a philosopher in a business school. *Philosophical Studies*, **85**(2–3): 119–33.

Bowie, N.E. 1999. *Business Ethics: A Kantian Perspective*. Malden, MA: Blackwell.

Brinkmann, U. and Seifert, M. 2001. Face to interface – the establishment of trust in the Internet: The case of e-auctions. *Zeitschrift für Soziologie*, **30**(1): 23–47.

Bromiley, P. 2004. *The Behavioral Foundations of Strategic Management*. Malden, MA: Blackwell.

Bromiley, P. and Cummings, L.L. 1995. Transactions costs in organizations with trust. In R. Bies, B. Sheppard and R. Lewicki (eds), *Research on Negotiations in Organizations*, Vol. 5: 219–47. Greenwich, CT: JAI Press.

Bussing, A. and Broome, P. 1999. Trust under telework. *Zeitschrift für Arbeitswissenschaft*, **43**(3): 122–33.

Bussing, A. and Moranz, C. 2003. Initial trust in virtualized business relations. *Zeitschrift für Arbeitswissenschaft*, **47**(2): 95–103.

Chiles, T.H. and McMackin, J.F. 1996. Integrating variable risk preferences, trust, and transaction cost economics. *Academy of Management Review*, **21**(1): 73–99.

Craswell, R. 1993. On the uses of 'Trust': Comment on Williamson. *Journal of Law & Economics*, **36**(April): 487–500.

Creed, W.E.D. and Miles, R.E. 1996. Trust in organizations: a conceptual framework linking organizational forms, managerial philosophies, and the opportunity cost of controls. In R.M. Kramer and T.R. Tyler (eds), *Trust in Organizations: Frontiers of Theory and Research*, 16–38. Thousand Oaks, CA: Sage Publications.

Cummings, L.L. and Bromiley, P. 1996. The organizational trust inventory (OTI): Development and validation. In R.M. Kramer and T.R. Tyler (eds), *Trust in Organizations: Frontiers of Theory and Research*, 302–30. Thousand Oaks, CA: Sage.

Currall, S.C. and Inkpen, A.C. 2000. Joint venture trust: Interpersonal, inter-group, and inter-firm levels. In D. Faulkner and M. De Rond (eds), *Cooperative Strategy: Economic, Business, and Organizational Issues*: 324–41. Oxford: Oxford University Press.

Currall, S.C. and Inkpen, A.C. 2002. A multilevel approach to trust in joint ventures. *Journal of International Business Studies*, **33**(3): 479–95.

Currall, S.C. and Judge, T.A. 1995. Measuring trust between organizational boundary role persons. *Organizational Behavior and Human Decision Processes*, **64**(2): 151–70.

Cyert, R.M. and March, J.G. 1963. *A Behavioral Theory of the Firm*. Englewood Cliffs, NJ: Prentice-Hall.

Darley, J. 1998. Trust in organizations: Frontiers of theory and research (Book Review Essay). *Business Ethics Quarterly*, **8**(2): 319–36.

Das, T.K. and Teng, B.-S. 1998. Between trust and control: Developing confidence in partner cooperation in alliances. *Academy of Management Review*, **23**(3): 491–512.

Dasgupta, P. 1988. Trust as a commodity. In D. Gambetta (ed.), *Trust: Making and Breaking Cooperative Relations*, 49–72. Cambridge, MA: Basil Blackwell.

Dean, J.W., Brandes, P. and Dharwadkar, R. 1998. Organizational cynicism. *Academy of Management Review*, **23**(2): 341–52.

Dirks, K.T. 1999. The effects of interpersonal trust on work group performance. *Journal of Applied Psychology*, **84**(3): 445–55.

Dyer, J.H. and Chu, W. 2003. The role of trustworthiness in reducing transaction costs and improving performance: Empirical evidence from the United States, Japan, and Korea. *Organization Science*, **14**(1): 57–68.

Ferraro, F., Pfeffer, J. and Sutton, R.I. 2005. Economics language and assumptions: How theories can become self-fulfilling. *Academy of Management Review*, **30**(1): 8–24.

Ferrin, D.L. and Dirks, K.T. 2003. The use of rewards to increase and decrease trust: Mediating processes and differential effects. *Organization Science*, **14**(1): 18–31.

Frank, R.H. 1988. *Passions Within Reason*. New York: W.W. Norton & Company.

Frank, R.H. 2004. *What Price the Moral High Ground? Ethical Dilemmas in Competitive Environments*. Princeton, NJ: Princeton University Press.

Frank, R.H., Gilovich, T. and Regan, D. 1993. Does studying economics inhibit cooperation? *Journal of Economic Perspectives*, **7**(Spring): 159–71.

Friedman, M. 1953. The methodology of positive economics, *Essays in Positive Economics*: 3–43. Chicago: University of Chicago Press.

Fukuyama, F. 1995. *Trust: The Social Virtues and the Creation of Prosperity*. New York: The Free Press.

Funk and Wagnalls Standard College Dictionary. New York: HarperCollins.

Gambetta, D. 1988. Can we trust trust? In D. Gambetta (ed.), *Trust: Making and Breaking Cooperative Relations*. Cambridge, MA: Basil Blackwell.

Ghoshal, S. 2005. Bad management theories are destroying good management practices. *Academy of Management Learning & Education*, **4**(1): 75–91.

Ghoshal, S. and Moran, P. 1996. Bad for practice: A critique of the transaction cost theory. *Academy of Management Review*, **21**(1): 13–47.

Gottschalk, P. 2000. Strategic knowledge networks: The case of IT support for Eurojuris law firms in Norway. *International Review of Law, Computers & Technology*, **14**(1): 115–30.

Granovetter, M. 1985. Economic action and social structure: The problem of embeddedness. *The American Journal of Sociology*, **91**(3): 481–510.

Hagen, J.M. and Choe, S. 1998. Trust in Japanese interfirm relations: Institutional sanctions matter. *Academy of Management Review*, **23**(3): 589–600.

Hardin, R. 1991. Trusting persons, trusting institutions. In R.J. Zeckhauser (ed.), *Strategy and Choice*, 185–209. Cambridge, MA: MIT Press.

Hardin, R. 1993. The street-level epistemology of trust. *Politics and Society*, **21**(4): 505–29.

Hosmer, L.T. 1995. Trust: The connecting link between organizational theory and philosophical ethics. *Academy of Management Review*, **20**(2): 379–403.

Hudson, R.L. and McArthur, A.W. 1994. Contracting strategies in entrepreneurial and established firms. *Entrepreneurship: Theory & Practice*, **18**(3): 43–60.

Husted, B.W. and Folger, R. 2005. Fairness and transaction costs: The contribution of organizational justice theory to an integrative model of economic organization. *Organization Science*, **15**(6): 719–29.

Jap, S.D. and Anderson, E. 2003. Safeguarding interorganizational performance and continuity under ex post opportunism. *Management Science*, **49**(12): 1684–701.

Jarvenpaa, S.L. and Leidner, D.E. 1999. Communication and trust in global virtual teams. *Organization Science*, **10**(6): 791–815.

Jarvenpaa, S.L., Knoll, K. and Leidner, D.E. 1998. Is anybody out there? Antecedents of trust in global virtual teams. *Journal of Management Information Systems*, **14**(4): 29–65.

Jones, G. 2001. Towards a positive interpretation of transaction cost theory: The central roles of entrepreneurship and trust. In M.A. Hitt, R.E. Freeman and J.S. Harrison (eds), *The Blackwell Handbook of Strategic Management*, 208–28. Malden, MA: Blackwell.

Jones, T.M. and Bowie, N.E. 1998. Moral hazards on the road to the virtual corporation. *Business Ethics Quarterly*, **8**(2): 273–92.

Jutla, D., Bodorik, P. and Dhaliwal, J. 2002. Supporting the e-business readiness of small and medium-sized enterprises: Approaches and metrics. *Internet Research – Electronic Networking Applications and Policy*, **12**(2): 139–64.

Kipnis, D. 1996. Trust and technology. In R.M. Kramer and T.R. Tyler (eds), *Trust in Organizations: Frontiers of Theory and Research*, 39–50. Thousand Oaks, CA: Sage.

Kostova, T. 1999. Transnational transfer of strategic organizational practices: A contextual perspective. *Academy of Management Review*, **24**(2): 308–24.

Kostova, T. and Roth, K. 2002. Adoption of an organizational practice by subsidiaries of multinational corporations: Institutional and relational effects. *Academy of Management Journal*, **45**(1): 215–33.

Kramer, R.M. 1999. Trust and distrust in organizations: Emerging perspectives, enduring questions. *Annual Review of Psychology*, **50**: 569–98.

Kramer, R.M. and Tyler, T.R. 1996. Whither trust? In R.M. Kramer and T.R. Tyler (eds), *Trust in Organizations: Frontiers of Theory and Research*, 1–15. Thousand Oaks, CA: Sage.

Lane, C. and Bachmann, R. 1996. The social constitution of trust: Supplier relations in Britain and Germany. *Organization Studies*, **17**(3): 365–95.

Lazar, F.D. 1997. Partnering – new benefits from peering inside the black box. *Journal of Management in Engineering*, **13**(6): 75–83.

Lazar, F.D. 2000. Project partnering: Improving the likelihood of win/win outcomes. *Journal of Management in Engineering*, **16**(2): 71–83.

Leana, C.R. 1999. Organizational social capital and employment practices. *Academy of Management Review*, **24**(3): 538–56.

Leeuw, F.L. 1997. Solidarity between public sector organizations – the problem of social cohesion in the asymmetric society. *Rationality and Society*, **9**(4): 469–88.

Lui, S.S. and Ngo, H.Y. 2004. The role of trust and contractual safeguards on cooperation in non-equity alliances. *Journal of Management*, **30**(4): 471–86.

March, J.G. 1994. *A Primer On Decision Making*. New York: The Free Press.

March, J.G. and Olsen, J.P. 1989. *Rediscovering Institutions: The Organizational Basis of Politics*. New York: The Free Press.

March, J.G. and Simon, H.A. 1958. *Organizations*. New York: Wiley.

McEvily, B., Perrone, V. and Zaheer, A. 2003. Trust as an organizing principle. *Organization Science*, **14**(1): 91–103.

McKnight, D.H. and Chervany, N.L. 2001. What trust means in e-commerce customer relationships: An interdisciplinary conceptual typology. *International Journal of Electronic Commerce*, **6**(2): 35–59.

McKnight, D.H., Choudhury, V. and Kacmar, C. 2002. Developing and validating trust measures for e-commerce: An integrative typology. *Information Systems Research*, **13**(3): 334–60.

McKnight, D.H., Cummings, L.L. and Chervany, N.L. 1998. Initial trust formation in new organizational relationships. *Academy of Management Review*, **23**(3): 473–90.

Mishra, A.K. 1996. Organizational responses to crisis: The centrality of trust. In R.M. Kramer and T.R. Tyler (eds), *Trust in Organizations: Frontiers of Theory and Research*, 261–87. Thousand Oaks, CA: Sage Publications.

Mitchell, L.E. 1999. Trust and team production in post-capitalist society. *The Journal of Corporation Law* (Summer): 869–912.

Möllering, G. 2001. The nature of trust: From Georg Simmel to a theory of expectation, interpretation and suspension. *Sociology*, **35**(2): 403–20.

Monge, P.R., Fulk, J., Kalman, M.E. and Flanagin, A.J. 1998. Production of collective action in alliance-based interorganizational communication and information systems. *Organization Science*, **9**(3): 411–33.

Nelson, R.R. and Winter, S.G. 1982. *An Evolutionary Theory of Economic Change*. Cambridge, MA: Belknap Harvard.

Noorderhaven, N.G. 1996. Opportunism and trust in transaction cost economics. In J. Groenewegen (ed.), *Transaction Cost Economics and Beyond*, 105–28. Boston: Kluwer.

Nooteboom, B. 1996. Trust, opportunism and governance: A process and control model. *Organization Studies*, **17**(6): 985–1010.

Nooteboom, B., Berger, H. and Noorderhaven, N.G. 1997. Effects of trust and governance on relational risk. *Academy of Management Journal*, **40**(2): 308–38.

Olson, G.M. and Olson, J.S. 2000. Distance matters. *Human–Computer Interaction*, **15**(2–3): 139–79.

Olson, G.M. and Olson, J.S. 2003. Mitigating the effects of distance on collaborative intellectual work. *Economics of Innovation & New Technology*, **12**(1): 27–43.

Parkhe, A. 1993. Partner nationality and the structure–performance relationship in strategic alliances. *Organization Science*, **4**(2): 301–24.

Pavlou, P.A. 2002. Institution-based trust in interorganizational exchange relationships: The role of online B2B marketplaces on trust formation. *Journal of Strategic Information Systems*, **11**(3–4): 215–43.

Perrone, V., Zaheer, A. and McEvily, B. 2003. Free to be trusted? Organizational constraints on trust in boundary spanners. *Organization Science*, **14**(4): 422–39.

Pizanti, I. and Lerner, M. 2003. Examining control and autonomy in the franchisor–franchisee relationship. *International Small Business Journal*, **21**(2): 131–59.

Ring, P.S. 1996. Fragile and resilient trust and their roles in economic exchange. *Business & Society*, **35**(2): 148–75.

Ring, P.S. 1997. Transacting in the state of union: A case study of exchange governed by convergent interests. *Journal of Management Studies*, **34**(1): 1–23.

Ring, P.S. and Van de Ven, A.H. 1992. Structuring cooperative relationships between organizations. *Strategic Management Journal*, **13**: 483–98.

Ring, P.S. and Van de Ven, A.H. 1994. Developmental processes of cooperative interorganizational relationships. *Academy of Management Review*, **19**(1): 90–118.

Sako, M. 1998. Does trust improve business performance? In C. Lane and R. Bachmann (eds), *Trust Within and Between Organizations*, 88–117. Oxford: Oxford University Press.

Saparito, P.A., Chen, C.C. and Sapienza, H.J. 2004. The role of relational trust in bank – small firm relationships. *Academy of Management Journal*, **47**(3): 400–410.

Sen, A.K. 1970. *Collective Choice and Social Welfare*. San Francisco, CA: Holden-Day.

Sen, A.K. 1977. Rational fools: A critique of the behavioral foundations of economic theory. *Philosophy and Public Affairs*, **6**(4): 317–44.

Shapiro, S.P. 1987. The social control of impersonal trust. *The American Journal of Sociology*, **93**(3): 623–58.

Sheppard, B.H. and Sherman, D.H. 1998. The grammars of trust: A model and general implications. *Academy of Management Review*, **23**(3): 422–37.

Sheppard, B.H. and Tuchinsky, M. 1996. Interfirm relationships: A grammar of pairs. *Research in Organizational Behavior*, **18**: 331–73.

Simon, H.A. 1997. *Administrative Behavior*. New York: The Free Press (1945).

Sutcliffe, K.M. and Zaheer, A. 1998. Uncertainty in the transaction environment: An empirical test. *Strategic Management Journal*, **19**(1): 1–23.

Whitener, E.M. 1997. The impact of human resource activities on employee trust. *Human Resource Management Review*, **7**(4): 389–404.

Whitener, E.M., Brodt, S.E., Korsgaard, M.A. and Werner, J.M. 1998. Managers as initiators of trust: An exchange relationship framework for understanding managerial trustworthy behavior. *Academy of Management Review*, **23**(3): 513–30.

Williamson, O.E. 1975. *Markets and Hierarchies: Analysis and Antitrust Implications*. New York: The Free Press.

Williamson, O.E. 1981. The economics of organization: The transaction cost approach. *American Journal of Sociology*, **87**(3): 548–77.

Williamson, O.E. 1985. *The Economic Institutions of Capitalism*. New York: The Free Press.

Williamson, O.E. 1993a. Calculated trust: A reply to Craswell's comment on Williamson. *Journal of Law & Economics*, **36**(April): 501–2.

Williamson, O.E. 1993b. Calculativeness, trust, and economic organization. *Journal of Law & Economics*, **36**(April): 453–86.

Williamson, O.E. 1993c. Opportunism and its critics. *Managerial and Decision Economics*, **14**(2): 97–107.

Williamson, O.E. 1996. Economic organization: The case for candor. *Academy of Management Review*, **21**(1): 48–57.

Young-Ybarra, C. and Wiersema, M. 1999. Strategic flexibility in information technology alliances: The influence of transaction cost economics and social exchange theory. *Organization Science*, **10**(4): 439–59.

Zaheer, A. and Venkatraman, N. 1994. Determinants of electronic integration in the insurance industry – an empirical test. *Management Science*, **40**(5): 549–66.

Zaheer, A. and Venkatraman, N. 1995. Relational governance as an interorganizational strategy: An empirical test of the role of trust in economic exchange. *Strategic Management Journal*, **16**(5): 373–92.

Zaheer, A., Lofstrom, S. and George, V.P. 2002. Interpersonal and interorganizational trust in alliances. In F.J. Contractor and P. Lorange (eds), *Cooperative Strategies and Alliances*, 347–77. London: Pergamon.

Zaheer, A., McEvily, B. and Perrone, V. 1998. Does trust matter? Exploring the effects of interorganizational and interpersonal trust on performance. *Organization Science*, **9**(2): 141–59.

Zak, P.J. and Knack, S. 2001. Trust and growth. *The Economic Journal*, **111**(April): 295–321.

8 Relying on trust in cooperative inter-organizational relationships

Andrew H. Van de Ven and Peter Smith Ring

Introduction

Slightly over 20 years ago with approximately 35 colleagues, we began a multi-year research collaboration into the dynamics of innovation.[1] It became known as the Minnesota Innovation Research Program (MIRP), coordinated by the Strategic Management Research Center of the University of Minnesota. Among the five critical concepts that helped guide our collective research efforts was the notion of transactions. We had come to see this concept as central to the innovation process because our review of several extant literatures revealed that innovation frequently was a product of inter-organizational collaborations, and the transactions that they produced. In addition, discussions with executives, managers, engineers and bench scientists at firms reputed to be among the leaders in the USA in fostering climates conducive to innovation led us to conclude that a study of the processes associated with innovation would require an investigation of the dynamics of collaborative efforts between groups of individuals and the firms, governmental agencies and non-governmental agencies that employed those individuals.

An explicit focus on the concept of trust did not surface in early discussions among MIRP investigators on what aspects of innovation to study. But as Ring and Rands (1989) moved more deeply into their study of the collaboration between 3M and NASA to employ the space shuttle as a vehicle for studying the effects of near zero gravity on a variety of experiments, it became apparent that reliance on trust was an underlying theme in the dealings between the various actors within the two organizations and in their interactions with each other (see, e.g. Ring 1996). And as the findings of the various research teams became more evident to the larger group of researchers who made up MIRP, it also became increasingly clear that what Ring and Rands were observing at 3M and NASA was not an idiosyncratic artifact of that collaboration.

As a consequence of our backgrounds and research interests, we undertook a synthesis of the findings of previous studies as they related to transactions (Ring and Van de Ven 1989).[2] As we were winding down our MIRP longitudinal field studies, we began to address the need to further refine our views on transaction governance and processes and take them before the larger academic community.

Our first effort, which involved a synthesis of the interactions between governance structures and transaction processes, met resistance from reviewers. Taking their guidance to heart, we began the development of two papers rather than our initial integrated effort. One dealt with governance. A second dealt with process. The fruits of our collaboration appeared first in the *Strategic Management Journal* (Ring and Van de Ven 1992) and two years later in the *Academy of Management Review* (Ring and Van de Ven 1994). By then the roles of trust in inter-organizational exchanges were becoming clearer to us and those views, although still in formative stages, were put forth in propositional terms.

Our view then and now is that there are contexts that give rise to compelling reasons to *rely* on trust in dealing with other people and institutions. We broadly defined trust as confidence in the goodwill of others not to cause harm to you when you are vulnerable to them (Ring and Van de Ven 1992). Like honesty, integrity and competence, we viewed trust as a deeply shared value and posited that reliance on it would frequently flow when the former two were also present in a relationship. We viewed trust both as a glue that bonded a wide variety of relationships and as essential to the basic fabric of many societies.[3] Thus many individuals rely on trust in dealing with institutions, organizations, strangers and friends in varying degrees and for different things. An ability to rely on trust also provides security and meaning to our relationships. It permits us to get on with day-to-day life without having to inspect and monitor all the uncertainties and inexplicable situations that we cannot control, but to which we are vulnerable.

Several trends are motivating a growing appreciation of the importance of trust in social and economic relationships. First, with the growth of relational contracting,[4] outsourcing, strategic alliances and networks, trust-based relationships are increasingly becoming an important organizing principle for doing business (McEvily et al. 2003). Second, in an increasingly global economy, the parties engaged in many business relationships are from cultures that rely on different bases of personal and institutional trust (Pearce 2001). Third, despite the immense appeal and importance of trust (Putnam 2002; Fukuyama 1995), there also is extensive evidence that trust is declining in many societies and organizations (Bruhn 2001).

These trends represent significant opportunities to advance our understanding of the diverse roles that reliance on trust can assume in modern economies and in the governance of economic exchanges.[5] They motivate a reexamination of some ideas about trust that we wrote about over a decade ago in two companion papers on the structures and processes of cooperative relationships between organizations (Ring and Van de Ven 1992; 1994).[6] This chapter reflects on those papers and subsequent work on trust. First, we summarize our initial views of trust, and discuss subsequent developments in the concept of trust, the contexts and contingencies surrounding the emergence of reliance on trust, and the consequences or performance outcomes associated with trust. We also look at empirical studies of trust that have been undertaken over the past decade and the implications of their findings for subsequent developments in scholarship on trust.

We then examine the evolution of trust in society. Social and technical change is producing more temporary, mobile and impersonal relationships (both between organizations and individuals associated with them). These trends threaten to undermine fragile long-term relationships based on *interpersonal trust*. One implication is that there seems to be greater reliance on *institutional trust*, where one relies on the security of rules, structures and organizations to buttress interpersonal trust. Another implication is that trust is often easier to breach than it is to build. No relationship is perfect, and most relationships are not expendable. As a result, seldom can parties terminate a relationship in the event a breach in trust occurs (as the literature implies). How can relationships continue when violations occur? We conclude by suggesting that an important research agenda is to examine forgiveness, repair and reconstruction of trust in relationships that have experienced a breach in trust among the parties.

The concept of trust and its evolution

When preparing our original articles, we concluded that the extant literature in the late 1980s offered two broad definitions of trust. The first reflected confidence or predictability in one's expectations. This definition takes a cognitive, information uncertainty, and risk-based view of trust. The second (which we adopted) defined trust as faith in the goodwill of others not to harm your interests when you are vulnerable to them. To our knowledge, this faith-based view of trust was novel to the management literature at the time. Our use of it 'legitimated' the concept among management scholars and opened up the way for a variety of other conceptual and empirical treatments of trust in the management literature.

Oliver and Ebers (1998) reviewed 198 articles that dealt with what we describe as cooperative Inter-Organizational Relationships (IORs),[7] and proposed that four basic research perspectives were at work: social network, power and control, institutional, and transactions cost economics (TCE). They concluded that trust played important but different roles in these perspectives.

TCE and social exchange theories were often compared as conflicting or complementary theories. Here trust has been viewed as promoting flexibility while hierarchical governance structures inhibit flexibility. Young-Ybarra and Wiersema (1999) obtained empirical support for this conclusion. They found that economic constraints from TCE were positively related to trust, while dependence was negatively related to trust.

We argued that the implications of trusting behavior, generally, had been ignored by TCE. While not the first to make the case, we were the first to offer a model that suggested how trust might matter in the context of the governance choices available to managers of IORs. This point was taken up and has been built upon consistently since then. For example, Möllering (2002) examined six perspectives on trust and IORs. Based on a study of 184 UK printing IORs, the TCE-based-argument was dismissed, while Bradach and Eccles's (1989) triadic forces of price, authority and trust received strong support.

Although assessments of the role of trust were being discussed in economics and philosophy (Baier 1986), our initial views of the concept of trust as goodwill were largely drawn from sociology. We relied on Dore's (1983) and Granovetter's (1985) formulations. Although we did not know it at the time, Dore's student – Mari Sako (1992) – was completing a doctoral study of British and Japanese interfirm relationships in which trust played a central role. She too relied on goodwill trust, and introduced the complementary concepts of contract and competence-based trust.

In our initial discussions of trust we also observed that other researchers took a more risk- or control-oriented view of trust, arguing that trust reduces risk (see, e.g. Arrow 1973; Fried 1982; Shapiro 1987; Williamson 1985; Zucker 1986). That view persists and is supported by empirical findings. For example, the more partners learn about each other, the more the uncertainties associated with their dealings decrease (Hyder and Ghauri 2000).

Our approach to trust implied that it could be fruitfully viewed as a multidimensional concept. But we said little beyond offering the competing goodwill and risk-/control-oriented perspectives on the definition of trust. Nor can we pretend that we had exhaustively reviewed the literature on trust. For example, we 'missed' the excellent collection on trust by Diego Gambetta (1988), the analysis by Bradach and Eccles (1989) exploring the triadic forces of price, authority and trust, and the important contributions of Butler (1991) and Larson (1992).

Others have since provided a rich body of conceptual discussions of the meaning of trust. Barney and Hansen (1994) classified types of trustworthiness into weak, semi-strong and strong forms. Our colleagues at Minnesota, Bromiley and Cummings (1995), undertook an extensive study of the properties of trust and developed a comprehensive instrument. McAllister (1995) explored distinctions between affect and cognitive-based trust. Hwang and Burgers (1997) derived several properties of trust, and demonstrated that trust supported cooperation through its impact on two main threats to cooperation, namely fear and greed. Ring (1997a) explored the roles of fragile and resilient interpersonal trust in inter-organizational relationships. Sheppard and Sherman (1998) examined four distinct forms of trust: shallow dependence, shallow interdependence, deep dependence and deep interdependence between parties. Further psychometric analysis found 16 subconstructs of trust (McKnight et al. 2002). Boersma et al. (2003) suggested that trust can be operationalized as competence-based trust and promissory-based trust. Trust has also been viewed as a form of social capital (Fukuyama 1995; Harvey et al. 2003; Nahapiet and Ghoshal 1998).

In sum, a significant body of scholarship on trust and its meaning in individual, organization and inter-organizational contexts has emerged in the past decade. In part this was stimulated by a series of special issues on trust in leading journals (e.g. *Academy of Management Journal*, 1997; *Academy of Management Review*, 1998; *Organizational Studies*, 2001; *Organization Science*, 2002) and a number of edited volumes and research monographs focused on the topic (e.g. Fukuyama 1995; Kramer and Tyler 1996; Misztal 1996; Lane and Bachmann 1998; Noteboom 2002).

What can we make of this literature defining trust? Rousseau et al. (1998) point out that in their assessment of the trust literature, although there is no single definition of trust, its composite elements (willingness to accept vulnerability, positive expectations regarding the intentions or actions of others) are found in most. These elements are entirely consistent with the approach that we followed in formulating our own initial views on trust. But we have found that subsequent operationalizations of the concept of trust have differed widely depending upon the disciplinary base of the researcher and the unit or level of analysis underlying the research being conducted. What is somewhat remarkable about these operational definitions is how few have been developed by setting out to rigorously investigate how a variety of economic actors actually employ the concept of trust in their daily conversations and actions, using these empirical results as the basis for instrument development. Butler (1991) and Bromiley and Cummings (1995) provide clear exceptions to this conclusion; yet their approaches are somewhat less relied upon than earlier formulations based in psychology designed to deal with a variety of interpersonal dynamics (not necessarily relevant to business contexts).

In our initial discussion of trust, we were concerned about its roles in governing economic exchanges between organizations. Consequently, we also explored its relationship to risk. Our definition of trust assumed vulnerability (a situation in which the risk of harm actually being done is present), so we were also concerned with what kinds of risks might be associated with economic exchanges that might lead to reliance on trust as a complement to, or substitute for, other forms of governance.

We assumed that risk and trust were concepts that the parties could think of separately, particularly in making decisions about cooperating with others and in the ways by which they might govern IORs (Ring and Van de Ven 1992). Das and Teng (1996; 1998; 2001) have significantly expanded on and extended this argument. Chiles and McMackin (1996) extended the arguments in developing a somewhat different model of trust in which risk neutrality took center stage. Mayer et al. (1995) also proposed a model of trust in which the role of risk was central.

One of the ways that we saw risk and trust as distinct concepts dealt with the problems that parties who are contracting with each other face *ex ante* in assessing how to deal with foreseeable risks *ex post*. We argued that *ex ante* parties rely on trust and then assume that the other, *ex post*, will deal with gaps in their contracts fairly, explicitly raising the issues of distributive and procedural justice but not exploring them further.[8]

In our 1992 *SMJ* article, we asserted that in addition to behavioral risk, IORs presented their managers with a variety of forms of risk: commercial, technological, engineering and managerial. Building on Williamson (1993) and Ring (1996; 1997a; 1997b), the role of behavioral risk has been extensively explored by Das and Teng (1996; 1998; 2001), who refer to it as relational risk and argue that it can be reduced by reliance on goodwill trust coupled with behavior and social control.

We also asserted that the degree of risk present in economic exchanges flowed from reductions in time, information and control. All three of these elements of risk have been explored. For example, Eriksson and Sharma (2003) explored the presence of risk in the decision-making routines of the parties. These had significant direct impacts on buyer–supplier cooperation, and were, in turn, affected by risks associated with the contexts of exchange. Mosakowski and Earley (2000) undertook an extensive investigation of the role that time plays in a wide variety of organizational and inter-organizational contexts. Hwang and Burgers (1999) also explored the role of time horizons in the context of IORs and demonstrated that trust and time jointly affect perceptions or risk. Brouthers and Brouthers (2003) found that differences in the entry modes employed by service and manufacturing firms in international contexts could be explained by the differing influences of risk and trust propensity.

Information-processing capabilities were found to enhance the ability of firms to assess partner trustworthiness, reducing the risk of misplaced trust (Carson et al. 2003). Dyer and Chu (2003) found that information sharing increases as perceptions of a partner's trustworthiness increases. Research by Ba and Pavlou (2002) demonstrated that reliance on trust mitigates information asymmetry by reducing transaction-specific risks. Sobrero and Schrader (1998), in a meta analysis of 36 empirical studies, concluded that mutual information sharing was related to the ability of the parties to cooperate in R&D endeavors, the nature of which inherently involves various kinds of risk we described in our 1992 article.

Dekker (2004) discussed control problems and their interrelationships with informal (trust-based) mechanisms in buyer–supplier relationships. Barthelemy (2003) describes the loss of control over activities as one of the central concerns associated with the growing reliance on outsourcing. Gallivan and Depledge (2003) offer a framework that recognizes that 'trust and control are not simple substitutes for each other. Rather, they form a dialectic, where it makes sense to consider each construct only in relationship to the other.' Gallivan (2001) argued that social and self-control, rather than reliance on trust, was more effective in enhancing performance in the virtual organizational context of open-systems software development. Das and Teng (1998; 2001) suggest a variety of ways in which control is related to risk and the roles that trust plays in governing IORs in which risk is present. Maguire et al. (2001) also argue that trust and control are closely related and make the case that the type of trust relied upon by parties may be a function of the potential loss of control they are attempting to forestall. In sum, each of the three antecedents of risk that we described in 1992 has been extensively researched and found to be associated with both risk and trust.

We assumed in our early work that parties to IORs would be *trustworthy*. Trustworthiness was reflected in open, other-regarding behavior. Barney and Hansen (1994) made significant extensions to this argument in their *SMJ* article outlining three forms of trustworthiness, and others have extended the ways in which it is possible to think about perceptions of trustworthiness. Becerra and Gupta's (2003) findings support these conclusions and Weaver and Dickson (1998) demonstrate that among IORs involving SMEs, parties were more likely to assume trustworthiness than not. A failure to live up to contractual obligations or socially imposed norms would lead to negative views of the relationship, even when financial performance met or exceeded expectations.

As this literature review suggests, our views on trust continue to evolve. Scholars have defined and examined trust in terms of behavior, cognition, emotion and faith. This coincides with the history of management thought, which can be viewed as a progressive quest to understand increasingly complex human and organizational phenomena.

Management theorizing in the 1950s and 1960s emphasized behavioralism, which was useful for explaining observable phenomena. For example, we can observe whether a person is trustworthy by observing whether the person cheats, steals, or lies. Fool me once, shame on you! Fool me twice, shame on me! The cognitive turn in the social sciences during the 1970s to 1980s was useful for explaining intentions, rational thinking (strategy) and sense-making. For example, a person is trustworthy if his or her intentions are honorable, other-regarding and fair. Behavioral and cognitive perspectives have their limits in explaining irrational or aberrant events and situations. As a result, in the 1990s scholars began to turn to emotion, affect and moods in people to explain irrational and impulsive psychotic behavior, such as envy, love, hate and greed. How affect impacts trust broadens the study of trust development (Williams 2001). But inexplicable phenomena remain. Some situations and events that occur in human and organizational relationships cannot be adequately explained on the basis of behavior, cognition, or emotion. Recently, some management scholars have begun to take their cue from religion to appreciate that in the final analysis humans rely on faith to reconcile inexplicable events that are beyond their control and to which they are vulnerable (Delbecq 1999). As with the evolution of management theorizing, our understanding of trust as a multidimensional concept is evolving to incorporate behavioral, cognitive, emotional and faith dimensions – each dimension addresses situations and events in relationships that cannot be explained by the other.

Empirical assessments of reliance on trust in IORs
In our companion articles, we set forth a number of propositions dealing with the development of trust in IORs. In addition to institutional contexts, these included:

- the parties' past histories of cooperation (with each other and with other partners);
- the degree of risk associated with their economic exchanges;
- the observance of norms of fairness (measured in terms of procedural and distributive justice);

- a willingness to follow norms of equity;
- the degree of personal embeddedness among and between partners to IORs; and
- stability in organizational roles.

Further, we argued that reliance on trust by the parties would be a factor in their negotiations, in their ability to learn, and in their ability to reduce the costs of transactions and the cost of governing relationships. Reliance on trust would also lead to increased flows of information between individuals and their organizations, the reduction of uncertainty, agency costs and opportunity costs, which, in turn, reduced the levels of formal safeguards the parties employed in dealing with each other (which, we argued, leads to increased managerial flexibility). Similarly, we argued that an ability to rely on trust in economic exchanges would be related to the choices the parties made in their approaches to governing their relationships.

Finally, there was the question of the nature of a relationship between reliance on trust and IOR performance. In an indirect way we asserted a positive relationship between the ability to rely on trust and performance by proposing that it reduced the risk inherent in an exchange, all other things remaining equal (Ring and Van de Ven 1992). We also asserted that performance would be related to the processes that the parties employed in negotiating, committing to and executing phases of their IORs (Ring and Van de Ven 1994). And in relating outcomes to trust, we argued in Ring and Van de Ven (1994) that over-reliance on trust invited opportunistic behavior which, in turn, might be met by an escalation of tit-for-tat-like responses involving increased reliance on formal safeguards that, ultimately, led to dissolution of IORs.

Since the publication of our papers, a significant number of empirical researchers have examined and found empirical support for these relationships between trust and its antecedents and consequences. It is not our objective to exhaustively review the empirical literature (but see, e.g., Zaheer and Harris 2005). However, a few comments on the overall findings from this research are in order.

With respect to the contexts surrounding reliance on trust, for example, Scheer et al. (2003) found that relationships between inequity and trust varied across cultures. Stewart (2003), building on the work of McKnight et al. (1998), added trust transfer to cognitive processes in demonstrating that intent to trust was a function of beliefs about trust. In their study of 615 Hong Kong firms with dealings in China, Child and Möllering (2003) provided empirical support for our arguments that institutional contexts have an impact on the willingness of parties to rely on trust. Similarly, Dahlstrom and Nygaard (1995) found that a high degree of institutional-based trust lowered levels of reliance on interpersonal trust.

To fully understand reliance on trust, Anderson et al. (1994) asserted the need to focus on the embedded context of relationships. Trust is context-specific (Lusch et al. 2003; Vaara et al. 2004). Chen et al. (1998) called for a culturally contingent model of cooperation. Rousseau et al. (1998) argued that reliance on trust is a matter of the culture of shared worlds; we trust persons who share our cultural values.

Gulati (1995) offered support for our proposition that the nature of the parties' prior relationships would be associated with their willingness to rely on trust. Batt (2003) found that satisfaction with exchange built on trust in his study of growers and market agents in Australia. Bankers involved in forming syndicates were found to favor past partners when forming new alliances, not just for knowledge of partners' reliability and capabilities, but also because of inertia (Li and Rowley 2002). Researchers have found that trust also has a number of indirect effects by enabling conditions – such as positive interpretations of another's behavior, procedural justice, and commitment – that are conducive to obtaining cooperation and higher performance (Dirks and Ferrin 2001). In their study of 119 buyer–seller relations, Perrone et al. (2003) demonstrated that trust is a function of role autonomy and discretion of agents.

Recently, the role that reliance on trust plays in the negotiations phase of IOR evolution has begun to be addressed. Naquin and Paulson (2003), for example, found that on-line negotiations were characterized by lower levels of interpersonal trust than were face-to-face negotiations. Direct effects of trust on organizations engaged in negotiation processes were observed by Dirks and Ferrin (2001). Ariño and Ring (2004) studied the role of trust and its associations with fairness in the context of a failed international joint venture negotiation. The direct effects that reliance on trust has on organizations include learning and knowledge sharing, according to Dirks and Ferrin (2001). Kale et al. (2003) provide empirical evidence that relational capital (based on mutual trust and interaction at the individual level) between alliance partners creates a basis for learning and know-how transfer across the exchange interface. •

A major focus of our two papers was the effect that trust would have on the cost of transacting and governing IORs. These views were dictated by a conscious decision to structure our arguments within the framework of an evolving theory of transaction cost economics that was having a significant impact on scholarship in the late 1980s and early 1990s (e.g. Williamson 1985; Kogut 1988; Hennart 1988). Although we were not the first to use the theory to explore issues related to trust and IOR dynamics, our 1992 *Strategic Management Journal* article was, at the time, the most explicit propositional statement of the governance and transaction cost implications of reliance on trust.

In the intervening years, a substantial body of research has explored these issues. For example, Dyer and Chu (2003) demonstrated in their study of US, Korean and Japanese automakers that an ability to rely on trust reduced transactions costs. Artz and Brush (2000) provided support for the proposition that an ability to rely on relational norms helped to lower the costs of exchange in buyer–supplier relationships involving original equipment manufacturers (OEMs). Brouthers and Brouthers (2003) found that trust was more critical to a choice of entry mode in IORs in service than in manufacturing industries. Trust in a supplier predicted support for a merger (Lusch et al. 2003).

Carson et al. (2003) found that as the information-processing capabilities of firms increased, so did their willingness to rely more on trust-based governance modes. Dyer and Chu (2003) in their study of US, Korean and Japanese automakers found that an ability to rely on trust was correlated with greater information sharing. In the Dirks and Ferrin (2001) study previously mentioned, the direct effects of trust on organizations included more open communication and knowledge sharing.

We also proposed that trust would be associated with conflict aversion. Experiments by Smithson (1999) demonstrate that conflicting sources of information generally are perceived as being less credible than those that derive from ambiguous sources. Conflict raises suspicions about whether sources of information are trustworthy or credible. If the sources disagree, then the judge is not only uncertain but must also disagree with at least one of the sources. Dirks and Ferrin (2001) also found that an ability to rely on trust produced creative conflict management approaches. Burt and Knez (1995) demonstrated the importance of 'third-party gossip' in understanding when people rely on trust in network contexts. Deeds and Hill (1999) found that healthy relationships (which Ariño et al. (2001) described as partners enjoying high levels of relational quality) were more effective in reducing opportunism than reliance on hostages or elaborate contingent claims contracts. Parkhe (1993) provided support for our proposition about the relationship between a willingness to rely on trust and a reduction in reliance on formal safeguards. We also argued that the direct effects of trust on organizations include greater flexibility; this was supported in the finding of Dirks and Ferrin (2001). Young et al. (2003) also found that trust promotes flexibility in IORs, and flexibility increases the productivity of entrepreneurial software companies (see also Young-Ybarra and Wiersema 1999).

In our arguments about relying on trust in IORs, we made no specific predictions about performance-related outcomes. Nonetheless, a sizable body of subsequent research has produced mixed findings on this issue. For example, the failure of the Sport7 joint venture, a fledging Dutch TV station, was linked to the entry of a new, less trusted actor in the business network (Sminia 2003). Trust is found to be one of several success factors for manufacturing networks (Scherer et al. 2003), prenatal IOR services in Quebec (D'Amour et al. 2003), children's mental health services (Rivard and Morrissey 2003), and supplier responsiveness in supply chain relationships (Handfield and Bechtel 2002). Trust also mediated communication/knowledge and technological outcomes in industry–university IORs (Santoro and Saparito 2003). Socially oriented trust was found to mediate relationships between client satisfaction and a variety of vendor characteristics in a study of 157 firms by Gainey and Klaas (2003).

In addition, several studies found trust to be unrelated to various indicators of IOR performance. In a study of 700 Sino-foreign joint ventures, asymmetric versus symmetric governance structures were not significantly related to profitability (Lee et al. 2003). So also, in a study of 53 collaborations in physics and sciences, trust was unrelated to performance (Shrum et al. 2001). In another study, the use of IT support for IOR knowledge management was explained by firm (and knowledge) cooperation between Norwegian and Australian law firms, while IOR trust was not a significant predictor (Gottschalk and Khandelwal 2002). And in a study of 164 small-firm alliances in Australia, trust was found to be important but not sufficient for alliance success; also important were strategic compatibility and appropriate governance structure (Hoffmann and Schlosser 2001).

Finally, several of our propositions have not been rigorously tested. For example, very little work has been done exploring the kinds of risk (other than behavioral risk) that frequently are associated with the kinds of economic exchanges conducted within IORs and how the negative impacts of these different sources of risk can be mediated when transacting parties are able to rely on trust. In our view, the impact of personal embeddedness on both the evolution of reliance on trust at an interpersonal level and on perceptions of trustworthiness remains under-explored. In short, there still are important gaps in a growing body of empirical work exploring relationships between reliance on trust and its antecedents and consequences.

The process of trust development
In our original arguments we generally focused on interpersonal trust, and we argued that in IORs reliance on trust takes place between individuals. In discussing the confidence that

an economic actor has 'in the goodwill of others not to cause harm when you are vulnerable to them . . .' at the organization level of analysis we rely, not on trust, but on other concepts. Depending upon the specific context, they include relational quality (e.g. Ariño et al. 2001), reputation (Ferguson and Deephouse 2000) and legitimacy (Olk and Ring 1997).

Rather than making assumptions about what transpires at an organizational level in decisions related to governance modes or contractual safeguards, however, we believe that the time has come to begin rigorous empirical testing of the following questions:

- Do executives, managers and employees actually trust the actions of organizations?
- Do they rely on that trust as substitutes for or complements to more formalized and elaborated forms of governance (e.g. equity joint ventures, elaborated levels of safeguards in written contracts)?
- Or do they rely on other concepts such as reputation or legitimacy when dealing with organizations?

We also encourage more empirical testing of the extent to which variance in governance modes, transaction costs and so on is more or less explained by the distinct (or interactive) contributions of reliance on trust (interpersonal or inter-organizational), reputation, legitimacy, or relational quality.

In our 1994 *Academy of Management Review* article, we offered a process model of the evolution of IORs, along with a set of propositions that describe the manner in which reliance on interpersonal trust might evolve over time. We argued that interpersonal trust building is a developmental process: 'It requires careful and systematic attention to the concrete processes by which personal relationships emerge between transacting parties' (Ring and Van de Ven 1994, p. 93).

Consistent with this argument, many studies have further explored how trust is created, learned and experienced. These studies have demonstrated that reliance on trust involves extensive investment, is reciprocal, and is constantly evolving. Ariño and de la Torre (1998) provided detailed insight into processes that led Coke and Nestlé to terminate their alliance, in part because each partner saw the other's behavior as being inequitable and opportunistic. Doz (1996) developed a model of IOR evolution in which learning played a central role, and his model provides a basis for thinking about how parties to economic exchanges can learn to rely on trust in dealing with each other. Kumar and Nti (1998) found that the ways partners assess and react to outcome discrepancies shape the developmental path of an IOR, and by implication the extent to which the parties will rely on trust in dealing with each other. Dyer and Singh (1998) and Hansen et al. (1997; 2001) extended these arguments in a more dynamic way by describing the kinds of capabilities firms would need to manage trust-based relational contracting processes. Ariño et al. (2002) provide an extensive discussion of the evolutionary dynamics of IORs, including issues related to the emergence of reliance on interpersonal trust. While stable relationships maintain equilibrium over time, divergence can lead to termination of the joint venture (Buchel 2002). Bell et al. (2002), for example, have found that violations of ability, integrity and benevolence all contributed to trust reduction, and early violations of trustee benevolence sensitized parties and contributed importantly to trust deterioration.

With the exception of the studies just reviewed, virtually all of the research on trust in IORs is based on cross-sectional studies that do not provide information about the temporal development of trust. We have very little empirical evidence about the evolutionary dynamics of interpersonal trust. Longitudinal research is required to observe how and why processes of trust develop over time. Scholars must begin to undertake longitudinal process studies if we are to provide managers with evidence-based models and principles for managing IORs to achieve their business and community-level strategies. Poole et al. (2000) provide detailed and useful methods for conducting such longitudinal process studies.

Changing contexts and assumptions of trust-based relationships
Thus far we have discussed scholarly advances to understanding the antecedents consequences and developmental processes of trust in IORs. As was the case in our 1992 and 1994 papers, most of this scholarship relied upon generally unstated assumptions about the role of culture and institutions that encourage people to rely on trust when managing and governing IORs. Three social and economic trends are making these assumptions explicit and are calling them into question. First, with the growth of relational contracting, outsourcing, strategic alliances and networks, trust-based relationships are increasingly becoming the organizing principle for doing business (McEvily et al. 2003). Second, despite the immense appeal and importance of trust, there is extensive evidence that trust is declining in many societies and organizations (see, e.g., Bruhn 2001; Rose et al. 1997. But see also Fukuyama 1995; Putnam 2002). Third, in an increasingly global economy the parties engaged in many business relationships are from cultures that rely on different bases of personal and institutional trust (Friedberg 2000; Pearce 2001). These trends represent significant challenges, as well as opportunities, for advancing our understanding of the roles that reliance on trust can play in the governance and management of economic exchanges.

The growth of IORs among organizations from different countries and cultures requires reexamination of the assumption that institutions provide recourse for parties to settle their disputes when violations of interpersonal trust occur. When parties cannot resolve differences through private ordering (using their own devices), those of us accustomed to the everyday presence of institutional guarantors (Commons 1950) naturally assume that all parties can resort to these kinds of institutions for the public resolution of disputes. This may be a valid assumption if the public institutions governing disputes between the parties to an IOR are judged to be trustworthy, legitimate and reliable. Pearce (2001) reports that under non-facilitative governments (those with weak, unpredictable, or hostile institutions, like China, and former communist countries in Europe), business managers have to depend more heavily on their personal relationships in order to obtain protection from threats that are more completely secured by facilitative governments (with strong institutions). She points out that 'although this reliance on personal relationships has been called trust-based authority, these relationships are not necessarily characterized by the warmth and supportiveness usually associated with that word. Rather, this is organizing based on mutual personal dependency rather than trusting relationships' (Pearce 2001, p. 54). Humphrey and Schmitz (1998) provide additional support for Pearce's observations in their assessment of the roles played by trust in interfirm relationships in the developing economies of the old Soviet Union.

Our focus on public ordering and the institutions that economic actors employ in its use in this chapter unduly narrows the range of institutions that can be employed in lieu of private ordering. We recognize that this is the case, as we did in our original articles. The fact remains, however, that other institutions can be relied upon by economic actors and are in fact used quite frequently. The role that trust plays in these contexts is well researched (see, e.g., Lane and Bachmann 1998; Biggart and Delbridge 2004; Ring 2004), but a more complete discussion of it is beyond the objectives of this chapter.

In our 1994 paper we proposed that 'the greater the transaction-specific investments made under conditions of uncertainty, the more the immediate parties stand to benefit from preserving the relationship' (Ring and Van de Ven 1994, p. 95). The internal resolution of disputes within an ongoing 'agreement' is often in the best interest of the parties involved. If parties resort to external institutional safeguards to resolve their disputes, the typical result will be the dissolution of the agreement being disputed, and, perhaps, of their ongoing business relationships. We noted, too, that over-reliance on interpersonal trust could also lead to an abuse of trust and that over-reliance on public ordering could produce similar results, citing the work of Granovetter (1985) and Shapiro (1987).

Underlying the caveats just noted was our assumption that human beings and their institutions are fallible. As we have observed, interpersonal trust is often easier to breach than it is to build. No organizational relationship is perfect, and most current business relationships are not expendable. As a result, seldom can parties terminate an organizational relationship in the event of a breach in interpersonal trust. But this raises one of the more interesting paradoxes of organizational relationships: they continue in the face of breaches of interpersonal trust. Our review of the literature reveals that too little attention appears to have been paid to forgiveness, repair and reconstruction of trust in relationships that have experienced a breach in trust among the parties.

The decline of trust
Ironically, and unfortunately, while the need to rely on trust and the benefits that flow from this are clear, there is extensive evidence that trust is declining in many (but not all) societies and within many organizations. Bruhn (2001, p. 3) describes the many polls and studies showing that trust and its allies – honesty, integrity and commitment – have been declining in the USA as well as in other countries over the past 50 years. Fukuyama (1995) notes a similar decline.

Others provide evidence that this is the case in the USA. For example, a national survey conducted in 1995 by the *Washington Post*, Harvard University and the Kaiser Family Foundation found that America is becoming a nation of suspicious strangers, and it is this mistrust of each other that is a major reason Americans have lost confidence in the federal government and virtually every other major institution – health professions, corporate business, education, churches and Wall Street (Brossard 1996).

Each succeeding generation that has come of age since the 1950s has been more distrusting of human nature. Today, nearly two in three Americans believe that most people can not be trusted; one-half say most people would cheat others if they had a chance, and that most people are looking out for themselves (Bruhn 2001).

Numerous reasons for the decline of trust have been offered. Watergate, the Berkeley and Watts riots, the Vietnam War, social and technical change, new configurations of the traditional family and generational differences have been described as loosening the social fabric of society, resulting in less caring, reduced social support and connectedness, reduced participation as citizens and, therefore, less social capital and trust (see, e.g., Fukuyama 1995).

These surveys pre-date the more recent corporate Enron-like scandals, sexual abuse in the Catholic Church, 9/11, terrorism, the war in Iraq, AIDS, SARS and the avian flu epidemic and so on.

Bruhn (2001, p. 35) also observes that

> Changes in the work environment over the past 2–3 decades have significantly altered how we trust organizations, our bosses and coworkers. In the past there was such a thing as lifetime employment. Corporations assumed responsibility for career development, and employees believed that their employer would act in their best interests. Having experienced massive restructurings, mergers, layoffs, outsourcing, growing wage disparities between executives and workers, excessive greed, employment has become more transactional, and employees know they are expendable.

These conditions appear to have significantly altered the landscape in which IORs emerged and evolved over the past two decades. If, as we argued, context is critical to understanding reliance on trust, what are the implications of these changes for IORs and those who manage them? And how have firms managed to cooperate with each other when their employees have increasingly been less trustful of the firms that employ them?

Let us start by defining what we perceive as the context in which many IORs will take place in the next decade. First, many more people will be perceived as less trustworthy, and the willingness of those with whom they do business to rely on interpersonal trust will be less evident. For example, as the world's economy becomes more global, those societies in which 'insiders' are perceived as being more trustworthy than 'outsiders' will discover that they are dealing with more 'outsiders'. Similarly, in economies in which familial ties were the basis for trust are likely to experience a reduced ability to rely on kinship ties.[9] Second, and as a consequence, IORs will experience more breaches of interpersonal trust. These breaches may not necessarily occur as a consequence of malfeasance. In fact, the breaches of trust may be inadvertent – a result of a lack of awareness that 'normal' behaviors are perceived as reflecting a lack of trust in 'business' relations when in fact they may have been intended to reflect a lack of trust in a social sense. Third, managers who, ordinarily, would respond by relying more on institutional sources of trust will have less confidence in those sources of trust. Or, as both Fukuyama (1995) and Putnam (2002) argue, managers will discover that they have less social capital to rely on in dealing with economic matters. In short, managers of IORs will find themselves in 'Catch-22' situations.

What might be done about this decline in trust when we need it the most? Management scholars offer three basic approaches: (1) do nothing; (2) work to improve institutional governance structures to deal more effectively with those who would abuse trust and act opportunistically; and (3) take steps to repair and reconstruct trust within ongoing interpersonal relationships.

The first option is to do nothing and accept the trends and situations as they are, even though they have become deplorable. There are, of course, grave consequences of doing nothing. According to Bruhn (2001, p. 33), 'At the individual level, a person who follows a life of distrust will find that his/her world is constantly narrowing. Usually chronically distrustful persons become cynical and depressed, and their behavior alienates them from others, leading to further social isolation.' Organizations and societies made up of substantial numbers of individuals acting on such a belief system will become increasingly dysfunctional. Therefore doing nothing is unacceptable and as such unlikely. The threat of allowing this first option to take hold across a broad spectrum of civil life is undoubtedly a factor in the rise of concern for the role that social capital plays in everyday economic and political (as well as social) life (see, e.g., Coleman 1988; Fukayama 1995; Nahapiet and Ghoshal 1998; Putnam 2002).

A second option is to address the design of institutions that are the legal structures and safeguards to provide support for parties that try to rely on trust, but find that those with whom they are dealing do not reciprocate. This requires re-examining a wide variety of institutional practices and policies.

For example, consider the consequences of just one contributing factor of increasing distrust – corporate layoffs. Wanberg et al. (2005) report that there were 8349 mass layoffs in 2001 in the USA, which led to 1.7 million individuals losing their jobs. Numerous psychological studies have documented the negative impact of job loss on the physical, mental and social functioning of unemployed workers and their family members (Leana and Feldman 1992). For example, studies demonstrate that job loss is associated with increased anxiety, depression, sleeping problems, alcohol disorders, divorce and child abuse (e.g. Dooley et al. 1996). Research suggests that job loss has a negative influence on every indicator of mental and physical health (e.g. Dooley et al. 1996; Leana and Feldman 1992). And those that remain employed evidence even less trust in the organizations that have laid off their friends and colleagues. There was a time when this phenomenon occurred almost exclusively within the USA, but in a global economy in which firms in labor-intensive industries increasingly have to move manufacturing to lower-labor-cost economies, 'layoffs' are visited on workers in countries in which lifetime employment within a single firm was assumed to be beyond the reach of the effects of globalization.[10]

This research raises a significant policy issue. Many years ago Reinhard Bendix (1956) pointed out that the history of business has been to 'internalize benefits and externalize costs'. To what degree should companies be allowed to externalize their human cost on individuals and society? Clean air, water and OSHA (Occupational Safety and Health Administration) laws have been established to curb pollution of our physical environment. Although we do not have the data, our guess is that costs of corporate abuses of human resources wrought on society far exceed the costs of those on our physical environment. These costs call attention to the need for a policy debate on the design of institutions and laws that curb corporate abuses of our human resources and their resulting pain and health care costs on former employees and society.

Legal systems and the institutional safeguards they provide are clearly needed to protect, enable and constrain behaviors that society values as fair and trustworthy. Ring (2004) offers a series of steps that could be taken by states to increase reliance on trust and reduce the costs of economic exchange in general. Among them are:

- reducing systemic governmental corruption, aggressively prosecuting individuals who abuse their public offices, thereby increasing confidence in institutional guarantors;
- increasing the level of robust competition within an economy, thereby providing economic actors with options to parties that cannot be trusted;
- increasing the amount of information available to economic actors and reducing information asymmetry, thereby reducing opportunities to benefit from opportunistic behavior;

- increasing requirements to bargain in good faith and providing remedies in the case of a breach, thereby increasing the incentives for parties to rely more heavily on interpersonal trust in *ex ante* stages of contract;
- making public more information on economic actors who are persistently opportunistic, thereby making it easier for individuals and organizations to avoid doing business with them;
- adequately supporting systems of justice when the stakes are high, dampening the benefits of opportunistic behavior while complementing, but not supplanting, social sanctions that already may be effective.[11]

In the final analysis, however, these kinds of interventions will never substitute for high-commitment interpersonal relations (Helper and Levin 1992). This brings us to our third option: repair and reconstruct trust within ongoing interpersonal relationships. As stated before, human beings and their institutions are fallible. No relationship is perfect, and most relationships are not expendable. With their 'backs against the wall', reasonable people often can and will work out their differences and failings. Even after serious violations, it is possible to reconstruct trust in relationships. Reconstruction can occur when the parties involved believe the relationship is worth salvaging, so they engage in a negotiation process that involves an extended period of time during which they assess the violation and the intent of the violator, and they offer an apology and render forgiveness.

The daughter of trust is forgiveness. The study of repair, forgiveness and reconstruction of relationships should be a high priority of organization and management scholars. Bruhn (2001, p. 30) discusses the act of forgiveness. 'Even though it may not be accepted by the other party, forgiveness always makes a difference to the forgiving individual and creates a permanent difference in the relationship, which over time, can lead to full conflict resolution and restoration of the relationship.' Healing begins with forgiveness (Schneiderman 1999). Authentic forgiveness includes the following characteristics:

- it is unconditional; it is offered to the other person regardless of the response;
- it is self-regarding as well as altruistic; forgiveness is offered for the well-being of the relationship and requires that the persons break free of old habits and feelings;
- it does not take place instantaneously; and
- it is not symmetrical; one party usually instigates the process and becomes the prime mover in restoring the relationship.

Schneiderman notes that if forgiveness is to be an effective intervention, full conflict resolution is necessary. Forgiveness is a transforming process that empowers the forgiver and forgivee (Kurzynski 1998).

We closed our 1994 *Academy of Management Review* article by observing that:

> as the uncertainty, complexity, and duration of economic transactions within and between firms increase, *it becomes increasingly important for scholars and managers to understand developmental processes of how equity, trust, conflict resolution procedures, and internal governance structures emerge and dissolve over time.* (p. 113, emphasis added)

We believe that developing this understanding is even more critical today than it was ten years ago.

Acknowledgements

We appreciate the useful suggestions of Reinhard Bahmann, Ned Lorez and Aks Zaheer on earlier drafts of this paper, and Julie Trupke in copy editing this chapter.

Notes

1. This investigation was funded by major grants from the National Science Foundation, the Office of Naval Research, and research contracts with other companies, many headquartered in Minnesota. MIRP's major findings were published in a trilogy of books by Van de Ven et al. (1989); Van de Ven et al. (1999); Poole et al. (2000). Findings also have appeared in a variety of academic journals.
2. Since 1972 Van de Ven had a stream of research and papers exploring a variety of aspects of inter-organizational relationships in the tradition of organizational sociology. Ring, a relatively new management scholar, had been a lawyer and legal scholar before beginning doctoral studies and had come to Minnesota with the aim of using his legal background as a platform for studying economic exchanges between firms.
3. See Bok (1979).
4. See Ring and Van de Ven (1992). The concept is one that relates to processes of negotiating a contract and the nature of the relationship that the parties enjoy. As Ring (2002) points out, the concept of a relational contract is one based in theory (e.g. Macneil 1974). No court in the USA has ever used the theory to support the claims of a party to a contract or its breach.
5. Trust is also critical to social relationships, but our focus in this chapter is on its role in economic exchange.
6. We are pleased to note that our papers have received considerable attention by scholars, not only in management, but also in a wide variety of disciplines. According to the Web of Science, as of June 2006 the 1992 paper in the *Strategic Management Journal* and the 1994 paper in the *Academy of Management Review* were cited in 318 and 360 papers respectively by other scholars.
7. Many other terms have been used to refer to cooperative inter-organizational relationships in the management literature, including: strategic business alliances, joint ventures, contractual relationships, buyer–supplier relationships and so on. Our use of the term IOR reflects the extensive prior research that organizational sociologists had conducted since the 1960s on IORs at the dyad, set and network levels of analyses (see, e.g., Galaskiewicz 1985).
8. Although there is an extensive literature dealing with the concepts of fairness/justice (see, e.g., Brockner 2002; Cropanzano and Greenberg 1997; Lind and Tyler 1988), very little work has been done towards integrating it within the literature on the dynamics of IORs. Ariño and Ring (2004) review the subsequent literature on justice theory in the study of alliances and report on the case of a failed attempt to negotiate an internal joint venture in which they employ justice theory in exploring reasons behind the outcome.
9. See Fukuyama (1995), particularly chapters 14 and 15, for a discussion of these kinds of 'institutions' and the relationships that they have with trust.
10. See, for example, Fukuyama's (1995) discussion of Japan in chapter 16.
11. See Biggart and Delbridge (2004) for an excellent discussion of various systems of exchange and the institutions that support them.

References

Anderson, J.C., H. Håkansson and J. Johanson (1994), 'Dyadic business relationships within a business network context', *Journal of Marketing*, **58** (4), 1–15.
Ariño, A. and P.S. Ring (2004), 'The role of justice theory in strategic alliance negotiations', paper presented at the annual meeting of the Strategic Management Society, San Juan, Puerto Rico.
Ariño, A. and J. de la Torre (1998), 'Learning from failure: Towards an evolutionary model of collaborative ventures', *Organization Science*, **9**, 306–25.
Ariño, A., J. de la Torre and P.S. Ring (2001), 'Relational quality: Managing trust in corporate alliances', *California Management Review*, **44**, 109–31.
Ariño, A., J. de la Torre, Y. Doz, G. Lorenzoni and P.S. Ring (2002), 'Process issues in international alliance management: A debate on the evolution of collaboration', in M. Hitt and J. Cheng (eds), *Advances in International Management*, **14**, 173–219.
Arrow, K. (1973), *Information and Economic Behavior*, Stockholm, Sweden: Federation of Swedish Industries.
Artz, K.W. and T.H. Brush (2000), 'Asset specificity, uncertainty and relational norms: An examination of coordination costs in collaborative strategic alliances', *Journal of Economic Behavior & Organization*, **41** (4), 337–62.
Ba, S.L. and P.A. Pavlou (2002), 'Evidence of the effect of trust building technology in electronic markets: Price premiums and buyer behavior', *MIS Quarterly*, **26** (3), 243–68.

Baier, A. (1986), 'Trust and antitrust', *Ethics*, **96**, 231–60.

Barney, J.B. and M.H. Hansen (1994), 'Trustworthiness: Can it be a source of competitive advantage?' *Strategic Management Journal*, **15** (S2), 175–90.

Barthelemy, J. (2003), 'The seven deadly sins of outsourcing', *Academy of Management Executive*, **17** (2), 87–98.

Batt, P.J. (2003), 'Building trust between growers and market agents', *Supply Management – An International Journal*, **8** (1), 65–78.

Becerra, M. and A. Gupta (2003), 'Perceived trustworthiness within the organization: The moderating impact of communication frequency on trustor and trustee effects', *Organization Science*, **14** (1), 32–44.

Bell, G.G., R.J. Oppenheimer and A. Bastien (2002), 'Trust deterioration in an international buyer–supplier relationship', *Journal of Business Ethics*, **36** (1–2), 65–78.

Bendix, R. (1956), *Work and Authority in Industry*, Berkeley, CA: University of California Press.

Biggart, N.W. and R. Delbridge (2004), 'Systems of exchange', *Academy of Management Review*, **29** (1), 29–50.

Boersma, M.F., P.J. Buckley and P.N. Ghauri (2003), 'Trust in international joint venture relationships', *Journal of Business Research*, **56** (12), 1031–42.

Bok, S. (1979), *Lying: Moral choice in public and private life*, New York: Random House.

Bradach, J.L. and R.G. Eccles (1989), 'Price, authority and trust: From ideal types to plural forms', *Annual Review of Sociology*, **15**, 97–118.

Brockner, J. (2002), 'Making sense of procedural fairness: How high procedural fairness can reduce or heighten the influence of outcome favorability', *Academy of Management Review*, **27**, 58–76.

Bromiley, P. and L.L. Cummings (1995), 'Transaction costs in organizations with trust', in R. Bies, B. Sheppard and R. Lewicki (eds), *Research on Negotiations in Organizations*, Greenwich CT: JAI Press, pp. 219–47.

Brossard, M.A. (1996), 'Americans losing trust in each other and institutions', *Washington Post*, 28 and 29 January, p. A1.

Brouthers, K.D. and L.E. Brouthers (2003), 'Why service and manufacturing entry mode choices differ: The influence of transaction cost factors, risk and trust', *Journal of Management Studies*, **40** (5), 1179–204.

Bruhn, J.G. (2001), *Trust and the Health of Organizations*, New York: Kluwer.

Buchel, B. (2002), 'Joint venture development: Driving forces towards equilibrium', *Journal of World Business*, **37** (3), 199–207.

Burt, R.S. and M. Knez (1995), 'Trust and third party gossip', in R. Kramer and T. Tyler (eds), *Trust in Organizations: Frontiers of Theory and Research*, Thousand Oaks, CA: Sage, pp. 68–89.

Butler, J.K. (1991), 'Toward understanding and measuring conditions of trust: Evolution of a conditions of trust inventory', *Journal of Management*, **17**, 643–63.

Carson, S.J., A. Madhok, R. Varman and G. John (2003), 'Information processing moderators of the effectiveness of trust-based governance in interfirm R&D collaboration', *Organization Science*, **14** (1), 45–56.

Chen, C.C., X.P. Chen and J.R. Meindl (1998), 'How can cooperation be fostered? The cultural effects of individualism–collectivism', *Academy of Management Review*, **23** (2), 285–304.

Child, J. and G. Möllering (2003), 'Contextual confidence and active trust development in the Chinese business environment', *Organization Science*, **14** (1), 69–80.

Chiles, T.H. and J.F. McMackin (1996), 'Integrating variable risk preferences, trust and transaction cost economics', *Academy of Management Review*, **21** (1), 73–99.

Coleman, J.S. (1988), 'Social capital in the creation of human capital', *American Journal of Sociology*, **94**, S95–121.

Commons, J.R. (1950), *The Economics of Collective Action*, New York: Macmillan.

Cropanzano, R. and J. Greenberg (1997), 'Progress in organizational justice: Tunnelling through the maze', in C.L. Cooper and I.T. Robertson (eds), *International Review of Industrial and Organizational Psychology*, New York: Wiley, pp. 317–72.

Dahlstrom, R. and A. Nygaard (1995), 'An exploratory investigation of interpersonal trust in new and mature market economies', *Journal of Retailing*, **71** (4), 339–61.

D'Amour, D., L. Goulet, J.F. Labadie, L. Bernier and R. Pineault (2003), 'Accessibility, continuity and appropriateness: Key elements in assessing integration of perinatal services', *Health & Social Care in the Community*, **11** (5), 397–404.

Das, T.K. and B.S. Teng (1996), 'Risk types and inter-firm alliance structures', *Journal of Management Studies*, **33** (6), 827–43.

Das, T.K. and B.S. Teng (1998), 'Between trust and control: Developing confidence in partner cooperation in alliances', *Academy of Management Review*, **23**, 491–512.

Das, T.K. and B.S. Teng (2001), 'Trust, control and risk in strategic alliances: An integrated framework', *Organization Studies*, **22** (2), 251–83.

Deeds, D.L. and C.W.L. Hill (1999), 'An examination of opportunistic action within research alliances: Evidence from the biotechnology industry', *Journal of Business Venturing*, **14** (2), 141–63.

Dekker, H.C. (2004), 'Control of inter-organizational relationships: evidence on appropriation concerns and coordination requirements', *Accounting Organizations and Society*, **29** (1), 27–49.

Delbecq, A.L. (1999), 'Christian spirituality and contemporary business leadership', *Journal of Organizational Change Management*, **12** (4), 345–9.

Dirks, K.T. and D.L. Ferrin (2001), 'The role of trust in organizational settings', *Organization Science*, **12** (4), 450–67.

Dooley, D., J. Fielding and L. Levi (1996), 'Health and unemployment', *Annual Review of Public Health*, **17**, 449–65.

Dore, R. (1983), 'Goodwill and the spirit of capitalism', *British Journal of Sociology*, **34**, 459–82.

Doz, Y. (1996), 'The evolution of cooperation in strategic alliances: Initial conditions or learning processes?' *Strategic Management Journal*, **17**, 55–83.

Dyer, J.H. and W.J. Chu (2003), 'The role of trustworthiness in reducing transaction costs and improving performance: Empirical evidence from the United States, Japan and Korea', *Organization Science*, **14** (1), 57–68.

Dyer, J.H. and H. Singh (1998), 'The relational view: Cooperative strategy and sources of interorganizational competitive advantage', *Academy of Management Review*, **23**, 660–79.

Eriksson, K. and D.D. Sharma (2003), 'Modeling uncertainty in buyer–seller cooperation', *Journal of Business Research*, **56** (12), 961–70.

Ferguson, T.D. and D.D. Deephouse (2000), 'Do strategic groups differ in reputation?', *Strategic Management Journal*, **21** (12), 1195–215.

Fried, C. (1982), *Contract as Promise*, Cambridge, MA: Harvard University Press.

Friedberg, E. (2000), 'Going beyond either/or', *Journal of Management and Governance*, **4**, 35–52.

Fukuyama, F. (1995), *Trust: The Social Virtues and the Creation of Prosperity*, New York: The Free Press.

Gainey, T.W. and B.S. Klaas (2003), 'The outsourcing of training and development: Factors impacting client satisfaction', *Journal of Management*, **29** (2), 207–29.

Galaskiewicz, J. (1985), 'Interorganizational relations', *Annual Review of Sociology*, **11**, 281–304.

Gallivan, M.J. (2001), 'Striking a balance between trust anti control in a virtual organization: A content analysis of open source software case studies', *Information Systems Journal*, **11** (4), 277–304.

Gallivan, M.J. and G. Depledge (2003), 'Trust, control and the role of interorganizational systems in electronic partnerships', *Information Systems Journal*, **13** (2), 159–90.

Gambetta, D. (1988), 'Can we trust?', in D. Gambetta (ed.), *Trust: Making and Breaking Cooperative Relations*, Oxford: Basil Blackwell, pp. 213–37.

Gottschalk, P. and G.K. Khandelwal (2002), 'Inter-organizational knowledge management: A comparison of law firms in Norway and Australia', *Journal of Computer Information Systems*, **42** (5), 50–8.

Granovetter, M. (1985), 'Economic action and social structure: The problem of embeddedness', *American Journal of Sociology*, **91**, 481–510.

Gulati, R. (1995), 'Does familiarity breed trust? The implications of repeated ties for contractual choice in alliances', *Academy of Management Journal*, **38** (1), 85–112.

Handfield, R.B. and C. Bechtel (2002), 'The role of trust and relationship structure in improving supply chain responsiveness', *Industrial Marketing Management*, **31** (4), 367–82.

Hansen, M., R. Hoskisson, G. Lorenzoni and P.S. Ring (1997), 'The transactionally intense firm: Leveraging relational capabilities', paper presented at the Academy of Management National Meeting, Management and Organization Theory Division, Boston, MA.

Hansen, M., R. Hoskisson, G. Lorenzoni and P.S. Ring (2001), 'Strategic capabilities: Leveraging interfirm relationships and trust', in T. Froehlicher, A. Kuhn and G. Schmidt (eds), *Competences Relationnelles et Metamorphoses des Organisations*, Paris: Editions ESKA, pp. 245–68.

Harvey, M.G., M.M. Novicevic, T. Hench and M. Myers (2003), 'Global account management: A supply-side managerial view', *Industrial Marketing Management*, **32** (7), 563–71.

Helper, S. and D.I. Levin (1992), 'Long-term supplier relations and product-market structure', *Journal of Law, Economics & Organization*, **8**, 561–82.

Hennart, J.F. (1988), 'A transaction costs theory of equity joint ventures', *Strategic Management Journal*, **9**, 93–104.

Hoffmann, W.H. and R. Schlosser (2001), 'Success factors of strategic alliances in small and medium-sized enterprises – An empirical survey', *Long Range Planning*, **34** (3), 357–81.

Humphrey, J. and H. Schmitz (1998), 'Trust and inter-firm relations in developing and transition economies', *Journal of Development Studies*, **34** (4), 32–62.

Hwang, P. and W.P. Burgers (1997), 'Properties of trust: An analytical view', *Organizational Behavior and Human Decision Processes*, **69** (1), 67–73.

Hwang, P. and W.P. Burgers (1999), 'Apprehension and temptation – The forces against cooperation', *Journal of Conflict Resolution*, **43** (1), 117–30.

Hyder, A.S. and P.N. Ghauri (2000), 'Managing international joint venture relationships – A longitudinal perspective', *Industrial Marketing Management*, **29** (3), 205–18.

Kale, P., H. Singh and H. Perlmutter (2003), 'Learning and protection of proprietary assets in strategic alliances: Building relational capital', *Strategic Management Journal*, **21** (3), 217–37.

Kogut, B. (1988), 'Joint ventures: Theoretical and empirical perspectives', *Strategic Management Journal*, **9**, 319–32.

Kramer, R.M. and T.R. Tyler (1996), *Trust in Organizations: Frontiers of Theory and Research*, Thousand Oaks, CA: Sage.

Kumar, R. and K.O. Nti (1998), 'Differential learning and interaction in alliance dynamics: A process and outcome discrepancy model', *Organization Science*, **9**, 356–67.

Kurzynski, J.J. (1998), 'The virtue of forgiveness as a human resource management strategy', *Journal of Business Ethics*, **17**, 77–85.

Lane, C. and R. Bachmann (1998), *Trust Within and Between Organizations*, New York: Oxford University Press.

Larson, A. (1992), 'Network dyads in entrepreneurial settings: A study of the governance of exchange relationships', *Administrative Science Quarterly*, **37**, 76–104.

Leana, C.R. and D.C. Feldman (1992), *Coping with Job Loss: How Individuals, Organizations and Communities Respond to Layoffs*, New York: Lexington Books.

Lee, J.R., W.R. Chen and C. Kao (2003), 'Determinants and performance impact of asymmetric governance structures in international joint ventures: An empirical investigation', *Journal of Business Research*, **56** (10), 815–28.

Li, S.X. and T.J. Rowley (2002), 'Inertia and evaluation mechanisms in interorganizational partner selection: Syndicate formation among US investment banks', *Academy of Management Journal*, **45** (6), 1104–19.

Lind, E.A. and T.R. Tyler (1988), *The Social Psychology of Procedural Justice*, New York: Plenum.

Lusch, R.F., M. O'Brien and B. Sindhav (2003), 'The critical role of trust in obtaining retailer support for a supplier's strategic organizational change', *Journal of Retailing*, **79** (4), 249–58.

Maguire, S., N. Phillips and C. Hardy (2001), 'When "silence = death", keep talking: Trust, control and the discursive construction of identity in the Canadian HIV/AIDS treatment domain', *Organization Studies*, **22** (2), 285–310.

Macneil, I.R. (1974), 'The many futures of contract', *Southern California Law Review*, **47**, 688–816.

Mayer, R.C., J.H. Davis and F.D. Schoorman (1995), 'An integrative model of organizational trust', *Academy of Management Review*, **20**, 709–34.

McAllister, D.J. (1995), Affection- and cognition-based trust as foundations for interpersonal trust, *Academy of Management Journal*, **38**, 24–50.

McEvily, B., V. Perrone and A. Zaheer (2003), 'Trust as an organizing principle', *Organization Science*, **14** (1), 91–103.

McKnight, D.H., V. Choudhury and C. Kacmar (2002), 'Developing and validating trust measures for e-commerce: An integrative typology', *Information Systems Research*, **3**, 334–59.

McKnight, D.H., L.L. Cummings and N.L. Chervany (1998), 'Initial trust formation in new organizational relationships', *Academy of Management Review*, **23**, 473–90.

Misztal, B.A. (1996), *Trust in Modern Societies*, Oxford: Polity Press and Blackwell Publishing.

Möllering, G. (2002), 'Perceived trustworthiness and inter-firm governance: Empirical evidence from the UK printing industry', *Cambridge Journal of Economics*, **26** (2), 139–60.

Mosakowski, E. and P.C. Earley (2000), 'A selective review of time assumptions in strategy research', *Academy of Management Review*, **25** (4), 796–812.

Nahapiet, J. and S. Ghoshal (1998), 'Social capital, intellectual capital and the organizational advantage', *Academy of Management Review*, **23** (2), 242–66.

Naquin, C.E. and G.D. Paulson (2003), 'Online bargaining and interpersonal trust', *Journal of Applied Psychology*, **88** (1), 113–20.

Noteboom, B. (2002), *Trust: Forms, foundations, functions, failures and figures*, Cheltenham, UK and Northampton, MA, USA: Edward Elgar.

Oliver, A.L. and M. Ebers (1998), 'Networking network studies: An analysis of conceptual configurations in the study of inter-organizational relationship', *Organization Studies*, **19** (4), 549–83.

Olk, P. and P. Ring (1997), 'Strategic alliances and firm-based legitimacy', *Corporate Reputation Review*, **1** (2), 128–32.

Parkhe, A. (1993), 'Strategic alliance structuring: A game theoretic and transaction cost examination of inter-firm cooperation', *Academy of Management Journal*, **36**, 794–829.

Pearce, J.L. (2001), *Organization and Management in the Embrace of Government*, Mahwah, NJ: Lawrence Erlbaum Associates.

Perrone, V., A. Zaheer and B. McEvily (2003), 'Free to be trusted? Organizational constraints on trust in boundary spanners', *Organization Science*, **14** (4), 422–39.

Poole, M.S., A.H. Van de Ven, K. Dooley and M.E. Holmes (2000), *Organizational Change and Innovation Processes: Theory and Methods for Research*, New York: Oxford University Press.

Putnam, R.D. (ed.) (2002), *Democracies in Flux: The Evolution of Social Capital in Contemporary Society*, New York: Oxford University Press.

Ring, P.S. (1996), 'Fragile trust and resilient trust and their roles in cooperative interorganizational relationships', *Business & Society*, **35** (2), 148–75.

Ring, P.S. (1997a), 'Transacting in the state of union: A case study of exchange governed by convergent interests', *Journal of Management Studies*, **4**, 1–25.

Ring, P.S. (1997b), 'Patterns of process in cooperative interorganizational relationships', in P. Beamish and P.J. Killing (eds), *Cooperative Strategies: A North American Perspective*, San Francisco: New Lexington Press, pp. 286–307.

Ring, P.S. (2002), 'The role of contracts in strategic alliances', in F. Contractor and P. Lorange (eds), *Cooperative Strategies and Strategic Alliances*, London: Elsevier Science, pp. 145–62.

Ring, P.S. (2004), 'Exchange systems, institutions and roles of states in producing and increasing reliance on trust and in reducing the costs of transacting', paper presented at Western Academy of Management International Meeting, Shanghai, China.

Ring, P.S. and G. Rands (1989), 'Sense-making, understanding and committing: Emergent transaction processes in the evolution of 3M's Microgravity Research Program', in A.H. Van de Ven, H. Angle and M.S. Poole (eds), *Research on the Management of Innovation: The Minnesota Studies*, New York: Ballinger/Harper Row, pp. 337–66.

Ring, P.S. and A.H. Van de Ven (1989), 'Formal and informal dimensions of transactions', in A. Van de Ven, H. Angle and M. Scott Poole (eds), *Research on the Management of Innovation: The Minnesota Studies*, New York: Ballinger/Harper Row, pp. 171–92.

Ring, P.S. and A.H. Van de Ven (1992), 'Structuring cooperative relationships between organizations', *Strategic Management Journal*, **13**, 483–98.

Ring, P.S. and A.H. Van de Ven (1994), 'Developmental processes in cooperative interorganizational relationships', *Academy of Management Review*, **19**, 90–118.

Rivard, J.C. and J.P. Morrissey (2003), 'Factors associated with interagency coordination in a child mental health service system demonstration', *Administration and Policy in Mental Health*, **30** (5), 397–415.

Rose, R., W. Mishler and C. Haerpfer (1997), 'Social capital in civic and stressful societies', *Studies in Comparative International Development*, **32** (3), 85–111.

Rousseau, D.M., S.B. Sitkin, R.S. Burt and C. Camerer (1998), 'Not so different after all: A cross-discipline view of trust', *Academy of Management Review*, **23** (3), 393–404.

Sako, M. (1992), *Prices, Quality and Trust: Interfirm Relations in Britain and Japan*, Cambridge: Cambridge University Press.

Santoro, M.A. and P.A. Saparito (2003), 'The firm's trust in its university partner as a key mediator in advancing knowledge and new technologies', *IEEE Transactions on Engineering Management*, **50** (3), 362–73.

Scheer, L.K., N. Kumar and J. Steenkamp (2003), 'Reactions to perceived inequity in US and Dutch interorganizational relationships', *Academy of Management Journal*, **46** (3), 303–16.

Scherer, E. (2003), 'Autonomy and integration in decentralized production', *Advances in Production Management Systems*, 206–17.

Schneiderman, G. (1999), 'An advisor's guide to forgiveness and the family', *Trust and Estates*, **13** (8), 30–3.

Shapiro, S.P. (1987), 'The social control of interpersonal trust', *American Journal of Sociology*, **93**, 623–58.

Sheppard, B.H. and D.M. Sherman (1998), 'The grammars of trust: A model and general implications', *Academy of Management Review*, **23**, 422–37.

Shrum, W., I. Chompalov and J. Genuth (2001), 'Trust, conflict and performance in scientific collaborations', *Social Studies of Science*, **31** (5), 681–730.

Sobrero, M. and S. Schrader (1998), 'Structuring inter-firm relationships: A meta-analytic approach', *Organization Studies*, **19** (4), 585–615.

Sminia, H. (2003), 'The failure of the Sport7 TV-channel: Controversies in a business network', *Journal of Management Studies*, **40** (7), 1621–49.

Smithson, M. (1999), 'Conflict aversion: Preference for ambiguity vs. conflict in sources and evidence', *Organizational Behavior and Human Decision Processes*, **79** (3), 179–98.

Stewart, K.J. (2003), 'Trust transfer on the World Wide Web', *Organization Science*, **14**, (1), 5–17.

Vaara, E., B. Kleymann and H. Seristo (2004), 'Strategies as discursive constructions: The case of airline alliances', *Journal of Management Studies*, **41** (1), 1–35.

Van de Ven, A.H., H. Angle and M.S. Poole (1989), *Research on the Management of Innovation: The Minnesota Studies*, New York: Oxford University Press.

Van de Ven, A.H., R. Garud, S. Venkatraman and M.S. Poole (1999), *The Innovation Journey*, Oxford: Oxford University Press.

Wanberg, C.R., T.M. Glomb, Z. Song and S. Rosol (2005), 'Job-Search persistence during unemployment: A ten wave longitudinal study', *Journal of Applied Psychology*, **90**, 411–30.

Weaver, K.M. and P.H. Dickson (1998), 'Outcome quality of small- to medium-sized enterprise-based alliances: The role of perceived partner behaviours', *Journal of Business Venturing*, **13** (6), 505–22.

Williams, M. (2001), 'In whom we trust: Group membership as an affective context for trust development', *Academy of Management Review*, **26** (3), 377–96.

Williamson, O.E. (1985), *The Economic Institutions of Capitalism*, New York: The Free Press.

Williamson, O.E. (1993), 'Calculativeness, trust and economic organization', *Journal of Law and Economics*, **36**, 453–86.

Young, G., H. Sapienza and D. Baumer (2003), 'The influence of flexibility in buyer–seller relationships on the productivity of knowledge', *Journal of Business Research*, **56** (6), 443–51.

Young-Ybarra, C. and M. Wiersema (1999), 'Strategic flexibility in information technology alliances: The influence of transaction cost economics and social exchange theory', *Organization Science*, **10** (4), 439–59.

Zaheer, A. and J. Harris (2005), 'Interorganizational trust for inclusion', in O. Shenkar and J. Reuer (eds), *Handbook of Strategic Alliances*, Thousand Oaks, CA: Sage, pp. 169–97.

Zucker, L.G. (1986), 'Production of trust: Institutional sources of economic structure', in L.L. Cummings and B.M. Staw (eds), *Research in organizational behavior*, Vol. **8**, Greenwich, CT: JAI Press, pp. 53–111.

9 The dark side of trust[1]

Martin Gargiulo and Gokhan Ertug

Introduction

Research on trust has seen a notable resurgence in the last two decades. Although there were some important contributions to the literature on trust after Deutsch's initial work (Deutsch, 1958; 1962), such contributions were sporadic until the late 1980s (for example, Kee and Knox, 1970; Zand, 1972; Luhmann, 1979; Barber, 1983). The influential article by Zucker (1986) and the collective volume edited by Gambetta (1988a) marked the beginning of the ongoing revival in research on trust. An increasing number of books (Fukuyama, 1995) and edited volumes (most notably Kramer and Tyler, 1995 and Lane and Bachmann, 1998), as well as special issues of the *Academy of Management Review* (Zaheer et al., 1998), *Organization Studies* (Bachmann et al., 2001) and *Organization Science* (McEvily et al., 2003) attest to the increasing interest in trust in general and in organizational settings in particular. Such efforts have resulted in an impressive body of research that encompasses both theoretical reflections and empirical studies.

Despite the diversity of approaches, practically all the existing studies stress the benefits trust can bring to the parties involved. This optimistic bias has been also noticed in related areas such as 'social capital' (Portes, 1998; Gargiulo and Benassi, 2000) and network forms of organizations (Podolny and Page, 1998). The lack of attention to this 'dark side' of trust has hampered the emergence of a more balanced and complete perspective on the nature and the effects of trust in general, and of what we will term 'excessive' trust in particular. Researchers often recognize that malfeasance may be more likely in contexts of high trust, but this acknowledgement rarely goes beyond a passing mention that has no bearing on the kernel of the discussion. Still less consideration has been given to the possibility that excessive trust may have negative effects for individuals and organizations even in the absence of malfeasance.

This chapter seeks to correct the optimistic bias that permeates the research on trust and to contribute to a more integrated theoretical approach to the effects of trust on outcomes that affect the well-being of the parties to a relationship. Specifically, we will argue that the detrimental effects of trust are closely linked with its purported benefits. First, trust diminishes information gathering and processing costs by reducing the need for monitoring and vigilance, but it can lead also to blind faith, which substantially increases the risk of malfeasance. Second, trust leads to greater satisfaction with and commitment to a relationship, but it can also lead to complacency and to the acceptance of less-than-satisfactory outcomes from such a relationship. Third, trust leads to expanded communication and information exchanges, but it can lead also to over-embedded relationships that create unnecessary obligations between the parties.

While the three types of detrimental effects discussed here may and do have empirical overlaps, we believe that it is useful to keep them analytically separate in so far as their effects on relational outcomes rest on distinct mechanisms. To undertake the discussion of each of these effects, however, it is necessary to conduct a brief review of the very concept of trust and of the main antecedents and consequences of trust highlighted in the literature. The definition of trust has occupied a considerable part of the discussion on the subject. Having some clarity on the notion of trust is essential to discuss its detrimental effects. Throughout the chapter, we will focus on organizational contexts, yet we will cite research in psychology and sociology selectively to the extent that it has had a noticeable impact on studies in organizational settings.

What is trust?

The definition of trust has occupied a considerable part of the literature on trust. The result of this preoccupation has been a number of disparate and *ad hoc* definitions based on equally different assumptions (Sheppard and Sherman, 1998). It was indeed this fascination with finding 'the' definition of trust that drove the editors of a recent special issue to state that perhaps the endeavor has claimed more attention than it deserves (McEvily et al. 2003). Yet this very lack of conceptual convergence makes it difficult to write an article on trust – or on the dark side of trust, for that matter – without clarifying some basic definitional issues and taking a clear stand in this respect.

Practically all definitions agree that trust is a belief that reflects an actor's expectations (the trustor) about another actor (the trustee).[2] This apparent agreement, however, conceals differences among numerous conceptualizations about the object, the nature and the preconditions of trust. Regarding the object of trust, the difference lies in whether it refers to the trustee's intentions or behaviors. Do we trust that someone intends to behave in a way that honors the trust we place in her, or do we trust that she will actually behave in such a way? A fruitful way to address this dilemma is to notice that the difference reflects the ability of the trustee to behave according to her intentions. A person may want to honor the trust we place in her but she may be unable to do so due to circumstances that are beyond her immediate control. Skill is one such circumstance. I can trust a friend's intentions to help me with my financial decisions, but I will not trust her advice unless I am convinced of her financial expertise. Although the trustor may find it easier to get information on the trustee's abilities than on her intentions, the dominant approach has been to include both the intentions and the ability of the trustee in the definition of trust (e.g. Mayer et al. 1995).

The second important definitional issue concerns the nature of the trustee's intentions. Here the relevant distinction is between expecting that the trustee intends to cooperate actively with the trustor or that she merely intends to behave in a non-harmful way. In other words, is trust based on the expectation that the trustee intends to refrain from acting in ways that could be detrimental to the trustor (even though such behavior may be to the trustee's benefit), or is trust based on the expectation that the trustee will actively help the trustor, even at the expense of her own benefit? While the second alternative may be required in some settings, we prefer to adopt the less restrictive approach and define trust based on the expectation that the trustee intends to behave in a way that is not detrimental to the trustor. Thus the trustor expects that the trustee does not intend to behave opportunistically, taking advantage of situations in which the trustee can derive benefits at the expense of the trustor.

The third definitional issue is somewhat implicit in the second, for it refers to the existence of opportunities to defect. Deutsch (1962) pointed out that trust is less likely to emerge in situations that offer few or no opportunities for the trustee to act in a way that can be harmful to the trustor (Malhotra and Murnighan, 2002; Molm et al., 2000). Such situations are characterized by a lack of interdependence between the trustor and the trustee, by the existence of binding contracts that constrain the trustee's behavior, or by the trustee's inability to defect. In these cases, the appropriate behavior of the trustee is secured by situational constraints. The trustor does not need to have any specific expectations about the intentions of the trustee. On the contrary, the lack of such constraints creates opportunities for defection and the trustor is less likely to risk entering exchanges unless he feels he can trust the trustee's intentions (Gambetta, 1988b; Kelley and Thibaut, 1978: 237). Trust, therefore, is more likely to emerge when defection is possible.

The previous discussion suggests that trust can be defined as the willingness of a party (the trustor) to be vulnerable to the actions of another party (the trustee) based on the expectation that the trustee intends and is able to perform in ways that will not harm the trustor in a particular situation, irrespective of the trustor's ability to control the trustee's behavior. This definition is consistent with those provided by Mayer et al. (1995) as well as by Rousseau et al. (1998).

The antecedents of trust

The literature identifies dispositional, relational and situational factors that can promote trust. Dispositional factors refer to the role of individual traits of the people involved and to the similarity (or dissimilarity) of such traits in promoting trust. Relational factors comprise both the history of direct interactions between actors and their indirect interactions through common third parties; they are essentially similar to what Zucker (1986) dubbed 'process-based trust'. Situational factors refer to the presence of uncertainty regarding the behavior of the parties – that is, the risk that a party may behave in a way that harms the other.

Dispositional factors acknowledge that individuals differ in their predisposition to trust others (Gurtman, 1992). In so far as an individual is highly predisposed to trust other people, one can expect that trust is more likely to emerge in the relationships entered by this particular individual. If both actors are highly predisposed to trust others, the likelihood for trust to emerge and to prosper in their relationship should be high (Becerra and Gupta, 2003).

Although dispositional factors typically refer to individual traits, researchers have stressed also the effects of the similarity of such individual traits in fostering trust. The vast literature on 'homophily' shows that trust is more likely to emerge between parties that are 'similar' along some relevant characteristics. Yet the nature and the salience of those characteristics are contingent upon social settings and thus may vary across cultures and across time, making it difficult to build normative theory on the effects of similarity on the emergence of trust. Scholars have tried to go beyond that limitation by building on the concept of in-group bias (Brewer, 1979), suggesting that trust is more likely to occur between actors who belong to the same category. Thus Zucker (1986) argues that people who have a shared attitude towards daily life and a mutual understanding of each other's perspectives are also likely to have common expectations about each other's behavior, which facilitates the emergence of trust. In a similar vein, McKnight et al. (1998) posited that individuals who are members of the same category tend to share goals and values, and to have positive perceptions about each other, which renders them more likely to trust group members than strangers. A recent seven-nation study by Huff and Kelley (2003) confirms that individuals place higher trust in people from their own national or ethnic group than in those who do not belong to such group.

Because actors who are members of the same group are more likely to share similar values, attitudes and behaviors, similar group membership can act as a signal that prompts same-group members to place higher trust in actors within their same groups. In this sense, same-group membership shapes the expectations about the other actor's behavior, facilitating the placement of trust. The classical example is Weber's (1946) essay on the Protestant sects and the spirit of capitalism in the USA, where he stresses that reputable sects only admitted members whose thoroughly checked conduct made them appear morally qualified beyond doubt (Weber, 1946: 305).

Relational factors are based on past direct or indirect experiences in which the behavior of the 'trustee' can be more accurately ascertained. The number of past direct interactions and the duration of the current relationship increase the communication and exchanges between the parties (Shapiro et al., 1992; Rempel et al., 1985), contributing to the emergence and consolidation of what Lewicki and Bunker (1995) called 'knowledge-based trust'. Kollock (1994) provides the most direct evidence in this respect. In an experimental study, he finds ongoing interaction and the number of past exchanges between a buyer and a seller lead to an increase in trust (Kollock, 1994: 336). This relationship held even when the quality of the good to be exchanged was known beforehand, hence eliminating uncertainty. In an empirical study of 175 cross-functional dyadic manager relationships, McAllister (1995) found that interaction frequency between managers increased the affect-based trust between those managers.

Although focusing mostly on third-party effects on trust, Burt and Knez (1995) also show evidence that confirms the direct effects of relational factors. They found that the probability of trust was positively associated to the frequency of interaction, duration and emotional closeness in the relationship between the parties. At the inter-organizational level, Gulati (1995) found that the number of previous alliances between two partners makes it less likely that future alliances between these partners will be equity based. Because equity-based alliances are costlier to exit, they provide a form of insurance against defection. Yet such alliances are also costlier to negotiate and to organize and – it is argued – were therefore more likely to be used when partners could not trust each other's intentions due to the lack of experience with each other.

Relational factors can also operate indirectly through common third parties. Burt and Knez (1995) present convincing evidence that trust – but also distrust – between two actors is significantly amplified by the presence of mutual contacts. More specifically, they found that mutual third parties that are equally close to both actors increase the probability of trust between those actors, whereas third parties that are closer to one of the actors than to the other increase the probability of distrust between the actors. To account for these findings, the authors invoke a mechanism by which third parties were active in disseminating information while seeking to do it in accordance with the opinions of his or her closer associate in the triad. These findings are consistent with field research in the New York apparel industry, in which Uzzi (1996: 679) found that 'embedded' ties (which are characterized by high levels of trust) result mainly from third-party referral networks, as well as from prior personal relationships. According to Uzzi, those pre-existing ties set expectations for trust between the actors and bring resources from those prior ties into the new economic exchange.

Situational factors take into account the context in which the relationship between the parties evolves. The development of trust is contingent upon the presence of uncertainty – that is, upon the risk that a party could behave opportunistically in ways that would harm the interests of the other party. When a party is unable to behave opportunistically due to situational constraints, her partner is unlikely to attribute the observed behavior to the party's trustworthiness. Conversely, if the party can defect but chooses to cooperate, her behavior can be taken as a sign of trustworthiness.

The relationship between uncertainty and trust has been depicted in a number of theoretical studies (e.g. Blau, 1964; Luhmann, 1979; Gambetta, 1988b). The strongest supporting evidence comes from experimental studies on exchange. Kollock (1994) ran a number of experiments where the quality of the exchanged goods was not known to the buyer before consummating the transaction. The buyer, however, could know beforehand whether there was variance in the quality of the goods offered by the seller. Buyers were significantly more likely to trust sellers in situations where the quality of the goods was uncertain – that is, when the seller had a choice on the quality of the goods offered in exchange. The result was independent of the frequency of transactions involving a particular seller. Indeed, even the partner with the lowest frequency of interaction in the uncertain category was perceived as more trustworthy than the partner with the highest frequency of interaction in the certain quality category. Malhotra and Murnighan (2002) investigated the effects of risk in the development of trust within a trust game experiment.[3] The authors manipulated the presence of two types of contracts regulating the exchanges. Binding contracts did not offer players any opportunity to exploit the other partner, whereas such opportunities did exist with non-binding contracts. The removal of a binding contract led to a significant reduction in the number of trusting choices subsequently made by the subjects. This was not the case with the removal of a non-binding contract, since the absence of exploitative behavior in this case conveyed information on the partner's intentions (see also Molm et al., 2000). These studies suggest that exchanges in which reciprocity cannot be taken for granted provide a more fertile ground for the development of trust than exchanges where such honoring is dictated by binding contracts, and thus the partner's behavior cannot convey information on her intentions.

To summarize, the development of trust is facilitated by individual characteristics that make people more likely either to trust others in general or to trust each other in particular, as well as by the frequency and intensity of their direct or indirect exchanges. Yet the effectiveness of these factors in fostering the development of trust is contingent on the presence of uncertainty regarding the trustee's behavior. Dispositional and relational factors act as signals on the likely behavior of the trustee in the future, whereas situational factors – specifically, opportunities for defection – are essential to interpret observable behavior as an indicator of non-observable intentions.

The behavioral consequences of trust

Trust has been associated with a number of observable behaviors. Although practically all the existing studies document an association between such behaviors and positive outcomes for one or both parties to a relationship, we will seek to present the behavioral consequences of trust in a neutral fashion. While this will not be always easy given the optimistic bias in the literature, our behavioral focus is essential for the aim in this chapter. Indeed, we will argue that while the behaviors prompted by trust are normally beneficial, too high levels of those same behaviors can cause negative outcomes. Following this approach, we identify three distinct behavioral consequences of trust. First, trust is associated with lower levels of monitoring, vigilance and safeguards towards the behavior of the trusted party. Second, trust is associated with higher levels of commitment to the relationship with the trusted party. Third, trust is associated with an expansion of the scale and scope of the exchange between the parties. We discuss each of these consequences separately.

Monitoring, vigilance and safeguards

The level of trust within a relationship is negatively related to the levels of monitoring and with the number of safeguards put in place by one or both parties to a relationship. As we argued earlier, the emergence of trust requires relatively low levels of monitoring and safeguards (Malhotra and Murnighan, 2002), yet the presence of trust also reduces the inclination to guard against opportunistic behavior through safeguards or monitoring (Bromiley and Cummings, 1995). In the same vein, McEvily et al. (2003: 97) have argued that trust is associated with lower levels of vigilance. Empirical evidence comes from both organizational and experimental studies. In a recent paper, Szulanski et al. (2004) show that trust in a party was associated with a reduction in the screening of knowledge received from that party. In a study of 71 teams, Langfred (2004) found that trust was a strong and significant negative predictor of monitoring. These studies are consistent with earlier research that uncovered a positive relationship between trust and the perceived accuracy of information received. Benton and his colleagues (Benton et al., 1969), as well as Roberts and O'Reilly (1974) found that trust in a partner was positively related to the perceived accuracy of information received from that partner.

Commitment

Trust has been associated with higher levels of commitment within a relationship, as well as with lower levels of conflict, which in turn lower the likelihood of exit. In an early experimental study of managerial decision-making groups, Zand (1972) found that trust in the current 'company' (here represented by the subjects' decision-making group) had a negative association with the intention to take a job in another company. In a longitudinal follow-up study of 125 alumni of a graduate business school, Robinson (1996) found that employees who had reported trusting their employer in the past were less likely to quit their jobs after a breach in the psychological contract by this employer (see also Tyler, 1994; Saparito et al., 2004). Brockner and his colleagues (Brockner et al., 1997) provided an important refinement to the relationship between trust and commitment, showing that this link cannot be fully explained by favorable outcomes. In a series of studies, the authors found that the positive association between trust and support for a supervisor was stronger in cases when the supervisor's decisions resulted in unfavorable outcomes for the trustor. Finally, Tyler and Degoey (1996) found that trust in a person occupying an authority position led to greater deference in response to actions taken by that person.

Consistent with these findings linking trust and commitment, scholars have shown also that trust leads to lower levels of conflict in relationships. De Dreu and his collaborators (De Dreu et al., 1998) report a negative association between trust and conflict in negotiating dyads, whereas Porter and Lilly (1996) show that high-trust teams have lower levels of intra-group conflict. These studies suggest that the level of trust within a relationship is positively related to the commitment to that relationship and negatively related to the level of conflict and to the likelihood of exit. Trust, in other words, introduces an element of stability in relationships.

Scale and scope of relationships
A third set of findings links trust to the expansion in the scale and scope of relationships. Specifically, this research shows that trust is associated with a number of observable phenomena such as greater and more open communication, multiplex relationships, as well as with greater and richer resource exchanges. The association between trust and enhanced communication has been documented for both interpersonal and inter-organizational relationships. At the interpersonal level, Zand (1972) and Boss (1978) found trust to have a positive effect on openness in communication in groups. Groups whose participants had more trust in each other were more open in voicing their ideas. At the inter-organizational level, Smith and Barclay (1997) found that trust had a positive effect on the openness of communication among alliance partners. In addition to improving the scale of communication between parties, trust also has a positive effect on the scope of communication. In a number of studies across different settings, researchers have documented that higher levels of trust lead to higher volumes of information transfer between the trusting partners (O'Reilly and Roberts, 1974; Roberts and O'Reilly, 1974; Dirks, 1999).

By improving both the scale and the scope of communication, trust results in thicker and richer exchange relationships, effectively 'expanding' the relationship between partners (McEvily et al., 2003). This theme is also elaborated upon by Brian Uzzi in a number of papers on embedded ties, characterized by high levels of trust (Uzzi, 1996, 1997; Uzzi and Gillespie, 2002; Uzzi and Lancaster, 2003). Specifically, 'information exchange in embedded relationships was more proprietary and tacit than the price and quantity data that were traded in arm's length ties' (Uzzi, 1997: 45). Embedded ties are also likely to account for a greater part of overall business volume, even if they are typically fewer than arm's-length relationships. In line with this argument, Tsai and Ghoshal (1998) found that perceived trustworthiness of the other unit led to greater exchange of resource between the units of a large multinational electronics company.

High-trust relationships are also more likely to result in multiplex ties – that is, in ties containing several economic or social exchanges between the parties. Indeed, this is an essential aspect of embedded relationships (Uzzi, 1996; Uzzi and Gillespie, 2002). A similar observation was also made by Ring and Van de Ven (1994), who observe that relationships originated in purely formal or economic concerns are often supplemented by informal personal ties governed by different norms and values. Multiplex ties may also exist among organizations, as they build on the trust present in one area of their exchange to facilitate the emergence of yet another area (e.g. Gulati, 1995; McEvily et al., 2003).

Our survey of the consequences of trust aimed to present these consequences as a list of observable behaviors or attitudes associated with the level of trust in the corresponding relationship. In principle, those behaviors can be either beneficial for or detrimental to the parties involved, and particularly to the trustor. However, an overwhelming majority of the research on trust interprets these findings in a positive fashion, focusing on the positive effects of trust on the parties to the relationship. While the focus of this chapter is on the detrimental effects of trust, we will provide first a brief overview of research that focused on the positive outcomes trust can have for one or more parties to a relationship, which will allow us to make clearer the contrast with the negative outcomes.

The benefits of trust

An impressive body of empirical research supports the claim that trust is beneficial for the parties involved in an exchange, at both the interpersonal and inter-organizational level. In one of the earliest experimental studies of the effects of trust, Zand (1972) studied the relationship between trust and problem solving. Manipulating the level of trust among group members, he found that members of high-trust groups achieve higher scores than low-trust groups in a number of dimensions, measured both through self-reports and by outside observers. Subsequent studies have gone beyond this general association between trust and performance to link benefits to the specific behaviors fostered by trust. We have classified the benefits associated with trust in three categories. First, trust lowers information-processing costs. Second, trust increases satisfaction with the relationship. Third, trust reduces uncertainty regarding the behavior of the other party. As we will see, each of these three types of benefits can be associated with the effects of the specific behaviors promoted by trust reviewed in the previous section.

Lower information processing costs

The effects of trust in lowering monitoring and in reducing safeguards has led scholars to propose that trust allows for economizing in information processing (McEvily et al., 2003; Luhmann, 1979). Because monitoring and safeguards are costly, trust-based relationships should be substantially cheaper to maintain than those in which trust is absent or kept to a minimum. This prediction has been confirmed in a number of studies focusing on buyer–supplier relationships. Pooling data from 344 buyer–supplier relationships in the automotive industry, Dyer and Chu (2003) found that a supplier's trust in the buyer is associated with lower costs of monitoring and enforcement after the transaction, as well as with increased information sharing and higher procurement productivity – measured by the dollar value of parts an procurement employee can purchase – as well as with performance – measured in terms of return on assets.

Increased satisfaction

The relationship between trust and satisfaction is perhaps the most robustly established finding in research on the consequences of trust. Muchinsky (1977) found organizational trust to be a significant and positive predictor of employees' satisfaction with their pay, co-workers, promotions, work and supervision. Driscoll (1978) also found that employees with higher levels of organizational trust were more satisfied with their jobs as well as with their participation in decision-making (see also Rich, 1997). In a similar vein, Schurr and Ozanne (1985) found that trust in the partner within buying–selling relationships was positively linked to satisfaction with that partner. Finally, Balasubramanian et al. (2003) found that the perceived trustworthiness of the broker predicted investors' satisfaction in two different samples of online investing.

The positive relationship between trust and satisfaction appears also in studies focusing on specific events. Thus Zand (1972) found an association between trust and satisfaction with a problem-solving meeting (also see Boss, 1978). Roberts and O'Reilly (1974) found that trust in their superiors was a significant predictor of employees' level of satisfaction with intra-organizational communication (see also O'Reilly and Roberts, 1974). Finally, Pillai and his colleagues (Pillai et al., 1999) show that trust mediates the relationship between leader behavior and employee satisfaction. While satisfaction might be highly subjective, a study that examined 175 cross-functional dyadic relationships between managers sheds light on some of the mechanisms that may underlie the positive link between trust and satisfaction. McAllister (1995) found that a manager who had high levels of affect-based trust in a colleague would engage more in need-based monitoring, attending to the other party's problems, trying to be of help, as well as engaging in more interpersonal citizenship behavior towards that colleague, factors that are likely to enhance performance and loyalty among the employees.

The link between trust, satisfaction and performance has also been established using more behavioral measures. In an empirical study of restaurants, Davis et al. (2000) found that establishments where the general manager was perceived as more trustworthy by the employees had higher sales, higher profits and lower turnover than those in which the manager was perceived as less trustworthy. Analyzing buyer–supplier dyads, Zaheer et al. (1998) found that the buyer's trust in the supplier was associated with lower levels of conflict and lower negotiation costs.

Lower uncertainty
The benefits of trust in inter-organizational relationships are also an important component in the stream of research led by Brian Uzzi and his colleagues (Uzzi, 1996; 1997; Uzzi and Gillespie, 2002; Uzzi and Lancaster, 2003). These empirical studies use qualitative and quantitative evidence showing that the sharing of sensitive, fine-grained, or proprietary information makes embedded relationships more adaptable and leads to tangible benefits such as a decrease in penalties due to late credit payments and increases in discount bonuses owing to early repayment of credits. Similarly, Noteboom et al. (1997) used data from supplier's reports on 97 supplier–buyer relationships to show that higher levels of trust were associated with lower perceived probability of loss that might result from the relationship, but not with the size of the loss if a problem were to occur. Zaheer et al. (1998) found that trust in the buyer–supplier relationship had a direct effect on the supplier's performance regarding competitive pricing, punctual delivery and high-quality supply, as assessed by the buyer.

This brief review of the empirical research on the benefits of trust illustrates the optimistic bias mentioned in the introduction to this chapter. When scholars do hint at potential problems associated with trust, they typically refer to 'distrust' and 'suspicion', as Kramer (1999) does in his recent review of trust and distrust in organizations. The notable exception is the research stream led by Uzzi and his colleagues. Despite sharing the optimistic tone on the benefits of high-trust embedded relationships, Uzzi and his colleagues clearly raise concerns about the possibility that embeddedness – and hence trust – may have a dark side that hinders performance. Specifically, Uzzi (1997) has argued that there is a curvilinear relationship between embeddedness and performance, which suggests that high levels of embeddedness may be actually detrimental for the parties involved. This brings us to the central concern of this chapter.

The dark side of trust
The possibility that trust could be associated with negative outcomes has seldom been explored in the literature, either theoretically or empirically (see Langfred, 2004 and Szulanski et al., 2004 for two recent exceptions). Yet scholars have repeatedly lamented the lack of systematic research on the 'dark side' of trust. In an article that appeared some

years ago, Zaheer et al. (1998: 156) were already encouraging research aimed at examining the 'downside' of trust in inter-organizational relations. Five years later, however, the same authors felt compelled to raise a similar concern in their article for the special issue of *Organization Science* devoted to the topic, suggesting that little progress had been made in this respect (McEvily et al., 2003: 100).

An important portion of the research on trust alludes to the potentially detrimental effects of trust, but those allusions rarely occupy more than a passing mention in the discussion of the limitations of the work or suggestions for future research. For example, Dirks and Ferrin (2001: 464) build on Granovetter (1985) to state that trust generates greater opportunities for both cooperation and malfeasance. In the same vein, Noteboom et al. (1997: 311) argue that trust also carries the risk of betrayal. Researchers seem to agree on the idea that trust can at times have negative consequences for one or more of the parties involved, but there is little conceptual clarity on how the effects of trust can become negative or on the nature of such negative effects. Mirroring this theoretical underdevelopment, there is also scant empirical evidence on the detrimental effects of trust. While most of the existing research has focused largely on the perils of 'insufficient' trust, our concern in this chapter is with the perils of 'excessive' trust.

Figure 9.1 depicts the relationship between levels of trust and benefits that guides our discussion in this chapter. Our main argument is straightforward: while the behaviors fostered by trust – lower monitoring, greater commitment, and greater scale and scope of exchanges – can (and typically do) result in significant benefits for the trustor, the net effects of such behaviors on benefits may become negative beyond some critical threshold. In so far as the level of trust in a relationship affects the level of those behaviors, we expect trust to have an inverted u-shaped relationship with the net benefits of trust.

Our concern in this chapter is to specify the mechanisms responsible for the downward slope of the curve. To this end, we draw upon the same three behavioral consequences of

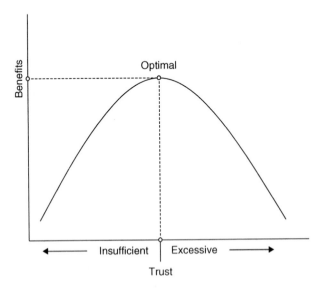

Figure 9.1   The relationship between trust and benefits

trust (monitoring, commitment and embedding) and argue that they can generate detrimental effects when the level of trust pushes those behaviors beyond a critical threshold. To present our arguments, we will compare the effects of 'optimal' versus 'excessive' trust, showing how excessive trust increases the speed at which the behaviors fostered by trust reach and eventually surpass a critical threshold beyond which the effects of trust turn negative. Specifically, we will discuss three ways in which excessive trust can bring about negative outcomes for the trustor. First, excessive trust can lead to 'blind faith'. This drives the trustor to reduce the monitoring of the behavior of the trustee beyond an optimal threshold, which increases both the risk of malfeasance and the potential damage such malfeasance might cause if it occurs. Second, excessive trust can turn commitment into complacency, which may impair the trustor's ability to react to declining performance by the trustee. Third, excessive trust can lead to a rapid expansion of a relationship beyond the optimal level determined by the interdependence and the uncertainty that characterize the initial exchange between the parties, creating unnecessary obligations that act as constraints for the trustor. We discuss these three ways to the dark side of trust separately.

Blind faith

As implicit in the definition adopted in this chapter, trust involves a cognitive 'leap of faith' regarding the future behavior of the trustee beyond the assurances provided by available information (Lewis and Weigert, 1985). Our survey of the consequences of trust has shown that this leap of faith results in lower levels of monitoring, vigilance and safeguards regarding the behavior of the trustee. By allowing the trustor to reduce the investment in these protective measures, trust reduces the associated information–processing costs (Luhmann, 1979), resulting in net benefits for the trustor. Yet the leap of faith implicit in trust can venture well beyond what is reasonable. This 'excessive' trust leads the trustor to remove safeguards and to reduce monitoring to levels that expose the trustor to malfeasance and that might even invite such malfeasance.

Figure 9.2 illustrates the link between trust and monitoring at different stages of development in the relationship. An actor typically reduces the monitoring of a partner's behavior as their relationship develops over time. Ideally, the reduction in monitoring must accompany the level of relationship development, which typically diminishes the uncertainty about the partner's intentions and prospective behavior. Yet the reduction in monitoring should not surpass an 'optimal' threshold, defined by the amount of damage the trustee could inflict on the trustor if he decides to behave opportunistically. Excessive initial trust, however, may increase the speed at which the trustor deactivates monitoring mechanisms and safeguards, reaching the minimum threshold at a relatively early stage of relationship development (t_1). At this point, the trustor has a deficit of monitoring represented by the segment *ab* on the vertical axis. This deficit increases as the relationship evolves, leaving the trustor increasingly exposed to malfeasance (Granovetter, 1985). This is the essence of the 'blind faith': while trust *always* implies a 'leap of faith' at the onset, excessive trust causes that leap to go well beyond what is reasonable given the nature of the exchange and the history of the relationship.

For simplicity, Figure 9.2 does not represent the possibility that excessive trust could cause a drop in the level of monitoring at the beginning of the relationship (point *c* on the vertical axis). Thus excessive trust can affect both the initial level of monitoring of the

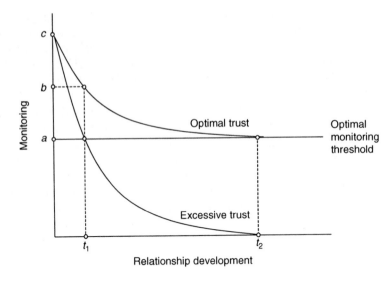

Figure 9.2   Monitoring and safeguards, by levels of trust

trustee's behavior as well as the reduction of monitoring through the development of the relationship.

The substantial reduction in monitoring caused by excessive trust increases both the opportunities for malfeasance and the amount of damage such malfeasance may cause to the trustor. The link between excessive trust and malfeasance operates through two complementary mechanisms. On one hand, reduced vigilance and safeguards render the trustor less able to detect or preempt malfeasance before it actually occurs. This is similar to Deutsch's (1958) notion of 'pathological trust', characterized by excessive gullibility and credulousness that may invite malfeasance. On the other hand, excessive trust puts the trustee in a better position to take greater advantage of the trustor if he wishes to do so. Indeed, because the trustee is more likely to have sensitive information about the trustor, the damage caused by malfeasance is potentially bigger (Granovetter, 1985). A similar argument was also developed by Lewicki et al. (1998), who argue that very high levels of trust can pave the way for subsequent exploitation unless they are tamed by some level of distrust – which they treat as a different dimension from trust. The authors argue that some level of distrust regarding certain areas or types of behavior limits the areas where a partner *can* be trusted (see also Shapiro, 1987; 1990). The trustor reduces his monitoring of certain aspects of the exchange, liberating resources to maintain adequate vigilance on the remaining aspects.

Malfeasance, however, is not the only way in which blind faith in the trustee may result in negative outcomes for the trustor. The reduction in monitoring and vigilance associated with excessive trust might also affect the quality of the information exchanged between the parties, leading to detrimental effects even in the absence of opportunistic behavior. Three recent empirical articles advance the idea that a minimum level of monitoring and vigilance might be a necessary condition for effective performance. In a study of 71 teams, Langfred (2004) shows that low levels of monitoring resulting from high trust can have negative effects on the performance of teams whose members have considerable autonomy. As the autonomy of the team members increases, so does the potential for coordination losses and process redundancy. Adequate levels of monitoring among team members can mitigate the negative consequences of autonomy (Saavedra et al., 1993). Because monitoring drops with trust, however, excessive trust may have a noticeable negative effect on performance in teams with highly autonomous members. Langfred (2004) furnishes three pieces of evidence in support of his argument. First, trust had an exponential negative effect on monitoring within a team. Second, members' autonomy had a negative main effect on performance. Third, the negative effect of members' autonomy was larger in teams with high levels of trust – and thus with lower internal monitoring.

Szulanski et al. (2004) also unveil the detrimental effects of excessive trust in a study on the effects of vigilance and monitoring on the accuracy of knowledge transfer within organizations. The authors assert that while the effect of trust between the source and recipient on the accuracy of the knowledge transfer is generally positive, this effect reverts to negative as knowledge ambiguity increases. The authors argue that an increase in uncertainty associated with the transfer of ambiguous knowledge requires more vigilance and monitoring on part of the recipient (Lewis and Weigert, 1985; McAllister, 1995; Lewicki et al., 1998). Because trust in the source lowers the recipient's tendency to engage in monitoring the accuracy of the information received, the quality of the transfer suffers. Using data from 122 transfers comprising 38 practices across eight companies, Szulanski et al. (2004) found that trust had the expected positive main effect on transfer effectiveness whereas the effect of causal ambiguity was negative. Yet the interaction between trust and causal ambiguity had a significant negative effect on transfer effectiveness. More specifically, the positive effect of trust vanished where causal ambiguity was one standard deviation above the mean and had an increasingly negative and significant net effect at two and three standard deviations above the mean.

An unpublished experimental study sheds light on the mechanism behind the effects uncovered by Langfred (2004) and by Szulanski et al. (2004). In this experiment, Sinaceur (2005) manipulated trust levels in negotiating dyads and measured its effect on information-seeking behavior and on performance. He found that high-trust dyads displayed significantly lower levels of information-seeking behavior, which in turn resulted in smaller gains for both parties to the negotiation.

To summarize: excessive trust can result in extremely low levels of monitoring and safeguards in a relationship, both of which facilitate opportunistic behavior by the trustee and reduce the trustor's ability to both detect opportunism and to control its negative effects. In addition, very low levels of monitoring impair the trustee's ability and willingness to seek and to analyze the behavior of the trustee, which reduces the alignment of interests and behaviors between the parties. Insufficient monitoring can cause direct harm to the trustor in case of malfeasance, but it can also prevent the trustor from obtaining the maximum benefits from the relationship. These two mechanisms contribute to explain the negative relationship between high levels of trust and benefits.

Complacency
Our review of the consequences of trust highlighted the positive relationship between trust, satisfaction and commitment to a relationship. Commitment facilitates the exchange of sensitive information, alleviates concerns of opportunism, and diminishes

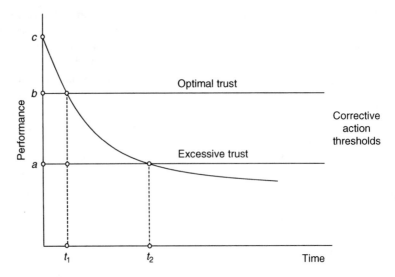

Figure 9.3   Corrective action before performance decline, by levels of trust

the likelihood of exit from a relationship (Uzzi, 1996; Saparito et al., 2004). Yet commitment may also result in relational inertia that traps an actor in an underperforming exchange (Gargiulo and Benassi, 2000). The result of this inertia is complacency. We argue that parties to a high-trust relationship are both less likely to perceive objective deteriorations in performance and will take longer to engage in appropriate corrective action once they acknowledge the deterioration.

Figure 9.3 depicts the theoretical relationship between trust and responses to declining performance. We assume that, beyond a certain threshold, a decline in performance triggers corrective actions aimed at either changing the performance of the partner or terminating the relationship – corresponding respectively to Hirschman's (1970) 'voice' and 'exit' responses to performance decline. Yet this threshold varies with different levels of trust, with optimal trust having a significantly higher threshold than excessive trust relationships. Excessive trust affects both the timing of the corrective action (from the 'optimal' t_1 to t_2) as well as the total decline in performance the actor sustains before taking corrective action. The cost of the 'complacency' prompted by excessive trust corresponds to the excess decline in performance from b to a, as well as to the negative effects such decline may cause during the t_1-t_2 period.

How does commitment become complacency? Two main mechanisms may be at work. The first is relational. High-trust relationships typically develop into an intricate set of mutual obligations and commitments (Uzzi, 1996), which should amplify the cost of corrective action. Before voicing concerns about declining performance to a highly trusted partner, the affected party may consider the negative effects that action might have on the relationship. Paradoxically, trust may make it more, not less difficult to address performance problems between partners. The second mechanism is cognitive. High-trust breeds strong bonds of familiarity and mutual understanding that greatly facilitate cooperation (Gulati, 1995). However, the same strong bonds may also serve as a filter for information and perspectives reaching the actors, generating a 'cognitive lock-in' that isolates them from the outer world (Grabher, 1993; Uzzi 1997). The ease of cooperation with familiar partners, and the uncertainty associated with entering an alternative relationship, raises the cost of investing in new relationships, effectively lowering the likelihood of exit. This 'relational inertia' (Gargiulo and Benassi, 2000) can make high-trust relationships extremely resilient to losses in their instrumental value. Relational inertia may be compounded by the weaker monitoring mechanisms described earlier, which make the affected party less likely to detect early signs of declining performance. The combined effects of relational and cognitive lock-in prompted by excessive trust push down the performance threshold for corrective action. Actors in such a situation are less likely to acknowledge the decline – perhaps brushing it aside as a 'temporary' setback – and will take longer to use corrective action, enduring more serious performance losses. In sum: excessive trust in one's partners delays the triggering of corrective action facing an objective performance decline, which causes larger and more sustained losses in benefits for the trustor before corrective action is ultimately engaged upon.

Unnecessary obligations
The third way in which excessive trust may have a detrimental effect is by leading one or both parties to take on obligations that go beyond what is required to secure the exchange that prompted the relationship in the first place (Wicks et al., 1998). Recall that trust is an efficient way to economize information–processing costs whenever an actor depends on another for a certain exchange and when there is uncertainty regarding the behavior of the other party (Luhmann, 1979; Gambetta, 1988b). To minimize that uncertainty, actors engage in actions that signal their willingness to reciprocate the cooperation of their partners. As discussed, these actions typically lead to an expansion of the scale and scope of the initial relationship. The higher the trust, the higher is the probability that the relationship becomes embedded in multiplex ties (Uzzi, 1996). While embedding may reduce the uncertainty surrounding the exchanges, it also creates obligations that constrain the behavior of the trustor. It is entirely possible that the relationship evolves beyond an optimal level of embedding determined by the uncertainty of the main exchange, creating unnecessary obligations for the parties. This is precisely the nature of the problem that Uzzi (1997) identified as the 'over-embedding' of economic transactions.

Figure 9.4 compares levels of obligations for optimal and excessive trust over different levels of relationship development. We assume that, for any given exchange, there is an 'optimal' embedding threshold. Beyond that threshold, the initial relationship becomes 'over-embedded', which can generate unnecessary obligations that have negative effects on performance (Uzzi, 1997). In a relationship with optimal trust, the actor approaches the optimal level as the relationship develops, but embedding (and thus obligations) stabilizes as it gets closer to the optimal level. In a relationship characterized by 'excessive' trust, however, the actors either rush into establishing mutual obligations at relatively early stages of their relationship or they establish higher levels of trust than are required by the nature of the relationship (Wicks et al., 1998). The intrinsic dynamic of embedded relationships rapidly makes the actors reach the optimal embedding threshold at t_1. At t_2, the point at which the relationship should have reached the optimal embedding threshold a, the excessive trust relationship would have reached a level of embedding corresponding to point b on the vertical axis. The segment ab in that axis captures the extent to which

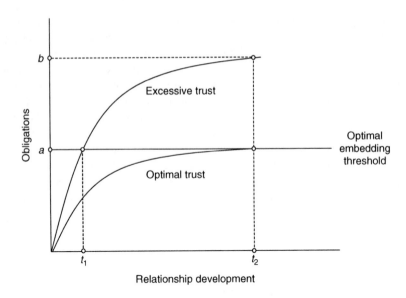

Figure 9.4 Relationship obligations, by levels of trust

the actors have incurred unnecessary obligations that commit resources and constrain their choices beyond what would have been optimal for their given exchange.

By accelerating and over-expanding the level of embedding in a relationship, excessive trust burdens actors with mutual obligations whose marginal effect in reducing uncertainty is smaller than the associated costs. These obligations are likely to result in an increased number of suboptimal exchanges, as the current partners would be preferred for new exchanges over otherwise valid alternatives. This, in turn, would further reduce the awareness of the existence and the capabilities of those alternative partners, consolidating the locking in of the actors into suboptimal relationships.

Unveiling the dark side of trust
This chapter has attempted to explain the dark side of trust by unveiling the mechanisms through which extreme levels of trust can have detrimental consequences for the parties. Our discussion has shown that while the behaviors prompted by trust are normally beneficial, extreme levels of those same behaviors can have negative effects. In doing so, we draw a direct connection between the detrimental effects of trust and its purported benefits. First, trust diminishes information-processing costs by reducing the need for monitoring and vigilance, but excessive trust can lead to blind faith, which substantially increases the risk of malfeasance and impoverishes the quality of information transfer between parties. Second, trust increases satisfaction by promoting commitment to a relationship, but excessive trust can lead to complacency and passivity in the face of inadequate outcomes from such a relationship. Third, trust reduces uncertainty by promoting greater scale and scope of communication, but excessive trust can lead to over-embedded relationships loaded with unnecessary obligations between the parties, trapping them into inadequate exchange schemes and consuming resources without bringing the associated benefits.

Figure 9.5 summarizes our argument linking the antecedents, behavioral consequences

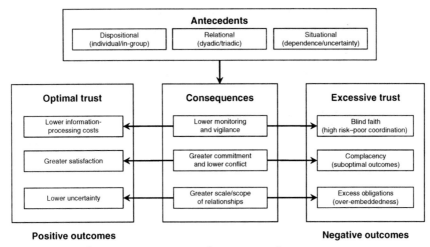

Figure 9.5   Antecedents, consequences and outcomes of trust

and outcomes of trust. Each of the three behavioral consequences of trust can lead to either positive or negative outcomes. We have linked negative outcomes to the notion of 'excessive' trust, in accordance with the idea that the level of trust has an inverted u-shaped relationship with benefits. We have argued that the negative outcomes associated with extreme levels of trust are prompted by the same behaviors that would typically cause benefits. Excessive trust, however, pushes such behaviors to levels that can leave the trustor without adequate vigilance and safeguards (blind faith), can dampen his capacity to react to performance decline (complacency) or can push him into accepting excessive obligations towards the partner (over-embeddedness).

Two comments on this figure are worth noting. First, the notion of 'excessive' trust (as opposite to 'insufficient' or 'optimal') is only identifiable by its consequences on observable outcomes. This implies that the researcher cannot establish beforehand what the optimal level of trust in a given setting would be. The researcher can estimate that optimal level from the available data, but this would be valid only for the specific context. Like most models that propose curvilinear relationships between the variables of interest, the theoretical insight of our model does not depend on the specific value of the optimal level for the independent variable, but rather on the fact that there *is* such an optimal level. Second, we do not venture any propositions linking specific antecedents to specific behavioral consequences (or outcomes) of trust. It is indeed possible that some antecedents have greater impact on specific consequences or outcomes, but we do not have at this point enough theoretical or empirical foundations to formulate such links. Rather, we advocate treating the association between the types of antecedents on one hand and behavioral consequences or outcomes on the other as an open question, using the results of empirical research to formulate additional hypotheses in this respect whenever convenient.

Our discussion of the ways in which excessive trust can cause negative outcomes suggests that research on the dark side of trust should attempt to include specific measures capturing the levels of monitoring, complacency and embeddedness in the relationships. Such measures would allow for testing both the effects of trust on the levels of these mediating variables, as well as the effects of such variables on outcomes. This emphasis on specific measures of the intervening variables is apparent in some recent papers (e.g. Langfred, 2004), but the bulk of the empirical research on trust has relied on measures of trust on one hand and outcomes on the other, without paying sufficient attention to – much less measuring – the intervening mechanisms. By drawing attention to the mechanisms, we hope our chapter can stimulate research in which the processes through which trust causes both negative and positive outcomes can be elucidated more thoroughly.

Lastly, we have not speculated about the specific circumstances or conditions that are likely to prompt actors into what we called 'excessive' trust. While an adequate exploration of those conditions would merit a chapter in itself, two possible hypotheses come to mind. First, extreme levels of trust can result from extreme values of the antecedents of trust. Dispositional factors contribute to the presence of trust in a relationship, but they also make people more vulnerable to malfeasance. An individual who is highly predisposed to trust others is also more at risk of exploitation by untrustworthy partners. It is one thing to meet someone from the same country while abroad; it is another to find out that he is actually from the same town, went to the same college and frequented the same health clubs we did. While it is entirely possible that every new joint affiliation increases the level of initial trust linearly, it is more likely that the level of trust increases exponentially with the level of the antecedent variables, at least up to a certain level. Moreover, in so far as similar affiliations are signals that can be manipulated by actors who do not intend to behave in a trustworthy manner, dispositional factors can facilitate malfeasance as much as they facilitate trust (Bacharach and Gambetta, 2001).

The extent to which dispositional factors may lead the trustor to dismantle safeguards and to reduce monitoring beyond a 'safety threshold' may depend on the wider context in which the trustor makes such decisions. While in this chapter we have discussed trust in the context of dyadic or triadic relationships, some scholars have also reflected on the 'public good' nature of trust (Fukuyama, 1995; Putman, 2001), stressing the level of trust an actor would have for any other actor within a given social system. Actors, it is argued, 'generalize' their knowledge of specific actors within that system to other players who are also members of that system, even though the trustor has not yet had direct or indirect experience of their behavior (Yamagishi, 2001). In systems with high levels of generalized trust, actors may need fewer dispositional elements to trust a potential partner, hence being more likely to incur excessive trust. As it is the case at the micro-level, macro-level (that is, system) trust can also fuel negative outcomes for the members of that system.

Second, extreme levels of trust may result from the interaction of multiple antecedents. Following the prior example, just imagine that we find out that the new acquaintance with whom we share a number of group affiliations is also closely associated with a number of our friends back home. Again, it is reasonable to expect that the joint occurrence of multiple common group membership and common acquaintances creates ideal conditions for high levels of trust to emerge from the onset in that relationship, especially if the context allows the parties to benefit from such trust (that is, interdependence and uncertainty are present). Thus we can expect significant interaction effects between antecedents on the level of trust in a relationship. Because high initial levels of the antecedents of trust make early emergence (or rapid development) of high levels of trust increasingly likely, the probability of observing the phenomenon we characterized as 'excessive' trust increases with the level of the antecedents of trust.

Conclusion

In this chapter, we discussed the possibility that trust may have a 'dark side' that results in undesirable outcomes. In doing so, we wanted to outline a research agenda often mentioned in passing but largely neglected by scholars who have worked on the origins and the effects of trust in organizational life. We have examined the detrimental consequences of 'excessive' trust by linking those consequences to extreme levels of the same behaviors responsible for the benefits of trust. In doing so, we have tried to rely on existing research that either suggests the possibility of detrimental effects of trust or tackles related issues that can serve as a platform to investigate such effects. While empirical research on the consequences of trust often assumes an implicit linear relationship between trust and a number of desirable outcomes or properties, our inquiry suggests that there are good reasons to believe that such a linear relationship does not correspond to reality. Rather, our discussion indicates that trust has a curvilinear relationship with desirable outcomes. This implies that there may be an 'optimal' level of trust and that additional investments aimed at enhancing trust may hinder the probability that benefits will accrue to the actors involved.

Challenging the implicit idea that there is a linear relationship between trust and desirable outcomes is in itself important, but the real value added in this respect lies in identifying the mechanisms through which the dark side of trust operates. Despite the limitations posed by the scant theoretical reflection and the even scarcer empirical evidence on the dark side of trust, our inquiry sought to shed some light on the mechanisms that are behind the potentially detrimental effects of trust, as well as to identify those effects in an empirically testable fashion. We hope that our necessarily limited contribution can help to correct the pervading optimistic bias in the research on trust, stimulating scholars to study also the ways in which trust can be detrimental. Trust is a good thing but there can be too much of a good thing too.

Notes

1. Research for this article was supported by INSEAD and partly funded by the Sasakawa Foundation. Direct all correspondence to Martin Gargiulo, INSEAD, Bd de Constance, 77305 Fontainebleau, France (martin.gargiulo@insead.edu) or to Gokhan Ertug (gokhan.ertug@insead.edu).
2. It is worth noting that 'trustor' and 'trustee' designate roles in an ongoing social relationship rather than specific actors. Indeed, the trustor becomes a trustee and vice versa in most social situations. This creates a reciprocation mechanism that is essential for the development of trust. According to Blau (1964), trust builds up initially through small exchanges that grow through reciprocation. This is the basic situation of the so-called 'trust game', in which actors take on roles of trustor and trustee sequentially and the game continues until one chooses to defect.
3. A trust game is a sequential game that starts with a trustor deciding whether to place trust in the trustee. If the trustor does not place trust in the trustee, the game is over. If the trustor place trusts in the trustee, the trustee can then choose whether to honor the trust or to defect. See Malhotra and Murnighan (2002: 541) for a detailed description.

References

Bacharach, M. and D. Gambetta (2001). 'Trust in signs', in K.S. Cook (ed.), *Trust in Society*, New York: Russell Sage Foundation, 148–85.

Bachmann, R., D. Knights and J. Sydow (eds) (2001), 'Trust and control in organizational relations', *Organization Studies*, **22**(2).

Balasubramanian, S., P. Konana and N.M. Nenon (2003). 'Customer satisfaction in virtual environments: A study of online investing', *Management Science*, **49**(7), 871–89.

Barber, B. (1983). *The Logic and Limits of Trust*. New Brunswick, NJ: Rutgers University Press.

Becerra, M. and A.K. Gupta (2003). 'Perceived trustworthiness within the organization: The moderating impact of communication frequency on trustor and trustee effects', *Organization Science*, **14**(1), 32–44.

Benton, A.A., E.R. Gelber, H.H. Kelley and B.A. Liebling (1969). 'Reactions to various degrees of deceit in a mixed-motive relationship', *Journal of Personality and Social Psychology*, **12**(2), 170–80.

Blau, P.M. (1964). *Exchange and Power in Social Life*. New York: Wiley.

Boss, W.R. (1978). 'Trust and managerial problem solving revisited', *Group & Organization Studies*, **3**(3), 331–42.

Brewer, M.B. (1979). 'Ingroup bias in the minimal intergroup situations: A cognitive motivational analysis', *Psychological Bulletin*, **86**, 307–24.

Brockner, J., P.A. Siegel, J.P. Daly, T. Tyler and C. Martin (1997). 'When trust matters: The moderating effect of outcome favorability', *Administrative Science Quarterly*, **42**, 558–83.

Bromiley, P. and L.L. Cummings (1995). 'Organizations with Trust', in R. Bies, R. Lemicki and B. Sheppard (eds), *Research on Negotiations in Organizations* (Vol. 5). Greenwich, CT: JAI Press.

Burt, R.S. and M. Knez (1995). 'Kinds of third-party effect on trust', *Rationality and Society*, **7**, 255–92.

Davis, J.H., F.D. Schoorman, R.C. Mayer and H.H. Tan (2000). 'The trusted general manager and business unit performance: Empirical evidence of a competitive advantage', *Strategic Management Journal*, **21**, 563–76.

De Dreu, C.K.W., E. Giebels and E. Van de Vliet (1998). 'Social motives and trust in integrative negotiation: The disruptive effects of punitive capability', *Journal of Applied Psychology*, **83**(3), 408–22.

Deutsch, M. (1958). 'Trust and suspicion', *Journal of Conflict Resolution*, **2**, 265–79.

Deutsch, M. (1962). 'Cooperation and Trust: Some Theoretical Notes', in M.R. Jones (ed.) *Nebraska Symposium on Motivation*. Lincoln, NE: University of Nebraska Press, 275–319.

Dirks, K.T. (1999). 'The effects of interpersonal trust on work group performance', *Journal of Applied Social Psychology*, **29**(6), 445–55.

Dirks, K.T. and D.L. Ferrin (2001). 'The role of trust in organizational settings', *Organization Science*, **12**(4), 450–67.

Driscoll, J.W. (1978). 'Trust and participation in organizational decision making as predictors of satisfaction', *Academy of Management Journal*, **21**(1), 44–56.

Dyer, J.H. and W. Chu (2003). 'The role of trustworthiness in reducing costs and improving performance: Empirical evidence from the United States, Japan, and Korea', *Organization Science*, **14**(1), 57–68.

Fukuyama, F. (1995). *Trust: The Social Virtues and the Creation of Prosperity*. New York: The Free Press.

Gambetta, D. (ed.) (1988a). *Trust: Making and Breaking Cooperative Relations*. New York: Blackwell.

Gambetta, D. (1988b). 'Can we trust trust?' in Diego Gambetta (ed.), *Trust: Making and Breaking Cooperative Relations*. New York: Blackwell, 213–37.

Gargiulo, M. and M. Benassi (2000). 'Trapped in your own net. Network cohesion, structural holes, and the adaptation of social capital', *Organization Science*, **11**, 183–96.

Grabher, G. (1993). 'The weakness of strong ties. The lock-in of regional development in the Ruhr area', in Gernot Grabher (ed.), *The Embedded Firm*. London and New York: Routledge, pp. 255–77.

Granovetter, M.S. (1985). 'Economic action and social structure: The problem of embeddedness', *American Journal of Sociology*, **91**, 481–510.

Gulati, R. (1995). 'Does familiarity breed trust? The implications of repeated ties for contractual choice in alliances', *Academy of Management Journal*, **38**(1), 85–112.

Gurtman, M.B. (1992). 'Trust, distrust, and interpersonal problems: A circumplex analysis', *Journal of Personality and Social Psychology*, **62**(6), 989–1002.

Hirschman, A.O. (1970). *Exit, Voice, and Loyalty*. Cambridge, MA: Harvard University Press.

Huff, L. and L. Kelley (2003). 'Levels of organizational trust in individualist versus collectivist societies: A seven-nation study', *Organization Science*, **14**(1), 81–90.

Kee, H.W. and R.E. Knox (1970). 'Conceptual and methodological considerations in the study of trust and suspicion', *The Journal of Conflict Resolution*, **14**(3), 357–66.

Kelley, H.H. and J.W. Thibaut (1978). *Interpersonal Relations: A Theory of Interdependence*. New York: Wiley.

Kollock, P. (1994). 'The emergence of exchange structures: An experimental study of uncertainty, commitment, and trust', *American Journal of Sociology*, **100**(2), 313–45.

Kramer, R.M. (1999). 'Trust and distrust in oganizations: Emerging perspectives, enduring questions', *Annual Review of Psychology*, **50**, 569–98.

Kramer, R.M and T.R. Tyler (eds) (1995). *Trust in Organizations*. Thousand Oaks, CA: Sage.

Lane, C. and R. Bachmann (eds) (1998). *Trust Within and Between Organizations. Conceptual Issues and Empirical Applications*. Oxford: Oxford University Press.

Langfred, C.W. (2004). 'Too much of a good thing? Negative effects of high trust and individual autonomy in self-managing teams', *Academy of Management Journal*, **47**(3), 385–99.

Lewicki, R.J. and B.B. Bunker (1995). 'Developing and Maintaining Trust in Work Relationships', in Tom Tyler and Roderick M. Kramer (eds), *Trust in Organizations: Frontiers of Theory and Research*. Thousand Oaks, CA: Sage, 114–39.

Lewicki, R.J., D.J. McAllister and R.J. Bies (1998). 'Trust and distrust: New relationships and realities', *Academy of Management Review*, **23**(3), 438–58.

Lewis, J.D. and A. Weigert (1985). 'Trust as a social reality', *Social Forces*, **63**(4), 967–85.

Luhmann, N. (1979). *Trust and Power*. Chichester: Wiley.

Malhotra, D. and J.K. Murnighan (2002). 'The effects of contracts on interpersonal trust', *Administrative Science Quarterly*, **47**, 534–59.

Mayer, R.C., J.H. Davis and F.D. Schoorman (1995). 'An integrative model of organizational trust', *Academy of Management Review*, **20**(3), 709–34.

McAllister, D.J. (1995). 'Affect- and cognition-based trust as foundations for interpersonal cooperation in organizations', *Academy of Management Journal*, **38**(1), 24–59.

McEvily, B., V. Perrone and A. Zaheer (2003). 'Trust as an organizing principle', *Organization Science*, **14**(1), 91–103.

McKnight, H.D., L.L. Cummings and N.L. Chervany (1998). 'Initial trust formation in new organizational relationships', *Academy of Management Review*, **23**(3), 473–90.

Molm, L.D., N. Takahashi and G. Peterson (2000). 'Risk and trust in social exchange: An experimental test of a classic proposition', *American Journal of Sociology*, **105**(5), 1396–427.

Muchinsky, P.M. (1977). 'Organizational communication: Relationships to organizational climate and job satisfaction', *Academy of Management Journal*, **20**(4), 592–607.

Noteboom, B., H. Berger and N.G. Noordhaven (1997). 'Effects of trust and governance on relational risk', *Academy of Management Journal*, **40**(2), 308–38.

O'Reilly, C.A. and K.H. Roberts (1974). 'Information filtration in organizations: Three experiments', *Organizational Behavior & Human Performance*, **11**(2), 253–65.

Pillai, R., C.A. Schriesheim and E.S. Williams (1999). 'Fairness perceptions and trust as mediators for transformational and transactional leadership: A two-sample study', *Journal of Management*, **25**(6), 897–933.

Podolny, J.M. and K.L. Page (1998). 'Network forms of organization', *Annual Review of Sociology*, **24**, 57–76.

Porter, T.W. and B.S. Lilly (1996). 'The effects of conflict, trust, and task commitment on project team performance', *International Journal of Conflict Management*, **7**(4), 361–76.

Portes, A. (1998). 'Social capital: Its origins and applications in modern sociology', *Annual Review of Sociology*, **24**, 1–24.

Putman, R.D. (2001). *Bowling Alone: The Collapse and Revival of American Community*. New York: Simon & Schuster.

Rempel, J.K., J.G. Holmes and M.P. Zanna (1985). 'Trust in close relationships', *Journal of Personality and Social Psychology*, **49**(1), 95–112.

Rich, G.A. (1997). 'The sales manager as a role model: Effects on trust, job satisfaction, and performance of salespeople', *Journal of the Academy of Marketing Science*, **25**(4), 319–28.

Ring, P.S. and A.H. Van de Ven (1994). 'Developmental processes of cooperative interorganizational relationships', *Academy of Management Review*, **19**(1), 90–118.

Roberts, K.H. and C.A. O'Reilly (1974). 'Failures in upward communication in organizations: Three possible culprits', *Academy of Management Journal*, **17**(2), 205–15.

Robinson, S.L. (1996). 'Trust and breach of the psychological contract', *Administrative Science Quarterly*, **41**, 574–99.

Rousseau, D.M., S.B. Sitkin, R.S. Burt and C. Camerer (1998). 'Not so different after all: A cross discipline view of trust', *Academy of Management Review*, **23**(3), 393–404.

Saavedra, R., C.P. Earley and L.V. Dyne (1993). 'Complex interdependence in task-performing groups', *Journal of Applied Psychology*, **78**(1), 61–72.

Saparito, P.A., C.C. Chen and H.J. Sapienza (2004). 'The role of relational trust in bank-small firm relationships', *Academy of Management Journal*, **47**(3), 400–410.

Schurr, P.H. and J.L. Ozanne (1985). 'Influences on exchange processes: Buyers' preconceptions of a seller's trustworthiness and bargaining toughness', *Journal of Consumer Research*, **11**(4), 939–53.

Shapiro, S.P. (1987). 'The social control of impersonal trust', *American Journal of Sociology*, **93**(3), 623–58.

Shapiro, S.P. (1990). 'Collaring the crime, not the criminal: Reconsidering the concept of white-collar crime', *American Sociological Review*, **55**(3), 346–65.

Shapiro, D.L., B.H. Sheppard and L. Cheraskin (1992). 'Business on a handshake', *Negotiation Journal*, **8**(4), 365–77.

Sheppard, B.H. and D.M. Sherman (1998). 'The grammars of trust: A model and general implications', *Academy of Management Review*, **23**(3), 422–37.

Sinaceur, M. (2005). 'Suspending judgments to create value: Suspicion, distrust, and trust in negotiations'. Unpublished doctoral dissertation. Stanford University, Stanford, CA.

Smith, J.B. and D.W. Barclay (1997). 'The effects of organizational differences and trust on the effectiveness of selling partner relationships', *Journal of Marketing*, **61**, 3–21.

Szulanski, G., R. Cappetta and R.J. Jensen (2004). 'When and how trustworthiness matters: Knowledge transfer and the moderating effect of causal ambiguity', *Organization Science*, **15**(5), 600–613.

Tsai, W. and S. Ghoshal (1998). 'Social capital and value creation: The role of intrafirm networks', *Academy of Management Journal*, **41**(4), 464–76.

Tyler, T.R. (1994). 'Psychological models of the justice motive', *Journal of Personality and Social Psychology*, **67**(5), 850–63.

Tyler, T.R. and P. Degoey (1996). 'Trust in organizational authorities: The influence of motive attributions on willingness to accept decisions', in Roderick M. Kramer and Tom Tyler (eds), *Trust in Organizations: Frontiers of Theory and Research*, Thousand Oaks, CA: Sage, 331–56.

Uzzi, B. (1996). 'The sources and consequences of embeddedness for the economic performance of organizations', *American Sociological Review*, **61**, 674–98.

Uzzi, B. (1997). 'Social structure and competition in interfirm networks: The paradox of embeddedness', *Administrative Science Quarterly*, **42**(1), 35–67.

Uzzi, B. and J.J. Gillespie (2002). 'Knowledge spillover in corporate financing networks: Embeddedness and the firm's debt performance', *Strategic Management Journal*, **23**, 595–618.

Uzzi, B. and R. Lancaster (2003). 'Relational embeddedness and learning: The case of bank loan managers and their clients', *Management Science*, **49**(4), 383–409.

Weber, M. (1946). *From Max Weber: Essays in Sociology* (trans. and eds Hans H. Gerth and C. Wright Mills). New York: Oxford University Press.

Wicks, A.C., S.L. Berman and T.M. Jones (1998). 'The structure of optimal trust: Moral and strategic implications', *Academy of Management Review*, **24**(1), 99–116.

Yamagishi, T. (2001). 'Trust as a Form of Social Intelligence', in Karen S. Cook (ed.), *Trust in Society*. New York: Russell Sage Foundation, 121–47.

Zaheer, A., B. McEvily and V. Perrone (1998). 'Does trust matter? Exploring the effects of interorganizational and interpersonal trust on performance', *Organization Science*, **9**(2), 141–59.

Zand, D.E. (1972). 'Trust and managerial problem solving', *Administrative Science Quarterly*, **17**(2), 229–39.

Zucker, L.G. (1986). 'Production of trust: Institutional sources of economic structure', in Barry M. Staw and Larry L. Cummings (eds), *Research in Organizational Behavior*. Greenwich, CT: JAI Press, Vol. **8**, 53–111.

10 Trust, codification and epistemic communities: implementing an expert system in the French steel industry

Richard Arena, Nathalie Lazaric and Edward Lorenz

Introduction

The aim of this chapter is to examine the relation between trust and knowledge codification in the context of the implementation of an expert system in the French steel company, Usinor. The Sachem (Système d'Aide à la Conduite des Hauts Furneaux en Marche) expert system project, which was designed to improve blast furnace control, was initiated by Usinor in the 1980s as part of a larger programme of knowledge codification and centralization. One of the objectives was to preserve knowledge and practices the company felt might face extinction during a period of massive layoffs that threatened to disrupt the traditional knowledge transfer patterns which had hitherto been carried out primarily via an apprenticeship system.[1]

At first glance, trust might seem largely irrelevant to the development of an expert system. Such systems, after all, involve the use of information technology by 'knowledge engineers' to transform largely tacit 'know-how' into a codified format that can subsequently be used as an aid in decision-making. The technical nature of such projects might suggest that they are largely neutral relative to problems of opportunism and trust.

We shall argue that trust was central to implementation of an expert system in the steel industry for three principal reasons that the project shared with most major efforts to codify and centralize knowledge in organizational settings: uncertain impact on decision-making power; causal ambiguity; and knowledge obsolescence (Johnson et al. 2002, pp. 251–7).[2] Knowledge codification was not politically neutral in the steel industry case for the basic reason that in organizational settings the distribution of knowledge is closely tied to the distribution of decision-making power. The right to make a decision in turn can bear on career opportunities and the longer-term distribution of profits. Questions of trust were inevitably raised in the steel industry because of the risk that management, or other individuals and groups, would attempt to seize upon the codification process as a means to increase their status and power relative to those that had revealed their hitherto largely tacit or non-explicit know-how.

The political dimension of knowledge codification in the steel industry was in turn closely linked to the problem of causal ambiguity. Blast furnaces are used for smelting and are capable of producing different grades of steel. The process involves coke, charred coal, various types of ore, hot air and gas being introduced into the furnace and then smelted. Dross is produced through a process of 'decarburization' and 'dephosphorization'. Since the resulting smelted scraps vary, melted metal must be analysed immediately in order to determine which gases should be added to it and at what temperatures.[3]

A number of problems can arise during this process, the most notorious occurring when ores do not tap properly and flow on one side of the tank. This happens when ores are insufficiently fluid and therefore create a kind of dome, preventing gases from moving up the furnace's throat. If intervention is limited in any way, ores and smelt scraps can suddenly sink back and cause a number of other problems, including obstructing the tuyères and triggering explosions or gas emissions.

Team operators responsible for the continuous control of the blast furnace must be able to solve problems and make quick decisions. While this ability depends on the integration of pieces of articulated knowledge, it largely takes the form of empirical know-how. Formal mathematical models describing the process have been produced but as yet no formal model describing the entire set of relevant chemical and physical reactions has been devised. Expert knowledge is consequently tied to particular individuals, but some of it inevitably defies articulation and is poorly reproduced and communicated. From the point of view of implementing an expert system, this implies not only a need to choose what knowledge will be codified but also a need to choose between the possibly conflicting beliefs of the experts concerning the efficiency or particular practices or solutions. Since validating some beliefs at the expense of others is not neutral relative to status and decision-making power, knowledge codification requires some generally accepted criteria for weighing and validating knowledge (Lazaric et al. 2003).

Knowledge obsolescence enters into these dynamics because implementing an expert system, as with other major processes of knowledge codification and centralization, is a process requiring considerable time and the problems tackled by the organization typically will change during the process. New knowledge representations come into play at both the individual and the collective levels, and new objectives concerning knowledge creation and accumulation emerge at the organizational level. For this reason, large investments in codifying certain practices and routines often prove in vain because the problems to be solved are no longer the same. Expert systems, if they are to provide a longer-term return on investment, have to be updated so as to continuously incorporate new non-explicit knowledge that emerges in the process of technical and organizational change. This implies a need for the longer-term commitment to project of those actors – operators, craftsmen, lower-level technicians – who arguably face the greatest risks in terms of potential loss of status within the organization. We would argue that in the absence of trust this commitment will not be forthcoming.

Defining trust

While the above discussion makes it plausible that trust-building was an essential part of the knowledge codification process in the French steel industry, it will nevertheless be useful to spell out the role of trust more precisely. What do we mean by trust and how does our notion of trust relate to the problems of uncertain impact on decision-making, causal ambiguity and knowledge obsolescence?

There is, of course, very little agreement in the literature on how trust should be defined. Moreover, discussions of trust are often riddled with distinctions or qualifying adjectives, such as 'weak' versus 'strong' trust, 'thin' versus 'thick' trust, or 'personal' versus 'institutional' trust. The use of these qualifiers can be explained by the fact that the meaning one attaches to trust in its vernacular use is strongly context dependent. The qualifiers serve to make explicit the distinctions that, in everyday language, are conveyed by the other words and phrases that are used in conjunction with the word trust. For example, if we say that X is not really trustworthy but that X can be trusted to fulfil his side of a contractual agreement, there is no contradiction. There is no difficulty in understanding that a distinction has been drawn between what one can expect from X in general and what one can expect from him in a particular contractual arrangement, given the incentives and constraints that he faces. This is the kind of distinction that is captured by the contrast between 'contractual' and 'goodwill' trust (Sako, 1998) or between 'weak' and 'strong' trust (Livet and Reynaud, 1998).

The multiple ways in which trust is contextualized in the literature raises the question of whether there is a set of properties that are common to the various uses of trust. Or, is it the case that we are dealing with a number of basically different concepts? We would argue that despite important differences, the various contextualized meanings of trust share the following three properties.[4]

1. When we say that an individual trusts, we invariably have in mind a tripartite relation of the following form:

    X trusts Y to do Z

    Y can be another person, an organization or an institution.
2. X is vulnerable in the sense that Y is a free agent and could conceivably act in ways that harm X. The intuition here is that without such vulnerability we do not consider the relation to involve trust. Of course, in any particular instance it may be that X fully expects Y not to act in ways that cause harm. This expectation could be based on any number of considerations, including what X knows about Y's interests or the constraints Y operates under. What is essential is that Y in his capacity as a free agent could act to cause harm (see Pettit, 1998).
3. X has reasons for his expectations regarding Y's behaviour and in this sense trust is justified.

In the case of Usinor's Sachem project, the basic tripartite relation we are interested in is between the blast furnace operators or experts (X) who are holders of tacit knowledge and the management team (Y) responsible for codifying at least some parts of their tacit knowledge and using it for implementing an expert system. Vulnerability (property 2) enters into the relation because of causal ambiguity and the operators' uncertainty over the impact of the knowledge codification process on their decision-making power and position within the organization. To the extent that an expert system succeeds in routinizing decision-making processes that previously depended on the tacit knowledge of skilled operators, it threatens to reduce their organizational usefulness. Thus, for the operators, a key question is whether to trust that management will develop and implement the expert system in a way that respects their interests and preserves their position within the organization (Z).

Property 3 requires that X has reasons for trusting Y and that trust is justified in this sense. This condition raises the general question of the foundations or sources of trust, about which there is a vast literature. One of the key distinctions made in this literature is between the micro- and macrofoundations for trust (Nooteboom, 2002; Williams, 1988). Microfoundations include such factors as perceptions of self-interest. That is, X may trust Y to do Z because of what he or she believes to be the case about Y's economic interests. Microfoundations may also include bonds of friendship or love between the two agents.

Macro sources include such factors as sanctions from some authority (the law, organization, or patriarch) which may constrain an agent's behaviour and make it more predictable. They may also include internalized norms of proper conduct which also serve to reduce uncertainty regarding an agent's likely behaviour.

The relative importance of micro- and macrofoundations will depend in part on whether Y is an individual or a collective entity (organization or institution). Microfoundations are especially relevant for interpersonal forms of trust (i.e. where Y is an individual). These sources may be established through an interactive learning process whereby X learns or discovers things that are relevant about Y's interests or normative values (Lazaric and Lorenz, 1998; Lorenz, 1993).

Where Y is an organization this sort of mechanism arguably is precluded, since organizations are not cognitive entities in the same way that individuals are and they do not in any obvious sense have reasons, self-interested or otherwise, for behaving in one way or another. This, however, does not mean that trust in an organization is purely inductive and based on a simple extrapolation of what has been observed of its behaviour and performance in the past. The sources of trust in an organization may be macro in nature. For example, we may trust an organization because of what we believe to be the case about its internal governance structure and how its incentives system sanctions employees' behaviour and encourages them to fulfil the requirements of their various functions and roles (see Lorenz, 2002).

Where does the case study at hand fit relative to the distinction between micro- and macrofoundations? We shall argue that trust in the case of the Sachem project combined aspects of both foundation mechanisms. Blast furnace operators came to trust the management team responsible for developing and implementing the expert system in part because of what they learned, through daily interaction, about managers' interests and objectives. For example, through such interaction the operators came to appreciate that management's objective was not so much to eliminate their expertise and organizational role as it was to transform and preserve it in the interests of improved enterprise performance. They also developed trust based on a macro mechanism involving the forging of a consensus between management and labour around a set of rules for validating beliefs in the knowledge codification process. The following sections describe the nature of these rules and how the consensus was established.

Trust and epistemic communities during knowledge articulation and codification

Articulation and codification of knowledge
In general, it is important to distinguish between 'tacit', 'articulable', 'articulated' and 'codified' knowledge. We argue that the knowledge of a person or an organization is articulable (and possibly may be articulated) when it can be made explicit by means of language. In the same vein, articulated knowledge is knowledge that has been rendered explicit through language. Language, in this context, refers to a system of signs and conventions that allow the reproduction and storage of knowledge in such a way that it can then be communicated and transferred between individuals.

The process of articulation involves the extraction of knowledge from the person holding it and the transformation of this personal knowledge into a generic form (Winter, 1987; Mangolte, 1997). One obstacle to this process is that the holder of personal knowledge may be unwilling to cooperate in divulging it. Another obstacle is more technical due to the fact that parts of knowledge that are held tacitly may defy articulation and remain poorly reproduced and communicated independently of the interests of the parties concerned. Finally, it is important to appreciate that the degree to which articulation will actually be pursued may differ radically between firms, depending on the associated costs and benefits accruing to the firm, the firm's strategic vision and the importance it places on the building of capabilities (Teece, 1998; Zollo and Winter, 2002).

Articulation should be distinguished from codification (Zollo and Winter, 2002) since as a rule only parts of the knowledge that have been articulated will be encoded on a particular medium: text, computer hard disk and so on. This distinction is crucial in the case of the Sachem project since, as we have observed, the initial articulation process revealed different and competing understandings of blast furnace technology. Correspondingly there was a need to establish choice criteria that were acceptable to the operators and technicians whose participation was critical for the success of the project. One way to understand this process of arriving at an organizational compromise is in terms of the creation of an 'epistemic community'.

The role assumed by an epistemic community is quite distinct from that of a 'community of practice' as discussed by Brown and Duguid (1991) and Lave and Wenger (1991). Communities of practice emerge spontaneously through the shared activity or practice of a group of agents. Around this shared practice the agents develop a common language and they come to share tacit knowledge. Such communities contribute to organizational performance notably through the way they serve to mobilize tacit knowledge in the interests of collective learning and problem-solving.

The cognitive functions of an epistemic community, on the other hand, are not limited to problem-solving based largely on the exchange of tacit knowledge, but extend to the realm of validating and disseminating explicit knowledge amongst a group of practitioners (Cohendet and Llerena, 2003). It is this fundamental difference between knowledge-sharing and knowledge validation that, in our view, distinguishes a 'community of practice' from an 'epistemic community'. As Haas (1992, p. 3) expressed it:

> an 'epistemic community' is a network of professionals with recognized expertise and competence in a particular domain and an authoritative claim to policy-relevant knowledge within domain or issue-area . . . This network has (1) a shared set of normative and principled beliefs, which provide a value-based rationale for the social action of community members; (2) shared causal beliefs, which are derived from their analysis of practices leading or contributing to a central set of problems in their domain and which then serve as the basis for elucidating the multiple linkages between possible actions and desired outcomes; (3) shared notions of validity – that is, inter subjective, internally defined criteria for weighing and validating knowledge in the domain of their expertise; and (4) a common policy enterprise – that is, a set of common practices associated with a set of problems to which their professional competence is directed, presumably out of the conviction that human welfare will be enhanced as a consequence.

While the notion of epistemic community was initially developed by Haas (1992) and others to analyse knowledge dynamics within broader professional and scientific networks, it can help us to understand the way individuals belonging to diverse groups and communities of practice within an organization come to accept the diffusion of their private knowledge and cooperate in the codification process. The emergence of an intra-organizational community whose members are tied together through subjectively shared 'criteria for weighing and validating knowledge in their domain of expertise' is not something that can be administratively mandated. The steel industry case suggests that such communities have to be constructed through a process of learning that involves trust-building (Lazaric and Lorenz, 1998; Moingeon and Edmonson, 1998). Moreover, in lieu of the problems of causal ambiguity and knowledge obsolescence, such communities remain more or less fragile structures open to reassessment on the part of the 'experts' whose participation is crucial to their survival. The process, we will suggest, begins with setting organizational rules for establishing legitimacy around the criteria used for validating knowledge and thus for achieving political compromise during the codification process (Lazaric, 2003).

Trust-building inside an organizational hierarchy: the Sachem project
The Sachem expert system had an impact on the social status and prestige of many of the company's practitioners, notably the blast furnace experts, whose practices had to be reviewed following the disclosure of their know-how. Securing the cooperation of the company's employees was extremely difficult in the circumstances and depended to a very large extent on the discretion of practitioners, but also on the ability of management to build trust around a set of rules and procedures for knowledge validation and codification.

   Usinor began building its epistemic community by carrying out a horizontal coordination exercise aimed at identifying the different ways in which the various communities of practice carried out similar tasks. The stage was concluded with the compilation of 'Xperdoc' (a kind of knowledge handbook), which was put together during the articulation and codification phase by a small group of experts, knowledge engineers and technicians. In 1987, the Sachem idea was born, mainly due to the efforts of some of the staff who believed that artificial intelligence could help memorize a large part of the knowledge held by experts. This idea was only implemented in 1990 under the supervision of Francis Mer, the company's top manager, who took a particular interest in this new tool in his efforts to improve Usinor's productivity. During the course of a year, over one hundred artificial intelligence applications were tested in collaboration with Usinor's R&D centre, IRSID. The implementation of artificial intelligence benefited from European subsidies and a 40-strong team spent five years working towards the creation of systems and their diffusion inside the group. Following this first stage, 17 technical solutions were selected, one of which was the Sachem project. This was first implemented in October 1996, following a long period of discussion within the company, which focused mainly on the following crucial questions: what kinds of knowledge should be articulated and stored? How should practices be selected? How can such practices be transposed into a new tool? How can the loss of tacit knowledge be avoided as the importance of articulated knowledge increases?

   In order to identify the 'best practices' and key know-how, 13 experts were chosen among those who had cooperated in writing 'Xperdoc'. Experts were selected according to know-how and location, in order to ensure a 'fair' representation of the various types of knowledge prevailing in the different plants (Sollac Fos, Dunkerque, Lorfonte Patural, etc.). The team worked with six knowledge engineers in order to extract the 'core know-how' and articulate it (400 interviews were conducted).

   It was this team that ultimately forged Usinor's epistemic community, and in the process ensured that the diversity of know-how found in the team was represented so as to avoid the emergence of a climate of distrust towards the ways in which knowledge was being articulated. Following an initial stage of translating the words or natural language of the 'experts' into codes, the stage of knowledge acknowledgement and validation was launched.

Blast furnace experts had to recognize their codified know-how, which had been radically transformed by computation. This stage was crucial, as it allowed experts to verify whether the codes did in fact represent what they had intended to articulate in the first place. Knowledge validation was a long and difficult stage as consensus had to be reached before it could be concluded. Individual meetings, which saw experts having one-to-one discussions with knowledge engineers, and a collective one, including all the experts, took place. Local know-how had been radically transformed as the 'knowledge engineers' had changed the way experts represented their own expertise. As it happened, parts of the general knowledge codified in the expert system had ceased to be meaningful to some of the experts, and the knowledge engineers designed a linguistic model (in natural language) in order to translate the code. The experts were thus able to recognize their own expertise and acknowledge it collectively. Similarly to the interpretative model, which had translated the experts' articulated knowledge into codes, the linguistic model converted codes into words. Different models had to be created because different levels of abstraction and local knowledge were required depending on their use.

The consequences of articulation and codification were very important because actual knowledge content changed drastically, forcing some blast furnace experts to modify long-standing beliefs and their usual interpretation of technical phenomena. One would expect some degree of resistance to this process. In fact, cooperation in the knowledge identification was successful partly because the blast furnace experts were acknowledged as the organizational knowledge carriers and their existing expertise was validated by the 'epistemic community'. But also critical was that the company relied on the experts to ensure the adaptation and continuous updating of the system in order to integrate ongoing changes and improve its daily performance. Let us explain this process in more detail.

Knowledge change and validation in the epistemic community
The process of articulation and codification entails a radical change in knowledge because it involves the selection of parts of all available know-how. Moreover, it affects the content of knowledge, as, in practice, the traditional expertise anchored in an expert's routines is alive. A first transformation occurs when experts put their practices and parts of their tacit know-how into words. This 'explicitation' creates articulated knowledge, which entails a first selection of know-how (see Nonaka and Takeuchi, 1995). Parts of know-how that are highly dependent on practices specific to particular plants cannot be articulated and resist extraction because of their ambiguity or by virtue of being highly personal. Experts' knowledge may be difficult to disembody:

> Experts generally know what to do because they have a mature and practiced understanding. When deeply involved in coping with their environment, they do not see problems in some detached way and consciously work at solving them. The skills of experts have become so much a part of them that they need be no more aware of them than they are of their own bodies. (Dreyfus and Dreyfus, 1986, p. 44)

A second transformation takes place when articulated knowledge is turned into code (Håkansson, 2002; Lazaric et al., 2003; Zollo and Winter, 2002). As technicians have their own ways of representing and selecting knowledge, parts of knowledge may be deemed useful simply because of the nature of particular technical parameters embedded in the expert system. In other words, the nature of the 'container' is far from neutral and can in fact change knowledge content by including unnecessary bits of know-how while excluding others. Consequently, the outcome is not a simple translation of existing knowledge into code but also a reformulation produced by the knowledge engineers and validated by the experts. Each stage of the process that takes place in the handover of live expertise and activated knowledge to the memory of an outsider and from one outsider to another entails a change in the preserved knowledge. This is neither a perfect equivalent nor a total substitute of the knowledge carried in the different memories.

Hatchuel and Weil (1992) argue that the container transforms knowledge content because each language has its unique ways of representing things. Repeated transmission through a variety of languages will always involve some losses as codes differ radically across languages. Moreover, articulation and codification are largely unpredictable because they are necessarily based on individuals' willingness to participate in a process that is likely to depart from their initial experience: most implemented codes differ substantially from the original individual representations of their particular technical problems. This is why the translation back into natural language and the validation by the experts that took place following the codification process was crucial to the project: it prevented experts from feeling they had lost their original know-how after they had passed it on to the knowledge engineer. As a blast furnace expert interviewed at the Dunkerque site acknowledged, 'The validation procedure implemented with the knowledge engineer prevented us from becoming frustrated and helped us understand why our know-how remained important even in its human form'. The application of this 'rule of validation' built inside the epistemic community paved the way for trust-building. In effect, the way experts cooperated in the construction of Sachem and their involvement in the process of extraction and articulation of their own expertise may appear curious to external observers. Several arguments can explain their cooperation. First, senior experts and operators were not insensitive to the argument that part of their own memory had to be preserved and communicated to others. Most of them were encouraged to transfer their know-how before reaching retirement and were proud to participate in the passing of knowledge to younger employees. Second, operators, technicians and blast furnace experts in the steel industry belong to the same 'community of practice' and blast furnace experts in particular are very powerful because of their long-standing experience. Their own legitimacy is entirely based on their personal knowledge and not their hierarchical grade. To the experts, participation in the Sachem project meant that the company acknowledged their empirical knowledge and validated their extensive work. The rule of validation was, in this context, perceived as a signal: an implicit acknowledgement of local knowledge and a formal validation of live expertise present in the company that had not always been clearly identified by the hierarchy before. However, although this process helped some experts get a better understanding of the power of their personal knowledge, it also highlighted the limits of their local know-how, because a part of their beliefs turned out to be either insufficiently reliable or only partially 'true'.

A good example is provided by beliefs concerning a phenomenon called fluidization involving an increase in temperature above the ores. At the Fos-sur-Mer plant, for example, some experts simply believed the process never occurred. Others attributed the observed increase in temperature to other causes. After the knowledge validation process, however, it was generally accepted within the community that fluidization occurred and that it preceded the descent of ores by an hour. This provides an example of how some kinds of knowledge can suffer from the selection process. Some prior beliefs were slowly redefined as a matter of course: what had been known to be true appeared to be only partly so due to the discovery of new causal links between technical events. The causal links connecting separate technical events, which used to be tacit and intuitive, were tested and proven in a more systematic manner. This does not mean that the articulation process resulted in a scientifically grounded understanding of the blast furnace, which still remains to be achieved. Nevertheless, it provided grounds for more robust beliefs and knowledge by changing the experts' and operators' local cognitive representations. Without a sufficient degree of confidence in this process of articulation involving lengthy discussions and cooperation among the experts, this change of prior individual and collective beliefs would have been difficult to implement, as habitual beliefs were questioned and practices and solutions were selected by the 'epistemic community' according to their reliability.

Training policy and trust-building

Before the introduction of the expert system, it took ten years of 'on-the-job training' to become a confirmed operator. Now only three years of work within the company are required to reach operational status, and five to become a confirmed operator. The new training policy has forced both experts and operators to reflect on their own know-how, as they now need to understand the ways in which they solve problems and justify their repertoires. This has transformed their knowledge and expertise, and while not eliminating know-how, has activated new pieces of detached knowledge, predominantly based on know-that.

The training policy contributed to the build-up of trust in a further important way in that it broadened the range of workers' skills and generalized them by preventing operators from passively reacting to the data produced by Sachem and by helping them understand their meaning. This process had the added effect of increasing the degree of cooperation between different generations of practitioners operating within the company and helping disseminate knowledge that was previously open only to those partaking in the long-established apprenticeship system. Finally, the fact that the workforce interpreted management's efforts as a positive signal that helped involve different parts of the company in the process of collective learning and that the effort encouraged the formation of a provisional but positive perception of management's intentions were two factors that proved crucial to the success of the process. In short, the training policy was extremely well perceived by the company's employees and played a crucial role in stabilizing mutual expectations in a context of high uncertainty.

The preservation of the blast furnace experts' legitimacy: knowledge maintenance and updating

The training policy was also implemented in order to avoid a 'cognitive prosthesis syndrome'. In other words, management had to ensure that both operators and experts remained constantly vigilant and active and did not become too confident in the new technological artefact. As an operator interviewed at the Foss-sur-Mer site observed; 'We are not going to systematically listen to its [the expert system's] recommendations, we are not going to be blind, we have our experience and our practice as "hand-rail". As the system is not locked in, we can interact with it, otherwise [when the system is locked in], I will not use it'.

In fact, Sachem requires feedback from its users and the blast furnace experts in order to be updated. As a result, the system's recommendations, which stem from its interpretation of the data (especially the identification of causal links between different events), and the operators' ultimate decisions are compared and scrutinized on a regular basis. All discrepancies between the system's commendations and the operators' ultimate actions are systematically analysed in order to detect divergences. This analysis allows the database to be enriched and updated. Parts of the tacit know-how that were not articulated by the operators and blast furnace experts and were considered insignificant during the first stage of articulation (in 1992) are gradually incorporated into the system. Updates are formalized in an annual meeting with the operators, foremen and experts. Experts play a crucial role in this context as they formalize and systematize the divergence analysis of users (operators) and introduce the new articulated knowledge, later turned into codes by the knowledge managers. In this way, the system's knowledge base is constantly enhanced by new articulated knowledge, a process that prevents it from rapidly becoming obsolete.

The constant activation of human skills is very important because, as Dreyfus and Dreyfus (1986) remind us, the coupling of human skills and machine capacity is crucial in order to trigger all the expert system's potentialities. Indeed, the expert system is not able to deal with new situations or solve new problems. Its ability is limited to the knowledge that has already been articulated. Without integrating new pieces of knowledge and codifying them, the system would become obsolete in the long run. All this means that the legitimacy of the blast furnace experts and their social status within the company are reinforced rather than diminished by the new technological tool and that the power of their expertise remains a key component of the new 'epistemic community' (see Fleck, 1998 for a similar discussion on this point).

However, the process of knowledge articulation and codification was confronted by important uncertainties because it entailed profound changes for the old 'communities of practice'. Trust and cooperation, in this context, were promoted by the way the importance given to the training policy and to the elaboration of organizational rules served to signal management's good intentions to operators. For example, the rule of validation that was established following the process of codification and the practice of examining any divergence between the expert system's recommendations and the operators' decisions acted as such a signal and created a climate of collective learning that gave an active role to the blast furnace experts. Such experts realized that the new system not only validated their existing empirical know-how, but also helped disseminate parts of their knowledge, thereby further enhancing their legitimacy. This process was also successful because the management did not impose a strict monitoring system and opted instead to create an 'epistemic community', a decentralized team that had a high degree of autonomy with respect to the hierarchy itself and that was accepted by the practitioners (despite the fact that it was precisely this team that was responsible for the substantial centralization of existing know-how through codification).[5]

Conclusion

The problems faced in creating an epistemic community in the context of the French steel industry are in many respects archetypical of the new governance challenges confronted by firms embarking on ambitious projects of knowledge management. Such projects typically cut across different communities of practices, each characterized not only by a common language and shared beliefs regarding problem solutions but also by shared expectations regarding norms of knowledge transmission and sharing. Thus creating an epistemic community faces a double challenge: one cognitive and linked to establishing shared cognitive frames across different communities, and the other normative and linked to the development of trust around standards of knowledge-sharing and validation.

The codification and articulation of knowledge are inherently linked to causal ambiguity (Szulsanski et al., 2004) and radical uncertainty, and for these reasons the process cannot be perfectly monitored. Nor can it be adequately governed by means of a complete contract. This inherently creates room for opportunism and vulnerability. In the steel blast furnace case, the holders of tacit knowledge could well have suffered from revealing part of their crucial tacit know-how. Overcoming this obstacle to cooperation and knowledge-sharing was linked to management's decision to create a decentralized 'epistemic community' responsible for the self-management of the codification process. Management opted for this solution because they recognized that they were dependent on the willingness of the 'experts' working within the 'epistemic community' to divulge their knowledge and to commit themselves to the project's goals. The choice of a decentralized self-managed structure helped to persuade the knowledge holders that management recognized the continuing value of their knowledge and expertise.

The training policy also played a positive role by demonstrating to the operators that the codification process amounted to more than a replication of existing knowledge. Knowledge holders could potentially benefit due to their role in updating the system, which required them to focus on activities that added value to the system. The permanent updating of knowledge inside the firm by the operators in the 'epistemic community' points clearly to the fact that they were the 'sense-makers' of this process. By demonstrating that their role goes beyond a simple enactment of knowledge codified in routines, it served to increase their status and prestige within the firm.

Notes

1. The discussion of the Sachem expert system is based on a case study carried out by N. Lazaric in 1998. See Lazaric (2003) and Lazaric, et al. (2003) for a more detailed description.
2. The notion of causal ambiguity has been proposed as an explanation for the imperfect imitability of organizational competences in resource-based theories of the firm. See Rumelt (1984) and Dierickx and Cool (1989).
3. For a fuller description of the process, see Lazaric et al. (2003, pp. 1830–33).
4. For an extended discussion of these definitional aspects, see Lorenz (2002) and Nooteboom (2002).
5. Paradoxically, this situation led to a degree of comfort that soon verged on excess confidence, thereby forcing the management to introduce procedures that required the staff to regularly review and question the formalized data. This shows how routinized behaviour can carry a risk. When not confronted by novelty, it can lead to an excess of confidence and thereby generate a degree of inertia that proves detrimental to its own evolution.

References

Brown, S. and P. Duguid (1991), 'Organizational learning and communities of practice: towards a unified view of working, learning and innovation', *Organization Science*, **2**, 40–57.

Cohendet, P. and P. Llerena (2003), 'Routines and incentives: the role of communities in the firm', *Industrial and Corporate Change*, **12**(1), 271–97.

Dierickx, I. and K. Cool (1989), 'Asset stock accumulation and the sustainability of competitive advantage', *Management Science*, **35**(12), 1504–11.

Dreyfus, H. and S. Dreyfus (1986), 'Why computers may never think like people', *Technology Review*, **89**(1), 20–42.

Fleck, J. (1998), 'Expertise: knowledge, power and tradability', in Williams R. Faulkner and J. Fleck (eds), *Exploring Expertise*, London: Macmillan, 143–72.

Haas, P.M. (1992), 'Introduction: epistemic communities and international policy coordination', *International Organization*, **46**(1), 1–35.

Håkansson, L. (2002), 'Creating knowledge – the power and logic of articulation' (what the fuss is all about), paper presented for the LINK conference, 1–2 November.

Hatchuel, A. and B. Weil (1992), *L'expert et le système*, Paris: Economica.

Johnson, B., E. Lorenz and B.-A. Lundvall (2002), 'Why all this fuss about codified and tacit knowledge?', *Industrial and Corporate Change*, **11**(2), 245–62.

Lave, J. and E. Wenger (1991), *Situated Learning: Legitimate Peripheral Participation*, Cambridge: Cambridge University Press.

Lazaric, N. (2003), 'Trust building inside the "epistemic community": some investigation with an empirical case study', in F. Six and B. Nooteboom (eds), *The Process of Trust in Organizations*, Cheltenham, UK and Northampton, MA, USA: Edward Elgar, 147–67.

Lazaric, N. and E. Lorenz (1998), 'The learning dynamics of trust reputation and confidence', in N. Lazaric and E. Lorenz (eds), *Trust and Economic Learning*, Cheltenham, UK and Northampton, MA, USA: Edward Elgar, 1–20.

Lazaric, N., P.A. Mangolte and M.L. Massué (2003), 'Articulation and codification of collective know how in the steel industry: some evidence in the French blast furnace', Research Policy, **32**, 1829–47.

Livet, P. and B. Reynaud (1998), 'Organisational trust, learning and implicit commitments', in N. Lazarick and E. Lorenz (eds), *Trust and Economic Learning*, Cheltenham, UK and Northampton, MA, USA: Edward Elgar, 266–84.

Lorenz, E. (1993), 'Flexible production systems and the social construction of trust', *Politics and Society*, Sept., 307–24.

Lorenz, E. (2002), 'Inter-organisational trust, boundary spanners and communities of practice', in B. Burchell, S. Deakin, J. Michie and J. Rubery (eds), *Systems of Production: Markets, organisations and performance*, London: Routledge, 60–73.

Mangolte, P.-A. (1997), 'La dynamique des connaissances tacites et articulées: une approche socio-cognitive', *Economie Appliquée*, **L** (2), 105–34.

Moingeon, B. and A. Edmonson (1998), 'Trust and organizational learning', in N. Lazaric and E. Lorenz (eds), *Trust and Economic Learning*, Cheltenham, UK and Northampton, MA, USA: Edward Elgar, 228–47.

Nonaka, I. and H. Takeuchi (1995), *The Knowledge-Creating Company*, Oxford: Oxford University Press.

Nooteboom, B. (2002), *Trust: Forms, Foundations, Functions, Failures and Figures*, Cheltenham, UK and Northampton, MA, USA: Edward Elgar.

Pettit, P. (1998), 'Republican theory and political trust', in V. Braithwaite and M. Levi (eds), *Trust and Governance*, New York: Russell Sage Foundation.

Rumelt, R. (1984), 'Towards a strategic theory of the firm', in R.B. Lamb (ed.), *Competitive Strategic Management*, Englewood Cliffs, NJ: Prentice-Hall, 556–70.

Sako, M. (1998), 'The information requirements of trust in supplier relations: evidence from Japan, Europe and the United States', in N. Lazaric and E. Lorenz (eds), *Trust and Economic Learning*, Cheltenham, UK and Northampton, MA, USA: Edward Elgar, 23–47.

Szulanski, G., R. Cappetta and J.-R. Jensen (2004), 'When and how trustworthiness matters: knowledge transfer and the moderating effect of causal ambiguity', *Organization Science*, **15** (September–October), 600–613.

Teece, D.J. (1998), 'Capturing value from knowledge assets', *California Management Review*, **40**, Spring, 55–79.

Williams, B. (1988), 'Formal structures and social reality', in D. Gambetta (ed.) *Trust: Making and Breaking Cooperative Relations*, Oxford: Oxford University Press, 3–13.

Winter, S. (1987), 'Knowledge and competence as strategic assets', in D.J. Teece (ed.), *The Competitive Challenge: Strategies for industrial innovation and renewal*, Cambridge, MA: Ballinger, 159–83.

Zollo, M. and S. Winter (2002), 'Deliberate learning and the evolution of dynamic capabilities', *Organization Science*, **13**, 339–51.

11 Trust attitudes, network tightness and organizational survival: an integrative framework and simulation model

Arjen van Witteloostuijn and Marc van Wegberg

Introduction

Anecdotal evidence suggests that dynamic high-growth firms run a large risk of not being able to honor trust. The boom and bust of the dotcoms and the Enron-type scandals provide examples of fast-growing firms that caused a breakdown of trust. This anecdotal evidence suggests that trust building and high dynamics may be conflicting conditions. Fast-growing firms respond to new opportunities. To this end, they may engage in transactions with new partners. New partners may make promises that are hard for them to honor. Without making promises, they will not be invited into a partnership. Once in the partnership, they may not have the resources or the incentives to make it a success. Lack of trust and lack of trustworthy behavior can be a problem with new partnerships. A firm that wants to engage in opportunities with new partners may have to take the risk of non-trustworthy behavior. There is a tradeoff between building trust and participating in a dynamic setting.

To realize its goals, an organization tends to need resources from other organizations. This can lead to a state of dependence which the resource-providing organization can opportunistically exploit. Opportunism diminishes the value of the cooperation, and may prevent cooperation where that would be optimal (Roy Chowdhury and Roy Chowdhury, 2001). If the partners in cooperation trust each other, they may be able to overcome the problems of opportunism. Trust can be defined as an expectation held by one trading partner about another that the other will behave in a predictable and mutually acceptable manner (Young-Ybarra and Wiersema, 1999). By creating a trusting relationship the firms may be able to solve the problems that might wreck an individual alliance. This chapter argues, however, that trust building comes at a cost. While it may protect an individual alliance, it may also limit the ability of a firm to engage in new relationships. A firm may be aware of profitable opportunities requiring partnerships that would harm its trust-building efforts with its existing partners. It may face a tradeoff between the quantity of opportunities it wishes to pursue and the quality of individual relationships that it undertakes.

Within its network of long-term contacts, a firm is flexible in terms of which contact to seek for a particular new project. In a dynamic market, new opportunities occur that create a demand for new partnerships. The question arises how a firm can develop enough trust in a new partner to enter into a partnership with it. The established firm may face a dilemma: it may have to choose between trust, a condition satisfied among its current partners, and entrepreneurship, which may call for new partners. A new partner is like an experience good: only after consuming the partnership is it possible to establish its quality – here, its trustworthiness.

This chapter argues that networking can help to diminish the risk. By repeatedly cooperating with a set of trusted partners, a firm can share information. Infrequently, a firm may enter into a partnership with an unknown firm. This enables it to participate in an innovation that requires a new combination of resources. It may find *ex post* that the new partner did not honor trust. The partner may not have had the required resources (adverse selection) or it may have been unwilling to provide the effort to use them properly (moral hazard). The established firm will share this information with the partners in its network. They will be once burned twice shy. The network acts as a screen, a filter of partnerships. Sharing the information with partners increases the sanctions against a new non-trustworthy partner. Each firm in the network can free-ride on the experience of its partners with the trustworthiness of new firms. Network filtering enables established firms to solve the dilemma. In most cases, they cooperate with partners they trust, either because of direct contact or because of information via their network, while occasionally they will experiment with a new partner. An entrant that honors trust will find this fact known throughout the established network. It will find many doors are open for it.

Theoretical perspectives in the literature on trust

Opportunism is a catch-phrase for several kinds of self-serving and non-truthful behavior. Various forms of opportunistic exploitation exist. Opportunism can occur *ex ante*, when a firm tries to be accepted as a partner by making promises that it is unable to honor (so-called adverse selection). Its resources may not be as valuable to its partner as it may have suggested in order to be accepted into the partnership. Another form of opportunism occurs *ex post*. Free-rider behavior can be a problem in any cooperation. A partner may not provide as much effort for the relationship as it appeared to promise beforehand (so-called moral hazard or the problem of hidden action). Moral hazard is difficult to avoid when one of the partners envisages the contact to be a unique event and exploits its knowledge of that fact.

A third kind of opportunism is when a firm gets more out of the transaction than agreed upon. Parallel to the problem of hidden action (moral hazard), there can be hidden benefit. For example, a firm may learn more from its partner than was agreed upon. A hidden benefit for the recipient can be beneficial to the originator, as it improves the ability of the firms to cooperate effectively. It may also, however, lessen the need for the recipient to cooperate with the originator. Learning from each other, including unintentional or hidden learning, leads to a convergence of the knowledge of the partners (Nakamura et al., 1996; Santangelo, 2000). Since both partners have less to contribute to each other, convergent learning tends to break up the alliance.

Partners in cooperation can solve some adverse selection and moral hazard problems by detailing their mutual expectations in explicit contracts. If a contract can specify the services to be provided, it protects the firm against both adverse selection and moral hazard. There are, however, many non-contractible aspects to cooperation. Some forms of cooperative behavior are difficult to specify *ex ante*, and may not be enforceable in court. This refers to relational aspects of cooperative behavior such as information exchange, mutual adjustment in the relationship, and willingness to solve each other's problems. In the case of an unforeseen contingency, a firm can take advantage of a contractual loophole to exploit its partner. The possibility of unforeseen contingencies, and the inability to contractually safeguard one's interests if these occur, would militate against engaging in the interdependent relationship.

Several theoretical frameworks explore the incentives for opportunism and the ways to contain opportunism. We explore issues of dynamics and trust in the context of three theoretical perspectives, namely game theory, organization theory (i.e. transaction cost economics and organizational learning), and alliance and network theory. Before presenting our integrative framework, we first briefly review these three perspectives on opportunism and trust. Here, we only focus on highlights relevant in the context of the current chapter's argument. Extensive reviews of the different theories can be found elsewhere in this *Handbook*.

Game theory
Game theory has analyzed the prisoner's dilemma where cheating is the individually rational course of action. Cooperative play leads to superior outcomes (payoffs) if it is reciprocated. Cooperative play is, however, vulnerable to incentives of individual players to opportunistically exploit each other. In a single-shot prisoner's dilemma game, defection (cheating or non-cooperative conduct) is the dominant strategy – that is, the unique Nash equilibrium. If one player acts cooperatively, the other can take advantage of that by defecting. It can take a free ride on the cooperative firm's efforts. Anticipating this outcome, both firms defect. The combined cheating by the players leads to a collectively sub-optimal outcome. The benefits of cooperative play are lost. This setting offers a fruitful context in which to analyze trust in transactional relationships (see van Witteloostuijn, 2003, for a recent overview and discussion).

In game theory, the general characteristic of players is that they maximize their objectives. They are indifferent to the means for achieving their goals. Cheating and trustworthy behavior are equally possible modes of conduct. Behavior is contextual: the context determines whether someone will cheat or honor trust. A game analysis shows how various types of context provide incentives for or against opportunism. This represents an analysis of 'calculative trust', that is, trust as a mode of behavior that is consciously chosen because of the expected payoffs (James, 2002). In a way, this type of game theory implies a dehumanized conception of behavior, ignoring the features of human beings of flesh and blood (Boone et al., 1999).

Game theory has identified conditions that coax players with a calculative sense of trust to display trusting behavior. These conditions have in common that they offer the players means to punish cheating or reward each other for honoring trust. The basic condition explored by game theory is repeated play. In a repeated context, the players recognize that making a costly contribution to the collectively optimal outcome today can be rewarded in the future by the promise of repeated contact. Opportunism is kept in check by the anticipation of future benefits. Their anticipation of future engagements with each other will stabilize their relationship and increase the chance of cooperative behavior. This in turn tends to increase their revenues (the payoffs of the game).

Support for this perspective can be found in Heide and Miner's (1992) study of the effects of industrial relationships on the degree of cooperative behavior. Heide and Miner (1992) call the expectation that a relationship is continued in the future 'extendedness'. They show that if partners in an industrial buyer–supplier relationship expect it to continue, they are more likely to display cooperative behavior. By cooperative behavior they mean flexibility to demands by the partner, information exchange with the partner, shared problem solving, and restraint in the use of power over the partner. In an ongoing relationship, partners are willing to provide extra effort in order to convince each other of their intent to support each other. The prospect of future benefits dominates over the lure of the short-run gains of cheating or opportunistic behavior.

In a dynamic economy, new opportunities emerge that may not be repeated in the future. Exploration in new directions may lead to several ventures with disappointing performance. An explorative joint venture may be a unique event. In game theory language, it can be a one-shot game. This raises the strategic conundrum: how to explore new directions without running into cheaters. There is growing literature arguing that games exist in a social context that can provide the necessary incentives for trusting behavior. The social context in which the interaction takes place will affect the cooperativeness of the game play.

A fascinating study that takes up the aspects of social context is by McGinn and Keros (2002). In an experiment, they show that a socially embedded relationship is more often cooperative than an arm's-length relationship. In particular, they show that if friends bargain with each other, they are more often cooperative than if strangers bargain with each other. This is an important finding, as they also find that the more cooperative the interaction is, the more likely it is that the bargaining is successful and the revenues are distributed more equitably. This so-called 'familiarity effect' is well known from the social psychology of games (van Witteloostuijn, 2003).

A second scenario for cooperation in a one-shot game is that being trustworthy can be a preference that some players have (Güth et al., 2000). They act cooperatively in a prisoner's dilemma game because their preference for trust is modified to express their desire to reciprocate the other player's cooperative intent. This strategy is only viable, however, if the other players can distinguish between trustworthy players and their untrustworthy (opportunistic) counterparts. The more players are willing to inform themselves of the nature of their partner, the more attractive it is to be a trustworthy partner. In this context, background features of the players matter a lot, such as their educational degree (Frank et al., 1993), ethnicity (Cox et al., 1991) or personality (Boone et al., 1999).

These two scenarios of cooperation in prisoner's dilemma games suggest the following insight. Social embeddedness and a preference for reciprocation are complementary to a trait of being trustworthy. There are two routes for this. First, a trusting relationship stimulates open communication and this in turn enhances cooperation. Second, the more transparent transactions are, not just to their participants but also to outsiders, such as potential transaction partners, the more it pays to act in a trustworthy, cooperative manner. If, however, a condition prevails of limited communication possibilities, a lack of social embeddedness, or a lack of information about the trustworthiness of individual players, then trustworthy behavior does not pay in these single-shot games.

A variation of the extendedness argument is that a relationship can be laterally extended, as opposed to extending it into the future. A relationship between two firms may be linked to other relationships they have with each other. A multi-channel contact theory recognizes that firms have multiple points of contact where they exchange threats and promises that may lead to more cooperative behavior (van Wegberg and van Witteloostuijn, 2001). Multi-market firms are a case in point. They have the opportunity to compete with each other in multiple markets (van Witteloostuijn and van Wegberg, 1992). Moves made in one market can elicit a response in another market. A non-contractual way to diminish opportunism consists of multi-channel extendedness – that is, a relationship is linked to other relationships in which a pair of firms is also vulnerable to opportunism.

The conclusion from this game-theoretic discussion is that opportunism can lead to cheating, particularly in the context of one-shot prisoner's dilemma games. Trust will be honored if the conditions of the game are extended in time (repeated play), breadth (multi-market competition games), or behavior (social context with multiple social links). The importance of social context and embeddedness points to organization theory as a complementary line of enquiry. It is to this theory – or, more appropriate: this set of theories – that we turn now.

Organization theory
Organization theory exists in many branches, two of which are particularly relevant in the context of the current chapter: transaction cost economics and the organizational learning perspective. Transaction cost economics is a static theory in that it relates conditions at one moment in time to the choice of cost-minimizing organization structure for a given transaction. The organizational learning perspective looks at organization structure in terms of an evolution due to learning, emphasizing dynamics. We discuss each in turn.

Transaction cost economics (TCE) can offer useful insights in this tradeoff between trust and dynamics. A transaction creates dependency for a partner when that partner makes investments that are specific to the transaction. Asset specificity exposes a firm to the possibility of opportunistic exploitation. A dynamic environment creates uncertainty that increases the transaction costs. It burdens the bounded rationality of decision makers by increasing the amount of future possibilities that need to be thought through and controlled for in long-term transactions between potential business partners. In the standard TCE theory, this condition stimulates a firm to provide for the transactions internally. However, if the firm does engage in a transaction with another organization, it exposes itself to the possibilities of opportunism. Dynamic theories of cooperation stress that to overcome cheating in a relationship, the partners need to engage in a prior period of trust building, mutual commitments and relationship bargaining (Blankenburg Holm et al., 1999; Bureth et al., 1997; Nooteboom et al., 2000; Zajac and Olsen, 1993).

Nooteboom et al. (2000) combine transaction cost theory and the resource-based view of the firm to explore how partners in industrial supplier–buyer relationships prevent short-term opportunistic exploitation of asset specificity. By creating mutual dependence between the buyer and the supplier, each reduces the incentives for the other to act opportunistically. They show that in the US car industry three mechanisms for mutual dependence hold sway. Specific investments make the supplier dependent, but by enabling the buyer to differentiate its products, they also make the buyer dependent. The buyer may exploit the supplier, for example by learning from it, but when using this knowledge it is likely to increase its dependence on the supplier. And, finally, in an ongoing relationship the partners build up mutual trust, which increases mutual dependence and stabilizes the relationship. Transaction-specific investments do make a firm vulnerable to opportunism, therefore, but the relationship can be structured in ways that help to overcome this fear for opportunism.

The *organizational learning perspective* distinguishes between exploration and exploitation (March, 1991). It is a dynamic perspective on organization. Exploitation refers to pursuing an existing course of action more intensively. Exploration means striking out in a new direction. While exploitation may run into diminishing returns, exploration tends to be risky. The choice between exploitation and exploration will affect the choice of which opportunities to pursue and which partners to cooperate with. In the context of exploitation, on the one hand, a firm may deepen existing relationships. It may extend and perpetuate collaboration with a limited number of partners such as subcontractors, distributors and customers. In this context, trust emerges. Exploration, on the other hand, may benefit from entering into partnerships with new partners. Many of these will turn out to be failures. Some new ventures will recover their costs. Only a few will be resounding successes that open new avenues of growth for the firm. The latter avenues will become fields for exploitation. Partners in exploratory ventures may be aware of each other's short-term goals. They may accept a termination of the venture on short notice as a real possibility. Both trust, in exploitation ventures, and opportunism, in exploration ventures, may be appropriate and accepted modes of behavior.

Theories of organizational learning have studied alliances. They suggest a link between trust, to increase inter-organizational learning, and dynamics, which results from learning. Organizational learning is a linchpin between trust and dynamics (Bureth et al., 1997). Firms need to engage in mutual commitments to build trust. Trust is a relational asset that stabilizes the relationship. It convinces the partners that they believe in the future of their cooperation. This can stimulate their learning. It helps the partners build up communication between them, which is necessary for learning to take place. Openness can create interdependence between both partners to a transaction, which may lessen opportunism (Nooteboom et al., 2000). Learning in turn is a form of dynamics. It enables the firms to develop new products and processes. The learning may have feedback effects on the relationship. If the learning creates generic, reusable, knowledge, the firm may abandon its partner to cooperate with new partners. If the learning, however, depends on mutual commitments, it may deepen the relationship. This specific focus on alliances is often combined with insights from network theory. Next, we briefly review relevant network-type of studies in this alliance area.

Network theory
The literature on alliances offers salient insights into how opportunism may lead to cooperation problems. It also discusses solutions that firms have developed, including ways to build trust. The upshot of this literature is that long-term relationships, socially embedded relationships and close groups of traders can sustain cooperative trusting behavior by transaction partners in the context of a network of ties. In this literature, different theories are applied, including the ones above, and new insights are developed. In the context of the current chapter, it suffices to discuss a number of insightful studies.

In the setting of a production joint venture, Roy Chowdhury and Roy Chowdhury (2001) argue that moral hazard of the alliance partners reduces the value of an alliance. The moral hazard consists of each firm's decision to provide fewer contributions (capital or labor) to the joint venture than would be collectively optimal. Each firm free-rides on the contributions made by the other firm. Free-riding reduces the value of the joint venture. Taking this into account, the two firms will cooperate only if their synergy is sufficiently large to outweigh the expected reciprocal free-riding. While they cooperate, they learn from each other. Due to imitative learning, their resources become more similar. This reduces the synergy that they have for each other. They may react to this by shutting down their joint venture. Imitative learning can undermine cooperation. A lack of trust (moral hazard) may thus cost the joint venture dear in the mid-term if their learning is imitative and synergy decreases over time. This line of reasoning relates to the organizational learning perspective.

In an empirical study on joint venture terminations, Kogut (1989) found that if the partners in the joint venture had other relationships with each other, such as other licensing, joint venture, or supply contracts, this tended to stabilize the joint venture. This embeddedness in a larger network may overcome adverse selection and moral hazard problems, and this in turn may explain its positive effect on joint venture durability. This is a multi-contact argument, with game-theoretic roots.

Long-term relations can build trust. If firms are already familiar with each other, they can make a fairly accurate assessment of the contribution that the other firm can make to a partnership. This is one reason for the finding that if two firms have cooperated in the past, they have a larger chance of allying in the future (Gulati, 1995). If partners provide mutual commitments, they are more likely to depend on each other in their relationship (Blankenburg Holm et al., 1999). In the initialization stage of a relationship, firms exchange views and communicate with each other to set the terms of their future engagement (Zajac and Olsen, 1993). By making these transactional investments early on, they can reap the benefits later by a value-creating cooperation. This is repeated-play logic.

If transactions occur between long-term partners, insiders in these networks face different opportunities than outsiders. Examples of trades among insiders are personal networks among Chinese businessmen. *Guanxi* is a personal network relationship that facilitates trades among insiders (Lovett et al., 1999). In a *guanxi* approach, the outsider is allowed only limited access to trades. Insiders trust each other. They need few safeguards for their transactions. As a result, transaction costs among insiders are low. Outsiders can be handpicked into the *guanxi* network after a probation period. If accepted, they become insiders after a while. Outsiders may feel discriminated against by these personal networks. Their exclusion can prevent potentially profitable trades from being undertaken. This is the familiarity effect.

These arguments suggest that in a repeated, continued, relationship firms find ways to overcome their adverse selection and moral hazard problems along the lines suggested by theory. It is in a new relationship, which may not be continued in the future, that these problems will surface. In a dynamic context, firms may want to engage in new relationships. These new relationships represent bets on new opportunities. If the new opportunity does not materialize, the relationship is expected to be terminated. The possibility of early termination reduces the extendedness of the relationship. This in turn will reduce the level of cooperative behavior, as Heide and Miner (1992) demonstrated.

In a dynamic market, industry or economy, there are many opportunities for new or improved products and services. While the opportunities may be exogenously given, it is up to companies to realize these opportunities. This may call upon firms to cooperate. By pooling their resources and building networks, firms can engage in new activities that they could not start up alone. Innovations often consist of new combinations, as Schumpeter famously argued. Networks of firms become the source of innovations, such as in the biotechnology industry (Powell et al., 1996). Cooperation may help firms increase the number of competitive actions they can undertake in the product market

(Young et al., 1996). Cooperation between an established firm and an upstart can help to overcome entry barriers (Kogut et al., 1995).

Integrative framework
On the basis of this overview, we now develop an integrative framework that combines the salient aspects of organization theory (particularly TCE and organizational learning) and network-type alliance studies into a game-theoretic foundation. Our framework combines two aspects. First, opportunities for new partnerships can be valuable but also risky. The risks are partly inherent to new opportunities and are partly due to the possibility of new partners being opportunistic. Second, firms exchange information about new partners in their contact network. This enables them to quickly spread information about a newcomer's trustworthiness. These two aspects suggest that firms use their contact network to screen new partners, in order to be able to respond to new opportunities and reinvigorate their network of trusted partners.

Opportunities and the risks of cheating
A new opportunity represents an imbalance between supply capabilities and customer needs. Environmental shocks, such as political or regulatory changes, can create disruptive changes. An 'Austrian' entrepreneur recognizes opportunities that were hitherto unattended to (Kirzner, 1997). Actions by companies, such as inventions, also create new opportunities. Cooperation with partners can enable a firm to respond to opportunities that it would have to pass by when acting alone. The partners are not sure in advance whether they will be able to combine their strengths successfully. Their bounded rationality in combination with uncertainty creates a potential for opportunism. Partners may use the cooperation as a cover to learn from each other. If they invest fewer resources in the cooperation than they appeared to promise, failure of the cooperation can be blamed on the uncertainty.

We identify two conditions that impact upon the firm's ability to respond to an opportunity. The first condition is the firm's network of long-term contacts. A firm without such a network is unable to respond adequately to opportunities with a high level of uncertainty and a high degree of dependence. A firm's existing network of long-term contacts helps it to identify new opportunities that it can respond to within its existing network. These opportunities combine elements of exploitation (of existing relationships) and exploration (new applications for its network).

The second condition that impacts upon the firm's ability to respond to new opportunities is its flexibility in collaborating with new partners. Before a firm can benefit from long-term relationships, it needs to undertake the risk of entering into new relationships. Working with a new partner requires various skills of the firm's management: the creativity to find new partners, the social skills to select appropriate partners, and the negotiation skills to set the terms of cooperation with a new partner. An inflexible firm is limited to opportunities that it can realize within its own organization. A firm with a limited flexibility can build up a network of relationships over time. While it prefers to use its existing network for new opportunities, it may infrequently engage in new relationships. The more flexible a firm is, the more it is willing to take up new opportunities beyond its existing network. It is more willing than less flexible firms to engage in market contacts or contractual relationships for these opportunities.

The more flexible a firm is, the more it creates a portfolio of relationships, with a variety of partners, new and existing ones. It needs to manage its long-term relationships on the basis of trust. These represent the exploitation motive from organizational learning theory. The firm also needs to engage in new relationships in order to enable exploration and renewal. These relationships are more likely to be opportunistic. A balancing act is needed, striking a happy medium between exploitation (old partners) and exploration (new partners). This happy medium is likely to be a moving target, changing with environmental shocks.

The discussion so far suggests that there are two limits on the discretion that a firm has to create this portfolio of cooperative ventures. The first is its flexibility in contacting new partners. The second is its existing trust relationship network. In order to safeguard the trust of its long-term relationships, it is limited in its ability to enter into new opportunities that would compete with its existing cooperative ventures. A large, long-term network of relationships both supports and limits the firm's ability to respond to new opportunities. It supports its ability to engage in trusting relationships for new opportunities with a high level of complementarity and high uncertainty. Figure 11.1 offers an illustration.

Flexibility on the horizontal axis in Figure 11.1 refers to a firm's willingness to cooperate with a new partner. It can be measured as the ratio of new to established partners within the current alliances portfolio of a firm. Dynamics refer to the ratio of pursuing new as opposed to existing opportunities. This is similar to the exploration/exploitation relationship in organizational learning theory. Performance (for convenience with dynamics on the vertical axis in Figure 11.1) refers to the long-term payoffs, such as the survival rate.

The story implied by Figure 11.1 is that the more flexible a firm is in its choice of new partners for new ventures, the more opportunities for cooperation it can respond to. Increasing the number of opportunities may not, however, improve performance. The performance of exploratory relationships with new partners tends to be more risky than the performance of mixed exploitation/exploratory ventures with existing partners. Cooperating with new partners makes the firm vulnerable to opportunism risks. Responding to opportunities with new partners may, moreover, have negative repercussions in the firm's existing network of relations. New exploratory ventures may compete with the firm's existing ventures. They may compete with the main product lines of the

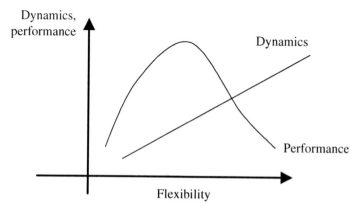

Figure 11.1   Flexibility, dynamics and performance

firm's existing long-term partners. Highly public conflicts with new partners may tarnish the firm's reputation with its existing partners. New partners can also crowd out established partners, which may unravel the firm's network of contacts.

To summarize this discussion, we posit our first *ceteris paribus* proposition, relating organizational survival to contact flexibility.

Proposition 11.1: Performance of firms (such as indicated by survival probabilities) has a hill-shaped relationship with the flexibility by established firms in accepting newcomers in their network.

Proposition 11.1 suggests that firms can either be too inert or too flexible. An unconditional plea for flexibility is counterproductive in the context of the subtle exploitation/ exploration balancing act (cf. Sorge and van Witteloostuijn, 2004; van Witteloostuijn et al., 2003).

Network transfer of trust
The trust attitude that a player has towards another player, and the latter's trustworthiness in honoring trust, improve with prior, lateral and future contacts among the players. Prior contacts build a reputation for trust. Future contacts give an incentive to sustain this reputation (the extendedness argument). Lateral contacts increase the stakes when an interaction backfires (multi-channel contact theory). Players can nurture trust in a network, population or cluster. A difference can exist between insiders and outsiders. The insiders have learned to trust each other (the familiarity argument). They are wary of outsiders. Outsiders need to be allowed to gain the trust of others before they too can become insiders.

A firm may be able to develop trust in another organization that it does not know directly. It may transfer the trust it has in a firm that it does know to the partners of that firm. The phenomenon that trust in a network partner is attached to a partner of the trusted entity is called 'trust transfer' (Stewart, 2003). The common partner acts as a conduit for trust transfer. In a *guanxi* personal network, for instance, family ties can act as conduits of trust transfer. In the absence of family ties, a firm can vouch for its contacts, and therewith introduce them to its partners.

Figure 11.2 builds on Figure 11.1 to show the impact of network tightness on dynamics and performance. The upward shift in the performance level represents the effect of a cohesive network. For any given level of contact flexibility (i.e. the ratio of new to established partners), a tighter network yields higher performance to the firm. New firms can more readily be trusted when a tightly interconnected contact network rapidly spreads their newly developing reputation to the established firms. This argument suggests our second proposition:

Proposition 11.2: Contact flexibility and network tightness interact positively with each other in their influence on performance (survival) of firms.

A simulation model of interaction, trust and newcomers
We explore the argument in a simple simulation model, based on game-theoretic and network logic, and including learning arguments. The model enables us to explore several dimensions of the trust and dynamics tradeoff issue. The model explores the conceptual relationships introduced in the previous section. In a dynamic environment, new

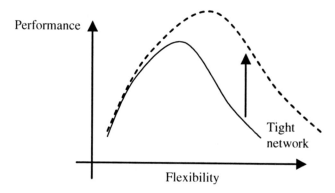

Figure 11.2   The effect of a contact network on performance

Table 11.1   Payoffs of the opportunity game

		Player 2: honor trust?	
		Yes	*No*
Player 1: honor trust?	*Yes*	(b, b)	(d, a)
	No	(a, d)	(c, c)

opportunities become available frequently. Moreover, these opportunities can be new in that they call for new combinations of firms. These opportunities create dilemmas for firms. Every firm tends to have some partners that it can trust. These tend to be the insiders in the industry. There are also, however, firms around that it does not know. In a dynamic setting, the latter may own resources that can be used for new products. But the former are more trustworthy. The importance of trust is to avoid cheaters who do not have the resources they claim to contribute (an adverse selection problem). The importance of dynamics is that by engaging in new relationships, a firm can find new uses for its resources, or find resources to match new ideas.

A game-theoretic foundation

We first present the setting in terms of game theory. Without a network, game theory can predict the specific outcomes. These outcomes are a benchmark for the simulation. Call $u_{i,t}$ the payoff of playing games by firm i in period t. The payoff is zero if the firm did not participate in a game in a given period. The payoff of an individual interaction represents a prisoner's dilemma. An interaction has the payoff structure depicted in Table 11.1.

These payoffs represent a prisoner's dilemma when $a > b > c > d$. In a static Nash equilibrium, the action (*Yes*, *Yes*) is Pareto efficient, but the actions '*No*' are dominant strategies and (*No*, *No*) is the unique Nash equilibrium. The highest payoff (a) comes from cheating on a trusting partner. Players would like to honor each other's trust, but know that each would like to abuse that fact by unilateral cheating. We assume that mutual cheating is a viable strategy ($c > 0$), but being cheated against is not ($d < 0$). Hence we have

Assumption 11.1 (prisoner's dilemma): $a > b > c > 0 > d$.

In a static game, the players will not cooperate due to the prisoner's dilemma. In a repeated game, if a firm honors trust it earns a payoff of b indefinitely, discounted at rate δ, which gives a discounted payoff of $b/(1-\delta)$. If the firm defects from that, it earns a in the first period and is punished for ever after that by retaliatory cheating. This gives the discounted payoff $a-c + [c/(1-\delta)]$. Firms will cooperate only if the former exceeds the latter – that is, if $[(b-c)/(1-\delta)] + c > a$. This suggests

Assumption 11.2 (cooperation in a repeated game): $\frac{b-c}{1-\delta} + c > a$.

Cooperation becomes less attractive if only a part of the population of players is able to honor trust. With a chance of β a firm is competent and can honor trust. With a chance of $1 - \beta$ it does not have the competence to honor trust, even if it wanted to, and always plays the *No* option in Table 11.1. If only the percentage β of the players is able to honor trust, the discounted payoff of following a cooperation strategy is reduced. It is intuitive that cooperation no longer pays if the following expression holds:

$$\beta\left(\frac{b-c}{1-\delta} + 2c - a - d\right) < c - d.$$

The simulation assumes that this condition holds. This gives

Assumption 11.3 (cooperation fails with too many cheaters): $\beta < \dfrac{c-d}{\dfrac{b-c}{1-\delta} + 2c - a - d}$.

The implication of Assumptions 11.1 to 11.3 is that cooperation is to be preferred among competent players (Assumption 11.2) in the repeated game (Assumption 11.1), but that in the wider population with incompetent players, cooperation is to be avoided (Assumption 11.3). The simulation needs to show whether in these circumstances the information network between competent players can help them avoid interactions with incompetent players, thus raising the gain from cooperation enough to make it the preferred strategy.

The simulation model
In each period, games are played. By chance, a meeting between companies i and j results in a valuable opportunity for cooperation. The chance that a pair of firms (i, j) have an opportunity to play a game is assumed to be the given probability γ, which indicates the dynamics of the industry. The higher γ, the more dynamic the industry is. A chance meeting to play is an interaction between the firms. If one (or both) of the participants in an interaction is a new firm, it enters the market.

The payoffs increase the fitness (viability) of a firm by the following fitness function:

$$f_{i,t} = f_{i,t-1} - \delta f_0 + u_{i,t-1}. \tag{11.1}$$

The parameter f_0 in Equation (11.1) is the fitness level of an upstart, and represents a benchmark for a surviving firm. If a firm has a negative fitness level, it exits the market. Potential entrants to the market have an asset stock of f_0. Each entrant has a honeymoon period, during which it does not exit, and its fitness is replenished up to f_0 if it falls below that level.

Firms decide about their action as follows. First, the strategies within a play are simple: a competent firm always cooperates, and an incompetent firm always cheats, provided that they entered into interaction. The incompetent firm has no alternative but to cheat, and the competent firm loses its reputation when it cheats. Second, decision making occurs before the game play, in the decision by each player whether or not to accept the invitation from the other firm to play the game – that is, to enter into the interaction. An incompetent firm, on the one hand, will accept every invitation to play. By Table 11.1, it can never lose as any payoff it earns is always positive.

Competent firms, on the other hand, always cooperate in any interaction to build a reputation. But doing so is costly when they meet a cheating firm (see Table 11.1). The uncertainty about competence makes it valuable for firms to learn about each other. To minimize losses from being cheated on – that is, the payoff level d – competent firms are discerning players. They reject many requests to play. They use the following decision-making routine whether or not to accept an invitation to interact. If firms interact in a period (t), they have $l_{ijt} = 1$, and $l_{ijt} = 0$ otherwise. If firm i has ever interacted with firm j before, then it has a memory of that history, expressed by $h_{ijt} = 1$, and $h_{ijt} = 0$ otherwise. Firms that have interacted in the past ($h_{ijt} = 1$) may have formed a link or contact. If two firms interact and both honor trust, they form a contact with each other. We indicate a contact between firms i and j by g_{ijt}, which equals 1 if there is a contact, and zero otherwise. A contact, once formed, continues indefinitely, in principle. It is broken only in two events: either by cheating or by exit, by one or both partners. The contacts of firm i constitute its egocentric network, G_i. The size of its egocentric network is the number of links that it has, k_i:

$$k_i = \sum_{j \in G_i} g_{ijt}. \tag{11.2}$$

If neither firm i nor its current network G_i know firm j (their histories with j are such that $h_{ijt} = 0$), it considers firm j to be a new firm. With a probability of α a competent firm that has an interaction with a new firm decides to accept the invitation to play the game. With a probability of $1 - \alpha$ it turns down the request. The parameter α represents the behavioral or contact flexibility that a firm is willing to trust a newcomer (cf. Figures 11.1 and 11.2). If an interaction opportunity emerges between two firms that know each other directly, and have ever experienced cheating, they refuse to accept the invitation to play. If they know each other indirectly, and one of them cheated on the other's contact partner, the invitation is also declined. Games are played only between incompetent players, therefore, between a competent player and a new player (at a probability of α), and between competent players that share a history of honoring trust.

The combination of opportunities that present themselves (at the probability of γ), the invitations that are mutually accepted, and the strategies that the pair of firms in an interaction play – that is, honor or cheat – determine their payoff (see Table 11.1). Their resulting payoffs, $u_{i,t}$, of *a*, *b*, *c* or *d* per interaction, respectively, are used to update their fitness levels (see Equation (11.1)). If new firms meet and honor trust, they form a contact. If one or both firms cheat, or if one exits, their contact is broken (i.e. $g_{ij} = 0$).

Running the simulation
The simulation makes 4000 runs. Each run tracks a market with entry, exit and co-operation during 200 time periods. There are 40 firms available. The payoffs are: *a* equals 7, *b* equals 3, *c* equals 1, and *d* equals -2. The initial fitness level f_0 is 20. The honeymoon period is 10 periods. The competence probability β is given at 0.34. The discount rate δ is 0.8. Assumptions 1 to 3 are honored by these values. We vary both the cooperation probability α and the industry dynamics parameter γ uniformly between 0 and 1.

Measuring network structure
At the end of each simulation run, we measure four indicators of network structure. These are network density, centrality, clustering and path length, all reflecting different aspects of network tightness (cf. Figure 11.2 and Proposition 11.2). In so doing, we introduce notions from network theory into our game-theoretic simulation. As a by-product of our simulation exercise, we will be able to explore whether different types of network tightness produce similar or dissimilar outcomes. On this, we do not have any *a priori* expectations, except for the general one implied by Proposition 11.2. We briefly return to this issue in the appraisal.

Network density D is the share of possible bilateral links that are actually formed. The total number of links is counted as $\Sigma_i^N k_i$ and divided by the total number of possible links. The latter equals $N(N-1)$ if there are *N* active nodes, each of which can link to $N-1$ other nodes.

Network centrality is the extent to which links are centralized among few nodes. One of the indicators for network centrality is degree centrality (Powell et al., 1996). It indicates the extent to which one firm has more links (a higher degree) than all others. This is measured as the sum total over the whole network of the difference between k_{max}, the highest degree in the network, and each individual degree: $\Sigma_i^N(k_{max} - k_i)$. This expression is normalized to a number between 0 and 1 by dividing it by its maximum value, $(N-1)(N-2)$, to give *C* for network degree centrality.

The *network clustering* coefficient *S* is the chance that if node *i* links to both *j* and *h*, *j* and *h* are linked together as well (Albert and Barabási, 2002). It is measured as the number of realized transitive links, with node *i* linked to both *j* and *h* and *j* and *h* linked to each other, as a percentage of potential transitive links where a firm *i* is linked to both *j* and *h*. In a random network, this equals the chance that any link is formed (between a pair of firms *j* and *h*), which equals the network density *D*.

A path p_{ijt} is the smallest number of firms needed to link any pair of firms (i,j) together in the network in period *t*. A pair that has a link with each other (i.e. where $g_{ijt} = 1$) has path length 1. If they are not directly linked, but they have a common partner, then the smallest (information) path between them is via that partner – that is, their path length is 2. If a pair of firms cannot be connected at all, for instance because they have no links, their path length is set at $N - 1$. The *network path length P* is the average path length over all possible pairs of active firms in the population. Hence we have

$$D = \frac{\Sigma_i^N k_i}{N(N-1)}, \quad C = \frac{\Sigma_i^N (k_{max} - k_i)}{(N-1)(N-2)},$$

(11.3)

$$S = \frac{\Sigma_{i \in M} \Sigma_{j>i} \Sigma_{h>j} g_{ij} g_{ih} g_{jh}}{\Sigma_{i \in M} \Sigma_{j>i} \Sigma_{h>j} g_{ij} g_{ih}} \quad \text{and} \quad P = \frac{\Sigma_{i=1}^{N-1} \Sigma_{j=i+1}^{N} P_{ij}}{\frac{1}{2} N(N-1)}.$$

Measuring outcomes

We measure performance as the survival rate – that is, as the number of competent firms that survive at the end of the simulation (cf. Propositions 11.1 and 11.2). Contact flexibility, the parameter α, and industry dynamics, the parameter γ, are givens in each simulation run. As said, we vary α and γ over different simulation runs.

Figure 11.3 shows the number of competent survivors in relation to network density (*D*). In the course of 200 time periods, entry tends to increase the total population up to the maximum of 40. The straight line in Figure 11.3 is the predicted relationship in a linear regression. The number of competent firms among them can both be a lot lower and a lot higher than the *ex ante* probability of β of 0.34 (which would translate to 14 firms out of 40). The higher the network density among the competent firms is, the larger the number of them that survive to the end of the simulation. The relationship between the network

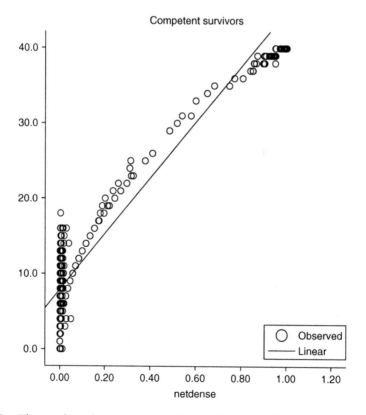

Figure 11.3   The number of competent survivors and network density (D)

Table 11.2   Regression analysis of survival on contact flexibility and network density

	1	2	3	4
Constant	11.113***	9.054***	4.908***	5.129***
$\alpha\gamma$	5.970***	27.101***	21.400***	18.276***
$(\alpha\gamma)^2$		−29.298***	−21.038***	−21.744***
D			36.709***	33.588***
$\alpha\gamma D$				32.859***
Adj. R^2	0.030	0.074	0.861	0.865

Note: Significance levels: *** $p < 0.01$. ** $p < 0.05$. * $p < 0.1$.

density and the survival of competent firms is that the denser the network is, the better it screens out cheaters from the new players. Hence it helps competent firms focus interactions on each other, thus increasing their fitness and driving out cheaters. This result is in line with Proposition 11.2.

Outcomes of the simulation
A regression analysis on the results of the simulation explores the network structure, in terms of the above four network tightness measures, that evolves from the simulated process. In Table 11.2, the number of competent survivors is regressed on contact flexibility and network density D. We take the compound parameter $\alpha\gamma$ as the indicator for contact flexibility: the higher $\alpha\gamma$ is, the more established firms are willing (α) and able (γ) to cooperate with newcomers. We take network density as the network tightness parameter, to start with. The dependent variable is the number of competent survivors at $t =$ 200. Note that the total number of suppliers after 200 periods is 40 with few exceptions of excessive exit.

Columns 1 and 2 in Table 11.2 show that the contact flexibility parameter $\alpha\gamma$ has the predicted curvilinear relationship with the survival rate. This provides support for Proposition 11.1 (see Figure 11.1). Column 3 shows that network density has a significant positive relationship with survival (see Figure 11.3 for an illustration). Network density interacts with contact flexibility to further increase survival (Column 4), which gives support for the interaction effect predicted by Proposition 11.2 and Figure 11.2.

There is some direct evidence that network density does indeed help established competent firms to screen new partners before accepting an invitation to interact. For all competent firms, we measure the share of their new contacts (new to the individual firm – i.e. $h_{ijt} = 0$) that are competent firms, called *NewCompetentRatio*. Without any ability to screen, this should be approximately β (= 0.34). With a network, established firms can boycott those new players that they learn from their network partners have cheated on them. This helps to increase the ratio of competent firms among new partners.

Figure 11.4 shows that almost any ratio is possible. There are markets where only cheaters survive, as their revenues are either *a* or *c*, which are both positive (see Table 11.1). In these cases, the ratio of competent firms among new partners is below their *ex ante* ratio, β. There are also cases where established competent firms attract new partners with a ratio of competent firms far above β. These tend to be the cases with relatively high network density levels. Hence, network density acts as a screen to weed out cheaters among new partners.

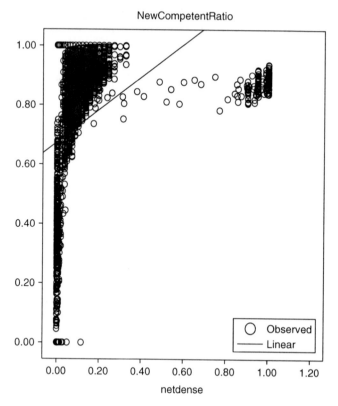

Figure 11.4   NewCompetentRatio in relation to network density D

Table 11.3   Regression analysis of survival on contact flexibility and network tightness

	1	2	3	4	5
Constant	7.527***	3.872***	4.569***	35.896***	28.725***
$\alpha\gamma$	7.638***	−20.885***	−47.320***	31.643***	117.555***
$(\alpha\gamma)^2$	−9.987***	19.350***	18.204***	−32.145***	−31.549***
C	25.203***				
S		14.610***	13.763***		
$\alpha\gamma S$			27.444***		
P				−0.823***	−0.615***
$\alpha\gamma P$					−2.496***
Adj. R^2	0.118	0.372	0.374	0.722	0.766

Note: Significance levels as for Table 11.2.

Table 11.3 presents the interaction effects with the other measures of network tightness. It shows only those that were significant. Columns 1, 4 and 5 show the predicted curvilinear relationship between survival and flexibility (the compound parameter, $\alpha\gamma$). Columns 2 and 3 on the network clustering parameter S reveal, however, a reversed curvilinear relationship. Network centrality has a positive effect on survival, but the overall predictive power (in Column 1) is small (adjusted R^2 of only 0.118). The interaction effect between contact flexibility and network clustering has the predicted positive effect on survival (Column 3). The less tight a network tends to be, the larger the path tends to be from one member in the network to another. A large path length has the predicted negative effect on survival (Column 4) and a predicted negative interaction effect with contact flexibility on survival (Column 5).

By and large, our simulation exercise provides support for Propositions 11.1 and 11.2. The exceptions are the reversed non-linear effect of contact flexibility on the survival rate if network clustering is introduced as our network tightness measure, and the non-significance of the flexibility * centrality interaction. Moreover, note that network density and path length are associated with substantially higher adjusted R^2 than network centrality and clustering, suggesting the former are more important than the latter in enhancing the network's role as a trust-screening device.

Appraisal

The aim of this exercise was to show that dynamics and trustworthy behavior are difficult to reconcile, requiring a subtle balancing act of exploitation (alliances with old partners) and exploration (alliances with new partners). Dynamic high-growth areas create opportunities for new relationships. New relationships can enable cheaters to prey on established honorable firms. Established firms either need to turn down some attractive opportunities or they need to accept the possibility of being cheated upon by opportunistic partners. The simulation model shows why networks arise between insiders who can trust each other. The dynamic process creates uncertainty, and firms need their network to collect information to reduce that uncertainty. Networking facilitates experiments: firms play with newcomers, and may discover that they are cheated on. They relay this information to their trusted network partners. The network increases the punishment power against cheaters. It acts as a screen to weed out cheaters before they can do too much harm. Protected by their network, established firms can afford to interact with newcomers, and play a cooperative strategy with them. As a result, newcomers can be integrated in the market and new opportunities can be realized. At an aggregate level, therefore, dynamics (uncertainty) and trusting behavior can go together, provided firms build a network of relationships.

Of course, this chapter was only able to lift the veil of the complex issue of trust attitudes, organizational learning and network tightness. Future research may further explore these issues by developing additional propositions. For example, our results reveal that the outcomes are not consistent across our four measures of network tightness. It remains to be seen what may explain this, and how robust these findings are. Ultimately, we hope that the propositions explored with the above type of simulation analyses are put to the test with real-world data. We believe that our integration of different theories – particularly game theory, organizational learning theory and network theory – in the context of a simulation model offers a powerful tool for developing and exploring new insights. However, by the end of the day, the ultimate test requires field work.

References

Albert, R. and Barabási, A.-L. (2002). Statistical mechanics of complex networks. *Reviews of Modern Physics*, **74**(1), 47–97.

Blankenburg Holm, D., Eriksson, K. and Johanson, J. (1999). Creating value through mutual commitment to business network relationships. *Strategic Management Journal*, **20**(5), 467–86.

Boone, C., De Brabander, B. and van Witteloostuijn, A. (1999). The impact of personality on behavior in five prisoner's dilemma games. *Journal of Economic Psychology*, **20**(3), 343–77.

Bureth, A., Wolff, S. and Zanfei, A. (1997). The two faces of learning by cooperating: the evolution and stability of inter-firm agreements in the European electronics industry. *Journal of Economic Behavior and Organization*, **32**(4), 519–37.

Cox, T.H., Lobel, S.A. and McLeod, P.L. (1991). Effects of ethnic group cultural differences on cooperative and competitive behavior on a group task. *Academy of Management Journal*, **34**(4), 827–47.

Frank, R.H., Gilovich, T. and Regan, D.T. (1993). Does studying economics inhibit cooperation? *Journal of Economic Perspectives*, **7**(2), 159–71.

Gulati, R. (1995). Social structure and alliance formation patterns: a longitudinal analysis. *Administrative Science Quarterly*, **40**, 619–52.

Güth, W., Kliemt, H. and Peleg, B. (2000). Co-evolution of preferences and information in simple games of trust. *German Economic Review*, **1**(1), 83–110.

Heide, J.B. and Miner, A.S. (1992). The shadow of the future: effects of anticipated interaction and frequency of contact on buyer-seller cooperation. *Academy of Management Journal*, **35**(2), 265–91.

James, H.S.J. (2002). The trust paradox: a survey of economic inquiries into the nature of trust and trustworthiness. *Journal of Economic Behavior & Organization*, **47**(3), 291–307.

Kirzner, I.M. (1997). Entrepreneurial discovery and the competitive market process: an Austrian approach. *Journal of Economic Literature*, **35**(1), 60–85.

Kogut, B. (1989). The stability of joint ventures: reciprocity and competitive rivalry. *The Journal of Industrial Economics*, **38**(2), 183–98.

Kogut, B., Walker, G. and Kim, D.-J. (1995). Cooperation and entry induction as an extension of technological rivalry. *Research Policy*, **24**, 77–95.

Lovett, S., Simmons, L.C. and Kali, R. (1999). Guanxi versus the market: ethics and efficiency. *Journal of International Business Studies*, **30**(2), 231–48.

March, J.G. (1991). Exploration and exploitation in organizational learning. *Organization Science*, **2**(1), 71–87.

McGinn, K.L. and Keros, A.T. (2002). Improvisation and the logic of exchange in socially embedded transactions. *Administrative Science Quarterly*, **47**, 442–73.

Nakamura, M., Shaver, J.M. and Yeung, B. (1996). An empirical investigation of joint venture dynamics: evidence from U.S.–Japan joint ventures. *International Journal of Industrial Organization*, **14**(4), 521–41.

Nooteboom, B., De Jong, G., Vossen, R.W., Helper, S. and Sako, M. (2000). Network interactions and mutual dependence: a test in the car industry. *Industry & Innovation*, **7**(1), 117–44.

Powell, W.W., Koput, K.W. and Smith-Doerr, L. (1996). Interorganizational collaboration and the locus of innovation: networks of learning in biotechnology. *Administrative Science Quarterly*, **41**, 116–45.

Roy Chowdhury, I. and Roy Chowdhury, P. (2001). A theory of joint venture life-cycles. *International Journal of Industrial Organization*, **19**, 319–43.

Santangelo, G.D. (2000). Corporate strategic technological partnerships in the European information and communications technology industry. *Research Policy*, **29**(9), 1015–31.

Sorge, A. and Witteloostuijn, A. van (2004). The (non)sense of organizational change: an essay about universal management hypes, sick consultancy metaphors, and healthy organization theories. *Organization Studies*, **25**(7), 1205–31.

Stewart, K.J. (2003). Trust transfer on the World Wide Web. *Organization Science*, **14**(1), 5–17.

Wegberg, M. van and Witteloostuijn, A. van (2001). Strategic management in the new economy: modern information technologies and multichannel contact strategies. In J.A.C. Baum and H.R. Greve (eds), *Multiunit Organization and Multimarket Strategy* (Vol. **18**, pp. 263–304). Oxford, UK: JAI.

Witteloostuijn, A. van (2003). A game-theoretic framework of trust. *International Studies of Management and Organization*, **33**(3), 53–71.

Witteloostuijn, A. van and Wegberg, M. van (1992). Multimarket competition: theory and evidence. *Journal of Economic Behavior & Organization*, **18**(2), 273–82.

Witteloostuijn, A. van, Boone, C. and Lier, A. van (2003). Toward a game theory of organizational ecology: production adjustment costs and managerial growth preferences. *Strategic Organization*, **1**(3), 259–300.

Young, G., Smith, K.G. and Grimm, C.M. (1996). 'Austrian' and industrial organization perspectives on firm-level competitive activity and performance. *Organization Science*, **7**(3), 243–54.

Young-Ybarra, C. and Wiersema, M. (1999). Strategic flexibility in Information Technology alliances: the influence of transaction cost economics and social exchange theory. *Organization Science*, **10**(4), 439–59.

Zajac, E.J. and Olsen, C.P. (1993). From transaction cost to transactional value analysis: implications for the study of interorganizational strategies. *Journal of Management Studies*, **30**(1), 131–45.

12 Learning about contracts: trust, cooperation and contract law
Simon Deakin

1. Introduction

The aim of this chapter is to explore the potential of evolutionary-theoretical approaches in the social sciences in understanding the role played by contract law in promoting cooperation and trust. A widely held view in the sociology of law is that legal rules and sanctions are marginal to contractual relations, and this has led to scepticism concerning the role which the legal system can play in supporting trust. This position rests on a series of empirical studies which are interpreted as having shown that the parties to business transactions make little use of either contract law or of formal agreements in their dealings with one another, relying instead on informal norms, tacit understanding and 'trust' (Macaulay, 1963; Beale and Dugdale, 1975; Collins, 1999: ch. 6). Against this, there are economic accounts of contract which see the law as directly influencing economic behaviour and outcomes. In the economic analysis of law, legal rules are understood to operate as surrogate prices in such a way to shape incentives (Veljanovski, 1996). 'Trust' simply denotes the presence of incentives for cooperation (Williamson, 1996). This position is based on certain well-known *a priori* assumptions about the capacity for rational action of economic agents.

These views are separated by a disciplinary divide which makes dialogue between them difficult. Economists are sceptical of the empirical studies since they rely on small sample sizes and so arguably do not generate statistically significant results (Hviid, 2000: 53). Sociologists, and lawyers writing from a sociological perspective, on the other hand, frequently criticize economic approaches for their 'reductionism' (Collins, 1999: 80). From their respective vantage points, both sets of criticisms ring true, but the gulf in understanding and approach does not bode well for our understanding of contractual phenomena.

A possible way forward towards a unified theoretical framework which is capable of generating a rich empirical research agenda is suggested by recent research on conventions and norms. Building on game theory, but increasingly moving beyond that paradigm by incorporating insights from evolutionary theory more generally, this body of work seeks to explain the emergence of norms and conventions on the basis of dynamic processes of learning and diffusion among a given population of agents. On this basis, generally shared understandings of acceptable or appropriate behaviour form the basis for coordinating action among boundedly rational agents. If these understandings are absent, then there is little that formal legal norms can do to promote cooperation. However, this is not the end of the matter, since the law can play a role in speeding up, or alternatively retarding, the process of diffusion of norms. In this regard, the body of legal doctrine which makes up 'contract law' (or any given part of it, such as the law relating to commercial sales or employment contracts) is a particular form of *coded information and knowledge* about solutions to problems of coordination. In other words, *contract law encodes learning about contracts*. The nature of the links between legal doctrine, on the one hand, and the body of extra-legal norms and understandings relating to contractual behaviour, on the other, is the key to how successfully the information and knowledge embodied in legal rules can be transmitted.

The aim of this chapter is to develop this argument further and explore its implications for our understanding of contract and of contract law. Section 2 below outlines the essential elements of the argument for seeing conventions as playing a central role in the economic order. Section 3 then seeks to extend existing arguments by showing how a role for the legal system can be conceptualized, and illustrates this approach by reference to empirical studies of contract process. Section 4 concludes.

2.   The role of conventions and norms in contractual cooperation

'Conventions' may be defined as units of shared information which provide a basis for coordinating the actions of individuals (Lewis, 1969). One illustration of this is the idea of 'focal points':

> People can often concert their intentions or expectations with others if each knows that the other is trying to do the same. Most situations provide some clue for coordinating behaviour, some focal point for each person's expectation of what the other expects him to expect to be expected to do. (Schelling, 1960, p. 57)

On this basis, a mere *regularity* can become a *convention* if everyone knows that it is; if everyone knows that everyone knows; and so on. In the technical language of game theory, highly stable conventions can be represented as a particular kind of steady state, a 'Nash equilibrium'. Game theory is concerned with how individuals behave in response to the behaviour of others, that is, with their *strategies*. A Nash equilibrium is a state in which no agent has an incentive to alter their strategy, given what they rationally expect the other agent(s) to do. Put slightly differently, it is a situation in which the strategy adopted by each player is the best response to the strategy which it is rational for the other to play in that particular environment.

The usefulness of conventions is illustrated by simple models of game of *pure coordination* and *equilibrium selection*. In a game of pure coordination, achieving a high pay-off depends entirely on being able to predict what the other party will do. However, the environment is such that the criterion of individual rationality provides no reliable guide to action. The classic example is of two drivers facing each other on the road in a foreign country for the first time. Neither driver has any grounds for knowing whether the other one will choose to drive on the left or on the right. If, however, the convention 'drive on the left' (or, as the case may be, 'drive on the right') is known to both, the parties can achieve a high (coordinated) pay-off and avoid a low (uncoordinated) one (see Figure 12.1).

There are two possible equilibria here: (left, left) and (right, right). They are both as good as each other in terms of the pay-offs to the players as individuals, and in terms of the aggregate well-being of the players. By contrast, in games involving the equilibrium selection problem, there are multiple equilibria with differing properties. The function of conventions here is to shift the parties' strategies from a sub-optimal outcome to one which enhances their joint well-being.

In the well-known prisoner's dilemma game (Figure 12.2),[1] it is individually rational for each party to 'defect', that is, to decline to cooperate, given that they would rationally

	Left	Right
Left	1, 1	0, 0
Right	0, 0	1, 1

Figure 12.1   Game of pure coordination (the pay-offs are expressed as (row, column))

	Cooperate	Defect
Cooperate	2, 2	0, 3
Defect	3, 0	1, 1

Figure 12.2   Prisoner's dilemma (the pay-offs are expressed as (row, column))

expect the other player to do the same. This expectation is rational since, for any given player, the strategy 'defect' results in a superior individual pay-off to the strategy 'cooperate', *whatever the other player does*. This is the inevitable result of the way in which the prisoner's dilemma game is set up. The environment in which the players find themselves is such that a sub-optimal outcome is sure to occur if each individual acts according to his or her own self-interest; hence the outcome of mutual defection is said to embody a 'unique' Nash equilibrium (see Binmore, 1994).

Other games can be imagined in which no such single strategy is dominant; outcomes necessarily depend on how the pay-offs are arranged. More fundamentally, the structure of the game can be altered in such a way as to build in the possibility of cooperation, which could be understood as an inherent behavioural trait, or as an embedded cultural phenomenon. The prisoner's dilemma, as a particular instance of a non-cooperative game, is no more 'realistic' than these alternative games. The interest of the prisoner's dilemma lies not in its realism, but in the possibility it provides for exploring the dynamics of a situation in which the expression of individual self-interest is radically opposed to the collective good.

This is why it makes little sense to try to insist that the players in the prisoner's dilemma surely must cooperate, since by doing so they could shift the outcome from a sub-optimal equilibrium (defect, defect) to a manifestly superior one (cooperate, cooperate). This would simply represent a different, and arguably less interesting, game, one in which the conflict between individual and collective well-being had been somehow abolished. This could be achieved by changing the background assumptions in some way, for example by making it possible for the parties to make a legally binding contract which was perfectly enforceable, or by altering their preferences so that the well-being of each one was inter-dependent with that of the other. These changes could be incorporated into the game easily enough by changes to the structure of pay-offs.

However, the point of the prisoner's dilemma is precisely that it asks us to consider whether cooperation can arise in a state of nature where contracting is impossible and legal enforcement does not exist: can it be used to show that conventions which support cooperation might emerge endogenously, that is, on the basis of nothing more than the bare ingredients of the interaction inscribed by the 'rules' of that particular game? The basic insight here is that spontaneous cooperation may indeed emerge if the game is played more than once, thereby giving rise to the possibility of defection in one round being punished in the next. More precisely, if the game is played *indefinitely* or *indetermin-ately*, a fragile but stable basis for cooperation can be established. If, on the other hand, both parties know the end point of the game, this form of cooperation begins to fall apart, since, by backwards induction, it becomes rational to defect not only in the final round (when the threat of retaliatory punishment has become meaningless) but, in anticipation of what will happen then, in all previous rounds.

Cooperation is not inevitable in the repeated prisoner's dilemma. On the contrary, it is just one of a number of equilibria which have been identified as being technically possi-ble when this game is played. Which equilibrium the parties arrive at depends on how far they play 'mixed strategies' (randomly altering their strategies over time), on the degree of error in their responses, and in the timing of these variations. To make further progress in understanding the origins of cooperation, it is necessary to introduce the additional idea of the 'evolutionarily stable strategy' or ESS. An ESS is a type of Nash equilibrium that sustains itself against alternatives under particular conditions. When the strategy is played by a certain critical mass of a given population of players, it becomes impervious to 'invasion'. For this to be the case, the strategy must be at least as good a reply to itself as any other strategy; and it must either be a better reply to itself than the alternative, or a better reply to the alternative than the alternative is when the alternative is playing itself (Hargreaves-Heap and Varoufakis, 1995; Sugden, 1998a).

Robert Axelrod's computer simulations, described in his 1984 book *The Evolution of Cooperation*, found that the 'naïve reciprocator' strategy of tit-for-tat was an ESS which thrived against alternative strategies in the sense just described (Axelrod, 1984). In tit-for-tat, one player cooperates until such time as the other player defects, and then subse-quently binds his or her strategy to whatever their opponent has just done. Once this pattern becomes established, the players' expectations become self-reinforcing, and a con-vention is thereby established. Tit-for-tat is not a *unique* ESS in the repeated prisoner's dilemma, and studies have shown that it is almost certainly not the best conceivable strat-egy for that game (Binmore, 1994: 197–203). However, the fundamental insight that *reci-procity* holds one of the keys to understanding the emergence and persistence of cooperation and, hence, in an extended sense, of social order, has an obvious resonance with empirical studies in a number of disciplines ranging from the study of animal behaviour to human anthropology. It also has clear importance for the study of contract law, where the importance of reciprocity has long been recognized in both the empirical and theoretical strands of relational contract writing (see, in particular, Macaulay, 1963; and Macneil, 1971, respectively).

The term 'reciprocal altruism', which was originally applied in evolutionary biology but has since entered wider use, describes a range of behaviour embodying tit-for-tat and related strategies (Trivers, 1985; see Zywicki, 2000). The term is somewhat misleading, since its conception of 'altruism' is firmly rooted in individual self-interest. Equally, the idea of 'gift exchange' with which it is associated can give the false impression that the process of transfer of resources is in some way gratuitous, when the opposite is the case. 'Reciprocal altruism', so called, implies that one party incurs a cost in order to confer a benefit on another, in the expectation that he or she will receive a benefit back in return at some future point. Repeated interactions and stable relations through time thus provide the basic conditions for the practice to develop. In addition, according to this point of view, there must be the possibility of 'punishment' for those who do not reciprocate the gains they have received, if only in the form of their exclusion from future trades.

The argument that reciprocal altruism generates a surplus which confers an evolutionary advantage on those groups that pursue this practice lies at the basis of the claim that some species, including human beings, are genetically 'hard wired' to engage in this practice (Zywicki, 2000). Such an argument takes us a long way from the rationality assumptions which most economists and, indeed, other social scientists use as a basis for understanding contractual phenomena, and it gives rise to highly controversial issues of evidence and proof. An argument that has greater relevance to attempts to understand the role of conventions in contractual cooperation makes use of the evolutionary metaphor, but transfers it from the genetic realm to that of 'culture', loosely understood as social institutions and practices. In this context, it is suggested that evolutionary processes operate on social practices so as to select against those that are less adaptive to their environment. In contrast to the genetic claim, which might properly be regarded as beyond the legitimate realm of social scientific inquiry, the 'cultural' version of the evolutionary argument is, arguably, one which social scientists are well equipped to investigate from both a theoretical and an empirical point of view.

The cultural version of the argument suggests that the effectiveness of a convention is a function of how widely it is observed and imitated, and this, in turn, depends on how well the practice which it embodies can be copied. Game-theoretical models may take us part of the way in understanding how it is that certain conventions become established and, in turn, how they are destabilized. This is the case with Peyton Young's pared-down model for the emergence of road traffic conventions (Young, 1996). Assuming that an individual's decision to drive on the left- or the right-hand side of the road is solely a function of what he or she observes other drivers doing, a well-established practice can tip over to its opposite depending on the memory of individual drivers and their propensity for random error. This is an illustration of the role played by information and norm 'cascades': the persistence of conventions of this type is linked to the number of agents following them because the pay-off increases the more agents follow the convention (Bikhchandani et al., 1998).

Social learning, then, may be thought of as a feedback mechanism through which particular practices become self-reinforcing. Through copying what others do, agents move towards conventions which are more successful without the need to know quite why the practice in question works for the best. Such conventions save on the transactions costs of continually searching for the 'right' solution (Warneryd, 1998). The process is one of 'blind' evolution because no one knows in advance that they are setting off on a 'superior path'; by definition, the path becomes 'superior' only in the light of what happens later (Gillette, 1998). Conventions of this kind, since they rest for their effect largely on the inertia created by habit and routine, may be neither efficient (in the sense of Pareto-optimal) nor especially just: widespread practices of sexual and racial discrimination offer an illustration.

The more 'optimistic' claim that 'efficient' conventions will emerge spontaneously rests on the controversial concept of group selection. This holds that conventions which support the well-being of the groups or societies which follow them will, for that reason, spread more rapidly, if not necessarily through the greater reproductive or genetic success of those groups (this argument is difficult to sustain given the indirect and poorly understood nature of the linkages between cultural and genetic selection), then at least through observation and copying by others of what are perceived to be successful strategies. The idea that group selection operates in the cultural sphere is one that has had a certain appeal in the social sciences, forming part, for example, of Hayek's critique of the regulatory state (Hayek, 1980). However, this again runs up against the problem that the rate of diffusion of a particular practice is not a simple function of the benefit which it confers upon its hosts; just as plausibly, it is determined simply by its copyability, that is, by the ease with which it can be observed, transmitted and imitated.

In both its 'optimistic' and its 'pessimistic' versions, convention theory seeks to offer a 'behavioural' economic account of norms which relies neither on an assumption of psychological internalization of altruism nor on a clear distinction between norms as mere regularities and norms as 'morally binding', nor on the exogenous, controlling effect of the law. The maintenance of the norm is incentive-compatible in the sense that it depends on the degree to which members of the relevant population interact among themselves, on the likelihood with which defection will be sanctioned in some way (which in turn depends on the nature of the information flows between individuals), and on the possibility of future gains from repeat trading. These elements are exemplified in Avner Greif's account of self-enforcing contracts among the Magribi traders of the eastern Mediterranean during the late Middle Ages (Greif, 1993). According to Greif, it was efficient for merchants to deal through overseas agents because to do so saved on the travelling time and costs of the merchant and made diversification possible, but it was also risky because of the danger of embezzlement by the agent. The solution emerged in the form of the Magribi traders' coalition which formed the basis for a 'multilateral punishment strategy' of agents who defected. Legal solutions were not available because effective court monitoring of contracts was impossible. As a result, an 'implicit' contract was 'agreed' in which the merchant indicated to the agent that future employment was conditional upon past conduct. If the merchant could show that the present value of being honest over future trades was higher than the value to be had from cheating now but being unemployed in future, the relationship could be maintained. The long-distance nature of the trade, however, also made it very difficult to identify 'cheating'. Merchants responded by ostracizing agents *alleged* to have cheated until such time as they compensated their 'victims'; agents in this position could be cheated against by other traders without fear of a similar sanction. The information mechanism was based on reputation within the Magribi community, and was sufficiently powerful for agents to forego legitimate short-term gains in order to avoid an *imputation* of cheating. It was cheaper to hire an honest agent in any one transaction, since this agent could offer his services for a lower wage (given his expectation of future dealing) than a (perceived) dishonest agent could; in this way, the norm was further reinforced.

Persuasive as this account is, it is essential to bear in mind that the trading coalition described by Greif emerged under very particular conditions. The Magribis were a culturally homogeneous group, bound together by religious and ethnic ties. Once the initial conditions for the norm were set, there was a strong incentive not to trade outside the group (so they did not trade, in practice, with other Jewish traders or in the Christian communities of the Mediterranean). The economic advantages of exclusive trading within the community sustained the social fabric only until the point at which the coalition was broken up by external political events, and the Magribis were assimilated into the wider Jewish community of the Mediterranean.

Greif's case study powerfully demonstrates how norms and conventions can grow up outside the reach of a largely ceremonial and practically ineffective legal system, while also demonstrating the precariousness of the trading system which these conventions sustained. But the focus in convention theory on the conditions for the emergence of social norms in something approaching a state of nature inevitably means that the nature of connections between the legal system and extra-legal norms has remained comparatively unexplored. There are numerous contexts in which the role of judicial interpretation and enforcement of contracts is a more active one than was the case with the Magribis. What can we learn from modern-day case studies of situations in which the law is capable of playing a more active role in policing contracts?

3.   Law, trust and social norms: insights from contemporary case studies

Where it does not depend on tight-knit communities, it might be supposed that the diffusion of information concerning solutions to coordination problems on the basis of imitation and observation alone would be a slow and haphazard process, with ample opportunities for errors, wrong turnings and inefficient lock-in effects. And yet highly complex forms of cooperation can be observed in many contexts where dense interpersonal networks of the kind identified in empirical work on contracts are simply not present. Nor is it obvious that 'punishment strategies' of the sort emphasized in the game-theoretical literature always or even as a general rule underlie such forms of cooperation. On the other hand, formal legal institutions are more or less ever present, albeit in a background role.

The socio-legal finding that legal forms and sanctions are often perceived as peripheral to contracting practice (Macaulay, 1963) is open to misinterpretation if it is read as implying the marginality or irrelevance of law, since it in no way rules out a wider role for law in assisting economic coordination. Indeed, it can be understood as inviting us to identify more precisely what that role is. Here, systems theory, or the theory of law as a self-reproducing or autopoietic system, usefully highlights the role played by law as a 'cognitive resource' or store of socially useful knowledge on which the parties can draw

(Carvalho and Deakin, 2006). According to this point of view, it is the role of formal institutions in standardizing and transmitting complex information (and *knowledge*, or
applied information) which makes it possible to widen the basis for trade beyond localized communities and thereby extend the scope of the division of labour. Moving beyond
a purely behavioural account of norms, systems theory emphasizes the role played by the
coding, through legal processes, of complex information and knowledge about the social
world (Teubner, 1992; Deakin, 2002; Luhmann, 2004). In the same way that behavioural
conventions save on the transaction costs of searching for the solutions to coordination
problems by repeated acts of observation and attempted imitation, the legal-institutional
phenomenon of coding transforms large quantities of information into a more readily
transmissible and digestible form.

The price mechanism is one example of this. In a competitive market, changes in prices
convey rich information about the relative scarcity of commodities in a way that is often
independent of the capacity of agents to access the sources of that information; they
may, and often will, be ignorant of the precise causes of scarcity. As Robert Sudgen suggests (1998b: 490), when a consumer is faced with the rising price of bread caused by a
distant harvest failure of which he is ignorant, he nevertheless 'knows all that he needs
to know in order to be induced to economise. The knowledge that the weather has been
bad for wheat growing exists in some people's minds, the knowledge that the price of
bread has increased exists in others; but the former has induced the latter'. Thus the
market is an institution through which 'changes in willingness to buy and sell are transmitted through the network of trading relationships'; it transmits information between
individuals who are not just in a relationship of repeat trading, but may not even be
known to each other (ibid.).

In the case of the legal system, the information contained in legal rules relates (among
other things) to means of solving coordination problems in particular contexts. Litigation
is one of the principal means by which this information is collected. Litigants, particularly in cases establishing a novel principle, are akin to 'norm entrepreneurs' who subsi-
dize the process of discovery of new rules for the benefit of society as a whole, in return
for the possibility of being the first to exploit a novel principle; they are 'repeat players'
who operate by amortizing current costs against expected future gains (Gillette, 1998).
Adjudication, in addition to holding out the prospect of returns for the litigants themselves, is also one of the means by which the outcomes of particular cases serve as guides
for conduct in the future. In this way, a theory of the efficiency of judge-made law has
been developed which is compatible with the precepts of public-choice theory: the private
incentives of particular interest groups to challenge rules through litigation ensure that
the system is purged of inefficient norms (Rubin, 1982).

An interest-group explanation of the law-making process is undoubtedly relevant here,
but, again, a choice-theoretic perspective does not tell the whole story. In particular, it
misses out the role played by processes internal to the legal system in ensuring the storing
and transmission of information: in evolutionary terms, the mechanism of (cultural)
inheritance. Systems theory suggests that this occurs through the translation of information about the social world into conceptual or dogmatic legal language, a task of
interpretation which is not confined to the individual judge but is shared by the legal community as a whole (Teubner, 1992; Luhmann, 2004). Hence *legal doctrine is a particular
kind of cultural transmission, which works by coding information and values into conceptual*

form, thereby assisting their wider dissemination both spatially and temporally. The processes which result in only certain disputes being litigated, only a fraction of these coming before a court for decision, and only a fraction in turn being reported and then analysed, possess an evolutionary character in the sense of selecting against those mutations which do not 'fit' with their environment. This process of conceptual formation is one in which the attitudes, beliefs and values of a society on what passes for conventional or 'reasonable' behaviour are continually being updated, refined and then transmitted to society by the legal system. However, in this perspective the criterion for the survival of particular ideas is their *interpretative fitness*, that is to say, their compatibility with the underlying conceptual unity and coherence of the legal system.

The effectiveness of law in providing a foundation for social order is to some degree, therefore, a function of its capacity for adaptation in the face of a changing external environment. In this context, Robert Sugden (1998b: 488), echoing Hayek (1960, 1980) and Leoni (1961), suggests that 'the system of common law is a spontaneous order, in which laws evolve as a result of the decisions of many different judges'. The body of doctrine created by this process is more effective in adjusting to changing social circumstances, he suggests, than is the case with precisely worded legislation. Not only can legislation not ensure its own permanence (since bodies empowered to change laws by these means can also repeal them), but very precise legislation is more likely to need revision since 'no legislator can foresee all circumstances' (Sugden, 1998b: 489).

However, it should not be supposed that legislation does not also encode information about solutions to coordination problems. The legislative process collects information through processes of interest-group lobbying, public investigation and parliamentary debate. Thus, like litigation, it contains elements of spontaneous order and is subject to selective processes by which certain rules are taken up and persist while others are discarded. In addition, legal rules derived from legislation also change over time without necessarily being formally repealed, thanks to judicial interpretations of statutes and codes; and these play a highly significant role in the evolution of legal doctrine in civil law systems just as they do in common law systems. Thus the claim that the common law is inherently more adaptable, and hence more efficient, than the civil law because it evolves in an incremental fashion to reflect changes in the wider economic environment (see Beck et al. 2003), is open to question.

One of the principal differences between the common law of contract and civilian systems lies in the different place accorded to the principle of good faith. However, this difference does not result from the supposedly greater capacity of the common law for juridical adaptation. Paragraph 242 of the German Civil Code, which embodies the principle of good faith in commercial transactions, is one of the principal examples of judicial innovation in the civil law. Paragraph 242 has come to acquire its current meaning largely as a result of shifts in judicial interpretation of commercial contracts, the most important of which occurred during the 1920s when the courts had to deal with the consequence of hyper-inflation for long-term agreements. It was in this context that paragraph 242 was interpreted as requiring parties to renegotiate long-term contracts which are subject to an unanticipated event, such as an unexpected rise in prices or fall in demand, in such a way as to go far beyond what would normally be permitted by the common law doctrine of frustration, which relieves the parties from future performance but only in a much more restricted range of circumstances (Dawson, 1983). Paragraph

242 and the good faith principle it embodies represent a particularly explicit formulation of the values of reciprocity in commercial relations. A commentator on paragraph 242 has said that it has the role of 'giving legal force to broad ethical values' (Leser, 1982: 138). In Italian contract law, similarly, the notion of good faith has been interpreted as meaning that performance of contractual obligations 'must take place with the loyal and honest cooperation of the parties to achieve the reciprocal benefits agreed in the contract. Only in that way can the contract play its part as a useful private mechanism in the context of the "social solidarity" which is the inescapable duty of all citizens under article 2 of the [1949] Constitution' (Criscuoli and Pugsley, 1991: 142). By contrast, the English courts have, notoriously, refused to countenance a general principle of good faith in commercial contracts, preferring to stress the autonomy of parties dealing 'at arm's length' (see McKendrick, 1995).

The economic impact of these different national legal frameworks for contracting has rarely been the subject of a systematic, comparative empirical analysis, but one such study was carried out by the author and colleagues as part of the UK Economic and Social Research Council's contracts and competition programme in the mid-1990s.[2] This project set out to examine how functionally similar transactions (contracts between 'original equipment manufacturers' and suppliers of component parts) were organized across the three national legal systems of Germany, Britain and Italy. It found considerable diversity in the form of contracts, their duration, and their substance. Contracts in Germany, in particular, tended to be longer term, spanning more than one exchange, and to make greater use of formal mechanisms of risk allocation, such as hardship clauses, than in the other two countries. It also found divergence in the willingness of parties to use legal action to enforce their contractual rights. However, it was the British firms, which most strongly stressed the virtues of contract informality, that were also the most likely to take legal action in response to non-performance. Resort to law was least likely in the apparently most highly juridified system, namely Germany.

A possible reading of these findings is that the indifference to legal aspects of contract described by Macaulay and later confirmed by Beale and Dugdale is not a universal feature of interfirm relations, but is specific to particular legal and business cultures. In the German and, to a lesser degree, Italian cases, it could be argued that the law was being used not as a second-best when trust broke down, but as a means of building trust in the first place. Under certain conditions, then, law and trust need not be antithetical.

Three levels of contractual regulation are relevant here: the body of commercial contract law, which is infused by the values of reciprocity derived from paragraph 242; the standard-form agreements for commercial dealing, which are laid down at industry level in Germany; and inter-party agreements at micro-level. These different levels are closely linked. Standard forms follow closely the guidance of the law on what amounts to performance in good faith; individual contracts, in turn, rarely depart from the template set at industry level. This is not to imply that the process of transmission is just one way, from the law down to the level of individual contracting; the process of litigation, which over a number of decades has resulted in several thousand decisions which have been reported and digested, ensures that information about what is occurring in commercial practice flows back up to the legal system.

There is a considerable contrast here with English commercial law. Parties are very much 'free to make their own agreements' in the absence of an overarching principle of good faith and relatively weak industry-level standard terms. During the period of the case study, standard-form contracts were disintegrating further in the industries being studied, as a result of the privatization of coal, gas and electricity; monopsony buyers, in the form of the old nationalized state corporations, had performed a similar role to trade associations in Germany in ensuring that standardized contract terms were followed. With their departure from the scene, long-established terms dealing with the balance of risk between main contractors and sub-contractors were swept aside in favour of agreements which shifted the risk almost entirely on to the latter.

In Italy, as in Germany, trade associations play an important role in setting and enforcing standards for commercial agreements. However, legal notions of good faith have limited relevance in commercial life, by virtue of the perceived ridigity and inefficiency of the court system. The principle of ethical dealing is reflected in trading standards which operate in particular regions or industries and which are linked to the roles played by local government and by trade associations. Artisanal associations act as a 'blend of trade association and government agency' (Best, 1992: 210) in providing a framework for interfirm cooperation. Among other things, they set 'benchmark prices' which serve to reduce negotiation costs, limit the opportunistic renegotiation of contracts and, by outlawing cut-throat competition, encourage firms to raise and maintain product quality (Dei Ottati, 1996).

Among the empirical findings of the ESRC-funded research on contracts was considerable evidence of differences in the way commercial parties regarded the legal system (Arrighetti et al., 1997; Deakin and Wilkinson, 1998). In Germany, respondents commented that their contracts were shaped by the general law as well as by the 'general conditions of business' applying in their industry. Both the Civil Code and the general conditions were seen to apply 'as a matter of course'. In Italy, firms were unable to estimate the costs and outcomes of legal action and did not rely extensively on contractual form to shape their relationship, apparently reflecting a court system perceived as slow, expensive and uncertain in terms of outcome. In Britain, there was a sectoral divide. Most mining machinery contracts were detailed and sophisticated, reflecting the legacy of nationalization in the coal industry; in the other sector studied, the manufacturing of kitchen furniture, it was common to find firms reporting that informal understandings were preferable to legally binding and/or written agreements.

This finding of clear inter-country differences, as already suggested, is enough to cast doubt on the widely held view that business contractors see the law as playing a peripheral role in contractual relations. It would seem that this is only the case in certain national and sectoral environments. In others, there is a much closer fit between formal legal and contractual mechanisms, and commercial practice. There is also evidence, from the contracts research just referred to, to suggest that in a system where the reciprocity norm is effectively diffused by virtue of this close 'fit', costs arising from contractual disputes are reduced. German firms were found to be much less likely to need to have resort to legal action for breach of contract than their British counterparts, while, within the British sample, the kitchen furniture manufacturers, who relied least on formal contractual documentation, were also the most likely to have to go to court to chase debts.

The work just described examined legal and social norms in the countries and industries in question at a particular point in time; in effect, it took a 'snapshot' of contractual practice which was only partially able to capture changes in the nature of norms. A later project carried out in Cambridge, concerned with insolvency procedures, was able to examine the process of the diffusion of commercial norms over time. This consisted of a case study of the 'London Approach', an informal process for assisting the restructuring and survival of public companies facing the threat of insolvency which, until recently, was sponsored and overseen by the Bank of England (see Armour and Deakin, 2001).

The London Approach represents a solution to a particular kind of coordination problem. The problem arises when large, publicly listed companies find themselves unable to meet repayments on the large, syndicated bank loans which represent one of the principal means by which they raise external finance. The issue is how to enforce a multilateral agreement among lenders for a 'standstill' on claims against the company so as to enable it to defer payment of its debts and carry out a restructuring that will avoid insolvency. The company is worth much less in the event of insolvency than if there is a successful 'workout' to restore it to financial health. However, an individual lender could halt the restructuring process by triggering insolvency proceedings if it calculates that, by doing so, it would be better off than it would be by taking part in the standstill.

The London Approach has been described as '[a] non-statutory and informal framework introduced with the support of the Bank of England for dealing with temporary support operations mounted by banks and other lenders to a company or group in financial difficulties, pending a possible restructuring' (British Bankers' Association, 1996:1). At stage 1, the debtor firm notifies its banks of financial distress; banks agree a standstill; and an accountants' investigation begins. At stage 2, a lead bank is nominated to coordinate the restructuring or 'workout'. According to the informal and non-legally binding rules of the London Approach, each bank shares in the gains (from avoiding insolvency) and costs (of the restructuring process) pro rata according to the nature of their exposure at the time the standstill began, but with 'superpriority' for new loans which are necessary to keep the debtor afloat.

The process is kept secret to preserve the reputation of the debtor company; the outside world may never know that its future was at risk. Formal contracts between the banks are rarely entered into, although it is common for them to be drawn up but left unsigned. Direct legal enforcement is therefore impossible. The process, it seems, is enforced through a number of extra-legal mechanisms. In particular, repeat trading among the banks and other City firms (legal and accounting professionals) that are involved in the process on a frequent basis provides a means for sanctioning free-riders. In addition, the Bank of England was, until recently, in a position to offer encouragement to potential defectors who could be invited to have 'tea with the old lady of Threadneedle Street', although there is no evidence of any direct pressure being brought to bear on companies in this way. Now that the Bank has, since 1997, given up its regulatory and supervisory role in financial markets (it ceded this function to the Financial Services Authority at the same time as its role as an independent central bank was strengthened), it is unclear whether the London Approach can be maintained, particularly given the entry of 'distressed debt dealers' and 'vulture funds' which specialize in buying up 'distressed debt' and, since they often operate from outside the City of London, may be less amenable to the pressures which have sustained the process until now (see Armour and Deakin, 2001).

The evolution of the London Approach has a life-cycle aspect to it. It began out of efforts to resolve particular corporate restructurings in the early 1970s; what worked in a small number of instances, on a trial-and-error basis, gradually became a model which could be applied more generally. By the mid-1990s it had become sufficiently widely known to be reduced to a published set of principles (British Bankers' Association, 1996), and for some of the details of its operation to be publicized (Kent, 1993, 1994a, 1994b, 1997). By the late 1990s, efforts were being made to adapt its use to other financial centres. But equally, the stability of its operation in the City was under threat, thanks to a significant change in the population of players in London's increasingly globalized financial markets. It remains unclear whether the new players will be persuaded that their own self-interest lies in participation in the London Approach.

The London Approach appears to represent a spontaneous, extra-legal solution to the coordination problem posed by the potentially conflicting interests of banks during a large-firm workout. Nevertheless, at every stage of its development, its evolution has been influenced by the legal and regulatory framework operating in the City of London. This is evident, first, in the absence of a debtor-in-possession law like the US Chapter 11; it is this that makes it possible for one creditor to precipitate value-destroying insolvency. Second, it seems that the development of the London Approach was 'seeded' by the particular role played by the Bank of England during a period of exceptional economic turbulence in the 1970s, when it was called on to deal with a number of bank failures and large-scale industrial rescues. Third, the Bank's specific (and in many ways anomalous) status, combining the functions of lender of last resort with those of financial regulator, appears to have been placed in a good position to grant credibility to the London Approach in its early years. Thus, notwithstanding the spontaneous elements in the emergence and stabilization of the London Approach, its trajectory was also tied up with the role of the Bank as a public institution charged with maintaining the effective functioning of London's financial markets.

4.   Conclusions: legal institutions, trust and contractual learning

This chapter has outlined some theoretical and empirical perspectives on the role of law and related public institutions in promoting the growth of conventions which serve as coordination mechanisms. An exclusive focus on the extra-legal dimensions of contractual practice misses the vital role which the legal system may play in assisting the diffusion of contractual learning and in the institutionalization of trust. Doctrinal legal rules operate as repositories of information and knowledge on how to solve coordination problems; legal processes of dispute resolution, adjudication and legislation serve to enhance the transmission and diffusion of this information. In performing this role, the legal system is assisted by institutional forms which span the public–private divide, such as trade associations, state corporations and regulatory authorities. The process is one of social learning, in the sense of the adaptation of normative systems to changes in the external environment. Feedback effects ensure that the direction of change is path-dependent and context-specific; particular solutions emerge and may persist thanks to the specificity of local conditions. Thus the empirical study of contracts, while it should be theoretically informed, must also be sensitive to the kind of local detail which institutional case studies are best equipped to capture.

Notes

1.   Binmore (1994: 102) explains the prisoner's dilemma as follows: 'The District Attorney knows that Adam and Eve are gangsters who are guilty of a major crime but is unable to convict them without a confession from one or another. He orders their arrest and separately offers each the following deal: "If you confess and your accomplice fails to confess, then you go free. If you fail to confess but your accomplice confesses, then you will be convicted and sentenced to the maximum term in jail. If you both confess, then you will

both be convicted but the maximum sentence will not be imposed. If neither confesses, then you will be famed on a minor tax evasion charge for which a conviction is certain." '

2. On the contracts and competition research programme see Deakin and Michie (1997). Arrighetti et al. (1997) set out the aims of the study of interfirm contracting referred to in the text. Around 60 in-depth interviews were carried out with firms in the three countries concerned and further interviews were undertaken with trade associations and other relevant parties. A semi-structured questionnaire was used to obtain a mix of quantitative and qualitative data, which were analysed in the papers just referred to.

References

Armour, J. and Deakin, S. (2001) 'Norms in private insolvency procedures: the "London Approach" to the resolution of financial distress', *Journal of Corporate Law Studies*, **1**: 21–51.

Arrighetti, S., Bachmann, R. and Deakin, S. (1997) 'Contract law, social norms, and inter-firm cooperation', *Cambridge Journal of Economics*, **21**: 171–95.

Axelrod, R. (1984) *The Evolution of Cooperation*. New York: Basic Books.

Beale, H. and Dugdale, A. (1975) 'Contracts between businessmen: planning and the use of contractual remedies', *British Journal of Law and Society*, **2**: 45.

Beck, T., Dermigüc-Kunt, A. and Levine, R. (2003) 'Law and finance: why does legal origin matter?', *Journal of Comparative Economics*, **31**: 653–75.

Best, M. (1992), *The New Competition*, Cambridge: Polity Press.

Bikhchandani, S. Hirshleifer, D. and Welch, I. (1998) 'Learning from the behaviour of others: conformity, fads, and informational cascades', *Journal of Economic Perspectives*, **12**: 151–70.

Binmore, K. (1994) *Playing Fair*. Cambridge, MA: MIT Press.

British Bankers' Association (BBA) (1996), *Description of London Approach*. London: mimeo.

Carvalho, F. and Deakin, S. (2006) 'System and evolution in corporate governance', in R. Rogowski and T. Wilthagen (eds), *Reflexive Labour Law*, 2nd edn. Deventer: Kluwer, forthcoming.

Collins, H. (1999) *Regulating Contracts*. Oxford: Oxford University Press.

Criscuoli, G. and Pugsley, D. (1991) *The Italian Law of Contract*. Naples: Jovene.

Dawson, J. (1983) 'Judicial revision of frustrated contracts: Germany', *Boston University Law Review*, **63**: 1039–68.

Deakin, S. (2002) 'Evolution for our time: a theory of legal memetics', *Current Legal Problems*, **55**: 1–42.

Deakin, S. and Michie, J. (eds) (1997) *Contracts, Cooperation and Competition: Studies in Economics, Management and Law*. Oxford: Oxford University Press.

Deakin, S. and Wilkinson, F. (1998), 'Contract law and the economics of interorganizational trust', in C. Lane and R. Bachmann (eds), *Trust Within and Between Organizations. Conceptual Issues and Empirical Applications*. Oxford: Oxford University Press, 146–72.

Dei Ottati, G. (1996) 'The remarkable resilience of the industrial districts of Tuscany', in F. Cossentino, F. Pyke and W. Sengenberger (eds) (1996) *Local and Regional Response to Global Pressure: The Case of Italy and its Industrial Districts*. Geneva: IILS.

Gillette, C. (1998) 'Lock-in effects in law and norms', *Boston University Law Review*, **78**: 792–842.

Greif, A. (1993) 'Contract enforceability and economic institutions in early trade: the Magribi traders' coalition', *American Economic Review*, **83**: 525.

Hargreaves-Heap, S. and Varoufakis, Y. (1995), *Game Theory: A Critical Introduction*. London: Routledge.

Hayek, F. (1960) *The Constitution of Liberty*. London: Routledge.

Hayek, F. (1980) *Law, Legislation and Liberty*. London: Routledge.

Hviid, M. (2000) 'Long-term contracts and relational contracts', in B. Bouckaert and G. de Geest (eds), *Encylopaedia of Law and Economics Volume III: The Regulation of Contracts*. Cheltenham, UK and Northampton, MA, USA: Edward Elgar, 46–72.

Kent, P. (1993) 'The London Approach', *Journal of International Banking Law*, **8**: 81–4.

Kent, P. (1994a) 'The London Approach', *Bank of England Quarterly Bulletin*, **33**: 110.

Kent, P. (1994b) 'The London Approach: distressed debt trading', *Bank of England Quarterly Bulletin*, **34**: 172–4.

Kent, P. (1997) 'Corporate workouts – a UK perspective', *International Insolvency Review*, **6**: 165.

Leoni, B. (1961) *Freedom and the Law*. Los Angeles: Nash.

Leser, H. (1982) 'The principle of good faith: Article 242 BGB', in N. Korn, H. Kötz and H. Leser (eds) (trans. T. Weir), *German Private and Commercial Law: An Introduction*. Oxford: Clarendon Press, 135–45.

Lewis, D. (1969) *Convention: A Philosophical Study*. Cambridge, MA: Harvard University Press.

Luhmann, N. (2004) *Law as a Social System*. Oxford: Oxford University Press.

Macaulay, S. (1963) 'Non-contractual relations in business: a preliminary study', *American Sociological Review*, **28**: 55.

Macneil, I. (1971) 'The many futures of contracts', *University of Southern California Law Review*, **47**: 691–816.

McKendrick, E. (1995) 'The regulation of long-term contracts in English law', in J. Beatson and D. Friedmann (eds), *Good Faith and Fault in Contract Law*. Oxford: Oxford University Press, 305–33.

Rubin, P. (1982) 'Common law and statute law', *Journal of Legal Studies*, **11**: 205–33.

Schelling, T. (1960) *The Strategy of Conflict*. Cambridge, MA: Harvard University Press.

Sugden, R. (1998a) 'Conventions', in P. Newman (ed.), *The New Palgrave Dictionary of Economics and the Law*. London: Macmillan, 435–60.

Sugden, R. (1998b) 'Spontaneous order', in P. Newman (ed.), *The New Palgrave Dictionary of Economics and the Law*. London: Macmillan, 485–95.

Teubner, G. (1992) *Law as an Autopoietic System*. Oxford: Blackwell.

Trivers, R. (1985) *Social Evolution*. Menlo Park, CA: Benjamin Cummings.

Veljanovski, C. (1996) *The Economics of Law: An Introductory Text*. 2nd edn. London: IEA.

Warneryd, K. (1998), 'Conventions and transaction costs', in P. Newman (ed.), *The New Palgrave Dictionary of Economics and the Law*. London: Macmillan, 460–65.

Williamson, O. (1996), *The Mechanisms of Governance*. Oxford: Oxford University Press.

Young, P. (1996) 'The economics of convention', *Journal of Economic Perspectives*, **10**: 105–22.

Zywicki, T. (2000) 'Evolutionary psychology and the social sciences', Law and Economics Working Paper No. 00–35, George Mason University School of Law.

PART III

CROSS-LEVEL APPROACHES

13 On the complexity of organizational trust: a multi-level co-evolutionary perspective and guidelines for future research

Steven C. Currall and Andrew C. Inkpen

During the past decade, scholars have made significant progress in the study of trust in organizational settings. For instance, significant theoretical advances have been achieved (e.g. Rousseau et al., 1998), as have empirical developments such as those published in special trust issues of *Organization Science* (McEvily et al., 2003) and *Organization Studies* (Bachmann et al., 2001). Despite this progress, however, 'trust remains an under-theorized, under-researched, and, therefore, poorly understood phenomenon' (Child, 2001: 274). The aim of this chapter is to spur research that moves beyond current theoretical and empirical approaches by using a multi-level and co-evolutionary framework for studying trust. We believe that trust researchers should devote greater attention to the complexity of trust and particularly its evolutionary nature. Our chapter is an attempt to explore the complexities of how trust evolves over time and how it is impacted by organizational context. This idea is consistent with the view of others such as Koza and Lewin (1998), who have argued that trust should not be viewed as a static construct. Also, we have argued elsewhere (Inkpen and Currall, 2004) that a co-evolutionary approach is useful for studying trust. We expand on those themes in this chapter.

Our thesis is this: it is possible to grasp the complexity of trust at one level (e.g. the interpersonal level) by examining trust at another level (e.g. the intergroup or inter-organizational level). As we will discuss in more detail later, Hackman (2003) recently argued that insights about a construct can be obtained when the researcher conducts analyses at one or more levels above or below the focal construct. With respect to trust, we suggest that the subtleties of the trust construct can be unearthed by understanding the organizational context of trust, which can involve, for example, explicating the impact of trust at one level of analysis on trust at another level of analysis. Indeed, we posit that trust at one level serves as the organizational context of trust at another level.

The plan of the chapter is as follows. We lay the foundation for our discussion based on a definition of trust that is suitable for exploring trust across the interpersonal, intergroup and inter-organizational levels. We then discuss a framework that can be used to think about trustors and trustees at different levels. The core of our argument comes next, where we posit linkages among trust at different levels and how trust at one level can affect trust at an adjacent level. We will refer frequently to the literature on joint ventures (JVs) and strategic alliances because a number of authors working in this area have addressed issues of trust at the interpersonal, intergroup and inter-organizational levels. And we will draw upon work that we have published on trust and JVs and alliances (e.g. Currall and Inkpen, 2002; Inkpen and Currall, 2004). Lastly, we conclude the chapter with several ideas that are intended to serve as guidelines for future research on trust.

A definition of trust that 'travels' across levels

As we have discussed elsewhere (Currall, 1992; Currall and Judge, 1995; Inkpen and Currall, 1997; Currall and Inkpen, 2002; 2003; Currall and Epstein, 2003), trust involves two principal concepts: reliance (Giffin, 1967; Rotter, 1980) and risk (Mayer et al., 1995; Rousseau et al., 1998). Therefore, we define trust as the decision to rely on another party (i.e. person, group, or organization) under a condition of risk. Reliance is action through which one party permits its fate to be determined by another. Reliance is based on positive expectations of, or confidence in, the trustworthiness of another party (Rousseau et al., 1998). Risk is the potential that the trusting party will experience negative outcomes, that is, 'injury or loss' (March and Shapira, 1987; Sitkin and Pablo, 1992), if the other party proves untrustworthy. Thus, risk creates the opportunity for trust (Rousseau et al., 1998).

Most conceptualizations of trust focus on the interpersonal level (Rousseau et al., 1998). Yet our definition of trust can be applied to persons, groups and organizations because all three entities make trust decisions and exhibit the measurable actions that follow from such decisions. In fact, it is common for organizational researchers to study decision-making by individuals (e.g. Bazerman, 2001), groups (e.g. Bar-Tal, 1990; Hackman, 2003), and organizations (e.g. Huber, 1990). Because persons, groups and organizations all are capable of making trusting decisions, our conceptualization of trust 'travels' (Osigweh, 1989) from the interpersonal to the intergroup to the inter-organizational level. So, the conceptual equivalence across levels is the following: under a condition of risk, a person's, group's, or organization's trust is signified by a decision to engage in action that allows its fate to be determined by another person, group or organization.

When referring to the parties involved in an interpersonal, intergroup or inter-organizational relationship, we find it useful to use the terms 'trustor' and 'trustee'. Designation of the trustor answers the question 'Who trusts?' Designation of the trustee answers the question 'Who is trusted?' Distinguishing between trustors and trustees has the advantage of avoiding confusion regarding levels of analysis and who is trusting versus who is being trusted (Mayer et al., 1995). We now turn to a presentation of a multilevel model of trust. After discussing this model, we will address linkages among trust at the interpersonal, intergroup and inter-organizational levels.

A multilevel perspective on trust

Some research on trust at multiple levels has been conducted in literature on inter-organizational relationships. For example, in writing on JVs, Barney and Hansen (1994) suggested that discrepancies can exist between interpersonal trust and inter-organizational trust within a JV because trust between partner organizations' managers may be strong although trust between partner firms is weak. Doz (1996) examined how alliances evolve and how trust at one organizational level impacts the development of trust at another level. Doney and Cannon (1997) empirically studied buyer–seller relationships and found that inter-organizational trust differed from interpersonal trust. Also in the buyer–supplier setting, Zaheer et al. (1998) empirically examined distinctions between inter-organizational and interpersonal trust. Jeffries and Reed (2000) focused on relational contracting among firms and explored the interaction between inter-organizational and interpersonal trust for the performance of inter-organizational relationships. Overall, however, the issue of trust and organizational levels has been under-explored and issues of similarities and differences in trust at the person, group and organization levels have received only limited attention (Currall and Inkpen, 2002).

Levels terminology

Before proceeding with a discussion of trust at multiple levels, a bit of terminology is in order. 'Level of theory', 'level of measurement' and 'level of analysis' are fundamental concepts in cross-level research (e.g. Klein et al., 1994; Rousseau, 1985). 'Level of theory' refers to the unit (person, group, or organization) the researcher seeks to explain and about which attributions and generalizations are made. For example, if one examines how trust between JV parent organizations may affect the JV's financial performance, then the unit of theory is the organization. Alternatively, if the focus is on trust as a factor affecting negotiations between individuals, then the unit of theory is the person. Level of measurement refers to the source of information such as individual interviews, group surveys, or organization-level archival records of organizational performance. Levels of analysis concern the statistical processing of empirical data.

A multilevel framework

We now return to trust and multiple levels. Currall and Inkpen (2002) proposed a three-level model of interpersonal, intergroup and inter-organizational relations. The aim of the model was to articulate the level of theory, as well as trustors and trustees, at the person, group and organizational levels. By articulating the level of theory, our aim in Currall and Inkpen (2002) was to provide for researchers a foundation for considerations regarding the level of measurement and the level of analysis in multilevel empirical research on trust.

An updated and amended version of the Currall and Inkpen (2002) framework is presented in Figure 13.1. The framework shows the three levels of trust. As depicted in the figure, model P→P refers to both the trustor and trustee as individual persons. Take, for example, the case of a JV or strategic alliance, in which a complex web of trust relations operates at the interpersonal, intergroup and inter-organizational levels. For example, in JVs three types of persons tend to be involved: business development executives in the parent organizations; operations managers in the JV itself; and the JV's board of directors, most of whom are top executives from the parent organizations. Relations among these individuals are important in shaping the partnership agreement between firms as well as in implementing and monitoring the JV. Variations of the interpersonal model are Model P→G. Using again the example of a JV, this is expressed in the form of a trustor as a single person and the trustee as a group of managers from the partner organization. Model P→F reflects a manager's trust in the partner organization as an entity. The figure shows that one can also envision trust between groups; on the diagonal of Figure 13.1, model G→G defines one group of managers from a JV partner firm as the trustor and another group of managers from a partner organization as the trustee. Model F→F represents inter-organizational trust, a common conceptualization in previous empirical studies of interfirm relations such as JVs and strategic alliances. Other variations of the P→P, G→G and F→F representations are shown in the off-diagonal cells of Figure 13.1.

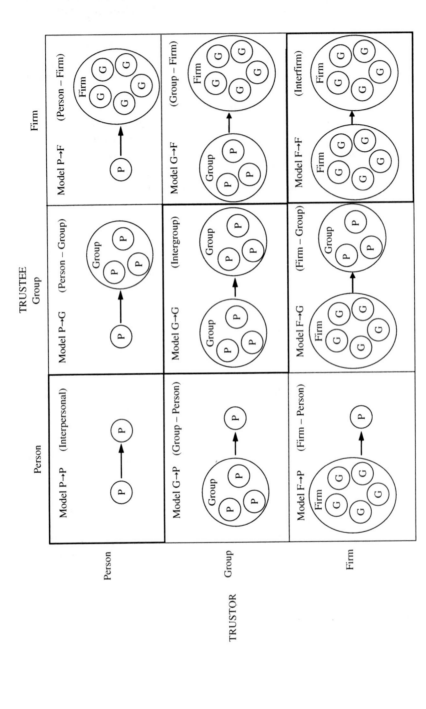

Source: Adapted from Currall and Inkpen (2002).

Figure 13.1 A multilevel perspective on trust

Development of trust and co-evolution of trust across levels
Much of the interplay of trust at the interpersonal, intergroup and inter-organizational
levels takes place during the development of trust. Currall and Epstein (2003) proposed
trust's evolutionary phases as shown in Figure 13.2. The diagram shows that early in a
relationship trust starts around the zero point of neither trust nor distrust because the
parties lack information about the trustworthiness of their counterpart. Development of
trust is often slow and incremental because parties tend to be reticent about trusting. This
is especially true of those whom we do not know or about whom we have uncertainty.
Trust building therefore follows an incremental pattern; one may trust in small ways first,
observe whether trust is upheld or violated, and then proceed with caution in trusting one
step at a time.

Over time, if trust-building actions are taken, the level of trust grows until it begins to
level off during the 'maintaining trust' phase. During this stage, the level of trust stays
roughly constant, if neither party takes actions that erode trust. If trust-violating events
occur, however, then the overall level of trust plummets into the 'destroyed trust' phase.
Herculean trust-building efforts must take place simply to return to the zero point and
even further efforts are then required to move into the positive trust domain.

Our main interest is the way that trust at one level may impact trust at another level
during the 'developing trust' phase. In this sense, trust serves as the organizational context
for trust at another level. This involves the co-evolution of trust at different levels, to
which we now turn.

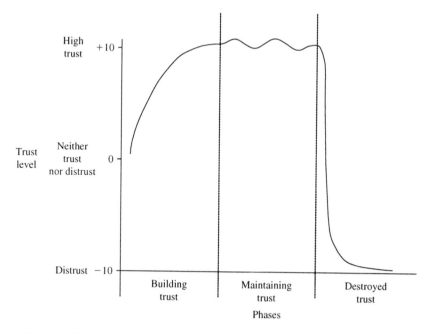

Source: Currall and Epstein (2003).

Figure 13.2   Evolutionary phases of trust

The co-evolution of trust across levels
What is 'co-evolution'? Lewin and Volberda (1999) identified five properties of co-evolutionary models of organizations: (1) multilevelness; (2) multidirectional causalities; (3) nonlinearity of relations among constructs; (4) feedback and interdependence between organizations; and (5) history dependence. In the present discussion, we focus primarily on multilevelness, multidirectional causalities (i.e. reciprocal relations) and history interdependence. In terms of multilevelness, we previously explained our multi-level framework for trust. With respect to multidirectional causalities, we will discuss in a moment how interpersonal, intergroup and inter-organizational trust affect each other in reciprocal ways. And, concerning history dependence, the interplay of interpersonal, intergroup and inter-organizational trust transpires over time. For example, interpersonal trust may develop as time passes to form intergroup trust, which may eventually expand to inter-organizational trust.

We believe that trust at one level can serve as an organizational contextual factor impacting the degree of trust at another level. A number of authors have written recently about organizational context (e.g. Heath and Sitkin, 2001; Johns, 2001; Rousseau and Fried, 2001). Johns (2001) has explained that organizational context 'can be characterized as cross-level effects in which a stimulus or phenomenon at one level or unit of analysis has an impact at another level or unit of analysis' (p. 32). Johns (2001, pp. 31–2) added:

> Cappelli and Sherer (1991, p. 56) define context in organizational behavior as the 'surroundings associated with phenomena which help to illuminate that [*sic*] phenomena, typically factors associated with units of analysis above those expressly under investigation.' Mowday and Sutton (1993, p. 198) define context as 'stimuli and phenomena that surround and thus exist in the environment external to the individual, most often at a different level of analysis'.

Central to our conceptualization is the interplay of interpersonal, intergroup and inter-organizational trust, especially during the developing trust phase. The linkages of the three levels are depicted in Figure 13.3, which posits, for example, that interpersonal trust between leaders from two organizations may serve as the organizational context for the development of trust between groups or trust between organizations. Conversely, a historical context of trust and partnerships between two organizations may foster the emergence of trust between groups of managers representing their respective organizations or interpersonal trust between two managers from the two firms. This reciprocal interplay of trust at the interpersonal, intergroup and inter-organizational levels over time is what we mean by the 'co-evolution of trust'. In other words, trust at one level will evolve over time and, in so doing, will serve as the organizational context for trust dynamics at other levels.

Fundamental to the ideas depicted in Figure 13.3 is the reciprocality of relations among interpersonal, intergroup and inter-organizational trust. Therefore, we return for a moment to the definitions of organizational context by Cappelli and Sherer (1991) and Mowday and Sutton (1993). We observe that they referred mainly to lower-level constructs being influenced by higher-level constructs. On the one hand, this makes sense, as in the case of the impact of organizational culture (an organizational-level construct) on the extent to which individual managers trust each other. On the other hand, however, we believe that a bi-directional emphasis is important whereby lower-level dynamics (e.g. the level of trust between CEOs of two companies contemplating a merger) also can influence higher-level relations (e.g. the legal structure of the terms of a merger contract).

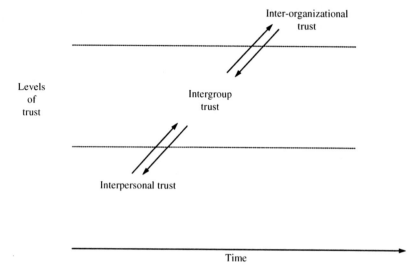

Figure 13.3   The co-evolution of trust across levels

Thus, we posit the existence of a bi-directional and reciprocal relationship among trust at the interpersonal, intergroup and inter-organizational levels, which is depicted in Figure 13.3. As further anecdotal support for the bi-directionality of lower-level to higher-level constructs, Johns (2001) cites the example of an individual whistleblower having a dramatic impact on an organization as a whole. Such instances have been observed in recent history, such as the case of Sherron Watkins, the whistleblower at Enron.

What determines the movement of trust across levels?
Numerous factors determine the movement of trust across levels. For example, trust at the interpersonal level can impact trust at the intergroup level, which, in turn, may influence trust at the inter-organizational level. Indeed, developmentally speaking, trust may have its origins in one-on-one relationships between managers but, over time, such trust may diffuse within an organization by fostering trust among groups. Furthermore, when individual JV managers trust one another, the strength of their relationship can lead to inter-organizational trust because these managers influence other managers, group dynamics (e.g. group cohesion or effective conflict management), and organizational structures and routines. Additional support for this logic is the fact that when a new JV is formed, information about the partner firm and its managers will be incomplete. A manager may be aware of prior relationships between the partner firms and may have been told 'our organization and the other organization have a strong relationship' (Inkpen and Currall, 2004). Also, controls such as legal recourse can create structural assurance beliefs about the managers involved in the JV (McKnight et al., 1998). For example, the specific language of the JV shareholder agreement may provide for legal action if the partner violates certain provisions. If a manager believes that legal recourse for the organization provides safeguards about the partner's future action, the manager will be more likely to trust counterpart managers (Inkpen and Currall, 1998; 2004). And intergroup trust may lay the foundation for

inter-organizational collaboration and partnerships. Conversely, distrust at the inter-group level may contaminate trust between two individuals or retard development of inter-organizational trust (Currall and Inkpen, 2002; Currall and Epstein, 2003).

Another factor that may cause trust to diffuse or travel from one level to another is that trust is an 'evidentiary' construct (Currall and Epstein, 2003). By that, we mean that it changes with evidence in favor of, or against, further trust. For example, Currall and Judge (1995) studied several psychological predictors of behavioral intentions to engage in trusting behavior such as one's attitude toward the trustee, social norms for (or against) trust, the extent to which the trustor has a trusting personality, and the degree to which the trustor believes that the trustee has been trustworthy in the past. Of these predictors, the perceived past trustworthiness of the trustee was the most significant determinant of intentions to engage in trusting behavior. This finding suggested that trustors are especially sensitive to evidence regarding a trustee's behavior and its impact on our assessment of his/her trustworthiness from one moment to another. Indeed, trustors are quite vigilant to the trustee's behavior and are constantly updating and recalibrating judgments regarding the degree to which another party can be trusted. In fact, when risk is great (i.e. when we have much at stake based on the trustee's trustworthiness or untrustworthiness), we may be hyper-vigilant regarding his/her behavior and its implications for our assessment of trustworthiness.

The implication of this dynamic is that trust between two individuals may be impacted by developments and information regarding the level of trust between two groups representing the partner firms, such that, if a counterpart group takes action that violates trust, this may sour the one-on-one relationship between two persons representing different firms. Along similar lines, if the board of directors of one partner firm issues a policy that is designed to withhold information from the other partner firm, groups or individuals may see this decision by the counterpart firm as evidence of untrustworthiness; hence intergroup or interpersonal trust may be contaminated.

Therefore, trust will move, or fail to move, from one level to another based on evidence regarding the trustworthiness of a trustee person, group, or organization. This is what makes trust a dynamic construct. It is not static because there is a constant flow of trust-related evidence based on a counterpart person's, group's, or organization's behavior. This information leads the counterpart to constantly update and recalibrate their assessment of the trustworthiness of the trustee.

What other factors might drive the downward flow from inter-organizational trust to intergroup or interpersonal trust? When inter-organizational trust exists in a new JV, the level of institutional resource commitment should play a key role in moving trust from organizations to groups to persons (Doz, 1996; Inkpen and Currall, 1998; 2004). Institutional commitment demonstrates the JV's legitimacy and strategic importance in the eyes of managers assigned to its operations (Inkpen and Currall, 1998). Such commitment may take the form of information technology infrastructure to foster communication among those working on the JV, dedication of stand-alone facilities to house JV personnel and operations, or dedicated facilitators (e.g. consultants) to mediate disputes between the firms or their representatives. These commitments facilitate the formation of trust between groups or persons because of the effective flow of information or because of munificence of resources available to groups or individuals. The idea of institutional commitment is akin to Zucker's (1986) notion of institution-based trust.

The movement of trust across levels also may be blocked (Inkpen and Currall, 2004). For example, in a situation of high competitive overlap between JV partner firms, the firms may feel compelled to write detailed contracts or policies that dictate terms and procedures concerning aspects of JV operations, which are designed to prevent diffusion of knowledge outside the JV. When knowledge flow is inhibited, it may have the unintended side effect of arresting trust development among groups of JV managers or between individual managers (Inkpen and Currall, 1998; 2004). Moreover, JV contracts and policies may involve the compartmentalization of information in certain domains (e.g. proprietary technology or marketing information). These 'don't tell' policies regarding certain types of information may inhibit the development of trust between managers from the JV partner firms because the act of withholding some information from their counterparts may raise suspicions in the counterpart regarding what else is being withheld.

Guidelines for future trust research

We conclude by suggesting several guidelines for trust researchers to consider in future theoretical and empirical work. Our hope is that these guidelines will prompt others to study the intricacies of the trust construct and how trust at the interpersonal, intergroup and inter-organizational levels co-evolve over time.

1.   Study the organizational context of trust by studying trust at other levels

There are several specific ways to explore the impact of organizational context on trust. First, attaining a deep understanding of the organizational setting in which we are studying trust will facilitate the development of hypotheses that tap the subtleties and complexities of trust. A deep knowledge of organizational context also facilitates the interpretation of empirical findings. Second, trust researchers should provide for readers details about the historical conditions and circumstances underlying trust between persons, groups and organizations. This will shed light on how strong or weak trust came to be. For instance, weak interpersonal trust between JV managers may be understood in the historical context of conflictual and acrimonious transactions between the JV parent firms. In this way, distrust at the inter-organizational level may explain why trust at the interpersonal level has failed to develop. Moreover, knowledge of historical conditions can assist the reader of research findings in drawing conclusions about the generalizability of empirical findings.

2.   'Bracket' trust by studying trust below or above it

In urging organizational researchers to conduct multilevel empirical analyses of organizational phenomena, Hackman (2003) drew upon the logic of the eminent physicist Freeman Dyson:

> Except in trivial cases, you can decode the truth of a [mathematical] statement only by studying its meaning and its context in the larger world of mathematical ideas . . . The progress of science requires the growth of understanding in both directions, downward from the whole to the parts, and upward from the parts to the whole. (Dyson, 1995, p. 32)

Applying this to the study of organizations, Hackman suggested that elusive explanations for empirical findings often can be found by conducting analyses at one level up or one level down from the phenomenon of interest, an approach Hackman refers to as 'bracketing'. Indeed, there is no guarantee that the most powerful explanatory variables operate at the same level of the phenomenon being studied; without a bracketing strategy, deeper explanations for a phenomenon may lie undetected.

But, how does the organizational researcher go about empirically mining for explanations at levels outside the level of the focal phenomenon? For example, how does one discover how intergroup trust impacts interpersonal trust? Here, Hackman (2003) advocates 'informed induction' whereby the researcher uses both qualitative and quantitative methods to study specific settings or cases as a way to formulate more general explanatory factors that may operate above or below the focal construct. (For discussions of the integration of qualitative and quantitative methods see, e.g., Cresswell, 1994; Lee, 1999; Currall et al., 1999; and Currall and Towler, 2002.) For instance, in seeking to uncover the historical origins of trust between two persons, the researcher might conduct interviews with members of groups to which the two persons belong. It may be that by studying group norms or rituals the researcher uncovers the reasons why two individuals from different groups trust, or do not trust, each other.

3.　*Triangulate trust measures*

Currall and Inkpen (2002) provided a detailed discussion of different approaches to measurement of trust at the person, group and organizational levels. We will not repeat that material here. Suffice it to say, however, that the complex nature of trust should be captured through simultaneous assessment at multiple levels – that is, by triangulating measures of trust. Triangulation involves use of multiple operational measures of a construct to better understand its properties. The use of triangulation enables researchers to examine the convergent and discriminant validity of trust measures. For example, when aiming to characterize an overall degree of trust within an organization, one may wish to assess both interpersonal and intergroup trust. Such analyses can shed light on the nature of trust by identifying similarities and distinctions across levels, which enhances the methodological rigor of our empirical work. By identifying where trust is strong and where it is weak, multiple measurements across levels will sharpen our knowledge of the role of trust in various organizational outcomes, such as collaboration, flexibility and financial performance.

4.　*Use longitudinal research designs to examine the co-evolution of trust across levels*

Many different organizational context factors can affect trust, such as communication effectiveness among individuals, demographic similarity among groups of managers, or resource complementarity among organizations. Yet our main thesis in this chapter was that an aspect of the organizational context of trust is the degree of trust or distrust operating at an adjacent level of analysis. Thus understanding organizational context involves cross-level relationships, namely, the interaction of the interpersonal, intergroup and inter-organizational and bi-directional linkages among them. Therefore, in addition to triangulating trust assessments by using measures at multiple levels, a fundamental element of understanding the co-evolution of trust is the use of longitudinal research designs whereby the researcher explores how trust dynamics at one level may, over time, be responsible for producing degrees of trust at adjacent levels.

Conclusion

We began this chapter by arguing that trust research should move beyond single snapshots of interpersonal, intergroup, or inter-organizational trust. Such reductionistic approaches do not do justice to the intricacies of trust or the degree to which it changes over time. Therefore, we call for a new era of trust research that shifts attention toward multilevel analyses of trust and the co-evolution of trust over time from one level to another. In other words, we have argued for a conceptualization of trust that incorporates the reciprocal and bi-directional linkages whereby trust at the interpersonal level may lead to intergroup trust, which may, in turn, spawn inter-organizational trust or vice versa. Such explorations of the co-evolution of trust across levels will yield a textured understanding of the intricacies of the trust construct, which, ultimately, will lead to more precise knowledge of the impact of trust on individual, group and organizational outcomes.

Acknowledgement
We thank Eden King for valuable comments on a draft of this chapter.

References

Bachmann, R., D. Knights and J. Sydow (2001), 'Special issue on trust and control in organizational relations', *Organization Studies*, **22**.

Bar-Tal, D. (1990), *Group Beliefs*, New York/Berlin: Springer-Verlag.

Barney, J. and M.H. Hansen (1994), 'Trustworthiness as a source of competitive advantage', *Strategic Management Journal*, **15**, 175–90.

Bazerman, M. (2001), *Judgment in Managerial Decision Making*, 5th edn. New York: John Wiley.

Cappelli, P. and P.D. Sherer (1991), 'The missing role of context in OB: The need for a meso-level approach', *Research in Organizational Behavior*, **13**, 55–110.

Child, J. (2001), 'Trust–the fundamental bond in global collaboration', *Organizational Dynamics*, **29**, 274–88.

Creswell, J. (1994), *Research Design: Qualitative and quantitative approaches*. Thousand Oaks, CA: Sage.

Currall, S.C. (1992), 'Group representatives in educational institutions: An empirical study of superintendents and teacher union presidents', *Journal of Applied Behavioral Science*, **28**, 296–317.

Currall, S.C. and M.J. Epstein (2003), 'The fragility of organizational trust: Lessons from the rise and fall of Enron', *Organizational Dynamics*, **32**, 193–206.

Currall, S.C. and A.C. Inkpen (2002), 'A multilevel measurement approach to trust in joint ventures', *Journal of International Business Studies*, **33**, 479–95.

Currall, S.C. and A.C. Inkpen (2003), 'Strategic alliances and the evolution of trust across levels', in M. West, D. Tjosvold and K. Smith (eds), *International Handbook of Organizational Teamwork and Cooperative Working*, New York: John Wiley and Sons, pp. 533–49.

Currall, S.C. and T.A. Judge (1995), 'Measuring trust between organizational boundary role persons', *Organizational Behavior and Human Decision Processes*, **64**, 151–70.

Currall, S.C. and A.J. Towler (2002), 'Research methods in management and organizational research: Toward integration of qualitative and quantitative techniques', in A. Tashakkori and C. Teddlie (eds), *Handbook of Mixed Methods in Social and Behavioral Research*, Thousand Oaks, CA: Sage Publications, pp. 513–26.

Currall, S.C., T.H. Hammer, L.S. Baggett and G.M. Doniger (1999), 'Combining qualitative and quantitative methodologies to study group processes: An illustrative study of a corporate board of directors', *Organizational Research Methods*, **2**, 5–36.

Doney, P.M. and J.P. Cannon (1997), 'An examination of the nature of trust in buyer–seller relationships', *Journal of Marketing*, **61** (2), 35–51.

Doz, Y. (1996), 'The evolution of cooperation in strategic alliances: Initial conditions or learning processes?', *Strategic Management Journal*, **17** (special issue), 55–84.

Dyson, F. (1995), 'The scientist as rebel', *The New York Review of Books*, 25 May, 31–3.

Giffin, K. (1967), 'The contribution of studies of source credibility to a theory of interpersonal trust in the communication process', *Psychological Bulletin*, **68**, 104–20.

Hackman, J.R. (2003), 'Learning more by crossing levels: Evidence from airplanes, hospitals, and orchestras', *Journal of Organizational Behavior*, **24**, 905–22.

Heath, C. and S.B. Sitkin (2001), 'Big-B versus Big-O: What is *organizational* about organizational behavior?', *Journal of Organizational Behavior*, **22**, 43–58.

Huber, G.P. (1990), 'A theory of the effects of advanced information technologies on organizational design, intelligence and decision making', *Academy of Management Review*, **15**, 47–71.

Inkpen, A.C. and S.C. Currall (1997), 'International joint venture trust: An empirical examination', in

P.W. Beamish and J.P. Killing (eds), *Cooperative Strategies: North American Perspectives*, San Francisco, CA: New Lexington Press, pp. 308–34.

Inkpen, A.C. and S.C. Currall (1998), 'The nature, antecedents, and consequences of joint venture trust', *Journal of International Management*, **4**, 1–20.

Inkpen, A.C. and S.C. Currall (2004), 'The co-evolution of trust, control, and learning in joint ventures', *Organization Science*, **15**, 586–99.

Jeffries, F.L. and R. Reed (2000), 'Trust and adaptation in relational contracting', *Academy of Management Review*, **25**, 873–82.

Johns, G. (2001), 'In praise of context', *Journal of Organizational Behavior*, **22**, 31–42.

Klein, K.J., F. Dansereau and R.J. Hall (1994), 'Levels issues in theory development, data collection and analysis', *Academy of Management Review*, **19**, 195–229.

Koza, M.P. and A.Y. Lewin (1998), 'The co-evolution of strategic alliances', *Organization Science*, **9**, 255–64.

Lee, T. (1999), *Using Qualitative Methods in Organizational Research*, Thousand Oaks, CA: Sage.

Lewin, A.Y. and H.W. Volderba (1999), 'Prolegomena on coevolution: A framework for research on strategy and new organizational forms', *Organization Science*, **10**, 519–34.

March, J.G. and Z. Shapira (1987), 'Managerial perspectives on risk and risk taking', *Management Science*, **33**, 1404–18.

Mayer, R.C., J.H. Davis and F.D. Schoorman (1995), 'An integrative model of organizational trust', *Academy of Management Review*, **20**, 709–34.

McEvily, W., V. Perrone and A. Zaheer (2003), 'Introduction to the special issue on trust in an organizational context', *Organization Science*, **14**, 1–4.

McKnight, D.H., L.L. Cummings and N.L. Chervany (1998), 'Initial trust formation in new organizational relationships', *Academy of Management Review*, **23**, 473–90.

Mowday, R.T. and R.I. Sutton (1993), 'Organizational behavior: Linking individuals and groups to organizational contexts', *Annual Review of Psychology*, **44**, 195–229.

Osigweh, C.A. (1989), 'Concept fallibility in organizational science', *Academy of Management Review*, **14**, 579–94.

Rotter, J. (1980), 'Interpersonal trust, trustworthiness and gullibility', *American Psychologist*, **35**, 1–7.

Rousseau, D.M. (1985), 'Issues of level in organizational research: Multi-level and cross-level perspectives', in L. Cummings and B. Staw (eds), *Research in Organizational Behavior*, Greenwich, CT: JAI Press, **7**, 1–37.

Rousseau, D.M. and Y. Fried (2001), 'Location, location, location: Contextualizing organizational research', *Journal of Organizational Behavior*, **22**, 1–13.

Rousseau, D.M., S. Sitkin, R.S. Burt and C. Camerer (1998), 'Not so different after all: A cross-discipline view of trust', *Academy of Management Review*, **23**, 393–404.

Sitkin, S.B. and A.L. Pablo (1992), 'Reconceptualizing the determinants of risk behavior', *Academy of Management Review*, **17**, 9–38.

Zaheer, A., W. McEvily and V. Perrone (1998), 'Does trust matter? Exploring the effects of inter-organizational and interpersonal trust on performance', *Organization Science*, **9**, 141–59.

Zucker, L.G. (1986), 'Production of trust: institutional sources of economic structure, 1840–20', in B. Staw and L. Cummings (eds), *Research in Organizational Behavior*, Greenwich, CT: JAI Press, **8**, 53–111.

14 Forms, sources and processes of trust
Bart Nooteboom

Introduction

Much has been written about trust, particularly outside economics, in sociology and management. In spite of this, much confusion and misunderstanding remains. Trust is full of paradox, as listed in Table 14.1. The purpose of this chapter is to untangle some of the confusion and to clarify the complexities of trust. The chapter draws on an earlier book (Nooteboom 2002), and gives a summary and an illustration of some central points; for further details and elaborations reference is made to the book.[1]

One important source of misunderstanding, related to Paradox 1 (see Table 14.1), is the confusion of trust as based on control (on the basis of self-interested behaviour) and trust as going beyond control (going beyond narrow self-interest). Can one speak of trust when one believes people will conform to expectations or agreements because they are contractually or hierarchically bound to do so, or because it is in their interest to do so, or only if they do so even though they have both the opportunity and the incentive not to do so? In other words, can trustworthiness go beyond self-interest? And if it does, is it then blind and unconditional? To clarify this, Nooteboom (2002) proposed a distinction between a wide notion of reliance, which includes control and incentives, and a narrower, stronger notion of trust, which goes beyond self-interest. As noted by Williamson (1993), if trust does not go beyond calculative self-interest, that is, control, it is not very meaningful. However, while Williamson argued that such trust cannot survive under the pressures of competition in markets, Nooteboom (2002) argued that it can, but that in doing so it does have limits, and these limits depend on pressures of survival. Trust and control are substitutes, in that with more trust there can be less control, but they are also complements, in that usually trust and contract are combined, since neither can be complete. Trust is needed, since contracts can never be complete, but it can go too far, since trust also can never be complete.

Table 14.1   Paradoxes of trust

Trust:
1. Goes beyond self-interest but has limits
2. Entails a state of mind and a type of action
3. May concern competence or intentions
4. Is based on information and the lack of it
5. Is rational and emotional
6. Is an expectation but not a probability
7. Is needed but can have adverse effects
8. May be broken and deepened by conflict
9. Is both a basis and an outcome of relations

Another source of confusion, related to Paradox 2 (see Table 14.1), is that some see trust as a (trusting) action, and then one can speak of people deciding to trust, while others see trust as a mental state, which one has or has not, and cannot decide to have. This can easily be resolved right away: trust is a state of mind, not an action, but it can lead to trusting action. One may decide to rely on people, even when not having trust in them.

A third source of confusion concerns what aspect of behaviour one can have trust in, related to Paradox 3 (see Table 14.1). One can trust the competence of people to conform to expectations, and their intentions to do so, to the best of their competence.

These confusions tend to invalidate much empirical research on trust, in which these distinctions and possible confusions were not taken into account. If, in a survey, one asks all-encompassing questions such as whether people trust others, it is left to the respondent to decide whether to interpret trust as a state of mind or an action, as being based on control or sources of trustworthiness that go beyond control, and as being directed at competence or at intentions. Since different people will make different interpretations, depending on their experience, the context and the framing of the question, the results will often be meaningless. More will be said about this later, with the police as an example.

A further source of confusion in Paradox 5, is that there are rational reasons for trust as well as emotional causes of it. Both occur, and the question then is how they are related. Considerable attention will be paid, in this chapter, to the psychological mechanisms of trust. Rational trust is based on information about someone, from which one infers their trustworthiness, but such information can hardly be complete, and one can hardly be sure about trustworthiness (Paradox 4). The person to be trusted (the trustee) probably does not even know when he/she may succumb to temptations or pressures of survival. Trust or mistrust are also governed by psychological tendencies, feelings and emotions, such as naïvety, fear, overconfidence, impulsiveness, enamouration and so on. Due to the open-endedness and incalculability of potential future behaviour, it is of dubious validity to model trust as a (calculable) probability (Paradox 6).

There is often a tendency to have too rosy a picture of trust, as being always good, and as going together with absence of conflict (Paradoxes 7 and 8; see Table 14.1). One may trust mistakenly and be open to great vulnerability. Trust may be so strong as to limit the flexibility and variety of economic relations that may be needed for learning and innovation. Precisely because there is trust, people may venture into intense conflict, and when that is resolved, trust is likely to deepen (Six 2004).

Finally, trust is not static. While it is needed as the basis for a relationship, it is also shaped by it (Paradox 9; see Table 14.1). Hence it should be seen as a process.

To clarify and elaborate on all this, this chapter will review the objects of trust, that is, things one can trust or rely on, sources of reliability and trust, resulting definitions of reliability and trust, the value of trust, its psychological mechanisms, its relation to contract, and its limits. As noted, most of this is derived from Nooteboom (2002), which is referred to for further details. The chapter ends with an application to the police, to give an illustration of how the different dimensions of trust come together in a specific case.

Objects of trust
Trust entails the acceptance of risk that arises from dependence, combined with lack of control. One can trust material objects (e.g. the car will start in the morning), empirical regularities or laws of nature (e.g. law of gravity), people, authorities, organizations,

institutions (e.g. laws), and higher powers (God). When the object of trust (what one trusts) is imposed, inevitable, beyond choice, as in the case of laws of nature, higher powers and many institutions (e.g. laws), one may speak of confidence rather than trust (Luhmann 1988). If one had trust in a judge, rather than confidence, this would suggest that one avoid judgement or select one's own judge.

Trust in people or organizations is called 'behavioural trust'. Behavioural trust has a variety of aspects: trust in competence (competence trust), intentions (intentional trust), honesty or truthfulness, resource availability and robustness, that is, limited sensitivity to outside disturbances. Competence trust refers to technical, cognitive and communicative competencies. On the firm level it includes technological, innovative, commercial, organizational and managerial competence. Intentional trust refers to the intentions of a partner towards the relationship, particularly the possibility of opportunism. Opportunism can have a passive/weak and an active/strong form. The passive or weak form entails lack of dedication or effort to perform to the best of competence. Dedication entails active participation, attention, and abstention from free-riding. The active or strong form of opportunism entails 'interest seeking with guile', in the words of Williamson (1975), with lying, stealing and cheating to expropriate advantage from a partner. Absence of such strong opportunism is called 'benevolence' or 'goodwill'. Thus intentional trust has two dimensions: trust in dedication and trust in benevolence.

In fact, the aspects of trust can be extended further. A systematic way of doing this is to ask and answer the question what kinds of things can go wrong in a relationship. Nooteboom (2002) did this on the basis of a multiple causality of action, derived from Aristotle.

Like people, organizations can be the object of trust, in both their competence and their intentions. We can trust an organization to behave responsibly in relation to its stakeholders and the environment. Of course an organization itself does not have an intention, but it has interests and can try to regulate the intentions of its workers to serve those interests. One's trust in an individual may be based on one's trust in the organization that person belongs to, for example because the organization has an interest in maintaining its reputation or brand name. Trust in an organization can be based on trust in the people in it. It can be affected by corporate communication, which aims to project a certain image. Trust in people and in organizations is connected by the functions and positions people have and the roles they play in their organizations (Ring and Van de Ven 1994). For personal trust to be transferred to the organization, trustworthy individuals must be backed up by their authority, position, bosses and personnel. Vice versa, for organizational trust to be transferred to individuals, the people involved should implement organizational interests and rules of trustworthy conduct.

Trust and control

Here, the focus is on intentional trust. In much literature, the explicit or implicit definition of intentional trust is a broad one: the trustor (A) trusts the trustee (B) if A accepts relational risk, that is, vulnerability to (active or passive) opportunistic actions of B, but expects that B will not in fact engage in such behaviour. In such a broad interpretation of the notion of trust, it would include 'control', defined as any instrument or condition that may mitigate relational risk. Control is often interpreted more narrowly as 'deterrence' (Maguire et al. 2001): in the case of opportunistic behaviour the partner would incur a penalty or a material loss. From Nooteboom (1996, 2002) the idea is adopted that there are three ways in which opportunism can be mitigated:

1. opportunity control: limitation of opportunities for opportunism, by restricting the range of a partner's actions, by contract or hierarchical supervision;
2. incentive control: limitation of material incentives to utilize opportunities for opportunism, due to dependence on the relationship, hostages or reputation effects;
3. benevolence or goodwill: limitation of inclinations towards opportunism, on the basis of social norms or personal relations.

Deterrence would include opportunity control and incentive control. Benevolence or goodwill goes beyond deterrence, with more intrinsic motives to limit opportunism.

Sources of reliability

Trust has rational reasons, based on inference of trustworthiness, and psychological causes, which block, affect or enable rational evaluation. For rational trust, based on inference of trustworthiness, we need to know what the sources of trustworthiness are. I adopt, with some modifications, a scheme from Nooteboom (2002), which was in turn adopted, with modifications, from Williams (1988), specified in Table 14.2.

Following Williams (1988), Table 14.2 distinguishes between 'macro' sources, which apply generally and impersonally, apart from any specific exchange relation, and 'micro' sources. The first arise from the institutional environment of laws, norms, values, standards, and agencies for their enforcement. They yield 'institution-based trust'. They are also called sources of 'thin' trust. This kind of trust requires that we trust those institutions to support or enforce trustworthiness of people and organizations. The 'micro' sources arise in specific relations, and are therefore personalized. They are also called sources of 'thick' trust. The distinction between macro and micro sources is also known as the distinction between 'universalistic' or 'generalized' sources versus 'particularistic' sources, made by Deutsch (1973: 55), and between impersonal, institutional and personalized sources made by Shapiro (1987) (see also Bachmann 2000). This distinction goes back to the work of Parsons. Social norms and moral obligations, including a sense of

Table 14.2   Sources of reliability (trustworthiness broadly interpreted)

	Macro: universalistic, institutional	Micro: particularistic, relation-specific
Self-interest		
Opportunity control	Contracts, legal enforcement	Hierarchy, managerial 'fiat'
Incentive control	Reputation	Dependence: unique partner value, switching costs, hostages
Altruism	Values, social norms of proper conduct, moral obligation, sense of duty, bonds of kinship	Empathy, routinization, benevolence, identification, affect, friendship

Source: Adapted from Nooteboom (2002).

duty, following Parsons and Durkheim, were proposed more recently by Bradach and Eccles (1984), Zucker (1986), and Dore (1983), among others. Fukuyama (1995) employed the term 'spontaneous sociability'.

Williams further distinguished self-interested and altruistic or 'other-directed' sources of cooperation. The self-interested sources are associated with the notions of deterrence and 'calculus-based trust' (e.g. Lewicki and Bunker 1996). In my reconstruction, taken from Nooteboom (2002), this includes opportunity control and incentive control. Limitation of opportunities has an 'outside form', to control outside partners, in contract enforcement. It also has an 'inside form', within an organization, in the exercise of 'hierarchy', with managerial 'fiat' under an employment relationship. Both entail monitoring of behaviour, to detect cheating as a cause for sanctions. The distinction between external contracts and internal hierarchy lies at the basis of the reasoning of transaction cost economics (TCE). In view of uncertainty and the consequent impossibility of complete contingent contracts, and the fact that with external contracting sanctions ultimately can only be imposed through the external authority of the law, internal control by hierarchy yields more opportunities to demand information for monitoring and to impose sanctions, under the general conditions of an employment relation.

In incentive control, partner B behaves well towards A because he is dependent on A for one or more of the following reasons: A has a unique, difficult-to-replace value to B, B faces switching costs as a result of relation-specific investments, partner A holds a hostage from B, or B has to protect his reputation. The notion of specific investments is derived from TCE, except that I consider the relation rather than the transaction as the unit of analysis, and hence speak of relation-specific, not transaction-specific, investments. I extend the notion of specific investments to include investments in relation-specific mutual understanding and in the building of relation-specific trust. The notion of hostage is also taken from TCE. It mostly takes the form of sensitive information that is of value to B, and is held by A, who can destroy, divulge or transfer it to a competitor of B, if B does not behave well. A hostage can also take the form of a minority share that A has in B, with the (typically implicit) threat of selling the shares to a firm that aims to take over B. It may also take the form of specialized staff of B, temporarily stationed at A, who could be poached by A.[2]

Calculation of self-interest includes reputation (Weigelt and Camerer 1988) and the assessment of future benefits of present cooperativeness ('shadow of the future'), as has been recognized by many (Telser 1980; Axelrod 1984; Hill 1990; Heide and Meiner 1992; Parkhe 1993). A reputation mechanism requires reporting and broadcasting of non-trustworthy behaviour. To forestall mere gossip, this often requires some agency to make reliable reports or to check their validity. This can be a trade, industry or professional association.

The 'altruistic' or 'other-directed' sources go beyond self-interested behaviour. Man is not only self-interested and opportunistic: in business also common honesty and decency are found (Macaulay 1963). This can yield voluntary compliance to an agreement that goes beyond self-interest (Bradach and Eccles 1984). This may be based on established, socially inculcated norms and values (macro), and empathy, identification, affect and routines developed in specific relations (micro). The first includes pressures of allegiance to groups one belongs to, or values and norms inculcated by socialization into those groups. On the micro side, empathy-based trust entails that one knows and understands how partners think and feel. It allows one to assess strengths and weaknesses in competence and intentions, to determine the limits of trustworthiness under different conditions

(Nooteboom 2002). Identification-based trust goes further: it entails that people think and feel in the same way, sharing views of the world and norms of behaviour. This may lead to affect- and friendship-based trust.

Routine-based trust, proposed by Nooteboom (2002), entails that when a relation has been satisfactory for a while, awareness of opportunities of opportunism, for oneself and for the partner, is relegated to 'subsidiary awareness' (Polanyi 1962). One takes the relation for granted and does not continuously think about opportunities to gain extra advantage.

As relations develop in time partners begin to understand each other better (empathy), and may then develop identification-based trust (McAllister 1995, Lewicki and Bunker 1996), and routine-based trust. This constitutes a relation-specific 'trust process'. Identification may go so far that one is not able or willing to consider the possibility of untrustworthiness. This may include cognitive dissonance: one does not want to face evidence of untrustworthiness because it conflicts with deep-seated convictions or feelings. Routine-based and identification-based trust can become excessive, causing rigidity of relations and blocking innovation.

The trust literature employs the notion of 'knowledge-based trust', which is also proposed as a stage in trust building (McAllister 1995; Lewicki and Bunker 1996). I find this a vague and confusing notion (Nooteboom 2002). Opportunity control (contracts), incentive control (dependence, hostages, reputation) and empathy are all based on knowledge of, respectively, the terms of a contract, the law and possible sanctions, uniqueness of partner value, hostage keeping, reputation, and how a partner thinks.

Definition of trust

The question now is whether we should adopt the wide definition of trust, indicated earlier, which would include deterrence (opportunity and incentive control) as sources of trust. Like Williams, many other authors have claimed that trust can go beyond deterrence, on the basis of 'goodwill' or 'benevolence', resulting from loyalty or altruism (Das and Teng 1998; Maguire et al. 2001; Lane and Bachmann 2000). Deterrence is felt to be foreign to the notion of trust: 'genuine' trust is based on other, more social and personal foundations of trustworthiness. Maguire et al. (2001: 286) claimed that if we do not include the latter, we conflate trust and power. As Williamson (1993) indicated, trust has no meaning if it does not go beyond calculative self-interest.

For these reasons, trust has been defined more narrowly as the expectation that a partner will not engage in opportunistic behaviour, even in the face of opportunities and incentives for opportunism (Bradach and Eccles 1984; Chiles and McMackin 1996; Nooteboom 1996). This narrower definition is felt to indicate better what most people would call 'real trust'. As suggested by Nooteboom (2002), this problem of definition has been and still is a source of major confusion and misunderstanding. Perhaps we should use different terms for the different notions: 'reliance' for the wide notion, including deterrence, and 'real trust' or 'trust in the strong sense' for trust that goes beyond deterrence, in benevolence.

The value of trust

Trust can have extrinsic value, as a basis for achieving social or economic goals. It can also have intrinsic value, as a dimension of relations that is valued for itself, as part of a broader notion of well-being or the quality of life. Many authors have pointed this out. People may prefer, as an end in itself, to deal with each other on the basis of trust. Most economists tend to think of value in exchange as something that exists independently of the transaction. As formulated by Murakami and Rohlen (1992: 70), 'The value of the relationship itself is typically ignored and the impersonality of the transaction is assumed.' In intrinsic utility, the exchange process itself matters, as does the economic surplus that the exchange yields.

When intrinsic, the value of trust can be hedonic or based on self-respect. Many people would prefer to have trust-based relations rather than relations based on suspicion and opportunism for hedonic reasons. For most people it is more agreeable or pleasurable to have friendly relations than to have to deal with animosity and suspicion. There is also an intrinsic motive of self-respect, based on adherence to internalized norms or values of decent or ethical conduct. There is also a more socially oriented motive, in the will to be recognized, valued and respected by others. Social recognition may be served by accumulating riches, power or glamour, but also by being trustworthy and trusting, and thereby demonstrating adherence to established values, norms or habits of behaviour. This may merge with the earlier motive of self-respect, while analytically it can still be distinguished. Fukuyama (1995: 358) traced the urge for recognition to Hegel: a struggle for recognition, 'that is, the desire of all human beings to have their essence as free, moral beings recognised by other beings'. As indicated, this does not necessarily lead to trustworthiness and trust. Philosophers have also postulated other urges, such as the will to power. The extrinsic, economic value of trust lies in the fact that it enables interaction between people and between organizations and can reduce transaction costs. The downside of trust is that it entails risk and can be betrayed, which may endanger the survival of a person or firm. There can also be too much solidarity, providing an obstacle to change and innovation.

The distinction between extrinsic and intrinsic value is analytical. They are not necessarily perceived as distinct. An important question is how they are related in the perception and behaviour of agents. Extrinsic value is instrumental, which entails calculation, and suggests a focus on self-interest, while intrinsic value can be non-rational, unreflective and other-directed. The question concerning their relation is related to questions whether and how calculative and non-calculative trust can be combined, and whether trustworthiness can go beyond self-interest.

Psychological sources

Trust entails acceptance of relational risk. This may be based on a rational evaluation of trustworthiness. However, such evaluation is mediated by decision heuristics, and next to rational evaluation trust is also based on instinct, inclinations, feelings and emotions. Evolutionary psychology suggests that a tendency towards 'give and take' (reciprocity), and accepting relational risk, is 'in our genes', since it was conducive to survival in the ancient hunter–gatherer societies in which humanity evolved. The variance of yields, in gathering edible plants, roots, nuts and so on, and the even greater variance in hunting, together with problems of durable storage, entails an evolutionary advantage of the willingness to surrender part of one's yield to others in need, in the expectation to receive from them when they are successful (Cosmides and Tooby 1992: 212). This would solve the problem, often noted in the literature, how in a sequential game of give and take the first move of giving, and thereby making a risky pre-commitment, is made (Simmel 1950; Luhmann 1979). The evolutionary argument suggests that we do this instinctively.

However, psychological mechanisms that were conducive to survival in evolution do entail biases that can lead to serious error (Bazerman 1998).

Here we should no longer talk of reasons but of causes of trust. However, the distinction I am making here may suggest a greater cleavage between rationality and emotion than is valid. Like many others, I believe that rationality and emotions are intertwined (Polanyi 1962; Merleau-Ponty 1964; Damasio 1995; Hendriks-Jansen 1996; Lakoff and Johnson 1999). I include in cognition not only perception and interpretation but also evaluation, that is, value judgements. Not only value judgements but also interpretations and even perceptions are emotion-laden. In the interpretative or hermeneutic view, our knowledge is constructed in mental categories, which include psychological mechanisms that may yield serious distortion.

Nevertheless, we can distinguish more or less rational inference of trustworthiness from less reflective causes of trust, based on affect of friendship or kinship, or on routinized behaviour. I follow Herbert Simon (1983) in recognizing the role of emotions in reason, to shift routinized behaviour from subsidiary to focal awareness. Emotions are rational in triggering reflexes or attention when survival requires it. However, they can yield error. They may lead us to jump to erroneous conclusions, and may produce prejudice. Evidence of untrustworthiness may be ignored as a result of cognitive dissonance. As Deutsch (1973: 159) put it:

> A person's perceptions of another will be determined not only by the information he receives from his direct experiences or from what others tell him, but also by his need to absorb this information in such a way as to prevent disruption of existing perceptions, cognitions, or evaluations to which he is strongly committed.

Decision heuristics

Social psychology offers a number of insights into the decision heuristics that people use. In a survey, Bazerman (1998) mentions the following heuristics:

- Availability heuristic: people assess the probability and likely causes of an event by the degree to which instances of it are 'readily available' in memory, i.e. are vivid, laden with emotion, recent and recognizable. Less available events and causes are neglected.
- Representativeness heuristic: the likelihood of an event is assessed by its similarity to stereotypes of similar occurrences. We recognize something according to the likeness of some focal features to those of a prototype, which may be a stereotype, and on the basis of that attribute other features from the stereotype that are not in fact present. This can easily yield prejudice.
- Anchoring and adjustment. Judgement is based on some initial or base value ('anchor') from previous experience or social comparison, plus incremental adjustment from that value. People have been shown to stay close even to random anchors that bear no systematic relation to the issue at hand. First impressions can influence the development of a relation for a long time.

One cannot maintain that these heuristics are irrational. In view of uncertainty and bounded rationality they may well be adaptive, that is, contribute to survival. Concerning the availability heuristic, note the importance of an emotion-laden perception of a suspicious event to trigger awareness of the routine and subject it to scrutiny, in focal awareness. Perhaps this is connected with the availability heuristic: we pay attention only when triggers are emotion-laden. If we did not apply such filters, our consciousness would probably be overloaded.

The representativeness heuristic is related to the role of prototypes in language and categorization. Since definitions can seldom offer necessary and sufficient conditions for categorization, and meaning is context-dependent and open-ended, allowing for variation and change, we need prototypes (Rosch 1978). A prototype represents an exemplar of a class that connects others in the class. Class membership is decided on the basis of resemblance to a salient case, or a typical case, which serves as a prototype. A prototype may turn into a shallow stereotype. However, the mechanism of attributing unobserved characteristics upon recognition of observed ones enables pattern recognition that is conducive to survival.

Concerning anchoring and adjustment, under uncertainty cognition does need such an anchor, and taking the most recent value of a variable, or a value observed in behaviour of people in similar conditions, with whom one can empathize, may well be rational. Trust can be seen as a default, in the sense that on the basis of past experience we assume trustworthiness unless we find new evidence that contradicts it. We adapt past guidelines for behaviour on the basis of new evidence. Incremental adjustment can be inadequate, but so can fast adjustment. Studies of learning and adjustment have shown that hasty and large departures from existing practices can yield chaotic behaviour (March 1991; Lounamaa and March 1987). Thus anchoring and adaptation may also be a useful and justified heuristic, in view of uncertainty. Nevertheless, these heuristics can yield errors.

The relevance of these heuristics to trust is clear, because they affect, or enable, expectation and attribution of trustworthiness. According to the heuristics, one would develop expectations, explain broken expectations, and attribute trustworthiness according to what is 'available' in the mind, stereotypes, existing norms or recent experience.

Another psychological phenomenon is that people are found to have difficulty in choosing between immediate gratification and long-term benefit, yielding a problem of 'the weakness of the will'. This has been explained in terms of people having multiple selves that are at odds with each other, or as a visceral drive competing with a rational inclination. Another interpretation follows the availability heuristic: immediate gratification is more 'available'. Studies of behaviour under uncertainty have shown that people may assess delay in gratification differently when it is near than when it is far ahead, and that sometimes discounting seems to take place not according to an exponential but according to a hyperbolic function. According to that function, the negative utility of a delay of gratification increases as the decision moves to the present. As a result, preferences may reverse at some point in time. The relevance of this phenomenon to collaborative relations is also clear, in the trade-off between loyalty to a partner, which may be in one's long-term interest, and the temptation to defect to another partner who offers more advantage in the short term. One may honestly think one is able to withstand that temptation in the future, and succumb to it when it nears. Again, we cannot unequivocally judge that this psychological mechanism is maladaptive. As noted also by Bazerman (1998), the impulse of temptation may also entail the vision of entrepreneurial opportunity, and too much repression of it may suppress innovation.

Framing

'Prospect theory' (Kahneman et al. 1982) has demonstrated that people are not risk-neutral, but can be risk-taking when a decision is framed in terms of loss, and risk-averse when it is framed in terms of gain. Framing entails, among other things, that in a relation people will accept a greater risk of conflict when they stand to incur a loss than when they stand to obtain a benefit. Related to this effect is the 'endowment effect': people often demand more money to sell what they have than they would be prepared to pay to get it. In the first case one wants to cover for loss. This may contribute to loyalty and stable relations, as follows. Relations typically end when one of the partners encounters a more attractive alternative, while the other partner wants to continue the relation. The first partner is confronted with a gain frame, the second with a loss frame. This may cause the second partner to engage in more aggressive, risky behaviour, to maintain the relation, than the first partner, who may be more willing to forego his profit and run less risk of a harmful separation procedure. One wonders what the adaptive rationale of this difference between a gain and a loss frame is, if any. Perhaps it lies precisely in the effect just mentioned: it reduces defection and thereby stabilizes relationships, which may have contributed to survival.[3] However, this is only conjecture on my part.

Earlier, I noted the importance for trust of empathy and identification, yielding the ability to dwell in (empathy) or share (identification) others' categories of understanding and motivations, as a function of conditions. Recall the definition of trust, above, as a four-place predicate: one trusts someone in some respect under certain conditions. It is part of trust, then, to understand another's cognition and motivation, as a function of conditions, in knowledge-based trust, to sympathize with them in empathy-based trust, or identify with them in identification-based trust. This is clearly related to the availability heuristic: 'availability' increases to the extent that one can understand behaviour, and sympathize or identify with it, or, on the contrary, abhor it. This affects both one's own trustworthiness, in the willingness to make sacrifices for others, and one's trust, in the tolerance of behaviour that deviates from expectations. One will more easily help someone when one can identify with his need. One can more easily forgive someone's breach of trust or reliance when one can sympathize or identify with the lack of competence or the motive that caused it. One can more easily accept the blame for oneself. One may sympathize with his action, seeing perhaps that his action was in fact a just response to one's own previous actions. Empathy and identification are both forms of affect-based trust, but in the latter affect is the strongest.

Another reason to attribute blame to oneself when someone else is in fact to blame is to reduce uncertainty or establish a sense of control. This works as follows. If it is perceived to be impossible or very difficult to influence someone's behaviour in order to prevent or redress damage from broken expectations, one may attribute blame to oneself. By doing that, one relieves the stress of feeling subjected to the power of others. For people with little self-confidence or a poor self-image, this is a move of desperation, and self-blame fits with the preconception one had of oneself. For people with self-confidence, self-blame may yield a sense of control: if the cause lies with oneself, one can more easily deal with it. Of course, that may be an illusion, due to overconfidence in oneself.

Another mechanism is that of a belief in a just world, which gives reassurance. By enacting justice, even anonymously, one confirms its existence by contributing to it, and thereby maintains a sense of security. However, when the sacrifice for another would be too high to accept, in the view of self-interest, then to avoid a self-perception of callousness one may convince oneself that his hardship is his own fault.

Yet another psychological mechanism is that in violation of rational behaviour, sunk costs, such as sacrifices made in a relationship, are not seen as bygones that should be ignored in an assessment of future costs and benefits. They are seen as sacrifices that would be seen as in vain if one pulls out after having incurred them. This yields what is known as non-rational 'escalation of commitment'. It is associated with cognitive dissonance: cutting one's losses and pulling out would entail an admission of failure, of having made a bad decision in the past. The phenomenon is confirmed in empirical research, which shows that when the decision to cut one's losses needs to be made by someone not involved in the initial decision, or when the threat of an admission of failure is removed, the rational decision to pull out is made. Again, one cannot say that this mechanism is always bad, because it also demonstrates perseverance in the face of setbacks, which can be a good thing, and is in fact a trait of many a successful innovating entrepreneur. This phenomenon can also be connected with the effect of a loss frame versus a gain frame, proposed in prospect theory. The person, or group, that made the initial decision experiences a loss frame, with the inclination to accept further risk in order to prevent acceptance of the loss. The decision maker who enters afresh experiences a gain frame, to make a decision that will offer profit in the future, regardless of past sunk costs, and will be less inclined to accept the high risk of continuing losses from sticking to past decisions. The mechanism of non-rational escalation can contribute to the continuation of a relationship where it is not beneficial.

Trust and contract: substitutes or complements?
How are trust and contract related? Are they complements or substitutes? If we interpret trust in the wide sense of reliance, it can be based on the assurance offered by contracts. Contract supports reliance. On the other hand, some social scientists argue that contract can be destructive of trust in the stronger, narrower sense. Unwanted side effects result mainly from the active use of contract in monitoring activities, threat or litigation, in other words deterrence. Such actions are argued to evoke conflict (Gaski 1984; Hunt and Nevin 1974; Lusch 1976), opportunism (Goshal and Moran 1996), and defensive behavior (Zand 1972; Hirschman 1970). As a result more coercion will have to be used (Goshal and Moran 1996), or in the words of Deutsch (1973: 88), 'Without the other's trust as an asset, power is essentially limited to the coercive and ecological (i.e. conditional) types, the types that require and consume most in the way of physical and economic resources.' As a result, Goshal and Moran argue that it may not always be desirable to specify and enforce a contract. The negative effects may not only materialize in the present, but also in future relationships. If a case is taken to court, the plaintive could seriously jeopardize a future relationship with that partner. If few alternative partners are available, the opportunity costs of this may be very high. Also, litigation may affect reputation, thereby jeopardizing potential future relations with others. Here, contract and trust are substitutes, or 'opposing alternatives' (Knights et al. 2001: 314).

I propose that some of these differences of opinion are only apparent, and are due to different interpretations of the notion of trust. If the argument is that trust in the wide sense of 'reliance' may be based on contract, this can be quite consistent with the argument that detailed contract specification and strict enforcement are in conflict with trust in 'the strong sense', going beyond control.

But even after correcting for such misunderstanding, trust and contact can still be seen as both complements and substitutes. If one accepts that due to uncertainty about future contingencies of contract execution contracts cannot be complete, especially in innovation, at some point one has to seek recourse to trust (in some sense). Trust, one might say loosely, begins where contract necessarily ends. Thus they are complements. On the other hand, intuition tells us that when trust is large, contracts can be limited. Thus they are substitutes.

Klein Woolthuis et al. (2005) conducted an empirical, longitudinal investigation of the relation between trust and contract during the evolution of collaborative projects in innovation, and found evidence for both substitution and complementarity. One finding, in favour of substitution, was in line with the argument of Lewicki and Bunker that first risk is mitigated by contracts, which later, as empathy develops, are replaced by trust. Another finding, in favour of complementarity, was that contracts may be extensive and complex under high trust for purely practical reasons of coordination in complex projects, or in other words for reasons of competence trust rather than intentional trust. Also, the drafting of a complex contract itself constitutes a relation-specific investment, which one does not want to engage in until sufficient trust has developed to make it likely to be worthwhile.

Limits of trust

Several authors suggest that goodwill does not operate independently from self-interest. Bachmann (in Lane and Bachmann 2000: 303) proposed that trust is a hybrid phenomenon, including both calculation and goodwill. According to Williamson (1993) it is impossible to reliably judge possible limits to other people's opportunism. Williamson claimed that if trust goes beyond calculative self-interest (in 'real trust'), it inevitably yields blind, unconditional trust, which is unwise and will not survive in markets. Pressures of survival under competition force firms to take advantage of others whenever they have the opportunity. In contrast, many social scientists maintain that such trust is viable, without necessarily becoming blind or unconditional, and is indeed pervasive, also in markets (Gambetta 1988; Helper 1990; Murakami and Rohlen 1992; Dyer and Ouchi 1993; Ring and Van de Ven 1994; Gulati 1995; McAllister 1995; Chiles and McMackin 1996; Nooteboom 1996). While in contrast with Williamson I maintain that trust beyond calculative self-interest can be viable, I agree that blind, unconditional trust is generally unwise in markets. There are generally limits to trustworthiness and trust. While trust is not always calculative, it is nevertheless constrained by possibilities of opportunism (Pettit 1995). Even the most loyal, committed and dedicated of people may succumb to the temptation of golden opportunities or pressures of survival. Firms may be subject to competitive pressure to such an extent that they cannot afford to accept any sacrifice for the sake of loyalty. Therefore there are limits within which people and firms may be worthy of real trust (Pettit 1995; Nooteboom 2002).

One way to model trustworthiness is in terms of a limited resistance to temptation towards opportunism. This may be modelled as a threshold for defection: one does not opportunistically defect until the advantage one can gain by so doing exceeds the threshold. This threshold may depend on implicit or explicit norms of conduct, and on competitive pressure. It is likely to adapt as a function of experience (Gorobets and Nooteboom 2005). Trust may then be modelled as based on a perception or assumption of such a constraint on a partner's opportunism.

Trust, being associated with the risk of things going wrong, is challenged when things do go wrong, or when 'trouble' arises (Six 2004). This does not necessarily entail a breakdown of trust. The question to be asked is why things went wrong. This could be due to outside accidents beyond anyone's control, a mistake, lack of competence, lack of effort, or opportunism. How does one assess what is the case? What motive and competence will one infer and attribute to the trustee, and what implications for action will one derive? An opportunistic partner would not admit his opportunistic motive, and will claim 'force majeure' if he can get away with that. This yields an argument for openness in trust relations (cf. Zand 1972), and the use of 'voice' (Hirschman 1970; Helper 1990): it may be better to admit a mistake, and timely so, in order to have the best chance of redressing it, than to run the risk of one's action being seen as a sign of opportunism (Nooteboom 2002).

Summing up, trust is a four-place predicate (Nooteboom 2002): a trustor (1) trusts a trustee (2) in some respects (3), under some conditions (4). We generally do not trust different people equally, we may trust a person in some respects but not in others, and we often trust people in some conditions but not in others. Trust generally has its limits because trustworthiness generally has its limits.

An illustration: trust in the police[4]

Trust by citizens in the police is of crucial importance for the legitimacy of the police itself, but also for external reasons: without such trust, people may lose trust in society more widely, and may be tempted to take the law into their own hands. Trust in the police is needed to maintain state monopoly of violence. The case of the police illustrates a number of features of trust. First, it illustrates the multi-level nature of trust. Trust in the police requires trust in individual officers as well as in police organization and underlying institutions of law and law enforcement, and these levels of trust should support each other. Mistrust in the police may spill over into mistrust of the social or political system as a whole. Conversely, lack of trust in politicians, or in a minister of justice, or in an interior minister, may spill over into mistrust in the police.

Surveys indicate that in the Netherlands citizens generally trust the police in their intentions but less in their competence. That is far from ideal, but it is much better than the reverse, with a competently corrupt police.

First, let us consider competence trust. That requires, first of all, that it is clear, to citizens and to the police itself, what can be expected of the police, and what the priorities are. What are the priorities of 'catching criminals', traffic control, protection, aid in disaster, and community service? How do people assess competence in each? Police service is partly an experience good, in which quality is assessed during the experience of direct contact, and partly a credence good, where the citizen is incompetent to judge quality even after contact. To the extent that competence cannot be judged, there is displacement from real but unknown factors to observable proxy indicators, such as the crispness of an officer's uniform, his manner and speech, and generally the authoritativeness that the officer exhibits, in calmness and self-confidence. When quality is difficult to judge, one will also seek judgement on the basis of outside information, such as gossip, reports in the media, or communications (e.g. on percentages of crimes solved) from the police itself. Public media may be biased, tending to report more on failures than on successes. Self-reports from the police may be suspect. As noted earlier, a reputation mechanism may require an independent agency to give trusted information (Shapiro 1987).

Next, let us consider intentional trust. Table 14.2 can be used as a tool for the analysis and design of its sources. Police officers are constrained in opportunities for opportunism by legal governance and bureaucratic control, but the effectiveness of this is limited by constrained opportunities for monitoring officers' conduct in the field. Monitoring and reporting by colleagues out in the field is limited by an ethic of mutual solidarity, needed for thick trust between officers, for mutual support under hazardous conditions. Incentive control is limited by one-sided dependence of the citizen on the police officer with his/her monopoly on violence: the citizen has limited opportunity for retaliation. Since one cannot choose to dodge the police, and one has no choice of officer, we may need to speak of confidence rather than trust. Attempts have been made to establish some countervailing power in the form of complaint procedures, which also enable a reputation mechanism. The force of reputation may be further enhanced by embedding a police officer in a local community, to yield a 'shadow of the future'. Building up understanding and reputation entails relation- or community-specific investments that will only be undertaken when there is a perspective of a more or less durable relationship.

Nevertheless, a fundamental asymmetry of dependence remains. Since instruments of both opportunity and incentive control have limited force, sources beyond self-interest are needed as a complement, in 'real' trustworthiness. One is the force of norms of conduct, which should dominate self-interest. This is, of course, what we call integrity. Another is empathy and routinization in relations. In routinization fair conduct has become a habit. Empathy entails that an officer should view the execution of his task from the perspective of the citizen. While sticking to legal and professional norms, the officer should try to act and explain his/her actions in ways that fit the intellectual and cultural 'absorptive capacity' of the citizen. Of course, one cannot expect that the citizen concurs with punitive action, but he/she should at least understand what is happening and what motivates police action. In terms of the social psychological analysis conducted above, officers should try to link with the citizen's repertoire of categories, and, if possible, to construe their own action as an adjustment with respect to the citizen's cognitive anchors, or to help citizens in the construction of adequate categories. There is an enormous potential here for the police to help prevent misunderstanding and grudges among foreigners and to aid in their integration in society. This is aided by a multi-cultural police force.

When empathy develops into identification it may go too far, with the officer compromising on the rules and norms out of identification with local citizen interests. Then, such an officer may have to be moved elsewhere. Thus citizen relationships need to be sufficiently durable to encourage investment in understanding and trust, but not so far as to yield excessive identification. In most activities in markets, agents are in a gain frame: they stand to profit from market exchange. A significant feature of police work is that citizens typically find themselves in a loss frame: criminals stand to lose their freedom and opportunity for criminal gain, and citizens are mostly encountered when they stand to lose personal safety or property. Hence the force of emotions, in the availability heuristic, is high. Threats of safety or property are likely to evoke mental frames of strong self-preservation, in flight, fight, revenge, panic and the like. The police officer should help to defuse the emotions involved. Emotions under the threat of loss detract from the reliability of citizen reports and complaints, reducing their worth as a means of governance (see above). It is all the more important, in such emotion-laden conditions, for officers to keep their cool, confidence, authority, fairness and empathy.

In sum, sources of reliability of the police are limited: hierarchical control is limited due to limits of monitoring, a highly one-sided dependence of citizens, limited opportunities for trust based on ongoing personal relations and routinized behaviour, while emotions and suspicions may run high due to citizens typically being in a loss frame. Thus reliability has to be based on legal control, procedures of accountability, press scrutiny to support a reputation mechanism, and, perhaps most important of all, integrity.

Conclusion

The notion of trust is filled with confusion and misunderstanding. One has to carefully distinguish between levels of trust: personal, organizational and institutional. Ideally, different levels of trust are mutually supporting: trust in people should be consistent with trust in the organization where they work, and should be supported by surrounding institutions. One has to distinguish between trust in different aspects of behaviour, particularly between trust in competence and trust in intentions. Concerning intentional trust, one needs to distinguish between a wide notion of trust, here called reliance, which includes control, of opportunities and incentives towards opportunism, and a stronger, narrower notion of 'real' trust that goes beyond calculative self-interest, on the basis of norms of conduct (integrity), or personal bonds of empathy or identification, or routinized conduct.

In view of this complexity of trust, survey questions asking people whether they 'generally' trust others, without specification or qualification, are so unreliable as to be useless and misleading. When answering the question, people may have in mind: trust in institutions, organizations or individuals; competence trust or (at least two kinds of) intentional trust; trust based on control or trust beyond self-interest; and trust under different kinds of circumstances. When asked about 'general' trust in the police, for example, people may trust the competence of individual officers, but distrust the competence of police bureaucracy. They may trust the intentions of the law, and the benevolence of most officers, but not their dedication. When asked about their general trust in the police, on which of these aspects will they focus to give their answers?

The notion of trust is filled with paradox. It can go beyond control and calculative self-interest but has its limits, depending on external pressures. Trust and control are both substitutes and complements. Trust entails lack of information but is also based on information. It can be rational, by inference of trustworthiness, but such inference is both limited and enabled by social-psychological heuristics that incorporate emotions.

Trust needs to be pieced together in its multiple dimensions to fit specific conditions. This was illustrated with the case of citizens' trust in the police. There, competence trust suffers from the fact that police service is to a large extent a credence good. Judgement of quality may then be sought in public reports on performance, preferably by some independent agency. It may also be sought in observed proxies of competence such as confident conduct and respectable manner and appearance of police officers. Trust in individual police officers should be supported by trust in police organization and related institutions, for example in their supply of sufficient means and training. Concerning intentional trust, hierarchical control is limited by weak direct monitoring of conduct. Citizens are subjected to one-sided dependence, so that there is limited incentive control by mutual dependence. Both problems can be redressed, to some extent, by complaint procedures. However, since control remains weak, trust should further be supported by norms of conduct (integrity), enhanced by selection, training and police culture, and empathy of officers with respect to citizens. Especially salient, perhaps, is that in interaction with the police, citizens often find themselves in a loss frame, which increases the emotional loading of contacts, and cognitive leaps to preserve self-interest. This reduces the reliability of compliant procedures and underlines the importance of a confident, correct manner, and empathy.

Notes

1. This book incorporates an earlier analysis from Nooteboom (1996).
2. Strictly speaking, this does not satisfy the condition of asymmetric value of a hostage: the poached worker is also of use to the poacher.
3. I do not wish to imply that stability of relations is always a good thing economically, in the sense that it is always conducive to efficiency and welfare. A certain amount of stability may be needed to recoup specific investments, which may in turn be needed to achieve high added value and innovativeness. However, relations can become too stable and exclusive and thereby yield rigidities. The question therefore is how to develop relations that have optimal duration: neither too short nor too long.
4. This section is based on a project commissioned by the Dutch Police.

References

Axelrod, R. (1984), *The Evolution of Cooperation*, New York: Basic Books.
Bachmann, R. (2000), 'Conclusion: Trust – conceptual aspects of a complex phenomenon', in C. Lane and R. Bachmann, *Trust Within and Between Organizations*, Oxford: Oxford University Press: 298–322.
Bazerman, M. (1998), *Judgement in Managerial Decision Making*, New York: Wiley.
Bradach, J.L. and R.G. Eccles (1984), 'Markets versus hierarchies: From ideal types to plural forms', in W.R. Scott (ed.), *Annual Review of Sociology*, **15**: 97–118.
Chiles, T.H. and J.F. McMackin (1996), 'Integrating variable risk preferences, trust and transacton cost economics', *Academy of Management Review*, **21** (7): 73–99.
Cosmides, L. and J. Tooby (1992), 'Cognitive adaptations for social exchange', in H. Barkow, L. Cosmides and J. Tooby, *The Adapted Mind*, Oxford: Oxford University Press: 163–228.
Damasio, A.R. (1995), *Descartes' Error: Emotion, Reason and the Human Brain*, London: Picador.
Das, T.K. and B.-S. Teng (1998), 'Between trust and control: Developing confidence in partner cooperation in alliances', *Academy of Management Review*, **23** (3): 491–512.
Das, T.K. and B.-S. Teng (2001), 'Trust, control and risk in strategic alliances: An integrated framework', *Organization Studies*, **22** (2): 251–84.
Deutsch, M. (1973), *The Resolution of Conflict: Constructive and Destructive Processes*, New Haven, CT: Yale University Press.
Dore, R. (1983), 'Goodwill and the spirit of market capitalism', *British Journal of Sociology*, **34**: 459–82.
Dyer, J.H. and W.G. Ouchi (1993), 'Japanese-style partnerships: Giving companies a competitive edge', *Sloan Management Review*, **35**: 51–63.
Fukuyama, F. (1995), *Trust, the Social Virtues and the Creation of Prosperity*, New York: Free Press.
Gambetta, D. (1988), 'Can we trust trust?', in D. Gambetta (ed.), *Trust: Making and Breaking of Cooperative Relations*, Oxford: Blackwell: 213–37.
Gaski, J.F. (1984), 'The theory of power and conflict in channels of distribution', *Journal of Marketing*, **48** (summer): 9–29.
Gorobets, A. and B. Nooteboom (2005), 'Adaptive build-up and breakdown of trust: An agent based computational approach', Discussion Paper 39, Centre for Economic Research, Tilburg University.
Goshal, S. and P. Moran (1996), 'Bad for practice: a critique of the transaction cost theory', *Academy of Management Review*, **21** (1): 13–47.
Gulati, R. (1995), 'Does familiarity breed trust? The implications of repeated ties for contractual choice in alliances', *Academy of Management Journal*, **30** (1): 85–112.
Heide, J.B. and A.S. Miner (1992), 'The shadow of the future: Effects of anticipated interaction and frequency of contact on buyer-seller cooperation', *Academy of Management Journal*, **35**: 265–91.
Helper, S. (1990), 'Comparative supplier relations in the US and Japanese auto industries: An Exit/Voice approach', *Business and Economic History*, **19**: 1–10.
Hendriks-Jansen, H. (1996), *Catching Ourselves in the Act: Situated Activity, Interactive Emergence, Evolution and Human Thought*, Cambridge, MA: MIT Press.
Hill, C.W.L. (1990), 'Cooperation, opportunism and the invisible hand: Implications for transaction cost theory', *Academy of Management Review*, **15** (3): 500–13.
Hirschman, A.O. (1970), *Exit, Voice and Loyalty: Responses to Decline in Firms, Organisations and States*, Cambridge, MA: Harvard University Press.

Hunt, S.D. and J.R. Nevin (1974), 'Power in a channel of distribution: sources and consequences', *Journal of Marketing Research*, **11** (2): 186–93.

Kahneman, D., P. Slovic and A. Tversky (eds) (1982), *Judgement under Uncertainty: Heuristics and Biases*, Cambridge, UK: Cambridge University Press.

Klein Woolthuis, R., B. Hillebrand and B. Nooteboom (2005), 'Trust, contract and relationship development', *Organization Studies*, **26** (6): 813–40.

Knights, D., F. Noble, T. Vurdubakis and H. Willmott (2001), 'Chasing shadows: control, virtuality and the production of trust', *Organization Studies*, **22** (2): 311–36.

Lakoff, G. and M. Johnson (1999), *Philosophy in the Flesh*, New York: Basic Books.

Lane, C. and R. Bachmann (2000), *Trust Within and Between Organizations*, Oxford: Oxford University Press.

Lewicki, R.J. and B.B. Bunker (1996), 'Developing and maintaining trust in work relationships', in R.M. Kramer and T.R. Tyler (eds), *Trust in Organizations: Frontiers of Theory and Research*, Thousand Oaks, CA: Sage Publications: 114–39.

Lounamaa, P.H. and J.G. March (1987), 'Adaptive coordination of a learning team', *Management Science*, **33**, 107–23.

Luhmann, N. (1979), *Trust and Power*, Chichester: Wiley.

Luhmann, N. (1988), 'Familiarity, confidence, trust', in D. Gambetta (ed.), *Trust: Making and Breaking of Cooperative Relations*, Oxford: Blackwell: 94–108.

Lusch, R.F. (1976), 'Sources of power: their impact on intrachannel conflict', *Journal of Marketing Research*, **13** (4): 382–90.

Macaulay, S. (1963), 'Non-contractual relations in business: A preliminary study', *American Sociological Review*, **28**: 55–67.

Maguire, S., N. Philips and C. Hardy (2001), 'When "silence = death", keep talking: Trust, control and the discursive construction of identity in the Canadian HIV/AIDS treatment domain', *Organization Studies*, **22** (2): 285–310.

March, J. (1991), 'Exploration and exploitation in organizational learning', *Organization Science*, **2** (1): 101–23.

McAllister, D.J. (1995), 'Affect- and cognition-based trust as foundations for interpersonal cooperation in organizations', *Academy of Management Journal*, **38** (1): 24–59.

Merleau-Ponty, M. (1964), *Le Visible et l'invisible*, Paris: Gallimard.

Murakami, Y. and T.P. Rohlen (1992), 'Social-exchange aspects of the Japanese political economy: Culture, efficiency and change', in S. Kumon and H. Rosorsky (eds), *The Political Economy of Japan, Vol. 3, Cultural and Social Dynamics*, Stanford, CA: Stanford University Press: 63–105.

Nooteboom, B. (1996), 'Trust, opportunism and governance: A process and control model', *Organization Studies*, **17** (6): 985–1010.

Nooteboom, B. (2002), *Trust: Forms, Foundations, Functions, Failures and Figures*, Cheltenham, UK and Northampton, MA, USA: Edward Elgar.

Parkhe, A. (1993), 'Strategic alliance structuring: A game theoretic and transaction cost examination of interfirm cooperation', *Academy of Management Journal*, **36**: 794–829.

Pettit, Ph. (1995), 'The virtual reality of homo economicus', *The Monist*, **78** (3): 308–29.

Polanyi, M. (1962), *Personal Knowledge*, London: Routledge.

Ring, P.S. and A. Van de Ven (1994), 'Developmental processes of cooperative interorganizational relationships', *Academy of Management Review*, **19** (1): 90–118.

Rosch, E. (1978), 'Principles of categorization', in E. Rosch and B.B. Lloyd (eds), *Cognition and Categorization*, Hillsdale, NJ: Erlbaum.

Shapiro, S.P. (1987), 'The social control of impersonal trust', *American Journal of Sociology*, **93**: 623–58.

Simmel, G. (1950), 'Individual and society', in K.H. Wolff (ed.), *The Sociology of George Simmel*, New York: Free Press.

Simon, H.A. (1983), *Reason in Human Affairs*, Oxford: Basil Blackwell.

Six, F. (2004), *Trust and Trouble: Building Interpersonal Trust within Organizations*, doctoral dissertation, Erasmus University Rotterdam, June.

Telser, L.G. (1980), 'A theory of self-enforcing agreements', *Journal of Business*, **53**: 27–44.

Weigelt, K., and C. Camerer (1988), 'Reputation and corporate strategy: A review of recent theory and applications', *Strategic Management Journal*, **9**: 443–54.

Williams, B. (1988), 'Formal structures and social reality', in D. Gambetta (ed.), *Trust: Making and Breaking of Cooperative Relations*, Oxford: Blackwell: 3–13.

Williamson, O.E. (1975), *Markets and Hierarchies*, New York: Free Press.

Williamson, O.E. (1993), 'Calculativeness, trust, and economic organization', *Journal of Law & Economics*, **36**: 453–86.

Zand, D.E. (1972), 'Trust and managerial problem solving', *Administrative Science Quarterly*, **17** (2): 229–39.

Zucker, L.G. (1986), 'Production of trust: Institutional sources of economic structure', in L. Cummings and B. Staw (eds), *Research in Organisational Behavior*, Greenwich, CT: JAI Press, vol. **8**: 53–111.

15 Levels of inter-organizational trust: conceptualization and measurement

Martyna Janowicz and Niels Noorderhaven

Introduction

The notion of trust has received increasing attention in recent years. It is pointed to as an important factor for understanding human nature and exchange relationships of market participants. In particular, trust is considered to be a variable of importance in inter-organizational collaborations (e.g. Gulati 1995; Madhok 1995). However, inter-organizational relations constitute a very specific context where those who frame the strategic intentions of collaborating organizations are often distinct from those who actually implement them – a consideration that is rarely reflected in research on inter-organizational alliances (Salk and Simonin 2003). This should be taken into account in studying inter-organizational relationships, especially since in such a context trust of individuals at different hierarchical levels is likely to differ in causes and consequences (e.g. Anderson and Narus 1990; Zaheer et al. 2002).

Research on trust in inter-organizational relationships is quite short of studies that go beyond one level of analysis (c.f. Doney and Cannon 1997). The few studies that do adopt a multilevel approach to studying inter-organizational trust often substantially vary in how they define levels of trust. In specific, various approaches differ in the level of aggregation at which the parties to the inter-organizational relationship, that is, the trustor and the trustee, have been conceptualized. This in turn finds reflection in divergent empirical treatments of trust at those levels and inconsistent findings in empirical research. Besides the various approaches offering unique strengths and weaknesses, of both theoretical and empirical nature, the issue of alignment between the level of theory and measurement in multilevel empirical studies needs to be considered (Currall and Inkpen 2002). In their recent work Currall and Inkpen (2002) point to the presence of misspecification in several of studies of inter-organizational trust, in particular the attribution of individual attitude (i.e. that of a key informant) to the firm (Currall and Inkpen 2002).

In light of the above, this chapter has two goals. First, we aim to explore the different levels of aggregation at which trust (on both the trustor's and trustee's part) in inter-organizational relationships has been conceptualized in the literature. To that end, we systematize and critically evaluate the extant approaches to the study of inter-organizational trust. We critically review Currall and Inkpen's (2002) claim of misalignment in a number of studies. Without dismissing the potential weight of the problem, we argue that the authors' conclusion with respect to the pervasiveness of the problem is predicated on two assumptions. One is that organization itself should always be the subject of trust, and the second is that the level data collection and measurement must by definition be the same. We challenge both the assumptions and show that lifting them may undermine the conclusions of Currall and Inkpen (2002).

Second, we build on the existing conceptualization of inter-organizational trust that views organizational trust as an attitude held collectively by all organizational members, and propose to take it further by considering the function of various types of organizational actors in the enactment of inter-organizational relationships. As we will further argue, trust at top management level is qualitatively different in its outcomes from trust at the level of lower-level managers and employees. While trust of top management boundary spanners influences the goals and parameters of inter-organizational cooperation, trust of lower-level boundary spanners working within the bounds of these parameters affects the extent to which these goals are met. Accordingly, we distinguish between strategic- and operational-level trust and define the former as trust held by top-level boundary spanners with respect to both their counterparts in the partner organization and the partner organization as such. Operational-level trust, as we define it, captures trust held by non-executive boundary spanners, again both towards their counterparts in the partner organization and towards the partner organization as a whole. These definitions assume that the subject of trust (i.e. the trustor) is always an individual, while the object of trust (i.e. the trustee) can be both an individual and an organization. The two levels of trust are thus distinguished according to who the trustor is and independent of who the trustee is.

In short, the contribution we hope to make with this study is twofold. First, we systematize and evaluate the extant conceptualizations of inter-organizational trust. Second, building on existing conceptualizations, we propose a more refined approach to defining inter-organizational trust, one that reflects the boundary spanners' organizational function. Accordingly, we begin by presenting the different approaches to defining levels of trust and consider their strengths and weaknesses. Next, the empirical issues involved in tapping trust at two levels are dealt with. We continue by discussing an alternative approach to identifying levels of trust. Conclusions follow.

Conceptualizations of inter-organizational trust

Trust defined

Although a relative consensus concerning the general conceptualization of trust has been reached, the definition of trust in the inter-organizational context remains problematic. The difficulty is related in particular to the question 'who is the subject of inter-organizational trust?' While some authors attribute trust to the organization as such, others argue that an organization itself cannot trust. The latter group argues that while it is conceptually consistent to view an individual both as an origin and an object of trust, the same is not true of an organization (Zaheer et al. 1998). Organizations are made up of and managed by individuals (Aulakh et al. 1996) and it is through them that interfirm relations come into effect (Inkpen and Currall 1997; Nooteboom et al. 1997). Therefore, it is not an organization itself that trusts, but rather the individuals who constitute it. The assumptions one holds with respect to the above issue bear heavily on the definition of inter-organizational trust one adopts.

Two broad approaches to defining trust can be distinguished: *behavioural* and *attitudinal*. The behavioural definition of trust holds that trust finds reflection in the decision to rely on another. Defining trust in terms of observable behaviour allows for extending the concept of trust to the level of a group or an organization (Currall and Inkpen 2002). Applying such a conceptualization, therefore, is possible (or even necessary) when the organization itself is assumed to be the subject of inter-organizational trust. For example, Currall and Inkpen (2002) adopt a behavioural conceptualization of organizational trust: 'the willingness to increase one's vulnerability to another whose behaviour is not under one's control . . .' (Zand 1972, p. 230), which is in line with their assumption that the organization as such is the subject of organizational trust; that is, trust is attributed to organization as an entity.

The attitudinal approach views trust as an expectation of the partner's reliability with regard to its obligations, predictability of behaviour, and fairness in actions and negotiations while faced with the possibility of behaving opportunistically (cf. Zaheer et al. 1998). While trust understood as a behaviour is attributable to an organization, this is not so for trust as an attitude. An attitude cannot be attributed to an organization, as it is an inherently individual-level phenomenon. Organizations do not have the ability to experience an attitude (Aulakh et al. 1996; Dyer and Chu 2000; Madhok 1995), but the individual agents that define their behaviour do. Therefore, application of an attitudinal definition of trust – 'the subjective probability that one assigns to benevolent action by another agent or group of agents . . .' (Nooteboom et al. 1997, p. 311) – is appropriate only when organizational members, rather than the organization as such, is assumed to be the subject of inter-organizational trust.

Yet the choice between the attitudinal and the behavioural definition of trust for the inter-organizational context is more than just a question of the subject of trust. It also has to do with the fundamental problem of how to infer the presence of trust in a relationship. Trusting behaviour of a party does not automatically imply the presence of attitudinal trust. The observed trusting behaviour may be driven by factors other than trust, for example lock-in or dependence on the partner (Nooteboom et al. 1997). Therefore behavioural trust is a much broader and more 'messy' concept than attitudinal trust. For that reason, in the context of this chapter we choose to subscribe to the attitudinal view of trust. We can afford to adopt such a definition of trust since the conceptualization of the levels of inter-organizational trust we subsequently propose hinges on the role of an individual in shaping an organization's behaviour.

Levels of aggregation

Having briefly considered the definitional issues related to trust in the inter-organizational context, we now take a closer look at the ways in which previous research has defined inter-organizational trust. The primary distinguishing feature of the different approaches appears to be the level of aggregation at which the parties to the relationship have been conceptualized. We thus propose to use it as a criterion for classifying the extant conceptualizations. The question of aggregation has to do with two issues: first with the question already mentioned above: where does the inter-organizational trust reside, that is, at the level of an individual or of an organization? The second question has to do with who is assumed to be the object of the inter-organizational trust; again the answer can be either an individual or an organization. Obviously symmetry need not be present: an individual can be assumed to trust an organization and an organization can be assumed to have trust towards an individual. In other words, for each conceptualization it is necessary to determine who is the trustor irrespective of who is the trustee and vice versa. Accordingly a two-by-two matrix can be sketched with the resulting four theoretical constructs. The vast-majority of the conceptualizations of inter-organizational trust to be found in the extant literature in one way or another make use of one or more of these four constructs (see Figure 15.1).

In the upper left quadrant – where both the trustor and the trustee are individuals – we find conceptualizations of what is commonly referred to as interpersonal trust (Currall and Judge 1995; Inkpen and Currall 1997; Jeffries and Reed 2000; Zaheer et al. 1998). This is the least controversial category as it captures trust present between individuals who happen to be members of two different organizations. In the lower right quadrant – where both the trustor and the trustee are organizations – we find conceptualizations of what is referred to as inter-organizational trust (Doney and Cannon 1997; Dyer and Chu 2000; Zaheer et al. 1998) or organizational trust (Jeffries and Reed 2000). Although most common, it is certainly not the only possible conceptualization of inter-organizational trust. In the upper right quadrant – where the trustor is an individual and the trustee is an organization – we encounter what is defined by Inkpen and Currall (1997) as firm-level trust, that is, a manager's perception of the partner firm's trustworthiness. Finally, in the lower left quadrant – where the trustor is an organization and the trustee is an individual – a conceptualization of trust where a (buying) firm trusts a (supplier) firm's sales person is to be found (Doney and Cannon 1997). The latter two conceptualizations are far less frequent than the former two treatments. Especially the organization-trusts-individual approach is quite rare, as reflected in the fact that we could identify only one study employing it.

| | | Who is trusted? (i.e. trustee) | |
		Individual	*Organization*
Who trusts? (i.e. trustor)	*Individual*	**INDIVIDUAL → INDIVIDUAL** e.g. Currall and Judge (1995) Inkpen and Currall (1997) Jeffries and Reed (2000) Zaheer et al. (1998) Zaheer et al. (2002)	**INDIVIDUAL → ORGANIZATION** e.g. Inkpen and Currall (1997) Nooteboom et al. (1997) Zaheer et al. (2002)
	Organization	**ORGANIZATION → INDIVIDUAL** e.g. Doney and Cannon (1997)	**ORGANIZATION → ORGANIZATION** e.g. Anderson and Narus (1990) Das and Teng (1998) Doney and Cannon (1997) Dyer and Chu (2000)* Jeffries and Reed (2000)* Zaheer et al. (1998)*

Note: * Indicates conceptualizations that treat organizational trust as a shared attitude of organizational members.

Figure 15.1 *Conceptualizations of inter-organizational trust*

Critical evaluation

Conceptualizations that involve an individual as a trustor (i.e. the upper two quadrants) are relatively unproblematic. First, there seems to be a widely accepted consensus concerning the conceptualization of interpersonal trust. Since both the trustor and the trustee are individuals, the theories of trust at the individual level are fully applicable here. Besides the relationship being based in an inter-organizational context – the two individuals being members of different organizations – there is not much that would make it unique or different. Similarly the conceptualization that holds an individual as a trustor and an organization as an object of that trust is largely uncontroversial. Doney and Cannon (1997, p. 36) comment that although 'some researchers disagree about whether organizations can be targets of trust, a large stream of literature emphasizes that people can develop trust in public institutions (Lewis and Weigert 1985) or organizations (Morgan and Hunt 1994), as well as individuals'. Trustworthiness can thus be a quality attributed to an organization (Inkpen and Currall 1997) and consequently one can talk of an individual's trust in an organization (Doney and Cannon 1997). From the empirical point of view conceptualizations that involve an individual as an object of inter-organizational trust (the upper two quadrants of Figure 15.1) are also relatively unproblematic. Data concerning trusting attitudes and/or behaviours of an individual boundary spanner towards its counterpart or the partner organization can be obtained in a relatively easy and reliable manner by way of an interview or a questionnaire.

In contrast, conceptualizations of trust that involve organization as a trustor (the lower two quadrants of Figure 15.1) are more problematic, both theoretically and empirically. Conceptually there are few attempts to tackle the question of what it means for an organization to trust. Many authors who adopt organization as the unit of analysis simply apply individual-level terminology and logic to the organizational level. However, theories of interfirm exchange that take trust to be a property of organizations without specifying the link between the micro and macro level are inaccurate, as they 'anthropomorphize the organization' (Zaheer et al. 1998, p. 142). In the strict sense of the word an organization cannot trust; only an individual can (Doney and Cannon 1997; Dyer and Chu 2000; Inkpen and Currall 1997; Zaheer et al. 1998).

In addition, obtaining reliable data on inter-organizational trust is more challenging if conceptualizations of such trust involve the organization as a trustor. As was argued earlier, when trust is attributed to an organization, only the behavioural definition of trust is appropriate. Currall and Inkpen (2002) posit that in such cases one should resort to investigation of agreements and corporate statements, as well as direct observation of the organization's actions that can be characterized as trusting. However, gathering organization-level data through direct observation is hardly feasible in a large-scale study. Additionally, the above-mentioned difficulty of knowing whether the trusting behaviour of the organization is actually a result of trust or of some lock-in or dependence on the partner needs to be taken into account (Nooteboom et al. 1997).

Alignment of theory and empirics

Any study that seeks to conform to the demands of conceptual and empirical clarity needs to ensure that it aligns the level of measurement with the level of theory (Klein et al. 1994). This is of particular relevance for the research on inter-organizational trust, where the potential for such misalignment is great. A mismatch between the level of aggregation of the theoretical constructs and the level that measures of inter-organizational trust represent diminishes the validity of hypothesis tests (Currall and Inkpen 2002). In other words, the data on inter-organizational trust used in a study have to reflect the same level of aggregation as the conceptualization of the trust they are intended to measure. At the same time, caution needs to be taken not to confuse the level of measurement with the level at which data are obtained. Both the above issues surface in a recent study of Currall and Inkpen (2002), in which the authors raise the issue of misspecification between the level of theory and the level of measurement in inter-organizational trust research.

The authors claim that by employing individual respondents to capture firm-level trust, a number of studies of inter-organizational trust attribute an individual attitude (i.e. of a key informant) to the firm and thus are marked by misspecification. Inasmuch as we recognize the potential problem of misalignment between level of theory and measurement, we also believe that the actual pervasiveness of the problem is much less pronounced than Currall and Inkpen (2002) seem to suggest. Specifically, in evaluating the particular studies, the authors make two implicit assumptions – one conceptual and one empirical. We argue that lifting these assumptions at least partly undermines the validity of their conclusions. First, in assessing the presence of misspecification Currall and Inkpen appear to use the yardstick of their own conceptualization of inter-organizational trust; in other words, they evaluate the empirical tools used in the studies with the conceptualization of inter-organizational trust they propose and not with the one proposed by the authors of the papers. We believe that in at least a few of the cases the misspecification is only apparent and disappears when the definition adopted by the original authors is considered.

For example, with respect to their own earlier study of inter-organizational trust (Inkpen and Currall 1997) the authors claim misalignment, based on the fact that data were sourced from a single informant. Such a conclusion may be correct if trust is attributed to the organization as a whole, that is, as in a 'firm's decision to engage in trusting actions toward the other firm' (Currall and Inkpen 2002, p. 490). However, the definition of organizational trust that the authors adopted in 1997 was as follows: 'trust in the partner firm in terms of an IJV [international joint venture] manager's perception of the perceived trustworthiness of the partner firm' (Inkpen and Currall 1997, p. 312). From that perspective, the use of a single respondent appears very much justified; the empirical treatment of trust is fully in line with the way it was conceptualized. A similar example is the study by Nooteboom et al. (1997, p. 312), which treated trust between organizations as 'relational risk with respect to a partner organization perceived by an individual who enacts the relation with the partner organization'. Again, the use of a single respondent appears to be fully justified when such a conceptualization is adopted. In sum, by benchmarking different studies against their own definition of inter-organizational trust, rather than the definition employed by the authors of the studies, Currall and Inkpen (2002) conclude that a number of them are marked by a misalignment.

Second, even if the conceptualization of trust as held by an organization is adopted, we do not deem all studies that rely on individual informants for data on interfirm trust to be by definition misaligned. The conclusions of Currall and Inkpen (2002) concerning the misalignment are based on the (empirical) assumption that an individual cannot be a source of data on group- or organization-level phenomena. We believe, however, that the level of measurement does not necessarily have to be identical to the level at which data are sourced. An individual respondent can be a reliable source of information that concerns the organization as a whole (cf. Geringer and Hebert 1991). Just as one can obtain a measurement of individual-level phenomena through direct observation or interviews, in the same way one can obtain organization-level measurement by observations or interviews. Obviously, it is not possible to interview an organization as such, yet it is possible to interview its well-informed members. Such data do not necessarily need to cause misalignment (assuming the organization is the level of theory) if the respondent is asked about matters that concern the organization as a whole.

That of course raises the issue of such data being reliable and representative for the organization. But, if the questions asked to the respondent deal with objective facts concerning the organization's behaviour (e.g. number of licences provided by the organization to the partner, the presence of conflict resolution provisions in the contract, etc.), then the use of an individual respondent seems more than justified. Data sourced from an individual would naturally be less reliable if they concerned the attitudes of the organizational members. In that case challenges involved in a cross-level approach, that is, obtaining organization-level data from an individual, are much greater, as 'reliance on key informants can give rise to problems of selection and perceptual agreement (Kumar, Stern and Anderson 1993)' and that 'informants' personalities, roles and experiences often result in perceptual disagreement (Kumar et al. 1993)' (Currall and Inkpen 2002, p. 481). However, the above concerns do not change the fact that the level of measurement and the source from which data are obtained are not one and the same. In sum, Currall and Inkpen's conclusion concerning the presence of misspecification is, in some sense, itself marked by misalignment – a misalignment between the level of measurement and the level of sourcing data.

Organization-level trust as a shared attitude
What the above discussion seems to suggest is that conceptualizations of inter-organizational trust that rely on an individual as a subject of trust are more sound theoretically and empirically than conceptualizations that attribute trust to an organization. Because of the difficulties related to ascribing trust to an organization, a conceptualization that defines organization-level trust as a shared attitude held collectively by members of a given organization has become quite prevalent (Dyer and Chu 2000; Jeffries and Reed 2000; Zaheer et al. 1998). On one hand, it accounts for the fact that trust is an inherently individual-level phenomenon and as such can be attributed to an organization only because it is made up of individuals. On the other hand, however, by aggregating the individual-level attitudes, it allows for ascribing trust to the organization as a whole. It thus provides a conceptual link between a trusting individual and a trusting organization in an inter-organizational context. Although very useful, we argue below that this conceptualization suffers from a couple of shortcomings, which the delineation of strategic and operational trust, we subsequently propose, seeks to cure.

Organizational trust as the shared attitude of individual organization members is likely to be heterogeneous; individuals' trust may stem from different sources, be of different strength and have different consequences. Hence the shared attitude of all organizational members may not be a very exact predictor of an organization's collaborative behaviour. First, it is usually only the boundary-spanning individuals of the collaborating organizations that interact with each other, rather than all members of the organizations. Trust held by those boundary spanners therefore would probably be of greater importance for the concept of inter-organizational trust than that of the non-boundary-spanning individuals. Second, boundary spanners (similarly to all other organizational members) occupy different positions in the organizational hierarchy, which determines their power and opportunity to affect various aspects of inter-organizational collaboration. By aggregating trust held by individuals playing different organizational roles in an effort to assess its impact on the overall behaviour of an organization in a collaborative context, the actual causal relationships might get overlooked.

For example, the structure of inter-organizational collaboration can be expected to be largely determined by top managers, who are the primary decision makers in organizations. Therefore trust held by those managers would probably be a more appropriate predictor of the collaborative structure compared to trust shared by all organizational members. Similarly, day-to-day implementation of the alliance tasks is much more a function of trust between operational-level employees of the partner organizations than of trust held by top managers. If they were included, trust under the explanatory variable would probably cloud the actual relationship. This is especially so since it is conceivable for the trust of the lower-level boundary spanners towards the partner organization (or some of its members) to be quite high, but for trust held by the top-level boundary spanners to be very low (or vice versa). In sum, if the shared attitude of organizational members is taken as a predictor of an organization's actions, the actual trust of a given group of organizational actors may get 'lost' (averaged out) in the overall measure of organizational trust. This could lead to distorted empirical results and incorrect conclusions. The significance and direction of a causal relationship in such a case would very much depend on what outcome was chosen as a proxy for an organization's behaviour – one decided upon by top managers or one determined by the collaborativeness of the operational-level employees.

Additionally, conceptualization of trust as held collectively by members of one organization towards the partner organization (Zaheer et al. 1998) is marked by some empirical limitations. The shared attitude of all organizational members towards the partner organization (or its members) is practically impossible to tap empirically, particularly in a large-scale study. Its literal measurement would in effect require interviewing every single member of the organization in question. Additionally, if one defines organizational trust as the attitude shared by organizational members towards the partner organization next to interpersonal trust, the former by definition encompasses the latter – the individual trustor is part of the trusting organization and the individual trustee is part of the trusted organization. The two constructs are not independent. Thus their effect should not be assessed simultaneously. In contrast, defining levels of inter-organizational trust in terms of trust held by individuals at different levels in organizational hierarchy, as proposed below, appears more pragmatic from an empirical point of view. The resulting measures of trust at different levels of analysis appear to be not only relatively independent but also easier to obtain in field research.

Strategic- and operational-level trust
The above discussion leads us to the following two conclusions. First, in order to bridge the conceptual gap between individual-level trust and the (inter-)organizational trust it is necessary to consider the individual as the subject of the organization-level trust. Second,

there is a need to look beyond the generalized concept of organizational trust and identify what function in the organization a particular individual trustor holds. Below, we elaborate on these two points and argue that in an inter-organizational context it is essential to distinguish trust at the strategic level from trust at the operational level.

Prior research has repeatedly stressed the importance of individuals and their relationships in trust between organizations (e.g. Gulati 1995; Inkpen and Currall 1997; Lewis and Weigert 1985; Macaulay 1963; Ring and Van de Ven 1994). It is because of the crucial role individuals play in organizations that the idea of trust, which in itself can only be attributed to an individual (Zaheer et al. 1998), may be extended to an organization. We can speak of 'organizations trusting each other' only because they are made up of and managed by individuals (Aulakh et al. 1996). It is through those individuals that the inter-firm relations come into effect (Aulakh et al. 1996; Inkpen and Currall 1997; Nooteboom et al. 1997). Therefore in considering trust between collaborating organizations, trust held by the individuals in boundary-spanning roles will probably be of greater relevance compared to trust of the non-boundary-spanning individuals. Building on this assumption, we further focus on the roles that organizational boundary spanners at different levels in organizational hierarchy play in shaping the course of organizational activities.

Extant literature stresses the systematically different roles and modus operandi of top managers compared to their colleagues at lower levels in the corporate hierarchy (e.g. Bower 1970; Mintzberg 1975; Ring and Van de Ven 1994; Zaheer et al. 2002). This is because different positions in organizational hierarchy are associated with specific expectations with regard to the position holder's contribution to the organizational tasks and thus with different roles of their incumbents (Floyd and Lane 2000). Organizational roles of individuals in turn affect their perceptions and mode of functioning. Zaheer et al. (2002, p. 348) state: 'individuals at different organizational levels view their respective worlds from different perspectives . . . individuals at higher and lower hierarchical levels . . . each see the world in *qualitatively different* [emphasis in the original] ways'. Differences pertain in particular to the level of uncertainty (Ireland et al. 1987), time horizons and risk. All these three dimensions are closely related to trust (Parkhe 1993; Zaheer et al. 2002).

Trust between individuals in an inter-organizational context has been argued to develop by virtue of the roles the actors perform in their organizations (cf. Ring and Van de Ven 1994). Since the roles of organizational actors vary significantly across the hierarchical levels, it is to be expected that the nature of trust across those levels would also vary (Zaheer et al. 2002). In particular, trust of boundary spanners at different hierarchical levels is likely to have distinct consequences for the collaborative relationship, due to their unique strategy-related roles. Top-level boundary spanners and those at lower hierarchical levels play different, though often complementary, roles with respect to the strategy-making process (cf. Floyd and Lane 2000; Hart 1992).

The process of strategy making can differ significantly across organizations. Depending on the strategy-making mode followed by an organization, the role of the top manager can range from that of a commander (i.e. formulating strategy) to that of a sponsor (i.e. recognizing initiatives emerging from below) (Hart 1992; Mintzberg 1978). Similarly, the roles of the lower-level organizational members can oscillate between those of good soldiers (i.e. executing plans formulated by top managers) and those of entrepreneurs (i.e. autonomously pursuing new initiatives) (Burgelman 1983; Hart 1992). Yet, although the range of potential roles that managers at a given level in organizational hierarchy play in the strategy-making process may be quite broad, there are, nevertheless, some distinct strategy-related roles specific to the different hierarchical levels.

Accordingly the roles of top management may be assumed to be dominated by decision-making tasks, like ratifying or directing, while those of the non-executive managers (middle and operating managers) encompass primarily communication of and reaction to information, for example implementing, facilitating, conforming or responding (Floyd and Lane 2000). This implies that the roles of strategic-level boundary spanners regarding an alliance are likely to be quite different from those of operational-level boundary spanners. Therefore, while the executive-level boundary spanners are well positioned to influence the cooperation policy of the organization, this is much less so for operational-level boundary spanners. That is also why in terms of attitudes those who frame the strategic intentions of an organization should be considered as distinct from those who actually implement them at the operational level (Salk and Simonin 2003).

Strategic-level trust
We have argued above that top managers, by virtue of their role as the primary decision makers, play qualitatively different roles in the functioning of their organizations from the lower-level managers. Specifically, from the point of view of their participation in the strategy-making process, top managers play two crucial roles in the collaborative context: that of initiating the alliance and that of shaping its structural context. First, top-level boundary-spanning individuals are strongly involved in recognizing and evaluating the potential benefits of collaborations with various partners (cf. Larson 1992). Trust at that level, therefore, is a factor contributing to the initiation of an alliance (Zaheer et al. 2002). Second, top managers 'play a crucial role in orchestrating and marshalling the resources and commitments that comprise the firms' collaborative strategies . . .' (Zaheer et al. 2002, p. 361). They are predominantly responsible for the shaping and manipulation of the structural context of the collaboration (cf. Burgelman 1983). Trust of the top-level boundary spanners, therefore, would be demonstrated in the collaborative arrangements of the alliance. In sum, strategic-level trust is crucially important in the partner selection and alliance formation stages of collaboration, thus finding manifestation primarily in the collaborative policies of the firm and the collaborative arrangements of the particular alliances. Admittedly in some special cases, top management trust may also be of importance in the subsequent stages of the collaboration. This, however, is likely to be the case when the collaboration encounters some unforeseen circumstances requiring an emergency intervention on the CEO's part to save the alliance (cf. Zaheer et al. 2002).

Considering the tasks and roles of the top managers, as discussed above, it is in the initial stages of the alliance's existence that their involvement can be expected to be greatest. The subsequent, everyday execution of the alliance tasks (with the exception of some extraordinary circumstances), in contrast, would largely be left to the responsibility of lower-level managers (Zaheer et al. 2002). The level of trust held by those actors, therefore, would have quite different consequences for the functioning of the alliance than trust held by the operational-level actors. In light of the above discussion, we conceptualize strategic-level trust as the shared attitude of the company's top boundary spanners towards the partner firm (cf. Inkpen and Currall 1997) and its members (cf. Gulati and Gargiulo 1999).

Operational-level trust

Compared to top managers, organizational actors at lower hierarchical levels play quite different roles in the strategy-making process. Specifically, boundary spanners of lower levels in an organizational hierarchy are responsible for the actual implementation of the collaboration (Doz 1996) and the efficient execution of its everyday tasks (Zaheer et al. 2002). By carrying out the operational tasks of the collaboration, they effectively link the two organizations across their boundaries (cf. Inkpen and Currall 1997). In contrast to top-level boundary spanners, lower-level boundary spanners have little influence on the collaboration policies of their organizations, but rather operate within their bounds (Zaheer et al. 2002). Trust between employees involved in the everyday implementation of the alliance, would thus have significant consequences for how the alliance unfolds over time (Zaheer et al. 2002). Trust at this level – operational-level trust – would therefore be manifested in the way the collaboration agenda set forth by the top management is implemented in the day-to-day operations of the alliance.

In line with the above and in contrast to strategic-level trust, we define operational-level trust between organizations as trust shared by the non-executive boundary spanners of the collaborating organizations towards the partner organization and its individual members. Currall and Inkpen (2002) define 'trust network' as the sum of interpersonal trust in a joint venture, that is, the trust present in all dyadic relationships of boundary spanners from the partnering organizations. Our definition of operational-level trust is broader than the trust network concept, however, because next to boundary spanners' trust towards their counterparts it additionally comprises the boundary spanners' trust towards the partner organization. Thus, similarly to the strategic level, both the partner organization and/or its individual members can be the objects of operational-level trust.

The question of the object of trust

The issue of the object of trust at the strategic and operational level requires a few words of comment. Although, as we argued earlier, only individuals should be considered to be subjects of interfirm trust, we believe that both individuals *and* organizations can be objects of trust (Perrone et al. 2003). As reflected in the definitions of trust at the two levels formulated above, we believe this to be the case at both levels of analysis. Inkpen and Currall (1997, p. 311) posit that '[a]lliance managers can foster trust by building one-to-one relationships with partner managers and by developing a familiarity with the partner's strategy, organization, and culture.' On one hand, thus, personal relationships among key individuals are pivotal in producing trust between collaborating firms (Bradach and Eccles 1989; Gulati 1995; Gulati and Gargulio 1999; Walker et al. 1997; Zaheer et al. 1998). On the other hand, however, inter-organizational trust should account for the relational risk with respect to a partner organization as perceived by an individual who enacts the relation with the partner organization (cf., Nooteboom et al. 1997).

Our conceptualization therefore assumes that an individual is the only subject of trust (i.e. a trustor) in an organization. The two levels of inter-organizational trust are delineated according to who is the trustor and independent of who is the object of trust (an individual or an organization). Previous research has shown that individuals without a problem distinguish between trust towards counterpart boundary spanners and the partner organization as a whole (e.g. Zaheer et al. 2002). However, in carrying out their responsibilities with respect to the inter-organizational collaboration, organizational boundary spanners (of either level) will probably be guided by the overall attitude towards the partner organization and their individual counterparts, rather than each of those objects of trust separately. Additionally, the effects of trust towards the partner organization and its individual members are unlikely to be independent; we expect that they would moderate each other. Thus although we do acknowledge that organizational actors can distinguish between trusting the partner organization or its specific members, we do not believe that this distinction has a bearing on the decisions they take. Rather, such decisions would be based on the overall evaluation of the trustworthiness of the partner organization *and* its individual members. There exists empirical evidence in support of our approach: trust in an individual manager of the partner firm has been shown to be a strong predictor of trust in the partner firm as a whole (Inkpen and Currall 1997; Zaheer et al. 1998).

Discussion

In sum, we argue that in considering interfirm trust, it is crucial to make a distinction between trust at the strategic level and trust at the operational level. This is due to the unique roles actors at those levels play in the strategy-making process, which in turn results in different consequences of trust at these two levels for the collaborative relationship. Specifically, we posit that strategic-level trust would be primarily operative at the strategy and policy-making levels, thus affecting the structural conditions of the alliance, while operational-level trust would play a major role in the effectuation of the inter-organizational collaboration, that is, the process of cooperation itself. Both of these types of trust, however, have an inter-organizational character and jointly constitute inter-organizational trust.

Schematically, our delineation of the two level of inter-organizational trust does not fit into any single quadrant of Figure 15.1 – locating it in the framework requires merging of the two upper quadrants of Figure 15.1 and introducing a horizontal division of the upper field (rather than a vertical one) – see Figure 15.2.

It is worth pointing out that although this operationalization bears some resemblance to the one offered by Zaheer et al. (2002), it is not the same. The authors do differentiate

		Who is trusted? (i.e. trustee)	
		Individual	*Organization*
Who trusts? (i.e. trustor)	*Individual*	Top-level INDIVIDUAL → INDIVIDUAL / ORGANIZATION Strategic-level trust	
		Operational-level INDIVIDUAL → INDIVIDUAL / ORGANIZATION Operational-level trust	
	Organization	ORGANIZATION → INDIVIDUAL	ORGANIZATION → ORGANIZATION

Figure 15.2   Strategic and operational level of inter-organizational trust

between levels in a hierarchy but only in terms of interpersonal trust, that is, between two individuals. Therefore, the two levels they identify would fit in the upper left quadrant of Figure 15.1. Our conceptualization, in contrast, cannot be simply placed in any single quadrant of Figure 15.1 (it cuts across two quadrants of the figure), as neither trust at the strategic nor operational level is of purely interpersonal character – it can have as its object another individual and/or the partner organization.

A criticism can be raised that our framework does not allow for the possibility that executive boundary spanners, next to their responsibility for setting the structure of the collaboration, may also be involved in the day-to-day implementation of the collaboration. Theoretically speaking, the trust they hold as top executives should affect their decisions concerning structure while the trust they hold as 'implementors' should affect the implementation of the collaborative tasks. However, it seems likely that in most cases the role of executives will be restricted to initiating and setting the structural conditions of the alliance and they will not have (much) opportunity to engage in the everyday implementation of the tasks of the collaboration. Thus, since the role of the top executives as organizational decision makers is likely to overshadow that of an operational organizational member, we did not consider it in our analysis.

Additionally, we wish to stress that in delineating the strategic and operational levels, it was not our intention to suggest that they are completely separate. First, we do not want to claim that individuals holding top management positions are qualitatively different from those at lower levels of the organizational hierarchy. Admittedly, individuals are subject to similar psychological processes and limitations, irrespective of their position in the organization. Second, both top-level and operational-level boundary spanners of any single organization are embedded in one organizational culture, which has been argued to affect the propensity of its members to trust and be trustworthy (Nooteboom 2002). Finally, elements of decision-making and implementation roles are likely to be found at every level and in practice overlap across levels is likely to be present (Floyd and Lane 2000). Moreover, the delineation of strategic and operational level is likely to vary considerably across organizations (cf. Floyd and Woolridge 1992). Notwithstanding all of the above, existing theory and empirical evidence suggest that positions across levels of organizational hierarchy differ fundamentally in the type of behaviour that is expected of their incumbents (Floyd and Lane 2000). Therefore the above considerations, in our view, would not undermine the argument that the ways in which top-level managers and lower-level managers are involved in the process of inter-organizational collaboration are distinct (by way of the organizational roles they play). The different nature of responsibility borne by individuals at both levels and the distinct character of decisions they are required to take are what constitutes the basis for the delineation of strategic and operational levels of inter-organizational trust.

Conclusions

Inter-organizational trust can be defined in various ways, depending on whether the trustor and the trustee are conceptualized as individuals or as organizations. Although none of the conceptualizations can be considered superior to others, problems arise when theories and concepts developed in one context are uncritically applied to another context. This has been a common occurrence with respect to trust between organizations being analysed in terms of interpersonal trust. It is thus essential to carefully consider what it means for an organization to trust and under what assumptions is it possible to make such an attribution. This also has consequences for the way trust in inter-organizational context can be measured. Validity of empirical results is at stake if the level of measurement is not aligned with the level of theory. In order to avoid such pitfalls one should be specific with regard to the definition of the inter-organizational trust concept employed in a particular study and make sure that the empirical measures correspond to the conceptual constructs in terms of level of aggregation.

We conclude that the conceptualization of organizational trust as an attitude shared by all organizational members is a useful response to the problem of attributing trust to an organization. However, we argue that it falls short of differentiating between organizational members whose trust by virtue of the roles they play in the organizations (boundary- versus non-boundary-spanning individual, top-level versus lower-level boundary spanner) is likely to have different consequences for the collaboration. This shortcoming in effect might be blurring our theoretical insight into the complexity of the inter-organizational context and obscuring the inferences about the impact of interpartner trust on various indicators of collaborative performance.

In light of the above we propose a refinement of the above conceptualization. Our fine-tuned definition of inter-organizational trust assumes that the *trustor* is always an individual, while the *trustee* can be either the partner organization as a whole or its individual members. Furthermore our approach to inter-organizational trust emphasizes the importance of the trustor's position in his or her own organization. Specifically, we argue two things. First, since it is organizational boundary spanners through whom interfirm relations come into effect, it is unnecessary to focus on trust held by this category of organizational actors, rather than all members of an organization. Second, since organizational actors at different hierarchical levels play different roles in the strategy-making processes, it is pivotal to demarcate trust of top-level boundary spanners from that of lower-level boundary spanners. Accordingly we propose to distinguish between operational-level boundary-spanning actors and strategic-level organizational boundary spanners and we suggest that inter-organizational trust at these two levels has unique consequences for interfirm collaboration.

Defining levels of inter-organizational trust in terms of trust held by boundary-spanning individuals at different levels in an organizational hierarchy, besides being based on solid theoretical grounds, also appears more pragmatic from the empirical standpoint. The resulting measures of trust at different levels of analysis are not only relatively independent but in addition would probably be easier to obtain in field research. If an individual is assumed to be the trusting party at both levels of analysis, then obtaining data concerning the level of trust at both levels from an individual is justified. From that perspective, well-positioned individual actors can be reliable sources of information concerning inter-organizational trust, both at the operational and at the strategic level (as we define them). This is an important issue, for if Currall and Inkpen's (2002) criticism were correct, large-scale survey-based studies of inter-organizational trust would pose practically insurmountable data requirements.

References

Anderson, J.C. and J.A. Narus (1990), 'A model of distributor firm and manufacturer firm working partnership', *Journal of Marketing*, **54**(1), 42–58.

Aulakh, P.S., M. Kotabe and A. Sahay (1996), 'Trust and performance in cross-border marketing partnerships: A behavioral approach', *Journal of International Business Studies*, **27**(5), 1005–32.

Bower, Joseph L. (1970), *Managing the Resource Allocation Process*, Cambridge, MA: HBS Press.

Bradach, J.F. and R.G. Eccles (1989), 'Price, authority, and trust: from ideal types to plural forms', *Annual Review of Sociology*, **15**, 97–118.

Burgelman, R.A. (1983), 'A process model of internal corporate venturing in the diversified major firm', *Administrative Science Quarterly*, **28**(2), 223–44.

Currall, S.C. and A.C. Inkpen (2002), 'A multilevel approach to trust in joint ventures', *Journal of International Business Studies*, **33**(3), 479–95.

Currall, S.C. and T.A. Judge (1995), 'Measuring trust between organizational boundary role persons', *Organizational Behavior and Human Decision Process*, **64**(2), 151–70.

Doney, P.M. and J.P. Cannon (1997), 'An examination of the nature of trust in buyer–seller relationships', *Journal of Marketing*, **61**(2), 35–51.

Das, T.K. and B.-S. Teng (1998), 'Between trust and control: Developing confidence in partner cooperation in alliances', *Academy of Management Review*, **23**(3), 491–512.

Doz, Y.L. (1996), 'The evolution of cooperation in strategic alliances: Initial conditions or learning processes?', *Strategic Management Journal*, **17**(special issue, summer), 55–84.

Dyer, J.H. and W. Chu (2000), 'The determinants of trust in supplier–automaker relationships in the U.S., Japan, and Korea', *Journal of International Business Studies*, **31**(2), 259–85.

Floyd, S.W. and P.J. Lane (2000), 'Strategizing throughout the organization: Managing role conflict in strategic renewal', *Academy of Management Review*, **25**(1), 154–77.

Floyd, S.W. and B. Woolridge (1992), 'Middle management involvement in strategy and its association with strategic type: A research note', *Strategic Management Journal*, **13** (special issue), 153–67.

Geringer, J.M. and L. Hebert (1991), 'Measuring performance of international joint ventures', *Journal of International Business Studies*, **22**(2), 249–63.

Gulati, R. (1995), 'Does familiarity breed trust? The implications of repeated ties for contractual choice in alliances', *Academy of Management Journal*, **38**(1), 85–112.

Gulati, R. and M. Gargiulo (1999), 'Where do interorganizational networks come from?', *American Journal of Sociology*, **104**(4), 1439–93.

Hart, S. (1992), 'An integrative framework for strategy-making processes', *Academy of Management Review*, **17**(2), 327–51.

Inkpen, A.C. and S.C. Currall (1997), 'International joint venture trust. An empirical examination', in Paul W. Beamish and Peter J. Kiling (eds), *Cooperative Strategies, North American Perspectives*, San Francisco, CA: The New Lexington Press, pp. 308–34.

Ireland, R.D., M.A. Hitt, R.A. Bettis and D.A. De Porras (1987), 'Strategy formulation processes: Differences in perceptions of strength and weaknesses indicators and environmental uncertainty by managerial level', *Strategic Management Journal*, **8**(5), 469–85.

Jeffries, F.L. and R. Reed (2000), 'Trust and adaptation in relational contracting', *Academy of Management Review*, **25**(4), 873–82.

Klein, K.J., F. Dansereau and R.J. Hall (1994), 'Levels issues in theory development, data collection, and an analysis', *Academy of Management Review*, **19**(2), 195–229.

Kumar, N., L.W. Stern and J.C. Anderson (1993), 'Conducting interorganizational research using key informants', *Academy of Management Journal*, **36**(6), 1633–51.

Larson, A. (1992), 'Network dyads in entrepreneurial settings: A study of the governance of exchange relationships', *Administrative Science Quarterly*, **37**(1), 76–104.

Lewis, J.D. and A. Weigert (1985), 'Trust as a social reality', *Social Forces*, **63**(4), 967–85.

Macaulay, S. (1963), 'Non-contractual relations in business: A preliminary study', *American Sociological Review*, **28**(1), 55–67.

Madhok, A. (1995), 'Revisiting multinational firms' tolerance for joint ventures: A trust-based approach', *Journal of International Business Studies*, **26**(1), 117–37.

Mintzberg, H. (1975), 'The manager's job: Folklore and fact', *Harvard Business Review*, July/August, 49–61.

Mintzberg, H. (1978), 'Patterns in strategy formation', *Management Science*, **24**(9), 934–49.

Morgan, R.M. and S.D. Hunt (1994), 'The commitment-trust theory of relationship marketing', *Journal of Marketing*, **58**(3), 20–38.

Nooteboom, Bart (2002), *Trust, Forms, Foundations, Functions, Failures and Figures*, Cheltenham, UK and Northampton, MA, USA: Edward Elgar.

Nooteboom, B., H. Berger and N.G. Noorderhaven (1997), 'Effects of trust and governance on relational risk', *Academy of Management Journal*, **40**(2), 308–38.

Parkhe, A. (1993), 'Strategic alliance structuring: A game theoretic and transaction cost examination of inter-firm cooperation', *Academy of Management Journal*, **36**(4), 794–829.

Perrone, V., A. Zaheer and B. McEvily (2003), 'Free to be trusted? Organizational constraints on trust in boundary spanners', *Organization Science*, **14**(4), 422–39.

Ring, P.S. and A.H. Van de Ven (1994), 'Developmental processes of cooperative interorganizational relationships', *Academy of Management Review*, **19**(1), 90–118.

Salk, J.E. and B.L. Simonin (2003), 'Beyond alliances: towards a meta-theory of collaborative learning', in Mark Easterby-Smith and Marjorie A. Lyles (eds), *The Blackwell Handbook of Organizational Learning and Knowledge Management*, Oxford: Blackwell Publishers, 253–77.

Walker, G., B. Kogut and W. Shan (1997), 'Social capital, structural holes and the formation of an industry network', *Organization Science*, **8**(2), 109–25.

Zaheer, A., B. McEvily and V. Perrone (1998), 'Does trust matter? Exploring the effects of interorganizational and interpersonal trust on performance', *Organization Science*, **9**(2), 141–59.

Zaheer, A., S. Loftrom and V. George (2002), 'Interpersonal and interorganizational trust in alliances', in Farok J. Contractor and Peter Lorange (eds), *Cooperative Strategies and Alliances*, Amsterdam: Pergamon, 347–77.

Zand, D.E. (1972), 'Trust and managerial problem solving', *Administrative Science Quarterly*, **17**(2), 229–39.

16 Does trust still matter? Research on the role of trust in inter-organizational exchange

Bill McEvily and Akbar Zaheer

What is the nature of inter-organizational trust? Is the concept even meaningful? If so, what role (if any) does it play in affecting the performance of interfirm exchange? These questions were at the heart of what motivated our study 'Does trust matter? Exploring the effects of inter-organizational and interpersonal trust on performance' (Zaheer et al., 1998). At the time of our study, there was considerable theoretical doubt and ambiguity about the influence of trust, an inherently individual-level concept, on exchange performance, an organizational-level outcome. Our goal was to provide some conceptual clarity on the topic and our approach was three-fold. First, we proposed a theoretical basis upon which interpersonal and inter-organizational trust could be conceptualized as related, but distinct constructs. We argued that whereas trust originates from individuals, the object of trust may be another person or entity, including a collective entity such as an organization. Thus, while interpersonal trust is the trust of one individual in another, inter-organizational trust is the collectively held trust orientation by members of one organization toward another organization. Second, we developed a theoretical model that related trust at the two levels of analysis, interpersonal and inter-organizational, to exchange performance. Our core proposition (summarized in Figure 16.1) advanced the idea that trust, both inter-organizational and interpersonal, enhanced performance by lowering the transaction costs of exchange. Third, we empirically tested our model with survey data from a sample of buyer–supplier relationships.

The results of our study empirically validated the notion of trust as existing at each level of analysis. While interpersonal trust and inter-organizational trust were strongly related, our discriminant analysis also confirmed that they were empirically distinct constructs. Consistent with this evidence, we also found that interpersonal trust and inter-organizational trust operate quite differently in affecting exchange performance. Specifically, we observed that inter-organizational trust was strongly related to lowered transaction costs and increased performance, while interpersonal trust was only indirectly linked to these outcomes through inter-organizational trust.

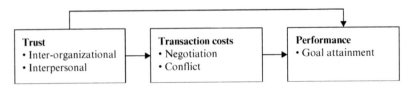

Source: Zaheer et al. (1998).

Figure 16.1   Performance effects of trust: initial theoretical model

The results of our study provided some initial evidence that trust improves performance of interfirm exchange by reducing transaction costs, but the findings were preliminary and raised a number of additional questions. Given that a number of other studies have since been published on the topic of trust and exchange performance, we are now able to address several of the questions that our initial study had raised. Our objective in this chapter is to review the subsequent research on trust in interfirm exchange relationships in order to: ascertain the degree to which the research has cumulated, summarize the key findings, establish how the literature has advanced both theoretically and methodologically, and identify key challenges that lie ahead. More generally, we are curious to know – does trust still matter?

To address these questions we conducted a review of recent research. We used the Web of Science database to identify studies related to our own. We identified a total of 91 published papers citing Zaheer et al. (1998). We then reviewed each paper to determine its topic and focus. We eliminated from further review those papers that did not address questions relating to the performance effects of trust in interfirm exchange and theoretical papers without an empirical component. After screening each paper we determined that a total of 16 were directly relevant to the topic of the role of trust in interfirm exchange.

We have intentionally limited the scope of our review to research that directly relates to the performance effects of trust and to trust at different levels of analysis. Our review provides a focused and in-depth discussion of research in this area and, based on the work reviewed, develops a theoretical model of the performance effects of trust. For a broader and comprehensive review, including the antecedents and nature of inter-organizational trust, see Zaheer and Harris (2005).

The remainder of this chapter summarizes our review of these studies. We begin by discussing research examining the performance effects of trust. Next, we consider studies that have specifically investigated the relationship between trust across levels in the context of inter-organizational exchange. We conclude the review with a discussion of key issues for future research.

Performance effects of trust

Since the publication of Zaheer et al. (1998) a number of other studies have investigated the relationship between trust and performance in the context of inter-organizational exchange. A key finding emerging from this growing body of research is that our preliminary results linking trust to performance have been corroborated across a number of different economic and organizational contexts. The precise form of the performance effect on trust varies quite considerably, however. We also observed that subsequent work extends in several important ways the basic theoretical model we initially proposed. In particular, recent research has built upon our model in three important ways (see Figure 16.2). First, subsequent research has considered causal mechanisms, additional to the transaction cost variables we had proposed, that *mediate* the relationship between trust and performance. Specifically, research has considered transaction costs, relational governance and transaction value as mediators, as shown in Figure 16.2. Second, recent studies have explored a variety of contingency factors that explain the conditions under which trust affects performance – that is, conditions that *moderate* the effect of trust on performance. In Figure 16.2 the vertical arrow between performance-enhancing

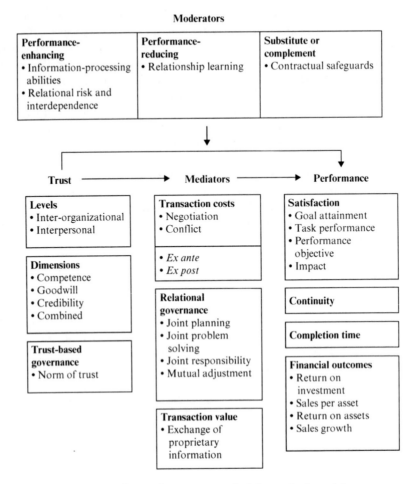

Figure 16.2   Performance effects of trust: expanded theoretical model

conditions, performance-reducing conditions, and factors that substitute for or comple-ment trust represents the moderators that have been studied. Third, current research has greatly expanded the *dimensionality* of both performance outcomes (satisfaction, conti-nuity, completion time and financial) and of trust (levels, dimensions and trust-based governance). Each of these three areas of research – mediators, moderators, and dimen-sionality of trust and performance – represent important advances and we use them to organize our review.

Mediators
The results of our initial study (Zaheer et al., 1998) broadly supported the thesis that trust influences transaction costs and performance, although the empirical findings we observed differed somewhat from the theoretical model we had proposed. Specifically, our results confirmed our prediction that trust lowers transaction costs, in the form of eased negotiations and reduced conflict, but the relationship between trust and performance

was not mediated by the reduction in these transaction costs as we had expected. Instead, we found a direct link between trust and performance, and no connection between transaction costs and performance. This pattern of results raised the obvious question of what accounts for the effect of trust on performance given our lack of support for one aspect of transaction costs (i.e. negotiation processes). One possibility is that transaction costs do indeed mediate the trust–performance relationship, but not in the way we had expected. Consistent with this idea, subsequent research has investigated the possibility that alternative specifications of 'transaction costs' mediate the relationship between trust and performance. We also speculated on two other possible mediating mechanisms, both of which have subsequently received research attention. First, we suggested that the eased negotiating process we observed might be part of a broader effort on the part of exchange partners to jointly manage and coordinate their relationship, an approach referred to as 'relational governance' in the transaction cost literature. Second, we raised the possibility that trust may affect performance through not only lowered transaction costs, but also increased 'transaction value'. We review the research in each of these areas next.

Transaction costs   Given the strong theoretical foundation linking transaction costs to performance, our lack of results for this relationship were surprising. Fortunately, research by Dyer and Chu (2003) pursued this question further by considering an alternative specification of transaction costs that included *ex ante* (search and contracting) and *ex post* (monitoring and enforcement) components, consistent with the theory. As these authors noted, while previous studies have combined the two forms of transaction costs, they need not be perfectly correlated. The results of Dyer and Chu's (2003) study of 344 auto suppliers in Japan, Korea and the USA supported the positive effect of trust on lowering *ex post*, but not *ex ante*, transaction costs. They further report evidence showing that suppliers' perceptions of a buyer's (i.e. automaker's) trustworthiness is negatively related to buyer transaction costs and positively related to buyer profit performance (10-year average return on assets). While the results were based on a very small sample from the buyer side ($n = 8$) and the buyer performance data precede rather than follow the trust data, this pattern of findings is consistent with the view that trust affects performance by lowering transaction costs, but only those transaction costs incurred *ex post*. Thus, trust appears to be more relevant during the execution of exchange agreements than during the search-contracting stage. This study makes an important contribution by both substantiating transaction costs as a key mediating mechanism in the trust–performance relationship, and providing a more precise understanding of the type of transaction costs that are most meaningful to this process.

Recent research has also supported the mediating role of conflict in the relationship between trust and performance. Shrum et al. (2001) examine 53 scientific collaborations in physics and find that trust is unrelated to performance. However, they conclude that trust is nevertheless important for the success of the collaborations because of its property of lowering conflict, although the researchers did not directly test for a relationship between conflict and performance. Interestingly, they did not find that prior relationships had higher trust than relationships without prior ties.

Research in this area could further build on the work thus far by adopting more robust research designs. In particular, it would be compelling to model the entire causal chain linking trust to transaction costs to performance with an integrated set of data (Dyer and

Chu examined some parts of the model with supplier data and other parts with buyer data) and with a more fully specified model of performance that is tested with a larger sample.

Relational governance   A closely related mechanism through which trust may influence performance is relational governance. Also referred to as bilateral governance, relational governance is a mode of organizing exchange that involves the integration of activities – such as decision making, planning and problem solving – across the relationship in an effort to reduce transaction costs (Macneil, 1980; Heide and John, 1990; Williamson, 1993; Zaheer and Venkatraman, 1995). Undertaking such close collaboration, however, requires a greater level of trust among exchange partners due to heightened risks (e.g. exploitation or appropriation of information) and interdependencies (e.g. reliance on a partner to provide resources or perform activities). From this perspective, trust is an enabling condition allowing exchange partners to pursue relational governance mechanisms that in turn improve the performance of the relationship.

Several studies have substantiated the idea that relational governance mediates the relationship between trust and performance. In a study of 164 buyer–supplier dyads from a cross-section of industries Johnston et al. (2004) found that supplier representatives' trust in buyer organizations was positively related to purchasing managers' assessment of relationship performance, through the bilateral governance mechanisms of shared planning and mutual adjustment ('flexibility in arrangements') for adapting to changes. Trust was also positively associated with joint responsibility, but the link between joint responsibility and performance was not supported. Using a measure of joint problem solving similar to that of Johnston et al.'s (2004) mutual adjustment, Claro et al. (2003) report similar results in their study of 174 Dutch suppliers. Specifically, these authors found that trust was positively related to joint planning and joint problem solving (resolution of disagreements), and that both of these relational governance mechanisms were positively associated with the supplier's growth in sales, but only joint problem solving was positively related to the supplier's perceived satisfaction with the relationship. Taken together, these studies provide consistent support for the effect of relational governance in mediating the relationship between trust and performance. An important extension of this work would be to link it to the work focusing on transaction costs as a mediator of the trust–performance link to address the questions of whether trust is an enabling condition of relational governance and in turn if relational governance lowers transaction costs.

Transaction value   In contrast to the view that trust affects performance by lowering transaction costs, Zajac and Olsen (1993) have suggested that it is through the enhancement of transaction value that trust results, in improved performance. Drawing on these ideas to interpret our results, we noted that trust may facilitate 'cooperation in the exploration of new information and coordination technologies, new market opportunities, and product and process innovation' (Zaheer et al., 1998: 155). Research by Dyer and Chu (2003) considered this possibility. Specifically, these authors report evidence from their study of auto suppliers indicating that trust increases the sharing of confidential and sensitive information (such as costs and proprietary technology) that creates value in the relationship, although they did not test for a mediated relationship between information sharing and performance.

These initial findings regarding the enhanced value created from trust are encouraging and suggest that additional research is called for to investigate whether trust does indeed promote collaboration in the areas identified and if the pursuit of these opportunities translates into value-enhancing performance outcomes such as innovation and learning (Lane et al., 2001). At the same time, the research thus far has just begun to explore the notion that transaction value is a key part of the reason why trust enhances performance. Clearly, there is ample opportunity for future research to consider more detailed and systematic models of transaction value that focus on collaboration processes, such as knowledge transfer (McEvily et al., 2003), and key outcomes such as innovation. We see this as one of the most important areas for future research and one where there is the greatest opportunity given the limited research to date.

Moderators

In addition to investigating different causal mechanisms linking trust to performance, recent research has also examined how the direct relationship between trust and performance is contingent upon several organizational and economic characteristics of the exchange relationship. Research has identified performance-enhancing conditions that further strengthen the positive effect of trust on performance, performance-diminishing contingencies that reduce the effect of trust on performance, and factors that can either substitute for or complement trust's effect on performance.

Performance-enhancing contingencies   Our basic theoretical model of the performance effects of trust implicitly assumed that the trustworthiness of a counterpart is perceived with a relatively high degree of accuracy and that exchange partners will be better able to sense and adapt to environmental changes due to superior information sharing. Recent research by Carson et al. (2003) relaxed these assumptions and allowed for the possibility of misplaced trust and varying abilities to interpret and respond to external change. Drawing on transaction cost theory, these authors argued that a key implication of the bounded rationality of decision makers is that the information-processing abilities of organizations will affect how accurately they assess a counterpart's trustworthiness and their ability to converge on common interpretations of environmental changes. In their study of 129 outsourced product R&D projects Carson et al. (2003) find that the positive effect of trust-based governance (use of trust to support *ex post* revisions to an incomplete contract) on task performance is larger when the R&D client has requisite information processing abilities (i.e. skills that are less tacit, skills that are related to the outsourced R&D task, and internal tasks that overlap with outsourced tasks). These findings suggest that in order to fully exploit the performance-enhancing potential of trust, it needs to be accompanied by the capability to accurately decipher a counterpart's trustworthiness and effectively adjust the exchange relationship to respond to unforeseen contingencies. This study also suggest that an important area for future research is to consider other organizational capabilities that are important for managing and exploiting trust-based relationships to achieve high performance.

The notion that environmental change affects the strength of the relationship between trust and performance is also the underlying premise of a second study investigating moderators of the trust–performance relationship. In a study of 255 international strategic alliances in China, Luo (2001) argues that long-term relationships such as alliances are subject to changes in the economic and social environment. Accordingly, the role of trust in enhancing performance is also likely to differ at different stages of the relationship. Consistent with these arguments, Luo found that the effect of trust on performance (return on investment) is amplified when the alliance is younger, as trust aids in overcoming the liability of newness and foreignness, and when market uncertainty is higher. The results also supported the notion that trust plays a stronger role in increasing performance (sales per asset and return on investment) when the reliance on resources, risk sharing, and reciprocal commitment between alliance parties is greater. Taken together the results of this study suggest that the effect of trust on performance is contingent upon the stage of the relationship and on environmental uncertainty. Future work in this area would benefit from the development of a theoretical model that integrates the broad set of factors moderating the trust–performance link. For instance, the factors studied by Luo seem generally to fall into the categories of the level of risk and interdependence inherent in a relationship, which have been identified as key conditions creating the need for trust (Rousseau et al., 1998). A study designed to test such a model would be beneficial.

Performance-reducing contingencies   In contrast to research focusing on how the performance effects of trust may be amplified by certain contingencies, work has also considered the conditions under which trust may diminish performance. Selnes and Sallis (2003) concur that sensing and responding to environmental change is critical for the performance of exchange relationships, and they argue that relationship learning plays a critical role in promoting effective adaptation. These authors view relationship learning as a joint activity between exchange partners involving the sharing, interpretation and integration of information into relationship-specific behaviors. Relationship learning is highly similar to the relational governance mechanisms (information sharing, joint problem solving and joint planning) that mediate the trust–performance relationship, and indeed Selnes and Sallis's (2003) study of 315 buyer–supplier dyads confirms the mediating role of these mechanisms. However, these authors also find that the positive effects of relationship learning level off and eventually diminish under high levels of trust. In these circumstances, there is a risk that exchange parties will be less inclined to share and seek out critical information and will become less objective, thereby limiting the ability of the parties to effectively adapt. This study makes an important contribution by demonstrating the limits to trust. Given that most research focuses on the positive outcomes of trust, identifying other conditions under which trust may adversely affect performance is an important area for research.

Substitutes or complements   Rather than treating the moderators of trust as either enhancing or diminishing performance, a third area of research on contingency factors allows for both possibilities. Lui and Ngo (2004) advance the perspective that trust and contractual safeguards are both important determinants of relationship performance, which may be mutually reinforcing in some cases and contradictory in others. Specifically, these authors argue that goodwill trust is a substitute, while competence trust is a complement, for contractual safeguards designed to protect against opportunism. Since goodwill trust reflects confidence in a partner's intention to fulfill obligations, safeguards would be unnecessary and the use of both trust and safeguards as a means to protect against opportunism would represent an inefficient allocation of resources. In contrast, competence trust reflects confidence in a partner's ability to fulfill obligations without regard to intentions, suggesting that safeguards would further enhance performance. In their study of 233 architecture–contractor alliances in Hong Kong, Lui and Ngo found that goodwill trust, competence trust and safeguards appear to be unrelated to performance (completion time and satisfaction) when considered independently. As predicted, however, the joint effects of trust and safeguards complement each other to improve performance in the case of competence trust and counteract each other to reduce performance in the case of goodwill trust. The results of this study add an important piece of evidence that helps reconcile the seemingly contradictory views of the performance-enhancing and -diminishing effects of contingency factors. Gallivan (2001), building on Das and Teng (1998), identifies other substitutes for trust. Specifically, he content-analyzes studies of Open Source Software (OSS), and concludes that trust is not a necessary condition for project performance. Rather, control of the conditions of collaboration, and of norms of behavior, obviate the need for trust in these virtual organizations.

We believe that examining the substitutes and complements for trust is a most promising approach for future research as it permits the integration of trust into broader models of exchange. Along these lines recent work by Poppo and Zenger (2002) tested the idea of relational governance as a substitute or complement for formal contracts within a broader transaction cost framework. Such an approach raises an interesting set of questions about the tradeoffs involved in treating trust as an efficient allocation of resources by recognizing that the creation of trust is not costless.

Dimensionality of trust

Another way that recent research has extended our 1998 study is by both expanding the dimensionality of trust and broadening the range of performance outcomes studied beyond our basic model of trust and performance. In our initial formulation, we treated trust as a unidimensional construct (at two different levels of analysis) and focused on a single indicator of performance, goal attainment. Adopting this approach provided us with a general sense of whether trust affects performance, but limited our ability to assess if the overall effect is driven by a particular form of trust and if the performance effect of trust is limited to a subset of outcomes. The fact that trust is intrinsically complex and multifaceted (Corazzini, 1977) and that interfirm relationship performance consists of multiple dimensions (Noordewier et al., 1990; Heide and Stump, 1995) raises the important question of 'Which dimensions of trust affect which performance outcomes?' Addressing this question is also important for assessing the robustness and generalizability of the trust–performance relationship.

Trust has been conceptualized and operationalized in many different ways (McEvily et al., 2003). Despite the heterogeneity in theoretical orientations, many agree that at its core trust is the willingness to be vulnerable based on positive expectations about another's intentions or behaviors (Mayer et al., 1995; Rousseau et al., 1998). Research on trust in the context of interfirm relationships has predominantly emphasized expectations regarding others' competence, goodwill, predictability and calculativeness. Overall, the findings are stronger for competence and goodwill than for predictability and calculativeness.

Competence Expectations about another's intentions or behaviors include 'technically competent role performance from those involved with us in social relationships and systems' (Barber, 1983: 9). This form of trust has also been referred to as ability (Mayer et al., 1995) and dependability or reliability (Rempel et al., 1985). Competence is considered to be a domain-specific form of trust based on the technical area within which an actor has a set of skills and expertise to perform certain tasks (Mayer et al., 1995). Several studies have investigated the link between competence trust and performance. In a comparative case study of ten virtual collaborative relationships between health care providers, Paul and McDaniel (2004) found that competence trust had a positive impact on health care delivery at remote sites. Lui and Ngo (2004) found that competence trust is related to alliance performance (although only in conjunction with contractual safeguards as discussed above). Further, Johnston et al. (2004) found that competence trust was positively related to the performance of buyer–supplier relationships (through its effect on bilateral governance, as noted above). Taken together, these studies provide fairly consistent findings for the relationship between competence trust and performance.

Goodwill   The idea that an exchange partner will look out for one's best interests is another critical component of trust (Ring and Van de Ven, 1992). Also referred to as 'benevolence' (Mayer et al., 1995), goodwill is the perception that a counterpart has positive intentions and motives. Some also describe goodwill trust in terms of fairness or refraining from behaving opportunistically given the chance (Anderson and Narus, 1990; Bromiley and Cummings, 1995). Interestingly, each of the three studies finding an association between competence trust and performance (i.e. Paul and McDaniel, 2004; Lui and Ngo, 2004; and Johnston et al., 2004) also support a relationship between goodwill trust and performance, suggesting that these two forms of trust are independent and mutually reinforcing (an issue specifically considered by Paul and McDaniel, 2004 and discussed below in the section on 'combinations'). In addition to these three studies, Pavlou (2002) also found that trust in the benevolence of a community of sellers was positively linked to transaction success in an online business-to-business marketplace. Based on these studies there seems to be broad support for goodwill as a dimension of trust that is related to performance.

Predictability   Predictability refers to the degree of consistency in intended behavior and the expectation that an exchange partner can be relied on to fulfill obligations (Anderson and Weitz, 1989). The recent study by Pavlou (2002) mentioned above also investigated the effect of predictability (referred to as credibility) on transaction success in an online, business-to-business marketplace. This study provides support for predictability as a dimension of trust that is distinct from other dimensions (i.e. goodwill) and as an antecedent of performance. Additional research that corroborates these initial findings and explores the potential relationships between predictability and other dimensions of trust would be valuable.

Calculativeness   One of the more controversial dimensions of trust is calculativeness (Lewicki and Bunker, 1996; Rousseau et al., 1998). This represents a highly rational view of trust that is based on consideration of the costs and benefits associated with making oneself vulnerable to a counterpart (Coleman, 1990). Williamson (1993) has taken issue with labeling such a belief as trust and has argued that it is more accurate to refer to such expectations as risk. Nevertheless, those who advocate consideration of calculativeness as trust maintain that there are conditions under which the evidence of failure to perform can be readily determined, but that there may still be limited or short-term exposure to vulnerability.

Paul and McDaniel (2004) found that calculative trust had a positive impact on health care delivery at remote sites in a comparative case study of ten virtual collaborative relationships between health care providers. These authors further found, however, that the effect of calculative trust is conditional upon the level of other forms of trust, an issue we discuss next. Given the limited evidence on calculativeness, and the important arguments leveled against the notion of calculative trust, we see this as an important area for future research.

Combinations   Although several different forms of trust have been considered, few studies have investigated the extent to which different dimensions of trust interact to affect performance. One noteworthy exception is Paul and McDaniel's (2004) comparative case study of ten virtual collaborative relationships referred to above. These researchers investigated the independent and combined effects of competence, goodwill (referred to as relational), and predictability (referred to as credibility) trust on relationship performance. They found that while all three forms of trust independently had a positive effect on health care delivery, trust forms also interacted in important ways. Specifically, Paul and McDaniel concluded that a neutral or positive assessment of the other party's competence is a necessary but not sufficient condition if performance is to be positive. Positive assessments of all three types of trust are necessary if performance is to be strongly positive. If any one type of trust is negative, then it is very likely that performance will not be positive. However, positive performance is still possible if at least one type of trust is positive and the others are neutral. In addition, the researchers found that calculative trust plays an accentuating role, implying that it tends to sharpen the differentiation delineated by competence trust. In contrast, goodwill trust plays an attenuating role where it tends to temper the differentiation delineated by the other types of trust. Overall, their study suggests that it is important to consider the combined effects of different forms of trust on performance. Additional research that corroborates the preliminary findings of this comparative case study would be valuable, particularly given the theoretical emphasis on trust as a multifaceted concept consisting of distinct, but related, components.

Trust-based governance   Carson et al.'s (2003) study is also relevant to the discussion of different forms of trust. Rather than studying trust *per se*, these authors examine the effect of what they call trust-based governance (use of trust to support *ex post* revisions to an incomplete contract) on the performance of outsourced R&D relationships. Carson et al. reason that trust-based governance is a relational norm that is valuable to supporting *ex post* renegotiations. Work by Poppo and Zenger (2002) similarly treats trust as an aspect of relational governance. Such a view shifts the role of trust in a model of exchange performance from being a behavioral orientation to a mechanism for governing relationships – akin to contracts, equity-based alliances, ownership and so on – based on social processes. This body of work raises an important theoretical question about whether trust (and norms) is best conceptualized as a mode of organizing, consistent with the relational governance literature, or as an expectation about a counterpart's behavioral orientation, consistent with the trust literature. One advantage of adopting trust as the 'relational governance' perspective is that it broadens the range of options available for measuring what is an inherently interpersonal-level concept at the inter-organizational level of analysis. Doing so, however, may come at the expense of stretching the concept of trust beyond its actual meaning. Clearly, this is an area that warrants additional research.

Dimensionality of performance

Like trust, the performance of interfirm exchange relationships has been conceptualized as multidimensional (Anderson and Narus, 1990; Noordewier et al., 1990; Heide and Stump, 1995). In particular, research to date has considered four key aspects of relationship performance: satisfaction, continuity, completion time and financial outcomes.

Satisfaction   Perhaps the most commonly used, and most heterogeneous, metric against which performance has been assessed is satisfaction with the interfirm exchange relationship. Anderson and Narus (1990) argue that satisfaction is an important consequence of interfirm exchange and is a close proxy for perceived effectiveness as well as other performance outcomes. Some have studied the effect of trust on satisfaction from the perspective of one exchange partner (i.e. a 'within-partner design'). For instance, in our initial paper, we related the purchasing manager's trust in the supplier contact and supplier organization to the purchasing manager's assessment of whether the supplier had fulfilled key goals (i.e. competitive pricing, timeliness of delivery, quality of supply). Along similar lines, Carson et al. (2003) considered the effect of trust-based governance on satisfaction, in terms of task performance (technological contribution, goal attainment, timeliness and innovativeness), from the perspective of clients in outsourced R&D relationships. Within-partner effects of trust on satisfaction were also found by Lui and Ngo (2004) in architect–contractor partnerships, by Claro et al. (2003) in flower supplier–distributor relationships, and by Pavlou (2002) in a study of industrial buyers in an online business-to-business marketplace. Mora-Valentin et al. (2004) adopted a similar approach, but considered the within-partner effects of trust on satisfaction for both parties to an inter-organizational relationship. In their study of R&D cooperative agreements between private firms and government-run research organizations they found that trust and satisfaction were unrelated for both research organizations and private firms.

Other studies have examined the effect of trust on satisfaction using a 'between-partner design': that is, one party's trust on the counterpart's assessment of satisfaction. For instance, Johnston et al. (2004) found that suppliers' trust of buyers is positively related (through relational governance) to buyers' assessment of satisfaction with the relationship and attainment of performance objectives (e.g. profitability, growth, innovation, costs, quality and service).

Still other studies used a 'combined-partner design' to examine the effect of trust on satisfaction. Along these lines, Selnes and Sallis (2003) related the joint trust of buyers and suppliers to their joint satisfaction (in terms of how worthwhile, equitable, productive and satisfying they found their relationship) and found both direct and indirect effects as described above. Similarly, Paul and McDaniel (2004) used coded qualitative data from both parties to virtual collaborative relationships between health care providers to create indicators of the level of trust and perceived impact (in terms of access, quality and cost) of the relationship, which were positively related as discussed above. Lane et al. (2001) use a multidimensional measure of international joint venture (JV) performance (such as goal attainment and profitability) using data from both JV parents and find a direct relationship of trust to performance. Relatedly, they did not find the expected relationship between trust and JV learning.

Clearly, there is a considerable amount of research supporting the relationship between trust and satisfaction – based on data from a single party, both parties and combined reports. The consistency in results across research designs and studies is encouraging. At the same time, a critical issue for future trust research relying on satisfaction as a measure of performance is to establish the connection to less subjective indicators of performance. Along these lines, the next three areas of performance we discuss represent attractive alternatives for providing more objective indicators of performance.

Continuity of relationship   A second way that the performance of an interfirm relationship has been assessed is by the willingness of the parties to continue doing business together in the future. Continuity is generally defined as the intention to extend the relationship into the future. Such a long-term orientation has been found to enhance performance (Noordeweir et al., 1990) and represents a commitment to the relationship (Anderson and Weitz, 1989). Two studies have examined the effect of trust on continuity. Pavlou (2002) found that industrial buyers' trust in a community of online business-to-business sellers was positively related to their expectation of future transactions with sellers. Similarly, in their study of R&D cooperative agreements between private firms and government-run research organizations, Mora-Valentin et al. (2004) found that trust and continuity are related for research organizations, but not for private firms. Taken together, these two findings provide some preliminary support for the effect of trust on the longevity of a relationship, but additional research corroborating these results and exploring how different dimensions of trust affect continuity is warranted.

Completion time   Another way of gauging the level of performance in interfirm relationships is completion time. This is a particularly important indicator of performance in relationships that are project-based. For instance, in Lui and Ngo's (2004) study of architect–contractor relationships, project delays result in labor and material cost overruns and revenue losses for the property developer. These researchers found that different forms of trust (goodwill and competence) interact with contractual safeguards to affect the likelihood of a project completing on schedule. This study provides a valuable addition to the range of performance outcomes considered and the effect of different dimensions of trust. Clearly, more studies that replicate such a finding would further enhance this finding, as would research that considers more fine-grained approaches to capturing completion time. For instance, indicators such as actual versus targeted number of days may provide a more meaningful indicator of performance in some contexts.

Financial outcomes   Clearly, financial outcomes are among the most relevant and compelling indicators of interfirm relationship performance, and recent research has begun to investigate the effects of trust on financial outcomes. Luo (2001) found that the general manager's trust in the partner firm interacts with relational risk and interdependence to increase sales per asset and return on investment in his study of international strategic alliances in China (summarized above). Similarly, Dyer and Chu (2003) found that automakers' assessment of supplier trustworthiness is positively related to automakers' pretax return on assets. And Claro et al. (2003) found that flower suppliers' trust in distributors is positively related (through relational governance) to suppliers' growth in sales. These initial studies linking trust to financial outcomes are encouraging, particularly the study by Luo (2001), which reported results from a relatively larger sample of relationships than the other studies and relied on archival, as opposed to self-report, financial data. Future research would benefit by considering the relationship between trust, financial outcomes, and other (subjective and objective) indicators of performance with an eye toward identifying tradeoffs and complementarities.

Trust across levels
In addition to examining the performance effects of trust, a second major contribution of Zaheer et al. (1998) was the explicit recognition that trust between organizations was a multilevel phenomenon. We went on to identify different trust concepts at the inter-organizational and interpersonal levels of analysis, to theorize about the consequences of each, and to measure the constructs and demonstrate that they were distinct, using discriminant validity and a second organizational respondent. The paper then tested the theorized relationships about the consequences of trust at the two levels of analysis. Results showed that inter-organizational, rather than interpersonal, trust was a predictor of exchange performance, but it operated directly, rather than through the mediators of reduced conflict and negotiation costs as we had theorized. However, the link between interpersonal and inter-organizational trust suggested that both levels of trust played a role.

Since the publication of our study, further theoretical and empirical development of the idea of multilevel trust between organizations has taken place, although researchers have dedicated relatively little attention to this important topic. One stream of research has further developed the theory of trust across levels of inter-organizational exchange. A second stream of empirical research has focused on the outcomes of trust across levels, in essence testing whether interpersonal or inter-organizational is the stronger of the two. A third research stream has further explored the relationship between trust at different levels, and has also begun to distinguish the significance of interpersonal trust between members of partner organizations at different hierarchical levels.

Theory of trust across levels
Symbolizing the first stream of research is a recent paper by Currall and Inkpen (2002), which theorized about multilevel trust in the context of international joint ventures (IJVs). These authors have argued that treating trust as a multilevel phenomenon is particularly relevant to IJVs due to the complexity of interactions which occur at the interpersonal, intergroup and interfirm levels. Based on this, they further suggest that trust occurs at all three levels (e.g. person to person, group to group), occurs across levels (person to group, organization to person, etc.), and trust at one level affects trust at other levels (interpersonal affects intergroup). It is worth noting that Currall and Inkpen's (2002) framework explicitly endorses the idea that organizations (and groups) can trust, in contrast to the position we took in our paper. Specifically, we argued that organizations themselves do not trust, since they would be inappropriately anthropomorphized in that case – rather inter-organizational trust is the 'collectively held orientation' of a group of organizational members toward another organization. However, Currall and Inkpen

(2002) directly challenge the assertion that organizations cannot trust. They argue that firms can in fact be construed as trusting if trust is conceptualized as an action rather than an expectation. Thus a firm's trusting actions toward another firm would constitute the inter-organizational trust of one firm *vis-à-vis* another. Curall and Inkpen (2002) go on to define three levels of trust – the firm, the group and the individual – and argue that measures at each level are, and should be, different. For example, within-group correlations should be used to aggregate group-level trust, and routines, such as corporate statements, may be used to measure firm-level trust. Taken together, Currall and Inkpen's (2002) multilevel theory presents a number of intriguing ideas, all of which remain to be empirically evaluated.

Outcomes across levels

A major empirical paper symbolizing the second stream of research, that of establishing the relative strength of trust at different levels of analysis, is a study by Luo (2001), who finds, in a study of Chinese joint ventures, that 'personal attachment' (which he sees as closely related to trust) creates a stable context within which inter-organizational trust is developed and routines institutionalized. He operationalizes 'attachment' only at the individual level, and finds that personal attachment has a direct effect on performance, which he contrasts with the finding for trust in Zaheer et al. (1998), where it is only the inter-organizational level that has a performance effect. However, since he does not directly evaluate trust in his model, the question remains whether personal attachment and trust are interchangeable. In addition, the findings for effects of interpersonal attachment on performance are difficult to evaluate relative to our findings for trust and performance given that neither inter-organizational attachment nor inter-organizational trust were examined along with personal attachment. With these additional effects included, the findings for personal attachment may differ.

Paul and McDaniel (2004) argue that their 'finding of a positive association between integrated interpersonal trust and performance . . . contradicts prior research' by Zaheer et al. (1998), which did not find support for the relationship. They suggest a methodological reason; their use of 'facet theory' relies on less restrictive data assumptions concerning linearity of relationships between variables than structural equation modeling. The research, however, also does not control for inter-organizational trust. The research design focused on interpersonal relationships only, not inter-organizational ones, and like the conclusions of Luo (2001), need to be considered with caution for that reason.

In contrast, Hagen and Choe (1998) have little trouble with the idea that organizations can trust. In particular, these authors cite the case of a bank trusting its borrowers even if the lending officers rotate. It may be interesting to ascertain the precise conditions under which inter-organizational trust and interpersonal trust are relatively more important in inter-organizational relationships. One possibility we raised, also mentioned in Hagen and Choe, is that the strength of the institutionalization patterns – in Hagen and Choe at the societal level, and in our study at the firm level – will moderate the higher-level relationship. The institutional bases of trust are strongly drawn upon in Bachmann (2001), who uses structuration theory and other sociological theories to argue that trust and power are alternate means of controlling inter-organizational relationships. He writes, 'Stable institutions reduce the risk of being betrayed in that they constitute a "world in common" with shared norms and solid standards of behavior' (2001: 346).

Relationship between levels

A third stream of research develops the notion of levels into a finer-grained analysis and develops the connections between the levels to a greater extent (see also Janowicz and Noorderhaven, chapter 15 in this book). Zaheer et al. (2002), in inductive research based on six case studies, theorize that all levels of interpersonal trust are not equally important – trust between CEOs matters to a far greater degree in affecting outcomes than does trust between boundary spanners at lower hierarchical levels. Further, the importance of interpersonal trust at different hierarchical levels changes as the interfirm relationship evolves – interpersonal trust at the top matters more in the early stages and, again, if things go wrong. The paper also details the connections between inter-organizational and interpersonal trust in a dynamic context as it is affected by low performance, reversing the causal link between trust and performance. If the interfirm relationship starts to underperform, inter-organizational trust drops first and thereafter induces a drop in interpersonal trust as well.

Discussion and conclusion

We began this review by revisiting the question we originally posed in our (1998) paper: does trust (still) matter? In other words, does subsequent research continue to support our initial findings that trust enhances inter-organizational performance? Also, does trust operate at multiple levels of analysis the way we had proposed? After an extensive review of the studies that have followed ours, we respond with a highly qualified 'Yes'. In the most optimistic sense, we find a number of studies have produced results that are consistent with our findings that trust enhances inter-organizational performance. However, from a more conservative perspective and given the methodological limitations with organizational research, it is difficult to point to any single exemplar, including our own, that unequivocally answers the question in the affirmative. While the pieces are coming together, the puzzle is not yet complete and the image not yet clear. Given this, the best we can do is to point to the weight of evidence that collectively supports the assertion that trust does in fact matter – at least some form of it, depending on other factors. Inevitably, though, a survey such as ours raises more questions than it answers. While we have pointed to the more specific ones in the body of the chapter, in this concluding section we raise some broader issues.

Internal validity

Possibly the most critical issue, as in all organizational research, is the methodological one of internal validity. Invariably, the methodological challenges of field research compromise internal validity enough that we are unable to unambiguously make the causal connection between trust and performance from any single study. In this regard, recent advances in experimental research, including on trust, are noteworthy. While some of these advances are taking place in our own or related fields, such as psychology, developments in experimental economics are also promising.

For instance, one clear exemplar of promising developments in experimental economics is the expanding body of research based on the trust (or investment) game (Berg et al., 1995; also see McEvily et al., Chapter 3 in this volume for a recent application). This game-theoretic paradigm has the benefit of capturing trusting behaviors in a way that is highly realistic and meaningful in terms of subjects' economic welfare. Moreover, given the controlled experimental context, alternative explanations and confounding effects can be ruled out. In addition, the standardized format of the trust game greatly facilitates the cumulation of findings across studies. At the same time, a drawback of the trust game is its limited ability to accurately replicate ongoing relationships that are embedded in an organizational and historical context.

Another important issue concerning internal validity, and one that seems to have become a standard recommendation in research on trust, is to call for future studies to conduct longitudinal research. It is a sad reality that despite the clear-cut causal strengths of longitudinal designs, in field settings such research is still relatively rare. Nevertheless, it remains an important and worthy goal. However, we also recognize that the obvious difficulties of doing longitudinal field research are compounded by short tenure clocks, long journal lead times, and the increasing non-research demands on faculty.

Another promising methodological direction for examining the development of trust over time is through the use of simulations (Axelrod, 1984). For instance, Lin and Li (2003) develop a simulation model of trust in an intra-organizational context that could be usefully adapted to the inter-organizational context. In general, we believe that researchers can profitably use data from existing empirical studies of trust in inter-organizational exchange to derive a set of realistic assumptions upon which to build a simulation model. While not without their limitations, simulations are useful for generating theory and identifying new and interesting relationships that can later be tested in field settings.

In sum, to strengthen the internal validity of research on trust in interfirm exchange we encourage researchers to look beyond our immediate field and recognize promising methodological developments in closely related fields. We also strongly recommend the value of combining methods. For example, one may start with examining an initial relationship in the lab, and look at the same or even the subsequent relationship in the field. We also want to stress the increasing importance of studying the effect of trust on performance over time. Given the lack of longitudinal studies thus far, the potential of such a study to make a valuable contribution to the field is considerable.

Cumulative research

Apart from internal validity, building a tradition of cumulative research is critical to advancing our field. We believe that there are two key issues hindering the development of a cumulative body of research. First, too many studies adopt measurement scales for trust afresh, reinventing the wheel each time. Although several well-developed and psychometrically validated scales now exist for measuring trust (e.g. Cummings and Bromiley, 1996), virtually no empirical studies use standard scales (for a review see McEvily and Tortoriello, 2005). These scales can be adapted as necessary for the specific context, but at a minimum, doing so will provide the field of trust research with a common starting point. Unless we begin to adopt a uniform approach to measuring trust it will be exceedingly difficult to compare findings across studies and draw general conclusions.

A second problem limiting the cumulation of research findings is the lack of studies that build on existing research. For example, as we have discussed earlier in this review, we believe that a number of studies may have prematurely concluded that interpersonal trust mattered for performance, noting that this was contrary to the findings of Zaheer et al. (1998). While we are by no means wedded to our findings, it is clear that in the absence of a control for inter-organizational trust, which is a major part of our initial model, such a claim is not well founded. The reason of course is that inter-organizational and interpersonal trust are related constructs, and the addition of inter-organizational trust into the model may render the effect for interpersonal trust non-significant. Thus it is important from the point of view of research cumulation to consider the factors that have been shown in previous research to affect performance, and to control for them before drawing strong conclusions.

In sum, in order for the field to make progress, studies are needed with a more consistent and standardized approach to trust measurement, and more systematic efforts at building on previous work. However, we also recognize that it is practically infeasible to control for all factors shown to be significant in previous research. We thus recommend a middle-range theory approach (Merton, 1957) where relationships that have shown conflicting findings are specifically examined, and factors that are closely related to the key factors are taken into account.

Top five research questions for future research
Building on the broad research issues we have identified above, we lay out below what we see as the fundamental theoretical and methodological questions that reflect current tensions at the frontier of research on inter-organizational trust. As we approach these research questions, an important issue to keep in mind is the criteria used to evaluate trust. Much of the research we have reviewed, including our own initial study, adopts the view that trust should be evaluated from the perspective of efficiency and transaction cost minimization. However, other criteria exist in the literature and warrant attention. For instance, from an embeddedness perspective (Granovetter, 1985), individuals are also driven to develop trust due to the social-psychological benefits derived from personal attachment or group membership. In addition, motivations of corporate social responsibility might play a role in promoting the development of trust in interfirm exchange (Banerjee et al., chapter 17, this volume; Jones and Bowie, 1998). Put differently, firms may choose to invest in trust in an effort to stay consistent with a socially responsible and ethical mission. Given these diverse views, it is important to consider the research questions we discuss below not solely from the perspective of trust as an efficiency-enhancing property of interfirm exchange. The questions that follow, presented in no particular order, chart out a research agenda for the future.

1. What kind of trust matters?   Organizations are inherently multilevel entities, which is part of what sets the field of organization theory apart from other fields of social science. Consequently, understanding the multilevel antecedents and consequences of phenomena is critical. In our original paper we took the position that inter-organizational and interpersonal trust both mattered to explaining exchange performance, although our evidence seemed to suggest that inter-organizational trust was the overriding driver. Few empirical studies in the area have simultaneously considered interpersonal along with inter-organizational trust to build on our findings and further explore the complex interplay between trust at the two levels of analysis. A fertile area of research lies in investigating the moderators and contingencies of the relationships between trust at each level and performance. Such inquiry will help answer the question of the conditions under which interpersonal trust matters more than inter-organizational trust.

A related issue concerns the different dimensions of trust, since trust is inherently complex and multidimensional (Corazzini, 1977). Dimensions include competence, goodwill, predictability and calculativeness, among others. Research has only begun to separate the antecedents and consequences of the different dimensions and components of trust, and additional work is needed in this area.

2. Can organizations trust? An elemental issue in this research area is whether organizations themselves can in fact trust. Our original paper takes the position that organizations cannot trust, since to imply that organizations can would be tantamount to anthropomorphizing the organization as a sentient entity. Rather, we viewed interorganizational trust as a collectively held orientation in one organization towards a partner organization. However, as noted previously, Currall and Inkpen (2002) directly challenge the notion that organizations cannot trust and see trust at the organizational level as embedded in routines and processes. Given their position, how can we reconcile a definition of trust based on expectations or psychological states with trust at the organizational level? Is it feasible for organizations to have expectations and psychological states? Other scholars too (see Janowicz and Noorderhaven, chapter 15, this volume) challenge the notion that organizations cannot trust and advocate the use of hierarchical levels to reflect trust at the organizational level. Accepting such an approach opens up the possibility for a wide range of research at the organizational level. Instead of relying solely on psychometric surveys, observing actions and behaviors of organizations provides an approach to ascertaining organizational trust and, moreover, to evaluating whether interorganizational trust is more properly conceptualized and measured in this manner.

3. Transaction costs or transaction value? An enduring, often referenced, but little researched question concerns the issue of transaction value versus transaction cost (Zajac and Olsen, 1993). Simply put, is it more accurate to suggest that trust lowers transaction costs or does it actually enhance transaction value? Or does it depend? Perhaps in some cases trust lowers transaction costs and in others it enhances transaction value. Much more work exists on the transaction-cost-lowering effect of trust than on its transaction-value-enhancing role. We suggest that contexts, contingencies and conditions need to be identified when and where trust plays one role or the other to a greater extent. A beginning in this regard is the work of Dyer and Chu (2003), but considerable scope exists for exploring this question further. For example, we were not able to identify any studies that examined innovativeness as a performance outcome of trust, which could be one example of the enhancement of transaction value.

4. Substitutes or complements? A promising direction for future research is identifying the substitutes and complements of trust. Issues around this question deal with both performance-enhancing and -diminishing effects of factors that complement trust, and thereby play the role of moderators in the relationships between trust and outcomes. However, considering complements of trust provides a way of linking trust to other governance mechanisms, such as contracts. Moreover, considering the substitutes to trust recognizes the costs of creating trust, treating it as a problem of optimal resource allocation and one that can be situated in a strong theoretical model of transaction cost governance, and thereby evaluated with an efficiency criterion (Poppo and Zenger, 2002).

As mentioned above, other criteria besides efficiency exist for evaluating the role of trust in governing exchange.

5. Is trust merely calculativeness?   Williamson (1993) leveled a serious critique about incorporating the notion of trust into theories of organization and, in particular, inter-firm exchange. In short, he argued that what people refer to as trust is really risk, and is calculative in nature. Trust, he maintained, in its pure, uncalculative state, should be restricted to intimate personal relationships, such as those with immediate family. While this position has attracted a great deal of attention, few have taken the critique seriously from an empirical standpoint. For instance, few studies explicitly incorporate risk as a control (see Saparito et al., 2004 for an exception). However, we believe that Williamson's critique warrants greater attention since trust and risk are closely related. Indeed, Rousseau et al. (1998) identified risk, along with interdependence, as a condition creating the need for trust. The threat of not taking Williamson's critique seriously is that much of what we are ascribing to trust may in fact be better explained by existing theories of risk.

At the same time, we believe that Williamson's position can be challenged on several grounds. For instance, although Williamson views trust and risk as synonymous, the organizational literature on trust sees the two concepts as theoretically distinct. Empirically, establishing the discriminant validity between trust and risk is an important area for future research. In addition, the organizational literature on trust argues that initially calculativeness prevails, but over time this form of trust is replaced with more relational forms of trust (see Rousseau et al., 1998; Lewicki and Bunker, 1996). Further, it can be argued that Williamson's analysis ignores temporal dynamics associated with trust. Williamson's argument is also inconsistent with the view that the lack of complete trust does not imply calculativeness, and that trust and calculativeness can co-exist (Bromiley and Harris, chapter 7 in this volume).

Concluding remarks

Does trust still matter? Based on our review, we would conclude that trust does indeed continue to be of great interest and concern to organizational researchers. At the same time, we believe that much important work remains to be done. The agenda that we have set out is undoubtedly challenging, but the insights to be gained from pursuing it are even greater.

Acknowledgements

We would like to thank Reinhard Bachmann and Jared Harris for helpful comments on an earlier draft of this chapter.

References

Anderson, J.C. and J.A. Narus (1990), 'A model of distributor firm and manufacturer firm working partner-ship', *Journal of Marketing*, **54**: 42–58.
Anderson, E. and B. Weitz (1989), 'Determinants of continuity in conventional industrial channel dyads', *Marketing Science*, **8**(4): 310–23.
Axelrod, R. (1984), *The Evolution of Cooperation*, New York: Basic Books.
Bachmann, R. (2001), 'Trust, power and control in trans-organizational relations', *Organization Studies*, **22**(2): 337–65.
Barber, B. (1983), *The Logic and Limits of Trust*, New Brunswick, NJ: Rutgers University Press.
Berg, J., J. Dickhaut and K. McCabe (1995), 'Trust, reciprocity and social history', *Games and Economic Behavior*, **10**: 122–42.

Bromiley, P. and L.L. Cummings (1995), 'Transaction costs in organizations with trust', in R. Bies, B. Sheppard and R. Lewicki (eds), *Research on Negotiation in Organizations*, Greenwich, CT: JAI Press.

Carson, S.J., A. Madhok, R. Varman and G. John (2003), 'Information processing moderators of the effectiveness of trust-based governance in interfirm R&D collaboration', *Organization Science*, 14(1): 45–56.

Claro, D.P., G. Hagelaar and O. Omta (2003), 'The determinants of relational governance and performance: How to manage business relationships?', *Industrial Marketing Management*, 32(8): 703–16.

Coleman, J.S. (1990), *Foundations of Social Theory*, Cambridge, MA: The Belknap Press.

Corazzini, R. (1977), 'Trust as a complex multi-dimensional construct', *Psychological Reports*, 40: 75–80.

Cummings, L.L. and P. Bromiley (1996), 'The organizational trust inventory (OTI): development and validation', in R.N. Kramer and T.R. Tyler (eds), *Trust in Organizations*, Thousand Oaks, CA: Sage.

Currall, S.C. and A.C. Inkpen (2002), 'A multilevel approach to trust in joint ventures', *Journal of International Business Research*, 33(3): 479–95.

Das, T.K. and B.S. Teng (1998), 'Between trust and control: Developing confidence in partner cooperation in alliances', *Academy of Management Review*, 23(3): 491–512.

Dyer, J.H. and W.J. Chu (2003), 'The role of trustworthiness in reducing transaction costs and improving performance: Empirical evidence from the United States, Japan, and Korea', *Organization Science*, 14(1): 57–68.

Gallivan, M.J. (2001), 'Striking a balance between trust and control in a virtual organization: a content analysis of open source software case studies', *Information Systems Journal*, 11(4): 277–304.

Granovetter, M. (1985), 'Economic action and social structure: The problem of embeddedness', *American Journal of Sociology*, 91(3): 481–510.

Hagen, J.M. and S. Choe (1998), 'Trust in Japanese interfirm relations: Institutional sanctions matter', *Academy of Management Review*, 23: 589–600.

Heide, J.B. and G. John (1990), 'Alliances in industrial purchasing: The determinants of joint action in buyer–supplier relationships', *Journal of Marketing Research*, 27: 24–36.

Heide, J.B. and R.L. Stump (1995), 'Performance implications of buyer–supplier relationships in industrial markets: A transaction cost explanation', *Journal of Business Research*, 32: 57–66.

Johnston, D.A., D.M. McCutcheon, F.I. Stuart and H. Kerwood (2004), 'Effects of supplier trust on performance of cooperative supplier relationships', *Journal of Operations Management*, 22(1): 23–38.

Jones, T.M. and N.E. Bowie (1998), 'Moral hazards on the road to the virtual corporation', *Business Ethics Quarterly*, 8(2): 273–92.

Lane, P.J., J.E. Salk and M.A. Lyles (2001), 'Absorptive capacity, learning, and performance in international joint ventures', *Strategic Management Journal*, 22(12): 1139–61.

Lewicki, R. and B.B. Bunker (1996), 'Developing and maintaining trust in work relationships', in R.M. Kramer and T.R. Tyler (eds), *Trust in Organizations: Frontiers of Theory and Research*, Thousand Oaks, CA: Sage Publications, 114–39.

Lin, Z. and D. Li (2003), 'Does competency-based trust benefit organizational performance? – A meso exploration using computer modeling', *Journal of Mathematical Sociology*, 27(4): 219–61.

Lui, S.S. and H.Y. Ngo (2004), 'The role of trust and contractual safeguards on cooperation in non-equity alliances', *Journal of Management*, 30(4): 471–85.

Luo, Y.D. (2001), 'Antecedents and consequences of personal attachment in cooperative ventures', *Administrative Science Quarterly*, 46: 177–201.

Macneil, I. (1980), *The New Social Contract: An Inquiry into Modern Contractual Relations*, New Haven, CT: Yale University Press.

Mayer, R.C., J.H. Davis and F.D. Schoorman (1995), 'An integrative model of organizational trust', *Academy of Management Review*, 20: 709–34.

McEvily, B. and M. Tortoriello (2005), 'Measuring trust in organizational research: Review and Recommendations', Working Paper, Carnegie Mellon University.

McEvily, B., V. Perrone and A. Zaheer (2003), 'Trust as an organizing principle', *Organization Science*, 14(1): 91–103.

Merton, R.K. (1957), *Social Theory and Social Structure*, New York: Free Press.

Mora-Valentin, E.M., A. Montoro-Sanchez and L.A. Guerras-Martin (2004), 'Determining factors in the success of R&D cooperative agreements between firms and research organizations', *Research Policy*, 33(1): 17–40.

Noordewier, T.G., G. John and J.R. Nevin (1990), 'Performance outcomes of purchasing arrangements in industrial buyer–vendor relationships', *Journal of Marketing*, 54: 80–93.

Paul, D.L. and R.R. McDaniel (2004), 'A field study of the effect of interpersonal trust on virtual collaborative relationship performance', *MIS Quarterly*, 28(2): 183–227.

Pavlou, P.A. (2002), 'Institution-based trust in interorganizational exchange relationships: the role of online B2B marketplaces on trust formation', *Journal of Strategic Information Systems*, 11: 215–34.

Poppo, L. and T. Zenger (2002), 'Do formal contracts and relational governance function as substitutes or complements?', *Organization Science*, 23: 707–25.

Rempel, J.K., J.G. Holmes and M.P. Zanna (1985), 'Trust in close relationships', *Journal of Personality and Social Psychology*, **49**: 95–112.

Ring, P.S. and A.H. Van de Ven (1992), 'Structuring cooperative relationships between organizations', *Strategic Management Journal*, **13**: 483–98.

Rousseau, D.M., S.B. Sitkin, R.S. Burt and C. Camerer (1998), 'Not so different after all: A cross-discipline view of trust', *Academy of Management Review*, **23**(3): 393–404.

Saparito, P.A., C.C. Chen and H.J. Sapienza (2004), 'The role of relational trust in bank–small firm relationships', *Academy of Management Journal*, **47**(3): 400–410.

Selnes, F. and J. Sallis (2003), 'Promoting relationship learning', *Journal of Marketing*, **67**(3): 80–95.

Shrum, W., I. Chompalov and J. Genuth (2001), 'Trust, conflict and performance in scientific collaborations', *Social Studies of Science*, **31**(5): 681–730.

Williamson, O.E. (1993), 'Calculativeness, trust and economic organization', *Journal of Law and Economics*, **36**: 453–86.

Zaheer, A. and J. Harris (2005), 'Interorganizational trust', in O. Shenkar and J. Reuer (eds), *Handbook of Strategic Alliances*, Thousand Oaks, CA: Sage, pp. 169–97.

Zaheer, A. and N. Venkatraman (1995), 'Relational governance as an interorganizational strategy: An empirical test of the role of trust in economic exchange', *Strategic Management Journal*, **19**(5): 373–92.

Zaheer, A., B. McEvily and V. Perrone (1998), 'Does trust matter? Exploring the effects of interorganizational and interpersonal trust on performance', *Organization Science*, **9**(2): 141–59.

Zaheer, A., S. Lofstrom and V. George (2002), 'Interpersonal and interorganizational trust in alliances', in F. Contractor and P. Lorange (eds), *Cooperative Strategies and Alliances: What We Know 15 Years Later*, Amsterdam: Elsevier.

Zajac, E.J. and C.P. Olsen (1993), 'From transaction cost to transaction value analysis: Implications for the study of interorganizational strategies', *Journal of Management Studies*, **30**(1): 131–45.

PART IV

TRUST AT THE LEVEL OF SOCIETY AND THE ECONOMY

17 An ethical analysis of the trust relationship
Sanjay Banerjee, Norman E. Bowie and Carla Pavone

Introduction

Discussions of trust and trustworthiness are under intense discussion in management. Both practitioners and academics are parties to the conversation. With respect to the analysis of these two concepts, especially in a business context, most discussants adopt either an economic analysis of the concept or a sociological analysis.[1] Jones and Bowie (1998) have argued that neither analysis fully captures the nature of the concepts. An economic account of trust looks at the conditions under which it is rational (in one's self-interest) to trust. The economic account also emphasizes the efficiency of trust. A growing literature of trust underscores its importance to economic life (e.g. Gambetta, 1988; Misztal, 1996; Rousseau et al., 1998; Smith et al., 1995). Trust seems to be beneficial to firms and organizations: it lowers agency and transaction costs (Frank, 1988; Jones, 1995), promotes efficient market exchanges (Arrow, 1974; Smith et al., 1995), improves cooperation (Mayer et al., 1995; Ring and Van de Van, 1992; Smith et al., 1995) and indeed enhances firms' ability to adapt to complexity and change (Korsgaard et al., 1995; McAllister, 1995). Trust also is described as an essential ingredient for innovation (Hosmer, 1994) and scientific collaboration.

Flores and Solomon (1998, p. 208) agree that a strictly economic definition of trust is inadequate and that, at its core, trust is an ethical concept:

> Economic approaches to trust, while well-intended and pointing in the right direction, are dangerously incomplete and misleading. Trust in business is not merely a tool for efficiency, although it does, as Nicholas Luhmann (1979) argues at length, have important implications for dealing with complexity and therefore efficiency. Moreover, it would hardly be honest to guarantee (as many authors do these days), that more trust will make business more efficient and improve the bottom line. Usually, of course, trust has this effect, but there is no necessary connection between trust and efficiency, and this is neither the aim nor the intention of trust. Indeed, trust as a mere efficiency-booster may be a paradigm of inauthentic trust or phony trust, trust that is merely a manipulative tool, a façade of trust that, over the long run, increases distrust, and for good reason. . . . Like many virtues, trust is most virtuous when it is pursued for its own sake, even if there is benefit or advantage in view. To think of trust as a business tool, as a mere means, as a lubricant to make an operation more efficient, is to not understand trust at all. Trust is, first of all, a central concept of ethics. And because of that, it turns out to be a valuable tool in business as well.

The sociological explanation of trust argues that trust arises from sociologically embedded norms that govern the relationship. However, in some cases people engage in trust when there are no stable norms that govern the relationship. As Jones and Bowie point out, virtual corporations provide one example. None the less we agree that the existence of norms is very important in understanding trust relationships. Our analysis is more concerned with the nature of those norms. Our main quarrel with the sociological account is that most social scientists ignore the essentially ethical elements in trust, trust relationships, and being trustworthy. We believe that moral or ethical norms play a crucial role in trust relationships.

The primary purpose of this chapter is to develop the ethical underpinnings of the trust relationship and to show how 'being trustworthy' is, in essence, a moral concept. Jones and Bowie point out that if one must know that trust will be in one's self-interest, then trust relationships may never get off the ground. In this chapter we emphasize the vulnerability that exists for at least one party in the trust relationship. If one is vulnerable, then one can never know in a particular instance if the other party will take unfair advantage of one's vulnerability. Thus one cannot know if participating in the trust relationship in this case is really in one's self-interest. In order to develop a principle for moral action in trust relationships, we identify the three essential ethical features of trust relationships. On the basis of that identification, we justify the following principle: unethical behavior in trust relationships is proving you are untrustworthy by reneging on or by deceiving the trustor of the fairness norms being applied to his or her vulnerability in this situation. Our discussion concludes by considering legitimate excuses when this principle is violated.

We begin by noting that 'trust' and 'trustworthiness' are not simply – or at least not usually – descriptive terms. They are normative concepts and often the normativity is ethical or moral. Thus to say that a person or organization is trustworthy is normally to praise or commend the person or organization. Also the word 'trust' often occurs in discourse about truth telling or contracts. This chapter will articulate why the terms 'trust' and 'trustworthiness' often have these moral connotations.

Given our claim that trust and trustworthiness often have moral dimensions, one might expect us to turn to the literature in philosophical ethics to guide us in our task. However, discussion of trust by moral philosophers has been extremely limited. There may be several causes of the paucity of the trust literature in philosophical ethics. First, ethical theorists are once again focused on metaethics. Metaethics is primarily about the definition of ethical terms and the possibility of the justification of ethical judgments. Issues of epistemology join with issues of metaphysics as philosophers discuss the ontological status of ethical judgments. Second, those philosophers whose work is primarily normative, including many applied ethicists, continue to work at the level of grand theory by applying theories such as Kantianism or utilitarianism to practical problems in medicine, law and business. There has been insufficient concern with bridge concepts such as 'conflict of interest', 'rights', 'fairness', 'of high character and trustworthiness' that often provide the most immediate justification for ethical judgments. In many instances, these bridge concepts do a better job of justification than respect for persons or the greatest good. Despite the relative lack of interest in trust by philosophical ethics, a comprehensive understanding of trust in management theory requires an ethical perspective. It is that ethical perspective that this chapter attempts to provide.

Analysis of the concept of trust

Before identifying the ethical essence of trust, one must begin with the perplexity that surrounds 'trust' and its associated family of concepts. Providing a definition of trust has become a very complicated affair. Indeed much of the academic literature on trust centers on definitional debates.

One dictionary definition of trustworthiness is 'meriting confidence for proved soundness, integrity, veracity, judgment, or ability' (Merriam–Webster, 2003). The definition contains two types of qualities. The first set is objective: soundness and ability. The company is either solvent enough to pay its bills or it is not. The factory either has the right equipment and skill sets to manufacture a truck or it does not.

The second, subjective set is more interesting from an ethical perspective: 'integrity', 'veracity' and 'judgment' are clearly ethical terms. The definition implies that both sets of qualities are abiding and context-independent. While this may be true of the trusted party's objective qualities, the subjective qualities are a function of the dynamics of the trust relationship. As a result, while the definition may be broad, there will be socially constructed limits to its application. The dictionary definition, however, does not do justice to the richness of the concept of trust.

Levels of trust relationships
Trust is often described as monolithic. In fact trust is multidimensional and multifaceted. Trust can be discussed on numerous levels and there are myriad types of trust relationships. As a simplifying device, we consider three levels of trust, as illustrated in Figure 17.1. Trust occurs at different levels of analysis: individual, organizational and societal. Trust may take place between entities at the same level (i.e. two different individuals, organizations or societies) or between different levels (i.e. between individuals and organizations). Nine different types of trust can be differentiated based on the potential

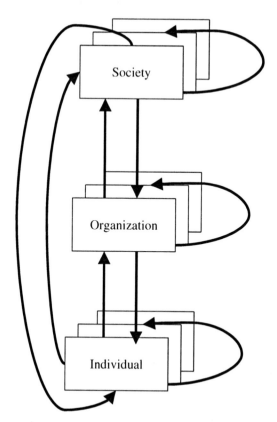

Figure 17.1   Three levels of trust

for trust relationships within and/or between each of the three social levels. Individuals can trust one another. Individuals may trust an organization, as when a patient trusts a hospital to provide competent care. And individuals may trust society, as when we trust society to assist us when a natural disaster such as a hurricane or flood strikes.

Organizations may trust an individual. For example: organizations trust their members to be loyal to the organization so long as it operates in a lawful and ethical manner. Organizations may trust one another: for example, manufactures may trust their suppliers to provide goods of high quality and suppliers trust manufacturers to pay them in a timely manner. Organizations also can trust society. For example, organizations trust society not to change the rules they operate under. They trust society to provide the requisite stability.

Finally, society may trust its citizens to be loyal and to pay their fair share of the burdens of cooperative social behavior. Despite a certain amount of cheating and monitoring, the US Internal Revenue Service still relies to a great extent on trust. Society also trusts organizations to live up to the purposes for which society allows them to operate. We should not forget that corporations are chartered in the best interest of society. Finally societies can even trust one another – to honor treaties, for example. Despite numerous examples of violations of trust, it behooves us to realize that trust permeates all levels of society. For purposes of this chapter, however, we will focus on the reciprocal trust relationships between individuals and organizations, with special emphasis on business organizations.

The situational ethics of trust relationships
One never simply trusts a particular person to do some particular thing during some particular time period. Trust always requires a general attitude, a proper context, a fabric of trusting experiences over time and an open-ended (but not unlimited) number of possibilities for trust (Flores and Solomon, 1997). The authors explain (pp. 63–4):

> If I trust you to answer the phone while I am in the shower I also trust you, presumably, not to insult the caller, not to read my private files while I'm gone, not to burn the house down, not to play your Alfred Hitchcock scenario on me in the bathroom, and so on . . . This is not to say, of course, that in trusting you to answer the phone I thereby trust you to do anything for me, even leaving aside questions of competence and special abilities. I trust you to answer the phone and would not trust you to give your life for me.

Furthermore, when one trusts a person, this need not entail any particular set of expectations. When a child trusts that he or she will be fed and protected, *by whom* remains a question. Or, when I reach London, I trust that there will be food at the airport, but I do not expect food from any particular person. Karen Jones (1996) captures this idea when she points out the expansiveness of trust. Such vaguely directed expectations are typical of basic trust (Flores and Solomon, 1997).

Trust is not simply a behavior (e.g. cooperation) or simply a choice (e.g. taking a risk), but is, at least in part, 'an underlying psychological condition that can cause or result from such actions' (Rousseau et al., 1998, p. 395). Trust is not even just a set of beliefs or expectations. Rather trust involves 'an affective attitude (Jones, 1996), an emotion, even a passion (in Baker, 1987)' (Flores and Solomon, 1997, p. 61). However, Jones (1996) points out that emotions are now recognized to be 'cognitive' in a number of important ways. Unlike Becker's (1996) overly harsh distinction between 'non-cognitive' emotions and cognitions (beliefs, expectations), trust should be understood as '*both* a set of beliefs and expectations and an emotional ("affective") attitude, and not as two separate components, but rather as having a single integrated emotional structure' (Flores and Solomon, 1997, p. 62).

Karen Jones (1996, p. 4) defines trust as 'an attitude of optimism that the goodwill and competence of another will extend to cover the domain of our interaction with her, together with the expectation that the one trusted will be directly and favorably moved by the thought that we are counting on her'. However, Jones's focus is on the trustor, not on the attributes of the trusted party. While she implies that being trustworthy means fulfilling the expectations of the trustor, in so far as they are appropriate and welcome, she does not offer a separate definition of trustworthiness. Notice that 'appropriate and welcome' cry out for ethical analysis. Flores and Solomon (1997, p. 53) make the important point:

> It seems to us obvious that they [trust and trustworthiness] are, in some nontrivial sense, two sides of the same coin . . . trustworthiness (perhaps like all virtues) means nothing in isolation, that is without trust, without anyone who cares or who is affected or who is trusting. Trustworthiness, in other words, is not a 'brute fact,' but an interpretation, or, if you prefer a social fact, dependent on collective acceptance.

In their review article, Rousseau et al. (1998) offer a composite definition of trust: 'Trust is a psychological state comprising the intention to accept vulnerability based upon positive expectations of the intentions or behavior of another' (ibid., p. 395). But this doesn't tell us much about trustworthiness – must one fulfill all the expectations (appropriate or not, agreed to or not) of the trustor in order to be trustworthy?

Unlocking the ethical essence of trust

Dennis Moberg defines trustworthiness as a 'trait of character that is respectful of the specific duties of ability, benevolence, and integrity toward others' (1997, p. 176). While he asserts that one can be too trustworthy (essentially by doing whatever anyone expects), he doesn't address how to evaluate these specific duties in terms of their appropriateness or limits. Notice, however, that Moberg's definition is straightforwardly ethical. In traditional terms, being trustworthy would identify a moral person.

In the context of everyday trust relationships, norms regarding how vulnerability in the trust relationship should be handled may even have unanimous agreement. However, we cannot emphasize enough the importance of transparency with respect to such norms. In the absence of such norms, the vulnerable party would be well advised not to trust. It should also be clear that violation of a mutually agreed-upon norm is a serious moral wrong on the same level as lying or breaking a contract.

Scholars appear to agree on certain fundamental issues related to trust. Trust is the willingness to be vulnerable under conditions of risk and interdependence; it's a psychological state of mind – not simply a behavior (e.g. cooperation) or simply a choice (e.g. taking a risk) that entails 'perceived probabilities' (Bhattarcharya et al., 1998), or simply 'confidence' and 'positive expectations' (e.g. Jones and George, 1998; Hagen and Choe, 1998; Das and Teng, 1998). Johnson-George and Swap (1982, p. 1306) assert that 'willingness to take risks may be one of the few characteristics common to all trust situations'. Also, other themes that come out of various studies – regardless of the discipline of the authors – are 'confident expectations' and a 'willingness to be vulnerable' (Mayer et al., 1995). Rousseau et al. (1998) synthesize the definition of trust – based on contemporary, cross-disciplinary collection of scholarly writings – as 'a psychological state comprising the intention to accept vulnerability based upon positive expectations of the intention or behavior of other' (p. 395).

But this definition is incomplete as it stands as can be seen by the question raised by Baier (1986, p. 234): 'what is the difference between trusting others and merely relying on them?' She explains, 'Trust . . . is reliance on another's good will' (ibid.), which resonates with the findings of Ring and Van de Van (1992) in organizational theory. In this case the added element when one moves from mere reliance to trust is an ethical element. What one is relying on is another's *good will*.

On the basis of this survey of the literature we are able to list the necessary conditions for a trusting relationship. These are:

1. Interdependence: at least one party in a trust relationship must be dependent on at least one other party in order to accomplish a goal.
2. Vulnerability: at least one party in the trust relationship is vulnerable to the opportunistic behavior of another party in the trust relationship.
3. Risk: as a result of this vulnerability, the interests of at least one party in the relationship are at risk.

We can then define a trust relationship as one of interdependence where at least one party is vulnerable to the opportunistic behavior of least one other party to the relationship but where nonetheless the vulnerable party voluntarily accepts the risks of its vulnerability.

The ethical component of the trust relationship
We are now in a position to identify the ethical component in the trust relationship. The ethical component arises from the vulnerability of the trusting party in the relationship to the goodwill of the other parties. *A trustworthy party is one that will not unfairly exploit vulnerabilities of the other parties in the relationship.* Ethics enters the picture when we need to decide what counts as an unjust or unfair exploitation of the vulnerability of one of the parties in the trust relationship. What counts as an example of excessive opportunism in that context? The non-vulnerable parties in the relationship have a moral obligation not to unfairly exploit the vulnerable parties.[2]

Fairness
Now that we have identified the ethical components in a trust relationship, we note that fairness is the key to determining the moral obligations in such a relationship. The trustee is not to take unfair advantage of the vulnerabilities of the trustors. What counts as fairness? The answer to this question can be determined by philosophical ethics and/or by investigation of norms of expectation (what people take as fair in these situations).

Many ethical accounts of fairness adopt the social contract perspective. The most well known and influential of these accounts is that of John Rawls (1971). A Rawlsian approach to fairness would ask what norms regarding the treatment of vulnerability would be accepted by all parties in the trust relationship. Those norms that could be publicly advocated and adopted by all the parties would be accepted as fair. Rawls believed that in order to arrive at a unanimous agreement one needed to reason as if one were behind a veil of ignorance and thus did not know specific facts about the case that would bias one in the selection of the norms of fairness. Once this personal bias was eliminated, the parties to the contract could develop norms of fairness.

We point out that this emphasis on norms of fairness is consistent with how people think and act in situations of vulnerability. Price gouging after a natural disaster like a blizzard or a hurricane is regarded as highly unethical and, under certain circumstances, is illegal as well. What explains the reaction? Recognition that merchants are taking unfair advantage of the vulnerabilities of those who have suffered through the natural disaster.

In his important book, *Passions within Reason*, Robert Frank (1988) has argued that people have norms of fairness that they use in everyday life. When behaving in accordance with these norms, they will often sacrifice what is in their rational short-term interest. Experimental evidence for this behavior is provided in ultimatum bargaining experiments (Kahneman et al., 1986; Güth and Tietz, 1985). In these games a person is offered $20 which he must divide between himself and another person. If the other person accepts the take-it-or-leave-it split, then both parties keep the $20 split according to the agreement. If the other person rejects the offer then nobody receives anything. The usual offer is a 50/50 split. When there is a radical inequality in the offer, the other person almost always turns it down. Neither set of actions can be explained on the basis of self-interest. Frank then defines a fair transaction as one in which the surplus of the transaction is divided approximately equally. On this line of reasoning, one party in a trust relationship exploits the vulnerability of another party to the transaction when that party takes much more than 50 percent of the surplus value gained from the trust relationship.

Trustworthiness as a social construct – some examples
Certainly there are general norms of fairness; the reasoning of Rawls and Frank is persuasive. But these norms become more nuanced when applied to specific cases. To put it another way, while fairness in the sense of not taking undue advantage of the vulnerabilities of the trustor may be an indicator of trustworthiness, the expectation is actually highly situational. For instance, the ongoing members of a card-playing group may consider each other deeply trustworthy for the things that matter in life, but that doesn't stop them from bluffing in a game of poker. A purchasing manager negotiating with a supplier may choose to misdirect the supplier about his or her top price. A job candidate may engage in impression management during an interview. In each case, the other parties not only expect the first person not to state the full truth, but this behavior does not undermine their perceptions of that person's fundamental trustworthiness. Instead, the lack of veracity is just part of the game.

Integrity can actually be something of a moving target. One manifestation of integrity may be to not take advantage of the vulnerabilities of others. However, aren't competition and capitalism all about taking advantage? Still, there are limits to this, as captured in the platitudes 'fight fair', or 'don't hit someone when he's down'.

This variability is best illustrated by the experience of investment firms located in the World Trade Center at the time of the 11 September 2001 attacks. Cantor Fitzgerald, Sandler O'Neill, and Keefe Bruyette and Woods each lost many employees – often their most senior executives and top experts. Before the attacks, these firms were all fierce competitors in a cut-throat industry, where the norm is to raid employees and poach business – to identify and exploit competitors' weaknesses in any way possible. Yet, in the immediate aftermath of 11 September, a different ethos prevailed. All three firms received help from competitors, suppliers and customers with real estate, technology, employee recruitment and market information – much of it *pro bono*. Competitors did not raid these firms for employees. Competitors (in conjunction with their customers) even included these firms in underwriting deals, so that the affected firms would have revenues while they rebuilt their businesses (Brooker, 2002; Cowan, 2002; Opdyke and Charles, 2001).

However, this ethos did not prevail once the firms were back on their feet, nor, it could be argued, did any of the parties expect it to. In fact, the old Wall Street norms of integrity again apply – the focus is on follow-through and doing what you said you would do. On Wall Street – in the absence of an extraordinary emergency like 11 September – you can be a ruthless competitor while still having high integrity – as defined in that setting.

Another example of situational integrity is when friends or spouses are also competitors. In this case, compartmentalization takes place. It would be untrustworthy for friends and spouses to share company secrets, but it would trustworthy for them to share personal secrets. It would be untrustworthy to take advantage of a friend's or spouse's vulnerable emotional state, but it would not violate trustworthiness to take advantage of a business vulnerability.

In his book on trust, Francis Fukuyama (1995) highlights the deep cultural differences between high-trust and low-trust societies, and the prosperity associated with social capital. Multinational firms face the challenge of dealing with the resulting conflicting cultural expectations of trustworthiness (Brenkert, 1998). For instance, it is a deeply held North American principle that firms should hire the 'best qualified' job candidate and select the 'best qualified' supplier. In each case qualifications are based on relatively objective measures, such as competence, experience and cost. At least in theory, personal relationships and obligations should not enter into the hiring or supplier decision – in fact, it would be considered unfair and untrustworthy to include such considerations. This contrasts sharply with business practices in much of Asia and Latin America, where personal relationship and obligations are paramount in business decisions – and not doing business on that basis would be a betrayal of trust (Kali et al., 1999).

Ethical principle for trust relationships
Despite the fact that the norms of fairness are situational and also tend to vary from society to society, we should not be excessively relativistic. If parties in a trust relationship are not to be duped or to be suckers, then some norms for managing vulnerabilities must exist, or else the trust relationship would never get off the ground. As we have seen, intuitive norms of fairness operate in US businesses. In situations of trust, the key is to eliminate information asymmetries regarding norms of fairness. If a vulnerable party enters into a trusting relationship with a different understanding from the stronger party of what will constitute exploitation of trust, he or she will be deceived. Deception regarding the norms of fairness is morally wrong.

The challenge, then, is how to determine the norms for trustworthiness in the face of the multiple relationships requiring trust in ordinary societal contexts. The categorical imperative may be to be trustworthy – but within the terms governing the situation. In many situations, the parties in a trusting relationship have an explicit or – more often – tacit agreement about their definition of trustworthiness. In other situations, that definition may not be commonly known or mutually agreed to. In those cases, the best a firm can do is to be explicit about what rules it is following – in effect to be trustworthy on its own terms.

Our conclusion from this discussion is that it is possible to endorse a moral principle for trust relationships: *Unethical behavior is proving you are untrustworthy by reneging on or by deceiving the trustor of the fairness norms being applied to his or her vulnerability in this situation.*

At the more micro level of everyday trust relationships, norms regarding how vulnerability in the trust relationship should be handled may be vague, unclear or contested. Thus we cannot emphasize enough the importance of transparency with respect to such norms. In the absence of such norms, the vulnerable party would be well advised not to trust. It should also be clear that violation of a mutually agreed-upon norm is a serious moral wrong on the same level as lying or breaking a contract.

Moral considerations from the perspective of those who trust
From the side of the party that is vulnerable, the ethical issue is when should one enter such a relationship; that is, when should one trust in order to achieve a mutually beneficial end? If a party has good reason to believe that its vulnerability will be exploited or that it will be unfairly taken advantage of, then there is not even a weak ethical obligation to enter into the relationship. However, in the absence of evidence of untrustworthiness, how should one behave? Should one adopt an attitude of optimal trust? Wicks et al. (1999) define the concept 'optimal' trust as a golden mean of excess (over-investment in trust) and deficiency (under-investment in trust) in human conduct. They say (p. 103):

> Optimal trust exists when one creates (and maintains) prudent economic relationships biased by a willingness to trust. That is, agents need to have stable and ongoing commitments to trust so that they share affect-based belief in moral character sufficient to make a leap of faith, but they should also exercise care in determining whom to trust, to what extent, and in what capacity. Optimal trust is an embedded construct, suggesting that it is determined in context and shaped by a variety of factors, such as the trustworthiness of the agent, local and broader social norms of the relevant social structure(s).

It should be noted that when Wicks et al. (1999) define optimal trust as a golden mean between excess and deficiency, they make trust into an Aristotlean virtue. We see nothing wrong in identifying a person who practices optimal trust as practicing a virtue. Our position here has support from other scholars. Flores et al. (1997) indicate that trustworthiness may be a virtue. As Hardin (1996) indicates, most of the positive benefits and moral virtues associated with trust are actually those of trustworthiness: 'That many accounts of trust are really accounts of trustworthiness therefore suggests that the moralizing of trust might be more reliably seen as a moralizing of trustworthiness. Certain standard moral theories, such as that of Kant or various virtue theories, could readily elevate trustworthiness to moral status' (p. 42). Hardin's view is consistent with our analysis.

Since we emphasize the contextual nature of trust and trustworthiness, it is important to explain how a virtue can both be universal and be applied contextually. Aristotle (1983) noted that the virtue of courage was the mean between two extremes (vices) – rashness and cowardice. Moreover, courage is a virtue that it is desirable that all people possess. However, Aristotle never thought that each person should possess courage in the same amount. A soldier is obligated to show more courage than a college professor. Thus a virtue can be both universal and context-specific.

If being trusting is an individual or organizational virtue, that does not mean that an individual or firm ought to trust when there is no basis for the trust. We repeat that there is no obligation to be trusting when the trusting party believes the other party will take unfair advantage of its vulnerability. But in situations that are more neutral, or where trust conditions might evolve, or where there is an opportunity to engage in a tit-for-tat strategy if a trusting opening move is met with exploitation of vulnerability, then it is a virtue to trust in those situations.

Trust in the larger ethical context
The importance of situational context can also be seen when we recognize that trust relationships that might benefit individuals and an organization may still not be good in the broader sense. The trust relationship at that level may be bad for society as a whole. When an organization and the individuals that compose it conspire to restrain trade and trust one another to keep their actions secret, that trust relationship is not ethical in the most comprehensive sense. Society is unfairly harmed by the trust relationship. Thus it is important to recognize that trusting relationships are not always moral relationships and that being trustworthy is not always laudatory. It is in recognition of facts like these that Immanuel Kant (1785) stated that the only thing good in itself is a good will. As Kant argued, everything else which is deemed good can be misused and thus not be considered good. Trust is no different in that respect.

Thus trusting relationships can be beneficial or harmful depending on the circumstance. Trust may not always be beneficial: trust based on a personal relationship promotes misallocation of capital (Brasch, 1973); trust or trust-like behavior can give rise to corrupt activities (Husted, 1994); trust in an intra-organizational context may exclude certain communities or groups, for example women (Kanter, 1977); and many current concepts of trust in organizations may 'tend toward cronyism' (Koehn, 1996). A pertinent question may be 'What is a trust-tied community without justice but a group of mutual blackmailers and exploiters?' (Baier, 1986, p. 253).

High trust among a dense network of family, friends and relatives hinders economically viable institutions and can give rise to 'crony capitalism' which is quite rampant in Southeast Asia, for example in Indonesia (McDermott et al., 1998). Furthermore, trusting without suspicion – that is 'saintly trust' – can be taken advantage of and promote abusive behavior. In an organizational context, too much trusting leads to insufficient monitoring, which in turn tends to encourage opportunists to steal from the firm with relative impunity (Becker, 1996; Flores and Solomon, 1998; Hardin, 1996). Also, as Husted (1998) mentions, 'trust may be a source of competitive advantage in business relationships (Barney & Hansen, 1994), however, to the extent that trust replaces rational economic criteria in decision-making, inefficiency and injustice may result' (p. 234). Trust can only be considered morally appropriate when it is placed in the larger social context. Thus nothing in our account of the ethics of trust indicates that the trust relationship is always ethically correct overall.

Excusing conditions

Whether reneging on trust is ethical or not is an interesting question and may not get a straightforward answer. Trust depends on the actors, rules of the game, and context. In general, reneging on trust is treated as unethical behavior. But specific cases often require more nuanced assessment. A trustee may renege on an implicit trust 'contract' for several reasons. First, he or she may simply be no longer *willing* to continue the trust relationship on its original terms. Second, he or she may not be *competent* to fulfill the implied terms of the trust relationship. Third, he or she may not be able to continue to fulfill the implied promise due to circumstances beyond his or her *control*. Each of these factors has a different ethical implication.

Lack of willingness clearly fails the ethical test. If the actor has voluntarily agreed to do the task, has the relevant skills, and knows the rules of the game, but just reneges opportunistically, we have a straightforward case of unethical behavior.

However, *lack of competence* may or may not be a valid excuse for violation of the trust principle. Competence includes both the skills required to fulfill the promise of the trusting relationship as well as knowledge of the 'rules of the game' of that relationship. When is low competence an excuse? This is an issue that goes back to Aristotle (1983). Generally speaking, low competence is an excuse so long as the person is not responsible for the incompetence. A drunk is incompetent but is arguably responsible for the condition of being drunk. Thus being drunk usually does not get one off the moral hook. Furthermore, if an incompetent party lacks the skills implied in a trust relationship, then he or she is morally required to inform the trustor before entering into the relationship. Finally, if the trusted party is initially competent, but circumstances change to require different or greater skills/resources than before, the party may ethically renege on the promises implied in the trust relationship.

Lack of control over external events may also be an excusing factor. In this case, although the trustee may be competent and willing, reasons beyond his or her control make it impossible to keep the promises implied in the trust relationship. When the trusted party has no control over the environment and thus reneges, the trusted party is not morally at fault. If the party has no control, he or she cannot be held responsible (as long as the party is not responsible for having no control). This conclusion is an instance of the principle in ethics that 'ought implies can'. To put it less cryptically, you can only have a moral obligation if it is causally possible for you to carry it out. Lack of control in this case is a legitimate excuse.

The interaction of these three factors – the willingness, competence and control of the trusted party – determines both the ethics and the outcomes of a trust relationship. Figure 17.2 depicts visually how these factors may affect each other. Let's see how this plays out in a number of situations. For example, if we assume that the trustee has control over the circumstances of the trust relationship, then Figure 17.2 can be rendered as a simple 2 × 2 decision matrix (see Figure 17.3). With control held constant, the two remaining factors are whether or not the trusted party is willing to keep to the implied trust contract and whether or not the trustee has the competence to fulfill the implied promise. Two elements can be considered in each box: whether or not the trusted party has engaged in ethical behavior as well as whether or not the trust promise has been kept.

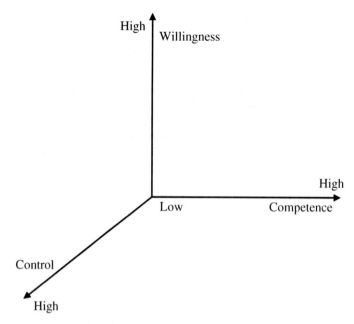

Figure 17.2   Interaction of willingness, competence and control

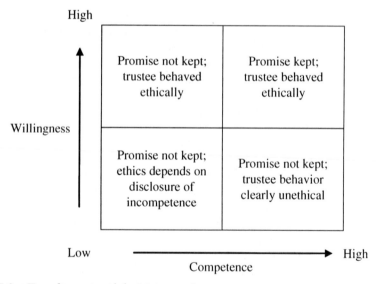

Figure 17.3   Two-dimensional decision matrix

When we incorporate control into the decision matrix, we can arrive at a more comprehensive framework (see Table 17.1) for determining when a trusted party has behaved ethically, even if the outcome of the trusted relationship is not positive. This framework varies the level of each of the three factors – competence, willingness and control – to arrive at a total of eight types of trusted relationships. This framework requires a few

Table 17.1   A framework for making an ethical assessment of a trust party's behavior

Competence	Willingness	Control	Outcome	Assessment
Hi	Hi	Hi	Promise kept	Ethical
Hi	Hi	Lo	Promise not kept	Ethical
Hi	Lo	Hi	Promise not kept	Clearly unethical
Hi	Lo	Lo	Promise not kept	Probably unethical (depends on disclosure of lack of control)
Lo	Hi	Hi	Promise not kept	Probably ethical (depends on disclosure of lack of competence)
Lo	Hi	Lo	Promise not kept	Probably ethical (assuming disclosure)
Lo	Lo	Hi	Promise not kept	Probably unethical (depends on disclosure of lack of competence)
Lo	Lo	Lo	Promise not kept	Possibly ethical, assuming disclosure

additional comments. First, we assume that a trusted party with high willingness to fulfill the trusted relationship is more likely to behave ethically. Therefore, we assume that situations with high willingness probably entail ethical behavior, even if lack of control or competence results in a negative outcome. Second, we assume that low willingness is more likely to lead to unethical behavior. Therefore, although lack of competence or control may be mitigating factors, we suspect that they are less likely to be disclosed.

Finally, this framework focuses on the ethics of the trusted party. Obviously, the trustor has certain responsibilities in the relationship as well. The trustor must take some steps to protect himself from being taken advantage of. If the trustor makes no attempt to determine the competence or willingness of the trustee, then there is a sense in which he or she brought it on him or herself. It is the practical responsibility of the trustor to conduct full due diligence and the ethical obligation of the trusted party to provide full disclosure.

Conclusion
This chapter began with an extensive survey and analysis of the various definitions of and approaches to trust and trustworthiness. We argued that a proper understanding of trust requires that we recognize the fundamental ethical components of trust, and especially trustworthiness.

We then defined the central terms as follows: a trust relationship is one of interdependence where at least one party is vulnerable to the opportunistic behavior of at least one other party to the relationship but where nonetheless the vulnerable party voluntarily accepts the risks of its vulnerability. It is this possibility that vulnerability can be abused that points to the ethical core behind trust. A trustworthy party is one that will not unfairly exploit vulnerabilities of the other parties in the relationship. We recognize that both of these terms are defined within a situational context and that who counts as trustworthy will vary across cultures. Finally, we provided a *prima facie* ethical principle for trust relationships: unethical behavior is proving you are untrustworthy by reneging on or by deceiving the trustor of the fairness norms being applied to his or her vulnerability in this situation.

We then concluded by pointing out circumstances in which we would relax our judgment that people have reneged in a way that was unethical. Those circumstances are based on the willingness, competence and control of the trusted party, and the degree to which those factors are disclosed to (or discovered by) the trustor.

Notes

1. We recognize that both psychology and organization science also provide accounts of trust. These accounts will be more fully discussed later in the chapter.
2. We recognize the possibility and indeed the likelihood of mutual vulnerability. In such a case the moral obligation is that no party unfairly exploit the vulnerabilities of the other parties. In cases of mutual vulnerability there are corresponding mutual ethical obligations.

References

Aristotle (1983), *Nicomachean Ethics*, Indianapolis, IN: Bobbs-Merrill.
Arrow, K. (1974), *The Limits of Organizations*, New York: Norton.
Baier, A. (1986), 'Trust and antitrust', *Ethics*, **96**(2), 231–60.
Baker, Judith (1987), 'Trust and rationality', *Pacific Philosophical Quarterly*, **68**, 1–13.
Barney, J.B. and Mark B. Hansen (1994), 'Trustworthiness as a source of competitive advantage', *Strategic Management Journal*, **15**(special issue), 175–90.
Becker, L.C. (1996), 'Trust as noncognitive security about motives', *Ethics*, **107**, 43–61.
Bhattacharya, R., T.M. Devinney and M.M. Pillutla (1998), 'A formal model of trust based on outcomes', *Academy of Management Review*, **23**(3), 459–72.
Brasch, John J. (1973), 'Trade credit and personalismo in Latin America', *Journal of International Business Studies*, **4**(1), 31–41.
Brenkert, G.G. (1998), 'Trust, morality and international business', *Business Ethics Quarterly*, **8**(2), 293–317.
Brooker, K. (2002), 'Starting over: When the planes slammed into the World Trade Center on Sept. 11, few companies were as hard-hit as a small, close-knit firm called Sandler O'Neill . . .', *Fortune*, **145**, 50.
Cowan, L. (2002), 'Rebuilding Wall Street: Survival test came early – Wall Street firms hit hardest by attacks make big changes', *Wall Street Journal*, Eastern edn, New York, C14.
Das, T.K. and B.S. Teng (1998), 'Between trust and control: Developing confidence in partner cooperation in alliances', *Academy of Management Review*, **23**(3), 491–512.
Flores, Fernando and Robert C. Solomon (1997), 'Rethinking trust', *Business & Professional Ethics Journal*, **16**(1–3), 47–76.
Flores, Fernando and Robert C. Solomon (1998), 'Creating trust', *Business Ethics Quarterly*, **8**(2), 205–32.
Frank, R.H. (1988), *Passions within Reason: The strategic role of emotions*, New York: Norton.
Fukuyama, F. (1995), *Trust: The social virtues and the creation of prosperity*, New York: Free Press.
Gambetta, D. (1988), *Trust: Making and breaking cooperative relations*, New York: Basil Blackwell.
Güth, Werner and Richard Tietz (1985), 'Strategic power versus distributive justice: An experimental analysis of ultimatum bargaining', in H. Brandstätter and E. Kirchler (eds), *Economic Psychology: Proceedings of the 10th IAREP Annual Calloquium*, Linz, Austria: R. Truaner.
Hagen, J.M. and S. Choe (1998), 'Trust in Japanese interfirm relations: Institutional sanctions matter', *Academy of Management Review*, **23**(3), 589–600.
Hardin, R. (1996), 'Trustworthiness', *Ethics*, **107**(1), 26–42.
Hosmer, L.T. (1994), *Moral Leadership in Business*, Homewood, IL: Irwin.
Husted, B.W. (1994), 'Honor among thieves: A transaction-cost approach to corruption in third-world countries', *Business Ethics Quarterly*, **4**(1), 17–27.
Johnson-George, C. and W. Swap (1982), 'Measurement of specific interpersonal trust: Construction and validation of a scale to assess trust in a specific other', *Journal of Personality and Social Psychology*, **43**, 1306–17.
Jones, K. (1996), 'Trust as an affective attitude', *Ethics*, **107**(1), 4–25.
Jones, T.M. (1995), 'Instrumental stakeholder theory: A synthesis of ethics and economics', *Academy of Management Review*, **20**, 404–37.
Jones, G.R. and J.M. George (1998), 'The experience and evolution of trust: Implications for cooperation and teamwork', *Academy of Management Review*, **23**(3), 531–46.

Jones, Thomas M. and Norman E. Bowie (1998), 'Moral hazards on the road to the virtual corporation', *Business Ethics Quarterly*, **8**(2), 273–92.

Kahneman, Daniel, Jack Knetsch and Richard Thaler (1986), 'Fairness and the assumptions of economics', *Journal of Business*, **59**(4), S285–S300.

Kali, Raja, Steve Lovett and Lee. C. Simmons (1999), 'Guanxi versus the market: ethics and efficiency', *Journal of International Business Studies*, **30**(2), 231–48.

Kant, Immanuel (1785), *Foundations of the Metaphysics of Morals*, reprinted in 1990, New York: Macmillan.

Kanter, R.M. (1977), *Men and Women of the Corporation*, New York: Basic Books.

Koehn, D. (1996), 'Should we trust in trust?', *American Business Law Journal*, **34**(2), 183–203.

Korsgaard, M., D. Schweiger and H. Sapienza (1995), 'Building commitment, attachment, and trust in strategic decision-making teams: The role of procedural justice', *Academy of Management Journal*, **38**(1), 60–84.

Luhmann, N. (1979), *Trust and Power: Two works*, New York: Wiley.

Mayer, R.C., J.H. Davis and F.D. Schoorman (1995), 'An integrative model of organizational trust', *Academy of Management Review*, **20**(3), 709–34.

McAllister, D.J. (1995), 'Affect- and cognition-based trust as foundations for interpersonal cooperation in organizations', *Academy of Management Journal*, **38**(1), 24–59.

McDermott, D., K. Linebaugh and J. Solomon (1998), 'Indonesia close to IMF pact to speed reform', *Wall Street Journal*, 15 January, A15.

Merriam–Webster (2003), *Merriam–Webster Unabridged*, Vol. 2003, Merriam–Webster Online.

Misztal, B.A. (1996), *Trust in Modern Societies: The search for the bases of social order*, Cambridge, MA: Polity Press.

Moberg, D.J. (1997), 'Trustworthiness and conscientiousness as managerial virtues', *Business and Professional Ethics Journal*, **16**(1–3), 171–94.

Opdyke, J.D. and G. Charles (2001), 'Rebuilding Wall Street: Wall Street rivals become allies', *The Wall Street Journal*, Eastern edn, New York, **238**(59), C1.

Rawls, John (1971), *A Theory of Justice*, Cambridge, MA: Harvard University Press.

Ring, P.S. and A.H. Van de Ven (1992), 'Structuring cooperative relationships between organizations', *Strategic Management Journal*, **13**, 483–98.

Rousseau, D.M.S., B. Sitkin, R. Burt and C. Camerer (1998), 'Not so different after all: A cross-discipline view of trust', *Academy of Management Review*, **23**(3), 393–404.

Smith, A. (1981), *An Enquiry into the Nature and Causes of the Wealth of Nations*, Indianapolis IN: Liberty Classics.

Smith, K., S. Carroll and S. Ashford (1995), 'Intra- and interorganizational cooperation: Towards a research agenda', *Academy of Management Journal*, **38**(1), 7–23.

Wicks, A.C., S.L. Berman and T.M. Jones (1999), 'The structure of optimal trust: Moral and strategic implications', *Academy of Management Review*, **24**(1), 99–116.

18 Trust and markets
Jens Beckert[1]

Markets are the core institution of capitalism. Without markets, no system of division of labor, even remotely as sophisticated as the one established today, could have developed. Without markets, no system of competition could have emerged that enforces the efficient production of goods and provision of services. Without markets, the distribution of material resources would need to be regulated by non-economic criteria.

While these consequences of market exchange have been widely acknowledged, it is much less well understood under what conditions markets can come into existence and thrive. One precondition is the supply of products that are in demand. Moreover, markets need at least some institutional safeguards that protect sellers and buyers from fraud, violence and free-riding. Economic sociologists (Granovetter 1985; Fligstein 2001) and institutional economists (Williamson 1975) have explored the institutional preconditions of markets in recent years, including the roles of state regulation, hierarchical organization, social networks and culturally anchored scripts and routines.

In this chapter I argue that the availability of exchangeable products and institutional provisions is a necessary but insufficient condition for the existence of markets. A further constitutive element of most markets is trust between the exchange partners. By trust I refer to each exchange partner's expectation[2] that his one-sided advance concession in a transaction will not be exploited by the other person through defection, although defection would generate extra profit for him.

Although trust (and mistrust) is a universal aspect of social relations, it only becomes an analytically important issue for market exchange under specific conditions. If the assumptions of standard microeconomic theory with respect to perfect information hold true, trust does not play a role in markets. All market participants have the relevant information regarding the characteristics of the product and know the intentions of their exchange partners. If these conditions, however, are not met; that is, if information regarding the product or service to be exchanged is incomplete and asymmetrically distributed, trust plays a crucial role in the prevention of market failure. The problems emerging from incomplete and asymmetrically distributed information have been analyzed in the economics of information and in game theory under such headings as the principal–agent problem, incomplete contracts, moral hazard and adverse selection (Arrow 1985; Stiglitz 1987). In sociology they are discussed based on the notion of double contingency (Parsons 1951; Ganßmann 2006).

Asymmetrical information gives rise to possibilities of strategic agency that is detrimental to the interests of one party in the exchange. The prevention of market failure demands that the party running the risk of being exploited can be convinced that the other party will not make use of this strategic option. Agency theory and game theory concentrate on changes in the incentive structure of the potential defector through hostages, credible commitments or monitoring. These institutional devices introduce a basis that eliminates defection as a rational strategy. While they undoubtedly play an important role in the integration of markets under conditions of asymmetrically distributed information and uncertainty, it is my contention in this chapter that they remain incomplete solutions to the problems at stake.

I claim instead that institutional safeguards only partially explain why market participants trust each other. In addition, we should pay special attention to the actions of the trust-taker that create an impression of trustworthiness. The way that trust functions is revealed in the study of the performative acts of the trust-taker, with which he tries to produce the appearance of trustworthiness and through which the trust-giver is motivated to his one-sided advance concession. Here, 'performative' implies the creation of an appearance of trustworthiness, through acts of self-presentation with which the trust-giver tries to persuade the trust-taker of the sincerity of his intention to cooperate. In terms of theory, it is only by emphasizing the performative act of the trust-taker's self-presentation that we can take a crucial characteristic of trust seriously; it is lost in those conceptions that stress institutions as a basis of trust relations. Trust can only be discussed meaningfully when it is not possible for the actors either to exclude the risk of exploitation or to calculate objective probabilities.

In what follows, I shall first critically discuss the different modes of explanation for the development of trust in markets provided by the literature on the subject. In the subsequent section, I shall develop a conception of trust that focuses on the self-presentation of the trust-taker. In the last part, I shall analyze the situational assumptions under which the self-presentations of the trust-taker obtain significance for market stabilization and discuss four strategies of performative production for the appearance of trustworthiness.

1.   Explanations of trust in market exchange

The existing literature on trust in economic exchange indicates that trusting behavior does not flow freely between individuals – this would be blind trust – but depends on social structural, institutional and cognitive preconditions that facilitate trust. Based on a review of trust research, six such 'facilitators' can be distinguished: tradition (Williams 1988; Fukuyama 1995), identity (Lewicki and Bunker 1996, 122ff.), power (Williamson 1975), norms (Parsons 1951; Weber 1958), institutions (Coleman 1990; Zucker 1986; Parsons 1951; Garfinkel 1963) and calculation (Dasgupta 1988; Kreps et al. 1982; Kreps 1990; Raub and Weesie 2000; Williamson 1993).[3] Researchers tend to view one of these facilitators or a combination of several of them as the answer to the puzzle why actors are willing to trust in market exchange.

Although these mechanisms do undoubtedly play an important role in market relations by contributing to the formation of reciprocal expectations, I contend that they don't yet do justice to the problem of trust facing market actors. They don't sufficiently take into consideration the contingencies that the trust-giver is exposed to due to the unforeseeable choices of the trust-taker. Theoretically and empirically, it seems implausible that the contingency of the trust-taker's behavior can in fact be fully reduced by the mechanisms cited.

That actors are so deeply ingrained in tradition that defection is not even considered as an option is an unrealistic assumption for modern societies and for most traditional societies as well. The same holds true for identity, that is, the precise mutual knowledge of the way the partners act.[4] Power and norms can be understood as a transformation of the dominant strategy so that the trust-taker chooses cooperation. Through this reinterpretation, however, the actual problem of trust in markets disappears. Moreover, despite social norms and hierarchical power structures, a violation of the norms by the trust-giver always remains a possibility. The reference to institutions is at least incomplete because, on the one hand, institutions cannot be instructive (or prescriptive) enough to set action guidelines for all contingencies; and on the other hand, institutions are controversial as distribution mechanisms for scarce resources, so there is no incentive for all actors to behave according to given expectations (Offe 1999, 65ff.). Also, with regard to the calculation of the exchange partner's intentions, it holds true for many exchange situations that, even with all attempts at calculation, a final doubt cannot be removed. If, however, we can calculate the exchange partner's choices, trust – as emphasized by Oliver Williamson (1993) – becomes a superfluous category.

Decision making under conditions of uncertainty with regard to the intentions of the exchange partner and incomplete contracts become ever more important in modern societies. Market relations in modern societies demand that risky advance concessions must be made without precise knowledge about the exchange partner, without relying on long-term relations, and despite only incomplete observation of his interaction with others. They must also be made in situations that are not extensively guaranteed by power or norms. The core of the problem of trust consists precisely in this 'middle condition between knowing and not-knowing' (Simmel 1992, 393), even when institutions, social norms, power and calculation of interest contribute to forming expectations. In consequence, a different conceptualization of the problem of trust in market relations is needed.

2.   The role of the trust-taker

The missing component in the discussed solutions to the trust problem consists of the turn to the performative acts of self-presentation by the trust-taker, which help in producing the willingness to trust in the situation itself. The focus on performative acts of the trust-taker demands an important shift in emphasis. Most research on trust brings the trust-giver to the center. This finds its justification in the intuitively offered interpretation of the sequence of games of trust, that is, that the trust-giver must be the initiator of the interaction, and the response of the trust-taker is only attached to it. There is, however, ample reason to focus on the trust-taker instead, as can be seen from Figure 18.1.

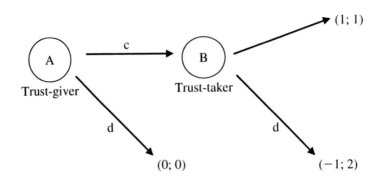

Source: Based on Dasgupta (1988).

Figure 18.1   The basic trust game

If the pay-offs of trust-taker and trust-giver are observed, it turns out that the trust-giver must be much more ambivalent toward the trust game than the trust-taker. The trust-giver can achieve a positive pay-off, but he also accepts the risk of exploitation, thus a negative pay-off. Not to get into the game of trust brings a neutral pay-off for him. The trust-taker, on the other hand, has a positive pay-off in any case, if only the advance concession of the trust-giver is achieved. Therefore, the trust-taker always has an interest in entering the trust game, independent of the intention of defection or cooperation.

Moreover, if the scope of action of trust-giver and trust-taker is considered, another difference emerges, which attracts interest to the trust-taker. The trust-giver is essentially confronted with the binary decision to accept the risk of defection or not; this depends on the estimation of the trustworthiness of the trust-taker, his own tendency for risk, and the potential loss in case of exploitation (Köszegi 2000, 6ff.). The actions of the trust-taker, on the other hand, aim at the production of trustworthiness. This not only opens a broad spectrum of possibilities of action that can achieve this goal, but these actions also sequentially precede the advance concession of the trust-giver. The advance concession of the trust-giver results from the production of the impression of trustworthiness by the trust-taker.

These two points have far-reaching consequences for understanding trust in market relations. That is, the focus now shifts to the contingent actions of the trust-taker, who has an unambiguous interest in the materialization of the exchange on the one hand, and on the other produces or at least can influence the trust-giver's advance concession with his own actions. Assuming that the trust-taker is aware of this central position in trust games, one can hypothesize that such games are primarily initiated by the trust-taker. Hence research on trust should orient its interest to the question of which repertoire of action evokes the impression of trustworthiness. This modified perspective on the structure of the trust game can be seen in Figure 18.2. Before the advance concession of the trust-giver is achieved, his willingness to trust has to be produced, for which the trust-taker must make an investment (α). This investment must be less expensive than the possible gain from a subsequent cooperative strategy, because otherwise the trust-taker would show an intention to defect. In case the game is terminated by the trust-giver, he has either a positive pay-off from obtained information – which must in any case be less than the utility

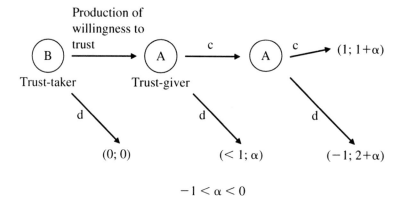

Figure 18.2   The trust-taker as initiator of the trust game

of further cooperation (<1) – or a loss.[5] In the next move, the game corresponds with the normal game of trust, except that the investments (α) for the production of willingness to trust have to be deducted from the trust-taker's pay-off.

3.   The impression of trustworthiness

An excellent starting point for the discussion of the creation of the impression of trustworthiness in markets by the trust-taker is the work by Michael Bacharach and Diego Gambetta on 'Trust in Signs' (2001). Bacharach and Gambetta study trust from a fundamental observation: it is not possible for the trust-giver to know whether the trust-taker does in fact have qualities of trustworthiness. These would be qualities such as honesty or good nature. All the trust-giver can perceive are signs in the behavior of the trust-taker, from which he draws conclusions about his actual trustworthiness. Such signs can be biological indications such as race, age, or skin color; but also concern clothing, body language, verbal expression, investments, or corporate logos. For this observation, Bacharach and Gambetta introduce the distinction between *krypta* and *manifesta*. *Krypta* stands for the actual qualities of the person, *manifesta* for the observed signals that form the empirical basis from which the trust-giver makes the decision for the first move in the trust game.

Without going into details of the very differentiated argumentation of the two authors, their observations allow us to see four central aspects of trust games, which are either not considered in the conceptions of the problem of trust cited above or are regarded only in a limited way.

1.   Attention shifts to the actions of the trust-taker, with which he sends signals of trustworthiness to the trust-giver and thus tries to provoke his advance concession. The sequence of games of trust starts with the trust-taker.
2.   To attain trust, the trust-taker must communicate signs that are interpreted by the trust-giver as signals of trustworthiness. Therefore, it is not enough for the trust-taker to have trustworthy qualities and intentions – for example, to be honest – but these must also be observable by the trust-giver in the form of visible signs. 'The deliberate use of signs, or signaling is a fundamental part of making oneself appear trustworthy' (Bacharach and Gambetta 2001, 155).
3.   The decision of the trust-giver to trust is seen as being based in the action situation itself. In the concrete decision-making situation, the trust-taker must communicate such *manifesta* to the trust-giver that convince him of his trustworthiness.
4.   The trust-giver cannot know whether the *manifesta* communicated by the trust-taker do in fact express the intention of trustworthy action. It is possible that the trust-taker communicates the signs with the deliberate intention to deceive the trust-giver in order to gain the pay-off from defection. It is possible to fake the existence of trustworthy qualities (*krypta*) with *manifesta*.

Bacharach and Gambetta (2001) link the conception of *krypta* and *manifesta* with the theory of signaling developed by Michael Spence (1973). Spence argued in the 1970s that signals could contain information relevant to decision making only when it is cheaper for the person who in fact has the signaled *krypta* to produce the signals than for the person who does not have the *krypta*.[6] An example of that are the signals studied by Spence for identifying good employees in the labor market. Important signals of job-seekers are school or university diplomas. But diplomas can be considered a differentiating signal only when it is easier for good employees to achieve the diploma than for bad employees. Otherwise, the diploma would contain no information about the quality of the employee and would be unsuitable as a criterion for selection.

By linking their conception of trust with the theory of signaling, Bacharach and Gambetta (2001, 158) describe the decision making of the trust-giver as at least bound-edly rational.[7] At least in some signals, the link between *krypta* and *manifesta* is not completely arbitrary (because of different costs linked with the production of *manifesta* for persons who have the *krypta* and those who do not), and signals with these qualities are consulted primarily by the trust-giver for the decision to be drawn into a one-sided advance concession.[8]

However, it is precisely this assumption, which is essential for the conceptualization of signals in game theory, that seems problematic for several reasons, requiring a much looser conceptualization of the relationship between *krypta* and *manifesta*. A first reason for this is empirical rather than theoretical, and can be seen in the increasing diversity of signals in modern economic structures, evoked by the pluralization of institutions, organizations and products, biographical options, cultural lifestyles and the internationalization of market relations. As a result, actors are confronted with such a plethora of signals as well as the rapid emergence of new signals that, because of limited cognitive capacities, their rational interpretation becomes increasingly difficult and improbable.

Second, the trust-takers can be assumed to be increasingly aware of the significance of the communication of *manifesta* for their success in motivating trust-givers to cooperate with them. This leads to the increase of investments in the production of *manifesta*. For the trust-giver, this means being confronted with an inflation of signals, which are increasingly less capable of being differentiated (see Offe 1999, 64f.). The problem of the relationship of signals and *krypta* is also discussed by Dasgupta (1988, 63–4), who pointed to the following possibility (contradicting Spence's assumption): the trust-taker who does not have trustworthy *krypta* may be in the situation of carrying out higher investments in the production of signs of trustworthiness than the honest transaction partner. This gives rise to a pooling equilibrium whereby the trust-giver cannot correctly judge the actual trustworthiness of the trust-taker from the signals that should indicate trustworthiness. It is not clear to the trust-giver whether the trust-taker is honest or dishonest.

Moreover, it is not only the trust-taker who is aware of the significance of signals to obtain trustworthiness. The trust-giver is also aware of the possibility of manipulating signals. This awareness is intensified by the media, which publish examples of the abuse of trust, hence making accessible disappointing experiences of other trust-givers beyond personal experience. As a result, the trust-giver inspects signals suspiciously and the production of the appearance of trustworthiness constantly demands ever more polished strategies.

As a consequence, the modeling of trust games based on game theory is theoretically problematic in assuming the possibility of rational interpretation of signals. Such games do not do justice to the fundamental uncertainty of the trust-giver, which also composes the core of any meaningful talk of trust. But what happens when only uncertain conclusions can be drawn from the *manifesta* with regard to the *krypta*? It follows initially that the trust of the trust-giver can easily be shaken. If no clear conclusions can be drawn from the signals for the trust-taker's intentions, a demoralizing oscillation of interpretation can result, the player will feel at one moment that he is being oversuspicious and should take the other at face value or, at worst, as someone who employs usual covers and, at the next, that a trap has been set for him. At one moment, he can feel that he has finally hit upon indicators that can't be faked, and the next moment, he can feel that this is exactly how the opponent wants him to accept these indications. (Goffman 1969, 69)

If this situation of double contingency is not to lead to a paralysis of action, in which every advantage of cooperative action is lost in advance, then despite the trust-giver's inevitable uncertainty, the view that the trust-taker will not exploit him must prevail. William James summarized this attitude of the trust-giver as the 'will to believe': 'Wherever a desired result is achieved by the co-operation of many independent persons, its existence as a fact is a pure consequence of the precursive faith in one another of those immediately concerned' (James 1897, 22). Trust can be described as the social mechanism that expresses the shutdown of the latent uncertainty of the trust-giver; trust works as a tranquilizer in social relations, enabling the trust-giver to remain calm despite the uncontrollable freedom of action of the trust-taker.

4. Trust and dramaturgic action

Yet the question of how trust-givers are convinced that their advance concession will not be exploited is not yet resolved. The rejection of an explanation of the trust-giver's willingness to trust based on rational calculation does not mean that the actors would not seek inferences (Thomas 1951) that assure them if they decide on the risky advance concession.[9] Trust-givers are usually not willing to attribute the results of their decisions simply to accident. It is my contention that an innovative way of explaining the assurance of the trust-giver lies with the trust-taker's performative acts of self-presentation, which are to convince the trust-giver of the credibility of the *manifesta*.

Anchoring trust in the performative acts of the trust-taker has already been discussed by Niklas Luhmann (1968, 37ff.), who sees trust based in the confidence of self-presentation. This idea is also considered in Anthony Giddens's discussions on trust. Giddens (1994, 187ff.) introduced the term of active trust to express the notion that modern societies are increasingly dependent on the discursive and dialogic engagement of potentially conflicting actors. Trust in abstract 'expert systems' (Giddens), the characteristic trust-takers for modern societies, demands the personal communication of trustworthiness at access points where the nexus of system and person takes place.[10]

Building on these works, Harald Wenzel (2001) developed a conception of trust that starts with the performative acts of the interacting agents and their definitions of the situation. Wenzel analyzes trust as a form of 'para-social interaction', in which, through the advance concession of the trust-giver, a successful game of trust is faked, yet is in fact produced only with the action of the trust-taker – through the fulfillment of trust. For this to happen, the trust-taker has to succeed in convincing the trust-giver of a definition of the situation that interprets it as cooperative; that is, he has to convince him of his trustworthiness. This 'enticement' of trust depends essentially on the trust-taker's performative self-presentation.

Like Giddens and Luhmann, Wenzel also refers to the concept of dramaturgic action introduced in the 1950s by Erving Goffman (1959). Goffman developed this term in analogy to the theater, where the actor on the stage has to give a credible expression to the character he embodies to the audience. This situation is considered paradigmatic for social interactions in which the actor tries to convey a certain impression of his character or his intentions (his *krypta!*) with the dramaturgical means of self-presentation. The projection of the self must produce the impression of authenticity – that is, the impression of the identity of *krypta* and *manifesta* – and represents the basis on which the trust-giver estimates the trustworthiness of the trust-taker. In the process, the trust-taker tries to produce the impression of trustworthiness, but the trust-giver decides on the actual trustworthiness of his behavior.

Various presumptions can be listed to realize the impression of trustworthiness. Luhmann (1968, 40) has already indicated that, in his performance of self-presentation, the trust-taker must deal with the expectations of the trust-giver in order to entice trust. Thus it requires an empathetic attitude of the trust-taker. It can also be assumed that the trust-giver's willingness to trust is oriented toward socially legitimated ways of action because, in case of damages by the trust-taker, the action can be justified in a face-saving way with regard to a third party: 'You would have acted the same way in my place!' In this sense, we can speak of a socially constructed fiction of trust. Moreover, Luhmann and Giddens indicate that presentations 'on stage' must express a confident control of the situation. This applies to the cheerfulness of flight attendants as well as to the confidence expressed by financial consultants about the future prices of the stocks just recommended for investment. These acts aim at assuring the trust-giver.

The concept of dramaturgic action emphasizes not only the decisive role of the trust-taker, but also offers an explanation for trust between actors who have no common history and therefore have to produce the appearance of trustworthiness in the situation. However, since the basis for the trust-giver's decision making is not in rational calculation, because self-presentation contains no unambiguous sign for trustworthiness, ultimately, for the trust-giver, it requires William James's 'will to believe' to realize the cooperative exchange. 'There are, then, cases where a fact cannot come at all unless a preliminary faith exists in its coming. And where faith in a fact can help create the fact' (James 1897, 25). It is in this deliberate act that the creative element of trust exists.

Going beyond Goffman, for Wenzel, self-presentations not only have the function of producing the impression of trustworthiness, but they also offer a common definition of the situation that prejudices the trust-giver's action. That is, the opening of the trust game leads to the moves of a gambit 'in which those involved gradually drift together finally to make the common action program irretrievably successful' (Wenzel 2001, 373). This can be illustrated by the implicit obligation to buy that one feels as a customer in a store, especially after a detailed consultation by a sales person. The performance of the sales person signals his/her expectation that there will be a purchase, and often the customer can resist this definition of the situation only against internal resistances. This is expressed in such sentences as, 'I'll think about it and come back', instead of a clear no. The explanation for this structuring effect of the first move, *pace* Harold Garfinkel (1963), is that actors normally take pains in social interactions to maintain at least the appearance of a smooth continuity in interaction.[11] We know that the trust-taker expects the one-sided advance concession from us. This expectation is also part of the definition of the situation. To violate it demands overcoming cognitive (or normative) resistances.[12]

5. The performative construction of markets

How can these considerations be applied to the question of the functioning of markets? The sociological conceptualization of markets sets out from a specific observation: market exchange depends not only on technology, institutional safeguards and an agreement between the exchange partners on the price of the goods to be exchanged. Instead, the presumptions of the willingness to engage in one-sided advance concessions in view of incomplete and asymmetrically distributed information are also problematic. Along with the economic problem of price, the social problem of the possibility of opportunistic behavior of the exchange partner must be resolved. The uncertainty with regard to the intentions of the alter ego makes markets precarious social structures that will implode when the willingness to trust is withdrawn. One central entrepreneurial function consists of the production and maintenance of the willingness for cooperation in view of the ineluctable freedom of the actors to behave opportunistically. While the sociology of markets in past years has referred especially to the significance of social networks (Burt 1992; Granovetter 1985, 2003; White 1981, 2002) and institutions (Fligstein 1996, 2001) for the solution of this problem, the performative commitment of the trust-taker has been widely overlooked. Thus, a significant aspect of the practice of markets has been omitted. Generating the appearance of trustworthiness by performative self-presentation is necessary in markets characterized by the following three features:

1. *Uncertainty with regard to the qualities of the goods (or services) to be exchanged* because of an asymmetrical distribution of information between principal (trust-giver) and agent (trust-taker). This is the case with products or services whose quality and value can be judged only imperfectly by the trust-giver. In this situation, the trust-giver is at the mercy of the claims of the trust-taker. The used car market (Akerlof 1970) is a relevant example, but many other transactions can also be cited – buying insurance, booking a vacation trip, or hiring an employee.
2. *Competition between the agents.* Because of the availability of rival and substitute products, trust-givers can choose between various trust-takers. The availability of many options for the trust-giver increases the uncertainty of whether the exchange with another agent would not be more advantageous. Because of limited cognitive capacity, this complexity can be reduced partially at most by the escalation of information. Trust is instead referred to in its function as a mechanism of tranquilizing which makes it bearable for the trust-giver to get involved with the trust-taker without having complete information. However, the result is also that there is an increasing competition for trust between the trust-takers, which appears in the escalation of such performative acts that aim at producing and maintaining the impression of trustworthiness and the commitment of the trust-giver.
3. *Short-term exchange relations.* If non-iterative games of trust increase (Wenzel 2001, 340ff.; Ziegler 1998, 427), in which tradition and identity lose significance for integrating exchange relations, the judgment of trustworthiness may rely more on signals partly produced in the situation.[13]

6.   Strategies of self-presentation in market relations

If these structural conditions prevail, what performative strategies can trust-takers use to achieve the integration of exchange relations? Four strategies of self-presentation for the production of the appearance of trustworthiness in market relations can be distinguished analytically.[14] On the one hand, the strategies aim at committing the trust-giver by increasing the (cognitive) cost of withdrawing from the relationship, and on the other at reducing the trust-giver's perceived risk of becoming the victim of exploitation. This succeeds to the extent that the trust-taker can convince the trust-giver that the actual *krypta* coincide with the communicated *manifesta*.

Commitment

In the strategy of commitment, the trust-taker intends to produce trustworthiness by erecting cognitive or normative barriers to withdrawal. Wenzel (2001) called this strategy a gambit. Examples of it are the visit of an insurance agent to the customer's home with which the trust-taker makes an advance investment. Like the exchange of gifts, these investments contain the expectation of reciprocity, which is to be fulfilled by the trust-giver with his advance concession. The strategy of commitment does not aim at reducing the trust-giver's perceived risk, but rather at erecting barriers to the termination of the interaction. The trust-taker's investment exercises a subliminal compulsion because it itself represents an advance concession, to which the norm of not disappointing trust applies (Luhmann 1968, 41). This explains the possible negative pay-off for both partners shown in Figure 18.2 (page 321), when the trust-giver's advance concession does not occur: while the trust-taker must make at least a small investment for the trust-giver's commitment, cognitive and normative costs of withdrawal may emerge for the trust-giver.

Congruence of expectation

In this strategy, the trust-taker uses the communication of signs to suggest a congruence of his qualities, ways of acting, and values with the expectations of the trust-giver. The suggested correspondence aims at evoking the judgment on the side of the trust-giver that he can indeed correctly interpret the signals sent by the trust-taker. Max Weber's (1958) discussion of 'strategic membership' of businessmen in certain churches or clubs in the USA, which aims at achieving trustworthiness in business dealings, is a classical example of the performative signaling of congruence. Empirical studies show that similarities of status, behavior and lifestyle of the trust-taker correlate with a higher trustworthiness (Plötner 1995, 156; Zucker 1986, 70ff.). The strategy is used not only in the relationship between customer and supplier, but also in job interviews, and in marketing aimed at differentiated target groups. 'Rituals of expectation congruence' are found in market relations in the communication of lifestyle, clothing, speech, national or ethnic affiliation, membership and so on.

Competence

By signaling competence, the trust-taker places himself 'between' the trust-giver and a situation perceived as uncontrollable by the trust-taker. Thus the trustworthiness of the trust-taker emerges by conveying the impression of control of the situation, which gives the trust-giver the impression of being in good hands. Typically, this strategy is found at points of access to expert systems, such as courts (attorneys), banks (financial advisers), hospitals (physicians), or transportation systems (pilots, flight attendants). Competence as a strategy of self-presentation by the trust-taker is to be expected in markets with information asymmetry, in which the trust-taker's ability matters. Maintaining the impression of competence makes the separation between performances 'on stage' and the activity 'backstage' necessary (Goffman 1959) to conceal any lack of professional control and human fallibility. The more convincingly the trust-taker conveys the impression of competence, the lower does the trust-giver perceive the risk involved in the situation. This is equivalent to the increase of trust in the trust-taker (Das and Teng 2001, 257–8).

Integrity
The strategy of integrity is closely connected with the strategy of competence, except that in the situation it is not the ability of the trust-taker that matters, but rather his authenticity, that is, the impression of an identity of *krypta* and *manifesta*. The communication of authenticity by the trust-taker changes the trust-giver's estimate of risk by diverting from the possibility of the trust-taker's insincere intentions of action. Current examples are the advertising campaigns for new issues of stocks (initial public offerings – IPOs) which aim not at explaining the economic indices of the enterprise, but rather at reassuring investors in view of the uncertain prospects of their investment. Thus, in Germany, show stars were used as actors in advertising campaigns for IPOs. Their perceived trustworthiness is transferred to the stocks of the enterprise offered. Because these actors have achieved a reputation, though in a completely different context, they are perceived as honest brokers, whose own willingness to invest is considered proof of the trustworthiness of the enterprise. Another example is the political stabilization of the agricultural market by the consumption of beef by leading European politicians in public, accompanied by the media, at the height of the mad cow disease crisis during the late 1990s. Here the authenticity of the statement of the harmlessness of consuming beef is made credible by a voluntary experiment on oneself.[15]

These four strategies of performative self-presentation aim at producing the appearance of trustworthiness, on the one hand, by 'drawing' the trust-taker into the situation (commitment), and on the other, by minimizing the risk perceived by the trust-giver of his one-sided advance concession. Thus the trust-giver's willingness to trust is also developed in the exchange situation itself. Even if, as shown earlier, the meaning of the trust-taker's self-presentation depends on the structure of the market situation, and willingness to trust cannot be constructed only on self-presentations, the establishment of perceptions of trustworthiness through signaling has thus far been an underestimated element of the stabilization of market relations. The issue here is not a theory of manipulation of the trust-giver, but rather the question of mobilizing the willingness to cooperate under conditions of uncertainty. In this sense, we can speak of the performative construction of markets.

7. Conclusion
This chapter develops an understanding of trust in market relations that brings the performative acts of trust-takers to center stage. It proceeds from a critique of the dominant analysis of trust games and the role of tradition, identity, power/control, institutions, calculation, and reputation for explaining trust. These considerations of trust are based too strongly on the possibility of control or the calculation of the actions of the trust-taker and thus do not do justice to the central quality of trust. This consists of the ineluctable uncertainty with regard to the action of the trust-taker. The idea of studying trust in market relations proposed here starts from the systematic examination of the structure of trust games, and thus shows the significant role of the trust-taker, which can be illuminated theoretically by the distinction between *krypta* and *manifesta* introduced by Bacharach and Gambetta (2001). With the arguments of incomplete information and asymmetrical distribution of information and the only equivocal conclusion of

underlying *krypta* from *manifesta*, I have, however, objected to the rational explanation of appearance of trustworthiness that Bacharach and Gambetta (2001) strive to achieve. Instead, willingness to trust and trust are understood much more strongly as contingent results of performative acts, which are not linked unambiguously with the intentions (*krypta*) of the trust-taker. The issue is not a theory of manipulation of the trust-giver, but rather the necessary reassurance of the trust-giver. The appearance of trustworthiness must be reached in the situation, in light of the trust-giver's knowledge of the contingency of the trust-taker's action. Only if successful will the trust-giver agree to provide the one-sided advance concessions.

The significance of institutions, norms, long-term relations and calculation to explain overcoming possible barriers to exchange is not to be challenged in any case. Trust in markets does depend on these mechanisms of market integration. However, trust cannot be reduced to them. The operation of these mechanisms themselves cannot be understood independently of the performative production of the willingness to trust. Only if I convince my exchange partner that I will live up to a specific norm, that I see the relationship as long term and that the purchase is indeed a sound decision can market exchanges be successfully completed. The creation of these beliefs is, however, accomplished in the situation. This is because the uncertainty entailed in the exchange cannot in fact be eliminated. All that actors can do is to reassure each other in their mutual intentions. Uncertainty remains irreducible in the market and is converted to certainty only through the completion of the transaction.

Notes

1. This chapter is based on my paper 'Vertrauen und die performative Konstruktion von Märkten' (2002). Parts of the chapter have been translated by Barbara Harshav.
2. In this chapter, 'expectation' refers to the beliefs an actor holds with regard to future actions of another person.
3. For a detailed discussion see Beckert (2002b).
4. See Giddens (1990), 33. However, it is possible to think of an explanation that does not accept the complete elimination of risk and thus is more appropriate to the problem of trust. Identification processes are achieved in iterative relations, but the trust-giver must also consider the possibility of exploitation by the trust-taker, since identification between two subjects can never be complete.
5. The result of the negative pay-offs for *both* actors in case the relationship is terminated before it achieves the advance concession of the trust-giver is discussed in Section 5.
6. As Bacharach and Gambetta (2001, 168) put it in direct reference to Spence, 'The main result of signaling theory implies that a manifestum m is secure against mimicry if and only if it is cheap enough for a k [*krypta*] to display and too expensive for an opportunist to display.'
7. Bacharach and Gambetta (2001, 174) discuss in great detail the possibilities of mimicry of signals and make no strict correlation between *krypta* and *manifesta*. But ultimately their theory aims at a *rational* explanation of trust, for which they have to maintain the assumption of the correlation between *krypta* and *manifesta*. To decide this is, ultimately, also an empirical question.
8. See also Raub and Weesie (2000) for the link between signaling theory and trust. Raub and Weesie develop a theory of how the trust-taker in a non-iterative game can motivate the trust-giver to the advance concession by a voluntarily produced hostage. Also for them, this hostage can be a reliable signal for the trust-giver only when the cost of signaling for the honest and dishonest trust-taker are different.
9. As Thomas puts it (1951, 5), 'It is also highly important for us to realize that we do not as a matter of fact lead our lives, make our decisions, and reach our goals in everyday life either statistically or scientifically. We live by inference. I am, let us say, your guest. You do not know, you cannot determine scientifically, that I will not steal your money or your spoons. But inferentially I will not, and inferentially you have me as your guest.' For the limits of the economic concept of calculation for understanding trust, see the excellent discussion of Möllering (2001), which relies primarily on Simmel, Luhmann and Giddens.
10. See Beckert (2002a), 263ff.

11. This may explain Köszegi's experimental observation (2000, 45) why trust-givers, after being exploited by a trust-taker, are still willing to cooperate with him. The trust-giver continues to define the situation as a cooperative game and tries to adhere to it despite the experience of disappointment.

12. In this respect, trust clearly accords with the gift exchange in which the first gift leads to a cycle of reciprocity, which creates its own assumptions. I am grateful to Axel Paul for this point.

13. Since the trust-taker's freedom of action also exists in the next round of the game of trust, it holds for trustworthiness, as it does for tranquilizers, that it must be 'taken' (communicated) again and again in order to maintain the effect. Trustworthy behavior is itself one form of the communication of trustworthiness. Thus Hirschman (1986, 142ff.) can describe trust as a good that increases with use.

14. The strategies may appear simultaneously.

15. The second example indicates that the strategy of integrity can be linked with the concept of credible commitments. Here, however, the guarantees and self-obligations offered by the trust-taker are not viewed from the point of view of rational calculation of costs, but rather in their *function as symbols* for the trust-giver. An example of this is the warranty for a used car, mentioned earlier. The significance of the warranty in the purchase seems initially to be that the risk to the trust-giver of his one-sided advance concession is removed, which changes the pay-off matrix represented in Figure 18.1 so that no negative pay-off for the trust-giver can emerge even if the trust-taker chooses to defect. This changed pay-off matrix increases the trust-giver's willingness and interest in a one-sided advance concession. This reading, however, is not precise. In fact, no one would buy a used car that can be assumed to lack the promised qualities, only because it is known that these qualities must later be provided by the seller at his own cost. The reason for this is that the material and emotional costs (e.g. in a legal debate) connected with it in fact do not lead to a full compensation, but can easily cause costs beyond the utility from the deal. Therefore, it seems important to interpret such guarantees also as a *signal* for authenticity. Thus, they help increase the trust-giver's willingness to trust; however, they do not allow unambiguous conclusions of the actual intentions of the trust-taker and do not necessarily change the pay-off matrix in the above mentioned way.

References

Akerlof, Georg A. (1970), 'The market for "lemons": Quality uncertainty and the market mechanism', *Quarterly Journal of Economics* **84**, 488–500.

Arrow, Kenneth J. (1985), 'The economics of agency', in J.W. Pratt and R.J. Zeckhauser (eds), *Principals and Agents. The Structure of Business*. Boston, MA: Harvard Business School Press, pp. 37–51.

Bacharach, Michael and Diego Gambetta (2001), 'Trust in signs', in K. Cook (ed.), *Trust in Society*, New York: Russell Sage, pp. 148–84.

Beckert, Jens (2002a), *Beyond the Market. The Social Foundations of Economic Efficiency*, Princeton, NJ: Princeton University Press.

Beckert, Jens (2002b), 'Vertrauen und die performative Konstruktion von Märkten', *Zeitschrift für Soziologie* **31**, 27–43.

Burt, Ronald (1992), *Structural Holes. The Social Structure of Competition*, Cambridge, MA: Harvard University Press.

Coleman, James (1990), *Foundations of Social Theory*, Cambridge, MA: Harvard University Press.

Das, T.K. and Teng, B.-S. (2001), 'Trust, control and risk in strategic alliances: An integrated framework', *Organizational Studies* **22**, 251–83.

Dasgupta, Partha (1988), 'Trust as a commodity', in Diego Gambetta (ed.), *Trust. Making and Breaking Cooperative Relations*, New York: Blackwell, pp. 49–72.

Fligstein, Neil (1996), 'Markets as politics. A political cultural approach to market institutions', *American Sociological Review* **61**, 656–73.

Fligstein, Neil (2001), *The Architecture of Markets. An Economic Sociology of Twenty-First Century Capitalist Societies*, Princeton, NJ: Princeton University Press.

Fukuyama, Francis (1995), *Trust. The Social Virtues and the Creation of Prosperity*, London: Penguin.

Ganßmann, Heiner (2006), 'Double contingency', in Jens Beckert and Milan Zafirovski (eds), *The International Encyclopedia of Economic Sociology*, London: Routledge, pp. 147–50.

Garfinkel, Harold (1963), 'A conception of experiments with "trust" as a condition of stable concerted actions', in O.J. Harvey (ed.), *Motivation and Social Interaction*, New York: Ronald Press, pp. 187–238.

Giddens, Anthony (1990), *The Consequences of Modernity*, Cambridge: Cambridge University Press.

Giddens, Anthony (1994), 'Risk, trust, reflexivity', in U. Beck, A. Giddens and S. Lash (eds), *Reflexive Modernization*, Stanford, CA: Stanford University Press, pp. 184–97.

Goffman, Erving (1959), *The Presentation of Self in Everyday Life*, Harmondsworth, UK: Penguin.

Goffman, Erving (1969), *Strategic Interaction*, Philadelphia, PA: University of Pennsylvania Press.

Granovetter, Mark (1985), 'Economic action and social structure. The problem of embeddedness', *American Journal of Sociology* **91**, 481–510.

Granovetter, Mark (2003), 'A theoretical agenda for economic sociology', in Mauro F. Guillén, Randall Collins, Paula England and Marshall Meyer (eds), *The New Economic Sociology*, New York: Russell Sage, pp. 35–60.

Hirschman, Albert O. (1986), *Rival Views of Market Society*, New York: Viking.

James, William (1897), *The Will to Believe*, New York: Longmans Green.

Köszegi, Sabine (2000), 'The trust building process in virtual organisations: An experiment', Working Paper OP 2000–01, Vienna: University of Vienna.

Kreps, David M. (1990), 'Corporate culture and economic theory', in J.E. Alt and K.A. Shepsle (eds), *Perspectives on Positive Political Economy*, Cambridge: Cambridge University Press, pp. 90–143.

Kreps, David M., P. Milgrom, J. Roberts and R. Wilson (1982), 'Rational cooperation in the finitely repeated prisoners' dilemma', *Journal of Economic Theory*, 27, 245–52.

Lewicki, R.J. and B.B. Bunker (1996), 'Developing and maintaining trust in work relationships', in R.M. Kramer and T.R. Tyler (eds), *Trust in Organizations: Frontiers of Theory and Research*, Thousand Oaks, CA: Sage, pp. 114–39.

Luhmann, Niklas (1968), *Vertrauen. Ein Mechanismus der Reduktion sozialer Komplexität*, Stuttgart: Ferdinand Enke Verlag.

Möllering, Guido (2001), 'The nature of trust: From Georg Simmel to a theory of expectation, interpretation and suspension', *Sociology*, 35, 403–20.

Offe, Claus (1999), 'How can we trust our fellow citizens?', in M.E. Warren (ed.), *Democracy and Trust*, Cambridge: Cambridge University Press, pp. 42–87.

Parsons, Talcott (1951), *The Social System*, Glencoe, IL: Free Press.

Plötner, O. (1995), *Das Vertrauen des Kunden*, Wiesbaden: Gabler.

Raub, W. and J. Weesie (2000), 'Cooperation via hostages', *Analyse und Kritik*, 22, 19–43.

Simmel, Georg (1992), *Soziologie, Untersuchungen über die Formen der Vergesellschaftung*, Collected Works, 11, Frankfurt: Suhrkamp.

Spence, Michael (1973), 'Job market signaling', *Quarterly Journal of Economics*, 87, 355–74.

Stiglitz, Joseph E. (1987), 'Principal and agent', in J. Eatwell et al. (eds), *Allocation, Information and Markets* (The New Palgrave), New York: W.W. Norton, pp. 241–53.

Thomas, W.I. (1951), *Social Behavior and Personality: Contributions of W.I. Thomas to Theory and Social Research*, ed. E.H. Volkart, New York: Social Science Research Council.

Weber, Max (1958), *The Protestant Ethic and the Spirit of Capitalism*, New York: Scribner.

Wenzel, Harald (2001), *Die Abenteuer der Kommunikation. Echtzeitmedien und der Handlungsraum der Hochmoderne*, Weilerwist: Vellbrück.

White, Harrison (1981), 'Where do markets come from?', *American Journal of Sociology*, 87, 517–47.

White, Harrison (2002), *Markets from Networks*, Princeton, NJ: Princeton University Press.

Williams, B. (1988), 'Formal structures and social reality', in Gambetta Diego (ed.), *Trust: Making and Breaking Cooperative Relations*, New York: Basil Blackwell, pp. 2–13.

Williamson, Oliver (1975), *Markets and Hierarchies*, New York: Free Press.

Williamson, Oliver (1993), 'Calculativeness, trust, and economic organization', *Journal of Law and Economics*, 36, 453–86.

Ziegler, Rolf (1998), 'Trust and the reliability of expectations', *Rationality and Society*, 10, 427–50.

Zucker, Lynne G. (1986), 'Production of trust, institutional sources of economic structure, 1840–1920', in B.M. Staw and L.L. Cummings (eds), *Research in Organizational Behavior*, 8, 53–111.

19 The economics of trust

Mark Casson and Marina Della Giusta

1. Introduction

Trust is widely recognized as an important component of a just society. It is less widely appreciated that trust also makes an important contribution to the economy. Trust not only improves the general quality of life, but improves productivity and economic performance too. Trust is an intangible asset. It is an important part of the invisible infrastructure, or social capital, of an economy (Putnam, 1993). The economic analysis of trust can inform a wide range of issues, which extend way beyond the traditional boundaries of economics as a subject area.

This chapter presents an economic perspective on trust. It analyses trust from a rational action point of view, incorporating emotions into decision-making processes. It examines the costs and benefits of trust, and shows how they can be compared with each other. It distinguishes different forms of trust, and identifies the particular forms that normally confer the greatest benefit to the economy.

It is sometimes suggested that economics has little to say about trust because issues relating to trust are excluded from the neoclassical general equilibrium (GE) model. This criticism is valid as far as it goes. It must be recognized, however, that the assumptions of the GE model are very strict compared with those which are required for rational action theory. It is rational action theory, rather than GE theory, which is the basis for this chapter.

It is also useful to draw attention to a couple of misleading remarks about the economics of trust in Fukuyama's influential discussion (Fukuyama, 1995). His claim that economists have not attempted to model trust is clearly erroneous, as the literature cited in this chapter demonstrates. In addition, he ignores the crucial economic distinction between trust mediated by formal legal institutions and trust mediated by moral and social mechanisms, moving back and forth between different meanings of trust at different stages of his argument. This leads him to characterize the competitive and individualistic culture of the USA as high trust and to play down the levels of trust in less competitive and more organic societies.

The particular form of institutionalism that underpins the present chapter is one that regards economic institutions as coordinating mechanisms. Comparative institutional analysis shows that there are many alternative sets of institutional arrangements which can be used to coordinate the economy. These are associated with different configurations of government, firms, banks, clubs and social networks.[1] All these different arrangements can be classified using a relatively small number of dimensions. When consistently applied, the distinction between high-trust and low-trust institutional arrangements emerges as one of the most important of these dimensions. The rational action approach allows the performance of different sets of institutions to be compared under different conditions, thereby identifying the circumstances under which high-trust principles will generate the best economic performance.

2. Why an economic approach? The contribution of economics to the study of trust

2.1 The role of scarcity

Economics is concerned with scarcity. The allocation of scarce resources is often taken as the defining topic in economics. It is not always recognized, however, that without scarcity, trust would not be an issue. Resources would be so abundant that everyone would have access to everything they required to satisfy their own needs without recourse to other people's resources. There would be no need to assert rights to resources because no one else would want them, since everyone would have sufficient resources of their own. Obligation would therefore be unnecessary, because there would be no rights to respect. The relative propensity of other people to honour obligations would therefore be of no consequence.

In a world without scarcity many of the everyday evils of a low-trust society would be absent. There would be no need for aggression, because it would not be worth the effort to take another person's goods by force. Stealth would be pointless, and so would deceit. On the other hand, social life would lose much of its point. Group activity would add no value, teamwork would be unnecessary, and even communication would become pointless. Trust would disappear as an issue because interdependence would become unnecessary; for example, telling the truth would not be an issue if there was no need for communication.

In practice, scarcity comes in many forms. Even if material resources are abundant, some resources appear to people to be superior to others. This applies to objects, but also to locations, and even to other people as well. In a vast and fertile land, natural undulations give some land better views that others and make it favoured for residence. Some land is on the sunny side of a hill and other land on the shady side, giving a higher crop yield. People then compete to occupy the best land, and once this happens land that is on a hill and therefore more easily defended becomes very desirable, as the history of warfare confirms.

Sexual partners are also believed to be scarce: some people are regarded as more attractive than others, and so attract competing suitors. As aggression can pay off in deterring sexual competitors, so dishonesty can pay off in concealing one's own physical defects or limitations, people start to show off by acting fitter and stronger than they really are. Even if everyone were regarded as equally physically attractive, it is possible that other characteristics would confer on some people higher status. Status creates an artificial scarcity by establishing categories – such as 'winner' – which automatically exclude the majority of people. Once the pursuit of status begins, people may start to cheat in order to win the game, thereby eroding trust even where real inequality is not an issue (Veblen, 1894).

Trust is therefore indispensable for the efficient allocation of scarce resources: when resources are scarce, people have a strong incentive to promote their own interests at the expense of other people. If, however, they are able to take account of the impact of their actions on other people, they will gain a reputation for being trustworthy. This means in turn that there will generally be a high demand for trust. However, supplies of trust are limited by the presence of other values, such as aggression, so that the number of people at any time who are known to be morally committed may be relatively small. Trust is therefore a scarce commodity.

The scarcity of trust has three main implications:

- In order to make the best use of available resources, the responsibility for the most important activities should be concentrated on the most reputable people. Special roles emerge which carry great responsibility, and reputable people are appointed to them. These roles essentially involve coordinating the actions of other less reputable people.

- It is important to ensure that everyone who is trustworthy gains a good reputation, so that the number of reputable people is as large as possible, given the amount of trust in the economy. Conversely, untrustworthy people must not be allowed to gain a reputation. Social mechanisms must be developed which make reputations as accurate as possible.
- The supply of trust should be increased where possible. Although trust is scarce, and its supply is fixed in the short run, the supply can be increased in the long run by encouraging more people to be trustworthy. If a group has a leader, then the leader can promote a value system conducive to trust and encourage people to commit to it. While the promotion of values incurs a cost, the benefits are sufficiently great that this is usually a worthwhile activity.

2.2   How does trust help to coordinate economic activity?

The need for trust arises in a wide range of contexts: from the default on a loan by an individual or an institution, to the delivery of bad-quality goods, to the breaking of contractual promises between firms or of electoral promises by a government (Hirschman, 1970; Akerlof, 1970; Axelrod, 1984; Khalil, 2003). It is useful to examine the types of obligation that arise in the context of economic exchange, and the corresponding need for trust.

2.2.1   Volatility and respect for individual property

Whilst economists have correctly emphasized the ubiquitous nature of scarcity, they have until recently paid little attention to the equally important issue of volatility. This is because the simplest models of scarcity rely upon equilibrium, and equilibrium is disturbed by volatility. To consider the implications of volatility it is therefore necessary to relax the assumption of equilibrium and allow for a regular stream of shocks. These shocks create a continuing need for coordination in order to adjust the use of resources to the new conditions.

Volatility is generated both outside the system – for example, through changes in the weather – and inside the system – for example, through innovation. We focus on external volatility first and consider internal volatility later.

Shocks are often localized, and are therefore best addressed by people on the spot who have local knowledge. Thus the power of decision-making needs to be delegated to a local level in order to deal effectively with local shocks. But under a delegated system people need to know who is responsible for what decision. Otherwise anarchy will ensue: some people will try to take the same decision, while other decisions will be entirely neglected, in which the case the *status quo* will be perpetuated by default.

Delegation therefore requires an authority system which specifies who is responsible for each decision that needs to be made. This creates an obligation for people to respect the system. While people have a right to take the decisions that have been allocated to them, they have no right to meddle in other people's affairs. Indeed, they have an obligation to respect other people's autonomy.

It is often convenient for people to consume the product of the resources nearest to them, which suggests that people who manage local resources should also have the right to the product. This transforms managerial authority into ownership. The owner of the resource controls its utilization and also has a claim on the product.

This arrangement is often commended on the grounds that it gives the owner a direct incentive to manage his resources efficiently. This argument is predicated on the view that the owner is selfish and potentially devious, and would not make the effort to manage the resource efficiently if he were not entitled to the product.

Where ownership arrangements are adopted, the authority system allocates responsibilities through property rights. However, these rights are of no significance if other people fail to respect them. Hence an obligation is created to respect property rights.

2.2.2   Specialization and the division of labour: honouring contracts   While volatility explains the need for decentralized authority, it does not explain interdependence through trade. A prominent feature of advanced economies is their complexity, and much of this complexity derives from the pattern of trade, and the information flows required to support it.

Some people have a natural aptitude for certain tasks, or have acquired an aptitude through education or experience. Overall output in an economy is increased if each person specializes in the activities in which they have comparative advantage. The same principle applies to the resources, such as land, which they own. To maintain balance in their consumption while specializing in production they need to exchange their surplus production with other people, thereby generating trade.

Trade in products involves an exchange of property rights. Each trader derives their right to the product from their ownership of the resource, and they exchange this right for other rights in the products that they wish to consume. Trade exposes people to significant risks, because a product may be supplied before payment has been made, giving the buyer an incentive to cheat. Conversely, a seller may cheat a buyer by disguising the poor quality of the product. The obligation to respect other people's property is therefore extended to an obligation not to cheat on trade.

The system is further complicated by the fact that it often pays for people to work in teams. Specialists in the same activity may combine to share a large facility, while specialists in different activities may find that they complement each other's skills.

Teamwork provides additional opportunities for cheating. Ownership of the output of a team is ambiguous since particular outputs cannot be accurately imputed to particular members. The ambiguity is normally resolved through a contract. One party – the employer – purchases the rights to the product in return for fixed payments to the employees (sometimes augmented by a bonus). The employer may work as part of the team, or be a specialist who manages the business. A group of shareholders may team up separately in order to finance production. The contractual obligations of employer and employee involve mutual promissory obligations. The employee agrees to act upon orders within certain limits, while the employer commits to pay wages and salaries. A paternalistic employer may also accept an obligation of care, involving the provision of welfare facilities and sick pay, while the employee may reciprocate: they work harder than necessary if they are treated well, but become disruptive if treated badly. The employment relationship therefore involves a wider range of obligations than ordinary product trade.

2.2.3　Finance: the obligation to repay　In an advanced industrial economy, workers are supported by durable capital equipment, whose purchase needs to be financed. Even in a simple mercantile economy based on trade in minerals and agricultural products, stocks of raw materials and work in progress need to be financed. Finance requires a high degree of trust because repayment is deferred – whether it is the payment of dividends or the redemption of a loan. Lenders can reduce their risks by holding collateral as a hostage against default, but nevertheless investment often involves unsecured loans. Large loans are often supplied by banks, which re-lend their depositors' funds. They also take a calculated risk with liquidity by hoping that not all their depositors will wish to withdraw their funds at the same time.

The obligation to repay is thus a crucial element of trust in advanced economies. The reputation of the banking system is crucial, because banks not only have to safeguard the interests of their depositors but maintain financial discipline over their borrowers too.

2.2.4　Negotiation: discouraging bluff and promoting compromise　It is tempting to generalize the notion of honouring contracts to say that economic efficiency demands complete honesty in trade. This is not the principle on which the market system works in practice, however. People are allowed to bluff in negotiations.

Consider a simple case in which a single commodity, such as a second-hand car, is to be sold by a seller who values it at v_1 to a buyer who values it at $v_2 > v_1$. Under a system of total honesty no relevant information would be withheld by either party. The buyer and seller would exchange their valuations. They might then invoke a principle of sharing benefits equally, resulting in a price equal to the average valuation: $p_1 = (v_1 + v_2)/2$.

Alternatively, they might share the information as before, but then decide to give the surplus to a charity. The price could be set at $p_2 = v_2$ on the understanding that the seller would give his profit $s = v_2 - v_1$ to a charity.

These principles are not widely used in practice: the obvious problem is that the seller may succumb to the temptation to overstate his valuation (e.g. claim that his costs are higher then they really are) while the buyer may understate the strength of his demand.

One solution is to waive the requirement for total honesty, and allow the buyer and seller to make initial offers on a purely strategic basis. The buyer quotes the lowest figure that he thinks the seller will accept while the seller quotes the highest figure that he thinks the buyer will pay. This can also produce the price p_1; if the seller correctly estimates the buyer's valuation and the buyer correctly estimates the seller's valuation, then the buyer quotes v_1 and the seller v_2. If the principle of 'splitting the difference' is then applied, the price becomes p_1.

Both 'share the benefit' and 'split the difference' involve a symmetrical treatment of the two traders, and it is therefore not surprising that they can produce the same outcome. However, the principle of splitting the difference is quite distinct from the principle of sharing the benefit because it is based on a principle of equal concession. It is applied to a process in which each person guesses what the other will accept, rather than states directly what they would accept themselves.

The principle of 'split the difference' implicitly assumes that there is room for concession. If the buyer justifies his bid of v_1 on the grounds that this is simply the least amount that he thinks the seller will accept, then no absolute dishonesty may be involved.

Although the buyer is withholding his own valuation, his statement about his belief concerning the seller's valuation may well be correct. Similarly the seller may be perfectly genuine in saying that he thinks that the buyer would pay as much as v_2. Dishonesty arises, however, if in order to strengthen his negotiating stance, the buyer says that he will not pay more than v_1, or the seller sells that he will not accept less than v_2. If negotiations continue after both the parties have made such statements, then it is clear that someone thinks that the other is lying, and if a concession is actually made by one or both of the parties, then it is evident that lying has actually taken place.

It is widely accepted in market economies that people do tell lies about what they are willing to pay. Such bluffing is usually accepted as an inevitable part of the negotiation process. The bluff referred to above involves describing an offer as the worst that you are prepared to accept when it is actually the best that you think you can get. The strategy is to force a concession from the other party while not making any concession yourself; it is the prospect of an asymmetric concession that motivates the false pretence.

An obligation to 'split the difference' can mitigate the problem of bluffing because both parties are then aware that they will be required to make concessions whatever they have said about their offers. In this case people may as well admit that their initial quote is the best that they think that they can get because then they do not lose credibility when they make a concession.

'Split the difference' does not solve all the problems associated with bluffing, however. It may encourage both parties to exaggerate their positions strategically, with the buyer claiming to believe that the seller can supply very cheaply while the seller claims to believe that the buyer is willing to pay a very high price. If the buyer exaggerates more than the seller, then the compromise price will be relatively low, whilst if the seller exaggerates more than the buyer, then the price will tend to be high. Thus whoever exaggerates the most gets the best deal. If both parties appreciate this, then the divergence between bids will escalate and the negotiations may founder; trust will disappear as the initial bids become absurdly exaggerated. This shows that the principle of 'split the difference' is most effective when it is combined with a principle that initial offers must be genuine estimates of what the other party is willing to pay.

Overall, therefore, a suitable ethic for negotiation is one in which neither party is required to state what the good is worth to them. Instead, each makes an offer based on an honest assessment of the best deal (from their point of view) that they believe that they can get, and the price is then fixed by splitting the difference. An obligation to make honest offers, and to be willing to compromise symmetrically, therefore promotes efficient negotiation of trade.

2.3 Reducing the need for trust: competition

It could be objected that the previous discussion has ignored the role of competitive forces in determining price. While there is some validity in this criticism, it must be recognized that certain types of competition can create more problems than they solve.

Competition can be analysed from either a static or dynamic point of view. The static point of view is similar to that adopted in GE theory. The idea is that any individual trade is embedded in a much wider set of all possible trades. There is no longer a single buyer and a single seller, but an entire spectrum of buyers and sellers. The power to determine price shifts from the individual traders to the market as a whole.

Each trader attaches his own distinctive value to the product. There is a continuum of valuations across different buyers, and another continuum across the sellers. Each seller negotiating with any given buyer believes that if this particular buyer does not wish to pay what is asked, then there is another buyer who will, and conversely, each buyer believes that if a seller refuses to accept his offer, then there is another seller who will.

Any change in market conditions will soon become evident as the process of negotiation proceeds. If a change in the environment reduces buyers' valuations, then sellers will discover a shortage of buyers at the previous price; their expectations of price will diminish, and they will lower their prices as a result. Conversely, if sellers' valuations are increased, then buyers' expectations of price will rise, and prices will increase. There is no point in anyone bluffing because no one can 'buck the market'. There is no scope for sharing a surplus or for making concessions, as there was before, because market forces now determine a unique equilibrium price. From a static point of view, therefore, competition reduces the need for trust.

2.4   Innovative intermediation: discouraging the threat of imitation

Despite its widespread use in neoclassical economics, the static theory of competition offers a poor account of the way that markets actually work. Indeed, the static theory is so unrealistic that static market adjustment is often portrayed as the work of a fictional character – the Walrasian auctioneer. The auctioneer intermediates the market by setting prices on a trial basis. By constructing trial balances of supply and demand he identifies the equilibrium price.

The Walrasian model contains one significant element of realism, however. Many markets, particularly consumer goods markets, are intermediated – though not by an auctioneer. They are intermediated instead by private firms. Some firms innovate new products and processes, creating entirely new markets in the process. Wholesalers specialize in carrying stocks which balance out short-term fluctuations in supply and demand, while retailers provide a convenience service to local customers.

These firms aim to benefit from volatility in the economy. They seek out profit by spotting changes which other people have missed. Innovators identify technological changes which can be embodied in new products and processes; wholesalers identify consumer trends, and adjust their stocks accordingly; while retailers spot new locations in which to establish stores.

Innovators incur significant costs in monitoring change in order to identify new opportunities. Much of the cost comes from the time spent collecting information. By the time they have acquired their information, heavy costs may have been sunk. Competition from imitators is a serious threat. Innovators need a significant profit margin in order to recover their sunk costs, but once their information has been discovered it is, in principle, available to everyone else as well at negligible cost. This means that they have to protect their plans through commercial secrecy. This may involve denying the information they possess.

The problem is not so much the selfishness of the innovator in his search for profit. Even if the innovator were an altruistic social reformer, he would still need to cover his sunk costs. It is rather the selfishness of the imitators that causes the problem, for it is this that creates the competition which leads the innovator to disguise, or even deny, the truth.

Altruists rarely imitate each other so closely that the innovator must resort to secrecy. Most altruists prefer to advertise their activities in the hope of winning other people over to their cause. When the common cause is simply earning a profit, however, then imitation becomes an attractive strategy.

To deter imitation, patent or copyright protection is often provided by the state. When patent protection is complete, an innovator has no incentive to withhold information or mislead other people. Politicians are aware, however, that patent protection may not only deter imitators, but deter the next wave of innovators too. Patent protection is therefore normally limited, both in time and in the scope of the innovation that it protects. Because patent protection is so limited, innovators sometimes continue to rely on secrecy, and so dishonesty becomes a complementary weapon.

In a purely profit-seeking culture, innovators are driven by a desire for profit, just like imitators. This raises the possibility that while innovation may generate a profit, it may not improve social welfare. Innovation may be progress, but it may be progress in the wrong direction. The fact that imitation creates problems for innovators does not mean that innovators are always an innocent party, for profit-seeking innovators may fail in their obligations of care to who those who are adversely affected by the changes they make. Innovation is often a painful and socially divisive process. One of the problems with motivating innovation through a selfish pursuit of profit is that it encourages the wrong sort of innovation. To reconcile profit-seeking innovation with social welfare requires a comprehensive system of property rights in which losers are compensated before the innovation goes ahead. If the costs of establishing such comprehensive property rights are too great, then a system of regulation is required as a substitute. Regulation is itself a blunt and costly instrument, but if society has failed to invest in a moral system capable of channelling innovation into socially beneficial projects, then it may well be better than no regulation at all.

3.   Alternative economic approaches to modelling trust

3.1   The neoclassical approach

In standard neoclassical theory people are assumed to be selfish and to maximize their material gains. They will therefore have an incentive to cheat, so sanctions are incorporated into contracts to prevent them from doing so. In this context, trust is useful only in so far as it reduces the costs associated with having to devise perfect contracts and enforceable sanctions, so trust is a purely instrumental non-material resource in which people will explicitly invest with the purpose of building a reputation for honesty. The latter in turn makes possible cooperative behaviour, and the emergence of stable structures for transacting.

More specifically, the neoclassical notion of trust refers to exchanges among individuals involving deferred compliance with (some of) the exchange agreements (as opposed to transactions on the spot), accompanied by insufficient information about other agents' choices. 'Trust is a particular level of subjective probability with which an agent assesses that another agent or group of agents will perform a particular action, both before he can monitor such action (or independently of his capacity ever to be able to monitor it) and in a context in which it affects his own action' (Gambetta, 1988, p. 217). The hypotheses on which such definition is based, and which define the behavioural hypotheses and therefore the boundaries within which transactions are treated in conventional neoclassical and game theory models can be summarized from a paper by Partha Dasgupta (in Gambetta, 1988) illuminatingly entitled 'Trust as a Commodity':

- In the absence of suitable punishment for breaking agreements, it is believed that the individuals involved in them will not have sufficient incentives to fulfil them (so that scarcity of trust derives in this context from the fact that people are assumed to be not naturally trustworthy).
- The threat of punishment must be credible. Given that at this stage a third party, in the form of another individual or institution, is required as enforcement agent, trust needs to be placed in the capability of such an agent.
- Trust among persons and agents is interconnected, because if trust in the agent vacillates, so does trust in the other person involved in the agreement.
- Trust is based on an expectation about choices made by another agent, and not about promises, which means that, in order to correctly form such an expectation, the other party's perspective has to be understood.

The definition of trust at which Dasgupta arrives on the basis of these premises is not dissimilar to the one presented above by Gambetta: trust consists of correct expectations about actions of others that have an influence on one's own choices. Trust is therefore a scarce non-material resource, and its value is in principle measurable, and described as being akin to the value of knowledge or information.

The need for trust in neoclassical economic theory stems from the impossibility of monitoring other people's behaviour, and the fact that the selfish individuals who cannot be monitored are aware of this, and recognize the opportunity it affords to cheat the other party. The solution is to devise enforceable contracts which modify incentives and thereby induce selfish people to behave in a socially responsible way.

Lack of trust accounts for one of the main results of static game theory: that individuals may fail to cooperate even if cooperative behaviour would benefit them, loosely referred to as the prisoner's dilemma. The rational decision of investing in trust (by creating a reputation of being trustworthy) is indicated as a building block for a healthy economic system, in that it allows transactions to occur.

An important way of modifying incentives is to embed a single encounter within a larger sequence of encounters. According to the theory of repeated games, trust may develop when individuals have repeated encounters and have memory of the outcomes of the previous ones. If encounters are repeated indefinitely, then there is always some future encounter in which a victim could punish a cheat. Even if honest behaviour involves a cost, under these conditions people may be willing to incur these costs in order to build a reputation (Dasgupta, in Gambetta, 1988). In particular, Kreps and Wilson (1982) demonstrate that in an infinitely repeated prisoner's dilemma game, uncertainty about the nature of the payoff to a player can produce a cooperative equilibrium. This means, for example, that traders will be more honest if they expect to trade with each other in the future.

3.2   The institutional approach
The approach in this chapter is more 'institutional' than standard neoclassical theory. Some forms of institutional economic theory, such as transaction cost theory, have been criticized for being too neoclassical because they place undue emphasis on coordination by markets and hierarchies and ignore informal methods of coordination based on networks of trust. This criticism has some force, particularly when applied to

Williamson's early work, where an emphasis on the ubiquity of opportunism leaves little room for trust to play a significant role in coordination. Although in his work the existence and importance of personal trust between individuals (based on absence of monitoring, and a favourable and forgiving attitude) is acknowledged, the attitude which is believed to be associated with the majority of transactions (involving individuals and institutions) is essentially enlightened self-interest, just as in neoclassical theory (Williamson, 1996).

It is argued here that this conception of trust is too narrow because it ignores the emotional dimension of trust. Recognition of emotions is perfectly compatible with the rational action approach, provided that emotions are considered as forms of utility or payoff rather than merely as a factor that distorts decision making (Casson, 1991, 1995; Della Giusta, 1999).

Institutional theory, as formulated in the works of David (1989), North (1990) and others (Smith Ring, 1997; Harriss et al., 1995), provides an explanation of the evolution of the beliefs and moral values of a society (incorporated into informal and formal institutions) through the stimulating role of organizations (which by spontaneously carrying out their activities alter the existing set of institutions). The institutional approach adopted in this chapter therefore takes a far more general approach to coordination, and emphasizes that people are not intrinsically selfish. It also recognizes the role of different types of leadership in facilitating altruistic activities.

Introducing the emotional dimension shows that morals as well as law can act as a basis for trust. Moral commitments frame the emotions that people generate as a result of the actions that they take. A person acting morally feels good about taking a socially responsible decision and feels bad about taking an anti-social decision. Anticipating how they will feel about the way they act, people acting morally win self-approval and avoid guilt. This makes them trustworthy, because they can be relied upon to take account of the impact of their actions on others. As a result, a reputation for trust can be built on the basis of making a visible moral commitment. People thus attribute intrinsic value to a reputation of trustworthiness.

Emotions are not incompatible with rational action, as is sometimes suggested. From a rational action perspective, pleasant emotions are goods while unpleasant emotions are bads: they enter into an individual's utility function in just the same way as any other good or bad, as explained in more detail below. People react emotionally to the situations in which they are placed. Emotions can be controlled by seeking out situations that are likely to generate good emotions and avoiding situations that are likely to generate bad ones. However, some situations are difficult to anticipate (e.g. accidents), while others are difficult to avoid altogether (e.g. going to work). Thus it is inevitable that people find themselves in bad situations in which they are aroused in an unpleasant way.

It is important to distinguish between responsive emotions and reflective emotions. Responsive emotions provide short-term rewards to particular reactions at a time when a person has been aroused. Typically, a responsive emotion stirs an individual to action. This action may be fairly basic – such as 'fight' or 'flight' – and it may be so quick that it is based on only very limited information. The effect of the reaction may be relatively harmless, such as jumping up to celebrate good news, or potentially harmful, such as hitting out at someone. Harmful actions may be damaging to oneself, or damaging to others, or damaging to both. Responsive emotions often create problems because they stimulate reactions that are inappropriate in a complex and sophisticated society. On the other hand, some responsive emotions can enhance a good experience too.

Reflective emotions arise in contemplative situations. They occur when people are relaxing and reviewing previous events. They relive incidents recalled from memory, and place them in perspective. People may congratulate themselves on certain actions which, on reflection, have advanced their personal interests, while regretting actions which have damaged them. The perspective does not have to be a purely selfish one, however. It may be a moral one instead. People either approve or disapprove of the actions that they took on the basis of the effects that they have had on other people. Approval raises self-esteem, and thereby generates a positive emotional reward, whilst disapproval reduces self-esteem and thereby generates an emotional penalty.

While people cannot avoid being aroused by situations in which they are placed, they can decide whether to inhibit the responses that would give them short-term satisfaction in order to benefit later when in contemplative mood. This decision is made before the situation is encountered by the individual. When in reflective mood, an individual decides whether they need to invest in greater self-control, by training themselves to inhibit certain responses that may have caused trouble in the past. In doing so they will take account of the long-term consequences of their future short-term reactions for both their material interests and their self-esteem. A rational calculation is made of the costs and benefits of greater self-control. The cost is the additional stress created by the inhibition of reactions, and the period of training that is required to strengthen inhibition. The short-term pleasure of the inhibited response is also lost. In return, however, the individual gains in terms of reputation. They can add to their reputation by improving their behaviour, as well as by safeguarding the reputation they already have.

Other things being equal, the net gain in reputation is greatest for individuals who have made a moral commitment. This is because they are concerned not only about their reputation with other people, but about their reputation with themselves, in terms of moral self-esteem. This means that they will invest more heavily in inhibition because it offers a greater total return. This in turn makes them more trustworthy. Thus morally committed individuals who invest in self-control increase not only the stock of prudential trust but also the stock of sacrificial trust within society.

4.   An economic theory of trust: combining reason and emotion

4.1   Defining trust

If a person we dislike acts in an inconsiderate way, we might exclaim 'Trust them to be selfish!' This does not mean that we would call them trustworthy – quite the reverse, in fact. It means that they are predictable. Predictability is a first meaning of trust.

If we were introducing a friend to someone, we might say 'You can certainly put your trust in them.' This normally means that they can be relied upon to honour their obligations. They will respect the rights that you hold, and also fulfil any promises they make. A propensity to honour obligations is a second meaning of trust.

In some cases it clearly pays a person to honour their obligations. In this case trust is underpinned by enlightened self-interest; it may be termed 'prudential trust'. In other cases, however, honouring obligations incurs a sacrifice for which there is no material compensation: this may be termed 'sacrificial trust'.

Considerable disagreement exists over the relative importance of law and morals in sustaining trust. In the present context, the law is an instrument of prudential trust, whilst morals are an instrument of sacrificial trust.

Another important distinction is between naïve trust and warranted trust. Naïve trust signifies a misplaced belief in the character of the other party, whereas warranted trust signifies, by contrast, a belief that is correct. In economic terms, warranted trust is an equilibrium concept, since expectations are fulfilled, and so there is no reason to change them. On the other hand, naïve trust is a disequilibrium concept because the expectations are not fulfilled and so need to be revised.

So far we have discussed cases of unilateral trust, in which one party trusts the other, but the feeling is not necessarily reciprocated. In mutual trust, conversely, each party trusts the other. While it is normally desirable that trust should be mutual, the economy can survive without mutuality, provided that intermediaries emerge to overcome the problems caused by lack of mutuality. It is therefore undesirable to make mutuality a defining characteristic of trust. It is better regarded as a special configuration with has highly desirable properties. Trust is therefore most usefully defined as a 'confident and warranted belief' that the other party will honour their obligations'. Confidence gives predictability, while the warranted nature of the trust ensures that the predictions are broadly correct.

4.2 Types of obligation

From an economic perspective, the depth of trust can thought of in terms of four main factors:

- the nature of the obligation;
- the size of the obligation, as measured by the value of the resources to which the obligation relates;
- the certainty of the obligation being honoured, as measured by the subjective probability that that there will be no default; and
- the reliability of the obligation, as measured by the actual frequency with which default occurs.

Six main types of obligation may thus be distinguished:

1. *Customary obligation.* The individual feels obliged to fulfil the reasonable expectations of another party. In particular, they feel obliged to follow laws or customs because they are aware that the other person may be relying on them to respect these laws and customs in order that their own plans turn out as expected. Respect for custom is a reflective emotion. People can reflect with pleasure on the contribution they have made to the maintenance of social order by observing customary courtesies of everyday life; conversely, they may become disillusioned if they observe widespread disregard for custom.

2. *Promissory obligation.* The individual has promised another party that they will behave in a certain way under certain conditions. The promise may form part of a legal contract, or it may be simply a verbal undertaking. Promissory obligation is also a reflective emotion. We know that we will feel guilty later if we have broken our promises. To avoid these feelings we may go to enormous lengths to construct

fanciful self-justifications, and to twist our recollections of events to shift the blame on to other parties.

3. *Reciprocal obligation*, reflecting a desire for mutuality. The individual feels obliged to respond to any action by another party which impinges upon them by performing a similar action which will have a matching effect on the other party. Reciprocal obligation is a responsive emotion, as its name suggests. Unlike reflective emotions, whose rewards may come long after an event, responsive emotions generate immediate reward: they urge us respond, and we feel satisfaction when we do so and frustrated when we do not. Reciprocal obligation is not purely responsive, however. Reflective reciprocity arises when we reflect on the benefits that we have received from other people's kindness, and decide that we would like to show our appreciation by offering something in return.

4. *Considerate obligation.* The individual feels obliged to take account of how their actions are likely to impinge on another person, whether or not they have given them any previous undertaking, and whether or not there is a custom governing their behaviour.

5. *Sympathetic obligation.* A sympathetic person feels obliged to help another person whose expectations have been disappointed, or whose expectations are likely to be disappointed if they do not intervene. Sympathetic obligation is different from considerate obligation because the obligation exists whether or not the sympathetic person has inadvertently caused the problem in the first place. Considerate obligation and sympathetic obligation both involve reflective emotions, but sympathetic obligation involves a significant amount of responsive emotion too. People who appear vulnerable and helpless excite sympathy, which can trigger an immediate response.

6. *Altruistic obligation.* An altruist wishes to help another person whether or not that person's expectations have been disappointed, and whether or not they have a specific need for care. They may even set out to raise the other person's expectations of what can be achieved, thereby increasing the demand for care. Altruistic emotion is more reflective than sympathetic emotion because it reflects a general attitude to society rather than a response to a particular person. Altruism is motivated mainly by general philosophical considerations, such as the view that everyone is morally equal and therefore has the same rights as everyone else. Sympathetic obligation, by contrast, is motivated by empathy with people in difficult situations.

The nature of the obligation that a person is willing to accept determines how trustworthy they are in different circumstances. Someone who recognizes customary obligations may be relied upon to behave in a non-violent and civilized way but, unlike a sympathetic person, they cannot be relied upon to help you if you are in difficulties.

Each type of obligation may be of a specific or general nature. A specific obligation is either a personal obligation towards a particular individual or a social obligation towards other members of their group, while a general obligation applies to society as a whole. Most types of obligation occur in both general and specific forms (see Table 19.1).

General obligations are often of an impersonal nature. Sometimes people may accept a general obligation but not a specific one, despite the apparent contradiction involved; thus a person may express a general obligation to society while being remarkably intolerant of individual members of that society.

Table 19.1   General and specific obligations of different types

Type of obligation	Specific	General
Customary	Individual keeps regular hours so that his friends know when and where he can be contacted	Individual keeps to the left when walking along corridors in order to avoid bumping into people
Promissory	Buyer makes contract with seller	New member of group swears allegiance at an initiation ceremony. Immigrant promises to be a good citizen
Reciprocal	Individual reacts to attack by 'an eye for an eye', and provides favours in return for gifts; they thereby maintain their relations with other people in a sort of homeostatic equilibrium	Individual undertakes public service to 'put back' into the system what they believed they have received. For example, an individual who received free education may do voluntary teaching
Considerate	Individual makes a careful study of his friend's needs in order that he can help them when required	Individual thinks carefully before he speaks or acts in order to avoid giving unnecessary offence to others
Sympathetic	Individual is dependable when coming to the assistance of friends in trouble	Individual is a 'Good Samaritan' who will help anyone he meets who is in difficulties
Altruistic	Parent supports child to help them realize their full potential	Citizen joins charity as a volunteer. Political activist dedicates their life to reforming society

4.3   Size of obligation

For any given type of obligation, trust is greater the larger the value of resources involved. An individual who can be trusted to repay a debt of £1000 cannot necessarily be trusted to repay a debt of £1 million. Everyone has a limit to the size of obligation they are willing to honour. For example, a sympathetic person may have limits to the amount of care they are willing to provide. A person who is willing to give small sums of money to street beggars may not be willing to make a substantial donation to a charity for street people if that would leave them relatively short of funds.

The limits of obligation are particularly evident where contracts are concerned. A customer who is given too much change may be sufficiently honest to return it to the shopkeeper, but the same person, as a homeowner, may be perfectly happy to dupe a buyer into paying hundreds of thousands of pounds for a house with a serious structural fault. In general, people seem to find it more difficult to honour obligations in exceptional situations which provide unusually large opportunities to cheat. This suggests that when people commit themselves to honouring obligations, there is an implicit restriction on the size of the obligation that are willing to accept. The significance of this restriction may not be appreciated until unusual circumstances arise. It appears that people can train themselves to be honest in regular dealings but can be caught out when they are confronted with a situation unlike any they have encountered before. Thus unanticipated circumstances are more likely than anticipated circumstances to precipitate dishonest behaviour.

4.4   Certainty and reliability
To be trusted is not the same thing as to be trustworthy. Trustworthiness is an objective characteristic of an individual in a given type of situation, but it cannot be directly observed. Trust is the attitude of another person towards them. Certainty expresses the confidence of the subjective belief held by the other person. If a person believes that the probability of another person cheating is only 1 per cent, then they are more certain in their trust than if they believe that the probability of cheating is 10 per cent. If the actual probability of cheating is 1 per cent, then the other person is more reliable than if it is 10 per cent. If the perceived probability matches the actual frequency, then the level of trust is warranted. Otherwise there may be unwarranted optimism or pessimism about the trustworthiness of the person concerned. If a person believes that someone who is reliable only at the 10 per cent level is actually reliable at the 1 per cent level, then their optimism is unwarranted, and conversely, if they believe that someone who is reliable at the 1 per cent level is actually reliable only at the 10 per cent level, then their pessimism is unwarranted.

Economic efficiency normally requires that trust be warranted. Unwarranted optimism leads to be people being cheated, and encourages dishonest people to deliberately seek out naïve and gullible people that they can take advantage of. There tend to be too many transactions of the wrong sort. Conversely, unwarranted pessimism discourages honest people from coming forward because they expect to be dismissed as frauds. This leads to too few of the right sort of transactions taking place.

4.5   Breadth of trust: reputation and reputation brokers
The number of people who hold the same confident belief about a particular person reflects that person's reputation. The typical individual knows only a small fraction of the people in their society, and only trusts a proportion of the people that they know. The people they trust are among family and friends, colleagues at work, fellow members of clubs and societies, and a few celebrities of whom they have heard favourable reports. Most ordinary people therefore have rather limited reputations, while a small number of celebrities have extensive ones.

Reputation is often specific. When people occupy specialized roles in society (see below), others are generally more concerned about how they play their roles than what they do when out of role. Thus a famous entertainer may be trusted to deliver value-for-money performances, while being distrusted in matters relating to their private life. In daily life, we often ask one person to help us in one way but not in another; one advantage of having a wide range of contacts is that help can always be obtained from a trustworthy source whatever the problem happens to be.

The efficient exploitation of a limited supply of trust requires that trustworthy people have wide reputations. These reputations will attract other people to deal with them instead of with people who lack reputation. Conversely, it is also desirable that untrustworthy people should have bad reputations that are as wide as possible so that people can actively avoid them.

An important role for trusted people is to act as reputation brokers; they spread accurate reputations by passing on their own assessments of people. If we are dealing with someone whom we are unsure whether to trust, we may turn to a reputation broker in the hope that they already know them. Older people who have accumulated a wide range of contacts are often well suited for this purpose. When very little at all is known about a person, it may be hard to know whom to ask about them, and so they may be asked to supply the names of reputable referees. In such cases the reputation of the referee is often more important than what they say about them. A simple endorsement from a highly respected person may carry greater weight than a more lengthy or detailed endorsement from a referee with less reputation.

People who lack reputation individually may be able to derive it from an institution to which they belong. Their institutional affiliation signals that they can be trusted. In dynastic societies, family affiliation may suffice; reputation is vested in the family name rather than in any particular member of the family. Schools and universities can also accredit their alumni – an important factor when there is competition between private educational institutions. This explains why references are often sought from institutions rather than from individuals. But where do institutions get their reputations from in the first place? Institutional reputation is often derived from the personal reputation of the founder. Institutions do not exist in timeless limbo – they have to be created, and personal initiative is required to do this. Some of the largest and strongest institutions are founded by committees or councils, which combine the reputations of the individuals involved.

Even in the absence of a formal institutional framework, a highly reputable person who leads a team or group of people may be able to transfer some of their personal reputation to those with whom they work. As explained below, reputation is often based on moral commitment, and reputable people are good sources from which to elicit commitments of the requisite kind. A person can gain reputation by explaining that they were influenced by a reputable individual who was the leader of their group. Reputable people can therefore not only act as reputation brokers, but as reputation builders too.

Even if an institution has no influence on its individual members, it may still enhance its members' reputation if it is highly selective. By setting tough professional examinations for prospective members, for example, an institution can accredit its members' technical competence. However, trust is difficult to assess by formal examination, and so if the institution lacks a distinctive ethos, it may find it difficult to accredit its members' trustworthiness. To enhance reputation for trust through selection, the institution needs to be able to show that it recruits from particularly trustworthy sources. In some firms, for example, there is a recruitment bias in favour of the children of existing employees. It is sometimes claimed that recruitment strategies of this kind can reinforce the reputations of long-standing paternalistic family firms (Rose, 2000).

Given that individuals derive part of their reputation from the groups to which they belong, it is important to distinguish between the internal and external reputation of the group. If a group leader emphasizes exclusive ties and in-group bonding at the expense of bridging with outsiders, then this will tend to strengthen the reputation of members with each other rather than with people outside the group. On the other hand, if the leader emphasizes fairness and impartiality, then it will tend to strengthen reputation outside the group.

Different types of group require different types of reputation. Military conflict, for example, makes soldiers heavily dependent on their colleagues for their safety and requires constructing the enemy as a completely distinct entity, and this brings internal reputation to the fore. In a professional practice, such as a legal partnership, however, individuals tend to work independently and to cultivate their own client base; this encourages external reputation building instead. There are a small number of cases in which both types of reputation are crucial. A medical team in a hospital, for example, is engaged in life-critical teamwork, but unlike the military situation it is the patient's life that is at risk. The patient has to trust the team, and they can only trust the team if the team members trust each other.

5.   Applications of the economic theory of trust

5.1   *Networks of trust*

Networks have two important roles in promoting trust, although these are not always distinguished properly. The first role is in spreading external reputation. Networking events such as parties, club meetings and other social gatherings allow people to update their knowledge of the reputation of people outside their own immediate group. They can make discreet enquiries about the creditworthiness of prospective business partners, or the reliability of potential subcontractors or employees. This allows them to manage the risk of dealing with untrustworthy people.

The second role of networks is in building internal reputation, whereby members of a team or group learn to trust each other better. When a group is formed, most members may only know the leader who recruited them. Unless there is a change in the situation, the leader will have to take responsibility for all coordination within the group because he is the only person that the ordinary members trust. The leader needs to use his influence to persuade them to trust each other. He does this by showing through example that he trusts them individually, and explaining his grounds for doing so. This explanation may centre on general rather than specific factors, such as a claim that everyone has been 'fired up' by a shared sense of mission within the group.

A trust-building leader can therefore transform a network of relationships centred on the leader as a hub into a complex of relationships linking every pair of members within the group. In geometric terms, the group is reconfigured from a hub, with the leader at the centre, connected to a set of solitary nodes, to a web in which every node is directly linked to every other node. In effect, therefore, every member of the group becomes a hub since, like the leader, they are connected to every other member of the group.

In a web configuration, the leader's node is indistinguishable from any other node. In fact, of course, the leader is distinguished by his special relationship with each of the ordinary members, which is reflected in the fact that he can make and break individual reputations within the group. The leader may also have a special administrative role, formulating collective strategies, and repairing breakdowns in relationships between particular pairs of individuals within the team.

Another important difference between a leader and the ordinary members of a group is that the leader is networked to the outside world through contact with the leaders of other groups. The leader belongs not only to his own group, but to another group of people who play a similar role in other groups. The leader of this group may in turn belong to an even higher-level group. At each level the leader builds up trust between his members by promoting their reputations within his group.

The network structures that underpin reputation are therefore hierarchical to a significant extent. However, it is the configuration rather than the relationship that is hierarchical: at each level the leader controls the reputation of the ordinary members, but he does not give them instructions as to how to behave. The leader has no power to interfere or meddle in a member's own group. The relationship between leader and follower is based on influence and endorsement, rather than conventional authority.

5.2   Investing in trust: encouraging moral commitment

The natural method of increasing trust, according to this view, is to encourage people to make moral commitments. From an economic perspective, strengthening moral commitment is the primary role of moral leaders. It is unrealistic to expect everyone to form their own view of society, and to determine the moral values that are required to address its problems. The complexity of this task calls for specialization. Moral leaders can carry out this specialized task, disseminating values and beliefs which are standardized across their followers. The followers of a particular leader form a social group. The followers accept the leader as an authority on all those moral issues that are too complex for them to arrive at a judgement for themselves.

Moral leaders require a wide reputation. They clearly need to be trusted, which means in turn that their own commitments need to be seen to be sincere. For this reason moral leaders are easily discredited when they fail to practise what they preach – even in their private life. Moral leadership is scarce. Building up a wide reputation for a deep moral commitment is not an easy task. Whereas in traditional society priests are the principal moral leaders, in a secular society based on market economics, politicians, artists, scientists and media celebrities also fulfil this role. The various sources of moral authority in an advanced economy are summarized in Table 19.2. The economic benefits of leadership include both the material benefits conferred by the superior coordination achieved in a high-trust society, together with the emotional benefits that are generated by higher levels of personal self-esteem.

Moral leadership is not the only way of increasing trust within society. Eliminating situations which arouse anti-social behaviour is another solution. However intensive the

Table 19.2   Source of moral authority used by leaders

Level of authority	Type of authority	Authority figures
Ultimate		
Traditional	Tradition	Ancestor
	Religion	Prophet, priest, scripture
Modern	Scientific experiment	Scientist
	Artistic expression	Artist
	Reasoned argument	Philosopher
Intermediate	Law	Legislator, judge, police
	Custom	Peer pressure
	Conscience	Self (contemplative)
	Celebrity role model	Statesman, entertainer, etc.
Local	Parent or teacher	Parent or teacher
	Employer or owner	Employer or owner
	Gang leader	Gang leader

moral leadership, people will always be weak-willed at times, and the obvious response is to take temptation out of their way. If the temptations cannot be removed, then giving people the opportunity to avoid them is another possibility. For example, if some people cannot resist the opportunity to gamble, even though they are using resources that belong to other members of their family, then a moral crusade against gambling that aims to strengthen self-control can be linked to legislation that either outlaws gambling or confines it to special areas which those who suffer from a compulsion can easily avoid.

5.3   Functionally useful moral values

Reflective emotions naturally reflect the fundamental moral values of the person who is reflecting. Reflection is a useful faculty, so far as coordination is concerned, when the moral system used for reflection encourages people to act in a manner that promotes coordination. With coordination as the objective, a set of functionally useful moral values may be derived – namely, values that will promote coordination when employed for reflective purposes.

The particular values that are most useful for coordination will depend on the nature of the economic environment, but there are certain core values that are useful in any economy which suffers from scarcity. Some of these values have already been noted:

- Respect for property
- Honouring contracts
- Repaying loans
- Negotiating on the basis of stated expectations about the other party's valuation rather than dishonest claims about one's own valuation
- Willingness to compromise in negotiation
- Directing innovation towards the solution of social problems
- Foregoing competitive imitation when this will leave a socially responsible innovator to sustain a loss.

While the first three of these are widely accepted as important, the last four are not. This is not because they are actively dismissed as unimportant, but because they are hardly ever given serious consideration. Most writers on the cultural basis of capitalism simply fudge the issue of whether honesty and integrity promote economic performance. The usual compromise position is to argue that people must tell the truth, but that confidentiality must be respected (which involves withholding the truth from others). It is also claimed that organizations should be 'transparent' while at the same time the right to privacy must be upheld. The way of rationalizing this position would be to say that there is only an obligation to tell the truth to those who have a need to know. Those who do not need to know do not have a right to enquire, and if they are impertinent enough to enquire, then it is legitimate, not only to refuse to reply, but to actively mislead them. The difficulty, of course, is in deciding who has a right to know what. In practice, it provides a licence to deny the right to know to those who have something to hide.

There are some other values that are said to improve performance which it is appropriate to mention at this point.

- *Work ethic.* If people work seriously at any task to which they are assigned, whether or not they are being monitored, then productivity will be high. If people are committed in their studies too, then they will also bring a high level of skill to their work. Ethic of work is a type of promissory obligation which is important for the economy.

- *Saving.* By sacrificing current consumption, investment can be financed which will contribute to long-term productivity growth. Emotions such as greed encourage people to seek immediate rewards, even when this may damage their own future consumption. Many people seem to have difficulty empathizing with their future selves – they cannot visualize themselves as old people needing to live on their accumulated savings – and so they spend even when enlightened self-interest would suggest that they should save. Others may be willing to save for their own benefit but not that of their children – they save for retirement cruises, but not to give their children 'a good start in life'. A value system that legitimates saving avoids a society's wealth being squandered through greed; it thereby ensures that accumulated wealth is transmitted from one generation to the next, and is augmented in the process.
- *Loyalty.* People who join an organization often benefit from training they receive. In a social group the benefit may derive from using the leader as a role model, and being able to study their actions at close hand. In a firm the benefit may derive from an apprenticeship, and so on. It is potentially damaging if people quit a group before they have had a chance to repay the group for its investment. The obligation to be loyal regulates this situation by encouraging attachment to be continued until intellectual debts have been repaid. Loyalty is an effective substitute for requiring employees to post bonds – a device that normally restricts employment opportunities to those with sufficient wealth to finance the bond.

While it might be thought that all these functionally useful values would be prominent in the value systems of successful Western market economies, it has already been pointed out that this is not in fact the case. For example, the tax systems in many countries impose 'double taxation' of savings by taxing both the interest and the income out of which people save. Welfare systems that employ means tests also have a built-in disincentive to save. In general, policy makers seem to have considered saving to be a much lower priority than in the late nineteenth century, when many savings banks were set up specifically to promote saving among the working classes. One explanation of the lack of emphasis on saving is that the steady inflation of property prices has made it very easy for homeowners to accumulate wealth. Another explanation is that social breakdown has weakened people's sense of obligation to their children, so that they no longer save to finance an inheritance. This in turn reflects the weakening of the loyalty ethic. The increasing concern over the adequacy of pensions suggests that a weakness in the savings ethic may eventually undermine economic performance. Similarly, a weakness in the loyalty ethic may damage the quality of parenting, reduce inherited skills, and undermine productivity.

6. Summary and conclusion

From an economic perspective, trust may be regarded simply as a special kind of belief. It is a belief that other people will honour their obligations. These obligations vary in degree from an open commitment to promote social welfare through to mere conformity with conventions.

Trust is most effective when beliefs are shared. Shared beliefs develop when people acquire a reputation for being trustworthy. It is possible to trust people that you do not know if you know that they belong to a group that has a corporate reputation. Reputation therefore helps to spread trust.

There are two main reasons why it is rational to trust others. The first is that once a reputation for trust has been required, it generally pays to keep it. This is particularly true if the reputation can be vested in an institution or a brand, and can be passed on (or sold on) to others. The second is that a moral commitment helps a person to acquire a reputation in the first place.

To acquire a reputation, it is normally necessary to do more than simply demonstrate a desire to invest in it. If someone is regarded as fundamentally selfish at the outset, then any action they perform can be construed as purely strategic, and therefore unlikely to be repeated in future. But if it is believed that they have a capacity for moral commitment, then it possible to construe their actions in another way. Moral commitment suggests that people will stick resolutely to the same pattern of behaviour. This allows people to acquire a reputation for moral commitment over time.

In the long run people can only acquire a reputation for moral commitment if such a thing as a capacity for moral commitment really exists; otherwise, the basic 'lie' would sooner or later be exposed. The question then arises as to how this capacity is to be explained. The answer is that people gain emotional rewards from honouring commitments to others. People enjoy both the excitement of responsive emotions and the peace of mind generated by reflective emotions, and not only the pleasures of material consumption.

People maintain a balance between these sources of enjoyment (or utility) – a balance that may differ between people. This balance involves giving appropriate weight to pursuing the reflective emotional rewards afforded by trustworthy behaviour. It also involves keeping anti-social responsive emotions under control. Otherwise a person will damage their reputation (which may harm their material living standards) and incur feelings of guilt (which will damage their enjoyment of reflection). People who attach appropriate weight to reflective rewards can therefore be trusted to honour their obligations in a wide range of different situations.

Some sorts of obligation are particularly conducive to the coordination of the economy. Economies are subjected to continual shocks, and so patterns of consumption and production are constantly having to change in order to adjust to new conditions. In a sophisticated society there is a division of labour in which different people specialize in different tasks. When patterns of consumption and production change, everyone has to adjust. The adjustments made by different people have to be harmonized, and so there is a need for coordination. Coordination can be effected by the negotiation of new contracts, or simply by actions taken in anticipation of what others will do. In other cases people watch out for problems to emerge and then take remedial action as quickly as possible.

Economists often suggest that contract is the paramount method of coordination, and that trust has economic value primarily because it facilitates the enforcement of contracts. The law, it is suggested, is an expensive mode of enforcement, and therefore trust mediated by social institutions is a more economical mode. In other words, social institutions are cheaper than legal institutions in maintaining the invisible infrastructure of the market economy. While this approach is basically sound, its focus on contracts as a coordinating mechanism is too narrow. There are many economic activities which cannot easily be coordinated by contracts, whatever enforcement mechanism is used. Sometimes informal contracts based on tradition and custom can replace them. In other cases, however, people simply have to try to anticipate how others will act, and stand in readiness to sort out problems as they arise. Coordination is effected through goodwill rather than a contract of any kind. The contribution of trust to economic performance is therefore wider than a purely contractual view of the economy would suggest.

Most of the functionally useful moral values that promote economic performance are traditional moral values favoured by the great organized religions, but there are some nuances which are not always fully appreciated. The most difficult moral challenge is to ensure that socially beneficial innovation is properly rewarded. This involves rewarding people who have spent their time investigating alternative ways of doing things. Modern market economies rely on the innovator appropriating their reward through their own initiative, but this may involve them in dishonesty in discouraging imitators. In some cases subsidies are provided, patents awarded and prizes given, but these do not always provide adequate compensation. On the other hand, there is also a risk that they may pay too much compensation, or create barriers to entry that deter later innovations.

The ambiguity over the economic relevance of traditional values such as absolute honesty to the organization of competitive markets casts a shadow over the moral legitimacy of the Western market model. Neoclassical models of competition, for example, reformulate the process of competition in such a distorted manner that trust ceases to be an issue. By illuminating these issues, the economic analysis of trust can make an important contribution to policy debate over the future of the Western market model in the twenty-first century.

Note

1. There is an emerging literature that tries to evaluate the economic benefits of belonging to 'networks of trust' (see Gomez and Santor, 2001; Sivramkrishna and Panigrahi, 2001; Haddad and Maluccio, 2003).

Bibliography

Akerlof, G.A. (1970), 'The market for lemons: Quality uncertainty and the market mechanism', *Quarterly Journal of Economics*, **84**, 488–500.
Axelrod, R. (1984), *The Evolution of Cooperation*, New York: Basic Books.
Casson, Mark (1991), *The Economics of Business Culture*, Oxford: Clarendon Press.
Casson, Mark (1995), *Entrepreneurship and Business Culture*, UK, Aldershot: Edward Elgar.
David, P.A. (1989), 'Path-dependence: Putting the past into the future of Economics', Discussion Paper, Stanford University, Stanford.
Della Giusta, Marina (1999), 'A model of social capital and access to productive resources', *Journal of International Development*, **11**, 921–34.
Fukuyama, Francis (1995), *Trust*, New York: Free Press.
Gambetta, D. (1988), *Trust: Making and Breaking Cooperative Relations*, Cambridge, MA: Cambridge University Press.
Gomez, Rafael and Eric Santor (2001), 'Membership has its privileges: the effect of social capital and neighbourhood characteristics on the earnings of microfinance borrowers', *Canadian Journal of Economics*, **34**(4), 943–66.
Haddad, Lawrence and John A. Maluccio (2003), 'Trust, membership in groups, and household welfare: Evidence from KwaZulu-Natal, South Africa', *Economic Development and Cultural Change*, **51**, N.3.
Harriss, John, Janet Hunter and Colin M. Lewis (eds) (1995), *The New Institutional Economics and Third World Development*, London: Routledge.
Hirschman, Albert O. (1970), *Exit, Voice and Loyalty: Responses to Decline in Firms, Organisations and States*, Cambridge, MA: Harvard University Press.

Khalil, E. (ed.) (2003), *Trust*, Cheltenham, UK and Northampton, MA, USA: Edward Elgar.
Kreps, D. and R. Wilson (1982), 'Reputation and incomplete information', *Journal of Economic Theory*, **27**, 253–79.
North, Douglass (1990), *Institutions, Institutional Change, and Economic Performance*, Cambridge, MA: Cambridge University Press.
Putnam, Robert (1993), *Making Democracy Work: Civic Traditions in Modern Italy*, Princeton, NJ: Princeton University Press.
Rose, Mary B. (ed.) (2000), *Family Business*, Cheltenham, UK and Northampton, MA, USA: Edward Elgar.
Sivramkrishna, Sashi and Ramakrushna Panigrahi (2001), 'An economic model of self-help groups: Policy implications for banks and NGO initiatives', *Journal of International Development*, **13**, 1119–30.
Smith Ring, Peter (1997), 'Processes facilitating reliance on trust in inter-organisational networks', in Mark Ebers (ed.), *The Formation of Inter-Organisational Networks*, Oxford: Oxford University Press.
Veblen, Thorstein (1894), 'The economic theory of woman's dress', *Popular Science Monthly*, **34**, 198–205.
Williamson, Oliver E. (1996), *The Mechanisms of Governance*, Oxford: Oxford University Press.

20 Trust, institutions, agency: towards a neoinstitutional theory of trust

Guido Möllering

Introduction

The notion that trust can be based on institutions has been widely accepted in the literature for many decades, if not centuries, in so far as sociologists and political scientists have sought to understand how social interaction requires – and produces – a reliable social order. It has also been adopted in certain parts of organization theory and management studies. For example, Reinhard Bachmann (1998) notes: 'The foremost problems relating to the analysis of trust seem to be connected to the understanding of the role of the institutional environment in which business relations are embedded' (p. 298). In this chapter, I aim to contribute to this literature by presenting fundamental concepts from sociological neoinstitutionalism that are particularly powerful for an institutional explanation of trust. By introducing concepts such as 'natural attitude' and 'institutional isomorphism' to the problem of trust, the difficult and, in my view, still under-explored question of how actors relate to institutions can be addressed. Admittedly, what I refer to as 'sociological neoinstitutionalism' here is just one specific and not even very coherent stream of literature in the broad range of institutional theories, unified only by some more or less direct connection with Powell and DiMaggio's (1991) *New Institutionalism* volume. However, this work is able to fill many of the holes left by other institutional approaches and, of course, by trust theories that do not take institutions into account at all. In management and organization studies, in particular, the focus has been on individual cognition or interpersonal social-psychological processes, merely acknowledging some influence of the 'environment' or 'context' without further theorization (see, for example, the contributions in Kramer and Tyler, 1996).

Sociological studies of trust, on the other hand, have tended to focus on the level of systems and institutions, attributing an almost marginal role to the trusting and trusted actors (Misztal, 1996). However, actors interpret and question institutions and do not merely reproduce them passively. Therefore, if a theoretically sound case can be made for why institutions can be a source of trust between actors, it also needs to be recognized again that institutions become an object of trust for the trustors who exercise agency in relying on them (or not). A closer examination of this issue is another aim of this chapter. Clearly, without trust in institutions those institutions cannot be the source of 'institutional-based trust' in other actors. Again, this problem has long been recognized, for example by Georg Simmel ([1907] 1990) or more recently by Susan Shapiro (1987), but a systematic treatment of what makes institutions trustworthy and how actors interpret and (thereby) come to trust institutions is still difficult to achieve, not least because it needs to evolve along with our advances and newly discovered challenges in institutional theory. I seek to contribute towards this end.

The previous point connects research on trust with recent discussions in institutional theory about questions of institutional change, institutionalization processes and the role of agency. The institutions to which trust relates are not immutable themselves. More importantly, rather than assuming a passive trustor who draws on institutions if and when they are established and reliable, actors are directly involved in the constitution of trust within and beyond the institutional context that they find themselves in. A third aim of this chapter is therefore to explore the new concept of 'active trust' which Giddens (1994b) has introduced more or less in passing and which the trust literature has not really taken on board yet, although most writers on trust would probably agree that trustors are not merely passive carriers of trust (or mistrust). Once again, conceptual foundations need to be filled whereupon further trust research can stand.

My argument here builds on the idea that trust is a matter of embedded agency where trustors and trustees, as actors, interpret the social context in which they are embedded (see also Bachmann, 1998; Möllering, 2005a). In so far as this context is institutionalized, trust may be rather 'normal' and reached quite easily by referring to institutionalized rules, roles and routines. However, trust remains ambivalent and ultimately dependent on the actor's leap of faith based on interpretation. Moreover, actors organize and enact the contexts they refer to. In this respect, trust is always more than just a social process or condition. It is also an idiosyncratic accomplishment, actively constituted in more or less institutionalized contexts.

A comprehensive definition of trust needs to take into account the rational, institutional and processual references that enable the leap of faith towards trust. Hence I define trust as a reflexive process of building on reason, routine and reflexivity, suspending irreducible social vulnerability and uncertainty *as if* they were favourably resolved, and maintaining a state of favourable expectation towards the actions and intentions of more or less specific others (Möllering, 2006). The first part of this definition highlights the rational element in trust, in other words: the idea that trust is a prudent choice based on an assessment of the trustee's trustworthiness (defined, for example, in terms of utility, benevolence, competence and/or integrity) at a particular moment in time and in a certain respect. This rationalistic view of trust is paradigmatic for much of the trust literature to date, but will not be discussed here, because I believe it is time (again) to look in more detail at other elements that are fundamental for a realistic understanding of trust. In particular, as outlined above, the roles of institutions and interpretation beyond passive behaviour and mechanistic calculation are not fully understood in trust research to date.

The need to find alternative explanations is evident, because rationalistic explanations regularly face the paradox that they are either explaining trust away or explaining everything but trust (James, 2002; Möllering, 2005b). For example, Oliver Williamson (1993) has a point when he insists that rational choice theorists such as James Coleman (1990) should not use the term 'trust' when what they really describe is 'calculativeness'. On the other hand, the non-rational aspects of trust, by definition, simply cannot be dealt with in rationalist theories (Nooteboom, 2002). For example, the problems described by game theory or principal–agent theory tend to be 'solved' by reference to trust, implying the relaxation or abandonment of the key rationalist assumptions of the original frameworks (Ensminger, 2001). Reason certainly plays a role in trust and I discuss this at length in another text (Möllering, 2006). In this chapter, however, I focus on one alternative approach derived mainly from one particular stream of sociological neoinstitutionalism which differs from the essentially rational-choice-oriented work represented, for example, in the publications of the Russell Sage Foundation Series on Trust (see Cook, 2001; or, more recently, Cook et al., 2005; Gambetta and Hamill, 2005).

To be sure, rational choice theory recognizes the role of institutions as parameters of individual decisions; and one may also find many empirical examples, especially in business, of situations in which the institutionalized legitimate form of action matches closely the behavioural assumptions made by rational choice theory (Bachmann, 1998). For example, managers are expected to justify their decisions in terms of a 'hard' cost/benefit rationale. In private, it is not considered inappropriate if the same managers go and buy a lottery ticket (an irrational decision since the expected value is clearly negative). However, this observation simply reinforces the need to apply a more general theory of institutions, in this case to questions of trust.

Specifically, I discuss trust in the light of the phenomenological roots of neoinstitutionalist theories. The rather uncommon idea of trust as institutional isomorphism is discussed in detail and with reference to constructs such as rules, roles and routines. This leads to an investigation of trust based on institutions, highlighting the idea that when institutions serve as a source of trust between actors, those institutions become objects of trust, too. The background to these considerations is that, because of its phenomenological roots, this neoinstitutionalist approach to trust does not deny agency (which would eliminate the relevance of trust). Rather, a more processual and interpretative perspective of embedded agency suggests itself. This will be presented in the final part of the chapter. More or less consciously, agents can contribute to the development of the trust-inducing contexts which, in turn, enable them to trust more easily. Anthony Giddens even describes 'active trust' as a contemporary kind of trust that needs to be constantly worked upon in the rather unstable contexts of late modernity.

At the very end of the chapter, before the conclusion, it is shown that the key idea that any kind of trust requires a leap of faith can be traced back to classic contributions by Georg Simmel. This leap of faith needs to be restored in trust research, because it delineates 'trust' from rational choice and, thereby, lends it its specific and original meaning. Research ignoring the leap of faith misses the essential element of trust and could therefore be superfluous (replicating earlier studies on risk-taking or social conditioning) or even misleading (suggesting an unrealistic level of certainty or invulnerability). A stronger emphasis needs to be placed on the key role of actors' idiosyncratic interpretation and suspension of doubt in trust, because trust implies an 'as-if' attitude which is ultimately realized at the actor level, notwithstanding the assumption that this important element of agency in trust is socially embedded. All of the points raised in this chapter are discussed more fully in Möllering (2006).

Trust as natural attitude
In this section, I will first explain how institutions can be sources of trust, emphasizing the taken-for-grantedness implied in institutions. I will discuss whether manifestations of trust depend on how much an actor can take for granted in interactions with others. Without denying the potential value of other institutional approaches, I will focus on theoretical perspectives grouped liberally under the label of sociological neoinstitutionalism (although several authors whom I cite would not normally be called neoinstitutionalists). According to Ronald Jepperson (1991),

institutions are socially constructed, routine-reproduced (ceteris paribus), program or rule systems. They operate as relative fixtures of constraining environments and are accompanied by taken-for-granted accounts. This description accords with metaphors repeatedly invoked in discussions – metaphors of frameworks or rules. These imageries capture simultaneous contextual empowerment and constraint, and taken-for-grantedness. (p. 149)

If we want to argue that taken-for-grantedness in particular enables trust, then such a neoinstitutionalist approach needs to recall its roots in phenomenology and, specifically, Schütz's concept of natural attitude. In this regard, Zucker (1986) is a rare but prominent example of a study of trust grounded firmly in neoinstitutionalist theory and, more importantly, explicitly in those phenomenological insights that make sociological neoinstitutionalism distinct from other kinds of institutional analysis. In Zucker's definition 'trust is a set of expectations shared by all those involved in an exchange', including both 'broad social rules' and 'legitimately activated processes' (p. 54). When actors involved in an exchange share a set of expectations constituted in social rules and legitimate processes, they can trust each other with regard to the fulfilment and maintenance of those expectations. By the same token, actors can only trust those others with whom they share a particular set of expectations. Either way, trust hinges on the actors' natural ability to have a world in common with others and rely on it. Zucker thus adopts a Garfinkelian perspective on trust which, in turn, in based on the phenomenological work of Alfred Schütz.

One central idea in Schütz's theoretical writings is that the actor's 'natural attitude' towards the world becomes the starting point for the analysis of social reality rather than being seen as the major obstacle for such analysis: 'The object we shall be studying therefore is the human being who is looking at the world from within the natural attitude. Born into a social world, he comes upon his fellow men and takes their existence for granted without question, just as he takes for granted the existence of the natural objects he encounters' (Schütz, 1932 [1967], p. 98). This natural attitude (sometimes also translated as 'attitude of daily life' or a similar expression) captures the observation that actors normally do not doubt the reality of their everyday world and can thus have a 'lifeworld'. Moreover, as part of the natural attitude, actors assume that other people's view of reality is not too different from their own. The accomplishment of 'reciprocal perspectives' (Schütz, 1970b, p. 184) is that the everyday world is largely a 'world known in common with others' or a 'common-sense world' (Garfinkel, 1963).

Schütz (1932 [1967]) reveals that a precondition for social interaction is taken-for-grantedness, which he defines as 'that particular level of experience which presents itself as not in need of further analysis' (p. 74). However, it is clear from his writings that he does not take the natural attitude as such for granted. Instead, he is also concerned with how actors retain the facility to interpret part of their lifeworlds with an attitude of doubt or curiosity (Garfinkel, 1963). The *epoché* of the natural attitude presents actors as rather skilful in handling the duality of familiarity and unfamiliarity in their stream of experiences (Schütz, 1970a; see also Endreß, 2001).

Harold Garfinkel (1963) draws on and interprets Schütz's concept of the natural attitude when he states that '[t]he attitude of daily life furnishes a person's perceived environment its definition as an environment of social realities known in common' and that it 'is constitutive of the institutionalized common understandings of the practical everyday organization and workings of the society as seen "from within"' (p. 235). The constitutive features of basic rules of a game serve Garfinkel as a heuristic to understanding stable social interaction: in particular, basic rules are constituted by three 'constitutive expectancies' (p. 190) by which players expect (a) the rules to frame a set of required alternative moves and outcomes, (b) the rules to be binding on all other players and (c) the other players to equally expect (a) and (b). Crucially, Garfinkel concludes that 'basic rules frame the set of possible events of play that observed behavior can signify' and 'provide a behavior's sense as an action' (p. 195), that is they literally define what can happen and has happened.

Garfinkel (1963, 1967) therefore sets out in his (in)famous breaching experiments to manipulate social interactions in such a way that the infringement of basic rules causes surprise, confusion, anomie and other kinds of strong irritation in the subjects of the experiments, thereby aiming to reveal the fundamental social structures that are ordinarily, routinely and tacitly referred to and reproduced in everyday life. He shows how actors quite actively 'normalize' and redefine events that fall outside of basic rules in order to maintain 'the game', in other words the perceived normality and stability of the social context (see also McKnight et al., 1998).

What makes Garfinkel's interpretation of the natural attitude particularly interesting for this study is that it includes a concept of 'trust' (mostly set in inverted commas by him) which I regard as fundamental to the natural-attitude view of trust: 'To say that one person "trusts" another means that the person seeks to act in such a fashion as to produce through his action or to respect as conditions of play actual events that accord with normative orders of events depicted in the basic rules of play' and 'the player takes for granted the basic rules of the game as a definition of his situation, and that means of course as a definition of his relationships to others' (Garfinkel, 1963, pp. 193–4). This means, on the one hand, that people trust each other if their interactions are governed by the three constitutive expectancies listed above. If this is the case, then trust can be regarded more generally as 'a condition for "grasping" the events of daily life' (p. 190). Moreover, though, compliance with basic rules and constitutive expectancies also means reliance on them. Trust in the natural attitude means interacting with others on the basis that everyone knows and accepts basic rules for the interaction.

Building on this, Lynne Zucker (1977; see also Zucker, 1983, 1987) notes that institutionalization can be seen as a *process* of defining social reality or as a *property* of an act as socially more or less taken for granted. For example, institutionalizing a ban on child labour is a process (re)producing social definitions of childhood and labour. And it depends on time and place to what degree such a ban has the property of being taken for granted. Thus Zucker emphasizes on the one hand that objective reality or social facts may persist even when they are not internalized, and on the other hand that the degree of institutionalization can vary from high to low (Jepperson, 1991). Highly institutionalized acts have ready-made accounts, meaning that they are easily legitimated, while less institutionalized acts are not so taken for granted and therefore will not influence the behaviour of others as strongly.

In Zucker (1986), however, she argues historically with reference to the economic structure of the USA in 1840–1920 that institutions have become more and more necessary and important. Viewing trust as a precondition for economic exchanges (Arrow, 1974), defining it with Garfinkel (1963) as a set of shared background and constitutive expectations, and noting certain similarities as well as dissimilarities with Durkheim's (1984) types of pre-contractual solidarity, Zucker (1986) identifies and examines three central modes of trust production, that is three different ways in which actors establish a world known in common and the rules for their interaction. First, 'process-based trust' is tied to past or expected exchanges between specific actors which can be first-hand or by reputation. These exchanges enable them to produce a basis for their interactions that cannot be extended outside of their relationship and are therefore not institutionalized. Second, 'characteristics-based trust' is produced through social similarity between actors, meaning that it is tied to persons possessing certain stable characteristics (for example, family background, ethnicity, sex) but already generalized to some degree, as externally ascribed characteristics activate expectations about common understandings. Third, 'institutional-based trust' describes sets of shared expectations derived from formal social structures represented, for example, by signals of membership of professions or associations, or by intermediary mechanisms such as bureaucracy, banking and legal regulation.

Hence, according to Zucker (1986), institutions can enable trust between actors and such trust can then even be institutionalized when the underlying shared expectations are relatively independent of time and space. Note, though, that in Zucker's account, and as pointed out similarly by Paul DiMaggio and Walter Powell (1991) and others, institutions as intermediary mechanisms are not seen (primarily) as a third-party guarantor and enforcer – as they would be in rationalist theories of trust – but as systems of rules and meanings that provide common expectations which define the actors as social beings.

Trust as institutional isomorphism
While the previous section has introduced the natural attitude as part of the conceptual foundations for the idea that trust springs from taken-for-grantedness, I borrow in this section the concept of isomorphism from neoinstitutionalist organization theory (specifically DiMaggio and Powell, 1983; Meyer and Rowan, 1977) to argue further that manifestations of trust may be explained to a considerable degree by institutionalization: the trustor A trusts (or mistrusts) the trustee B in a certain matter because it is natural and legitimate to do so and 'everybody would do it'. For similar reasons, trustee B will honour the trust (or not). Note that, in this pure sense, the question of the utility of trust is detached from the institutionally required acts.

The last point just noted reflects the provocative claims by John Meyer and Brian Rowan (1977) who argue 'that the formal structures of many organizations . . . dramatically reflect the myths of their institutional environments instead of the demands of their work activities' (p. 341). According to these authors, myths are rationalized, impersonal prescriptions with rule-like specifications about the appropriate means to pursue prescribed purposes. Moreover, myths are highly institutionalized, which means that they are taken for granted as legitimate and beyond the discretion of individual actors. On the one hand, Meyer and Rowan (1977) identify isomorphism as the process of adapting (systems of) action to match and imitate institutional requirements. On the other hand, this is seen as mere 'dramatic enactments of the rationalized myths pervading modern societies' (p. 346). In other words, myths are only complied with on the surface; a legitimate façade is constructed, 'decoupled' from the actual action. Translating this argument from formal organizational structures to trust, the question arises whether seemingly trustful interactions may equally be little more than dramatic enactment and ceremony. It could thus be the case that actors are not really trusting or trustworthy, but the same sequence of action unfolds as if they were. They put up 'façades of trust' (Hardy et al., 1998) while their trust is actually 'spurious' (Fox, 1974). However, Meyer and Rowan's (1977) concept of isomorphism introduces an instrumentalism that separates the actor level too much from the institutional and societal level and therefore runs the risk of losing major phenomenological insights that are fundamental to neoinstitutionalist theories.

Paul DiMaggio and Walter Powell (1983) manage to alleviate this problem by distinguishing between different types and mechanisms of isomorphism. Starting with Hawley's (1968) basic definition of isomorphism as a constraining process that forces one unit in a population to resemble other units that face the same set of environmental conditions, one type of isomorphism can be labelled 'competitive', according to DiMaggio and Powell. It subsumes on the one hand population ecology explanations (for example Hannan and Freeman, 1977) that attribute the similarity of units in a population to the evolutionary superiority of their properties. On the other hand, competitive isomorphism can also subsume instrumental imitation, in other words the deliberate copying of other units which are doing well. In terms of trust, competitive isomorphism would thus mean that in certain contexts actors generally trust each other because this practice has emerged as more successful than not trusting. In other contexts, distrust may have been selected over time as a more efficient practice than trust. (Note that the theory underlying the concept of competitive isomorphism assumes rational utility maximizers and/or disinterested evolutionary forces, leaving little room for agency.)

The other, more open, and hence for the present discussion more relevant, type of isomorphism distinguished by DiMaggio and Powell (1983) is called 'institutional isomorphism' and is subdivided for analytical purposes into three mechanisms: coercive, mimetic and normative isomorphism. First, coercive isomorphism stems from external pressure to conform in order to gain legitimacy. The pressure may be implicit or explicit and the sanctions against nonconformity may be more or less severe, but this mechanism is mainly one of avoiding a lack of legitimacy. It matches Meyer and Rowan's (1977) argument that avoidance of coercion means enacting and upholding objective myth and ceremony, decoupled from subjective content and utility. Whether coercive isomorphism should be categorized as institutional is debatable. Zucker, for example, argues that 'applying sanctions to institutionalized acts may actually have the effect of deinstitutionalizing them' (Zucker, 1977, p. 728). The need for coercion gives rise to doubts about the validity of the legitimation for the respective institution (see also Zucker, 1987). For trust in particular, the idea of trusting or being trustworthy just because of external pressure is not seen as a durable basis for social interaction (except in rationalist accounts). The idea of trust as coercive institutional isomorphism may still apply, though, if the external pressure is predominantly latent but gives 'structural assurance' (McKnight et al., 1998, p. 479).

The second mechanism of institutional isomorphism identified by DiMaggio and Powell (1983) is mimicry ('mimetic processes', p. 151) or 'modelling' (Galaskiewicz and Wasserman, 1989). An actor imitates, implicitly or explicitly, the behaviour of another. This mechanism applies especially in contexts of high uncertainty and ambiguity where legitimacy can be obtained by doing as everybody else, or a recognized referent, does. The act as such is detached from its utility and reduced to the question of 'appropriateness' (March and Olsen, 1989). Considering trust according to this logic, actors who do not know if it is prudent to place or honour trust will do whatever (relevant) others would normally do in this situation.

Third, normative isomorphism entails the general principle that socialization instils particular cognitive bases and legitimations in the actor subject to them (DiMaggio and Powell, 1983). This mechanism comes closest to the idea of a natural attitude and the view that institutions frame how actors can grasp their lifeworld and relate to it in their actions. Role expectations are learned and fulfilled because they go hand in hand with the actor's self-image or identity and 'what such a person must do'. Once actors have internalized norms and accepted roles associated with a part of their lifeworld, they enact those roles mostly implicitly but at times also explicitly. This produces isomorphism in the sense that all actors who play the same institutionalized role will do so in a standard, recognized, legitimate way. Trust as normative isomorphism would thus mean that actors who have been socialized to place or honour trust in certain types of situation will conform to this expectation, because otherwise they would be going against their own nature or against the objective reality of society (Zucker, 1986). Interestingly, this conformity means at the same time that the actor is able to maintain self-respect and integrity, that is, a favourable identity or self-image. This view of isomorphic, unquestioned trust can explain, for example, manifestations of trust that cannot be explained by calculativeness.

Rules, roles and routines
Although there is currently no established neoinstitutionalist school of trust research and the above sections only identify a few concepts that it might entail, the trust literature contains many relevant references to rules, roles and routines as bases for trust. Some of this literature will be reviewed briefly in this section in order to show that arguments building on notions of natural attitude and institutional isomorphism are not uncommon. For example, if the main problem of trust, accordingly, is not opportunism but the ability to engage in meaningful interaction in the first place, then contract law, trade associations and technical standards are social institutions that embody systems of rules for interaction and thus a basis for trust, if rules are understood as cultural meaning systems (Lane, 1997). A similar logic applies to the idea that trust can be based on roles. For example, when Bernard Barber (1983, p. 9) identifies the 'expectation of technically competent role performance' as one key element of trust, he already presupposes institutionalized roles or what he calls 'shorthand ways of referring to complex patterns of expectations among actors' which make it possible to trust (or distrust) a role incumbent. The 'swift trust' in temporary systems described by Debra Meyerson, Karl Weick and Roderick Kramer (1996) is a special but highly illustrative example of how reliance on clearly defined roles makes trustful interactions possible even when these interactions are relatively isolated and transient as, for example, in project work: 'If people in temporary systems deal with one another more as roles than as individuals . . . then expectations should be more stable, less capricious, more standardized, and defined more in terms of tasks and specialities than personalities' (p. 173). Thus roles carry the taken-for-granted expectations on which trust can be based.

The concept of role is also central to Adam Seligman's (1997) social-philosophical analysis of trust, but in his framework reliance on role expectations merely gives 'confidence', whereas the problem of 'trust' only arises in the face of role negotiability: 'Trust is something that enters into social relations when there is role negotiability, in what may be termed the "open spaces" of roles and role expectations' (pp. 24–5). Seligman claims that pervasive role negotiability is a defining aspect of modernity and stems from the proliferation of roles, ensuing dissonances and gaps in (no longer) taken-for-granted definitions of roles. While Seligman's account thus points to the limits of the institutional approach, the unconditionality that for him characterizes trust may not be too different from the Schützian natural attitude, where actors play an active part in interpreting their lifeworlds, normalizing events and socially constructing reality. At least Seligman supports the view that role expectations are a basis for confidence. If we assume further that all roles may in principle be negotiable but cannot be negotiated all at once, then Seligman's 'confidence' and 'trust' have to go hand in hand, requiring a kind of Garfinkelian constitutive expectancy that at any given moment in time most role expectations will not be negotiated. After all, even Garfinkel's experiments would not have 'worked' in the sense of producing meaningful findings if he and his students had breached all rules and roles at once, which would be difficult to imagine anyway.

Finally, routines are introduced here as a third heuristic alongside rules and roles in order to lend the notion of trust based on institutions' greater plasticity. Routines are regularly and habitually performed programmes of action or procedures. They may or may not be supported by corresponding (systems of) rules and/or roles, and they represent institutions inasmuch as they are typified, objectivated and legitimated, not senseless repetitions, although their sense is mostly tacit and taken for granted while they are performed (Scott, 2001). As with rules and roles, 'the reality of everyday life maintains itself by being embodied in routines' (Berger and Luckmann, 1966, p. 149). Similarly, Anthony Giddens (1984) points out: 'Routine is integral both to the continuity of the personality of the agent, as he or she moves along the paths of daily activities, and to the institutions of society, which are such only through their continued reproduction' (p. 60). By implication, the placing and honouring of trust itself is seen as part of the routine. For example, most parents will not fret every morning when their child leaves for school, because entrusting the child to the care of bus drivers, teachers and others is part of a daily routine. However, this brings up a higher-order problem of trust again: trust in the reliability of the routine in continuously producing the same (range of) outcomes and, more importantly, trust in the motivation and ability of the actors involved not to deviate from the programme of action – for whatever reason. Agency cannot be explained away (Feldman and Pentland, 2003).

In sum, rules, roles and routines are bases for trust in so far as they represent taken-for-granted expectations that give meaning to, but cannot guarantee, their fulfilment in action. However, this explanation has to be incomplete, because a neoinstitutionalist view affords both the trustor and the trustee a non-passive role in challenging, changing and cheating the institutions, albeit not all of them all at once and all the time. This notion of agency (Beckert, 1999; DiMaggio, 1988) will be addressed later, but first I should perhaps pursue the simpler issue that a trustor who trusts on the basis of institutions needs to have trust in those institutions, given that they cannot be assumed to be infallible and immutable.

Trust in institutions

Lynne Zucker's (1986) 'institutional-based trust' is conceptually interesting and, according to her, empirically vital because it implies that a trustor can trust a trustee without establishing 'process-based trust' in a personal relationship. However, as Jörg Sydow (1998) argues, this makes institutions an object of trust, too, and not only a source.

An analytical distinction therefore has to be drawn between the influence that institutions have on the trustor–trustee relationship on the one hand and the trust that actors have in the institutions on the other (see also Bachmann, 1998). This latter notion of trust in the system, in particular at the societal level, has been the main area of interest in a significant part of the trust literature, notably political-science-oriented work, such as Barber (1983), Dunn (1988), Coleman (1990), Fukuyama (1995), Putnam (1995), Sztompka (1999), Warren (1999) and Cook (2001), as well as those studies analysing trust items in large-scale surveys like the General Social Survey in the USA (for example Paxton, 1999; Glaeser et al., 2000). Niklas Luhmann's (1979) observation that 'the old theme of political trust . . . has virtually disappeared from contemporary political theory' (p. 54) no longer applies.

In this regard it is interesting to note that Barbara Misztal (1996) presumes that the concern for trust in the social sciences has been – from the classics to the present day – above all else a search for the bases of social order, that is, a dependable social system. The requirement of 'trust in the system' is already evident for Hobbes's Leviathan just as much as for Locke's social contract (see for example Dunn, 1988). What this means in modernity and beyond the question of government has been expressed by Georg Simmel ([1907] 1990), who in his discussion of the transition from material money to credit money notes that 'the feeling of personal security that the possession of money gives is perhaps the most concentrated and pointed form and manifestation of confidence in the socio-political organization and order' (p. 179). Niklas Luhmann (1979) introduces his concept of 'system trust' by reflecting on money, too, and supposes that an actor 'who trusts in the stability of the value of money . . . basically assumes that a system is functioning and places his trust in that function, not in people' (p. 50). According to Luhmann, system trust builds up through continual, affirmative experiences with the system. It grows and persists precisely because it is impersonal, diffuse and rests on generalization and indifference.

Interestingly, Luhmann suggests that abstract systems should have inbuilt controls which can be maintained by experts. Actors do not need to trust in an impenetrable system as a whole but 'only' in the functioning of controls. In stark contrast to Susan Shapiro (1987), Luhmann does not see an infinite regress of controlling the controls and thus the danger of a spiral of distrust. Moreover, according to Luhmann, system trust also rests on the actor's assumption that everybody else trusts the system, too. While the assurances of experts and others thus give a 'certainty-equivalent', system trust overall means confidence in an unavoidable, disinterested and abstract entity (Luhmann, 1988).

Luhmann does not address a point implicit in his trust concept which I regard as crucial, namely that trust is essentially not so much a choice or, in Luhmann's less rationalistic terminology, a selection between one course of action (trusting) or the other (distrusting), but between either accepting a given level of assurance or looking for further controls and safeguards. System trust (and also personal trust) fails or cannot even be said to exist when this state of suspending doubt is not reached. The 'inflationary spiral of escalating trust relationships and the paradox that the more we control the institution of trust, the more dissatisfied we will be with its offerings', attested by Shapiro (1987) for modern societies, where 'the guardians of trust are themselves trustees' (p. 652), are only set in motion if the response to a need for trust is always the installation of more controls, instead of being satisfied at some point that the system apparently 'works'. In particular,

Anthony Giddens (1990) captures more lucidly than Luhmann how actors can have trust in abstract systems or institutions. He describes the 'access points' where the actor experiences the system by interacting with other actors, typically experts, who represent the system. Patients, for example, develop trust (or distrust) in the medical system to a large extent through their experiences with doctors and other medical professionals such as nurses and midwives who represent and 'embody' the institutions of medicine (see Parsons, 1978; and more recently McKneally et al., 2004; Brownlie and Howson, 2005; Lowe, 2005).

However, as Luhmann pointed out, too, the object of system trust is indeed the system as such, but since it is impossible for individual actors to comprehend the system, they can only assure themselves of its proper functioning through the re-embedded performances of experts who refer to and represent a particular system. Giddens (1990) goes further than Luhmann (1979) and places a different emphasis, because he does not see the role of experts primarily in controlling the system but in bringing it to life. According to Giddens (1990), if trust in systems is 'faceless' and trust in persons involves 'facework', then systems obtain a 'face' at their 'access points', which sustains or transforms 'faceless commitments' (p. 88). This interplay of disembedding and re-embedding is not unproblematic, which Giddens demonstrates by describing, on the one hand, how carefully system representatives design their performances in order to quell doubts about the system's functioning while, on the other hand, actors pragmatically accept the system but also retain an attitude of scepticism. Trust in an institution means confidence in the institution's reliable functioning, but this has to be based mainly on trust in visible controls or representative performances rather than on the internal workings of the institution as a whole.

Institutions can be seen as bases, carriers and objects of trust: trust between actors can be based on institutions, trust can be institutionalized, and institutions themselves can only be effective if they are trusted (see also Child and Möllering, 2003). While this is perfectly in line with sociological neoinstitutionalism, it has become apparent in the course of this chapter that this approach reveals, but does not fully explain, how actors achieve the natural attitude, the acceptance of normality, the assumption of good faith and similar notions that actually point towards the imperfection of institutions. Hence a more elaborate development of this approach will also have to face the questions which currently plague neoinstitutionalism. For example, consider the discussions about the 'institutional entrepreneur' (DiMaggio, 1988) as an actor who plays an outstanding role in reflexively creating, preserving and changing specific institutions (Beckert, 1999). Can a corresponding role be conceived for a kind of 'trust entrepreneur' who actively shapes context in a trust-enhancing manner?

Active constitution of trust
So far, I have stressed the actor's reliance on institutions, implying a rather passive role for trustors. In the following sections, I will argue that all trust – even when it is based on taken-for-granted institutions – is not just passive but requires an as-if attitude on the part of the trustor which renders irreducible social vulnerability and uncertainty unproblematic. And in less institutionalized contexts, trust becomes even more a kind of 'active trust' (Giddens, 1994b) in the sense of the trustor actively engaging in a process of trust development. This process may be started 'blindly'. However, trustors need not foolishly or heroically enter into such a process but may rather begin the trust-building process with

small steps. Over time, trust then evolves with the relationship, ideally in a self-reinforcing fashion. An important aspect of the process is whether the actors can negotiate through familiarization between familiarity and unfamiliarity. The concept of active trust highlights furthermore that trust should be seen as a continuous process of reflexive constitution which requires mutual openness and intensive communication. The trust literature to date mainly sees trust as an active choice in given circumstances. The following sections go beyond these notions by identifying ways in which actors actively influence the circumstances for their trusting choices. There is a 'creative element' (Beckert, 2005, p. 20) in trust.

To start with, 'blind trust' can actually be quite functional: unintentional, coincidental behaviour may trigger a process of desirable interactions that could not have been willingly produced as easily. Moreover, Russell Hardin (1993) makes repeated reference to the idea of strategic 'as-if trust' alongside trust based on encapsulated interest. Accordingly, imagine an actor who thinks that trust would be desirable but cannot rationally trust the potential trustee yet. This actor may *nevertheless* choose to feign trust with the aim of building up genuine trust. Hardin envisages 'as-if trust' to be used when the trustor only has a vague notion that a trustful, cooperative relationship with the potential trustee could be beneficial. However, it is difficult to determine within a rational choice framework how much non-rationality will be rational for the actor in such an uncertain context, meaning that it is hard to judge rationally when it is rational to be non-rational (Good, 1988, p. 42). Trust therefore remains atleast partly non-rational itself: the trustor *just does it*. Not the rational validity of expectations and generalizations as such but their availability in the first place is what makes trust functional. 'Trust begins where prediction ends' (Lewis and Weigert, 1985, p. 976) and all that matters is that trust emerges *at all*. Actors may choose to trust blindly in order to overcome rational or institutional vacuums and paradoxes.

Hardin (1993) clearly presents the strategy of as-if trust as a temporary solution which enables a process whereby the trustor can gradually cease to feign trust because genuine trust develops. Moreover, if trust generally is functional in that it reduces social complexity, it does not necessarily mean that trust has to reduce complexity immediately or completely. Instead a 'principle of gradualness' (Luhmann, 1979, p. 41) can be followed. Trust is generated and extended step by step, beginning with relatively small steps. This implies that trust building requires time and may be rather tentative. This was already seen by Peter Blau, who thought of trust as evolving and expanding gradually in parallel to social associations from minor initial transactions: '[T]he process of social exchange leads to the trust required for it in a self-governing fashion' (Blau, 1968, p. 454; see also Blau, 1964).

A possible explanation for the mechanism identified by Blau is given by Dale Zand (1972), who presents a 'spiral reinforcement model of the dynamics of trust' (p. 233). Accordingly, high initial trust will lead the actor A to disclose information, accept influence and reduce control, which the other actor B perceives as positive signs of trustworthiness that increase B's level of trust and induce similarly open behaviour. This reinforces A's initial trust and thus leads to further trusting action, reinforcing B's trust and so forth. In other words, expectations of trust and the resultant action would be a typical example of a self-fulfilling prophecy. This perspective of trust based on positive experience matches Lynne Zucker's concept of 'process-based trust' (already mentioned above). Zucker (1986) states that process-based trust is 'tied to past or expected exchange such as in reputation or gift-exchange' and informed by 'a record of prior exchange, often obtained second-hand or by imputation from outcomes of prior exchange' (p. 60). Actors establish an exchange history analogous to the traditional giving of gifts and counter-gifts (Mauss, [1925] 1954; Blau, 1964), which involves a trust-inducing time lapse and a formation of mutual expectations of reciprocity.

The notion that trust develops gradually and grows with mutual experience in relationships over time is also captured very instructively in a well-known model by Roy Lewicki and Barbara Bunker (1996). They describe three types of trust that serve to illustrate the stages of trust development over time. They argue that in the first stage of a new relationship 'calculus-based trust' is required. It rests on calculative reasoning about the other's incentives to maintain the relationship and the deterrents preventing him from breaking trust. Where calculus-based trust proves to be valid, the actors may get to know each other better and understand each other's needs, preferences and priorities more generally so that in the second stage 'knowledge-based trust' develops which 'is grounded in the other's predictability – knowing the other sufficiently well so that the other's behavior is anticipatable' (p. 121). Interestingly, Lewicki and Bunker point out that not all relationships develop knowledge-based trust on top of calculus-based trust: some relationships will stabilize just on a calculus level, though many relationships reach knowledge-based trust because the getting-to-know-each-other is almost inevitable. A few relationships may even evolve after some more time to the stage of 'identification-based trust' where the 'parties effectively understand and appreciate the other's wants' and 'each can effectively act for the other' (p. 122). Although calculus and knowledge are still present as bases for trust, identification with the other's desires and intentions becomes the perceptual paradigm for the actors. Lewicki and Bunker illustrate that trust does not simply grow stronger over time, but the 'frame' in which the actors consider trust changes as trust develops, so that the issues faced at an early stage should be very different from those in a long-established, identification-based trust relationship.

Although there are important differences between the process concepts of trust proposed by different authors discussed in this section, and although it may be debatable whether the stages and phases of trust development will follow exactly the patterns suggested, an overall conclusion common to all of these contributions can be drawn: actors do not need to trust each other fully right from the beginning of a relationship, because they can engage experimentally in a kind of as-if trust which may gradually produce proper trust. While such a process may simply emerge, the more interesting possibility is that actors may actively produce mutual experiences with the aim of testing whether a trust relationship is feasible, but without being able to know in advance the associated benefits and risks. It follows, again that an essential feature of trust and its development must be the actor's ability to 'just do it' and overcome, at least momentarily, the irreducible uncertainty and vulnerability in social exchanges.

Familiarity, unfamiliarity and familiarization
According to Luhmann (1979), 'trust is only possible within a familiar world' (p. 20) and, in line with the neoinstitutional approach, the presence of many familiar elements in an interaction context positively influences the actor's ability to confer or deny trust (Luhmann, 1988). The concept of familiarity recalls the discussion on trust and institutions presented earlier, because familiarity essentially represents taken-for-grantedness

and the 'natural attitude' that actors have towards their lifeworld. However, the main point of interest here is how actors deal with and overcome unfamiliarity and how they may be able to develop trust (gradually) in contexts of low familiarity through a process of familiarization.

Familiarity in Alfred Schütz's terms (1970a) 'demarcates, for the particular subject in his concretely particular life-situation, that sector of the world which does from that which does not need further investigation' (p. 61). Objects regarded as familiar are 'beyond question' and thus 'taken for granted'. Familiarity, requires the natural attitude as it 'presupposes the idealizations of the "and so forth and so on" and the "I can do it again"' (p. 58). Another way of interpreting familiarity, according to Schütz, is to say that it expresses 'the likelihood of referring new experiences, in respect of their types, to the habitual stock of already acquired knowledge . . . by means of a passive synthesis of recognition' (pp. 58–9). In other words, even a new object can be sufficiently familiar to the actor if it can be recognized as typical. This indicates, however, that familiarity implies the unfamiliar, too, at least in two respects. First, 'the now unquestioned world . . . is merely unquestioned until further notice' (p. 61), meaning that all that the actor is subjectively familiar with could in principle be questioned. Second, unfamiliarity is not just something that actors can choose to direct their attention towards and question if and when they please, but rather something that actors cannot avoid because 'unfamiliar experience imposes itself upon us by its very unfamiliarity' (p. 28) and becomes thematic and topical whether the actor likes it or not, especially in processes of social interaction. Schütz does not see the actor as locked into the natural attitude, but as able to respond constructively to 'imposed relevance' when prompted to in the stream of experience. If trust builds on familiarity, then the good news from Schütz is that unfamiliarity need not automatically mean distrust as long as the actor uses his capacity of familiarization to increase his familiarity when necessary.

Like Schütz, Luhmann (1988) sees an intimate connection between the familiar and the unfamiliar, because the underlying distinction can re-enter its own space in what I would label a process of familiarization: 'We can live within a familiar world because we can, using symbols, reintroduce the unfamiliar into the familiar' (p. 95). However, 'we know in a familiar way about the unfamiliar' (p. 95), which means that Schütz's 'imposed relevance' of the unfamiliar can only be dealt with in familiar terms. Thus familiarization shifts the boundaries of familiarity *from within*. Unfamiliarity only renders trust impossible when the actor fails to engage in familiarization.

Trust in this sense relies on both familiarity and familiarization. Hence trust requires familiarity, but the two concepts must not be confused (Luhmann, 1988). Rather, according to Luhmann (1979), they should be seen as 'complementary ways of absorbing complexity and are linked to one another, in the same way as past and future are linked' (p. 20). In familiarity, past experiences are condensed and their continuity assumed, which makes future-oriented trust possible: 'But rather than just being an inference from the past, trust goes beyond the information it receives and risks defining the future. The complexity of the future world is reduced by the act of trust. In trusting, one engages in action as though there were only certain possibilities in the future' (p. 20). This can be interpreted to mean, on the one hand, that familiarization is a kind of hindsight that can strengthen the familiarity base for trust. However, on the other hand, I would claim that familiarization is very much future-oriented, too, so that trust in general and active trust in particular may be described as the familiarization of the future: trust 'risks defining the future', as Luhmann puts it in the above quote.

Adam Seligman (1997) develops an elaborate argument on the relationships between trust, familiarity and the conditions of modernity which connects in many places with Luhmann's work but gives a very different perspective. He states that familiarity commonly means the actor's ability to impute the values that condition the actions of another actor and thus enables the first actor to have expectations towards the second (Seligman, 1997, p. 69). However, he emphasizes throughout his book the 'unconditionality' of trust as its essential feature, because 'it involves one in a relation where the acts, character, or intentions of the other cannot be confirmed' and it means 'a vulnerability occasioned by some form of ignorance or basic uncertainty as to the other's motives' (p. 21). The freedom of the other and his very otherness are the object of trust. The trustor expects not to be harmed, but lacks the means to verify his expectations. Having expressed the clear position that unconditional trust cannot be based on conditioning familiarity, Seligman offers a surprising twist later on when he introduces the idea that, put simply, familiarity in modernity can encompass unconditionality and thus serve as a mechanism that produces system confidence and enables trust. In other words, the actors in modern societies are familiar with the fact that other individuals are to a greater or lesser extent unknowable and unconditionable and therefore *need* to be trusted. Familiarity in modernity, then, also means accepting mutual unconditionality without thereby removing it. Thus familiarity is required in forming trusting expectations; familiarization creates familiarity; trust represents a kind of familiarization with the future; but the future, in the sense of the other's eventual actions and intentions, remains unknowable. Within this general position, it is now possible to appreciate the significance of the inspiring comments on 'active trust' by Giddens (1994b), for whom 'familiarity is the keynote to trust' (Giddens, 1994a, p. 81) in traditional societies, but who, like Luhmann, Seligman and many others, observes an erosion of familiarity as a stable basis for trustful interaction in post-traditional societies and envisages the active constitution of trust by late-modern actors.

Reflexive constitution and continuous communication

Giddens (1994b, pp. 186–7) introduces the term 'active trust' very briefly and somewhat casually but nevertheless captures by it an interesting view of the particular mechanisms involved in building trust in late modernity. Where perceived trustworthiness and contextual confidence become increasingly difficult, active trust may be a way out, but it 'has to be energetically treated and sustained' (p. 187). Without yet calling it 'active trust', Giddens refers to central ideas behind this concept in some of his earlier writing. For example, Giddens (1990) points out that trust needs to be 'worked upon' (p. 121; see also Giddens, 1991). Active trust implies a reflexive process of trust development, which requires continuous communication and openness (see also Beckert, 2002). In a manner of speaking, this makes every move a first move, because the basis for the relationship and trust needs to be constantly reproduced in order to result in a stable or at least continuous relationship. Active trust therefore recognizes the autonomy of the other, i.e. the freedom to honour or exploit the trust. More and more often, actors have 'no choice but to make choices' (Giddens, 1994b, p. 187) from what they know to be imperfect decision bases. This, however, brings the true nature of trust to the fore, because trust would be 'frozen' if it were based on compulsion and is only really trust in the face of contingency (Giddens, 1994a, p. 90).

'*All* trust is in a certain sense blind trust', as Giddens (1990, p. 33, emphasis in original) asserts provocatively, and thereby emphasizes probably the most essential feature of trust. First, however, it should be noted again that Giddens does not associate the blindness of trust with passivity on the part of the trustor. On the contrary, trust 'has to be worked at – the trust of the other has to be won' (Giddens, 1991, p. 96). Such active trust 'presumes the opening out of the individual to the other' (Giddens, 1990, p. 121) in the absence of external supports for trust (Giddens, 1992). Familiarity has to be continuously and reflexively created. Thus active trust reflects contingency and change in an ongoing process of reflexive constitution.

Giddens's conceptualization of trust does not contradict his theory of structuration (Giddens, 1979, 1984), but he does not draw specifically on this theoretical framework when he discusses trust. That it might be quite instructive to do so is demonstrated by Sydow (1998), who conceptualizes trust in terms of a modality in the duality and recursiveness of structure and (inter)action. The constitution of trust, according to Sydow's structuration perspective on trust building (see also Sydow and Windeler, 2003; Sydow, Chapter 21 in this volume), involves the development of interpretative schemes, resources and norms to which the actor refers in trustful and trustworthy interaction, thereby (re)producing the social structure of signification, domination and legitimation in which the phenomenon of trust is constituted and to which further action will refer. Charles Sabel's (1993) notion of 'studied trust' fits very well with the mechanisms described by Sydow and also with Giddens's concept of active trust (Beckert, 2002). Sabel emphasizes the actor's ability to actively work on trust by challenging entrenched interpretations and redefining the social context in such a way that the trust required for cooperation becomes possible (see also Maguire et al., 2001; Möllering, 2006).

Such a view implies, of course, a processual perspective whereby trust only materializes in reflexive social practices which, over time, mostly reproduce trust but may always change it as well, either intentionally or unintentionally. While a 'structuration theory of trust' is effective in describing the constitution of trust and leaves room for the crucial 'unconditionality' (Seligman, 1997) of trust, it cannot explain clearly how this latter aspect is handled within trust. In other words, additional concepts are required to understand how actors can live with the fact that the ongoing process of structuration itself is open-ended – *despite* or rather *because of* the actor's agency, which represents the irreducible social contingency without which trust would be neither required nor possible but which the trustor treats *as if* it were resolved. Giddens (1990, 1991) himself highlights in connection with the concept of trust a kind of 'suspension of reflexivity' akin to the suspension of doubt within the natural attitude. Active trust in particular is always a kind of trust-in-the-making which requires the trustor to go down an essentially unknowable path. This suspension needs to be looked at more closely.

Suspension: the leap of faith

Trust is only reached if the prospective trustor can cope with the irreducible social vulnerability and uncertainty that rests in the trustee's principal freedom to either honour or exploit trust. The fact that trust is therefore 'risky' has been taken far too lightly. This means that writers on trust commonly point to the element of risk (or uncertainty) in trust, but they seldom explore how actors deal with this in practice. I regard this as an important omission, because actually, as will be explained in this final section, the crucial achievement of trust is that in trust the possibility that it might be exploited or based on corrupted 'good reasons' is suspended but not eliminated. Such a view is rare in the literature on trust, but where it can be found it can mostly be traced back to a few inspiring passages in the work of Georg Simmel (Misztal, 1996; Möllering, 2001).

Simmel does not regard mere weak inductive knowledge as proper trust (Giddens, 1991). Within trust there is a 'further element of socio-psychological quasi-religious faith' (Simmel, 1990, p. 179). In the same source, Simmel confesses that he finds this element 'hard to describe' and thinks of it as 'a state of mind which has nothing to do with knowledge, which is both less and more than knowledge'. He expresses this element of faith as 'an assurance and lack of resistance in the surrender of the Ego' which may rest upon particular reasons, but is not explained by them. Trust combines weak inductive knowledge with some mysterious, unaccountable faith: 'On the other hand, even in the social forms of confidence, no matter how exactly and intellectually grounded they may appear to be, there may yet be some additional affective, even mystical, "faith" of man in man' (Simmel, 1950, p. 318).

Niklas Luhmann (1979) adopts Simmel's notion of trust as a 'blending of knowledge and ignorance' and remarks that 'trust always extrapolates from the available evidence' (Luhmann, 1979, p. 26). However, Luhmann overlooks Simmel's concern with the element of unaccountable faith, although he describes the rationale for action based on trust as above all 'a movement towards indifference: by introducing trust, certain possibilities of development can be excluded from consideration' (ibid., p. 25). And in line with Simmel he notes: 'Although the one who trusts is never at a loss for reasons and is quite capable of giving an account of why he shows trust in this or that case, the point of such reasons is really to uphold his self-respect and justify him socially' (p. 26).

Luhmann's trust concept includes many elements that resemble Simmel's transcendental ideas of trust as an operation that goes beyond that which the actor can account and control for. As Poggi (1979) notes, Luhmann argues that 'successful responses to the problem of complexity . . . typically do not eliminate complexity, but rather reduce it: that is, make it "livable with" while in some sense preserving it' (p. x). Interestingly, Poggi also suggests that Luhmann could have used the Hegelian notion of *Aufhebung*: the dialectical principle of synthesis transcending thesis and antithesis, thereby simultaneously preserving and rescinding them (Hegel, [1807] 1973). And indeed Luhmann argues that trust involves 'a type of system-internal "suspension" (*Aufhebung*)' (Luhmann, 1979, p. 79).

Giddens (1990), unlike Luhmann, recognizes that Simmel believes that trust differs from weak inductive knowledge in so far as it 'presumes a leap to commitment, a quality of "faith" which is irreducible' (Giddens, 1991, p. 19). This commitment would often be characterized more by the habitual and passive acceptance of circumstances than by an active leap (Giddens, 1990, p. 90). The latter, however, is typical for the 'active trust' in late-modern societies (Giddens, 1994b). Giddens (1990) argues that the suspension that enables trust has to be learned in infancy through the ambivalent experience of love from caretakers on the one hand and the caretakers' temporary absence on the other, whereby the infant develops the ability to reach a state of trust which 'brackets distance in time and space and so blocks off existential anxieties' (p. 97). This trust as a kind of skill learned in infancy remains essential as actors grow up to become adults. According to

Giddens, the faith in the loving caretaker's return 'is the essence of that leap to commitment which basic trust – and all forms of trust thereafter – presumes' (p. 95). The infant's anxiety can be generalized to the problem of ignorance that actors face in any social encounter with others whose actions and intentions they cannot fully know or control (Giddens, 1991). Trust, as the 'solution', requires faith in the sense of a more or less active leap to commitment.

This brings us to Luhmann's (1979) remark that trust is an 'operation of the will' (p. 32). Trust goes beyond that which can be justified in any terms by the actor, but the actor exercises agency through his will to either suspend uncertainty and vulnerability or not. Luhmann's reference to 'will' in the context of trust and suspension inspires a closer a look at William James's essay on 'The Will to Believe', a pragmatist approach to the theme of faith which Jens Beckert (2005) has also identified as highly instructive for understanding trust. James ([1896] 1948) defends the actor's right to believe – in religious matters but also generally, for instance in social relations – even when there is no conclusive evidence. Such a belief would be called faith: 'we have the right to believe at our own risk any hypothesis that is live enough to tempt our will' (p. 107). Note that by introducing the condition that the hypothesis has to be 'live enough', James points out that actors should not be allowed to believe anything but that 'which appeals as a real possibility to him to whom it is proposed' (p. 89). Implicitly, he thus refers back to his essay 'The Sentiment of Rationality' (James, [1879] 1948) and major principles of pragmatist philosophy. In this earlier source, he says that faith is 'synonymous with working hypothesis' (p. 25). The ability to have faith is distinctly human, according to James, and he defines faith as follows: 'Faith means belief in something concerning which doubt is still possible; and as the test of belief is willingness to act, one may say that faith is the readiness to act in a cause the prosperous issue of which is not certified to us in advance' (p. 22).

From the standpoint of James's pragmatism, faith requires the 'sentiment of rationality', in other words the actor's genuine but not conclusively justifiable conviction that what he believes is 'true' in the pragmatist sense of being useful, giving expectations and (thus) enabling action. This sentiment produces the 'will' to believe. Faith in these terms matches exactly that element in trust which – like a 'tranquilizer' (Beckert, 2005, p. 18) – allows the trustor to have favourable expectations towards the actions and intentions of others whose behaviour cannot be fully known or controlled. I call this element 'suspension' (Möllering, 2001, p. 414), meaning the 'leap of faith' that brackets ignorance and doubt, thereby enabling the trustor, at least momentarily, to have expectations as if social vulnerability and uncertainty were resolved. Note that the 'as if' implies genuine faith here and is therefore radically different from Hardin's notion of strategically feigned 'as-if trust' (see also Möllering, 2006). In suspension, a complex notion of simultaneously powerful and vulnerable agency is acknowledged.

Conclusions and implications

In this chapter, I have investigated three main questions from the perspective of sociological neoinstitutionalism and related approaches. What does it mean to say that institutions are a basis for trust? How can we deal with the issue that institutions are both sources and objects of trust? And what is the role and significance of agency in the constitution of trust? By way of conclusion, I summarize my answers to these questions.

First, institutions are a basis for trust between actors, because they imply a high degree of taken-for-grantedness which enables shared expectations even between actors who have no mutual experience or history of interaction. In the first instance, this approach is based on the phenomenological assumption that actors are 'looking at the world from within the natural attitude' (Schütz, 1932 [1967], p. 98), relying on 'constitutive expectancies' (Garfinkel, 1963, p. 190) and the validity of institutionalized rules, roles and routines. However, this approach does afford the actor an active role in interpreting – and questioning – institutions.

Second, because actors are not seen as passive reproducers of structure, institutional-based trust between actors requires that the institutions on which such trust is based are 'trusted' themselves. In other words, institutions are both a source and an object of trust. Here, the notions of 'system trust' (Luhmann, 1979) and 'trust in abstract systems' (Giddens, 1990) come into play, conceptualizing how actors develop confidence in institutions. While there cannot be absolute certainty, actors learn about the reliability of institutions through direct experience and through mediated demonstrations that institutions 'work'. However, once again agency is at the core of this version of a neoinstitutional theory of trust, because actors are involved more or less consciously in processes of institutionalization and may seek to influence institutions in an entrepreneurial way.

Third, the last point shows that the significance of (institutionally embedded) agency in the constitution of trust lies in the assumption that actors (re)produce collectively the institutional framework which then serves them as a source for trust (in other actors), but becomes an object of trust (in institutions), too. The notion of 'active trust' (Giddens, 1994b) captures this creative and processual aspect of trust most clearly and points to the key theoretical finding that agency on the part of the trustor implies a leap of faith that needs to be made in the face of irreducible social uncertainty and vulnerability. If this need of 'suspension' could be rendered obsolete by institutions or rational cognition, then trust would be deterministic and, therefore, a pointless category.

In the process of answering the above questions, I have re(dis)covered some conceptual foundations for trust which can be found relatively far back in the literature by looking at the details of some seminal writings that inform neoinstitutional approaches to trust. Most of these are clearly not part of the mainstream of trust research in the social sciences, not even in areas where institutional theories have gained a certain prominence. All the more, the concepts outlined here, such as the natural attitude, isomorphism, routines, active trust, familiarization and suspension, should be seen as core elements of trust rather than fringe considerations. What makes trust unique is not just the vast variety of potential trust bases – none of which should be overlooked lightly – but, more importantly, the fact that trust is a phenomenon capturing how actors use their embedded agency to deal with the irreducible social vulnerability and uncertainty without which one would not speak of 'trust'.

Acknowledgements
This chapter combines central passages from Chapter 3 to 5 in my book *Trust: Reason, Routine, Reflexivity* (2006). I thank Elsevier for giving me permission to use those passages here. A previous version was presented at the Academy of Management Annual Meeting in Honolulu, 5–10 August 2005 after a double-blind review which provided useful suggestions for improvement, as did the feedback received at the conference. I thank Aks Zaheer and an anonymous reviewer for their helpful comments in preparing the chapter for this

handbook. I am also grateful to many colleagues for invaluable advice and encouragement. Specifically, I thank Patrik Aspers, Reinhard Bachmann, Jens Beckert, John Child, Chris Grey, Christel Lane, Philip Manow, Geny Piotti and Jörg Sydow.

References

Arrow, K. 1974. *The Limits of Organization*. New York: Norton.
Bachmann, R. 1998. 'Conclusion: Trust – conceptual aspects of a complex phenomenon'. In C. Lane and R. Bachmann (eds), *Trust Within and Between Organizations*: 298–322. Oxford: Oxford University Press.
Barber, B. 1983. *The Logic and Limits of Trust*, New Brunswick, NJ: Rutgers University Press.
Beckert, J. 1999. 'Agency, entrepreneurs, and institutional change: The role of strategic choice and institutionalized practices in organizations', *Organization Studies*, **20**(5): 777–99.
Beckert, J. 2002. *Beyond the Market: The Social Foundations of Economic Efficiency*. Princeton, NJ: Princeton University Press.
Beckert, J. 2005. *Trust and the Performative Construction of Markets*. MPIfG Discussion Paper 05/8. Cologne: Max Planck Institute for the Study of Societies.
Berger, P.L. and Luckmann, T. 1966. *The Social Construction of Reality*. New York: Doubleday.
Blau, P. 1964. *Exchange and Power in Social Life*. London: John Wiley.
Blau, P. 1968. 'Interaction: Social exchange'. In D.L. Sills (ed.), *International Encyclopedia of the Social Sciences*: 452–8. New York: Macmillan.
Brownlie, J. and Howson, A. 2005. 'Leaps of faith and MMR: An empirical study of trust'. *Sociology*, **39**(2): 221–39.
Child, J. and Möllering, G. 2003. 'Contextual confidence and active trust development in the Chinese business environment'. *Organization Science*, **14**(1): 69–80.
Coleman, J.S. 1990. *Foundations of Social Theory*. Cambridge, MA: Harvard University Press.
Cook, K.S. (ed.) 2001. *Trust in Society*. New York: Russell Sage Foundation.
Cook, K.S. Hardin, R. and Levi, M. 2005. *Cooperation Without Trust?* New York: Russell Sage Foundation.
DiMaggio, P.J. 1988. 'Interest and agency in institutional theory'. In L.G. Zucker (ed.), *Institutional Patterns and Organizations*: 3–22. Cambridge, MA: Ballinger.
DiMaggio, P.J. and Powell, W.W. 1983. 'The iron cage revisited: Institutional isomorphism and collective rationality in organizational fields'. *American Sociological Review*, **48**(2): 147–60.
DiMaggio, P.J. and Powell, W.W. 1991. 'Introduction'. In W.W. Powell and P.J. DiMaggio (eds), *The New Institutionalism in Organizational Analysis*: 1–38. Chicago, IL: University of Chicago Press.
Dunn, J. 1988. 'Trust and political agency'. In D. Gambetta (ed.), *Trust: Making and Breaking Co-operative Relations*: 73–93.Oxford: Basil Blackwell.
Durkheim, E. [1893] 1984. *The Division of Labour in Society*. London: Macmillan.
Endreß, M. 2001. 'Vertrauen and Vertrautheit – Phänomenologisch-anthropologische Grundlegung'. In M. Hartmann and C. Offe (eds), *Vertrauen: Die Grundlage des sozialen Zusammenhalts*: 161–203. Frankfurt: Campus.
Ensminger, J. 2001. 'Reputations, trust, and the principal agent problem'. In K.S. Cook (ed.), *Trust in Society*: 185–201. New York: Russell Sage Foundation.
Feldman, M.S. and Pentland, B.T. 2003. 'Reconceptualizing organizational routines as a source of flexibility and change'. *Administrative Science Quarterly*, **48**(1): 94–118.
Fox, A. 1974. *Beyond Contract: Work, Power and Trust Relations*. London: Faber & Faber.
Fukuyama, F. 1995. *Trust: The Social Virtues and the Creation of Prosperity*. London: Hamish Hamilton.
Galaskiewicz, J. and Wasserman, S. 1989. 'Mimetic and normative processes within an interorganizational field: An empirical test'. *Administrative Science Quarterly*, **34**(3): 454–79.
Gambetta, D. and Hamill, H. 2005. *Streetwise: How Taxi Drivers Establish Their Customers' Trustworthiness*. New York: Russell Sage Foundation.
Garfinkel, H. 1963. 'A conception of, and experiments with, "trust" as a condition of stable concerted actions'. In O.J. Harvey (ed.), *Motivation and Social Interaction*: 187–238. New York: The Ronald Press Company.
Garfinkel, H. 1967. *Studies in Ethnomethodology*. Englewood Cliffs, NJ: Prentice-Hall.
Giddens, A. 1979. *Central Problems in Social Theory: Action, Structure and Contradiction in Social Analysis*. London: Macmillan.
Giddens, A. 1984. *The Constitution of Society*. Berkeley, CA: University of California Press.
Giddens, A. 1990. *The Consequences of Modernity*. Stanford, CA: Stanford University Press.
Giddens, A. 1991. *Modernity and Self-Identity*. Cambridge, UK: Polity Press.
Giddens, A. 1992. *The Transformation of Intimacy*. Cambridge, UK: Polity Press.
Giddens, A. 1994a. 'Living in a post-traditional society'. In U. Beck, A. Giddens and S. Lash (eds), *Reflexive Modernization*: 56–109. Cambridge, UK: Polity Press.

Giddens, A. 1994b. 'Risk, trust, reflexivity'. In U. Beck, A. Giddens and S. Lash (eds), *Reflexive Modernization*: 184–97. Cambridge, UK: Polity Press.

Glaeser, E.L., Laibson, D.I., Schenkman, J.A. and Soutter, C.L. 2000. 'Measuring trust'. *Quarterly Journal of Economics*, **115**(3): 811–46.

Good, D. 1988, 'Individuals, interpersonal relations and trust'. In D. Gambetta (ed.), *Trust: Making and Breaking Co-operative Relations*: 31–48. Oxford: Basil Blackwell.

Hannan, M.T. and Freeman, J.H. 1977. 'The population ecology of organizations'. *American Journal of Sociology*, **82** (5): 929–64.

Hardin, R. 1993. 'The street-level epistemology of trust'. *Politics & Society*, **21**(4): 505–29.

Hardy, C., Phillips, N. and Lawrence, T. 1998. 'Distinguishing trust and power in interorganizational relations: Forms and façades of trust'. In C. Lane and R. Bachmann (eds), *Trust Within and Between Organizations*: 64–87. Oxford: Oxford University Press.

Hawley, A. 1968. 'Human ecology'. In D.L. Sills (ed.), *International Encyclopedia of the Social Sciences*: 328–37. New York: Macmillan.

Hegel, G.W.F. [1807] 1973. *Phänomenologie des Geistes*. Frankfurt: Suhrkamp.

James Jr, H.S. 2002. 'The trust paradox: A survey of economic inquiries into the nature of trust and trustworthiness'. *Journal of Economic Behavior & Organization*, **47**(3): 291–307.

James, W. [1896] 1948. *Essays in Pragmatism*. New York: Hafner Press.

Jepperson, R.L. 1991. 'Institutions, institutional effects, and institutionalism'. In W.W. Powell and P.J. DiMaggio (eds), *The New Institutionalism in Organizational Analysis*: 143–63. Chicago, IL: University of Chicago Press.

Kramer, R.M. and Tyler, T.R. (eds) 1996. *Trust in Organizations: Frontiers of Theory and Research*. Thousand Oaks, CA: Sage.

Lane, C. 1997. 'The social regulation of inter-firm relations in Britain and Germany: Market rules, legal norms and technical standards'. *Cambridge Journal of Economics*, **21**(2): 197–215.

Lewicki, R.J. and Bunker, B.B. 1996. 'Developing and maintaining trust in work relationships'. In R.M. Kramer and T.R. Tyler (eds), *Trust in Organizations*: 114–39. Thousand Oaks CA: Sage.

Lewis, J.D. and Weigert, A. 1985. 'Trust as a social reality'. *Social Forces*, **63**(4): 967–85.

Lowe, P. 2005. 'Embodied expertise: Women's perceptions of contraception consulation'. *Health*, **9**(3): 361–78.

Luhmann, N. [1968, 1975] 1979. *Trust and Power: Two Works by Niklas Luhmann*. Chichester: Wiley.

Luhmann, N. 1988. 'Familiarity, confidence, trust: Problems and alternatives'. In D. Gambetta (ed.), *Trust: Making and Breaking Co-operative Relations*: 94–107. Oxford: Basil Blackwell.

Maguire, S., Philips, N. and Hardy, C. 2001. 'When "silence = death", keep talking: Trust, control and the discursive construction of identity in the Canadian HIV/AIDS treatment domain'. *Organization Studies*, **22**(2): 285–310.

March, J.G. and Olsen, J.P. 1989. *Rediscovering Institutions: The Organizational Basis of Politics*. New York: Free Press.

Mauss, M. [1925] 1954. *The Gift: Forms and Functions of Exchange in Archaic Societies*. Glencoe, IL: Free Press.

McKneally, M.F., Ignagni, E., Martin, D.K. and D'Cruz, J. 2004. 'The leap to trust: Perspective of cholecystectomy patients on informed decision making and consent'. *Journal of the American College of Surgeons*, **199** (1): 51–7.

McKnight, D.H., Cummings, L.L. and Chervany, N.L. 1998. 'Initial trust formation in new organizational relationships'. *Academy of Management Review*, **23**(3): 473–90.

Meyer, J.W. and Rowan, B. 1977. 'Institutionalized organizations: Formal structure as myth and ceremony'. *American Journal of Sociology*, **83**(2): 340–63.

Meyerson, D., Weick, K.E. and Kramer, R.M. 1996. 'Swift trust and temporary groups'. In R.M. Kramer and T.R. Tyler (eds), *Trust in Organizations*: 166–95. Thousand Oaks, CA: Sage.

Misztal, B.A. 1996. *Trust in Modern Societies*. Cambridge, UK: Polity Press.

Möllering, G. 2001. 'The nature of trust: From Georg Simmel to a theory of expectation, interpretation and suspension'. *Sociology*, **35**(2): 403–20.

Möllering, G. 2005a. 'The trust/control duality: An integrative perspective on positive expectations of others'. *International Sociology*, **20**(3): 283–305.

Möllering, G. 2005b. 'Rational, institutional and active trust: Just do it?' In K.M. Bijlsma-Frankema and R. Klein Woolthuis (eds), *Trust under Pressure: Empirical Investigations of Trust and Trust Building in Uncertain Circumstances*: 17–36. Cheltenham, UK and Northampton, MA, USA: Edward Elgar.

Möllering, G. 2006. *Trust: Reason, Routine, Reflexivity*. Oxford: Elsevier.

Nooteboom, B. 2002. *Trust: Forms, Foundations, Functions, Failures and Figures*. Cheltenham, UK and Northampton, MA, USA: Edward Elgar.

Parsons, T. 1978. *Action Theory and the Human Condition*. New York: Free Press.

Paxton, P. 1999. 'Is social capital declining in the United States? A multiple indicator assessment'. *American Journal of Sociology*, **105**(1): 88–127.

Poggi, G. 1979. 'Introduction'. In N. Luhmann, *Trust and Power*: vii–xix. Chichester: Wiley.

Powell, W.W. and DiMaggio, P.J. (eds) 1991. *The New Institutionalism in Organizational Analysis*. Chicago: University of Chicago Press.

Putnam, R.D. 1995. 'Bowling alone: America's declining social capital'. *Journal of Democracy*, 6(1): 65–78.

Sabel, C.F. 1993. 'Studied trust: Building new forms of cooperation in a volatile economy'. In R. Swedberg (ed), *Explorations in Economic Sociology*: 104–44. New York: Russell Sage Foundation.

Schütz, A. [1932] 1967. *The Phenomenology of the Social World*. Evanston, IL: Northwestern University Press.

Schütz, A. 1970a. *Reflections on the Problem of Relevance*. New Haven, CT: Yale University Press.

Schütz, A. 1970b. *On Phenomenology and Social Relations*. Chicago, IL: University of Chicago Press.

Scott, W.R. 2001. *Institutions and Organizations*, 2nd edn. Thousand Oaks, CA: Sage.

Seligman, A. 1997. *The Problem of Trust*. Princeton, NJ: Princeton University Press.

Shapiro, S.P. 1987. 'The social control of impersonal trust'. *American Journal of Sociology*, 93(3): 623–58.

Simmel, G. [1907] 1990. *The Philosophy of Money*, 2nd edn. London: Routledge.

Simmel, G. [1908] 1950. *The Sociology of Georg Simmel*. New York: Free Press.

Sydow, J. 1998. 'Understanding the constitution of inter-organizational trust'. In C. Lane and R. Bachmann (eds), *Trust Within and Between Organizations*: 31–63. Oxford: Oxford University Press.

Sydow, J. and Windeler, A. 2003. 'Knowledge, trust, and control: Managing tensions and contradictions in a regional network of service firms'. *International Studies of Management and Organization*, 33(2): 69–99.

Sztompka, P. 1999. *Trust: A Sociological Theory*. Cambridge: Cambridge University Press.

Warren, M.E. (ed.) 1999. *Democracy and Trust*. Cambridge: Cambridge University Press.

Williamson, O.E. 1993. 'Calculativeness, trust, and economic organization'. *Journal of Law and Economics*, 36 (2): 453–86.

Zand, D.E. 1972. 'Trust and managerial problem solving'. *Administrative Science Quarterly*, 17(2): 229–39.

Zucker, L.G. 1977. 'The role of institutionalization in cultural persistence'. *American Sociological Review*, 42 (5): 726–43.

Zucker, L.G. 1983. 'Organizations as institutions'. In S.B. Bacharach (ed.), *Advances in Organizational Theory and Research, Vol. 2*: 1–43. Greenwich, CT: JAI Press.

Zucker, L.G. 1986. 'Production of trust: Institutional sources of economic structure, 1840–1920'. In B.M. Staw and L.L. Cummings (eds), *Research in Organizational Behavior, Vol. 8*: 53–111. Greenwich, CT: JAI Press.

Zucker, L.G. 1987. 'Institutional theories of organization'. *Annual Review of Sociology*, 13, 443–64.

21 How can systems trust systems? A structuration perspective on trust-building in inter-organizational relations

Jörg Sydow

Introduction: towards a realistic perspective on trust

Trust, in persons as well as in social systems, is generally regarded as economically most valuable. While only a very few voices question the overall beneficial value of trust (e.g. Kern 1998; Jeffries and Reed 2000; Langfred 2004), most think that trust in persons, organizations and institutions saves on transaction costs (e.g. Ring 1997; Zaheer et al. 1998; Dyer and Chu 2003). Even more importantly, trust can be used as an 'organizing principle' (McEvily et al. 2003) in order to cope with interdependence and uncertainties within and between modern organizations. As such trust is considered to enable strategic actions that would not be possible otherwise because it 'bridges' risks (Luhmann 1979). This enabling effect of trust, which ultimately requires a 'leap of faith' from the trustor (Lewis and Weigert 1985; Möllering 2006), is particularly obvious when knowledge-sharing becomes possible and a relation-specific investment that would not be feasible otherwise emerges as economically attractive. As a consequence, trust is sometimes even considered as one of the foundations of organizational competitive advantage (Barney and Hansen 1994). Trust, then, is an attribute of an organization rather than of an individual. Prevailing theories of trust take this into account. Some of them even explain how trust in social systems emerges but all fail to explain how, as always required in cooperative inter-organizational relationships, systems can trust systems.

Moreover, most of them provide an either under- or oversocialized view and, thus, not a realistic understanding of trust-building in organizations and in inter-organizational relationships. Christel Lane (1998) contrasts the undersocialized conception of calculative trust which dominates the economic literature with the more normatively based, yet often highly oversocialized conception that springs from some sociological theories. However, 'to posit common values and norms as the *sole* basis of trust is as one-sided as the notion of calculative trust' (Lane 1998: 8). Convincingly, she therefore pleads for a more balanced understanding of trust in and between organizations. This is particularly important in inter-organizational relationships, no matter whether trust is considered as a substitute for market and hierarchical forms of governance (Powell 1990) or as complementary to price and authority (Bradach and Eccles 1989). While there are other approaches towards a more balanced, history-sensitive and, hence, realistic conceptualization of trust (e.g. Luhmann 1979; Hardy et al. 1998; Reed 2001), this chapter will draw almost exclusively on structuration theory by Anthony Giddens (1984) in order to develop a realistic, processual and balanced perspective on trust-building in and between organizations.

Such a conceptualization requires not only the analysis of trust as a medium and outcome of multidimensional organizational structuration processes (see also Mayer et al. 1995; Rousseau et al. 1998), but also a thorough differentiation between trust in persons on the one hand and trust in systems on the other (Luhmann 1979). Such a multi-level approach to organizational and inter-organizational trust (see also Barney and Hansen 1994; Zaheer et al. 1998; Currall and Inkpen 2002), which should complement the multidimensional analysis described below, is not only necessary with regard to persons and systems as possible objects of trusting, but also as individual and collective actors respectively may be more or less *actively* trusting. Giddens (1990: 34) assumes such a differentiation when he defines trust as 'confidence in the reliability of a person or system, regarding a given set of outcomes or events, where that confidence expresses a faith in the probity or love of another, or in the correctness of abstract principles'. Furthermore, a realistic understanding of trust in and of persons as well as in and of systems requires – from a structurationist perspective that emphasizes tensions and con-tradictions in social life – that we analyze trust in organizational and inter-organizational settings, not in isolation, but with reference to knowledge, control and power (see also: Bachmann 2001; Das and Teng 2001; Inkpen and Currall 2004). While these are often hastily assumed to simply be a substitute for trust, a structuration perspective offers a more complex, again more realistic picture of their sometimes subtle interrelationships.

This chapter, hence, will first introduce structuration theory – which has been applied most recently to 'correct' the thrust of strategic management theories (Pozzebon 2004) and to develop a more processual and embedded understanding of organizational resources (Duschek 2004; Feldman 2004) – as a theory of trust-building in inter-organizational relationships, by presenting trust as both an ingredient and outcome of structuration processes. Second, it will carefully distinguish between personal trust and system trust, although both are, of course, recursively related. Building on such a dis-tinction and clarification, the chapter will argue how organizational and even trans-organizational systems may be conceived as not only trust-receiving, but also as trust-giving, and how the multidimensional analysis of this process can be conducted. Third, the complex and quite intriguing interplay between trust on the one hand and knowledge, control and power on the other will be outlined from a structuration per-spective before suggesting some implications for building trust in inter-organizational relations and for trust research in inter-organizational settings.

The main impetus of the chapter in practical terms is a plea for a more trust-sensitive management of organizations and inter-organizational relations that, above all, acknow-ledges the conceptual differences as well as the subtle interplay between personal and system trust. Such a realistic perspective sharply contrasts with the rather straightforward 'trust management' that still dominates 'practice guides' on trust-building and overlooks these distinctions and interactions. The main implication of the structuration perspective for trust research will also be stated. Given the limitations of a book chapter, preference will be given to enhancing the more general understanding of trust-building in inter-organizational relationships from a structuration perspective at the cost of a detailed analysis of the diverse and often conflicting facets of the phenomenon.

Trust as a medium and outcome of structuration

Trust has been defined in many ways (e.g. Mayer et al. 1995; Rousseau et al. 1998; Möllering 2006), but there are at least three common understandings. First, every con-ception of trust, no matter whether it is conceived as an attitude or a behavior, has to acknowledge the relational character of the construct and the risks principally involved in trusting relationships. For trust is based upon positive expectations about interdependent behavior that may not actually be met by the exchange partner, so that the trustor's interests are violated. Second, trust may be given with regard to the competence of an agent (competence-based trust) or it may extend to his or her benevolence, goodwill or integrity (goodwill trust) (c.f. Mayer et al. 1995). It is this latter quality that makes trust particularly valuable for economic and organizational analysis, for dependency on the actions of others – and, hence, vulnerability – is an everyday feature of organizational and inter-organizational life. And third, any conceptualization has to recognize that trust is as much a condition or ingredient as an outcome of action. This is particularly true of cognitive-based trust, but does also apply to affect-based trust, which 'is rooted in emotional attachment and care and concern for the other party's welfare' (Jeffries and Reed 2000: 875, referring to the work of Lewis and Weigert 1985). However, rather than focusing on actions *per se*, a structurationist perspective would center around 'social practices', that is, on interactions in which agents repeatedly refer to social structures and thereby reproduce or transform these very structures. These structures, according to the theorem of the 'duality of structure' (Giddens 1984), which is central to structuration theory, are considered as both enabling and constraining the social interactions within this process of structuration in which trust is indeed not only an outcome, but also a medium of structuration.

In order to describe this process of structuration more precisely, Giddens (1984) distinguishes three dimensions of both action and structure. First, in communicative actions, agents (via interpretative schemes) refer to rules of signification such as views and understandings shared in an organization or an inter-organizational network, while, second, in sanctioning behavior, agents (via norms) refer to rules of legitimation such as honesty and tolerance. In doing so, agents reproduce or transform these two aspects of structure. In influencing ongoing interactions more or less powerfully, agents (via facilities), third, refer to resources of domination, like a lead in operative knowledge or an authoritative right attached to a certain social position. Again, agents, by referring to these resources, reproduce or transform this third aspect of structure. In consequence, structuration theory offers an abstract, but very processual, perspective on trust and trust-building that, on the one hand, does not neglect the role of structure as is common in many undersocialized conceptions. On the other hand, it does not downplay the role of action and overstate the role of structure either, which is common to many oversocialized conceptualizations of the trust-building process.

For the constitution of trust within and between organizations, this implies that agents can develop an expectation towards the behavior of a trusted person or system if, and only if, they are able to refer in their interactions to structures that enhance the trust-building process. With regard to rules of signification, these are, above all, views, images and understandings shared between either individual or collective actors. With regard to rules of legitimation, it is important to consider that the respective structures strengthen open communication, fairness and justice, tolerance and so on. And with regard to resources of domination, the fact that trust-building requires and consumes authoritative and allocative resources and, for that reason, causes opportunity costs, seems to be particularly relevant. Once fragile or even robust trust has emerged, it is necessary that these rules and resources are reproduced in a trust-enhancing manner and, eventually, developed further in social interactions (cf. Sydow 1998: 37–9). In consequence, trust itself becomes a valuable (authoritative) resource that is a potential basis for organizational competitive advantage and allows those who control it to powerfully intervene into ongoing interaction sequences.

Being not only a condition or ingredient, but also an outcome of social practices, trust – or trustworthiness as the latent characteristic of the trustee, as worthy of being trusted (Barney and Hansen 1994) – may itself be analyzed in terms of the three aspects of action and structure differentiated above. Thus trust in and between organizations may be conceived as a rule of signification, as a rule of legitimation and/or as a resource of domination. If trust constitutes a rule of signification in a particular organization, for instance because a high-trust organization is believed to significantly reduce transaction costs and to open up new possibilities for strategic action, agents are more likely 'to refer to this rule via a scheme which helps to interpret the social world as a trusting context of action' (Sydow 1998: 39). And by referring to this rule *in praxi*, agents tend to reproduce this structure of signification though it may well be based on an illusion. Similarly, organizational or inter-organizational trust may be seen as a rule of legitimation to which agents refer via social norms in order to sanction a particular trusting or distrusting behavior positively or negatively. If an action is sanctioned positively and if a social system is characterized by other, yet related norms (e.g. reciprocity, openness and fairness), this rule is likely to enhance trust-building in and between organizations. Again, this only applies if agents refer to these norms in their practices. Finally, as already indicated, trust relations within and among organizations may be conceived as an authoritative resource which, according to Giddens (1984), offers the possibility of influencing and eventually dominating others. Agents refer to this resource in their interactions via facilities or instruments of power and, in consequence, widen their scope of organizational or inter-organizational action. As mentioned before, however, agents should not overlook the fact that some trust-building activities require substantial resources (e.g. transaction-specific investments) and repeated reference to the structural properties of systems before being effective. Trust in systems makes actions by individual and collective actors feasible that would not be possible otherwise, especially in 'radical modern societies' (Giddens 1990).

Trust in systems – trusting systems – systems trusting
Since Lynne Zucker's (1986) compelling historical analysis of trust development in the US economy, at the latest, the role of social systems and institutions has been on the agenda of trust research in organization and management studies. Zucker distinguishes between 'process-based trust', which develops from concrete experiences of interactions on the one hand and 'characteristics-based trust', which is independent of a concrete social or economic exchange on the other. Following Sydow (1998), the sources of this latter kind of trust may be either personal characteristics (such as age, sex or belonging to a particular ethnic community) or system characteristics (such as the organizational image, reputation or size). However, the type of trust which, due to a relative failure of process- and characteristics-based trust in a world with greater spatial and social distances, has gained more and more relevance over the years is the so-called 'institutional-based trust'. This kind of trust not only transcends the concrete exchange experience, but is also independent of the characteristics of the interacting partners (Zucker 1986). Very important sources of institutional-based trust are, for example, legal national frameworks and industry-based

business associations (Lane and Bachmann 1996), but also the socio-cultural background, which becomes particularly obvious in cross-border cooperation (Child and Möllering 2003). Such institutional-based trust, like trust in technical and social systems (cf. Giddens 1984), requires confidence in abstract principles and procedures, and not only – and not even primarily – in the individuals with whom one interacts: 'institutions cannot be effective bases for trust, if they are not trusted themselves' (Möllering 2006: 72–3).

Trust research in organization and management studies today widely acknowledges the role of social systems and institutions in the emergence of trust within and between organizations. For instance and on an organizational level, it has been found that organizational boundaries act effectively as 'information envelopes, such that the more valuable the information produced, the more its dissemination is limited' (Zucker et al. 1996: 108). Also, the relevance of trust in systems such as organizations (as objects of trust) has been demonstrated, not least in the literature on inter-organizational relationships and networks (e.g. Sydow 1998; Zaheer et al. 1998; Jeffries and Reed 2000; Nooteboom 2002). This, in particular, allows for differentiating between interpersonal and inter-organizational trust: while interpersonal trust may often be a seedbed of inter-organizational trust, inter-organizational trust, due to institutionalization by means of abstract principles, may be high in some cases, although the trust relationships between concrete 'boundary spanners' (Adams 1980) are weaker. Conversely, inter-organizational trust may be rather low despite high interpersonal trust, because the individuals have not been successful in transferring their trust in each other to the organizational level. This strict distinction between personal and system trust is, among others, reflected in recent trust research arguing that the 'determinants' of interpersonal trust on the one hand and inter-organizational trust on the other may well be different (e.g. Barney and Hansen 1994; Sako and Helper 1998; Zaheer et al. 1998; Blois 1999).

In all cases of trust in organizations or organizational trustworthiness, it is useful to think of organizations as corporate actors (Coleman 1990), that is, as collective actors with a systems identity that, for this very reason, can be trusted with respect to and held responsible for its actions so that the likely situation in 'cooperative inter-organizational relationships' (Ring and Van de Ven 1994) is that systems trust systems. This means that organizations cannot be only objects, but also subjects of trusts; i.e., they can be considered as being more or less trusting. In inter-organizational relationships, the trustees are typically other organizations. However, as will be argued in the following paragraphs, trust in and of social systems such as organizations or inter-organizational networks results from complex structuration processes in which individual actors and social systems interact in a subtle way.

Systems as objects of trust can be understood from a structuration perspective that neither neglects the importance of human agency nor of system structures. More precisely, it comprises social systems such as organizations (and this is even more true of rather loosely coupled inter-organizational networks), not as static and homogeneous entities, but rather as dynamic and fragmented systems in which knowledgeable agents pursue different interests (Sydow and Windeler 1998). However, the structural properties of an organization, its formal hierarchy as well as its informal culture, contribute to the coordination of their interactions. To do so, these structural properties have to be enacted and reproduced by the individuals in their role as organizational actors. Perrone et al. (2003), for instance, demonstrate that organizational (*sic!*) properties, in their case the degree of role autonomy of purchasing managers acting as boundary spanners, indeed make a difference to the trust-building process. The authors find that these managers will be trusted to a greater extent by supplier representatives 'when they are free from constraints that limit their ability to interpret their boundary-spanning roles' (ibid.: 422). The reason for this limited or even negative impact of 'too much' structure upon trust is that the trustee's actions may be interpreted as responses to control rather than signs of trustworthiness.

Despite this particular finding, the structural properties of an organization that contribute to coordinated interaction among organizational members may also increase the trustworthiness of an organization. This is likely to be the case when the organization is structured in an 'appropriate' manner. Trust in individual organizational members may then actually decrease if they behave in a way that is not consistent with the organization's practices. Despite this inappropriate behavior, the system may continue to be trusted if the organization is considered likely to sanction this kind of behavior in an appropriate manner, eventually even by dismissing organizational members.[1]

Anyhow, the (hierarchical) structure and culture of an organization have not only to be enacted by management, but also to be acknowledged by subordinates, that is, by more or less all members of an organization or the subsystem that is responsible for managing a particular inter-organizational relationship. Similarly, the organizational culture has to be perceived and expressed in daily interactions by the organizational members, not only by top management. It is only then that these structures (in structurationist terms a culture also represents a structure) 'guide' the expectations and actions of organizational members and, finally, the expectations and actions of an organization in a way that other agents can confidently rely on – at least with respect to a given set of outcomes or events.

Following Giddens's definition of system trust, this requires confidence that expresses a faith in 'the correctness of abstract principles' (Giddens 1990: 34). Though these structural properties 'guide' the actions of organizational members towards a more or less collective trusting behavior (Nooteboom 2002), others can never be certain that an organization – as a corporate actor – will act in a particular way. The consequent risk involved is, as mentioned in the introduction to this chapter, constitutive for trust in general and for trust in a social system such as an organization or a network of organizations in particular.

Though it is somewhat harder to think of organizations as subjects of trust or as trusting rather than being trusted or trustworthy entities, structuration theory suggests that the more or less active trusting of a social yet more or less dynamic and fragmented system can be understood in a similar way. The problematic anthropomorphization of organizations and other social systems, however, can be avoided if the role of individuals in this systemic process of trust-building is clarified. Again, structural properties of an organization, the culture and climate of an organization that favors open communication, for instance,[2] make it much more likely that organizational members will act in a way that enhances trust-building in an inter-organizational relationship, by means of generous information disclosure or active knowledge transfer, for example. While a dispositional or emotional element may well be involved when an individual actor trusts others (Erikson 1963; Rotter 1967; McEvily et al. 2003) or an organization, this is not possible in the case of an organization as a trustor. However, dispositions and emotions of individual organizational members, boundary spanners in particular, matter a great deal in inter-organizational processes when they refer to the structural properties of the organ-ization or other social systems that allow for these dispositions and emotions to be put into practice.

In more operational terms, a kind of 'collectively-held trust orientation towards the partner firm' (Zaheer et al. 1998: 143) may emerge when organizations trust, because of such structural properties guiding the behavior of organizational members. Again, the other organization – a networked system supplier or research institute, for example – can never be completely certain that the individual members of the focal organization, and thus the organization itself, will act in a particular way. This enables us to think of an organization actively trusting while some organizational members may well distrust the system supplier and/or the research institute as an organization, not to mention single members of these organizations. One reason for this kind of 'deviant' behavior is that according to the omnipresent 'dialectic of control' (Giddens 1984) – a second theorem central to the theory of structuration – actors, collective and corporate included, can always act otherwise, no matter how precise the rule or coercive the situation is. Even a well-established collectively held trust orientation towards the partner organization may, because of the influence of the CEO or another influential individual, for instance, rapidly turn into a non-trusting or even a distrusting attitude and behavior.

The picture becomes even more realistic, but also more complex and contingent, when the social context of the two organizations – the system supplier and its customer, for example, trusting each other within one inter-organizational relationship – is taken into account. Increasingly, this context is conceptualized as either an inter-organizational network or even as an 'organizational field' which comprises 'those organizations that, in the aggregate, constitute a recognized area of institutional life: key suppliers, resource and product consumers, regulatory agencies, and other organizations that produce similar ser-vices or products' (DiMaggio and Powell 1983: 143). Some of these organizations may or may not be linked to the focal two organizations in a (trusting) way that constitutes an inter-organizational network – which then forms the immediate environment of the dyad. From a structuration perspective, neither this immediate environment nor the wider context is conceived as being somehow 'external' to the organizations. Rather, just as organizational members in their interactions refer to structural properties of their organ-ization, they also refer to those of the network or field. Among those field properties that become 'enacted' (Weick 1969) and are most relevant for trust-building between organ-izations are not only the legal framework and other institutions like industry associations or professional standards, but also the similarity of the domains of the collaborating organizations and the level of competition derived from this homogeneity. For there is ample evidence that trust-building processes in a competitive and fluid environment are much more difficult to trigger and to sustain than in a more cooperative and stable context (see the example of transitional economies such as China, e.g. Child 1998; Child and Möllering 2003).

This structurationist conception of trusting systems and systems trusting does not, of course, as already indicated, exclude the parallel existence of either distrust in persons or distrusting persons – and vice versa. Since organizations and inter-organizational rela-tions result from complex structuration processes in which several more or less powerful individuals interact as organizational members, some, in particular actors in less central organizational roles, may well deviate in their interactions from the trust/distrust relationships on a systems level. That is, an organization may be trusted, and may itself actively trust, even though not necessarily all organizational members are trustworthy or do trust. On the other hand, even a majority of individual organizational members may trust and be trusted by others on a personal level, without the organization trusting or being trusted as an abstract social system. An example cited in a recent study of a strategic alliance between a pharmaceutical and a biotechnology company draws an even more complex and dynamic picture:

> Some [members] put their trust in the repeated assurances of one individual (while remaining vigilant of the organization), whereas others . . . appear to have placed their confidence in the pharmaceutical company's reputation. Trust and vigilance seem to have been aimed at multiple levels inside a single organization. Moreover, the two were dynamic. Vigilance yielded to trust as operational issues were successfully addressed and compromise helped deflate conflict, but trust (when violated) gave way to vigilance. (de Rond and Bouchikhi 2004: 64)

Given the resulting scope of possible contingencies, one may nevertheless expect that the more important and influential the individuals trusted/not trusted or trusting/distrusting are for the structuration of the respective organization (e.g. top managers in contrast to subordinates) or for the structuration of the focal inter-organizational relationship (e.g. boundary spanners in contrast to people acting in the technical core of an organization), the less likely is the parallel existence of trusting and distrusting relationships on a personal and system level. Nevertheless, a thorough investigation of trust relationships between organizations requires the analysis of both interpersonal *and* inter-organizational relationships as well as of their subtle and rather complex interplay (see also Zaheer et al. 1998; Jeffries and Reed 2000).

From a structuration perspective, the interplay between these two levels can be conceptualized somewhat more precisely. Trust and trust-building can and should not only be analyzed with respect to the three dimensions of action and structure (communication, sanctioning, power, and signification, legitimation, domination respectively), but also as a process of – in Giddens's terms – 'dis- and reembedding'. For trust is attributed to abstract systems (or parts of them) through 'the "lifting out" of social relations from local contexts of interaction and their restructuring across indefinite spans of time-space' (Giddens 1990: 21). This disembedding, which is guided by the structural properties of the organization, the network and/or the field, is complemented by a process of reembedding in which agents, boundary spanners in particular, interact face to face. This reembedding face-to-face work, in which agents also refer to the structures of the organization and the organizational field, usually takes place at certain 'access points' (ibid.: 85) which are typically to be found at the boundaries of organizations. In organizations interacting in vertical relationships, like supply chains, these access points are most prominently to be identified in the purchasing and marketing departments. Due to an increased outsourcing of knowledge generation, they are nowadays also to be located in the R&D department and some other organizational subsystems. This trend, together with increased collaboration with competitors in horizontal relationships, leads to even more distributed access points that may be found in almost every subsystem of an organization. The consequence of this development is that the coordination becomes more complex, also within organizations and not least with respect to trusting and being trusted.

Interpersonal trust between such boundary spanners of different organizations or sub-systems which start to partner may foster the development of inter-organizational trust via such disembedding processes. However, existing trust between the two or more organizations may, in turn and in a process of reembedding, also structure the development of trust on an interpersonal level. Again, from a structuration perspective it is sensible to assume subtle and recursive relationships between personal and system trust which, however, do not necessarily support, but may also undermine each other (Jeffries and Reed 2000). What is clear, however, is that not only the number of access points has increased over the years but that interactions between boundary spanners become more frequent once an alliance or joint venture has been created (e.g. Inkpen and Currall 2004). In consequence, interpersonal and inter-organizational relationships, which are simultaneously shaped by knowledge, control and power, become more and more important for the trust-building or -destroying process.

Trust, knowledge, control and power – complex relationships
While Giddens has defined trust as confidence in the reliability of a person or system regarding a given set of outcomes or events, he conceives 'knowledge' as providing 'accurate or valid awareness' (Giddens 1984: 90). This knowledge is mainly gained by 'reflexive monitoring' (ibid.) and sediments in what he calls the practical or discursive consciousness of the agent, all important elements of his 'stratification model of the agent', a third important concept of structuration theory. According to this model, agents mainly act on the basis of their practical consciousness or 'tacit knowledge' (Polanyi 1967). This is particularly the case when they act routinely in situations well known to them. Despite the fact that agents are not always able to explain their actions and/or to grasp the conditions under which they act and produce intended and unintended consequences, they are knowledgeable, that is, able to apply their knowledge *in praxi*.

This knowledgeable agent, as generally emphasized by the extensive literature on organizational knowledge and learning (e.g. Dierkes et al. 2001), may also be a social system such as an organization or even an inter-organizational network. When knowledge is gained and/or transferred from a practical to a discursive level, the degree of reflexivity, of a person or a system respectively, is assumed to increase. Reflexivity means that 'social practices are constantly examined and reformed in the light of incoming information about those very practices, thus constitutively altering their character' (Giddens 1990: 38). Trust, individual as much as organizational, is not naïve faith, but based upon such reflexive monitoring and, thus, exhibits some degree of reflexivity. Even high initial trust tends to evolve not from naïve belief, but from relevant knowledge about the integrity of the exchange partner or other institutional cues, which allow for categorization processes and enable an individual or organization to trust another without first-hand experience (Meyerson et al. 1996; McKnight et al. 1998). This initial trust may not only delimit the usage of control right from the beginning of a relationship, but also enable experiential learning about, from, and with another actor – a joint venture partner for instance – that would not be possible otherwise. Only then may trust, control and learning co-evolve so that partners develop a thorough understanding of each other and each other's behavior that continues to underlie the collaborative process (Inkpen and Currall 2004). This interpretative understanding, however, will only be effective in triggering and sustaining a trust-building process if it is supported by appropriate rules of legitimation and necessary resources of domination.

Often knowledge is thought to substitute for trust, but Georg Simmel (1950: 318) has already stated convincingly: 'The person who knows completely needs not to trust; while the person who knows nothing can, on no rational grounds, afford even confidence.' From a structuration perspective, this statement can be extended to social systems and specified with respect to (knowledge about) the structural properties of the very systems, that is, rules of signification and legitimation on the one hand and resources of domination on the other, and the communications, sanctioning behavior and powerful interventions in ongoing interactions whereby agents refer to these structures. Especially under the condition of highly reflexive coordination that is typical of formal organizations (Giddens 1984) and, increasingly, managed inter-organizational relationships, trust presupposes the existence of some knowledge of the respective structures and interactions in general and of the capability and the goodwill of an acting individual or a collective agent in particular. The growing knowledge intensity of economic activities may thus imply only more reliance on trust (cf. Adler 2001).

In this respect, 'knowledge-based trust' (Sheppard and Tuchinsky 1996) seems to be a very relevant form of trust and a common feature of (inter-)organizational life. The gaining of a common understanding and some familiarity, that is, knowledge about shared expectations and norms, is often necessary for trust to develop (cf. Zucker 1986 and, for the phenomenological roots of her argument, Möllering, Chapter 20 in this volume). In some cases, this familiarity may even result from vigilance. Some of this knowledge is likely to result from the fact that 'members of an organization actively probe their counterparts to see if they can maintain or increase their level of trust' (McEvily et al. 2003: 99). However, increasing knowledge of one kind or the other does not simply transform trust into certainties. Rather, 'many of the uncertainties which face us today have been created by the very growth of human knowledge' (Giddens 1994: 185). Under no circumstances does knowledge render trust superfluous, because both practical and discursive knowledge is always imperfect, even if it enables the development of more global trust from rather local or specific forms of trust. In this respect, trust is typically based upon knowledge as 'overdrawn information' (Luhmann 1979: 32), that is, information interpreted to an extent that exceeds its original meaning and/or area of application. It follows that the relationship between knowledge and trust – beyond the simple fact that some doubt-raising knowledge may of course also destroy trust or even lead to mistrust, and beyond the fact that trust, via its risk-bridging potential, can also provide access to additional sources of knowledge – is significantly more complex and full of tensions and contradictions. As will become clear presently, this also applies to the relationships between trust on the one hand and control and power on the other.

A structuration perspective acknowledges and helps to understand these complex relationships by focusing on social practices in which trust, knowledge, control and power are not only an important outcome, but also a medium of structuration, and that they interact with regard to the three dimensions of the social. While especially economic theories view trust and control as antithetical attributes of (inter-)organizational relations (e.g. Cummings and Bromiley 1996; James 2002), or consider trust as an inappropriate construct altogether (e.g. Williamson 1993), the practice-based approach provided by structuration theory again draws a more complex picture (cf. Sydow and Windeler 2003; Möllering 2005; 2006). For instance, trust may well emerge from the specification of contracts (e.g. Lorenz 1999), which is usually considered a means of control (e.g. Uzzi 1997), especially so when a relationship develops (e.g. Ring and Van de Ven 1994). For contracting may well be an object of inter-organizational learning, that is a means to increase mutual understanding and a knowledge repository (Mayer and Argyres 2004).

Control, again following Giddens (1984), implies monitoring and influencing or steering actions and events in quite a reflexive way that, at least by intention, fits the interests of those who exercise control. But due to the contingent reproduction of social systems, control, like knowledge, is always imperfect – however powerful an actor may be. Even if control is assured by formal contracts and severe sanctions, one cannot escape the dialectic of control implicated in social practices. From a structuration perspective, the relationship between trust and control is indeed as complex, subtle and contradictory as that between trust and knowledge. Apart from the fundamental role of knowledge in the process of creating trust and control, control can, for example, generate trust in a very direct and often overlooked way. This 'control-based trust' (Sydow and Windeler 2003) is likely to occur when the control measures applied show that the actions, procedures, or results do occur as expected – that is, when the trust given turns out to be justified. Whatever the result of monitoring this process, however, control will and cannot make trust entirely superfluous.

Obviously, if not operated in a trust-sensitive way, control can also undermine trust in a very direct manner. Das and Teng (2001: 263) argue that this is particularly likely in the case of behavior and output controls, while the more opaque social control – which 'influences people's behavior through creating shared goals and norms' and 'increases mutual understanding' – is considered by them as enhancing rather than undermining trust (see also Inkpen and Currall 2004). In turn, some control may be directly based on existing trust in and between organizations which justifies reference to 'trust-based control' (Sydow and Windeler 2003). That is, trust is assumed to open up additional possibilities of control, not least ample opportunities for social control. Das and Teng (2001: 265) point out that competence trust and goodwill 'will enhance the effectiveness of all control modes (behavior, output, and social) in an alliance', while a high level of trust may well render control superfluous in other social settings.

Like knowledge and control, power is also often regarded as a substitute for trust (e.g. Luhmann 1979; Bachmann 2001). Again, social praxis which, from a structuration perspective, is always imbued with power, seems to be more complicated. For instance, 'power can be hidden behind the façade of "trust" and the rhetoric of "collaboration", and used to promote vested interests through the manipulation of and capitulation by weaker partners' (Clegg and Hardy 1996: 679; see also Hardy et al. 1998). Not surprisingly, powerful organizations have been found to be more inclined to be trusting, while the less powerful tend to be less confident of the trustworthiness of their exchange partners, even if the relationship has proceeded smoothly (Young and Wilkinson 1989). And if a trusting relationship is sustained, this gives the dominant organization even more power and opportunities to reproduce trust as an important component, not only of the rules of signification and legitimation, but also of the resources of domination. If exercised in a certain rule-conforming manner, power is even likely to not substitute or destroy, but to enhance trust and, thus, to lead to an even more powerful position *vis-à-vis* another organization. The mechanism of positive recursiveness in a nutshell: trust increases power, and power offers the opportunity (*sic!*) for developing even more trusting relations, however only if the powerful action remains within the confines of certain rules of signification and legitimation (cf. Sydow 1998: 38). This escalating recursiveness of trust is path-dependent, whereby any serious understanding of path-dependency points to a process of self-reinforcement and of gaining momentum that implies at least some irreversibility. Whether or not this process turns tentative or fragile forms of trust into more durable and resilient forms of trust – or indirectly into more direct forms of power and control based on 'better' knowledge – is an open question and the answer depends upon structural properties of the systems relevant to the constitution of interpersonal and inter-organizational trust on the one hand and upon the practices of agents – not least of managers – referring to these system properties in their interactions on the other.

As implied in this argument, the complex interplay of trust, knowledge, control and power could and should be analyzed on a personal as well as on a systemic level (cf. Sydow and Windeler 2003 for details), for trust in persons and trust in systems should be conceived as two distinct constructs, even though they are mutually constituted in complex and overlapping structuration processes (see also Zaheer et al. 1998). While the interrelatedness of knowledge, trust, control and power at the systemic level is quite similar to that at the personal level, there are at least two special characteristics distinguishing these processes at the systems level from those at the personal level. First, the interplay between knowledge, trust, control and power at the system level is the medium and result of more or less coordinated interactions and relations among individual agents. In other words, it signifies a structural property of systemically coordinated practices. These practices, and their respective sets of rules and resources, go well beyond the actions and relations of a particular individual. System trust, therefore, refers to forms of trust that agents invest in the validity and correctness of abstract principles and procedures in and of social systems (or in the technical systems they use in such systems), no matter whether they represent a firm, a network, or a field. System trust is – if at all – only partly based on personal trust, that is, on trust in an individual person. Rather, system trust often necessarily abstracts from personal trust by trusting in the validity and correctness of abstract principles and procedures. Thus system trust includes trust in the control of these very principles and procedures by the system – including the selection and control of technologies as well as of persons (cf. Sydow and Windeler 2003). Second, knowledgeable agents, managers in particular, interrelate the constitution of system knowledge, trust, control and power with personal knowledge, trust, control and power through a continuous process of disembedding and reembedding occurring in particular at the access points already mentioned. In general, the interrelatedness of knowledge, trust, power and control as ingredients of structural properties of the social system enables and restrains the capability of agents to act. This makes the management of tensions and contradictions between knowledge, trust, power and control one backbone of the effective management of organizations and, in particular, inter-organizational relationships. By acknowledging these complex, subtle and quite contradictory relationships in face of the complex interplay between the personal and system levels *in praxi*, 'trust adopts a new, more reflexive quality' (Sydow and Windeler 2003: 82; see also Child and Möllering 2003).

Implication for trust research and management
Trust emerging in and between organizations is always 'in a certain sense blind' (Giddens 1990: 33). Otherwise, to speak of trust would not be justified. This blindness alone makes any kind of intentional 'trust management', especially if based upon supposedly

hands-on instruments, difficult and unrealistic – if not impossible. An alternative and more realistic and theory-based recommendation would be that agents in general and strategically placed executives in organizations and hub firms in inter-organizational networks in particular adopt a trust-sensitive approach towards managing organizations and inter-organizational relationships. Though it is helpful to think of system trust as being independent of the interactions of individuals in the first place, it has to be recognized that these very individuals are involved in complex disembedding and reembedding processes – in which strategically placed actors are particularly likely to make a difference to the production and reproduction of system trust.

Managing organizations and inter-organizational relationships, though typically considered as more reflexive than most other activities, is – like these other actions – rooted mainly in the practical consciousness of the agent. Together with the importance of unacknowledged conditions and the unintended consequences of actions, also much emphasized by Giddens's structuration theory in general and his stratification model of the agent in particular, this fact causes managerial action to always include not only reflexive, but also non-reflexive moments. The implied limitation to the intentional management of trust is for at least four reasons particularly true with respect to building and maintaining trusting inter-organizational relationships.

First, both personal and system trust are often, though not always, a by-product of otherwise intended action. Since any intentional trust management runs the danger of destroying rather than building trust, cultivating trust seems to be much more adequate. Second, almost every managerial action has implications for trust on both complexly interrelated levels. Thus, rather than pleading for a specialized 'trust management', management should reflect on more or less every one of its actions with regard to their implications for organizational or inter-organizational trust. Third, in sharp contrast to social systems that, like organizations, are defined by Giddens (1984) by their extremely high level of reflexivity, inter-organizational relations *in praxi* have not always received the reflexive attention they deserve, especially in an increasingly networked world. This is also true with respect to inter-organizational trust. Fourth, inter-organizational relations, due to a lack of institutionalization in general and of hierarchical authority in particular, are both more in demand and more difficult to manage in a trust-sensitive way than organizations. Think, for instance, of the difficulties in controlling the behavior of boundary spanners, who often work much of their time in a partner organization.

If this analysis is correct, trust-building in inter-organizational relationships, though under no circumstances requiring a maximization of reflexivity, offers quite substantial opportunities as well as necessities for a somewhat (*sic!*) more reflexive approach:

> Trust-sensitive management, here of inter-organizational relationships in particular, requires a close reflexive monitoring of any action with respect to its impact upon trust, whereby the object of monitoring is the necessity of trust as well as the foundation of trust relations. . . . Thereby they should pay special attention: (1) to the processes, characteristics, and institutions which enhance not only trust in persons, that is, interpersonal trust, but also in organizations; and (2) to the disembedding and reembedding processes at work in the constitution of inter-organizational trust. Not least (3) they should reflect upon the structural properties which enhance the constitution of inter-organizational trust on the level of the network as well as on other levels of analysis. (Sydow 1998: 54)

In addition, (4) agents in general and managers in particular should be aware of the tensions and contradictions implied in the complex relationships between knowledge, trust, control and power. For even more than the everyday understanding of trust (which sometimes turns out to be quite naïve), these complex relationships are often not well understood either in theory (cf. de Rond and Bouchikhi 2004) or *in praxi*. And a better understanding would be helpful for more effective trust-building in inter-organizational relationships.

For trust research, this perspective implies not only having to be clear about different levels and their interaction in theorizing and developing or choosing adequate trust measures that are aligned to these levels (see Gulati 1995; Currall and Inkpen 2002), but also specifying the processual understanding of the interplay of action and structure developed in this chapter and applying it to the broad variety of quite distinct forms of inter-organizational relationships. Only then does it become transparent how interpersonal trust interacts with inter-organizational trust and how trust travels from one level to another.

Acknowledgements

This chapter was written during my 2004/05 sabbatical leave to the University of Arizona, Tucson. I thank the Eller College of Management for providing me with the necessary working facilities and the Deutsche Forschungsgemeinschaft (DFG) for a generous travel grant. I am also grateful to the editors and to one anonymous reviewer for their extremely useful comments on an earlier version of this chapter. Though the chapter does not explicitly refer to my own empirical research into inter-organizational networking in the fields of financial services, airport authorities, new and old media, and photonics, my understanding of trust constitution has profited a great deal from these studies. I therefore thank the numerous practitioners in these fields for sharing their views with me.

Notes

1. Of course the reverse case is also possible. Interpersonal trust between boundary spanners may be high even though inter-organizational trust is low (Currall and Inkpen 2002, who include group trust as a third-level contruct). In this case, organizational-level trust does not profit from the high level of interpersonal trust, because the organizational members are, for instance, considered as atypical for the organization or only trustworthy because they permanently violate organizational rules.
2. See Schneider (1990), for example, or Becerra and Gupta (2003), who demonstrate the relevance of communication frequency for trust-building processes in organizations.

References

Adams, J.S. (1980) Interorganizational processes and organizational boundary activities. In: Cummings, L.L. and Staw, B.M.: *Research in Organizational Behaviour*, 321–55. Greenwich, CT: JAI.
Adler, P. (2001) Market, hierarchy, and trust: the knowledge economy and the future of capitalism. *Organization Science* 12 (2): 215–34.
Bachmann, R. (2001) Trust, power and control in trans-organizational relations. *Organization Studies* 22 (2): 337–65.
Barney, J.B. and Hansen, M.H. (1994) Trustworthiness as a source of competitive advantage. *Strategic Management Journal* 15 (special issue): 175–90.
Becerra, M. and Gupta, A.K. (2003) Perceived trustworthiness within the organization: The moderating impact of communication frequency on trustor and trustee effects. *Organization Science* 14 (1): 32–44.
Blois, K.J. (1999) Trust in business to business relations: An evaluation of its status. *Journal of Management Studies* 36 (2): 197–215.
Bradach, J.L. and Eccles, R.G. (1989) Price, authority and trust: From ideal types to plural forms. *Annual Review of Sociology* 15: 96–118.

Child, J. (1998) Trust in international strategic alliances: The case of sino-foreign joint ventures. In: Lane, C. and Bachmann, R. (eds): *Trust within and between Organizations*, 241–72. Oxford: Oxford University Press.

Child, J. and Möllering, G. (2003) Contextual confidence and active trust development in the Chinese business environment. *Organization Science* **14** (1): 69–80.

Clegg, S.R. and Hardy, S. (1996) Conclusions: Representations. In: Clegg, S.R., Hardy, C. and Nord, W.R. (eds): *Handbook of Organization Studies*, 676–708. London: Sage.

Coleman, J.S. (1990) *Foundations of Social Theory*. Cambridge, MA: Harvard University Press.

Cummings, L.L. and Bromiley, P. (1996) The organizational trust inventory (OTI): Development and validation. In: Kramer, R.M. and Tyler, T.R. (eds): *Trust in Organizations*, 302–30. Thousand Oaks, CA: Sage.

Currall, S.C. and Inkpen, A.C. (2002) A multilevel approach to trust in joint ventures. *Journal of International Business Studies* **33** (3): 479–95.

Das, T.K. and Teng, B.-S. (2001) Trust, control and risk in strategic alliances: an integrated framework. *Organization Studies* **22** (2): 251–83.

de Rond, M. and Bouchikhi, H. (2004) On the dialectics of strategic alliances. *Organization Science* **15** (1): 56–69.

Dierkes, M., Berthoni Antal, A., Child, J. and Nonaka, I. (2001) (eds) *Handbook of Organizational Learning and Knowledge*. Oxford: Oxford University Press.

DiMaggio, P.J. and Powell, W.W. (1983) The iron cage revisited: Institutional isomorphism and collective rationality in organizational fields. *American Sociological Review* **48**: 147–60.

Duschek, S. (2004) Inter-firm resources and sustained competitive advantage. *Management Revue* **15** (1): 53–73.

Dyer, J.H. and Chu. W. (2003) The role of trustworthiness in reducing transaction costs and improving performance: Empirical evidence from the United States, Japan, and Korea. *Organization Science* **14** (1): 57–68.

Erikson, E.H. (1963) *Childhood and society*. 2nd edn. New York: Norton.

Feldman, M.S. (2004) Resources in emerging structures and processes of change. *Organization Science* **15** (3): 295–309.

Giddens, A. (1984) *The Constitution of Society*. Cambridge: Polity.

Giddens, A. (1990) *The Consequences of Modernity*. Cambridge: Polity.

Giddens, A. (1994) Risk, trust, reflexivity. In: Beck, U., Giddens, A. and Lash, S. (eds): *Reflexive Modernity*, 184–97. Cambridge: Polity.

Gulati, R. (1995) Does familiarity breed trust? The implications of repeated ties for contractual choice in alliances. *Academy of Management Journal* **38** (1): 85–112.

Hardy, C., Phillips, N. and Lawrence, T. (1998) Distinguishing trust and power in inter-organizational relations: forms and façades of trust. In: Lane, C. and Bachmann, R. (eds): *Trust Within and Between Organizations*, 64–87. Oxford: Oxford University Press.

Inkpen, A.C. and Currall, S.C. (2004) The coevolution of trust, control, and learning in joint ventures. *Organization Science* **15** (5): 586–99.

James Jr, H.S. (2002) The trust paradox: A survey of economic inquiries into the nature of trust and trustworthiness. *Journal of Economic Behavior & Organization* **47** (3): 291–307.

Jeffries, F.L. and Reed, R. (2000) Trust and adaptation in relational contracting. *Academy of Management Review* **25** (4): 873–82.

Kern, H. (1998) Lack of trust, surfeit of trust: some causes and consequences of the innovation crisis in German industry. In: Lane, C. and Bachmann, R. (eds): *Trust Within and Between Organizations*, 203–13. Oxford: Oxford University Press.

Lane, C. (1998) Introduction: Theories and issues in the study of trust. In: Lane, C. and Bachmann, R. (eds): *Trust Within and Between Organizations*, 1–30. Oxford: Oxford University Press.

Lane, C. and Bachmann, R. (1996) The social constitution of supplier relations in Britain and Germany. *Organization Studies* **17** (3): 365–95.

Langfred, C.W. (2004) Too much of a good thing? Negative effects of high trust and individual autonomy on self-managing teams. *Academy of Management Journal* **47** (3): 385–99.

Lewis, J.D. and Weigert, A. (1985) Trust as a social reality. *Social Forces* **63** (4): 967–85.

Lorenz, E. (1999) Trust, contract and economic cooperation. *Cambridge Journal of Economics* **23** (3): 301–15.

Luhmann, N. (1979) *Trust and Power*. Chichester: Wiley.

Mayer, K.J. and Argyres, N.S. (2004) Learning to contract: Evidence from the personal computer industry. *Organization Science* **15** (4): 394–410.

Mayer, R.C., Davis, J.H. and Schoormann, F.D. (1995) An integrative model of organizational trust. *Academy of Management Review* **20** (3): 709–34.

McEvily, B., Perrone, V. and Zaheer, A. (2003) Trust as an organizing principle. *Organization Science* **14** (1): 91–103.

McKnight, D.H., Cummings, L.L. and Chervany, N.L. (1998) Initial trust formation in new organizational relationships. *Academy of Management Review* **23** (3): 473–90.

Meyerson, D., Weick, K.E. and Kramer, R.M. (1996) Swift trust and temporary groups. In: Kramer, R.M. and Tyler, T.R. (eds): *Trust in Organizations*, 166–95. Thousand Oaks, CA: Sage.

Möllering, G. (2005) The trust/control duality: An integrative perspective on positive expectations of others. *International Sociology* **20** (3): 283–305.

Möllering, G. (2006) *Trust: Reason, Routine, Reflexibility*. Amsterdam: Elsevier.

Nooteboom, B. (2002) *Trust: Forms, Foundations, Functions, Failures and Figures*. Cheltenham, UK and Northampton, MA, USA: Edward Elgar.

Perrone, V., Zaheer, A. and McEvily, B. (2003) Free to be trusted? Organizational constraints on trust at the boundary. *Organization Science* **14** (4): 422–39.

Polanyi, K. (1967) *The Tacit Dimension*. Garden City, NY: Doubleday.

Powell, W.W. (1990) Neither market nor hierarchy: Network forms of organization. In: Staw, B.M. and Cummings, L.L. (eds): *Research in Organizational Behavior* vol. 12, 295–336. Greenwich, CT: JAI Press.

Pozzebon, M. (2004) The influence of a structurationist view on strategic management research. *Journal of Management Studies* **41** (2): 247–72.

Reed, M.I. (2001) Organization, trust and control: A realist analysis. *Organization Studies* **22** (2): 201–28.

Ring, P.S. (1997) Processes facilitating reliance on trust in inter-organizational networks. In: Ebers, M. (ed.): *The Formation of Inter-organizational Networks*, 113–45. Oxford: Oxford University Press.

Ring, P.S. and Van de Ven, A.H. (1994) Developmental processes of cooperative relations between organizations. *Strategic Management Journal* **19** (1): 90–118.

Rotter, J.B. (1967) A new scale for the measurement of interpersonal trust. *Journal of Personality* **35** (1): 651–65.

Rousseau, D.M., Sitkin, S.B., Burt, R.S. and Camerer, C. (1998) Not so different after all: A cross-discipline view of trust. *Academy of Management Review* **23** (3): 393–404.

Sako, M. and Helper, S. (1998) Determinants of trust in supplier relations: Evidence from the automotive industry in Japan and the United States. *Journal of Economic Behavior and Organization* **34** (3): 387–413.

Schneider, Benjamin (1990) (ed.) *Organizational Climate and Culture*, San Francisco, CA: Jossey-Bass.

Sheppard, B.H. and Tuchinsky, M. (1996) Micro-OB and the network organization. In: Kramer, R.M. and Tyler, T.R. (eds): *Trust in Organizations*, 140–65. London: Sage.

Simmel, G. (1950) *The Sociology of Georg Simmel*, trans. and ed., K.H. Wolff. New York: Free Press.

Sydow, J. (1998) Understanding the constitution of inter-organizational trust. In: Lane, C. and Bachmann, R. (eds): *Trust Within and Between Organizations*, 31–63. Oxford: Oxford University Press.

Sydow, J. and Windeler, A. (1998) Organizing and evaluating interfirm networks – A structurationist perspective on network processes and outcomes. *Organization Science* **9** (3): 265–84.

Sydow, J. and Windeler, A. (2003) Knowledge, trust and control: Managing tensions and contradictions in a regional network of service firms. *International Studies of Management & Organization* **33** (2): 69–100.

Uzzi, B. (1997) Social structure and competition in interfirm networks: The paradox of embeddedness. *Administrative Science Quarterly* **42**: 35–67.

Weick, K.E. (1969) *The Social Psychology of Organizing*. Reading, MA: Addison-Wesley.

Williamson, O.E. (1993) Calculativeness, trust, and economic organization. *Journal of Law and Economics* **36** (2): 453–86.

Young, L.S. and Wilkinson, I.F. (1989) Characteristics of good and poor interfirm relations. *European Journal of Marketing* **23** (2): 109–22.

Zaheer, A., McEvily, B. and Perrone, V. (1998) Does trust matter? Exploring the effects of inter-organizational and interpersonal trust on performance. *Organization Science* **9** (2): 141–59.

Zucker, L.G. (1986) Production of trust. Institutional sources of economic structure. In: Staw, B.M. and Cummings, L.L. (eds): *Research in Organizational Behavior* vol. 8, 53–111. Greenwich, CT: JAI Press.

Zucker, L.G., Darby, M.R., Brewer, M.B. and Peng, Y. (1996) Collaboration structure and information dilemmas in biotechnology: Organizational boundaries as trust production. In: Kramer, R.M. and Tyler, T.R. (eds): *Trust in Organizations*, 90–113. Thousand Oaks, CA: Sage.

22 Trust and/or power: towards a sociological theory of organizational relationships
Reinhard Bachmann

1. Introduction

This chapter deals with trust and power as mechanisms to coordinate expectations between social actors. It will be shown that trust is an effective means to control social relationships between individual and organizational actors. Depending on different forms of trust and power, which are largely determined by the institutional business environment in which relationships are embedded, both mechanisms engage in different combinations with one another. Each of these combinations has their specific consequences with regard to the level of trust that will prevail in business relationships.

This chapter will proceed as follows: first, the nature of trust as a social phenomenon will be examined (Section 2). Then (Section 3), the insights gained through this analysis will be transferred to relationships between business organizations which are viewed as a specific type of social exchange. In the next section of this chapter (Section 4), power will be introduced and analysed as a 'combinable functional equivalent' to trust that is equally effective in coordinating expectations and controlling relationships, both at the general level of social exchange and at the level of economic relationships between firms. Following from this step of the argument, the intricate interlinkages between 'interactional' forms of trust and power, on the one hand, and 'institutional-based' forms of trust and power, on the other hand, will be analysed (Section 5). This will be the central part of the theoretical argument presented in this chapter. Here, it will be argued that in environments where a low level of regulation prevails, trust and power, that is, 'interactional' trust and power, have a tendency to be alternative forms of coordinating relationships. In business systems that are characterized by a high level of regulation, by contrast, the then dominant forms of trust and power, that is, 'institutional-based' trust and power, typically occur in close combinations with one another, where power has a considerable potential to foster the development of trust between social actors. In the first case, it will be shown, the overall level of trust is relatively low in business relationships, whereas it tends to be high in the second case. This chapter will then (Section 6) provide some links to the relevant empirical literature which prepared the ground for the theoretical approach presented here. The final section of this chapter (Section 7) will suggest a conceptual and empirical research agenda which builds on the theory that is presented in this chapter.

2. The theory of trust

From a theoretical point of view, the question of how expectations and interactions among social actors can be coordinated and controlled is most interesting. This is a fundamental question in all social sciences which – depending on the epistemological approach that is taken to answer it – creates paradigmatic divisions of conceptual perspectives. Very much in contrast to this, in the 'real' world ordinary people are rarely bothered by such fundamental issues. There are, of course, some spectacular cases where social actors fail to communicate and misunderstand each others' motives and interests. But in the vast majority of social relationships, actors' behaviour follows widely accepted routines that are deeply integrated into large and strongly differentiated social systems and contexts. Against this background, it is not surprising that, as a matter of fact, social relationships between individual and collective (i.e. organizational) actors can be controlled highly effectively. It is a problem that in the empirical world is almost always already solved before any philosophical questions and problems may set in.

None the less, theoretical reasoning is anything but negligible. It is important as it holds the key to understanding the logic of the social systems in which actors' behaviour is embedded and to predicting how actors are likely to behave in specific circumstances in the future. Thus it does make sense to ask such questions which social *praxis*, in its everyday operational mode, seems to ignore so generously.

The theoretical approach to the problem of coordinating social actors' expectations and controlling their interactions can perhaps be best understood by reference to a mind experiment focusing on one simple question: What is – to put it in a Kantian terminology – the 'condition of the possibility' that social actions can neatly link into one another, so that contextually embedded long strings of coordinated interactions can emerge in the social world? The answer to this question – in general terms – is not complicated at all. There 'must' be social mechanisms at work that allow for this possibility and in fact make sure that, under normal circumstances, social actors can coordinate expectations and control their interactions. Following Luhmann (1979), trust can be seen as one of these mechanisms. Trust, in other words, may be understood as such a fundamental social mechanism that allows for coordinated interactions and thus indeed for the possibility that highly differentiated social systems can emerge in the empirical world. Power, significance, incentives or legitimacy may be seen as other mechanisms, equally fundamental and deep-seated in social actors' relationships (Giddens 1984; Bradach and Eccles 1989).

In Luhmann's systems-theoretical perspective, trust is a mechanism to reduce unstructured complexity and uncertainty. In his seminal work on trust (1979), he argues that social actors need to be able to make specific assumptions about each others' future behaviour. Rather than being caught up in situations where any behaviour of the *alter ego* is equally likely at any point in time, social actors 'must' be able to identify and select possibilities of each others' future behaviour that are more likely than others. If that was not the case, the social world would seem far too 'complex' and uncertain to be made sense of by any potential actor, and individual as well as collective actors would probably in most cases not be able to interact at all. Mechanisms such as trust, Luhmann argues, provide possibilities to select one or a small number of expectations as regards the *alter ego*'s future behaviour that can be assumed to be relatively likely to be actualized, while all the rest of the uncountable other possibilities that actors would in theory have to take into account because of the principle of freedom of human beings are simply ignored. The criterion for this selection process may be grounded in nothing but a momentary feeling and be completely arbitrary. What is important here is only the fact that a selection process does take place in that one actor chooses to make some very specific assumptions about another actor's future behaviour, and that a paralysing situation of ultimate uncertainty is thus turned into a situation where expectations can be coordinated and interactions are controllable. This is enough to put social actors in the position to start a relationship. The *alter ego* who realizes that a trustor engages in such a selection process will then also be able make specific assumptions about the other party, and a social relationship – and indeed a widespread social system – can emerge on the basis of coordinated mutual expectations and interactions. This is why trust is such a fundamental mechanism in all social contexts. If one party (i.e. the trustor) makes such specific assumptions about another party's (i.e. the trustee's) future behaviour, this actor reduces 'complexity' in that he or she simply selects one or a small number of positive assumptions about the other actor's future behaviour in the face of an – in principle – infinite number of other possibilities. In this situation a trustor has no guarantees that his or her assumptions will prove to be justified. But this is not the point here; rather it is indeed an intrinsic characteristic of trust that guarantees do not exist. The only important issue here is that a social actor (i.e. the trustor) suspends his or her possible doubts and acts 'as if' there were 'good reasons' to assume that the other actor (i.e. the trustee) will behave trustworthily. The literature calls this a 'leap of faith' (Möllering 2006).

A trustor, in other words, offers a 'pre-commitment' (Luhmann 1979). He or she simply assumes that the trustee will not behave opportunistically and exploit his or her vulnerability. If the trustee does not respond to this offer, this may well be the end of what could have become a trust-based relationship, just before it started to develop. It is by no means necessary that the trustee also agrees to act as a trustor and to establish reciprocal trust in a relationship, but he or she has to decide actively to take on the role of the trustee, who equally makes specific assumptions about the trustor's future behaviour. Someone who is recognizable as a trustor is likely to behave in a predicable manner and therefore a specific code of communication is chosen between the two parties. Not everything is possible at any future point in time between the two actors. Rather, a trustor has chosen to limit his or her repertoire of action, as has the trustee. On the basis of reduced 'complexity', meaningful and coordinated interaction can occur and although none of the actors has complete certainty with regard to one another's future behaviour, they can establish a highly efficient way of interacting with each other.

Trust is a prime mechanism to coordinate expectations and control interactions. It facilitates interactions which might otherwise not be possible and it greatly simplifies life for social actors, if one social actor only makes the first step and offers a trust-based relationship. Up to this point, this certainly seems to be straightforward and simple to do and understand. However, this is where the crucial questions arise. The trouble with trust is that it requires acceptance of risk. It absorbs uncertainty, that is, situations where anything can happen at any time, but it produces risk, which would not exist if a potential trustor was not prepared to invest trust in a relationship. In other words, trust transforms uncertainty into risk; that is, trust can turn out to be justified and beneficial for the trustor or indeed misplaced if the trustee chooses not to conform with the trustor's expectations. None the less, considerable progress is made when, from the point of view of the trustor, only two options exist: the trustee can behave either trustworthily or opportunistically. This is a situation that is incomparably better than a situation where an actor faces an unlimited number of possibilities as regards the other actor's future behaviour.

Risk, however, is unavoidable for any trustor. Where there is no risk, trust cannot exist, nor is it needed. Only if the available information is incomplete and imprecise can trust bridge knowledge gaps or be used to extrapolate from the given information. This is simply the nature of trust. In Luhmann's words, placing trust in another actor is like overdrawing a bank account. Similar to spending more money than one owns, trust draws on information which is not in stock. But as any business person knows, sometimes a little loan can be incredibly useful to start a profitable business. Under these conditions, trust necessarily is a 'risky investment' (Luhmann 1979), but in many cases it pays off in business as well as in other types of social exchange.

Even though a trustor needs to tolerate risk, he or she would of course want to be able to roughly assess the risk that he or she has to bear. A potential trustor thus seeks reasons as to why he or she should believe that the amount of risk that is involved in a trust investment remains within certain limits and can thus be deemed acceptable. Despite the fact that risk is not altogether avoidable for the trustor, it makes a lot of sense for him or her to at least have a rough idea of what could happen if the worst scenario comes true. Although it is grossly misleading to assume that a trustor can ever 'calculate' the risk that is involved in a trust investment, as Rational-Choice-based theories of trust suggest (e.g., Coleman 1990), any serious trustor seeks to avoid 'blind trust' and understandably is keen to know that even in the worst case he or she will survive without intolerably high damage.

At this point in the argument, it obviously seems most interesting to ask what can provide such 'good reasons' for a trustor to believe that the risk he or she is prepared to run is acceptable, especially in the face of benefits that may come through a well-placed trust investment. Luhmann (1979) gives a clear answer to this question. He suggests that the existence of legal norms can assure someone who is willing to make a trust investment that the risk that comes with this decision does not exceed a certain level of tolerability. However, it is important to note that Luhmann's solution does not imply that the sanctions that are attached to legal norms should be activated in order to minimize the inherent risk of trust. Rather, he believes that legal norms can channel social actors' behaviour in such a way that conflicts are avoided. Possible sanctions need to remain latent, if legal norms are to do their job effectively. Long before any conflict arises, legal norms 'persuade' social actors to align their behaviour with certain commonly accepted rules and thus can be conducive to providing exactly those reasons that a potential trustor needs in order to positively assess the inherent risk of a trust investment. If open conflict arises, legal norms have failed to do their job effectively and they then certainly make no contribution to developing trust in a social relationship. Legal norms, from Luhmann's point of view, provide what Garfinkel has called a 'world-in-comon' in that they establish commonly known and accepted rules of behaviour. Where these exist, the inherent risk of trust is low enough for potential trustors, who then have good reasons to actually make the decision and indeed invest trust in a relationship.

Luhmann's theory of trust can be summarized as follows. The first step is a potential trustor's pre-commitment. He or she simply chooses to assume that the trustee will behave trustworthily. This reduces uncertainty and brings both the trustor and the trustee into a position where they can develop a relationship based on coordinated interaction. To sell off uncertainty by means of trust means to buy in risk, which is much easier to handle but needs to be low enough to be tolerable. Where commonly accepted rules of legal and social behaviour exist, it seems likely that social actors will orient their behaviour to them, which minimizes the inherent risk that a trustor has to bear when deciding to invest trust in a relationship. Thus, one can conclude, trust is significantly more likely to occur where reliable rules of behaviour make potential trustees' future behaviour more predictable than it would be if these rules did not exist.

3.   Trust in organizational relationships

If this approach to understanding the theoretical foundations of trust holds good, the role of trust in business relations, as a sub-category of social relationships, can be understood in very similar terms. Relevant legal norms appear as contract law in the context of inter-organizational relationships and as labour law in intra-organizational relations. These norms, where they exist and are accepted in daily practice, can provide precisely those 'good reasons' which are needed to encourage potential trustors to invest trust in their relationships with business partners rather than drawing on another functionally more or less equivalent coordination mechanism, for example power or monetary incentives.

Examining the development of trust in business relationships more closely reveals that – as in any other form of social relationships – it is not only legal norms that can serve as a facilitator of trust. More informal behavioural norms and technical standards can equally channel economic actors' behaviour into certain patterns, which makes their behaviour more predictable than it would be if these rules were not in place. For example, the existence of procedural ISO norms and product-related technical standards in the engineering sector can effectively reduce the risk of low product quality in a situation where a buyer firm considers establishing a trust-based relationship with a supplier firm (Lane 1997). Also, it can be argued that a national business system which has a rigorous and reliable system of education and vocational training in place encourages 'competence trust' (Sako 1992) in that job applicants' and employees' certified and documented skills seem more reliable than claims of expertise that individuals may make depending on their mood or personality traits. Equally, to give another example, powerful industry associations, in which a large majority of firms of a given industry are active members, can exert a strong influence on the social rules of acceptable and unacceptable business behaviour and thus become a prime source and facilitator of trust between individuals and organizations in a specific industry as well as the relevant business system as a whole. All these sets of legal and more or less formal social rules are to be seen as elements of the national, sectoral, supra- or infra-regional business system's 'institutional framework' in which business relationships are embedded (Granovetter 1985).

Irrespective of whether these rules and norms are legal, social or technical in nature, they have a latent potential to sanction non-compliant behaviour and can thus reduce the possibility of opportunistic behaviour on the part of potential trustee. This is one of the most important reasons why they exist and why they can encourage trust in business relationships. Like legal norms, social and technical norms are essentially not meant to be used in order to sanction a trustee's possible 'misbehaviour'. What is much more important is that they produce shared knowledge and a common understanding of what is appropriate behaviour in relationships between individual and/or organizational actors. Thus business partners' behaviour becomes relatively predictable and the risk of trust being grossly misplaced is reduced considerably. Institutional arrangements that represent and control commonly accepted rules of behaviour can, in other words, be seen as a key factor where the level of trust in a specific business system is under review. Cultural factors, that is, more general and implicit norms of behaviour, may also play an important role (Fukuyama 1995; Hofstede 1991), but institutional factors must be seen as of greater importance if individuals and organizations are deemed to be knowledgeable social actors.

Notwithstanding the above argument, trust can be developed in different ways and, depending on these production modes, different forms of trust are generated in business relationships as well as in other forms of social exchange. In the argument presented so far in this chapter, emphasis has been placed on 'institutional based trust' (Zucker 1986) or 'system trust', as some scholars (Luhmann, Giddens) prefer to say. This is a form of trust that is constitutively developed by reference to the institutional arrangements that exist in a given business system. Besides this form of trust, however, trust can also occur as what may be called 'interactional trust'. This is a form of trust that constitutively draws on the particular characteristics of social actors ('characteristic based trust', in Zucker's terminology) or experiences made at the level of relationships by the involved social actors, be they individuals or organizations. 'Interactional trust' rests on social actors' reliability, integrity and communicative skills and does in principle not need powerful institutional arrangements to be developed effectively. In this case, much more than commonly accepted norms and rules, it is the social actors themselves who, in a particularistic manner, develop trust in their relationships.

The latter form of trust undoubtedly plays an important role in business and in other social relationships. However, overly relying on 'interactional trust' has a number of significant disadvantages. In order to develop it, social actors may have to bear considerable costs, emotionally, financially, and in terms of time that is required to build a sufficient amount of trust in a relationship. Above all, the number of social actors to whom relationships based on 'interactional trust' can be developed and nurtured over a longer period of time is quite limited. Especially in business relationships, where asset-specificity is low, these costs and restrictions are often unacceptable and social actors will have to consider other ways of coordinating their expectations and controlling their interactions effectively. If, for example, a buyer firm that is dealing with a supplier firm of simple, cheap, and globally available inputs had to develop trust on the basis of experiences with one another, or characteristics such as shared ethnic background, this would in most cases appear to be quite irrational and economically not viable (Barney and Hansen 1994).

The limitations of the mode of trust production are very convincingly demonstrated in Zucker's famous article (1986). With reference to the American economy of the nineteenth and early twentieth centuries, she argues that at a certain stage of growth, the socio-economic system could no longer primarily rely on 'characteristic-based' or 'experience-based' trust. In order to further grow, the national business system had to increasingly draw on 'institutional-based' trust. Commonly accepted rules and standards of business behaviour became a prime source of trust in business relationships. Industry associations, nation-wide legal and technical standards as well as other elements of the institutional framework of the American socio-economic system more and more replaced or at least complemented 'interactional trust' in business relationships. Without any direct costs on the part of the social actors involved in a specific relationship, trust in the form of 'institutional-based trust' became a commodity that could be mass-produced on the basis of reliable institutional arrangements. Government-controlled economic agencies and regulations, the growing importance of trade associations and other factors contributed to establishing an institutional framework of the business system which facilitated the production of 'institutional-based trust'. This could be seen as a major step to economic modernization, allowing many business transactions to take place that would not have occurred otherwise. With regard to the economic system's further differentiation and growth, this was a vital development which came at some collective cost. But it relieved business partners from always having to develop trust at the interactional level, which overall is also much more costly for the business system as a whole.

4. Trust and power

Trust is generally a very important resource in organizing individual and organizational relationships efficiently. In business relationships it can save transaction costs (Dei Ottati 1994; Zaheer et al. 1998) and in other social relationships it can equally reduce complexity and save enormous monitoring efforts, time, emotional and other forms of expenditures. Often, there may be 'functional equivalents' that can replace trust as a coordination and control mechanism or other mechanisms that can complement and significantly strengthen the potential of trust as a mechanism to coordinate expectations and to control interactional dynamics. Sometimes, however, trust is the only possible coordination mechanism, and interactions would not be deemed controllable and thus simply not take place if trust was not available.

Clearly, trust also has disadvantages. It can suddenly break down, and if this happens it is very difficult to restore. Trust is a fragile mechanism, and where actors feel betrayed they do not easily give a relationship a fresh start, even when viewed in a rational manner this might be a good option. Betrayed trust, in other words, does not just leave social actors without trust. Rather, it produces distrust between them which often makes it difficult merely to re-establish a neutral basis for future social exchanges. Also, there are many situations where trust seems too costly or even impossible to establish in the first place. If, for example, 'institutional-based trust' is no viable option because the institutional arrangements of a given business systems are weak, patchy and unreliable, and the interactional form of trust production would take too much time and effort, then trust may appear to be no option at all.

Considering these disadvantages of trust, it seems more than fortunate that trust is not the only coordination and control mechanism in business and other social relationships. As already touched upon above, power appears as one of the most useful other 'combinable functional equivalents' to trust in many situations. Under certain circumstances, power is no doubt a most useful tool, and indeed the better option. Despite the fact that it has a much lower reputation if it is viewed from a normative point of view, it seems to function quite similarly to trust. If it is looked at from an analytical perspective, the differences are relatively small. In Luhmann's conceptual framework (1979; 1984), which is committed to a non-normative view, power appears as a social coordination and control mechanism which – like trust – operates on the basis of a selection process. Social actors who exert power over others select specific assumptions about their future behaviour in the face of other possibilities.

In this respect, there is no great difference between power and trust. While trust usually starts with a potential trustor's 'positive' assumptions about a potential trustee's future behaviour, a claim of power often builds on a 'negative' hypothetical assumption which the powerful actor presents to the subordinate actor as a possibility of behaviour that he or she should avoid. Sometimes, however, it can also be the other way round. A potential trustor may choose a 'negative' hypothetical assumption about a potential trustee's behaviour and decide to see it as unlikely to occur, while a powerful actor may select a specific 'positive' option as regards the subordinate actor's future behaviour and persuade the subordinate actor to comply with this assumption.

On closer inspection, it is not only the case that trust and power can both be reconstructed as mechanisms based on processes in which social actors select specific assumptions about another actor's future behaviour. There are also other similarities that are worth considering in this context. For example, a claim of power – similar to trust – inevitably involves risk. Drawing on Hegel's philosophy, Giddens (1984) and other authors have referred to this phenomenon as the 'dialectics of power'. In this perspective, it appears that power can also break down quite easily. If a supposedly powerful actor makes a power claim which is not credible and simply ignored or rejected by the supposedly subordinate actor, power can immediately vanish, leaving the allegedly powerful actor without any power and often without many good alternative options.

Although there are also some important differences between power and trust, both mecahnisms are relatively similar as a means to facilitate coordinated expectations and to control the dynamics of interactions. Often trust may seem the preferable coordination and control mechanism. Where a social actor is not in a position to make a credible power claim because he or she has no or not enough 'authoritative' (immaterial) or 'allocative' (material) resources of power (Giddens 1984) available to refer to, he or she may be left with little choice and invest trust in a relationship even when the risk that comes with it is relatively high. In other situations, social actors may have large resources of power and not bother too much about the option of investing trust. They may simply utilize their power in order to efficiently facilitate decisions that could otherwise not be taken, or at least not as swiftly and effectively.

In practice, trust and power often occur in combinations and the question is only which of the two mechanisms is dominant in coordinating expectations and controlling interactions. A relationship may in the first place be based on trust, but also draw on power where trust has its limitations and vice versa. For example, a buyer firm may trust its supplier with regard to the quality of parts and material delivered by this firm as long as there is not too much at stake in terms of the consequences of possibly faulty inputs in the final product. However, it may use power where the delivered parts and material, if faulty and undetected, can cause significant damages to the end-product. Also, there are cases conceivable where – to use the same example again – a buyer firm in normal circumstances uses its power to make its supplier compliant with certain specifications that are required in terms of the quality of parts and material, and then change to trust where its power seems worthless. The latter may be the case where the quality of parts and material can only be assessed long after the end-product has been delivered to the customer.

The question of whether trust or power dominates a business relationship – like any other type of social relationship – is a matter of availability of these mechanisms and social actors' preferences that they build in the face of the given social context. It is unrealistic to assume that social actors always base their decisions on rationalistic calculations, as Rational Choice theorists (e.g., Coleman 1990), at least heuristically, tend to assume. At the same time, social actors do not usually behave completely irrationally when they make their decisions. Rather, they consider their options in the light of the social environment in which their interactions are embedded. The latter largely consists of cultural and, in particular, institutional arrangements, as discussed above. Luhmann, Giddens and also Coleman agree that there are institutional arrangements in which it is in a social actor's interest to behave trustworthily, and others in which they tend to refrain from doing so. The difference in these three theoretical approaches is only that institutions 'channel' the behaviour of social actors in Luhmann's and Giddens's view while Coleman, based on his assumption of 'hyperrational' social actors, suggests a quite deterministic impact of institutional arrangements on social actor's decisions.

If it seems realistic to argue that social actors consider their resources and risks when either deciding to invest trust or use power in their social relationships, then institutional arrangements can be deemed highly relevant factors. Clearly, not everyone has resources of power available and many potential trustors find the risk of trust not bearable where no reliable institutional order is in place while 'interactional trust' is costly to establish, especially when a one-off transaction is considered with a potential business partner. Then, if no other coordination and control mechanism can fill the gap, the consequence might well be that no social exchange is possible. No doubt, psychological dispositions and cultural factors may also have their relative influence on social decisions. But more than these, particularly in business contexts, it seems that institutional arrangements are highly predictive of whether social actors will invest trust or fall back on power. These are the most likely options that decide upon the quality of business relationships.

5.   Trust or power?

Earlier in this chapter, an important distinction was made between trust developed in the course of social interaction ('interactional trust') and trust developed between social actors who interact in the face of strong institutional arrangements ('institutional-based trust'). No doubt, in the case of power, the same distinction can be made. Then, 'interactional power' and 'institutional-based power' are to be distinguished. 'Interactional power' is a form of power which depends on the social actors that are involved in a power-based relationship. In order to exert interactional power, an individual or organizational actor refers to his, her or their resources of power and lets them be material (e.g., money, property etc.) or immaterial (e.g., reputation, skills etc.). In the case of 'institutional-based power' social actor that exert power in the course of their action constitutively refer to institutional arrangements that grant them a social position in which they can make and enforce decisions, even if these are not based on a collective agreement, or entitles them to claim scarce material resources that are not available to everyone. In the latter circumstances, similar to trust, power exists and is exerted 'in the face of' strong and reliable institutional (i.e. 'hierarchical') arrangements that put a social actor into a powerful or a subordinate position. Where this is the case, power appears in the form of 'institutional-based power'.

If this makes sense and it holds true that, depending on how trust and power are developed, trust, on the one hand, can either be interaction-based or institution-based, and power, on the other hand, can equally be based on interactions or institutions, then the possible interrelatedness between trust and power deserves a more detailed review. Above, it was only argued that trust and power can occur at the same time, while it is usually one of these two coordination mechanisms that is dominant in a social relationship. However, this seems to be only half of the story that can be completed in light of the distinction between the two possible forms of power.

In principle, four combinations of the two forms of trust and the two forms of power are conceivable, and it might well be argued that empirical cases can be identified where 'hybrid' combinations (i.e. 'institutional-based trust' combined with 'interactional power', or 'interaction-based trust' combined with 'institutional-based power') occur

(Bachmann and van Witteloostuijn 2002). However, the generic and empirically typical combinations are different and can be described as follows.

On the one hand, trust and power can appear in their interactional forms. In this case, they tend to be alternative options. At least, whether trust or power is the dominant coordination and control mechanism in a relationship is often not difficult to establish. Either a relationship is more based on trust or more based on power where the interactional forms of trust and power are relevant. Social actors tend to be relatively clear about which mechanism ultimately governs their relationships. They might trust one another to a certain extent but prefer to use their individually available resources of power if critical situations occur. Equally, it could be that they use their power resources which they can command but change to trust where their resources can no longer credibly underpin their power claims.

On the other hand, trust and power can occur in their institutional-based forms. Where these circumstances are present, trust goes hand in hand with power. It can even be argued that close combinations of trust and power are then unavoidable. Power that social actors derive from institutional contexts, which grants them a powerful position within hierarchical arrangements, is often a very strong facilitator of trust, rather than a form of alternative option. In other words, where a social actor who exerts power can refer to institutionalized rules which he or she is following in making his or her decisions, the subordinate actor will have relatively 'good reasons' to believe that he or she can trust the powerful actor. This is much more the case in these circumstances than when 'interactional power' prevails. Thus it can be concluded that while interaction-based forms of trust and power have a tendency to be become two different options although they can also be combined to some extent to strengthen each other, institutional-based forms of trust and power are sometimes so strongly intermingled that it can be difficult to say what is actually the dominant coordination and control mechanism in a relationship. Here, strong and reliable institutions are the source of power that is highly conducive, if not a precondition, to producing a high level of trust in individual and organizational relationships.

Linking this proposition with Luhmann's approach to analysing trust confirms the insight that this systems-theoretical conceptualization of trust is much more oriented to 'institutional-based trust' than 'interactional trust'. In this perspective, business systems that are characterized by strong institutional arrangements, such as reliable legal norms and other social norms of business behaviour, appear to produce a powerful social order in which social actors find each other's future behaviour relatively predictable. The latter amounts to saying that under these conditions social actors have more 'good reasons' to invest trust in their relationships to other individual and organizational actors than in circumstances where there is no powerful and collectively maintained institutional order, and where power, should this be the dominant mode of coordination and control, can only be drawn from privately available 'authoritative' or 'allocative' resources.

Despite the fact that the theoretical argument presented in this chapter is generally geared to understanding 'institutional-based trust', it is also important ignored that this is not the only form of trust and that numerous business relationships, irrespective of the institutional environment in which they are embedded, rely more strongly on 'interactional trust' than on 'institutional-based trust'. Notwithstanding the fact that the process of developing 'interactional trust' is relatively slow and presupposes considerable efforts on the part of the social actors involved in a relationship, it specifically plays a most important role in systems that build on an individualistic culture and lack strong forms of institutional arrangements. Where the institutional framework of the business system is weak and patchy, 'interactional trust' may sometimes appear as the only viable form of trust that can effectively govern business relationships. But in this case there is also an understandable need more often than not to change to power or at least to increase the weight of power – which then is interactional power – in business relationships. If that was not the case, a critical lack of coordination of expectations and control of interactions would be looming, leading to chaotic patterns of social communication and exchange. Therefore, as a matter of necessity, weakly regulated business systems are generally characterized by a significantly higher level of power, that is, 'interactional power', than more strongly regulated systems. The latter are typically building on a relatively high level of trust, and the literature usually describes them as 'high trust systems' (e.g., Fukuyama 1995; Hofstede 1991).

6. The wider research context

These theoretical conceptualizations of trust and power link to the contemporary political economy literature, which provides various notions of how to analyse different types of business systems and – often in a comparative view – examines a wide range of empirical aspects (Whitley 1992; 1999; Lane 1995; Sorge 1996; Crouch and Streeck 1997; Hall and Soskice 2001). However, compared to this literature the theoretical approach presented above draws more on genuine sociological theory and tries to get to grips with the social coordination and control mechanisms that underlie the processes that lead to different forms of cooperation between individuals and organizations. In this respect, on the one hand, it digs deeply into the micro-processes of business behaviour. But, on other hand, the above theoretical argument also places particular emphasis on the institutional level of business systems. 'New Institutionalism' in sociological theorizing (e.g., Powell and DiMaggio 1991; Scott 1995), which specifically draws attention to social phenomena that exist beyond the micro-level of analysis, has inspired the presented approach significantly.

In a more specific context, the strand of literature that focuses on Anglo-German comparisons also plays an important role here. In this tradition of research it was consistently found that the German socio-economic model is based much more on trust than its Anglo-Saxon counterpart. Fox (1974) was one of the first contributors to this body of literature. While his analysis examined industrial relations, other scholars later added more levels of analysis, including management styles (Stewart et al. 1994) and institutional arrangements (Lane 1995) that characterize these two business systems. This research, however, is – similar to parts of the political economy literature – rather descriptive and has not too much to say where theoretical explanations are in demand.

A very direct link between empirical research and the theoretical argument presented in this chapter exists through the author's involvement in a multidisciplinary project on 'vertical contracts' that was carried out in Cambridge in the mid-1990s. In the context of this research, which focused on the quality of supplier relationships in Germany, the UK and Italy, different forms and developments of trust were identified and could be explained by reference to the specific institutional characteristics of the business systems in which relationships were deeply embedded (e.g. Lane and Bachmann 1996; 1997;

Arrighetti et al. 1997; Deakin and Wilkinson 1998; Deakin, Chapter 12 in this volume). For example, it could be shown that contracts between business organizations varied significantly across the countries studied and had different functions within the business relationship. Broadly speaking, detailed contracts and other ways of referring to general rules of business behaviour were common and conducive to building trust in the German case. By contrast, a higher level of informality in contractual relations in the UK led to a consistently lower level of trust in business relationships. A number of other factors, such as, for example, the role of industry associations, was also looked at. In this context, the same pattern emerged: in the German case, trade associations were found to be very powerful. They defined the social rules of business behaviour and could effectively control an industry's 'general terms of business' (Lane and Bachmann 1996). This form of power (i.e. 'institutional-based' power) was conducive to building trust at the level of exchanges between social actors. In the UK, industry associations were found to be relatively weak and far from being able to represent their industry as a whole. They were not in a position to define the rules of acceptable business behaviour and hardly contributed to the development of trust between firms. The Italian case, in many ways, was consistent with this finding but as such represented a hybrid model of trust development, somewhere between the UK and Germany.

These results considerably extends the perspective taken by many contributions that are based on a one-dimensional understanding of trust, usually seeing trust as an intrinsically individual phenomenon. Also, it contrasts sharply with the socio-legal tradition of research. The latter (Macauly 1963; Beale and Dugdale 1975) had always insisted that trust resides 'beyond contract' and implied that extensive references to legal rules were detrimental to building trust in inter-organizational relationships. According to our comparative research, this may be the case in a certain environment. But the fact that many studies, including the named ones, are only looking at the Anglo-Saxon context makes them largely blind to what we call 'institutional-based trust'. Then no doubt trust seems to be predominantly 'interactional trust', which in the theoretical framework presented above is indeed more difficult to reconcile with business partners' strong references made to legal norms and powerful rules of social behaviour. Under these conditions, social actors tend to develop individualistic forms of 'goodwill trust'. But they find little reason to invest institutionally based 'competence trust' (Sako 1992) because the degree of institutional regulation is too low in this business context to effectively reduce the inherent risk of trust. Thus it is not completely wrong to say that trust can hardly build on detailed contracts, but it is only a specific form of trust ('interactional trust') for which this is true in a certain type of business environment (i.e., the Anglo-Saxon system). However, this is only a part of the story. 'Institutional-based trust' is a different form of trust which flourishes, for example, in the German and indeed in most continental European business systems. This form of trust goes hand in hand with strong general rules of behaviour, be they of legal or social quality. Also, this insight seems largely to hold true when it is transferred to intra-organizational relationships. In the latter case, to a large extent the internal 'institutional inventory' of the organization (Bachmann 2003b) can be seen as the equivalent to the external institutional framework, having similar effects on the development of trust in social relationships within the organization.

In contrast to trust, the analysis of power has not attracted very much attention in the recent organizational literature. Since the heyday of the Labour Process Debate in the 1970s, few scholars have remained interested in this phenomenon (e.g., Rainnie 1993). However, it appears important to somewhat counterbalance the enormous interest in trust in the current organizational literature to better understand trust itself as a vital coordination mechanism within business relationships. In the above-mentioned Cambridge study, the analysis of trust moved centre-stage in the course of this research project. This study also paid little explicit attention to the phenomenon of power as a 'combinable functional equivalent' to trust as regards the problem of coordinating expectations and controlling interactions in organizational contexts, although some hints, such as the much greater number of 'adversarial' relationships in the UK (Lane and Bachmann 1996; 1997), sparked interest in more in-depth analyses of the role of power in coordinating and controlling exchanges between individual and organizational actors. Only on the basis of further theoretical work carried out against the background of this empirical study's results could it then be shown how closely power is interlinked with trust and that the forms and combinations of trust and power make the big difference between countries, supra- as well as infra-national regions with regard to the quality of inter-organizational relationships (Bachmann 2001).

7.   The research agenda

The theoretical approach outlined above calls for applications and empirical testing which has been started (e.g. Bachmann 2003a; 2003b; Clases et al. 2003) but is far from being completed. In the final section of this chapter some important items for a research agenda to examine blind spots and the tacit hypotheses underlying this theoretical approach will be discussed. The unanswered questions require empirical research which is quite specific and goes well beyond the exploratory approaches on which many of the existing studies on trust are based. At the same time, some important theoretical issues remain to be clarified.

One of the central questions that needs further investigation concerns the relationship between individual actors' behaviour and collective (i.e. organizational) actors' behaviour. This is an issue which is debated in detail, for example, in Zaheer et al. 1998 (also see McEvily and Zaheer, Chapter 16 in this volume). In the theoretical framework presented here, for the sake of simplicity it is assumed that collective actors can trust other actors in the same sense as when individual social actors invest trust in relationships. Zaheer et al. (1998) confirm that 'interpersonal' and 'inter-organizational' trust are strongly related but they also found that it is only inter-organizational trust that has direct effects on performance by way of lowering transaction costs. If this is the case, then it must be concluded that 'interpersonal' and 'inter-organizational' trust operate in different ways, which deserve further investigation. While McEvily and Zaheer (in this volume) refer to an interesting study by Dyer and Chu (2003) which suggests discerning different forms of transaction costs which could be lowered either by 'interpersonal' or 'inter-organizational' trust, this does not fully explain the relationship between individual and collective actors' trust in exchange partners and how, if at all, these forms of trust can be transformed into one another.

Related to this issue is the problem of individual versus collective trustees. A considerable part of the literature suggests that 'system trust', 'impersonal trust', 'organizational trust' and even 'institutional trust' are terms which should be used when the 'object' of trust is an organization rather than an individual person (e.g. Sydow 1998). This concerns an issue that is also not examined in the theoretical approach presented here. Generally, this theoretical framework suggests using the term 'institutional-based trust' (as opposed to 'interactional trust') when social actors, independent of whether they are individuals or organizations, trust another actor in the light of a given institutional environment in which interactions are embedded. Institutions are seen as mediators of social actors' decisions to either invest trust in a relationship or refrain from doing so. If the 'object' of trust is an organization, questions arise that are similar to the questions concerned when the subject of trust (i.e. the trustor) is a collective actor. In this context the central research question concerns the relationship between individual and collective trustees and, again, the problem of how, if at all, one of these forms of trust can be transformed into the other.

If it is true that trust and power can best be understood as a means to coordinate expectations and interactions between individuals and organizations, or – to put it differently – to control interactions and organizational processes, then it is important to find out more about other possible mechanisms which may also play a role in this context. For example, incentives, be they monetary or linked to social status, should be considered as an equally basic coordination mechanism. Bradach and Eccles (1989) suggest a view that draws on a transaction cost economics perspective, seeing 'prices', 'authority' and 'trust' as three basic governance mechanisms. This might be worth relating more to sociological theory, which makes the market ('prices') understandable as one of at least three fundamental mechanisms to control social behaviour so that differentiated social systems can exist on the basis of the effective coordination of actors' expectation and interactions.

More comparative work is needed to confirm the theoretical approach presented above. In particular, other countries than those studied in the empirical research that fed into this approach should be included to see whether this framework is robust when used in other cultural and institutional contexts. The question of how directly the level of institutional regulation determines the relationship between trust and power is central here. There might well be factors which produce a more complex picture when this approach is tested in culturally diverse non-European countries or in smaller European countries which have a more hybrid institutional framework than Germany and the UK. Bachmann and Witteloostuijn (2002) contains some ideas as to how empirical projects could be designed to study relationships in Ireland (suggested as a derivative of the UK socio-economic system) and the Netherlands (suggested as heavily influenced by the German business model).

In methodological terms the bulk of existing literature is heavily based on formalized trust inventories (Rotter 1967; McAllister 1995; Cummings and Bromiley 1996; Gillespie 2003), experiments or qualitative case studies drawing on open questions and flexible interview guidelines. In both cases the problem of data validity is difficult to tackle and the most sophisticated statistical analysis cannot resolve this problem. Given the fact that trust is such a multi-faceted phenomenon, which respondents tend to understand in different ways, the problem of internal and external validity should be taken seriously. Future research on trust needs to enlarge its methodological tool case and especially add more sophisticated methods that are common in social psychology. For example, 'repertory grids' (Clases et al. 2003) may provide a promising methodological approach to further understand the meaning that the studied social actors themselves attach to concepts such as trust and power.

References

Arrighetti, A., Bachmann, R. and Deakin, S. (1997), 'Contract law, social norms and inter-firm cooperation', *Cambridge Journal of Economics*, **21**(2): 329–49.

Bachmann (2001), 'Trust, power and control in trans-organizational relations', *Organization Studies*, **22**(2): 337–65.

Bachmann, R. (2003a), 'The role of trust and power in the institutional regulation of territorial business systems', in Fornahl, D. and Brenner, T. (eds), *Cooperation, Networks and Institutions in Regional Innovation Systems*, Cheltenham, UK and Northampton, MA, USA: Edward Elgar: 58–81.

Bachmann, R. (2003b), 'Trust and power as means of coordinating the internal relations of the organization – A conceptual framework', in Nooteboom, B. and Six, F. (eds), *The Trust Process in Organizations. Empirical Studies in the Determinants and the Process of Trust Development*, Cheltenham, UK and Northampton, MA, USA: Edward Elgar: 58–74.

Bachmann, R. and van Witteloostuijn, A. (2002), 'Institutional and inter-personal forms of power and trust as means of co-ordinating and controlling trans-organizational relationships', paper presented at the 18th Egos Colloquium, Barcelona.

Barney, J.B. and Hansen, M.H. (1994), 'Trustworthiness as a source of competitive advantage', *Strategic Management Journal*, **15**: 175–90.

Beale, N. and Dugdale, T. (1975), 'Contracts between businessmen: Planning and the use of contractual remedies', *British Journal of Law and Society*, **2**: 45–60.

Bradach, J.L. and Eccles, R.G. (1989), 'Price, authority and trust: From ideal types to plural forms', *Annual Review of Sociology*, **15**: 97–118.

Clases, C., Bachmann, R. and Wehner, T. (2003), 'Studying trust in virtual organizations', *International Studies of Management and Organization*, **33**(3): 7–27.

Coleman, J. (1990), *Foundations of Social Theory*, Cambridge, MA: Harvard University Press.

Crouch, C. and Streeck, W. (eds) (1997), *Political Economy of Modern Capitalism*, London: Sage.

Cummings, L.L. and Bromiley, P. (1996), 'The Organizational Trust Inventory (OTI): Development and validation', in Kramer, R.M. and Tyler, T.R. (eds), *Trust in Organizations: Frontiers of Theory and Research*, London: Sage: 302–30.

Deakin, S. and Wilkinson, F. (1998), 'Contract law and the economics of interorganizational trust', in Lane, C. and Bachmann, R. (eds), *Trust Within and Between Organizations. Conceptual Issues and Empirical Applications*, Oxford: Oxford University Press: 146–72.

Dei Ottati, G. (1994), 'Cooperation and competition in the industrial district as an organization model', *European Planning Studies*, **2**: 463–83.

Dyer, J.H. and Chu, W.J. (2003), 'The role of trustworthiness in reducing transaction costs and improving performance: Empirical evidence from the United States, Japan and Korea', *Organization Science*, **14**(1): 57–68.

Fox, A. (1974), *Beyond Contract: Work, Power and Trust Relations*, London: Faber and Faber.

Fukuyama, F. (1995), *Trust. The Social Virtues and the Creation of Prosperity*, New York: Free Press.

Giddens, A. (1984), *The Constitution of Society*, Cambridge: Polity Press.

Giddens, A. (1990), *The Consequences of Modernity*, Cambridge: Polity Press.

Gillespie, N. (2003), 'Measuring trust in working relations: the behavioral trust inventory', paper presented at the Academy of Management Conference, Seattle, WA.

Granovetter, M. (1985), 'Economic action and social structure: The problem of embeddedness', *American Journal of Sociology*, **91**: 481–510.

Hall, P.A. and Soskice, D. (eds) (2001), *Varieties of Capitalism. The Institutional Foundations of Comparative Advantage*, Oxford: Oxford University Press.

Hofstede, G. (1991), *Cultures and Organizations: Software of the Mind*, London: McGraw-Hill.

Lane C. (1995), *Industry and Society in Europe: Stability and Change in Britain, Germany and France*, Aldershot, UK and Brookfield, VT, USA: Edward Elgar.

Lane C. (1997), 'The social regulation of inter-firm relations in Britain and Germany: Market rules, legal norms and technical standards', *Cambridge Journal of Economics*, **21**(2): 197–215.

Lane, C. and Bachmann, R. (1996), 'The social constitution of trust: Supplier relations in Britain and Germany', *Organization Studies*, **17**: 365–95.

Lane, C. and Bachmann, R. (1997), 'Cooperation in inter-firm relations in Britain and Germany: The role of social institutions', *British Journal of Sociology*, **48**: 226–54.

Lane, C. and Bachmann, R. (1998), *Trust Within and Between Organizations: Conceptual Issues and Empirical Applications*, Oxford: Oxford University Press.

Luhmann, N. (1979), *Trust and Power*, Chichester: Wiley.

Luhmann, N. (1984), *Soziale Systeme*, Frankfurt: Suhrkamp.

Macauly, S. (1963), 'Non-contractual relations in business: A preliminary study', *American Sociological Review*, **28**(2): 55–67.

McAllister, D.J. (1995), 'Affect- and cognition-based trust as foundations for interpersonal cooperation in organizations', *Academy of Management Journal*, **38**(1): 24–59.

Möllering, G. (2006), *Trust: Reason, Routine, Reflexivity*, Amsterdam: Elsevier.

Powell, W.W. and DiMaggio, P.J. (eds) (1991), *The New Institutionalism in Organizational Analysis*, Chicago, IL: Chicago University Press.

Rainnie, A. (1993), 'The reorganization of large firm subcontracting: Myth and reality', *Capital and Class*, **49**: 53–73.

Rotter, J.B. (1967), 'A new scale for the measurement of interpersonal trust', *Journal of Personality*, **35**(4): 651–65.

Sako, M. (1992), *Prices, Quality and Trust. Inter-firm Relations in Britain and Japan*, Cambridge: Cambridge University Press.

Scott, R.W. (1995), *Institutions and Organizations*. Thousand Oaks, CA: Sage.

Sorge, A. (1996), 'Societal effects in cross-national organization studies: Conceptualizing diversity in actors and systems', in Whitley, R. and Kristensen, P.H. (eds), *The Changing European Firm. Limits to Convergence*, London: Routledge: 67–86.

Stewart, R., Barsoux, J.-L., Kieser, A. Ganter, H.-D. and Walgenbach, P. (1994), *Managing in Britain and Germany*, London: Anglo-German Foundation.

Sydow, J. (1998), 'Understanding the constitution of interorganizational trust', in Lane, C. and Bachmann, R. (eds), *Trust Within and Between Organizations. Conceptual Issues and Empirical Applications*, Oxford: Oxford University Press: 31–63.

Whitley, R. (ed.) (1992), *European Business Systems*, London: Sage.

Whitley, R. (1999), *Divergent Capitalisms: The Social Structuring and Change of Business Systems*, Oxford: Oxford University Press.

Zaheer, A., McEvily, B. and Perrone, V. (1998), 'Does trust matter? Exploring the effects of interorganizational and interpersonal trust on performance', *Organization Science*, **9**(2): 141–59.

Zucker, L. (1986), 'Production of trust: Institutional sources of economic structure, 1840–1920', *Research in Organizational Behavior*, **6**: 53–111.

Index